EOIN O'DUFFY

EOIN O'DUFFY

A Self-Made Hero

FEARGHAL McGARRY

OXFORD
UNIVERSITY PRESS

OXFORD

UNIVERSITY PRESS

Great Clarendon Street, Oxford OX2 6DP

Oxford University Press is a department of the University of Oxford.
It furthers the University's objective of excellence in research, scholarship,
and education by publishing worldwide in

Oxford New York

Auckland Cape Town Dar es Salaam Hong Kong Karachi
Kuala Lumpur Madrid Melbourne Mexico City Nairobi
New Delhi Shanghai Taipei Toronto

With offices in

Argentina Austria Brazil Chile Czech Republic France Greece
Guatemala Hungary Italy Japan Poland Portugal Singapore
South Korea Switzerland Thailand Turkey Ukraine Vietnam

Oxford is a registered trade mark of Oxford University Press
in the UK and in certain other countries

Published in the United States
by Oxford University Press Inc., New York

British Library Cataloguing in Publication Data

Data available

Library of Congress Cataloging in Publication Data

Data available

Typeset by Newgen Imaging Systems (P) Ltd., Chennai, India
Printed in Great Britain
on acid-free paper by
Biddles Ltd., King's Lynn, Norfolk

ISBN 0–19–927655–2   978–0–19–927655–4

1 3 5 7 9 10 8 6 4 2

Preface

I was travelling to Dublin on the Belfast train recently, editing a final draft of what would become this book, when an elderly man got on at the border town of Dundalk. After politely enquiring what I was working on, he declared, with real conviction, that the subject of my biography should have been shot. His father, it transpired, had fought in the Irish Civil War under Frank Aiken, and the son had preserved some of the hatreds of that time. On another occasion, following a stormy debate on the rights and wrongs of Irish intervention in the Spanish Civil War hosted by the University Philosophical Society in Trinity College Dublin, the secretary of the Phil told me that he had once asked a former leader of Fine Gael what he thought of his party's founding president. The former taoiseach had replied that he didn't really know much about the man, nor did his party. In their own way, both responses are indicative of how Eoin O'Duffy now tends to be remembered, or not remembered as the case may be. The reaction which I have most often encountered is derision.

Perhaps this is why, despite his remarkable career and his important role in the formative years of the Free State, it has taken so long for a biography to appear. In contrast to O'Duffy, most of the leading lights of revolutionary Ireland belonged to a political tradition or, at the very least, left behind a band of supporters who felt it necessary to defend their legacy regardless of how dubious that legacy might appear to others. Fighting about the past, after all, remains an important aspect of Irish politics, and popular interest in that past helps make Irish history a particularly interesting field of study. It was to be one of the many ironies of O'Duffy's life that someone who devoted so much time and effort to cultivating his own reputation would be remembered as one of the most egregious figures of modern Ireland.

This book may not alter O'Duffy's unfortunate reputation, but it does attempt to restore some complexity to the way in which he is understood and remembered. His life can be neatly divided into three acts: but for the final one, he would have been assured of an important legacy in Irish history as a patriot and state-builder. The first part of this book (Chapters 1–4) traces his gradual emergence, through the classic route of GAA activism, as one of the leaders of the republican movement. During the second phase of his career as

Garda commissioner between 1922 and 1933 (Chapters 5–7), O'Duffy played the role of reactionary rather than revolutionary. The final, tragic, act (Chapters 8–11)—which begins with his suitably dramatic dismissal from his post by his political nemesis Eamon de Valera—was characterized by fascism and failure.

However, this book charts the continuities as well as the changes. O'Duffy's narrative arc, in contrast to that of any half-decent dramatic hero, was not characterized by adversity, acquisition of self-knowledge, and eventual resolution. Although repackaged in various forms—including cultural nationalism, republicanism, and fascism—his ideas, motives, and behaviour varied little throughout his life. While he could easily (and reassuringly) be dismissed as a pathetically flawed figure, a third-rate demagogue who hung on to the coat-tails of Mussolini, Franco, and Hitler, it was the same person who was appointed chief of staff of the IRA, commissioner of the Garda Síochána, general officer commanding the National Army, leader of the political opposition, and spent most of his career basking in public approval.

Rather than dismissing him as an unrepresentative anomaly, this book argues that O'Duffy's acquisition of power and status was partly a consequence of his successful invention of a persona which reflected, if in a highly distorted and exaggerated form, the values of the society and times in which he lived. Ultimately, of course, this proved unsustainable, as do all projects built on myth and deception. Although the General is best known for his brief political career, this book devotes as much attention to cultural and psychological aspects of his life as to the political: like most of his generation, his revolutionary fervour was motivated more by a vision of a Catholic Gaelic nation than republican political thought. As a cultural zealot who exploited the forces around him with varying degrees of success, O'Duffy's *modus operandi* renders him a useful prism through which to explore some of the key themes of twentieth-century Irish history, including the importance of language, religion, sport, morality, sexuality, and identity in public and private life.

I have attempted to understand O'Duffy not only in the context of Monaghan, revolutionary Ireland, and its complex relationship with Britain but also the wider phenomena of inter-war fascism, international anti-communism, and the politics of fear. This biography has been informed by and, I hope, will add to our understanding of, the psychological attractions of nationalism, ethnic identity, and cultural insecurity, forces which remain potent factors in world history. Biographies of Irish patriots often—and sometimes even appropriately—focus on courage, self-sacrifice, and idealism.

These figure in O'Duffy's story but so, too, do more problematic issues which illuminate some of the darker aspects of a period characterized by violence and hatred as well as idealism and conviction. After all, can we really understand modern Ireland without considering such themes as invention, intolerance, hypocrisy, and the abuse of power?

F. McG.

Acknowledgements

I have accumulated many debts since setting out to write this book: first, as a lecturer at the Department of Modern History at Trinity College Dublin; then, as a recipient of an Irish Research Council for the Humanities and Social Sciences Government of Ireland post-doctoral research fellowship attached to the Department of History at NUI Maynooth; and, finally, during its completion as a member of the School of History at Queen's University in Belfast. I am grateful to my colleagues and students at each institution, particularly David Fitzpatrick, who has remained a source of advice and encouragement, and Vincent Comerford, whose support and kindness made my time at Maynooth so rewarding. Sean Connolly, David Hayton, and the late Martin Lynn have made me feel very welcome at Queen's. Martin, a mentor and friend, is greatly missed.

Patrick Maume, Enda Delaney, and Peter Hart generously took the time to read this book, improving it with many sharp insights and suggestions. They, and other friends and colleagues, including Mike Cronin, Terry Dooley, Diarmaid Ferriter, Brian Hanley, Liam Kennedy, Albert Moncusi, Querciolo Mazzonis, William Murphy, and Sean O'Connell, have been generous with their time and ideas over the past years. Giulia Cecere and Anne Klatt provided expert translation. Paul Bew, Richard English, and Roy Foster provided welcome advice and support. Nicholas Allen, Joost Augusteijn, Marie Coleman, Al Connolly, Tim Pat Coogan, Fred Corcoran, Anthony Cronin, Anne Dolan, Bishop Joseph Duffy of Clogher, Patrick Duffy, Sean Duffy, Brian Fallon, Patrick Long, Liam McEniffe, Uinseann MacEoin, Michael MacEvilly, Maurice Manning, Filipe Ribeiro de Meneses, Risteárd Mulcahy, Patrick Murray, Eunan O'Halpin, Margaret Ó hÓgartaigh, Des O'Rawe, Rob Stradling, and David Timmons suggested sources, responded to queries, or otherwise provided assistance.

I wish to thank the following institutions and their staffs for access to their collections and their professionalism: the Archivio Centrale dello Stato (Rome), the Archivio Storico Diplomatico del Ministero degli Affair Esteri (Rome), the Archivo General Militar (Ávila), the Archivos del Ministerio de Asuntos Exteriores (Madrid), the Cardinal Ó Fiaich Memorial Library and Archive (particularly Crónán Ó Doibhlin), the Garda Síochána Museum (particularly Inspector John Duffy), the Imperial War Museum, the Irish Military Archives (particularly Victor Laing), Monaghan County Museum (particularly Padraig Clerkin and Noel Breakey), the National Archives of Ireland (particularly Catriona Crowe), the National Archives (London), the National Library of Ireland (particularly Noel Kissane and Collette O'Flaherty), the Public Record Office of Northern Ireland, the main library and special collection libraries at Queen's University (particularly Deirdre Wildy), and the UCD Department of Archives (particularly Seamus Helferty). I would like to thank also Anne Gelling and Kay Rogers at Oxford University Press for all their help and Sally McCann for her excellent copy-editing.

My greatest debt is to Selina, my family, and my parents for their support. This book is dedicated to the memory of my grandmother, Moya Corcoran, who remained a great admirer of the General ever since their paths crossed at the Eucharistic Congress of 1932.

F. McG.

Belfast
July 2005

Contents

List of Plates   xiii
List of Abbreviations   xv

 1. Joy to my youth   1
 2. The best man in Ulster   25
 3. War to the death in Monaghan   47
 4. The coming man   74
 5. The flower of the young manhood of Ireland   115
 6. Preaching the gospel of national virility   141
 7. Red terror   170
 8. The Irish Mussolini   200
 9. Hoch O'Duffy!   234
10. The third greatest man in Europe   270
11. Ireland's Quisling   316

Epilogue   343
Notes   351
Select bibliography   412
Index   417

List of Plates

1 Pulling the strings: the first known photograph of O'Duffy with Monaghan's triumphant 1914 hurling team (© Monaghan County Museum).

2 O'Duffy flanked by Tom Ennis and Emmet Dalton, salutes as Free State forces enter Portobello Barracks in 1922 (© RTE Stills Library).

3 An intense-looking Commissioner O'Duffy with Garda headquarters staff including his cousin Patrick Walsh, c.1922 (courtesy of the National Library of Ireland).

4 The blessing of the force, c.1922 (courtesy of the National Library of Ireland).

5 Cruising: the General, looking dapper in customised formal wear, c.mid-1920s (courtesy of the National Library of Ireland).

6 One of many portraits to appear in the Garda periodical, c.mid-1920s (courtesy of the National Library of Ireland).

7 O'Duffy, with minister for justice Kevin O'Higgins, at the Phoenix Park depot, c.mid-1920s (© RTE Stills Library).

8 The General, surrounded by fellow Gaels, enjoys a GAA match, c.early 1930s (courtesy of the National Library of Ireland).

9 A sketch by the celebrated artist Seán Keating (courtesy of the trustees of the Keating estate). Another Keating portrait of the General resides in McKee Barracks.

10 O'Duffy, miscellaneous actors, and the Irish Olympic delegation at MGM studios in Hollywood, 1932 (courtesy of the National Library of Ireland).

11 The General toured the Middle East shortly after his removal by de Valera in 1933 (courtesy of the National Library of Ireland).

12 O'Duffy and followers give the raised-arm salute, c.1933 (courtesy of the National Library of Ireland).

13 The General addresses a Blueshirt meeting in County Cork, *c*.1934 (courtesy of *The Irish Examiner*).

14 O'Duffy addresses an audience from the balcony, *c*.1934 (courtesy of *The Irish Examiner*).

15 A Blueshirt parade in rural Cork, *c*.1934 (courtesy of *The Irish Examiner*).

16 O'Duffy poses with members of CAUR's 'fascist international' (including the leaders of the Austrian Heimwehr, Norwegian Nasjonal Samling, Romanian Iron Guard, and Spanish Falange).

17 On the circuit: O'Duffy, and other aspiring demagogues, sign autographs for admirers at a Blackshirt rally in the Netherlands, 1935 (courtesy of the National Library of Ireland).

18 The General poses in the uniform of the Irish Brigade, *c*.1937 (© Monaghan County Museum).

19 Putting on a brave face: the Irish Brigade leadership, 1937 (courtesy of the Public Record Office of Northern Ireland: D/1625/6). The General is seated between his second in command, NCP stalwart Dermot O'Sullivan and prominent Blueshirt Padraig Quinn. The sinister Tom Gunning is seated second from far left.

20 An ailing O'Duffy addresses the NACA, *c*.1943 (courtesy of the National Library of Ireland).

List of Abbreviations

Organisations, officials, and titles

AAA   Amateur Athletics Association (UK)
ACA   Army Comrades Association
AOH   Ancient Order of Hibernians
BUF   British Union of Fascists
CGS   Chief of the general staff, National Army
CI   County inspector
DD   *Dundalk Democrat*
EOD   Eoin O'Duffy
G2   Army intelligence directorate
GAA   Gaelic Athletic Association
GHQ   IRA General Headquarters
GOC   General officer commanding
IAAA   Irish Amateur Athletics Association
IAAAF   International Amateur Athletics Federation
IBA   Irish Brigade Association
IFG   Irish Friends of Germany
IG   Inspector general
IRA   Irish Republican Army
IRB   Irish Republican Brotherhood
NACA   National Athletic and Cycling Association
NCP   National Corporate Party
NDA   National Defence Association
NUI   National University of Ireland
O/C   Officer commanding
RIC   Royal Irish Constabulary
RUC   Royal Ulster Constabulary
TD   Teachta Dála [Dáil Éireann deputy]
UIL   United Irish League
YIA   Young Ireland Association

Archives and records

AB   Archivo de Burgos
AGMA CGG   Archivo General Militar (Ávila), cuartel general del
                Generalísimo
ASMAE   Archivio Storico Diplomatico del Ministero degli Affari
                Esteri (Rome)
BMH WS   Bureau of Military History witness statements
CO   Colonial office (London)
D/FA   Department of foreign affairs
DJ   Department of justice
DT   Department of the taoiseach
HO   Home office (London)
IWM SCW   Imperial War Museum, Spanish Civil War collection
MAE AB   Archivos del Ministerio de Asuntos Exteriores (Madrid),
                archivo de Burgos
MAI   Military Archives of Ireland
MCM   Monaghan County Museum
NAI   National Archives of Ireland
NLI   National Library of Ireland
ODP   O'Duffy papers
PRO   Public Record Office, London (now The National Archives)
PRONI HA   Public Record Office of Northern Ireland, home affairs
                series
UCDA   University College Dublin Archives
WO   War office (London)

1

Joy to my youth

There is no sweeter sound to the ear of an Irish-Irelander than that of the hard-clipping hurley, or the swift step of the Gaelic footballer in pursuit of the game.[1]

OWEN Duffy, who would become better known as Eoin O'Duffy, was born in Cargaghdoo, near Castleblayney, in County Monaghan on 28 January 1890. Cargaghdoo, known locally as 'the Horseshoe', was an impoverished rural townland of less than one hundred people, one-third of whom were illiterate. Most of its inhabitants belonged to three extended families: the Meegans, Walshs, and Duffys; the latter, interrelated, families combined in feuds against the Meegans, regarded as interlopers from Connaught.[2] Eoin's father, also Owen Duffy, was a subsistence farmer who eked a living from 15 acres of boggy land that he had inherited from his father, Big Peter, in 1888.[3] He and his wife, Bridget Fealy, who grew up and died in the same part of Monaghan, had seven children: Peter, James, Alice, Mary, Red Frank, Black Pat, and, the youngest, Owen. They were known locally as the Peadar Mores, after the original Big Peter, and given nicknames according to the hue of their hair to distinguish them from the many surrounding Duffys.

The family background was typical of late nineteenth-century Monaghan, a predominantly rural county where the great majority of inhabitants lived off the land. Three-fifths of the county's farmers, including Owen Duffy, lived on holdings with a rateable value of less than 15 pounds: outside Connaught, only five counties had higher rates of rural poverty. Emigration was high. More people had left Monaghan between 1851 and 1901 than lived there in 1911. Castleblayney rural district, where the Duffys lived, had the highest emigration rate in the county. Aside from its poverty, Monaghan was distinguished by its position on the country's religious borderlands where the Catholic south gave way to Protestant-dominated Ulster. Three-quarters of its population of 71,000 were Catholic. The remainder were Presbyterians and Church of Ireland Protestants, the latter comprising a smaller landed élite. Monaghan's religious minority dominated the administrative, professional, and commercial life of the county although, after the local government reforms of 1898, every clerical and professional position in the patronage of the country council was soon in Catholic hands.[4]

Aside from trade and employment, there was little interaction between Catholics and Protestants, who attended different schools, joined different societies, and voted for rival parties. In some parts of the county, such as the Protestant village of Drum, a more thorough form of segregation existed. The sectarianism which constituted such an inescapable fact of life of O'Duffy's youth had been widespread since the late eighteenth century in south Ulster 'where, almost uniquely, Catholics and Protestants both constituted significant elements within the population'.[5] Local Catholics believed that 'Unionists always considered themselves to be superior people. They had been superior since the Plantations and they were determined to hold on to that superiority. The other inhabitants of the island, in their view, were an inferior sort of race, not to be trusted with any responsibility. They were simply the Paddy MacMahons and the Hughie Duffys while the Unionists were known as the Mr Boyds and Mr Wilsons.'[6] Conversely, Protestants perceived themselves as the victims of discrimination: 'Whenever a place is going to which a salary is attached...the principle acted upon is that no Unionist need apply.'[7] The sectarianism of Monaghan society, which intensified during the third Home Rule crisis of 1912–14, would exert considerable influence on O'Duffy's political outlook.

Local politics reflected these sectarian factors—Catholic nationalists dominated the county's local bodies after 1898 and elected both its MPs—as well as the social hierarchy of the time. Monaghan's Catholic MPs came from its tiny number of professionals rather than its more numerous commercial, farming, and labouring classes. Most Catholics, regardless of class, gave their allegiance to one of the Irish Parliamentary Party's grassroots organizations, the United Irish League (UIL) or the Ancient Order of Hibernians (AOH). After 1908 a small minority supported Arthur Griffith's more nationalist Sinn Féin party, but the county's large Protestant minority served to discourage nationalist disunity at elections. Sectarian tensions were also reflected by the high level of political mobilization in Monaghan.[8] The 5,000 strong membership of the UIL represented over twice the national average, while only two counties (neighbouring Cavan and Leitrim) had a higher per capita membership in 1913.[9] In addition, there were over 2,000 Hibernians in 46 lodges by 1916.[10] A Catholic fraternity with many similarities to the Orange Order (including its sashes, bands, parades, and predominantly Ulster membership), the 'Hibs' functioned as a constituency organization for the Irish Party, an 'approved society' which administered national insurance, and a defender of Catholic interests. In theory, the UIL and AOH co-operated in the interests of John Redmond's Irish Party; in practice, they clashed over such issues as the selection of candidates for general elections. Both organizations flourished in the decade before 1916. The strengthening of cultural nationalism in this period was also demonstrated by the growth of the Gaelic Athletic Association (GAA) and the Gaelic League.

In Monaghan, as elsewhere, nationalist politics were dominated by the Irish Party. Such was its dominance, no parliamentary seat was contested in the county between 1895 and 1910.[11] But, underlying the party's superficial hegemony, local politics in Monaghan were complex and fragmented. There was a strong tradition of nationalist factionalism, attested to by John McKean's victory over the Redmondite candidate in 1910, a result which provoked parades, jubilation, and riots. Many of his supporters, it was believed, were among the first to support Sinn Féin after 1916.[12] Local loyalties, family traditions, and long-standing grievances were as important electoral factors as political policies. As one man recalled: 'Old people used to say to my mother "Such a person was a Fenian, such a person was a land leaguer or such a person was a Castle hack" . . . The people marked out as Fenians included the Go McDermotts, the Stack Finnegans and the Stud Martins.'[13] But in the Duffy household, as on most farms, the order of business for discussion was 'births, deaths, marriages, the weather, the crops and . . . Home Rule'.[14] His family's politics, if any, are unknown but O'Duffy once claimed to have been a Hibernian in his youth.[15]

Aside from the bare details which can be gleaned from state records such as the census, little is known about O'Duffy's childhood or his family history, a fact which is in itself revealing of his humble background. He came from a class, and a place, where people lived in relative poverty, leaving behind few records of their existence. The only substantial source for his childhood is his unpublished autobiography, which, although self-serving and unreliable, provides some interesting details and useful clues to his self-image. His folksy reminiscences depict the traditional poor but happy childhood: 'God did give joy to my youth. I had enough of eating, enough of laughing and dancing and singing. If I had a sorrow here and there, a head sore from a cuff, muscles sore almost beyond bearing with farm work that seemed too great, well, I have been none the worse of it since.'[16] One of his earliest responsibilities was to bring his mother to town on the 'ass-cart' on market day: 'when she sold her eggs, butter and chickens, and went to buy the week's groceries I stabled the ass, and toddled off to listen to everything and peer at everything in the town'.[17]

He was raised in a pious household, an austere and impoverished environment much like that evoked in the writings of the Monaghan poet Patrick Kavanagh, where social standing was 'measured in terms of high-crop-yields, pre-marital chastity, and regular attendance at Mass and confession'.[18] In his memoir, O'Duffy described a peasant Catholic tradition of devotional rituals dating back to pagan customs and moral certainties which would exert a lifelong influence: 'When my father came ceremoniously on the ploughed lea at the dawn of a fine Spring day, a spotless white sheet arranged about him to sow the corn, it was my job to carry the seed to him, after it had been sprinkled with holy water.' The Rosary was said nightly without fail: 'many a cuffing, often quite undeserved, I was given for creating distractions'.[19] Among other arcane customs, red tape was tied to the tails of cows and, on May Day, flowers strewn at the byre door 'to dissuade anyone with the evil eye from taking the butter off the milk'. The biennial two-week mission at Lough Egish was a much-anticipated event:

Every Catholic in the parish 'made' the mission—the aged and sick being visited by the missioners in their own homes. Sometimes Protestants went to hear the sermon at the 'close', which was usually preached out in the open because of the huge crowds. Many of us too attended the missions at Broomfield...which were conducted by the Redemptorist Fathers from Dundalk. The Redemptorists were great at telling terrifying stories, and were unequalled in striking the fear of God into our hearts.[20]

Weddings, dances, and wakes provided the main diversions from the monotony of rural life. Except where death had been exceptionally violent or sudden, young people travelled to wakes from miles around: 'Songs, tricks and all sorts of simple harmless amusements were introduced. The relatives would not of course participate, but neither would they offer any objection. Nobody liked a dull wake. A "king" was chosen, usually some local "wit", and it was his duty to see that everyone was pleased. He was assisted by two attendants, and if his comic instructions were not obeyed they would use their belt to chastise the timid.'[21] Weddings were even more raucous, particularly when uninvited neighbours organized a 'kettling' for the married couple, who 'would find the house surrounded by boys and girls from far and near, who would "serenade" them with songs, music, hornblowing and yelling for hours'.[22] A less good-humoured form of kettling was directed at families who occupied 'evicted farms': 'Hornblowing was only part of what they suffered. They never came of course to wakes or kaileys or dances. None of their neighbours spoke to them, none would buy or sell with them, lend them a box barrow or a pitch fork . . . When we walked up the road past a grabber's house we kept our faces averted; we would not show so much friendliness as even to glance at his gate.'[23] Rural life was also enlivened, if not excessively, by barn dances: 'Often too there would be a "join"—everyone giving sixpence—to purchase a quarter cask of porter for the men, and soft drinks (cordial) for the youngsters. Nobody got more than one jug of stout, and there was no intoxication.'[24] Many of the customs related by O'Duffy, such as the fife and drum parades and 'wee bonfire night' and 'big bonfire night' when dances were held at the crossroads, resembled those of the local Protestant community. In later life, O'Duffy would contrast the wholesome simplicity of his idyllic, and idealized, childhood with the racier temptations of post-war Ireland.

O'Duffy attended the nearby Laggan national school, graduating to the more highly regarded school in Laragh, where he developed an interest in Irish culture. Gaelic language and folklore, increasingly the preserve of the older generation, had long been in decline in Monaghan. Although—like most people in Cargaghdoo—his family did not speak Irish, O'Duffy began attending the Gaelic League's night classes, improving his knowledge by visiting the homes of native speakers in Farney.[25] He claimed that it was through reading poetry in school that he was first drawn into 'the current of national thought' and, belying his subsequent image as a Monaghan bruiser, recollected 'a time when I felt myself fast becoming a member of the literary set'.[26] He kept a diary from an early age, and claimed to have won prizes for the stories which he sent to the *Weekly Freeman*'s 'Uncle Remus club'. His education was also put to use at home: 'Every Saturday night I read to the neighbours as they sat around my father's hearth in a pleasant haze of tobacco and turf smoke the full reports in our local paper the "Democrat" of important business transacted in important style by the 'Blayney Board of Guardians, and, of course, the proceedings in the local Petty Sessions Court.'[27] After coaching from an elderly 'will-drawer', O'Duffy took over his duties. He also wrote his neighbours' letters to America: 'the news was given in the following exact order:—weddings, christenings, deaths, the weather, the crops, the cattle, and then any special items such as the arrival of a new Curate'.[28]

O'Duffy's bucolic reminiscences are interspersed with occasional but unmistakable hints of a less happy childhood. He grew up in poverty on a 'one-horse farm': 'The produce raised on it by the incessant toil of my father and all of us, was not sufficient to keep clothing upon us, and food in our stomachs, as well as pay the rent to Stockdale, and the rates to Scott, who called with clock-like regularity.'[29] With a rateable annual valuation of 7 pounds, the farm was insufficient for the family's needs. His father and brothers farmed conacre land—small patches of land rented in return for labour—and worked on the roads to make ends meet.[30] Born eight years after his closest sibling, O'Duffy was raised like an only child, forming a close attachment to his mother, who, he admitted, spoiled him: 'I spent the first four years in the Irish country boy's traditional petticoats. I still remember the uneasy feeling I had when my first trousers arrived from town...I did not understand then either why mother was so strangely unenthusiastic, even unhappy, looking at this evidence of my advance from childhood days to full boyhood.'[31] Given this close bond, he was devastated by her slow death from cancer. The rest of his family being otherwise occupied, it fell to him to nurse her through her illness: 'Mine was the task of keeping the turf ablaze in her room, and of bringing her what little food she would have. Slowly though, the smile she had for me as I strutted about my sick-room duties grew fainter, her eyes more tired.' Alone, aged only 12, he witnessed her death, even signing the death certificate.[32] The impact of the loss of his mother, whose ring he would wear for the remainder of his life, was deepened by his father's lack of affection: 'While mother lived father appeared to take but little interest in my existence. The other members of the family being much older brought in a little money and were regarded as assets, but I was a liability.'

After her death, his father took a 'rough but kindly' interest (possibly more the former than the latter given his minimal contact with the male members of his family after leaving home).[33] His brother Peter died shortly after emigrating to the Unites States, while Red Frank and Jim 'stole away' to Glasgow. Black Pat, who inherited the family small-holding, was the only other son to remain in Ireland.[34] O'Duffy struggled at school due to a severe stammer: 'I had become so sensitive that I sought to keep silent in the background...I eventually conquered the painful stuttering that was wont to make me grow red-faced while the less kindly of my schoolmates hid their grins with difficulty.'[35] An unpublished biography, written by O'Duffy's acolyte, Liam Walsh, also conveys the impression of an unhappy childhood:

A taciturn boy, or youth as he now was, he was shy and lonely; yet he was fired with ambition even in those early days, and worked hard to fulfil his determination to excel in everything he undertook. He never liked to be beaten, and one might nearly say he was not too punctilious in his means of outmanoeuvring anything that savoured of opposition...He was always a serious lad with a remarkable memory, a characteristic which so marked him in later years.[36]

As was often the case with the youngest sibling in rural families, O'Duffy was encouraged to remain in school by his father and parish priest in order to pursue a career as a teacher, one of the more prestigious occupations open to someone of his background. In 1909 he sat the king's scholarship examination for St Patrick's college in Drumcondra, securing a place in the second of its three divisions.[37] However, because the restricted number of openings for teachers meant that a place was not assured that year, he successfully applied for a clerkship in the county surveyor's office in Monaghan town.[38] His new job brought him into contact with local politics, in particular two prominent nationalists who would exert a benign influence on his early career. Thomas Toal, whom O'Duffy greatly admired, served as county council chairman for forty-four years. He was a supporter of the Gaelic League, the Gaelic Athletic Association, the Irish Party, and, in later years, Sinn Féin and Fine Gael. The county manager, Denis Carolan Rushe, an enthusiastic Gael and local historian, encouraged O'Duffy during his early days with the council and later sheltered him when on the run.[39]

The position, paying 1 pound per week, was a comfortable one: 'I considered myself well able to afford luxurious lodgings and I fear I aroused some little envy by putting up at the Provincial Hotel owned by an old friend of the family.'[40] O'Duffy soon mastered the rudiments of surveying, proving himself 'a highly efficient young fellow' in the eyes of the council. In 1910 he decided to pursue a career as a surveyor. A great believer in self-improvement, he studied by night to qualify as an assistant surveyor, coming fifth in the national local government board examination in 1912. When a vacancy arose in Clones and Cootehill rural district, O'Duffy, backed by a testimonial from Dr McKenna, bishop of Clogher, was appointed.[41] A local councillor recollected the occasion:

O'Duffy was a clerk, not a qualified engineer. The pick of the clerks became assistant engineer, or surveyor. I was in my shop at home. This young fellow arrived on a bicycle with knickerbockers and cap, on a summer day and introduced himself as O'Duffy. 'I want your vote, I'm going for the job of assistant surveyor. I can't get a proposer. I know if I get a proposer I will get it. None of the men below, even Toal will propose me. You being married to a parishioner of my own might support me.' I proposed him and he got it.[42]

He later secured the additional post of engineer, increasing his wages to over 100 pounds.[43] O'Duffy was a capable, hard-working, and ambitious young man. He enjoyed his work, taking pride in the condition of his roads and his refusal of the offers of braces of grouse and brown envelopes from local con-tractors which then, as in more recent times, secured preferment for council contracts: ' "A little present for the lad-een" one of those benevolent people would call it. Bottles of the "home brew" were offered to me, for poteen was made on a fairly large scale in the area. As I was a prefect in the Pioneer Total Abstinence Association, the poteen had no great allure.'[44] The bribery attempts stopped, O'Duffy claimed, after he shamed the worst offenders at a public meeting.

One of the truest Gaels in Ireland

In 1912 O'Duffy moved to Newbliss to take up his new position. He spent the next decade living in Newbliss and nearby Clones, forming a stronger attachment to this part of Monaghan than his own. His recollection of happy years as a boarder 'under the watchful eyes and loving care' of the Tummon family suggests that he found a happier home life than the one he left behind.[45] Clones, a market town of 2,400 people, was situated in west Monaghan's drumlin belt, a short distance from the Fermanagh border. It was an important junction on the Great Northern Railway, the point where the Dundalk to Omagh and Belfast to Cavan lines intersected. Although some pockets of squalor existed, Clones was moderately prosperous. In terms of property and influence, the town—which had witnessed sectarian rioting in the nineteenth century—remained a Protestant stronghold. Given some of the events which would follow, it is worth noting that Clones lay within a part of Ulster characterized by long-standing sectarian tensions. Nearby Rosslea, for example, had witnessed an infamous clash between Land Leaguers and Orangemen in 1883, and the wealthy Protestant families of the area, such as the Saundersons and the Ernes of Crom Castle, had produced some of Irish Unionism's leading politicians. During the revolutionary period, Clones would be scarred not only by sectarian violence but partition, which saw the town lose most of its natural hinterland. Five of the eight roads leading from Clones ran immediately into Northern Ireland.[46]

It was also in Clones that O'Duffy renewed his childhood involvement in the Gaelic League and, although far from fluent, began teaching beginners' Irish classes. Founded in 1893, the League was devoted to the revival of Gaelic, which it sought to achieve through its incorporation in the national curriculum and by promoting classes and other social events. Some nationalists initially regarded its arrival in Monaghan in 1895 with suspicion. One leading organizer was accused of being 'a spy from Dublin Castle', while many locals, with peasant pragmatism, felt Irish was 'nearly done away with' and that 'one language was enough for them'.[47] After the local bishop was won round, however, the League soon became sufficiently well established to organize the local *feiseanna* and *aeridheacht*, which O'Duffy had attended as a child. Local children competed for prizes, submitting essays on such subjects as the 'Best collection of Irish surnames in use' or 'The best list of Irish words in common use in English'.[48] It was at these functions that O'Duffy first saw such figures as Patrick Pearse, Alice Milligan, and Eoin MacNeill, who were at the forefront of the revival of cultural nationalism and, in later years, separatism.

By promoting Irish, the League sought to strengthen national identity or, as Douglas Hyde famously put it, de-anglicize the Irish people. Despite declaring itself non-political, the League attracted the interest of advanced nationalists as well as cultural enthusiasts. Its supporters in Monaghan—priests, teachers, and professionals prominent among them—included Home Rulers, Sinn Féiners, and Fenians. Opinions differ as to its politics. One local claimed that 'Religion or politics had nothing to do with membership. The Protestants learned Irish in Lossetts school and competed at the Feis.'[49] A local historian, however, stated that 'local Protestants kept out of the movement and they ignored the feiseanna'.[50] The League's ethos did not appeal to many Protestants. After failing to establish a branch in Castleblayney, one disappointed organizer recorded that patriotism was 'at a very low ebb among the men and women of this little West British town'.[51] So far as O'Duffy was concerned, 'Gaelic League classes in those days meant not only learning the language but practising Irish patriotism. We all vowed to encourage Irish, and nobody would risk the scorn of his classmates by turning up in clothes made outside Ireland instead of in good Irish tweeds, by riding a bicycle other than a Pierce or a Lucania. Few of us smoked, but those who did only used Irish made cigarettes.'[52]

Although the League introduced O'Duffy to a burgeoning cultural nationalist ethos, he makes no great claims to any incipient separatist outlook in his autobiography. Along with his family and neighbours, he 'laughed heartily at the songs and skits against the R.I.C. which were always a popular feature' at local *ceilidhthe*: 'The RIC we felt were representative of this oppression our age-old nation was suffering...they were the tools of tyranny.' He described their 'fiercely pro-Boer' enthusiasm—'Paul Krueger had all our admiration'—during the war in South Africa, an event which many of his generation recalled as central to the emergence of a more radical nationalism. But, as for many people, the allure of the Gaelic League was more social than political: 'none of us would indulge in foreign rag-time at all. We had merry Irish music, cheerful Irish songs. As I recollect it, the Gaelic League class was the brightest institution in the country.'[53] O'Duffy was no different from the other 'energetic and moderately successful men whose careers provided inadequate scope for their talents and ambitions' in pre-independence Ireland.[54] His experiences support the view that the cultural revival was driven by the large body of educated lower middle class men and women whose social and economic aspirations were stifled under British rule.[55]

The League formed part of a wider revival of cultural nationalism which embraced literature, music, dancing, and sports. It was the latter which increasingly provided the focus of O'Duffy's interests. In 1910, shortly after his appointment to the county surveyor's office, he joined the Harps' Gaelic football club. Despite going on to play a prominent role in Irish sports, O'Duffy rarely participated in them: 'I kicked football as a boy on McKean's Meadow with my schoolmates at Laragh, but I was bigger than I was skilful ... the comradeship I enjoyed was off the field rather than on it. Only once was I given a place on a team, and then it was because someone else had failed them at the last moment.'[56] Notwithstanding his lack of sporting prowess, O'Duffy was attracted by the social and cultural aspects of an organization which offered a young man in a new town opportunities for friendship, respectability, and social advancement. Later in life, he would reflect that it was in 'these years in Newbliss and Clones I made the staunchest friends I have—among my Councils, my road staffs, in the Gaelic League, in the Gaelic Athletic Association, and later in the Irish Volunteers.'[57]

Like many Gaels who graduated to separatism, O'Duffy would later depict his cultural activism as the first step on his revolutionary career. As Cahir Healy put it: 'He saw more clearly than most of us the real ideals that lay behind the work he was propagating. Ireland and her independence was the hidden goal to which all roads led.'[58] O'Duffy's career would appear to reinforce the view, one subsequently endorsed by nationalists and Gaels, that the cultural revival precipitated the emergence of separatism. As *The War of Independence in Monaghan*—an orthodox nationalist account—put it:

Independence had gone first, then the land, then the language. By 1900 the Irish way of life was doomed. All things English were being accepted without question as superior while the Irish 'province' quickly began to sport itself with English games, amuse itself in English music-halls, delight itself with English songs and pride itself in British victories. The people had forgotten ... its glorious past and looked forward hopefully to a happy future under Home Rule. The slave was glad to be conceded the rights of being a serf again.[59]

Against this rising tide of apathetic anglicization, the Irish Ireland movement infused O'Duffy's generation with patriotism. This new sense of Irish identity

undermined the Irish Party's moderate nationalism, paving the way for the rise
of republicanism: 'The spirit of the nation was slowly fanned back to
life...Gradually this distinctiveness sought political expression.'[60] In recent
decades this mechanistic interpretation has given way to a more complex
analysis of the period between the fall of Parnell and the Easter Rising, which
places greater emphasis on the resilience of the constitutional nationalist tradition until the radicalizing impact of the Ulster Volunteers, the threat of partition, and the Great War.[61] Nonetheless, the relationship between the Gaelic
revival and the new nationalism—although more complex than many Gaels
would allow—remains important, as is demonstrated by the inextricable link
between O'Duffy's revolutionary career and his GAA activism.

The GAA was founded in 1884 by a seven-member committee, which
included four Fenians. In the period in which O'Duffy joined, the Irish
Republican Brotherhood (IRB) retained considerable influence within the
movement, which offered it the same sort of opportunities as the Gaelic
League. However, the emergence of the GAA also reflected a wider international phenomenon whereby sport, previously 'regulated by regional custom,
haphazardly organised and locally focussed', became 'codified, centrally
administered, and organised on a national basis'.[62] By 1908, 800 clubs had been
established throughout Ireland and, although most Gaels joined to play sports
rather than make a political statement, the GAA began to exert an important
influence by popularizing a nationalist ethos which was militantly anglophobic
if not explicitly revolutionary.[63]

This ethos was illustrated by its ban on the playing, or even watching, of
English sports such as association football, and the exclusion of Crown forces
from its membership. But, although the GAA strengthened the identification
of Irish nationalism with Catholicism and anglophobia, it was a cultural rather
than a political movement: 'to see it as a nursery of revolutionaries is to stretch
a point very far'.[64] Like the Gaelic League, it reflected Irish society more than
it shaped it. Pre-war nationalist politics continued to be dominated by the Irish
Party, which assimilated the cultural rhetoric of Irish Ireland in the same way
that it had subsumed potential challenges from the AOH and UIL.[65] Nonetheless, the ideology of cultural nationalism strengthened a potentially revolutionary spirit, and the complex relationship between cultural identity, nationalism, and the shaping of separatist mentalities is illustrated by O'Duffy's
journey from Gael to guerrilla.[66] The non-ideological aspects of the GAA for
future revolutionaries would also prove important. The GAA provided a
network of like-minded people through which ideas could be disseminated,
contacts made, and support mobilized, serving 'not only as a recruiting

ground...but as an apprenticeship for national organisers'.[67] O'Duffy's apprenticeship would lay the foundation for his emergence at the head of the republican movement in Monaghan.

O'Duffy recalled that his career in sports administration 'began rather surprisingly. When I arrived at Greenan's Cross on 21st September, 1912, to conduct my Irish class and ceilidhe there, I was informed by the County Board's chairman, the late Patrick Whelan, that earlier in the day I had been appointed honorary secretary of the Board.'[68] The county board had gone through several secretaries in the previous year. It was an onerous post which involved affiliating teams to the county board, arranging fixtures, and settling endless rows about disputed results, biased referees, poached players, and unpaid fines. O'Duffy proved so successful that he was appointed secretary of the GAA's Ulster provincial council two months later, following Whelan's recommendation of him as 'an Irish speaker, an ardent supporter of the GAA and ... most energetic young man'.[69] O'Duffy accepted the post, promising 'to do his best to keep the flag of the Gael flying in the province of Ulaid'. The separatist *Gaelic Athlete* was soon lauding him as 'the life of the game not only in Monaghan, but all over Ulster', while the *Dundalk Democrat* considered him 'one of the truest Gaels in Ireland'.[70]

O'Duffy earned his reputation as 'a gifted and dynamic organiser' by tackling the organizational and financial disarray within the GAA in Monaghan.[71] His approach is illustrated by his annual report for 1913, which announced the affiliation of eighteen new clubs and proposed numerous improvements for running the county leagues, increasing revenue, appointing impartial selectors, and reducing the number of delayed games which did much to deter spectators. He even donated his expenses to offset the county board's deficit, a characteristic example of the generosity with which he threw himself into his work, before modestly concluding that his 'lengthy epistle has already tired your patience, but my desire to see our county take a high place in the ranks of the GAA is my apology for trespassing this far'. In response, the chairman 'said he had put all other athletes in the shade; he was a model for them all. Although their junior he was showing most of them the way.' O'Duffy declined re-nomination, but was eventually persuaded to remain, prompting the press to enthuse that 'a more capable or more enthusiastic Gael does not exist'.[72]

He proved an equally successful provincial secretary. His 'very elaborate report' to the Ulster convention the following week outlined 'a year of unparalleled success', evidenced by an increase in affiliated clubs from 63 to 96. By 1914, the figure had reached 111, while Monaghan won both the hurling and football provincial championships, an achievement O'Duffy attributed to the new unity within the county organization:

I always believed that if Monaghan presented a united and determined front we would be hard to beat, and when we met Louth at Dundalk in the All Ireland semi-final I felt the dawn had come. Monaghan's brilliant display on that occasion delighted everyone who witnessed it—every player selected took the field, interior jealousies and dividing lines vanished, and a spirit of enthusiasm and true sportsmanship prevailed . . . Discipline, harmony and good fellowship were the prevailing features from that forward, and the team took the field on every occasion since exactly as selected.[73]

This was an allusion to the reforms which he had introduced in the selection of the county team. Previous selection committees had been haphazardly appointed, allowing the stronger clubs to stack the county team with their own players while lesser ones boycotted it.

O'Duffy's assertiveness in promoting Gaelic sports was also demonstrated by his 1914 report. Complaining that 'the game of the foreigner is promoted to the exclusion of our native pastimes' in the diocesan seminary, he suggested a deputation to Bishop McKenna: 'I am sure the students themselves, being sons of Gaels as they are, will co-operate . . . we should leave no stone unturned in the matter, and if we fail the public can judge for themselves.' O'Duffy received fulsome praise for his efforts: 'He certainly made matters hum . . . not alone in Monaghan but throughout Ulster . . . His relentless energies and self-sacrifice in the cause were worthy of anything they could do for him.'[74] His resignation as county secretary in 1914 was much regretted:

Those of us who follow Gaelic football know the hopeless and disorganised state Monaghan was in when Mr. O'Duffy took up the secretaryship . . . That Monaghan are Champions of Ulster is due solely to the untiring and indefatigable efforts of Mr. O'Duffy. He saw that the best men in the county were selected without fear or favour, and when selected he ensured they travelled, and he travelled with them. Wherever our County team was engaged, there was the Secretary encouraging them to victory.[75]

The local press agreed that the 'the principal credit for Monaghan's advancement is due to his untiring work and energy. A Gael out and out, Mr. O'Duffy was the heart and soul of the GAA in Monaghan.'[76] His acceptance of the position of vice-chairman allowed the plaudits to continue: 'Mr O'Duffy came on the scene at a time when the GAA was at a very low ebb in Monaghan, but the martial instinct of the indomitable and unconquerable Gael was strong in his soul, and by his resistless energy he had taken a noteworthy part in placing Monaghan in the vanguard of Ulster Gaeldom.' Another board member agreed that 'O'Duffy was a Gael of unflinching courage, and with it he fired his followers to an enthusiasm that was invincible.'[77]

Such martial rhetoric is striking, given O'Duffy's later activism. There were certainly similarities between O'Duffy's roles in the GAA and IRA, both of which involved constant travelling, organizing, encouraging activity where little existed, promoting co-operation between rival parishes, and mediating local disputes. It was an immense advantage to O'Duffy in his latter role that he knew, and was known to, the young Gaels of Ulster. There were similarities also between descriptions of the young GAA organizer and the later revolutionary. His admirers emphasized his energy, organizational abilities, and commitment. He devoted a remarkable amount of his time to the cause, travelling widely and rarely missing a meeting. He was generous in his support, donating, for example, the O'Duffy silver cup for the provincial junior championship.[78] But the weaknesses for which he was later criticized were also present. He was over-sensitive to 'fault finding in the Press', and incapable of allowing a perceived slight to pass (a characteristic Richard Mulcahy described as his 'primadonnism'). On one occasion, for example, he declared that a letter by 'Gael' critical of the county board should have been signed 'Traitor'.[79] On another, he rounded on his ungrateful players: 'the county team was spoiled by him, who put himself to much inconvenience to make travelling easy for them and paid expenses out of pocket that he wouldn't get back on many occasions for six months. He wouldn't guarantee they would be spoiled by him any more.'[80] Such sensitivity, verging on petulance, was something of a handicap in Monaghan's GAA circles, where relatively trivial disputes could provoke bitter personal abuse, often focusing on one's west British proclivities.

O'Duffy combined tireless devotion to his causes with a less attractive domineering tendency. Although widely lauded for his efforts, his overbearing influence alienated some. This, coupled with an element of what Liam Walsh described as his 'boyish unscrupulousness', led to unfortunate confrontations such as his intervention in the Toal cup final in 1916, when his home team, Clones, lost to Clontibret. Deciding that the referee had prematurely ended the game, O'Duffy refused to present the cup to the winning captain and rescheduled a replay closer to Clones.[81] A more serious incident occurred in 1915, when Cavan beat Monaghan by a single point in the Ulster final. After Monaghan supporters complained about the encroachment of spectators on the pitch and the disallowal of a goal by the Cavan umpires, O'Duffy demanded that the result be overturned.[82] Cavan denied any wrongdoing but its failure to send a representative to the subsequent Ulster council meeting allowed Patrick Whelan, the Ulster council president (and head of the Monaghan county board), to approve

O'Duffy's request.[83] The GAA central council later overruled the decision, a rare display of central power which reflected the scale of O'Duffy's stroke. The controversy was still rumbling in 1917, when Cavan threatened to leave the Ulster council on the grounds of its domination by O'Duffy and Whelan.[84]

O'Duffy's utilitarian views on the relationship between sport and nationalism also provide an early indication of his drift towards cultural chauvinism. He was one of the most uncompromising defenders of the ban on 'foreign' games, a stance he justified on patriotic grounds: 'The bulk of the opposition to the GAA has been so far that nobody has a right to dictate what games others should play. The Association, of course, does not dictate. It seeks to aid Irish youth in playing national games in preference to games which because of alien origin and atmosphere tend to injure their proper sense of nationality.'[85] Believing that English sports were deliberately fostered as part of a process of anglicization—'the object being, of course, to shatter our individuality and to blend us in the Empire'— O'Duffy viewed the GAA as 'an integral barrier against the processes of paganism and denationalisation'.[86] He was an outspoken opponent of the Irish Amateur Athletics Association, whose members he regarded as 'sycophants of the Crown'.[87] Such views were not unusual within the GAA, which had been established partly due to a fear of declining national identity. Its first patron, Archbishop Croke, had famously lamented the debilitating effects of England and her 'fashions, her accents, her vicious literature, her music, her dances, and her mannerisms, her games also, and her pastimes'. This 'potent identification of foreignness with immorality' formed an important aspect of O'Duffy's mentality.[88]

Such exclusivism should be seen in the context of 'generations of English and Anglo-Irish condescension towards "priest-ridden", "backward" Ireland'.[89] The relationship between the denigration of rival sporting codes and cultural insecurity was illustrated by the county board's description of association football clubs as 'the nation-killing enclaves patronised by the adherents of society imitation', and its determination to break through the 'shoneen lines' of 'West Britonism'.[90] Although O'Duffy resented the accusation that his stance was motivated by bigotry, the ban reinforced sectarianism.[91] The discovery of a soccer match between Protestant grammar school pupils and Catholic children in Carrickmacross, for example, was denounced as 'a terrible disgrace to our Gaelic movement'.[92] When O'Duffy learned that a county player had participated in the game, he withheld his Ulster championship medal as punishment for disgracing his team 'by playing the foreign abomination'.[93] The ban was an important device in the construction of an exclusivist nationalist consciousness, a definition of Irishness entailing much narrower cultural, linguistic, and religious criteria than previous definitions of national identity.[94] Like the cultural nationalist movement itself, the ban reflected a process of invention more than revival. As R. V. Comerford has observed: 'Tennis and cricket were no more foreign than tea-drinking, train engines, [or] rosary beads . . . Definition of the Nation by selective rejection is one of the key ways in which nationalists (as also their opponents) contribute to nation-invention.'[95]

Notwithstanding his lifelong criticism of the politicization of sport, O'Duffy's interest in sport was inherently political. Throughout his life, he used the term 'non-political' in the narrowest possible sense, meaning something not identified with a specific party as opposed to a national movement or ideology:

> politics and nationality are different. The GAA is non-political, although a great National Organisation, formed to preserve and cultivate our national pastimes, to lift up the youth of the country from the pit of moral and national degradation into which it had fallen, to recover our lost individuality, and to make our young men more thoroughly and essentially Irish and self-respecting and to have athleticism and patriotism inseparably associated.[96]

The corollary of O'Duffy's belief that the GAA represented 'a complete breakwater against a tide of apathy and anti-nationalism in Ireland's athletic affairs' was his tendency to equate indifference to Gaelic sports with opposition to nationalism: 'Sooner or later, people who disparage or are apathetic to our national games, to our dances, music and language, will shed the veneer—no matter how important they may seem in the national life.'[97]

Gaelic sports fulfilled many useful functions for nationalists. By providing a tangible link to the past, even an invented one, cultural nationalism sated a pressing psychological need in the post-famine era of dislocation and modernization—a period involving rapid social change which contemporaries often viewed as anglicization—and by doing so helped to legitimize contemporary nationalism.[98] O'Duffy shared this need for cultural authenticity, solemnly tracing the lineage of the 'games that are anciently and utterly Irish' from Lugaw of the Long Arm in 3000 BC, through Queen Tailte, the Firbolgs, and the *ard-fheis* at Tara to the ancient kings of Ireland, who were famed 'for their dexterity in wielding the caman'.[99] He resented the suggestion that the revival of Gaelic sports owed anything to the popularity of association football and rugby: 'Some people imagine that England is the home of football and that the present Gaelic game is an offspring of Soccer. Nothing could be farther from the truth. There are records to prove that football is of Celtic origin and that the present Soccer game is only that particular style adopted by England

and her garrison in this country. There was football played in Galway in 1527, and the first record we have of the game being played in England was nearly 150 years later.'[100] He speculated that William Webb Ellis, the boy from Tipperary who famously grabbed the ball during a football match at Rugby school, 'was consciously emulating Gaelic footballers he has seen in his homeland, and that Rugby, like Soccer, is thus another anglicised form of an Irish game'.[101]

Another important issue for nationalists was the perceived role of the GAA in the physical and moral improvement of the native population, more specifically the imagined ethnically and culturally pure indigenous race known as Celts or Gaels. After the Monaghan–Cavan final of 1916, for example, the *Dundalk Democrat*'s Gaelic columnist challenged

any other Association, society, or body to get together voluntarily a gathering of over 5,000 young men and women and afterwards truthfully chronicle that not an untoward incident occurred, not an appearance of drink, not an obscene expression . . . the Gaelic field has no charm for the dull, effeminate, good-for-nothing, loafer; they are conspicuous by their absence, they are elsewhere. That our Association only provides attraction for the manly, the virtuous, the temperate—in short, for those imbibed with the higher instincts of the Celt.[102]

O'Duffy's belief that sport was crucial to the well-being of the national community was central to his lifelong devotion to it: 'The Gaelic games not only develop muscle and mind, but help to preserve the individuality of our race.'[103] Such ideas, accompanied by an assumption of national superiority, were commonplace in this period. The GAA annual, for example, observed that 'the Irish Celt is distinguished among the races, for height and strength, manly vigour and womanly grace . . . despite wars, and domestic disabilities, the stamina of the race has survived almost in pristine perfection'. The ideal Gael was 'a matchless athlete, sober, pure in mind, speech and deed, self-possessed, self-reliant, self-respecting, loving his religion and his country with a deep and resistless love, earnest in thought and effective in action'.[104] Ironically, much of this rhetoric was imported from England, where team games had come 'to be revered as an essential element in the pedagogy of character formation' and 'the quintessential masculine expression of nationality and/or imperialism' by the late nineteenth century.[105]

It also formed part of a broader discourse in early twentieth-century Europe, one which was underpinned by the growth of ideas such as eugenics, social Darwinism, and racial conceptions of nationalism.[106] National fitness was increasingly promoted by patriotic sports associations of all political complexions; just as British intellectuals used Anglo-Saxon sporting superiority

to rationalize imperialist jingoism, the cult of the Celt was deployed to reinforce nationalist claims.[107] Ireland's failure to compete under its own flag at
the Stockholm Olympic Games in 1912, and thereby prove 'that its people
possess the physical qualities necessary for their preservation and . . . recognition as a separate national entity', troubled those Gaels who believed that 'the
doctrine of the survival of the fittest holds as good today as at any time in
history'.[108]

The most influential source of this rhetoric, as Mandle has observed, was
Britain: 'Much of what the GAA regarded as distinctive about the meaning of
its games was merely the result of the substitution of "Ireland" for "Britain" or
"England".'[109] Given the GAA's success in appropriating this imperialist sporting ethos, it was unsurprising that the thinking of Gaels like O'Duffy reflected
that of muscular Christians like Thomas Arnold, the celebrated headmaster of
Rugby School. British public school boys, no less than Monaghan Gaels, were
encouraged to be physically fit, aggressively religious, and, above all, manly.
Manliness was a concept which 'should not be confused with what today is
called machismo, since it encompassed a raft of attributes including honour,
duty, sacrifice, honesty, and of course physical strength and endurance. Good
character was supposed to arise from a strong will, which was in turn a sign of
a healthy mind. Since the health of the mind and that of the body were inextricably linked, Victorians assumed that by looking after the body the will could be
strengthened.'[110] A concern about the physical deterioration of the national
stock also formed part of this phenomenon. O'Duffy contrasted the degeneration of British army recruits with the vitality of the Gael: 'the GAA, with its
amateur and national outlook, will continue as an unbreakable barrier against
professionalism or any similar menace to our national virility'.[111] He would
later attribute the IRA's physical superiority to the GAA: 'Hardened and
vitalised by Gaelic games, our men could wear the enemy out in speeding
across country, in braving the weather's worst rigours of rain or cold through
long nights and tiring days.'[112]

Although such ideas represented a significant strand of Irish Ireland
thought, they also formed part of a wider phenomenon. Tom Garvin has noted
how religious assertiveness and an obsession with the native language and
moral fibre of the population were characteristic of rural societies challenged
by modernization, and how opportunistic patriots in such societies often val-
ued culture and sport not for their own qualities so much as their potential in
mobilizing political support.[113] As will become evident, O'Duffy's ideas about
sport, and the underlying concerns which informed them, would play a central
role in his leadership of the IRA, Garda Síochána, and Blueshirts.

Fighting the ghost of a dead enemy

O'Duffy's rise through the ranks of Gaeldom occurred during a period of radical political change. It was not until 1918 that Sinn Féin's electoral victory transformed Irish politics, but the Irish Party's problems had been apparent for some time. Rather than crowning its long struggle for Home Rule, the introduction of the Government of Ireland bill in 1912 unleashed the forces which proved its undoing. The Irish revolution was set in train by Edward Carson's Ulster Volunteers, established in 1913 with the intention of using violence to prevent the implementation of Home Rule. Some southern separatists claimed to admire Carson's revolutionary precedent, but the view from Monaghan, where 5,000 Protestants signed the Ulster Covenant and 1,800 men enrolled in the Ulster Volunteers, looked rather different.[114] The creation of the latter force inevitably provoked the formation of the IRB-dominated Irish Volunteers in November 1913. A meeting held the following January to establish a company in Monaghan town included O'Duffy among its attendance of priests, politicians, and Gaels. AOH and UIL representatives, who regarded the new militia with undisguised suspicion due to its Fenian links, were also present. Speaking on behalf of local Redmondites, the chairman of Monaghan county council made it clear that their support was contingent on the Volunteers' loyalty to the Irish Party.[115] The president of the Volunteers, Eoin MacNeill, responded in an appropriately conciliatory fashion, commending Redmond's efforts to win Home Rule but insisting on the necessity of the militia to ensure its enactment.

The meeting demonstrated the radicalizing impact of events in Ulster. MacNeill described the opportunity granted them 'by the action of their opponents' as 'a special favour from God almighty'. The county secretary, a friend of O'Duffy, enthused: 'People never dreamt that the day would come when . . . the young men of the county could assemble in a public meeting to band themselves together in a military force . . . Any person who was not willing to join the Volunteer force was certainly a coward.' Such sentiments were underpinned by an awareness of the formidable level of local Unionist paramilitary organization, which was strongest in the religious borderlands where sectarian conflict appeared most likely.[116] Long-held sectarian grievances also played their part, the county council chairman recalling 'the time when his father would not get one perch of ground in the district where he lived not while there was any Orangeman to take it'. O'Duffy, who did not speak at the meeting or join the resulting organizing committee, appears to have been an interested but passive witness to this significant revolutionary moment.

Civil war became increasingly likely in 1914. In January the inspector general warned that political unrest in Ulster was growing 'more serious as time advances'.[117] The Curragh mutiny in March demonstrated the unlikelihood of Britain implementing Home Rule by force, while the landing of 25,000 loyalist rifles in Larne the following month further raised the stakes: 'the big traders' private cars in Monaghan were seen early the next morning coming home after delivering the guns'.[118] Nationalists, including John Redmond, who seized nominal control of the Irish Volunteers in June, flocked to the organization: in one month alone the number of companies in the county jumped from 4 to 17.[119] The police identified Patrick Whelan, justice of the peace, coroner for north Monaghan, and O'Duffy's GAA mentor, as the 'prime mover in the county', while the support of other Gaels for the new militia was demonstrated by the holding of Volunteer parades in GAA grounds.[120] In May, by which time Monaghan was dotted with training camps and armed volunteers on manoeuvres, the inspector general reported that 'the condition of the province could hardly be surpassed in gravity except by open insurrection'.[121] But, while the inspector general regarded the Ulster Volunteers as 'a body of unquestionable value as a military Force', he believed that 'scarcely any' of the Irish Volunteers were 'armed or disciplined or properly drilled'.[122] Equipped with less than a hundred rifles—one-fifth of which, the police noted, were stashed in Whelan's house—the militia was also politically divided between Redmondites and advanced nationalists.[123]

By the summer of 1914, Carson had mobilized 85,000 Ulster Volunteers, almost one-third of Ulster's male adult Protestants, while the Irish Volunteers mustered another 150,000 men. British power in Ireland, the inspector general warned, had never been weaker since the Act of Union: 'Events are moving. Each county will soon have a trained army far outnumbering the police, and those who control the Volunteers will be in a position to dictate to what extent the law of the land may be carried into effect.'[124] But, just as civil war loomed upon the horizon, the crisis was averted by the sudden outbreak of the Great War. Redmond and Carson immediately professed their loyalty to the Empire, postponing their grievances in the imperial (and their own) interest. Asquith's Liberal government placed Home Rule on the statute book in Westminster, with the proviso that the Ulster question would be settled before its implementation after the war's conclusion. In Monaghan, the county inspector reported a complete transformation: 'the bitterness between Unionists and Nationalists which has existed during the past 12 months has been obliterated by the sudden and great danger to the Empire'. Tyrone's county inspector—who had recently reported that 'hatred between Catholic and Protestant was never in my memory half so deep'—could not recall 'such good feeling between Catholics and Protestants.'[125] Volunteering dwindled as thousands of Irishmen rushed to the colours. For those who preferred a quieter (and, given the booming wartime agricultural economy, prosperous) life, volunteering held little purpose except potentially to mark one out for conscription. Moreover, as the county inspector dryly observed, although most people in Monaghan 'want Britain and the Allies to beat the Germans', relatively few wished 'to risk their lives in helping [them] to do so'.[126]

Where did O'Duffy's allegiances reside during this critical period? Although his attendance at the Volunteers' inaugural meeting might be seen as evidence of a separatist outlook, 'republicanism was still a fringe ideology in 1913', and most Irish Volunteers remained Home Rulers.[127] As a GAA official, O'Duffy regularly mixed with prominent separatists like J. J. Walsh and Harry Boland. He attended the GAA's central council meeting in City Hall on Easter Sunday, one day before the rising, but is unlikely to have known of the insurrectionists' well-guarded plans. However, the evidence, although inconclusive, suggests that he sympathized with their aims. Shortly before the rebellion, O'Duffy had helped to establish Dail Uladh, a cultural body distrusted by some local nationalists due to its separatist sympathies.[128] Despite his suspect northern provenance, he was described by the separatist journalist Seamus Upton as 'a Gael to his finger tips, and a Nationalist to his core'.[129] But although he moved in circles where support for separatism was prevalent, neither press nor police sources indicate any active involvement on his part before 1917. Moreover, O'Duffy, who enjoyed nothing more than rehearsing his national record, never claimed any such involvement. He was a follower rather than a leader during this period, one of the many nationalists who responded to the wave of radicalization which swept the nation after Easter 1916.

The local and national events which shaped O'Duffy's decision to become a revolutionary, however, can be traced. The Great War postponed, but failed to resolve, the Irish crisis. In the long run, it further radicalized politics by widening the gulf between constitutional nationalists and separatists. Redmond's support for the war divided the great majority of National Volunteers from a radical minority who viewed England's difficulty as Ireland's opportunity. (Monaghan's faction-prone nationalists anticipated the national split.)[130] Denounced by the Redmondite *Dundalk Democrat* as a 'little knot of discontented, sour, sore-headed cranks, critics and mischief makers, incapable of anything but making an unpleasant noise', the Irish Volunteers would have remained an isolated minority had the war ended quickly.[131] But the longer the war dragged on, the more the Irish Party's difficulties became apparent. From its very inception, the threat of conscription had provoked fear among nationalists.[132] Carson's inclusion in the cabinet in the summer of 1915 increased such fears, by which time the *Dundalk Democrat* was becoming increasingly concerned about 'the cranks and factionists who direct their efforts towards promoting discord in Irish national politics'.[133] The newspaper identified a widening gulf between Irish Party supporters and O'Duffy's restless generation:

We can understand young men who know nothing about the political history of the past forty years—there are unfortunately many such—misunderstanding the position of the Irish Party . . . The trouble with them is that they allow themselves to be influenced by feelings of hatred (natural enough in Irish patriots of a bye-gone day) against something which they call 'England'—a something that no longer exists. They are wasting their time, and worse than wasting it, fighting the ghost of a dead enemy.[134]

By late 1915 the *Democrat*'s editorials betrayed a real fear of separatism.[135] A revealing chain of events, anticipating the events of the following year, illustrated the volatile atmosphere. In November Edward Phelan, a nationalist solicitor, organized a meeting in Carrickmacross to set up a home defence corps, as other neighbouring towns had done. Without warning, the meeting—which included constitutional nationalists—was stormed by a hostile crowd, who succeeded in gashing Phelan's head with a rock. The sudden eruption of violence seemed inexplicable. One man attributed it to a rumour 'that the shopkeepers in town were going to dismiss their assistants to compel them to join the army. That's the kind of nonsense that got about. We had the men who have a stake in the country at the meeting, and all classes and creeds were represented.'[136] The police responded ineptly, failing to identify the assailants but arresting three youths for singing nationalist songs.[137] This disturbance was followed by the first local commemoration of the Manchester Martyrs in years, at which a young Dublin schoolmaster, Patrick Pearse, urged the shedding of blood for Irish freedom.[138] The well-attended meeting, which was organized by a parish priest, led one Redmondite councillor to concede that 'the Sinn Fein movement had a great hold in Carrick'.[139]

By January 1916 local separatists were sufficiently emboldened to re-establish a company of the Irish Volunteers.[140] The release of the three clumsily arrested 'martyrs' provided the opportunity for its first public demonstration—a torchlight parade through the town, headed by a phalanx of armed men and priests. Fr Bernard Maguire, the parish priest of Inniskeen, declared the occasion a small but significant turning-point: 'Hitherto they had no clearly defined opposition camp, except the Orange camp. Now they had the [nationalist] people in two sections—the men who were absolutely right and those who were absolutely wrong...A day would come when those who were now opposed to them would be glad to creep into the movement by the back stairs'.[141] Sinn Féin, the county inspector warned, was now 'spreading rapidly'.[142]

Although not immediately apparent, the impact of the Easter Rising would soon dramatically accelerate this trend. As in much of the country, Eoin MacNeill's countermanding order ensured that none of the Volunteer companies in Monaghan participated in the Rising.[143] Moreover, the county inspector reported that 'The feeling of the people generally towards the rebels at the time was that they were guilty of a mad act as the rebellion was causing great loss of life and destruction of property and had no chance of success.'[144] Indeed, he had been cheered by a crowd when he read a telegram announcing the shelling of Liberty Hall and the arrival of British troops.[145] Local bodies, led by the county council, competed to denounce the rebellion, which the *Dundalk Democrat* condemned as 'an act of madness'.[146] A priest in Carrickmacross buoyed his congregation with the 'good news' that the 'Sinn Féin rebellion has been crushed and its leaders are being executed.'[147]

However, the more nuanced views expressed by Carrickmacross board of guardians, most of whom would indeed creep into Sinn Féin by the back stairs, were more representative. Eddie Kelly ridiculed the 'weak-spirited' local separatists for failing to participate in the rebellion: 'everyone should approve of the action of the authorities in shooting these rebel leaders—because that is what they are, only a handful of foolish Revolutionists'.[148] There was some sympathy for 'the young gassons that were led into it' but, when one representative expressed surprise at seeing 'educated gentlemen mixed up with Jim Larkin's crowd', another retorted: 'Educated gentlemen! They are a lot of impractical dreamers. The men that thought to engineer the fight with a few rifles against the present-day munitions of war must be impractical dreamers.' The board attributed the trouble to young men, students, the Gaelic League, 'professional men and University men and men over University Colleges', and 'hot-headed revolutionaries and socialists'. One Redmondite indignantly declared: 'In the future we are going to know who will lead, and we won't let every Tom, Dick and Harry place himself in a position to do it.' It was a revealing response. The old order regarded Sinn Féin, a term which embraced anyone who sympathized with the Rising, as a threat emanating not only from extreme nationalists but the younger generation, the intelligentsia, social upstarts, and the discontent. But no less revealing was the unspoken implication behind the criticism of the rebels, not for having fought but for having done so without the possibility of victory.

In Monaghan, as elsewhere, it was the British response that proved decisive. The arrest of local separatists, few, if any, of whom had been involved in the rebellion, was counter-productive, but it was the treatment of the rebel leaders which proved crucial.[149] As one Sinn Féin sympathizer recalled: 'Easter Week came and the people were stunned, the Sinn Feiners more than anyone else...No one could understand what had happened...Keenan, a leading Hib, put his head across the hedge and said "What do you think of your Sinn Féiners now?" My brother James, who thought that Pearse was mad, replied "They made their protest against the right of England to rule this country at any rate".' It was the executions, he recalled, that changed everything: 'The one mistake that Lloyd George made was to execute them. Instead of spies they now became Tones and Emmets.'[150] Nationalist anger at the rebels, and calls for their punishment, gave way to resentment against Britain. At the heart of this response was ambivalence about the Irish Party and Home Rule itself. Self-government within the Empire was supported because it was considered the only pragmatic policy, not because of any hostility to independence, which was widely regarded as a preferable but unrealistic aspiration. However, it was now felt, as the county inspector noted, 'that the rebellion had done more than years of constitutional agitation to convince the Government of the urgent necessity for Home Rule'.[151] There was, as yet, no widespread conversion to separatism, but the seeds of revolution had been sown, a revolution which O'Duffy would lead in Monaghan.

2

The best man in Ulster

From the national games the Volunteers turned to the national struggle for independence. Their Irish–Ireland ideals illuminated them in battle as in play, but they shouldered rifle instead of caman, wore bandolier instead of jersey.[1]

DESPITE its importance in his emergence as a national figure, little has been written about O'Duffy's involvement in the War of Independence. Local histories acknowledge his role as the driving force behind the IRA, but offer few details as to how this dominance was achieved or to what effect. The speed of his ascent to the leadership of the republican movement in Monaghan caught many, including the authorities, by surprise. Most historians merely note that O'Duffy enjoyed a good war until his organizing abilities brought him to the notice of GHQ. But for O'Duffy, as for most of his revolutionary generation, the 'four glorious years' remained the pivotal event of his life, a formative period which functioned as a source of idealism, inspiration, and legitimacy. The importance of O'Duffy's identification with the values of the Gael was noted in the previous chapter. This chapter considers an equally important dimension of his self-image and public persona, his self-perception as a soldier, which would exert a significant influence in his subsequent career. His idealization of military values was symbolized by his habit of carrying a military cane, an affectation unusual enough to attract comment, and the fact that throughout his career O'Duffy was known simply as 'the General' to his followers.

Organization

O'Duffy attributed his decision to join the Irish Volunteers—'the happiest day of my life'—to his GAA background and the intervention of Michael Collins:

I had been attending a match in Croke Park in November 1917 and afterwards the secretary, the late Luke O'Toole, brought me to his home. There he introduced me to Collins. Within the hour I had been admitted into the ranks of the Volunteers. The first question he addressed to me, in his earnest, brief, businesslike yet cheerful manner, was about the strength of the GAA in Monaghan. Then he said he had heard of my work. The Volunteers were not so strong in Monaghan as they should be, or, for instance, as the GAA clubs were. Would I help? I would, and said so. When Collins talked of national matters, few young Irishmen could resist the infection of his enthusiasm. The upshot was that I went back to Monaghan a Volunteer and within a short time had recruited virtually every able-bodied member or supporter of the GAA into Volunteer activities.[2]

However, his letter to Cathal Brugha, the Dáil minister for defence, provides a more prosaic account of his early revolutionary career:

I joined the Volunteers in May 1917, and became Section Commander in Clones Company, the only Company then in Co. Monaghan. In September 1917 the Company became 20 strong, and on a new election of officers taking place, I was appointed Captain. I then got directly in touch with G.H.Q. and acting on their instructions I succeeded in forming Companies at Newbliss and Scotstown convenient to Clones. These Companies were formed into Battalions of which I was appointed Commandant. Early in 1918 I succeeded in forming outposts at Carrickmacross, Ballybay, Castleblayney and Monaghan...thus forming the nucleus of five Battalions...On the 1st August the Brigade was established, and I was unanimously elected Brigadier. Three months after its establishment the Brigade consisted of 56 Companies and 5 Battalion Councils, and a Brigade Council fully staffed. Each of the above Companies was organised by myself alone and unaided.[3]

Aside from the final boast, this version is substantially accurate. O'Duffy, almost certainly a Volunteer before meeting Collins, retrospectively dated his enlistment to their first meeting. Throughout his career, O'Duffy would depict himself as a protégé of Collins and the heir to his political legacy. He was certainly the former. He claimed, without much exaggeration, that from their first meeting 'not a week passed, whether in prison or out of prison, no matter what trials he endured that I did not hear from him or see him.'[4] Nor is there any doubt about Collins's opinion of O'Duffy. After the latter's incarceration in 1918, Collins inquired of Austin Stack: 'do you see Eoin O'Duffy? He's another hellish loss. The best man by far in Ulster.'[5]

When O'Duffy joined the Irish Republican Brotherhood (IRB) and Sinn Féin is less clear; there is no record of his involvement in the latter before 1918.[6] Dublin Castle noted: 'Although of considerable importance, very little seems to be known about this man prior to 1918; apparently he did not attract attention in whatever work he was engaged upon, and it would seem that it was only in or about January or February 1918 that the Police had reason to report on his movements.'[7] O'Duffy was, by inclination, more active on the military side of the movement and his later political prominence was a consequence of his influence within the Volunteers and IRB. His initiation into the latter, which presumably occurred when he first met Collins in November 1917, was witnessed by another leading brother, Seán Ó Murthuile: 'Collins had in mind the possibility of O'Duffy being a useful man in the IRB Councils as well as Irish Volunteers Councils, and I was invited by Collins to the first interview he had with Eoin.'[8] O'Duffy's subsequent rise to national prominence was due in no small part to the patronage of Collins, who reorganized the IRB into the secretive élite of the republican movement.

His progress within the Volunteers also owed much to his background in the GAA, which, he claimed, provided the backbone of the force: 'So far as Monaghan is concerned, the Volunteers minus the GAA organization would have been negligible... The GAA had gathered and trained the manpower along the right lines, physical and mental; the Volunteer organization brought it into the front lines when the time came.'[9] In reality, the degree of co-operation between both organizations was much exaggerated by O'Duffy, who, like many separatist Gaels, depicted them as virtually synonymous. But although many Gaels continued to support constitutional nationalism before 1918, the GAA did function as a source of popular resistance to the authorities. Following the Easter Rising, but before he joined the Volunteers, O'Duffy took a leading role in the campaign against the recently introduced amusement tax, one of several minor confrontations which, although ostensibly justified by self-interest rather than politics, served to identify the GAA with militant opposition to British authority.[10] O'Duffy was, at the same time, outraged by any allegations of politics in the GAA. At one county board meeting he condemned the commission of inquiry into the rebellion for describing the GAA as a political organization: 'This is a falsehood. I have been at hundreds of meetings... and I never yet heard a word of politics.' The GAA was not anti-British, merely 'anti foreign games and anti those who encourage them in this country'. Denouncing the authorities' desire to 'suppress our national pastimes', O'Duffy condemned the arrest of prominent Gaels as 'an outrage which demands investigation'.[11]

On a more practical level, the GAA provided O'Duffy with an ideal recruitment network. One local Volunteer estimated that they 'owed 70–80% of their organisation to the GAA. First hop take Eoin O'Duffy, the greatest and very foremost of all. Second hop take Phil Marron. Third hop take Dan Hogan . . . Most of O'Duffy's contacts were through the GAA.'[12] Hogan, a clerk in Clones train station and a celebrated county player, would become O'Duffy's right-hand man. There was a noticeable overlap between the leadership of the GAA and the republican movement, as evidenced by the prominence of such figures as Patrick Whelan, Dr Conn Ward, and P. J. O'Daly.[13] O'Duffy's experience as Ulster secretary also proved invaluable: 'he knew every parish, town, village and corner of the county and indeed his knowledge of the surrounding counties was uncanny. He was quite familiar with all national activities over a wide area. He knew all the young men and made it his business to meet selected individuals at the most unlikely places.'[14] The local GAA team would often form the nucleus of a Volunteer company. In the summer of 1918, for example, Francis Tummon asked O'Duffy to enrol his group of friends in the IRA. O'Duffy travelled to Wattlebridge to address the boys before their weekly training session:

On this particular Sunday there were about thirty boys of all ages but only about twenty assembled to listen to O'Duffy . . . In his talk, lasting roughly twenty minutes, O'Duffy outlined the objects of the Volunteers, how the organisation was built up and their ultimate aim, namely the overthrow of British rule in Ireland. Finally, he said that anyone present who was not prepared to use force should not join the Volunteers. His words left a lasting impression on me and, I'm sure, on all present. There were at least half a dozen who listened to O'Duffy on that Sunday afternoon but never joined the Volunteers. The practice game of football from which we were summoned to listen to Gen. O'Duffy was resumed, but the foundation of a company was laid.[15]

The GAA also provided separatists with meeting places during the period when Sinn Féin struggled to gain a foothold. In February 1917 the county inspector observed that O'Duffy's club was 'decorated with Sinn Fein colours & portraits of rebel leaders executed after the rebellion—GAA influence is causing disaffection to spread amongst the young men of Clones'.[16] In June he reported that the 'GAA is the most active political organisation & it has actively associated itself with the Sinn Fein movement which through its football matches it has great opportunities of extending.'[17] Such opportunities included waving 'Sinn Fein flags in a provocative way', and singing 'Easter Week & other seditious songs' en route to matches.[18] GAA matches also provided a cover for IRA activities.[19] The RIC noticed a new trend as teams named after separatists replaced those named after constitutional nationalists.[20] In 1918 the Carrickmacross Emmets split when a section of the team seceded to form the Carrickmacross Redmonds, while, by 1921, the O'Duffy Gaels had taken to the field.[21]

Sinn Féin flourished in Monaghan during the summer of 1917. By the end of the year there were 35 *cumainn*, 5 more than the largely inactive UIL and only 13 less than the more resilient AOH.[22] Its policy, however, remained vague— little more than admiration for the 1916 rebels and hostility towards the Irish Party—reflecting the inchoate nature of the movement before the convention of October 1917. The Redmondite *Dundalk Democrat* carried a surprisingly benign, if patronizing, report of the party's first meeting in Monaghan town in October, which attracted several thousand 'fine young men and women, well dressed and well behaved'.[23] O'Duffy was presumably among the Volunteer contingents armed with hurleys. The *Democrat* attributed the new movement's popularity to 'the ignorance of the average man under 30 of the revolution that has been effected in the condition of Ireland during the past half century by the constitutional methods which he is taught to despise'. Another large rally in Carrickmacross was attributed to the poison introduced by T. M. Healy's earlier campaign against the Irish Party.[24]

But it was not only the young and bitter who supported Sinn Féin. Its organizers were prominent among 'the Catholic clergy, the teachers, professional men, tradesmen and smaller farmers'. Shopkeepers, large farmers, and others belonging to 'the respectable people' remained loyal to the Irish Party.[25] Local Volunteers also emphasized this class divide, if in exaggerated form: one republican claimed that his company 'was made up mostly of servant boys who worked in Planters' houses'.[26] But many within the most respectable section of society did back the new party. Twenty priests attended Sinn Féin's first public meeting, much to the irritation of the Redmondite press.[27] The party also drew support from the Irish Ireland movement and public servants. One nationalist complained: 'nearly all I have met have been Government servants, or sons of policemen. Their fathers smashed our heads with their batons in the Land League days ... and now their sons want to smash the party that emancipated us.'[28] However, it was not only public servants but clerks, local body officials, and the lower middle class generally who supported Sinn Féin: in terms of his age and social, economic, and cultural background, O'Duffy was highly representative of this new movement.[29]

Throwing himself into revolutionary activism with the same energy and commitment that he had invested in the GAA, O'Duffy quickly established himself as the leading republican in Monaghan. His (now lost) diaries, Liam Walsh noted, demonstrated 'the extraordinary energy of this apparently tireless worker. Night after night he was engaged on some mission or another, and it is frequently recorded where he attended three or four different functions in the same night ... they included drill parades, route marches, arms classes, Company, Battalion and Brigade Council, Sinn Fein and Cuman na mBan meetings.' During his frequent visits to GHQ in Dublin he 'interested himself in every possible function of a national character which he could conveniently attend'.[30] A serial committee-joiner, O'Duffy belonged to a remarkable array of social, sporting, cultural, and professional bodies: 'I was at one period honorary secretary in my spare time of no fewer than ten voluntary organisations. Not only did I need to work sixteen hours a day, but I had to suffer irregular meals and widely varying hours of sleep.' He commenced a life-long habit of compiling a 'timetable of tasks and appointments for every week, and for every day'.[31] It was a life-style which demonstrated his voracious appetite for public life as much as his commitment to republicanism; in later life, his craving for public exposure would verge on the obsessive.

Authority came easily to O'Duffy, his idealization of military life evident in his bearing and demeanour which imitated the obvious role model of the British officer. A photograph of a uniformed O'Duffy in *Hue-And-Cry* was accompanied by a caption describing him as 'Clean-shaven, but now may have a small reddish moustache; smart-looking; speaks well, brown eyes, long thin nose, pale complexion, thin face, slight make, 5 feet 9 inches high, about 30 years of age: walks with long strides and swings his arms'.[32] Even in these early years he cultivated a stern public persona at odds with his more garrulous personality. Walsh observed that his neat dress, 'shrewd look and expressionless face, and the dominance which he so naturally attained over his comrades, gave the impression he was cold and heartless, but it was not so, for beneath it all there was kindness and understanding'.[33] (His intense gaze—often taken as a sign of intelligence—is captured in Leo Whelan's portrait of the IRA's GHQ staff.) Walsh claimed that O'Duffy, while not universally popular, won his men's support through his exercise of leadership and loyalty.[34]

This assessment is supported by the testimony of the many Volunteers who were interviewed by three local priests in the 1960s for a local history of the war. Their unpublished and remarkably frank interviews, known as the Marron papers, form the most valuable source for this period of O'Duffy's life. Although many of the veterans had come to support Fianna Fáil and the General had become a discredited figure, few criticized his leadership.[35] One recollected

he never forgot a face or the name that went with it and he was painstaking to a detail. It was his habit to call as many Volunteers from various parts to a central point for a lecture on tactics ... punctuality was important but a roll call was not necessary because O'Duffy knew every volunteer by name & his company before his lecture was far advanced. At these meetings volunteers were encouraged to discuss their problems and to ask questions.

Another remembered him as 'a great organiser. No half-way measures with him. He would take no excuses.'[36] His abilities were conceded by subsequently hostile sources like Dr Conn Ward, his intelligence officer, who assessed him as 'a very good organiser [but] too emotional & erratic—not very intelligent'.[37]

O'Duffy typified the archetypal IRA officer familiar from War of Independence memoirs: driven, self-disciplined, and austere. During 'this period of his life he was never seen with a cigarette in his mouth and did not know the taste of intoxicating liquor'.[38] His piety was attested to by annual pilgrimages to Lough Derg and winter retreats at the Jesuits' Milltown Park.[39] A young boy recalled the atmosphere on his father's remote farm which served as an IRA safe house: 'They used just arrive over the hills from nowhere. O'Duffy kept aloof & spent his time typing in the parlour ... There was always plenty of Holy Water around & Rosaries said before going off but never any drink.'[40] A strict disciplinarian, he demanded high standards from his men. One recalled that he 'was careful to advise all units to avoid public houses and people who were in the habit of frequenting such Beer Shops'.[41] Another claimed: 'If you went into a public house he would sack you at once.'[42] James McKenna recollected that his battalion's monthly meetings 'usually dealt with training, the procuring of firearms, and the suppression of illicit distillation. General O'Duffy insisted on strict temperance in the ranks of the volunteers.'[43] Such views were not unusual in Irish Ireland and separatist circles where alcohol was often linked to Redmondite and British immorality, but the zealousness of O'Duffy's early attitude to drink, coupled with his later descent into alcoholism, raises the distinct possibility of a family background of alcoholism.

By 1918 O'Duffy had become the driving force behind the IRA, endlessly touring the county, generating enthusiasm, establishing new companies, and placing older ones under his authority. Packie Coyle, like many IRA men, testified that O'Duffy 'took me into the Volunteers'.[44] Jimmy Kirke 'did not join anything till O'Duffy came'.[45] One Sunday, Tom Carragher recalled, 'someone whispered "Be at Pat Ward's tonight" ... this was the night the Broomfield crowd were started or rather re-organised by O'Duffy'.[46] Patrick Corrigan described the initiation, a ceremony invariably conducted by O'Duffy:

The man who really put Monaghan into action was Owen O'Duffy. He swore us in in a vacant house. He said 'Possibly some of you will be shot in this business. Maybe you'll

shoot somebody. The men of Cork and other counties are fighting the British. They
want to spread the war over the whole island. The British cannot attend to all the
ambushes. Let us draw them here—an ambush here at least every week or fortnight.
Anyone afraid to take part, go home.'[47]

Despite claiming little interest in politics, O'Duffy became secretary of Sinn
Féin's north Monaghan *comhairle ceanntair* in 1918. His authority within both
wings of the republican movement was reinforced by his membership of the
IRB. Although O'Duffy would become a leading Brother, succeeding Collins
as supreme council treasurer in 1921, he rarely alluded to the organization. Similarly, few of the Fenian interviewees in the Marron papers acknowledged its
existence, let alone its influence. Some IRA officers claimed not to have learned
of its existence until the treaty, while even lowly IRB men appear to have been
unaware of its influence.[48] One IRA officer felt there was 'no usefulness in the
organisation . . . We could hear things that were likely to happen in the IRA
but as far as that went we would also get to know the same information in the
Volunteers.'[49] Those who declined to join were more suspicious of its influence.
Francis O'Duffy, an IRA officer and Sinn Féin councillor, did not see the need
for a secret society: 'when Eoin O'Duffy announced that all Volunteer officers
were to take an oath of allegiance to the Dail, I enquired publicly if officers were
to regard this oath as superseding any other undertaking they might already
have given, and O'Duffy gave a definite assurance to that effect. I hoped that
this would put an end to the IRB organising among the Volunteer officers, but
I was mistaken.' Soon after, two of his key men were given 'an instruction in
Eoin O'Duffy's handwriting' to join the IRB. The reluctant officers were supported by their captain: 'I pointed out that since Volunteer officers were bound
to obey orders from their "superior" officers in the Volunteers and had sworn
allegiance to the Dail, they could not conscientiously take an oath to obey their
unknown superiors in another organisation.' He believed that 'many of the
officers were members . . . This might be expected from the influence which
Eoin O'Duffy exercised in that area.'[50] He was right. The key figures on the
brigade staff, including O'Duffy's deputy, Dan Hogan, were IRB men. Those
who were not, such as Dr Conn Ward, had resisted pressure to join.[51]

What was the purpose of this secret organization? Patrick McGrory, the
brigade quartermaster, who was appointed an IRB organizer by O'Duffy,
claimed that its function 'was to control and stiffen the Volunteer Company
and through the Volunteers to control and stiffen the Sinn Fein Club.'[52] The
IRB's influence was both facilitated and necessitated by the disorganized
nature of the Volunteers in 1918: 'Headquarters remained a shadowy institution, its influence largely exercised through the fraternal web of the IRB, spun

by Collins and his associates in Dublin. Despite an increasingly elaborate hierarchy of brigade and battalion staffs, company officers and support services, most of the local companies were still loose bands of neighbouring adolescents as in 1914.'[53] In an army where captains were elected rather than commissioned, and often for their social status or sporting prowess rather than military ability, the assertion of authority and discipline proved problematic. Just as the IRB strengthened Collins's authority over his regional commanders, it allowed O'Duffy to draw his subordinates into closer conspiratorial loyalty.

Despite McGrory's comment, Brian MacMahon's memoir illustrates that the IRB could be used to blunt, as well as sharpen, resistance. The latter's battalion was led by P. J. O'Daly, an assistant county surveyor, who resisted pressure from O'Duffy to adopt more aggressive tactics. Eventually, O'Duffy offered MacMahon O'Daly's command:

> I had called on several friends who knew the position in the Battalion, on the way down, and had been advised by all without exception not to touch the job. They said that all but three of the eleven Company Captains were for all practical purposes Daly's employees in so much as they were foremen on the Direct Labour road's scheme and he, as Civil Engineer for the area, was their boss. He had an even firmer hold on them through having brought all of them into the IRB of which he was the local head, and they were under oath to obey him. I was told that a meeting of the local IRB was always held on the nights previous to Battalion Council meetings and that the business of the following night was discussed and decided upon at each IRB meeting, so that, no matter who became O.C., Daly would still control the Battalion by majority vote.[54]

MacMahon declined the offer without mentioning the IRB (already a 'sore point' as O'Duffy 'had several times invited me to join and had asked my elder brother, also a member, to put pressure on me to join'). Despite the offer, MacMahon was under no illusions about O'Duffy's loyalty to the IRB: 'I knew O'Duffy all my life, as we were born and reared within a stone's throw of each other, and close friends until the IRB question intervened somewhat. We had several heated arguments as to the validity of the Brotherhood or its necessity, and I should have known then that if I should ever come up against the IRB I could not rely on his support.' MacMahon instead accepted the position of adjutant but felt that O'Daly—who regarded him as O'Duffy's 'spy'—used the Brotherhood to stymie his effectiveness. His candid account illustrates how the strength of local rivalries and weakness of conventional command structures underpinned the IRB's importance.

Aside from organizing and establishing his authority over Volunteer units, O'Duffy's main concern in this early period was to find some form of activism to occupy their enthusiasm. Early activities—forming fife and drum bands, painting banners, and parading—tamely mimicked the AOH.[55] The series of by-elections which preceded the 1918 general election did much more to invigorate the movement. O'Duffy's Volunteers were mobilized for the by-elections in south Armagh (January 1918), east Tyrone (April 1918), and east Cavan (June 1918). Their policing of the streets on election day, described with military precision by O'Duffy, challenged the RIC's authority and demonstrated the new movement's exciting confrontational style:

Wednesday, April 3 1918. General mobilisation of Volunteers at 7 a.m. Republican Police appointed for the different streets of the town. Took charge of George's Street, Barrack Street, Sinn Fein Committee Rooms and three Polling Booths in Courthouse with companies of Volunteers from Donaghmore, Tullyallen, Moy, Clones and Newbliss. On continuous duty from 7 a.m. to 4 p.m. General mobilisation of foregoing Companies to march to Coalisland, where they were reinforced by local Company of Volunteers and three Companies of Fianna na hEireann. Paraded the town and cleared streets of disorderly crowds... Returned to Barracks with local men and returned at 2 a.m. after inspecting the guard on Ballot Papers.[56]

The *Dundalk Democrat* viewed such displays as poor form: 'the Sinn Feiners on the eve of the poll have had recourse to the last desperate expedient of trying to overawe the voters by a display of political violence. For no other purpose than this have hundreds of young men been brought from far corners of Ireland and paraded about the constituency in military formation, armed openly with hurleys, and under leadership and direction of persons clad in the strange uniforms of the Sinn Fein Volunteers.'[57] The newspaper was delighted by Redmond's success in Armagh and Tyrone, although Arthur Griffith's victory in Cavan proved its celebratory (and now decidedly anachronistic) ballad, 'South Armagh has killed Sinn Fein', premature.[58]

Despite the alarming precedents of 1914 and 1916, these bold displays often met with a patronizing response. The *Democrat* thought the 'most amusing part of the whole performance was a number of youths parading the town with a white cloth fastened around one arm, with the letters "I P" engraved thereon. One of the youths when asked why he was wearing it replied with a solemn countenance that he was one of the "Irish Police," and, pointing to another lad, said he was in charge and was a head constable.'[59] A local judge, faced by an intransigent republican in the dock, displayed a similar attitude:

It is all very well for people to say they won't recognise the courts... I think that the policy that is pursued by the political party to which the prisoner belongs, or did belong, is the silliest policy that could possibly be imagined. Supposing you had no court of law in the country you would have absolute chaos... I regard it as play-acting.

Really if we Irish had not largely lost our sense of humour we would laugh at it. It is so utterly ridiculous and nonsensical there would be a burst of laughter all over the whole country at this flag carrying and gasconading that is going on.[60]

Such condescension may have been intended to deflate Sinn Féin's growing self-confidence but some complacency seems clear. Republican activities would appear less ridiculous as ever more effective methods were devised for subverting British authority.

Defiance

The evolution of IRA activism has been described as a transition from public defiance to guerrilla warfare.[61] There was little violence between republicans and their enemies—the British authorities and Irish Unionists—in 1918. The movement consolidated its strength, absorbing and intimidating potential rivals. Public drilling grew more widespread as the Volunteers increased in numbers and confidence. Drilling, the inspector general noted, provided excitement, discipline, 'an arrogant spirit, and a sense of power amongst the young men engaged in it, which is very embarrassing to the Police'.[62] It forced the RIC to choose between turning a blind eye to open provocation or arresting republicans, thereby making 'heroes out of nobodies' and provoking 'savage indignation among countless families which had previously supported the new movement, if at all, only out of herd instinct'.[63] In March, a constable discovered 'men apparently drilling in the Clones GAA Football grounds. When he came close the men began to play hurley.' Clones Volunteers also marched to nearby Newbliss to counter an AOH meeting. During the same month Sinn Féin 'held two dramatic entertainments' in Clones: 'seditious songs were sung' and the police were humiliatingly refused admittance 'though they offered payment'.[64] In April, the conscription crisis provoked by the passing of the Military Services Act destroyed what remained of the Irish Party's credibility. Sinn Féin's anti-conscription meetings, offering 'a favourable opportunity to stampede the public into their ranks', were held throughout 'all the towns and most of the villages' in the county.[65]

The ineffective pattern of British repression, irritating enough to provoke support for Sinn Féin but insufficiently robust to suppress it, was becoming evident. The conscription and 'German plot' crises were followed by the banning of unscheduled public gatherings. In Monaghan, where GAA matches were broken up but Orange Order parades tolerated, the Redmondite press blasted Dublin Castle's 'imbecility'.[66] For O'Duffy, such repression presented an opportunity to demonstrate the injustice of British rule. He organized Gaelic League *aeridheacht* (festivals), which were obligingly broken up by the police, and refused to apply for a permit for the Cavan–Armagh football final on 7 July.[67] When the players and supporters found the pitch occupied by police and soldiers, O'Duffy had to be restrained from storming the field. At the GAA county convention the following month he complained about the RIC's harassment, chastising those counties which co-operated with the authorities. In response, the Ulster council endorsed O'Duffy's refusal to apply for permits and agreed to hold unlicensed matches in as many parishes as possible on 4 August.[68] After this proposal—and similar ones from elsewhere—won the approval of the GAA central council, over 100,000 Gaels participated in Gaelic Sunday, an event 'which became part of the mythology of Irish nationalist defiance'.[69] In response, the authorities ceased enforcing the regulation.

This politicization of the GAA was resented by Redmondites. The *Dundalk Democrat* complained that local games had 'descended more and more into the troubled sea of politics until they were simply recognised as so many Sinn Fein demonstrations'.[70] Evidently sharing this view, the RIC charged O'Duffy and Dan Hogan on 14 September with 'illegal assembly' following a game between the Clones Kaffirs and Newbliss Hottentots.[71] A diary kept by O'Duffy during his incarceration in Belfast Prison has survived. He found his first weeks on remand difficult, due to the poor food, monotony, and constant surveillance: 'Lying awake on such a bed, in such a cell, in the darkness of the night gruesome thoughts of previous occupants of the cell—perhaps murderers etc. would enter your mind, but one gets hardened to these things.'[72] On his return to Clones for his trial on 29 September, he received a hero's welcome, being mobbed by supporters at every train station in the county.

As we entered Clones it was evident we were in for a lively time. Immense crowds gathered in all directions, the platform was packed with Military, police D.I.s & an immense crowd. As we alighted from the train we were torn from the police & affectionately greeted particularly by the ladies. Neither Mr. Hogan nor myself being ever too attentive to the ladies, we were non-plussed by such loving embraces, both now & during our short stay in Clones. Beside the station some thousands had lined up—people being present not only from Co. Monaghan but from Cavan & Fermanagh.[73]

They were driven to the courthouse, pursued by a raucous crowd singing the 'Soldier's Song'. O'Duffy, speaking in Irish, refused to recognize the court. The case was straightforward enough:

Constable Maguire deposed that with Constable Ryle he followed a crowd on bicycles from Clones to Clontibret to attend a football match. At Newbliss on the return journey, the crowd dismounted and stacked bicycles, after which they drank water. O'Duffy then went back through the ranks and talked to them. Witness described various orders done by the using of a whistle by Hogan, who at Cootehill was referee of the football match. The witness described some marching done about Glynch on the road from Newbliss to Clones, when by orders the cycling corps went on some by-roads and then returned after which they went to Clones, to the residence of Mr. O'Duffy, where they dispersed by command given in Irish.[74]

The authorities should have arrested O'Duffy for a more conventional case of drilling. The inability of the police, 'well-fed gentlemen with heavy uniforms and mounted on heavier official machines', to keep up with the 'athletic Clones lads' provoked derision.[75] O'Duffy feigned shock at being arrested for using a whistle ('like any cycling club'), while the bishop of Clogher complained in his Lenten pastoral of youths being 'sentenced to terms of imprisonment for displaying such skill in the control of a group of cyclists as not to constitute a danger to themselves or others, by mounting and dismounting to whistle signals'. Arrests were still unusual in this period, but the RIC, who were keen to stamp out drilling, had identified O'Duffy as 'the only openly active Sinn Feiner' in Monaghan.[76] O'Duffy was unperturbed. He had deliberately goaded the police by refusing to apply for match permits ('although milder counsels in the GAA were inclined towards acceptance'), ostensibly on the grounds that it would recognize 'a non-existent British right to control Irishmen playing Irish games', but in reality to further his policy of using the GAA to increase popular support for republicanism.[77] O'Duffy's depiction of his prosecution (for drilling *after* the game) as police harassment of the GAA was characteristic of his tendency to conflate opposition to the Volunteers with hostility to the GAA. He told a GAA convention that 'he felt proud it was for GAA activity he was taken away', and revised the circumstances of his arrest by claiming that he had been arrested for holding GAA matches without a permit. This remains the accepted version in local and GAA histories.[78]

Having refused to put up sureties for good behaviour, O'Duffy was sentenced to two months' imprisonment. On their return to Belfast Prison, he and Hogan received 'a bit of a lecture as to how foolish we were in not accepting bail' from the governor, before proceeding to the more welcoming Sinn Féin wing:

As we arrived loud cheers could be heard on all sides and the 'new arrivals' received a warm reception . . . What a different atmosphere this place has to the remand side. Not a criminal to be seen. About 160 of the cream of Ireland gathered together, all intelligent, robust & exemplary young men, whose only crime is intense love of country, & irresistible desire to secure the freedom of their mother land. Everyone appears happy here—even the warders. There is a feeling of independence.[79]

The rationale for incarcerating together 200 of the country's most committed republicans on short sentences with free assembly was not obvious. O'Duffy attributed the liberal régime to Thomas Ashe's death in custody: 'a coach & fours was driven through the prison regulations, & our men have practically received their own terms'. Prisoners were allowed to receive food from Cumann na mBan and offered facilities (which O'Duffy accepted) to continue their outside employment. The governor's authority collapsed almost entirely when the outbreak of influenza sweeping the country struck the prisoners (including O'Duffy), forcing him to leave cells open at night and supply 'brandy with the greatest liberality'.[80] In prison, friendships and alliances were formed and feuds begun: Austin Stack fell out with Michael Brennan, grumbling about 'people who tried to get special treatment for Clare men on all occasions'.[81] Despite his later reputation as the Free State's steely authoritarian, O'Duffy's future boss, Kevin O'Higgins, was one of the wildest inmates, prominent among

a crowd of water-throwers who caused great annoyance to many other prisoners. They often stood with cans of water on the top balcony and emptied them down on people passing below . . . A 'no-collar' brigade was formed and men went round the prison taking the collar and tie off anyone whom they found wearing them. Some little friction arose with the authorities because on one occasion a warder was seized and the collar taken off him. The result of the activities of the 'no collar' brigade was the formation of a society . . . wearing their shoes and trousers but nothing else except collars and ties round their bare necks. One friendly warder spoke to me about this incident and told me how humiliated he was at seeing men going around the yard like half-naked savages, as he said, 'with all them Orange warders looking at them'.[82]

Boxing matches, concerts, and dances broke the monotony on Sundays and festive occasions. O'Duffy, a leading member of 'the Prison Cuman-na-mBan', enjoyed the revelry:

The 'make-ups' of the 'ladies' was amusing. The bed sheet was appropriated as petticoat, & the blanket or quilt as a skirt, the hair of the mattress as flowing locks with the towel as head adornment. A shirt took the place of a blouse, & other articles of cell 'furniture' appropriated as adornments. A most interesting programme of song & dance followed, & I had the privilege of contributing in full dress 'The Hole in Her Stocking'.[83]

Gracing a dance 'in entirely new turn out' a fortnight later, O'Duffy was gratified to discover a paragraph in the prison journal 'devoted to my costume & head dress'.[84] He also excelled in the tradition of practical jokes, appointing himself prison doctor:

all new arrivals are brought into my 'Dispensary' for examination. It is necessary to anticipate the real prison doctor in the matter so that the joke may look the thing. To

give the thing colour I have arranged that a warder (in the know) should stay inside
with me...The disguise has always been so good that I have not yet got discovered.
It was a treat to witness the broad smiles on the prisoner's faces as I ordered the warder
to procure eggs for these gentlemen's breakfast, their choice of roast or chop for
dinner etc.

His daily routine revolved around morning prayers, parades, officers' classes,
Gaelic lessons, and the evening rosary. O'Duffy enjoyed prison life, notwithstanding occasional irritations such as the pilfering of 'a pound of sugar and a
sweet cake' and the difficulty of 'south of Ireland Irish the d—for a northerner
to follow'.[85] He wrote to one friend: 'Well, I was never in better form myself.
I realise now that I worked too hard when at home, & the rest will do me
good...it is really a privilege to be associated with a body of young men so
high-souled & exemplary.'[86] The camaraderie of prison life, combined with
the more serious revolutionary education which took place, strengthened the
bonds between the prisoners and their commitment to the cause. Prison
provided a useful, if over-leisurely, opportunity for the republican élite to
contemplate their movement and the future Irish state. Ernest Blythe's prison
notebook recorded the subjects assigned for study, ranging from Stack on
German politics to O'Duffy on transport policy.[87]

O'Duffy's jail diary, in contrast, contains little of political insight, confirming
his frequent assertions of his lack of interest in politics. It does, however, convey
a sense of the centrality of the Gaelic language and, even more so, the rituals of
Catholicism to his ideological outlook. For example, he recorded how many
prisoners received Communion: on 22 September he noted that a 'Large number of prisoners are weekly Communicants...there is no daily mass in the
Prison & consequently no facilities for Daily Communion.' The following Saturday was devoted to confession to mark the anniversary of the hunger-striker
Thomas Ashe, who died while being force-fed in Mountjoy prison. The Protestant *gaelgoir* (Irish speaker) Blythe, delivered an oration on 'the dead martyr's
life' with 'particular emphasis on Thos. Ashe's devotion to the Irish Language &
its significance in the future of our country's history'.[88] O'Duffy approv-
ingly noted that every prisoner received Communion the following morning:
'The celebrant announced before commencing Mass, that he was offering up
the Mass for the happy repose of the soul of the late Thos Ashe & for the success
of the cause for which he gave his life, & for which he died—the Sacred cause
of Irish Freedom. It was touching to witness the effect of this pronouncement
on the faces of the prisoners.'

Imprisonment did not distract O'Duffy from events in Monaghan.
Competition for the north Monaghan nomination in the imminent general

election had become intense and somewhat acrimonious. Among the interested parties were Seán MacEntee and Dr Conn Ward (destined to become O'Duffy's life-long local rival). O'Duffy's letter to one local republican indicated, if coyly, his own interest:

Is North Monaghan squared up yet or is anyone chosen definitely? I suppose you heard that the doctor withdrew in my favour. He says he never intended to oppose me & had he been at the meeting he would not have allowed his name to go forward. When I heard how they carried on, I wrote J. O'Daly and Mr Whelan telling them on no account would I allow my name to be mentioned further in connection with the matter. It is represented to me that unless I go forward the constituency is lost, so that I do not really know what to do. I have absolutely no ambition nor desire for the job, nor never had, & I would prefer to do a month here anytime as make one speech. Like yourself I am no orator, & I hope never will be. I do sincerely hope the thing will be settled up somehow at once. We must be a laughing stock for the other side. Unless there is a unanimous decision now, the result will be detrimental to the movement.[89]

O'Duffy had mastered the undemanding rhetoric of republican politics: as Collins confided to Stack, the prison O/C: 'I'm having a quiet laugh within myself at the political eagerness of some of the "I'm only a fighting man" fraternity'.[90] Having consulted Stack, O'Duffy sought the nomination.[91] Despite his imprisonment, a highly desirable criterion for selection, he failed to win it, but he was at least able to spike his rival by backing the eventual winner, Ernest Blythe, when it was decided 'to bring in a stranger to whom there was no local objection'.[92]

O'Duffy was released on 19 November 1918, shortly before the general election. Imprisonment had seen him join the revolutionary élite on the inside, while bestowing him with popularity and notoriety on the outside. He was met from the train by supporters, and pleased to discover that 'whistle-and-run' had become a popular children's game: 'Parents even provided their children with whistles so that the police should have no excuse for forgetting how and why those two man had been imprisoned.'[93] Disillusioned and unaccustomed to contesting elections, the Irish Party proved unequal to Sinn Féin's determined challenge. Months before the election, the *Dundalk Democrat* noted the contrast between the Irish Party's inactivity and the enthusiasm of its rivals, who were busy raising campaign funds, selecting candidates, and scrutinizing the electoral register.[94] It complained also that the 'clerical canvass against the Irish Party...was unremitting'.[95] O'Duffy's Volunteers provided an additional advantage: 'On polling day an army of Sinn Fein motor cars was let loose on the constituency. Bodies of strange men equipped with bludgeons and hurley sticks appeared on the scene...where their presence intimidated aged

Nationalists.'[96] The losing Irish Party candidate complained that 'he had been beaten by a neglected register, by imported mobs, by misrepresentation and lying the most gross and intimidation the most widespread'.[97]

Although such transgressions were well-established features of the Irish electoral tradition, the republicans' efforts surpassed those of their opponents. One Volunteer candidly recalled: 'We got voters and intimidated others'.[98] Among other intimidating incidents, the county inspector reported that hurley-wielding 'Peace Patrols' took up positions outside polling stations.[99] Hibernians, where they held the upper hand, behaved in a similar manner. A Sinn Féin activist who attempted to hold a meeting outside Ballyocean Catholic Church recalled that 'stones were thrown at us, men advanced with sticks, and though we had a few supporters, they had to run for their lives'. Another meeting was abandoned when the local priest was refused a hearing by a 'howling crowd' led by the AOH's Arthur Treanor. O'Duffy would not forget such incidents.

Volunteers were also run out of Drum, to the delight of its Protestant population:

> Just after dark another squad came in from Clones town,
> In command of Owen O'Duffy the village to surround,
> But like their other leaders he is just another bum,
> For he left their comrades to their fate in the famous town of Drum.
>
> The Orange boys came marching in not meaning any harm,
> But when they met the Clones Boys they struck them with alarm,
> They took their flags and hurley sticks just while you'd lick your thumb,
> And chased them like a flock of sheep from the famous town of Drum.[100]

Unionists recalled that 'O'Duffy's motor was smashed and he had to run for his life', an inconvenience he would become accustomed to during his subsequent political career.[101] Nonetheless, the republican candidates won comfortably in Monaghan, a victory the *Dundalk Democrat* churlishly attributed to the votes of Unionists, 'illiterate women', 'female voters drawing separation allowances', and other despised groups. In reality, Sinn Féin won over half the total poll and two-thirds of the nationalist vote in the county.[102] Nationally, the republicans won 73 seats against the Irish Party's paltry 6, while the Unionists took 26. Supported by this democratic mandate, Sinn Féin convened an Irish parliament, Dáil Éireann, and declared independence in January 1919. Established by democratic means, the Republic would be defended by violence.

In Monaghan, as in much of the country, the drift from sporadic violence to disorder was gradual. Poorly armed, and constrained by a substantial minority of hostile Unionists and resentful Hibernians, O'Duffy focused on organizing the ever-expanding Volunteer units and improving his brigade's intelligence and command structures. Violence remained rare, but intimidation of the IRA's enemies gathered pace. A wide-scale boycott of the RIC had begun in the summer of 1918, one pragmatic Sinn Féin leader urging republicans not to interfere with armed police but to 'let them have it when they were unarmed'.[103] In the summer of 1919 the RIC stood by impotently while republicans attacked an AOH dance in Castleblayney.[104] In December a constable was attacked and disarmed near Castleblayney. Policemen, and their wives, began receiving death threats. Others were forced at gunpoint to swear oaths to resign.[105] Most effective, however, was the policy of ostracizing the RIC, a predominantly Catholic force whose members had previously been well respected. They were shunned by their neighbours, who refused to exchange greetings, sit beside them at church, or conduct business with them.[106] Many chose to resign, the inspector general noted, rather than live 'boycotted, ostracised, forced to commandeer their food, crowded in many instances into cramped quarters without proper light or air, every man's hand against them, in danger of their lives and subjected to the appeals of their parents and their families to induce them to leave the force'.[107]

In many areas, the strategy of ostracization preceded that of assassination, a policy much discussed in Monaghan. The *Dundalk Democrat* called on the Dáil, some of whose deputies were uneasy about such tactics, to disassociate itself from these killings.[108] Some local priests also counselled restraint. The inspector general drew attention to a significant incident in Carrickmacross: 'when the Parish Priest in the course of religious instruction in his Church condemned the murderous attacks on the police whose character he defended, one local Suspect stood up and walked out and another interrupted the Clergyman'.[109] O'Duffy did not yet support the policy of assassination. When the county crown solicitor discovered he was to be rearrested, he pleaded for his continued liberty:

I know that he is opposed to assassination and has so far prevented the shooting of policemen in this county though he may for all I know have taken part in the Ballytrain Barrack attack. I can myself quite understand that you may fail to see a distinction and personally I consider blowing up a barrack and ambushing a policeman to be both crimes but I am able to at least understand the O'Duffy type of mind which considers shooting policemen in a barrack 'war' and shooting them on the road murder. I am certain that if O'Duffy be arrested at present all restraining influence re the extremists in the county will be removed and assassinations are likely to commence. I am not writing this at random but on evidence I have gathered from Sinn Feiners who are opposed to violent methods.[110]

Not only did O'Duffy oppose the killing of policemen, he cultivated contacts with friendly, frightened, or otherwise susceptible RIC men. Diligent policemen were intimidated out of their jobs, while their less enthusiastic colleagues—such as Sergeant Doherty of Emyvale barracks—were urged to remain in their positions. O'Duffy even ordered fake attacks to boost the credibility of shirkers and sympathizers.[111] Aided by his intelligence officer, Dr Conn Ward, O'Duffy built an effective intelligence network. His most valuable informant was his cousin and childhood next-door neighbour, Patrick Walsh, a district inspector in Donegal who regularly visited the RIC depot in Dublin where he 'picked up a lot of general information there—plans, location (suspected) of wanted men, spies to be sent into certain areas, and the import-ant police code-numbers for the month or fortnight'.[112] Ward recalled that valuable intelligence was also supplied by post-office clerks: 'I had agents in Monaghan Post Office and other post offices who intercepted messages, letters, telegrams, etc. and passed them on to me for decoding...[we] had even the postmen organised. Often an intercepted message was delivered to me for perusal or decoding by a postman in uniform. Collins supplied me with an enemy code—it often changed each month—and the rest was a matter of time.'[113] Raids on police despatches and post offices allowed O'Duffy to identi-fy his enemies and read the latest reports on his activities.[114] Seized mail was read by O'Duffy and his staff, rubber-stamped with the inscription 'Censored by the IRA', and re-posted.[115] This intelligence network deterred potential informers and restricted the police's ability to cope with the republican threat. Indeed, a police report of a raid on O'Duffy's house in September 1919 suggests the force was rendered ineffective before serious violence was directed against it:

O'Duffy was present when the search was made & when 5 revolvers & 108 rounds of revolver ammunition were found. O'Duffy remarked to Sergt. Wray who made the seizure that he supposed this would mean trouble to which the Sergt. replied that he supposed so. Only two police were present & only 3 others in Clones & consequently it was not safe to arrest O'Duffy.[116]

Despite his notoriety, it was not until after this raid that O'Duffy was forced on the run and, even then, he continued to draw his salary from the council. In February 1921, the Unionist councillor Colonel Madden (better known to nationalists as 'Dirty Buttons'), complained that O'Duffy had not been seen for months: 'I am being told that he is what is called technically "on the run".' The council's response was unsympathetic. The republican-dominated body accepted its surveyor's assurances that O'Duffy's roads were the best in the county (prompting one councillor to interject that 'He seems to be "on the run" from one job to another').[117] Madden returned to the subject with even less success the following month:

'Who pays him?' queried the Colonel.
Secretary—The county pays him.
Col Madden—Who hands the money to him?
Secretary—The cheque is sent to him.
Mr Marron—Why is the Colonel so anxious about this man. Is he looking for information?
Dr Ward—...He could not possibly perform his work owing to the activity of the British forces in this country. He thought they should appoint a man to do it and continue to pay Mr O'Duffy. He thought that was the least they ought to do for a man hounded out of his work.[118]

O'Duffy's revolutionary duties, which included overseeing the destruction of the roads he was paid to repair during the day, continued to be subsidized by the council. Indeed, the level of repairs required earned him a bonus.[119] He also found time to establish an auctioneering business with Dan Hogan, based, as a circular to Sinn Féin *cumainn* illustrates, on a crude appeal to sectarianism: 'It is not our desire to interfere in any way with the business of any Catholic auctioneer now practising, but every day we see Catholics placing their sales in the hands of non-Catholic Auctioneers who are the avowed supporters of the British garrison.'[120] His ownership of a car and ability to purchase 25 pounds' worth of 'Republican Bonds' marked him out as prosperous by local standards. Like many rural republican leaders, O'Duffy was a hard-working, canny, and ambitious individual who would also have prospered in normal times. Richard Mulcahy would later remark, in a not entirely approving manner, that O'Duffy 'had a handling of all types of money'.[121] Life on the run allowed O'Duffy to dedicate more of his time to the IRA as well as his business interests. By 1920, it took him over three weeks, spending two nights with each company, to inspect just one of the five battalions under his command.[122] He led a peripatetic existence, endlessly inspecting IRA companies and seeking refuge in isolated farmhouses, safe houses, and friendly hotels. In Monaghan town he stayed with Mrs Clare, an RIC sergeant's widow with 'an easy and discerning manner of dealing with the police'.[123]

Despite his many commitments, O'Duffy remained active in the GAA, serving as a county coach and sitting on a committee to revise GAA rules during the height of the conflict.[124] He intensified his campaign against garrison games in late 1919, writing to the *Anglo-Celt* to condemn the government's harassment of the GAA and 'the sneers of that superior section of the people who regarded Irish games beneath them because they did not bear an English hall-mark'.[125] He accused the government of using 'bribery and corruption' to popularize soccer in order to 'make the world believe that the people of Ulster are different from the rest of Ireland, and that we are so endeared to the Empire as to ape even her habits and customs'. He cited several examples. The chairman of the Belfast Soccer League offered two Clones GAA players '£5 per match and a good time' to switch codes. The Donegal county board secretary was offered £50 to defect to the Irish Football Association. A Clones soccer team, composed 'largely of ex-soldiers', had received 'free outfits and . . . high class cuisine—much better than Gaels could provide'. O'Duffy insisted that this campaign would not weaken the GAA—'on the contrary, it will awaken the spirit and strengthen the backbone of our Ulster people and the irresistible voice of young Ireland'—but warned that it would bring 'to the surface some unexpected shoneenism'. He concluded by calling for a boycott of soccer:

it is the game of the British Garrison, the atmosphere surrounding it is anglicised, and no one can contradict me when I say that the enemies of Irish Freedom patronise and finance it. Ireland asks her sons to play and support our National games; the friends of the Empire ask you to play and support Soccer—make your choice, and for goodness sake do it at once. We welcome every Irishman to our fold who has a pride in the ancient traditions of our race and who, to preserve our individuality, is prepared to cast aside everything which means to make us slaves to the mannerisms of an alien race.

His tirade provoked a sarcastic response from 'Clones Celtic Player' who did not see what 'the days of the Firbolgs' had to do with soccer, and questioned why youths with little interest in Gaelic sports should not play soccer:

Mr. O'Duffy's letter deliberately connects politics with sport; why, I do not know. I have never regarded Soccer as an English game, and Mr. O'Duffy well knows it is as much an international pastime or game as billiards, cards, swimming, running . . . Mr. O'Duffy apparently does not believe in any person remaining neutral: if you are not for him, you are against him . . . Mr. O'Duffy yearns for freedom in the realms of politics, yet he would deny it to even the 'natives' in the realms of sports. For aught I know, this great sports man may now, in his seclusion be perfecting some new indoor game to take the place of those foreign and very antiquated games—'billiards' and 'solo-whist', and, if he succeeds, devotees of the two latter games may shake in their shoes.[126]

The campaign illustrated O'Duffy's relentless determination to subordinate sport to political ends. Given the importance of sport in disseminating British imperial values, and the belief, shared by many leading Gaels, that such values were intended to sap Irish national identity, this conflict between 'native' and 'anglicized' sports was inevitable.[127] O'Duffy's intention was not merely to widen divisions between Catholics and Protestants but also between republicans and constitutional nationalists. It was a cultural equivalent of the political campaign against Redmondites, intended to remove the middle ground between supporters of Sinn Féin and British rule. The campaign served much the same purpose as the GAA's ban and its exclusion of public servants who had taken the oath of allegiance (a recent measure which had led O'Duffy to announce the expulsion of his erstwhile mentor, Patrick Whelan).[128] Finally, by strengthening local support for republicanism, and depicting its political rivals as pro-British, it helped to legitimize the violence which was soon to follow.

3

War to the death
in Monaghan

For me war has no horrors. I am not a bit afraid of war.[1]

By the spring of 1920, the Monaghan brigade was ready for action. Its first operation, the destruction of Ballytrain barracks on 15 February, would prove the most successful. O'Duffy and his brigade staff planned the attack 'in the most minute detail'.[2] After setting up a number of roadblocks, and cutting the surrounding telegraph and telephone lines, a large force of Volunteers silently occupied Ballytrain, a quiet village in rugged, hilly, country, north-west of Carrickmacross.[3] At 2 a.m. they opened fire from several buildings surrounding the barracks. O'Duffy had assumed that its small garrison of six men would quickly capitulate but, as one of the constable's wives later revealed, they were unable to 'because of the tension between the two sergeants. Lawton was a Catholic and Graham was a Protestant. Neither of them would suggest surrender lest the other would boast afterwards that he would have held out but for his comrade's cowardice.'[4] Undeterred, the well-drilled Volunteers set to work:

All the men engaged in this early morning attack wore masks. They carried either revolvers or rifles and were led by a tall thin man [O'Duffy] who gave orders through a megaphone, addressing the leaders of the various gangs by numbers. This tall leader, with another man [Hogan], did all the talking. Several times they called loudly to the police to surrender, and the only reply received was a continuance of the rifle firing...[5]

A council ganger and team of quarry-blasters, who worked under O'Duffy on the roads, began digging under the foundation of the barracks' gable wall.

Despite hearing the ominous scraping of picks, the policemen refused to surrender.[6] Volunteers kept the barracks under fire while Ernie O'Malley, a visiting GHQ organizer, provided 'a display of the correct method of throwing a hand grenade'.[7] When the mine was set, James McKenna recalled, O'Duffy 'gave them three calls through a megaphone . . . "they replied each time with a rifle shot" '.[8] O'Duffy then urged the policemen to take cover at the opposite side of the barracks.[9] The explosion reduced the gable wall to rubble, collapsing the first floor upon the dazed policemen who surrendered immediately. According to McKenna: 'When we reached the police they said "Thank God we are safe," "you gave us a good chance," "It was our own fault".' Constable Roddy recalled that O'Duffy 'asked if anyone had been shot, and when I said "No" he replied, "There's none of our men shot either. I am glad there is no life lost. We didn't come to do any injury, but merely for the arms."' O'Duffy congratulated them on their resistance—'Ye made a good fight'—but demanded to know why they had not surrendered. Sergeant Lawton replied: 'We had no notion of giving in till we had to.'[10] Sergeant Gallagher, who was seriously wounded, was given a first-aid kit of dubious value ('a little linen purse containing some lint and religious emblems'), while O'Duffy exchanged a few words in Gaelic with Lawton. He took the opportunity to lecture the police, telling 'them that at the general election the people had voted for freedom. The police were acting against the will of the Irish people. He appealed to them to leave the force and join their brother Irishmen.' Retrieving the RIC's weapons and ammunition from the rubble, his men headed home.[11] Having ordered them to make themselves conspicuous at mass the following morning, O'Duffy returned to Newbliss where he spent the night at a priest's house.[12]

The skilfully executed raid confirmed O'Duffy's promising reputation at GHQ, which had sanctioned the operation. It had a significant local impact, encouraging Volunteers and boosting recruitment and activity.[13] By forcing the closure of vulnerable barracks in Scotstown, Tydavnet, Emyvale, and Smithboro, the raid left much of rural Monaghan unpoliced, shaking the morale of RIC men and Unionists. Even in towns like Clones, one Volunteer recalled, it now became 'the practice of the IRA to parade the streets of the town at night and the R.I.C. remained within their barracks during the hours of darkness'.[14] In retrospect, perhaps the most striking aspect of the first major action of the war in Monaghan was the lack of ruthlessness, even chivalry, displayed by both sides, a quality which would be conspicuous by its absence by 1921. The attack was inevitably followed by a series of police raids which netted many Volunteers during the following month.[15] O'Duffy was arrested at a meeting of the GAA's Ulster council in Armagh, although it was widely believed that he had invited his arrest in order to start a hunger strike in Belfast prison to support the ongoing protests in Wormwood Scrubs and Mountjoy.[16]

On his return to Belfast, O'Duffy, now an IRA leader of some stature, joined the prisoners' military council, pressing for a hunger strike to protest against their arrest without charge or trial. It began on Monday 26 April, when over a hundred prisoners delivered an ultimatum to the governor demanding their unconditional release. They remained sufficiently healthy to complete a handball tournament on Tuesday, but O'Duffy ordered the men to bed that evening after a prisoner collapsed during the Rosary. On Wednesday, following the transfer of the prison O/C and fifty-four republicans to another jail, O'Duffy took charge. He immediately halted the deportations by pointedly informing the doctor that he would be held personally responsible should any of these prisoners die.[17] The doctor, remembered as 'a kind and considerate old man', began discharging the ailing prisoners. The governor appeared no less keen to avoid confrontation with his 'determined' but 'orderly and obedient' charges.[18]

By the end of the week the authorities' resolve had crumbled, an outcome assisted by pressure from Dr MacRory, bishop of Down and Connor, who visited the prisoners daily, urging them 'to continue our fight and to stand or fall by our principles'.[19] Phil Marron, the prison handball champion who had earlier promised his mother that the strike would 'end in death or victory', wrote: 'There are 44 of us here in the one ward, in the very best of spirits but very very weak, however we will be all right in a few days and expect to make our triumphal march home in the beginning of next week.'[20] They had achieved a symbolically important victory: 'Our fight is won and we have proved ourselves to be Irishmen. Our success is wonderful propaganda in the city of Belfast and after a little while the Joe Devlinites will be Sinn Feiners.'[21] In contrast, the authorities' lack of resolve compounded the demoralization of the RIC. When O'Duffy returned to Clones a week later, he was formally welcomed by the county council (an increasingly republican body since the general election had revealed which way the wind was blowing), which expressed its appreciation for his courageous opposition to injustice: 'He had been arrested for no crime as far as they knew, and he had fought a manly battle.' Agreeing that they 'had a hard fight against injustice', O'Duffy 'hoped they would now be able to carry on the work'—the nature of which he left unspecified.[22]

He had been released just in time to participate in the June local elections, of particular importance as the respectable performance of constitutional nationalists in the earlier (urban) election, the first held under proportional representation, had allowed Sinn Féin's critics to argue that it did not speak for nationalism.[23] A pragmatic combination of intimidation and organization prevented this reoccurrence. As one nationalist candidate from Inniskeen, who withdrew after he was raided by armed republicans, complained: 'There is not much freedom or self-determination about that kind of thing.'[24] By the following week every nationalist candidate in south Monaghan had withdrawn from the election.[25]

Republican control of the county council demonstrated the increasingly blurred distinction between Sinn Féin's functions and those of the IRA. In effect, the coercion of republicans drove the political wing underground, ensuring that more decisions were made by the IRA. It was O'Duffy who arranged which republicans would stand for election. He preferred young candidates who did not own property that might be seized when the council refused to forward the rates to the local government board. Some were apolitical Volunteers, but many were veteran Redmondites who simply switched sides. Hence, the traditional complaints of jobbery continued to be heard, but from Hibernians rather than republicans.[26] Given the circumstances, it was not the most democratic of bodies—as one councillor recalled: 'Before the meeting of the Co. Council was held, the Sinn Fein members held a meeting in St. Macartan's Hall where Father McNamee instructed us how to vote. That is we were to repudiate the British local government and to stop paying the rates to them . . . Only man to oppose it was Colonel Madden (Dirty Buttons).'[27] Issues affecting military matters were decided solely by O'Duffy.[28]

Victory in the local elections allowed Sinn Féin to implement Arthur Griffith's strategy of establishing rival structures of administration. The tricolour was raised over the courthouse, and the county council proclaimed its allegiance to the Dáil.[29] O'Duffy chaired a meeting of local bodies to establish arbitration courts under the auspices of the Dáil, an initiative which quickly sidelined the crown courts.[30] Both magistrates and witnesses failed to attend petty sessions in Carrickmacross and Castleblayney the following month, while sessions in Shercock and Cootehill were cancelled after their cases were 'transferred' to the republican courts.[31] Monaghan assizes were adjourned when the plaintiff explained that 'his life would not be worth very much' if he continued with the case.[32] The *Dundalk Democrat* often highlighted the coercive aspect of the republican courts.[33] In August, for example, a man charged with assaulting a republican who had 'subjected him to annoyance for refusing to vote for MacEntee' was abducted for ignoring the ruling of the Dáil court. During the same week, two men accused of assaulting their female companions after a dance were abducted and forced to choose between deportation or a fine.[34]

The inspector general claimed 'that the great mass of the population would be relieved to see an end put to them'.[35] The *War of Independence in Monaghan*, however, stated that they 'quickly established a reputation for justice', although republican judges were too reluctant to convict without reliable evidence.[36] In contrast, one of the actual judges recalled that if a Volunteer officer 'was satisfied of the accused's guilt . . . conviction was taken for granted', regardless of whether any evidence was produced.[37] Prosecutions for crimes as diverse as theft, wife desertion, and infanticide occurred.[38] One IRA warder recollected that his 'prisoners were there for stealing sheep, clothes, bicycles and for sexual misdemeanours'.[39] Criminal prosecutions presented greater difficulties than did arbitration cases as judges had to resort to fines, exile, and other unconventional punishments due to the impracticality of imprisonment. The prosecution of Protestants, who were forced to swear an oath to the Republic, also provoked resentment.[40] But notwithstanding the inevitable abuses, many republicans felt the courts were a successful improvisation. Their popular, if not universal, acceptance demonstrated the Dáil's credibility and the weakness of British authority. The RIC greatly resented the government's toleration of the courts, which 'do more than anything else to undermine the authority of the Crown in this county, and to drive loyal persons to seek protection in the Sinn Fein fold'.[41] However, their subsequent suppression also proved problematic: 'The S.F. courts died out when the war got hot. The IRA tried people on their own.'[42] One Volunteer complained that his commandant, P. J. O'Daly, 'loved to preside at midnight courts, to take witnesses out of bed at all hours and to use Volunteers to do it. He loved the sense of power it gave him.'[43] These less accountable trials, often presided over by O'Duffy, would result in several dubious executions.

Sinn Féin desperado

O'Duffy had drawn up plans to reorganize the Volunteers while in prison, and it was shortly after his release that the RIC began to record the county's state as disturbed: 'Co. Monaghan is getting an evil reputation. The Sinn Feiners there stop at nothing but murder.'[44] One of the IRA's most common activities was raiding for *poitín*, which became more available as lawlessness grew. The IRA fined the *poitín*-makers of the remote mountain districts, destroying or seizing their stills for display outside churches. These actions won support, particularly from wives and mothers, but also antagonized people in areas where poitín-making had become a way of life.[45] Publicans were ordered to close their bars on time, fined if drunks were found on their premises, and forbidden to serve 'the tramp class'. During Terence MacSwiney's hunger strike, O'Duffy banned 'all dances and other entertainments'.[46] Such measures reflected both the prevalence of alcoholism in rural areas and the IRA's puritanical ethos. O'Duffy warned that Volunteers of any rank who succumbed to the 'Drink Evil' would have to leave the county 'within 7 days or be shot'.[47] Like the establishment of the republican courts, the IRA's appropriation of the RIC's policing duties allowed it to assert its authority over the community while challenging the power of the state.

A police report described one such midnight raid by O'Duffy and twenty armed men in Lisnaskea in July 1920: 'The owner of the house, who was in bed, heard a noise outside his door, and a voice shouting "Open the Door". The owner on asking who are you was told to "open the door. We are the Irish Volunteers" and without waiting for the door to be opened the raiders burst it in.'[48] A search of the house yielded 18 pounds of sugar. The owner was brought outside and tied up with other prisoners while the raids continued. O'Duffy returned with 'one other prisoner, a bottle of whiskey, an arm of a still, and a piece of a worm', releasing the men after they pledged to never make poitín again. The district inspector reported that the victim, who had recognized O'Duffy, was willing to give evidence 'but if he does so he cannot live in the country as he would be murdered'. He recommended a charge of burglary as it would 'degrade and humiliate them more than a charge of unlawful assembly'.[49] Despite the interception of this report by the IRA, the county inspector urged prosecution, but he was overruled by the deputy inspector general, who noted that the victim 'may be in some danger already owing to the loss of the file but nothing to what he would be in if this Sinn Fein desperado Owen O'Duffy was arrested'. The police offered the victim money to leave the area and decided to rearrest O'Duffy on an old charge but, despite several close shaves, they failed to catch their elusive prey, who was spotted, among other disguises, in 'woman's clothes' and 'clerical garb'.[50]

The IRA's other principal activity was raiding for arms. O'Duffy told Cathal Brugha that his brigade had received only one rifle from GHQ, the other eighty-four having been 'captured from the British or Ulster Forces'.[51] In reality, most of these weapons were seized from their Protestant neighbours. In June 1920 the county inspector identified O'Duffy as the ringleader behind the widespread arms raids.[52] A police report described one such raid during the same month. At 3 a.m. on 9 June the door of Robert McAdoo's house near Clones was forced open by several dozen men:

Ten men entered and went straight to McAdoo's bedroom shouting 'hands up', covered him with revolvers and demanded his arms ... They arrested McAdoo and took him about 1½ miles into a field where they put him on his knees and made him swear that he would not divulge the names of the raiders. McAdoo states that Owen O'Duffy of Clones was in command of this party & gave all orders as regards searching & read a document to him in the house to the effect that he was to hand over all arms in his possession to them. O'Duffy ... also administered the oath. O'Duffy was wearing a mask—a handkerchief tied across his face ... McAdoo told him on his way from the house to take off his mask that he knew him well.

McAdoo, described as a 'weak-minded' Protestant, was willing to testify against O'Duffy despite believing 'it will mean his death at their hands', a prediction which seemed all the more prescient after his statement was intercepted by the IRA.[53] The county inspector, however, decided that O'Duffy could not be arrested without a military force being drafted into Clones, a remarkable admission of his lack of authority.[54]

Under pressure to halt the raids owing to their unpopularity, O'Duffy secured GHQ's permission for a one-off county-wide raid on 31 August.[55] Volunteers swapped areas with other companies to prevent their identification. Their choice of targets reflected the increasingly sectarian nature of the conflict: raids were reported on 'nearly every Unionist home in the Churchill, Monaghan town, Newbliss, Clones, Ballybay and Carrickmacross areas'.[56] While it was obviously easier to capture arms from Protestant civilians than from the RIC, the raids were also motivated by sectarian tensions and the Volunteers' resentment of Protestant support for the authorities: 'They gave information concerning the IRA to Crown forces and maintained a most hostile attitude to everything republican.'[57] The raids formed part of a broader pattern of intimidation which included Hibernians and other active Redmondites.[58] One list of targets illustrates the range of grievances underlying much revolutionary violence.

We did five houses:

 i Master McGroder—always pro-British
ii Maguire from Cavan, an ex-RIC man living at the Crossroads. He struggled and did not give up the gun till his wife fainted.

iii McWilliams, a Protestant who occupied a house once owned by Corrigan, a Ribbonman, who was evicted in early Land League times.

iv Kimmins or Cummins, a Protestant, occupying a house and farm from which a Ribbonman Marron had been evicted.[59]

O'Duffy was criticized by some of his own men for the general raid, which provoked resentment among the wider community. One Volunteer conceded that 'We got very little arms . . . as the Unionists had handed in their firearms to the police before the raid took place.'[60] Another deemed it 'partly a failure'.[61] It also produced the brigade's first fatalities. Three Volunteers were killed during the raid, while a fourth died soon after.[62] They were buried secretly: 'it was not considered good policy to publish our casualties'.[63] Local Protestants, many of them isolated in rural nationalist areas, were outraged. Some fought back despite the size of the raiding parties (in some cases reportedly up to 200 men).[64] Jock Hazlett of Kilnadrain was shot in the neck by raiders.[65] Col Madden's daughter was shot during a raid on Ardan House in Clones.[66] In contrast, one Protestant, whose 'dog was very friendly with the raiders' received a polite apology for the disturbance, while another paid 'tribute to the pleasant way that the raiders visited him. They came and parted on the happiest terms.'[67]

More than any event up to that time, however, the raid increased sectarian tensions.[68] One Volunteer complained that it 'did more harm than good as it made the Unionists and Hibernians more antagonistic than ever. After this in predominantly Unionist areas the armed Orangemen or B men paraded the roads every night.'[69] Volunteers were also outraged by their own casualties, which were seen as evidence of 'how determined the Protestants were to use their arms'.[70] Its repercussions illustrated the cyclical nature of much of the violence which would follow. Bernard Marron, an IRA man shot dead as he raided the McCaul farm, was avenged a fortnight later in a second midnight raid by 100 masked men. James McCaul was shot in the chest and his son, Patrick, was abducted and ordered to leave the country.[71] In October, Michael Kelly, a Catholic hackney-driver, was murdered by Unionists as a reprisal for the arms raid.[72] In March 1921 an elderly Protestant farmer from Drumgarra and his son were murdered to avenge Patrick McKenna, who had been killed while raiding their farm:

Somewhere about 2 o'clock on Tuesday morning—a bitterly cold morning with a drizzling rain succeeding the sleety showers of the early night—the Fleming household was aroused by a crowd of armed civilians estimated at between forty and fifty, who demanded admission, calling on William Fleming and his son to come out at once.

The men rose from bed, and the old man shouted back that they would not surrender. They were then called upon to hand out the shotgun for which the elder man had obtained a permit. This the Flemings refused to do. Thereupon the house was set on fire. With the smoke suffocating the old woman and the children...Fleming and his son opened up the door and handed up the gun. Neither man was fully dressed...bareheaded and barefooted—they were escorted from the house, through a bye-road some perches from the house...They were placed against the ditch by the armed men and a volley of shots directed at them. Robert fell mortally wounded. A big discharge from a shotgun—probably the weapon which had been handed up—caught him in the lower jawbone. The side of his neck was almost blown away...The father was seriously wounded. He was shot in the back and stomach. Though very seriously wounded, he crawled back to the outhouse and there, in the presence of his mother and children, lay on the floor and covered himself with hay.[73]

A 'quiet, inoffensive man, a Unionist in politics, but not mixing much in political matters', William Fleming 'had been very friendly with all around' until the death of McKenna.[74] The arms raids continued for some months— the killing of Thomas Hill, a popular Protestant farmer, provoked further outrage—until public pressure took effect, with even the republican-controlled county council calling for an end to them.[75]

As brigade O/C, it was O'Duffy's responsibility to control local units and prevent a descent into communal violence. One Volunteer recalled that he did act as a restraining influence:

At Tullyvara a Hibernian, Keenan, was arrested and charged with assaulting a Volunteer...A girl at Cullaville had her hair clipped for courting an RIC constable whom she later married. This was the state of the country in 1919. The authority of the British Government had collapsed but the Volunteer movement in this area had not yet realised who the real enemy were...O'Duffy called for stricter discipline. He criticised some previous activities. He pointed out clearly that our real enemies were the British Government and their spies, the RIC. At the same time it was up to the Volunteers to maintain law and order in the area. Anyone who was not prepared to obey orders was free to leave the meeting.[76]

This restraining role became crucial in the final year of the conflict, as the number of unjustifiable incidents increased. A teaching inspector, for example, was abducted because his views on history did 'not coincide with Irish ideas'.[77] An IRA officer complained that one of his companies was 'more interested in raiding their neighbours than in fighting'.[78] O'Duffy continued to criticize such behaviour. He prevented one company from killing local Protestants to avenge Michael Kelly's death.[79] Another Volunteer remembered him 'insisting that they were to act solely under orders'.[80]

Was O'Duffy responsible for directing a campaign of sectarian violence? Given the county's demographic composition, sectarian conflict was inevitable regardless of who led the IRA. O'Duffy's views on Protestants, as on most issues, were inconsistent and contradictory. He denied accusations of bigotry, pointing to his amicable relationship with Unionists:

Often on the evening of the 'twelfth' of July—annual festival day of the Orangeman— I would visit Rockcorry, after the 'walk' with its fiery orations and defiant drumming, and join the Chairman and other members of the Cootehill Rural District Council in their revellings. Though the 'Boyne Water' and 'Derry Walls' were rendered with much gusto, they enjoyed equally if not better their Surveyor's recital of 'Orange and Green' and 'The Man from God Knows Where'.[81]

Yet, like most Irish republicans, O'Duffy was essentially a Catholic nationalist; aside from opposition to British rule, his ideological outlook was defined by the importance of Gaelic culture, Catholicism, and the right of a supposed Irish race to self-determination. At the same time, he rejected the notion that he adhered to a sectarian conception of nationalism, and welcomed oddities like *gaelgoir* Protestant patriot Ernest Blythe into the fold.

The ambiguous position of Unionists within this world-view was never resolved: Protestants were clearly not part of the Irish nation as O'Duffy conceived of it, yet he understood that republican ideology embraced Protestants within the Irish nation. This irresolvable dilemma reflected the tensions between the civic nationalist rhetoric of republicanism, which dated back to Wolfe Tone and the United Irishmen, and its ethnic nationalist reality (a tension which remains to this day). O'Duffy fell back on the usual arguments to square the circle: that the assimilative powers of the Gael would eventually absorb the alien planter; that Unionism was an artificial ideology; that Protestants were victims of a false consciousness, or even misunderstood nationalists. The latter theory necessitated a remarkable degree of self-delusion. O'Duffy implausibly asserted that 'Many Protestants were in the best of my corps', and that this religious diversity 'was not in any way peculiar to Monaghan'. After 1920, O'Duffy would blame Britain's partition of Ireland for the 'invisible border in the minds of Irishmen', rather than seeing the former as a consequence of the latter. Throughout his life, a tendency to emphasize 'the natural national unity among Irish people who to the outsider seem poles apart' would alternate with belligerent demands for war on the north. This contradictory outlook was shared by republicans of much greater intellect. De Valera often claimed that 'the natural Irishness of the northerners' would flourish when British rule ended, while on other occasions denouncing Unionists 'with undisguised hostility as aliens'.[82]

O'Duffy generally strived to keep a lid on sectarian violence but there were significant exceptions. His support for the Belfast boycott, which began in the summer of 1920 as a protest against the mass expulsion of Catholics from the shipyards, raised sectarian tensions. Commercial travellers from Belfast were expelled and local shopkeepers were warned not to deal with Belfast firms. Despite some nationalist unease, the boycott was extended to those Protestant traders who refused to support the campaign on economic or political grounds. The boycott's inconsistencies were highlighted by an incident when Castleblayney's board of guardians demanded that its officials accept the Dáil's authority or face dismissal. Observing that a resolution against the imposition of political tests by the Orangemen of Belfast was passed at the same meeting, the *Dundalk Democrat* asked: 'Could self-contradiction go further?'[83] The boycott's local appeal was based on self-interest as well as solidarity, nationalist traders welcoming the opportunity of breaking the dominant position of their Protestant competitors.

Even before it was authorized by the Dáil in September 1920, O'Duffy strongly backed the boycott, ensuring that Monaghan was the only county where it was effectively enforced.[84] The IRA picketed Protestant stores, harassed Catholics who patronized them, and demanded fines to remove traders from their blacklist. Delivery vans from Belfast were burned. Trains carrying northern goods were raided and the rail-tracks sabotaged. These attacks were also intended to prevent the predominantly Protestant workforce of the Great Northern Railways from carrying troops or military supplies. Workers who did not co-operate were abducted and forced to sign pledges to refuse such work. Henry Macklin, who kidnapped a train driver, recalled that 'O'Duffy held a court martial on him. He was so full of sorrow in the way he asked pardon that O'Duffy let him go with a caution never to appear around Monaghan again. And he never did.' A less co-operative worker was shot.[85]

Although emotionally satisfying, disruption of cross-border trade reinforced partition in the long run. Indeed, the boycott provides an interesting line of demarcation on republican attitudes to the north. Ernest Blythe complained about his cabinet colleagues' ignorance of the north when Collins won approval for this 'most ridiculous and short-sighted proposal'.[86] When Desmond FitzGerald complained to the supposedly progressive Countess Markievicz about the sectarian nature of her boycott publicity, the Countess replied that she 'found that the religious is much more effective than the political plea where Republicanism has not been thoroughly crystallised', a revealing sentiment which O'Duffy would have understood.[87] In Monaghan, the boycott intensified sectarianism to the point that the RIC warned that violence 'is likely to occur on the slightest provocation'.[88] In February 1921, the county inspector predicted conflict between the IRA and the Ulster Special Constabulary along the Monaghan–Fermanagh border.[89] These tensions would come to a murderous climax in the small border village of Rosslea.

War to the death

In Monaghan, as elsewhere, the final six months of the conflict were the most violent. The IRA killed eighteen people between January 1921 and the truce, compared to only three during the previous two years. What lay behind this escalation of violence and how responsible was O'Duffy? Two, more or less simultaneous, trends accounted for the deaths: first, a decision was made to assassinate crown forces; and, second, the IRA demonstrated a new willingness to kill its civilian enemies. O'Duffy's ruthlessness, and probably that also of GHQ, contributed to both trends. Having warned his men that the struggle would be intensified, and offered them the opportunity to leave, he ordered all five battalions to attack crown forces from the first day of 1921 with the intention of killing them rather than merely seizing their weapons.[90]

An ambush in Ballybay on New Year's Day killed a Black and Tan and a civilian.[91] Two days later, an RIC sergeant was wounded. Three weeks later, two constables 'were found lying dead on the road in pools of blood . . . riddled with bullets'. Another died soon after.[92] In May 1921 Constable Perkins was killed by an ambush which, the inspector general noted, demonstrated the IRA's improving tactical expertise.[93] O'Duffy planned and ordered most of these operations but, as one Volunteer explained, it was not his intention to kill as many policemen as possible: 'we only attacked those who were particularly obnoxious in their efforts to destroy us'.[94] Nevertheless, from having previously restrained his men, O'Duffy ruthlessly urged them on, as an incident recalled by a Scotstown IRA officer illustrates:

O'Duffy came round on a Friday and ordered us to shoot Sergeant Wilaghan at Urbleshanny chapel on Sunday at first mass . . . There were three Catholics in the barracks and twelve of the Tans always came to the foot of the avenue when the other three would be at Mass. We had sixteen men and scouts, and we were well armed. We were at the chapel at daylight and some of the men were in position. Some of our men did not like it and raised objections saying the congregation would stampede and that it would end badly, and none of them liked fighting at the chapel. So we called it off.[95]

This escalation of violence formed part of a national trend after the arrival of the ill-disciplined Black and Tans and more efficient Auxiliaries had placed the IRA under severe pressure. O'Duffy's rhetoric hardened: in late 1920 he urged 'war to the death in Monaghan against the enemy who has threatened to wipe out the Young Republic', ordering that officers showing 'any wea[kness] whatsoever at reprisals or threats of reprisals by [the] enemy shall be scrapped at once, no matter of what rank or how useful otherwise'.[96] A similar ruthlessness was displayed by Dan Hogan, who was much admired by his men for his military ability and devotion to the Rosary, and sometimes credited as a greater military influence than O'Duffy. Dr Conn Ward recalled: 'Bloody Sunday affected him and [he] wanted to get using [the] gun at all opportunities.'[97] (Hogan's brother, Mick, had been murdered by British soldiers while playing football in Croke Park.)

This new policy provoked some opposition. One priest appealed to the young men of Corduff to consider their actions:

I understand, from more sources than one, that Mr. O'Duffy is prepared to shoot those who oppose him. At the risk of being shot, I do not hesitate to tell him that this course of action is indiscreet, and that he will not be allowed to play fast and loose with the souls and bodies of our young men and the homes of our people without, at least, one voice being raised against it. It can scarcely be called courage for young men with arms in their hands to ambush soldiers and policemen, fly when they have murdered them and leave civilians who have no weapons except those which Nature gives them to the mercy of an enraged soldiery. Until such time as the Officers at the head of the Volunteers display ordinary prudence, I call upon any Volunteer for whose eternal salvation I am responsible to leave them, and to refuse to obey orders.[98]

O'Duffy forwarded this appeal to Collins, claiming that the priest, a former Sinn Féin supporter, had been intimidated by the Black and Tans. Collins replied that it 'amounts to an argument against the Flying Columns. I think physical force is necessary.' There were many other local priests who agreed. British intelligence, which intercepted this correspondence, thought such appeals would have 'little effect on the minds of the rebels'.

The fate of Rosslea illustrates the interrelated factors underlying the escalation of violence, which included the provocative behaviour of the Specials, the cyclical nature of sectarian violence, and O'Duffy's determination to confront challenges to his authority. There are many accounts of what occurred at Rosslea but most agree that the trouble originated with a belligerent Protestant trader named George Lester. In February 1921 it was reported that Lester, after receiving a threatening letter, called on local Catholics and 'threatened reprisals should anything happen him or his property'.[99] Other accounts also claimed that 'a B-man called Lister' had fired on a priest.[100] According to James McKenna, the final provocation occurred when Lister 'held up and searched at least two boys whom he suspected of being despatch carriers for the IRA'.[101] McKenna reported that when 'O'Duffy heard of Lester's action, he ordered me to have Lester shot. Within a short time Lester was fired on from the market house at about 8.30 a.m. when he was removing the shutters from his shop windows. He crept into his shop, and in due course recovered from his injuries.'

The Specials retaliated by invading Rosslea on 23 February, sacking the Catholic part of town.[102] An outraged O'Duffy told GHQ: 'Every Catholic house was fired into and several women and children had narrow escapes. In some cases an effort was made to burn them alive... We cannot allow this wanton conduct to go unpunished. Am I right in assuming I have a free hand in this matter?'[103] He called his officers together to plan a reprisal. While the meeting was still in progress, Dan Hogan returned from Dublin, informing O'Duffy that Collins had given him 'a free hand in the reprisals'. Resolving that they should kill four B Specials and burn down sixteen houses, O'Duffy divided the targets between three battalions.[104] The territory was unfamiliar to most Volunteers, but local youths who worked as seasonal labourers for Rosslea's Protestant farmers led each raiding party to its target.[105]

The raid occurred on the night of 21 March. Fourteen houses were torched and three Protestants, two of them Specials, were killed.[106] Samuel Nixon was the first to die:

their residence was completely circled by Sinn Feiners, who opened a deadly fire on all the apartments save that occupied by the children, and her husband had both arms broken while lying in bed. Being practically unconscious, he had no alternative but to surrender. He was dragged from the house and shot dead in the presence of his wife who clung to him and implored the raiders not to take his life. It was while trying to protect her husband that his wife had the top of her finger blown off. She was unable to get the body into the house, and was found beside it when neighbours arrived at daybreak.[107]

William Gordon, a caretaker on the Madden property, was killed next when Volunteers opened fire through his window. Finally, Joseph Douglas, who was not a Special and presumably a victim of mistaken identity, was dragged from his mother's house and executed by the roadside.[108] Some Protestants put up a fierce resistance. James McKenna was struck by the reaction of one older man: 'I said if you had kept your sons at home from the sack of Rosslea, we would not be here tonight. He replied heatedly, "You thought you could have it all your own way when you shot Lester." His attitude surprised me & seven armed men around him.' The county inspector recorded one near lapse in discipline: 'In one of the Rosslea cases when the men came out of their house on surrendering the raiders wanted to shoot them but a leader said 'If you shoot them, I'll shoot you, they did no more than they were entitled to do in defending themselves.'[109]

Although sectarian murder was no longer a rarity, the *Dundalk Democrat* expressed the revulsion felt by many at the brutality of what occurred in Rosslea:

We are here face to face with the 'civil war' of which people have so often talked carelessly, not realising either the real danger or the meaning of such a conflict. We wonder do those who talked of 'letting North and South fight it out' still hold, after reading this tragic story, that this is a desirable method of settling the Irish Question. If this thing spreads—which God forbid—nothing can save Ireland from a hideous war of extermination in which Catholic and Protestant will suffer as have those of Rosslea.[110]

The hatred between both communities was illustrated by the lack of regret felt by some Volunteers over four decades later: 'From what we heard they were a pain of bad boys and richly deserved what they got.'[111] There were no IRA fatalities, although several men were wounded and captured. The scale of the reprisal, one Volunteer recalled, 'had the effect that General O'Duffy desired'.[112] Local Unionists advised against further reprisals, conceding that the raid 'was mainly directed against Unionists who are members of the B class of the Special Constabulary'.[113] In the longer term, however, it intensified sectarianism along the border, an outcome which the county inspector believed was deliberate: 'the I.V. leaders finding that they have been losing their influence with the rank & file on political grounds are reopening the sectarian question to try to recover their lost position'.[114] Although the raid was primarily retaliatory in motive, the circumstances surrounding the reoccurrence of violence in Rosslea the following year suggests that the killings, which strengthened the IRA's credentials as defenders of the Catholic community, were also intended to reinforce republican authority over the nationalist community.

Like all brigade operations, the attack was carefully planned by O'Duffy. However, the fact that he did not participate in it raises questions about his role in the fighting. O'Duffy would later claim that he 'took charge of practically every operation myself'.[115] But, although he planned most operations, there is little evidence that he participated in many. O'Duffy was not the only IRA leader whose role was primarily organizational, but there can be few to have claimed such a prominent role in combat in proportion to their actual one. In later life, he would often drew attention to his military exploits. In 1926, for example, the *New York Evening Post* enthused: 'Three times he was wounded. You will look in vain for the index finger of his right hand, shot off in one of his numerous engagements.'[116] Dublin Castle recorded, with a touch more scepticism, that he was 'Supposed to have been wounded in different ambushes, and had index finger of left hand blown away.'[117] Yet none of the accounts in the otherwise comprehensive Marron papers mentions a single occasion when O'Duffy was involved in open conflict (although several refer to the precautions he took for his own safety). Aside from the attack on Ballytrain barracks, directed from beyond the line of fire, and the occasional midnight raid, there is no evidence that O'Duffy fired a shot in anger. The finger lost for Ireland, according to one Volunteer who encountered O'Duffy with 'one of his hands heavily bandaged', was an unintended casualty of war: 'He had an accident with an automatic pistol'.[118] Dr Paddy McCarville, a member of the north Monaghan flying column who amputated the remaining stump, also insisted that it 'had nothing to do with fighting'.[119]

The significance of the heroic reputation which O'Duffy successfully cultivated, while in some respects undeserved, should not be dismissed, given its importance at the time and throughout his later career. It ensured that he was respected, even feared, by his men and the local population, as no doubt did his power over life and death in Monaghan. His acceptability as chief of staff in the eyes of the IRA's restless regional commanders in 1922 rested partly on his uncompromising military reputation. On countless subsequent occasions, O'Duffy would exploit his war record to defend himself from criticism, undermine his opponents, or motivate those who served under him. That he exaggerated his fighting credentials should not detract from his skilful exploitation of them to bolster his genuine leadership qualities.

Keeping our own weak ones right

During the final months of the conflict, O'Duffy displayed greater ruthlessness towards his own men as well as the enemy. He forgave mistakes but punished the careless and weak. After a Corduff Volunteer allowed a priest to compromise an ambush, O'Duffy disarmed his company and sentenced the Volunteer to death following a court martial: 'Hanratty left the country and never returned.'[120] Castleblayney company was also scrapped after it failed to mobilize for an ambush.[121] An Anyalla Volunteer recalled a similar incident when an informer named Hugh O'Neill was sentenced to death: 'O'Duffy... went to his house but failed to find him anywhere.'[122]

The case of Patrick Larmer provides a more tragic example. Larmer was carrying despatches for the IRA when he stopped to join a game of pitch-and-toss outside Rockcorry church. After the group was searched by a passing military patrol, Larmer was arrested and divulged the names of other Volunteers in his company, who were soon arrested.[123] After he was released from Belfast's Victoria barracks, Larmer returned home and made a full confession to his officers, claiming to have confirmed only what the Tans already knew.[124] Some of his comrades, like John McGahey, were inclined towards sympathy: 'Larmer was an intelligent country boy who unfortunately for everybody concerned was timid and easily scared... His only fault was his weakness in yielding to threats under torture by the Tans'.[125] Sensing 'an intention to find him guilty' before the court martial, McGahey sought O'Duffy out to urge him not to kill the boy: 'I got a feeling that my pleadings were having the desired effect on O'Duffy when Dan Hogan arrived on the scene and intervened in a manner most aggressive towards myself. I have felt since, that only for Hogan's untimely arrival, I could have succeeded in influencing O'Duffy to spare Larmer's life. I failed.'

Another IRA officer, Jim Sullivan, had similar misgivings that same evening:

I attended a Brigade meeting which was held at Tullycorbett at which General O'Duffy and Dan Hogan attended. When the meeting was over I was preparing to leave when O'Duffy noticed the fact and told me to wait. He then informed me that Larmour [*sic*] was to be court-martialled. During this conversation something happened or was said which gave me the impression that Larmour was to be shot. I protested against shooting him and O'Duffy said it would be an example and a warning to the others. I replied that it would be very bad to take a young life as a warning. I said that I believed that Larmour told the Tans nothing but what they already knew. I also stated that I was with young Larmour on his first night out on a Volunteer operation when we had more men than arms to go round, and I asked for volunteers to man the arms we had and that Larmour was the first to step forward... He was then executed... [126]

For Volunteers who knew nothing about those who were executed, except the rumours which left no doubt as to their treachery, these 'British spies' deserved no sympathy. For others, such as McGahey, the regret remained evident decades later: 'I am convinced that his execution was much too drastic... I feel that his memory deserves this vindication from me.'

Such ruthlessness must be seen in context. Order could not be maintained without discipline, and three local Volunteers had previously been sentenced to death because of an informer.[127] O'Duffy's chilling rationale, that the execution would serve as 'a warning to the others', was the motive behind many of the executions he ordered—not only those of IRA men but Redmondites, Protestants, and other enemies of the Republic—in this period. This was not a phenomenon unique to Monaghan: as Peter Hart has noted, British military and intelligence successes in early 1921 had led a shaken IRA to recover lost ground 'by tightening its security and its hold on host communities'.[128] At the end of a month which had seen O'Duffy order the raid on Rosslea, as well as the executions of Larmer and another youth, the county inspector warned that the IRA was 'starting on a new scheme for murdering all opposed to them and punishing any one acting against them with death'.[129]

Given the threat represented by informers, a threat magnified by the political and religious demography of the county, the policy of executions was, from a republican perspective, a logical and necessary one. One senior republican estimated that only 20 per cent of south Monaghan's inhabitants were 'out and out supporters of the IRA'. Another 35 per cent were 'mild supporters', but almost 33 per cent were rabid Hibernians or Unionists.[130] The latter represented the enemy within, elements which could not be won over but could be frightened into submission. Ex-servicemen, pedlars, poitín-makers, and other outcasts also came under suspicion amidst the climate of fear which gripped Monaghan as dumped corpses turned up with increasing frequency. In remote areas, one IRA officer recalled, 'old men with land war and even Fenian memories' were 'very suspicious of strangers and even of some of their neighbours whose families had been under suspicion generations earlier. We were often warned "Look out for them, the black blood of the "Sthag" [informer] is in them."'[131] Particular areas, usually AOH strongholds, were regarded as suspect: 'There were plenty of spies in Tydavnet and Truagh parishes'.[132] Patrick Corrigan recalled the first local execution:

The Tans dropped off young men along the roads who posed as IRA men. In January 1920 one of these came to our district. He stayed in a vacant house and asked after the IRA. He was introduced and asked many questions about the locality. He suggested stoning the windows of the Redmondite supporters . . . I smelt a rat. I assembled the other offices and after a day, we arrested him. We found papers on him showing that he was a British soldier. His name was Joseph Gibbs. We shot and buried him on a hillside . . .[133]

Gibbs may have been a spy, a soldier, an ex-serviceman, or a vagrant. The conflict in Monaghan, as in other areas, unleashed not only communal hatred between the two communities but against perceived enemies within.[134] Corrigan participated in another shooting in April 1921: 'We arrested a pedlar...We shot and wounded him. He was also a British soldier, named McCabe from Armagh. These actions had the effect of keeping "our own weak ones" right. We had South Monaghan safe.'[135] John McCabe, an ex-soldier and pedlar of religious emblems, was found trussed up in a stable near Tullyvaragh with a sign inscribed 'Convicted spy, IRA'.[136] He had been abducted from Carrickmacross, permitted to confess his sins to a priest, and then shot in the head, back, and legs. The Volunteers involved were amazed to learn that this 'enemy espionage agent' survived despite being 'riddled with bullets'.[137] The county inspector, however, could not explain the shooting: 'No reason is known for the attempt on him. He was not in communication with the Monaghan police & in his occupation he does not seem to have made enemies.'[138]

McCabe's was one of several dubious shootings in this period. Henry Carr, an elderly farmer from Corvoy, had been found by neighbours 'lying in a pool of blood on the road' a fortnight earlier. He had been abducted from his home in the early morning of 25 March and taken to a nearby crossroads where he was shot six times in the head, chest, knee, leg, and shoulder: 'The usual notice was found beside the body—"Shot by IRA. Spies beware".'[139] Carr, who died two days later, was described as 'One of the old school of Nationalism and a man of some political knowledge, he expressed his opinions freely and fearlessly and these were well known to everybody.' Neither the *Dundalk Democrat* nor the police could explain his death: 'The old man lived alone & was generally well liked. On a raid about six weeks ago his home was visited & he chatted with the military officer. Beyond this he has had no communications with the Crown forces.'[140] However, one Volunteer claimed that a letter from Carr to the local military barracks had been discovered in an IRA raid on the mail. Local Volunteers, disguised as crown forces, had then interviewed Carr, executing him after he revealed his guilt.[141] Carr may have been a spy, as the IRA claimed, or simply an outspoken Irish Party supporter. He was the first of a series of Redmondites executed after the alleged discovery of incriminating letters.

The executions continued. On 17 April Kitty Carroll, an impoverished *poitín*-maker, was discovered by the roadside at Duffy's Cross, Tydavnet, with the usual sign: 'Spies and informers beware. Tried, convicted and executed by IRA.'[142] Carroll had previously been fined by both the IRA and the RIC.[143] Not only had she refused to pay the fines, she had continued to distil *poitín* and sent a letter to the RIC, intercepted by republicans, informing on her competition. A Volunteer recounted that 'following a court-martial by the IRA she was summarily executed and labelled as a spy'.[144] In contrast to the unproven allegations of spying levelled against the executed Redmondites, the IRA's account was confirmed by the county inspector: 'Seeing others also making poteen she sent out a letter to the police telling about them. This letter was captured on the raid on the mails and Kitty was taken out of her house 16/17 April, marched a mile away and shot dead. The usual IRA notice was forthcoming but this also is believed to be a case of sheltering behind their terrorism.'[145] The charge of spying appears to have been a convenient rationale for the execution of an obvious and antisocial security risk, someone, in the words of one Volunteer, who 'was scarcely normal and was not sufficiently intelligent to cloak her activities'.[146] Like most of the IRA's civilian victims, she was a person of no social consequence: a middle-aged Protestant spinster who lived with her senile parents and 'weak-minded' brother in a little cabin on 'a few acres of wretched mountain land'.[147]

How responsible was O'Duffy for these executions? Referring to Carroll's murder, Terence Dooley observed: 'No evidence was found to suggest that this crime was ordered to be carried out by the local leaders of the IRA; neither is there any evidence to suggest that the perpetrators were brought to justice or even reprimanded . . . this would suggest that local IRA units did more or less as they liked, and that in a county such as Monaghan, where Protestants had traditionally held the upper hand, IRA policy was dictated to a certain extent, not by a national cause but by a desire to exact revenge at a local level.'[148] Dooley's argument is sound, but questions remain about O'Duffy's complicity. Although unauthorized murders were inevitable, it seems unlikely that as strict a disciplinarian as O'Duffy lacked the authority to prevent the dramatic escalation of executions in these final months of the conflict. In Carroll's case, the fact that she reportedly received a court-martial points to the involvement of a senior officer. O'Duffy had also recently ordered that *poitín*-makers be exiled or shot, although the execution of women contravened IRA policy and was an unusual enough occurrence to provoke condemnation, including from Westminster.

O'Duffy's responsibility for the broad policy of executions is confirmed by his involvement in the death of three Hibernians during this period. The most controversial of these was the killing of Francis McPhillips, whose corpse was found alongside that of Larmer. McPhillips, a Catholic youth, was abducted from his mother's farm by five masked men at 4 a.m. on 9 March. After a court martial, which O'Duffy presided over, he was brought to a laneway and shot.[149] The process took some time, as O'Duffy had difficulty procuring a priest willing to hear his confession.[150] He was discovered with a notice pinned on his breast declaring 'Tried, convicted and executed by the IRA'.[151] Local Volunteers insisted that he was killed for informing. His mother claimed it was because he was a member of the AOH.[152] The county inspector, who acknowledged the circumstances behind Larmer's execution, claimed there was 'no reason known for the murder of McPhillips'.[153]

Seamus McPhillips, who researched the executions of the three Hibernians killed during this period, noted that it was believed locally that McPhillips was killed for passing information about republicans to his Presbyterian neighbours, a deed which was uncovered when an IRA raid on the mail produced an incriminating letter.[154] It was claimed that McPhillips, like Carr, inadvertently revealed his guilt to IRA men posing as RIC officers.[155] Whatever the truth—and the common elements involved in each appear suspicious—the killing divided the local community for decades. Some republicans had believed it unnecessary: Johnny McKenna had pleaded for his life on the grounds that he was 'inoffensive and innocent'.[156] In 1934, when O'Duffy returned to Monaghan as president of Fine Gael, he unwisely raked up the killing. Irritated by the AOH's support for Fianna Fáil, he hinted that the blame lay elsewhere: 'The AOH should be careful of their new found friends in Monaghan. Things had happened in the parish of Aghabog. It was singular that some people should attribute to him many things that happened ... There were certain people in that hall that night who had appealed against the shooting in Aghabog: there were certain people prominent in another organisation who had ignored that appeal.'[157]

O'Duffy's reopening of such a sensitive issue for political purposes was deeply resented, as was his crude attempt to deflect the blame onto his Fianna Fáil rival, Dr Conn Ward. His speech prompted Fr Maguire, the Aghabog parish priest who had heard McPhillips' final confession, publicly to accuse O'Duffy of responsibility for the execution:

After the court-martial the boy was brought to me. I was convinced then, and since I have got no evidence to change my opinion, that the boy should not have been put before the squad, I appealed to his guard to have the sentence revised, but I was told that it was final. I suggested that the boy should be sent out of the country and that the course should meet the case ... To my judgement the deceased was deserving of every human consideration, because he was generally acknowledged as not up to the normal mental standard. Moreover, it was commonly stated then and since that local bitterness influenced the evidence and court-martial decision.[158]

His death, as Fr Maguire hinted, was bound up with the bitter tensions between local Hibernians and republicans. The AOH, in contrast to the moribund UIL, had remained a vibrant movement, as had been demonstrated by the beatings meted out to republicans during the 1918 election campaign. Its condemnation of the IRA's policy of assassinating policemen led republicans to suspect that the Hibernians could not be trusted and, ultimately, to accusations of spying. In November 1920 Michael O'Brien, a 24-year-old farmer from Bawn, had become the first Hibernian victim of the IRA. He was shot, it was believed locally, because on returning home from Shercock fair with his Protestant neighbours he had recognized some armed IRA men in a ditch outside O'Duffy's safe house and called out their names.[159] The AOH national secretary, however, complained to the Dáil's minister for defence that O'Brien and another Hibernian, Arthur Treanor, were shot because 'they refused to join or support the IRA'.[160] The motives behind O'Brien's death remain unclear, but there is stronger evidence that O'Duffy ordered the execution of the third Hibernian victim for political reasons.

Treanor, in contrast to most of the IRA's victims, was a prominent member of the community. He owned two farms and sat on the north Monaghan UIL executive, board of guardians, and rural council. His corpse was discovered on 25 June 1921: 'The hair was singed, showing that the person or persons who fired were close to their victim. From the position in which he was found it would appear that he was in a kneeling posture, and that after the fatal shot he fell forward on his face. A label attached to the body alleged that he had given information to the police.'[161] Treanor, it will be recalled, had been an outspoken opponent of Sinn Féin during the 1918 election. He had also been involved in an altercation with republicans in council chambers when a vote of sympathy was proposed for the late Lord Mayor of Cork, Terence MacSwiney. He was subsequently fined by the IRA but refused to pay, instead leaving the country. Shortly before his death he had returned home, his wife paying the fine when the farm was raided. Assuming he was safe, Treanor returned to his house the following night but was abducted by the IRA.

The evidence for his guilt was the usual: 'A cheque was enclosed in a letter to a man named Arthur Treanor. This cheque came from Dublin Castle in payment for his information to Dublin Castle about the local IRA. The man was subsequently shot as a spy. He was a notorious British supporter from the time the Volunteers first started. The cheque was definite evidence.'[162] However, a local IRA captain recalled that 'Treanor was intelligent and shrewd and more difficult to involve'.[163] Another Volunteer claimed that he was targeted because he was 'several times seen calling to Monaghan and Aughnacloy barracks. He was warned more than once but persisted.'[164] Four decades later, Dr Conn Ward confirmed that Treanor had fallen under suspicion because of his hostility to Sinn Féin and his friendship with members of the RIC. When the IRA raided his house, however, they had found nothing except unpaid bills, which were taken as evidence of his innocence. Ward claimed that, despite the lack of evidence and the fact that his wife was told that he had been given a reprieve, O'Duffy had ordered the execution.[165]

Corpses continued to be discovered in ditches, back lanes, and roadsides. On 1 April 1921 a Protestant postman named Hugh Duffy was found in a laneway shot in the brain, heart, and lungs. He had been given a bogus telegram to deliver. IRA volunteers stated that the 'order was given for Duffy's liquidation' because he was one of a group of B Specials who were 'particularly active against the IRA'.[166] The county inspector (no less biased a source than the IRA interviewees) believed otherwise: 'He was acting in the absence of the regular postman who was sick & though he had so acted for years it is believed that those who opposed his appointment thought that this was a good time to use the terror of the IRA name to remove him.'[167] The reasons for many of these killings will never be known. While it is clear that few, if any, people were shot solely because of their religion, the high proportion of Protestants among the IRA's civilian victims suggests that capital punishment was far more likely to be meted out to Protestants who provoked hostility or suspicion than to Catholic transgressors.[168]

Although these executions cast the darkest shadow over O'Duffy's good war, they did not damage his local standing nor his subsequent career. On the contrary, his ruthlessness enhanced his reputation among republicans, most of whom believed the executions were justified. Referring to the treatment of the local Hibernians, *The War of Independence in Monaghan* claimed that 'a small number continued to hinder the national effort and some went as far as to help the common enemy. Therein lies much of the tragedy and the embarrassing memory of some of the events of these days.'[169] It adopted an equally pragmatic attitude towards the killing of the other 'spies' despite the (undisclosed) findings of the authors' own research:

It has often been said that some of the spies who were executed were in fact innocent. At least some of them may have been executed on evidence that would not satisfy an ordinary jury in normal times. These were not normal times, however. The deaths of these spies may have brought disrepute on certain sections of the IRA. Nevertheless they had a chastening effect on the population, and were a dire warning to any Irishman who might be tempted to sell his fellow-countrymen or endanger their lives. If any of the executed spies was really innocent, then his friends will know that his death was due to exceptional circumstances and that his death, like the deaths of many of the men who executed him, was for the good of his country.[170]

This 'chastening effect' was understood by IRA men who fought a war in an area where half the population did not support them. As one Volunteer explained: 'the ruthless cutting down of informers broke' the enemy's 'grip on outcasts inclined to give information to obtain sops or privileges for themselves'.[171] Underpinning the preventative rationale behind the executions, the censoring of mail, the fire-bombing of those who fraternized with the authorities, and the questioning and searching of inhabitants of 'mixed districts' was the IRA's belief (one shared by British officers and Specials) that ordinary people would submit to the more menacing force. As one IRA man recalled: 'stopping people in broad daylight had a disconcerting and a demoralising effect on the local "B" men, and it kept the Nationalist population in such areas who were not republican from taking any chances to fraternise or curry favour from local Unionists'.[172] Such methods were not unique to guerrilla warfare in Ireland or elsewhere.[173] While Tom Garvin has noted that Tipperary republicans privately conceded that the outcome of republican violence was the intimidation of informers and civilians generally rather than the breaking of British power, the two were obviously interconnected: in contrast to earlier periods of unrest, the authorities received little information.[174] As Richard English observed: 'These killings, and the public depositing of the placarded bodies, suggested to the population a menacing combination of IRA intelligence and brutality. This was symbolic violence used to chilling effect, and it formed one of the main strands of Republican activity in the Revolutionary years.'[175] O'Duffy shared the paradoxical tendency of many republicans to idealize rural peasants as the backbone of the Irish nation while, at the same time, harbouring considerable reservations about the sturdiness of the national vertebrae.[176] He understood that without such violence republicans would have struggled to impose their will on the community, and that the effective suppression of internal dissent was one of the principal distinctions between successful and unsuccessful revolutions.

How does O'Duffy's war add to our understanding of revolutionary violence in Ireland? This reconstruction of the role of a key guerrilla commander highlights the importance of individual leaders in organizing the IRA, co-ordinating its activities, calibrating the range and intensity of its violence, and mediating between competing pressures, whether from above (GHQ), below (Volunteers, republican politicians, and local Catholics), or the enemy (police, soldiers, and Specials). Considered in conventional terms, little of note happened in the revolutionary backwater that was Co. Monaghan between 1919 and 1921. A recent history of the War of Independence noted that, aside from the attack on Ballytrain, there were 'only three notable actions' in

Monaghan, resulting in the death of one policeman and the wounding of three Auxiliaries.[177] But this is to miss the point, forcefully made in Hart's study of Co. Cork, that much of the violence of this period was not directed at armed combatants. In Monaghan, as elsewhere, many of the conflict's victims did not belong to armed organizations.[178]

Despite the legendary accounts of crossroad ambushes, immortalized by ballads and deeply entrenched in the popular memory of the Tan War, few people were killed in open combat: 'Executions, assassination and murder were much more common than battles, and death was more likely to come at point-blank range, on doorsteps and ditches, than in a firefight.'[179] Consider, for example, O'Duffy's terse entry in an otherwise expansive monthly report detailing his brigade's unsuccessful attempts to engage the enemy: 'The following executions, of which details have been forwarded to the D/Information, were carried out by our forces during month: 1 traitor, 4 informers, and 2 death sentences for killing of our men'.[180] The brutal methods by which republicans prevailed in the Irish War of Independence were not as far removed from the recent Northern Ireland conflict as many southern politicians like to believe.

Consideration of all of those who were killed, rather than merely those in uniform, raises unsettling questions about the motives underlying revolutionary violence. O'Duffy's men killed over twenty people, approximately half of whom were civilians. As Peter Hart has empirically demonstrated, the violence between 1919 and 1921 constituted not only a war of national liberation but also 'a power struggle, not just between revolutionaries and states but also between and within communities. Both north and south, this violence was primarily directed at minority groups with the aim of uprooting, expelling, or suppressing perceived enemies within.'[181] Historians have questioned whether Hart's research accurately reflects events elsewhere or, for that matter, in Cork.[182] Aside from the Monaghan IRA's greater propensity to kill its nationalist rivals, the pattern of violence in Monaghan appears little different from that high-lighted by Hart's research on Cork, where over 200 civilians were killed in the course of the revolution: 'the main target group was the Protestant minority, followed by ex-soldiers, tinkers and tramps, and others seen as social or political deviants'.[183] Alongside the drive for independence, the struggle for domination of the nationalist community, sectarianism, and even murkier factors played some role in republican violence.

However, these findings need to be assessed in context. Cork and Monaghan were relatively unusual in having substantial Protestant minorities. The IRA in Monaghan, and in the surrounding south Ulster borderlands, was even more unusual in having a well-armed, state-supported, and violent loyalist paramilitary opponent in the form of the Special Constabulary. Republican violence in Monaghan was inevitably more sectarian than much of the rest of the country, which tended to be dominated by one side or the other, and should not be seen as representative of patterns of violence elsewhere.[184] Given the demographic mix, moreover, the level of violence in Monaghan was much lower than might have been expected: Rosslea proved the exception rather than the rule. If O'Duffy was responsible for some of the questionable murders which took place under his command, he was also responsible for the relative restraint demonstrated by the IRA during this period.

There were other reasons why the wave of violence which gripped Monaghan during the spring of 1921 did not tarnish O'Duffy's reputation. Intimidation, fear, polarization, sectarianism, and guilt ensured that the motives, participants, and circumstances behind the killings remained obscure, allowing an uneasy veil of silence to descend after the war's end. A rare exception was provided by a remarkably frank editorial in the *Dundalk Democrat*, a Redmondite paper which was qualified to speak on behalf of those who experienced the revolution as a period of fear and oppression rather than exhilaration and liberation:

From January to June over a thousand human lives were taken in the prosecution of that night-time war. Some of the victims were men who took their lives in their hands as combatants. Many were harmless and innocent people, the victims either of the ruthless methods employed or of circumstances incident to such a 'war'. Each accused the other of murder; and unquestionably the candid historian will feel constrained to apply that term to deeds as to which contemporary records thought it best to utter no verdict. There was of course little open fighting. Men were shot down on the country roads, in city streets, in their homes, in railway trains, on the threshold of the house of God. Every such shooting was the prelude to a bloody reprisal … in such conditions, mere suspicion seals many a death warrant. Nor is it improbable that private vengeance exacted its toll over cover of civil turmoil.[185]

Despite the bitterness of the civil war—and rare exceptions such as the McPhillips controversy—neither side exploited the executions for political gain. Resentment festered throughout the lifetime of the victims' families but few people sought to reopen the wounds of the past. Some of those executed may have been spies. Even if not, Hibernians, Protestants, and others on the receiving end of republican violence had to live in the new state, one in which O'Duffy as Garda commissioner would describe the erection of a memorial to the executed Hibernians as an act of anti-government agitation.[186]

By the spring of 1921 O'Duffy had proved himself one of the most effective IRA leaders in Ulster. Even the exacting GHQ organizer Ernie O'Malley described him as 'energetic and commanding'.[187] Although relatively few casualties were inflicted on crown forces in comparison to counties like Cork, the Monaghan brigade was the most violent in Ulster and the third most lethal outside Munster.[188] O'Duffy later boasted that he had moulded an efficient brigade amidst unpromising conditions, tying down large numbers of the enemy: 'we had 3 companies of Auxiliaries, 1,500 military and 360 RIC in the Brigade [area] with a regiment of cavalry operating against us . . . We had no unsuccessful operations, every bullet finding its mark.'[189] These claims were characteristically exaggerated, but in a conflict where local initiative and effective organization were the deciding factors in the levels of violence between active and inactive counties, O'Duffy deserves much of the credit for Monaghan's performance.[190] This was also the view from GHQ. Richard Mulcahy, IRA chief of staff, recalled that O'Duffy 'took barracks and generally was active. There was a time when we brought him in on organisation work when there wasn't very much he could do in the area.'[191] He was an obvious choice for promotion when it was decided to divisionalize the IRA in March 1921. O'Duffy had earned his place among the nation's revolutionary élite.

4

The coming man

The only pleasure in freedom is in fighting for it.[1]

THE bitterness and disillusionment provoked by the treaty split and Irish Civil War would exert a greater influence on O'Duffy's subsequent career than the preceding years of unity. At the same time, these troubled years also constituted a period of rapid political advancement for O'Duffy. Within less than a year of his appointment as commandant of the 2nd northern division in March 1921, O'Duffy's membership of the inner circle of the revolutionary élite had been confirmed by his multiple roles as chief of staff of the Irish Republican Army, treasurer of the Irish Republican Brotherhood, and Dáil Éireann politician. It would not be the last occasion that the career of O'Duffy, whose importance within the republican movement stemmed from his organizational abilities rather than his personal or political skills, would thrive during an atmosphere of disorder and crisis.

Promotion

The IRA's reorganization into divisions was intended to decrease the army's dependence on GHQ, reduce the number of officers under GHQ's direct supervision, and address the problem of inactive areas by encouraging co-ordination between brigades.[2] O'Duffy was initially reluctant to accept his new command, comprising Co. Tyrone and part of Derry, on the grounds that he might 'lose my grip' over his own county. He did so only after Mulcahy assured him that he 'would retain nominally & to a certain extent actually my inspectorship over Monaghan'.[3] His grip was tightened by the appointment of Dan Hogan as his replacement, and his continued authority over Monaghan county council.[4] O'Duffy was unimpressed by his new command, complaining to GHQ about his men's lack of discipline and 'absolute ignorance of the care and use of arms'. The commandant of the worst battalion was 'the principal poteen-maker in the county . . . and the majority of the officers and men followed in his footsteps . . . The priests & people are disgusted with the IRA in this area—in fact the only decent self-respecting young fellows are those outside the IRA.' His remedy was 'drastic punishment', beginning with the dismissal of every officer in the offending battalion.[5] By May O'Duffy had reorganized every battalion, establishing his division on a 'fairly well organised footing'.[6] He was in regular contact with the commanders of the 3rd and 4th northern divisions, and pushing for regular meetings of the northern commanders to co-ordinate the war in Ulster.[7]

O'Duffy's efforts were rewarded by his promotion to the influential post of GHQ director of organization, a position once held by Collins, in place of the ineffective Bob Price.[8] The organizational and administrative talents which accounted for his rapid ascent were not always appreciated by other commanders. Oscar Traynor, O/C Dublin brigade, recalled that Mulcahy 'was always terribly impressed by reports. He once shown me reports by Owen O'Duffy . . . "Isn't that a magnificent report," he asked? It was all 1. 2. 3. 4. a. b. c. d. "Now what strikes me about the man", I said, "is that he must have plenty of time on [his] hands" . . . This is about a month or six weeks before O'Duffy is appointed.'[9] The ability to file helped to separate the men from the boys in the IRA: the two men he would work most closely alongside in GHQ, Michael Collins and Richard Mulcahy (both graduates of the British Post Office), shared his background and administrative abilities.[10] In terms of his good—but not excellent—education, Irish Ireland credentials, and administrative skills, O'Duffy was representative of the republican élite. The numerous, well-educated, and socially frustrated lower middle classes from which they derived formed the main participants and beneficiaries of the Irish revolution: the most capable and ambitious among them would rise from humble origins to national leadership during this rapid period of 'exciting meritocratic flux'.[11]

O'Duffy's appointment placed him at the nerve centre of the IRA during a crucial period. Despite earlier successes by Collins's celebrated intelligence network, GHQ was fighting for its survival by the summer of 1921. Seán Ó Murthuile contrasted the British military command—'trained strategists who worked together within walls of steel directing operations through the means

of all modern appliances and aided by a most expensive intelligence system'—
with the IRA's general staff, who

could only meet once in a while for decision and consolidated action, they being
compelled to direct their respective branches from miserable secluded offices over
shops in the less frequented parts of Dublin, relying entirely upon couriers to keep in
touch and to direct operations. One day we would hear of a raid on one of Collins' many
such offices, another day it would be a descent on the office of Gearoid O'Sullivan…
They, in most cases, escaped arrest, and settled in some other part of the City where
operations were begun afresh.[12]

Life on the run in Dublin presented different challenges from Monaghan, but
O'Duffy handled the pressure well. On one occasion, Joe Sweeney, commandant of the 1st northern division, spotted several Auxiliaries while walking
through the capital with him: 'I said to O'Duffy "Is your description not circulated around the town?" He said "It is, but the best thing to do is to walk on".
So we walked down by the auxiliaries two months before the Truce. Then he
took me down to his office on the quays.'[13] But it was not only IRA leaders who
were feeling the pressure. Mounting international criticism, public disquiet in
Britain, and the British army's desire to conclude the war before another winter of conflict created an appetite for peace among both sides. The results of the
general election for the southern House of Commons in May 1921, which
returned all of Sinn Féin's candidates (including O'Duffy) unopposed, reinforced London's belief that a political settlement was necessary. But, despite the
growing rumours of peace talks, the sudden announcement of a truce on 11 July
took many by surprise.

Most people responded with relief and jubilation; in some areas crowds
spontaneously gathered around bonfires to celebrate the first night of freedom
from the threat of violence. The truce was greeted with less enthusiasm in other
quarters. One Monaghan IRA officer described his men's response as 'a mixture
of satisfaction and disappointment—disappointment that the possible end
had come before we had achieved anything worthwhile, and joy in the hope
that, even should negotiations break down, we would now have a chance of
getting properly armed and meeting the Tans on level terms.'[14] A similar
ambivalence was eloquently expressed by another Monaghan Volunteer:

To say that we were jubilant would be untrue. It was more bewilderment. Through the
years of the struggle, the hangings and executions and sufferings had engendered in us
something unchristian. Our lust to kill had not been satisfied. During the period of the
Truce, the politicians and respectables took over. It was they who interpreted our
dream, the dream we fought for. It was they who decided the terms to which we must

agree. In the mind of every soldier was a little republic of his own in which he was the hero. But his dream was shattered. The process-server that he once made easy to talk to was back in business, the same gripper, the same sheriff with the same old laws while the little hero was back at his plough.[15]

The violence and aspirations of revolution proved easier to unleash than contain. Leading IRA men like Frank Aiken and Ernie O'Malley confidently anticipated a resumption of hostilities.[16] This view was not shared by GHQ's officers, who had a better understanding of the IRA's vulnerable position. Seán Ó Murthuile believed that it would have been 'impossible to carry on for much longer . . . the Truce was regarded as a blessing'.[17] O'Duffy's contribution to the treaty debates indicated that he, like Collins and Mulcahy, shared this assessment.

The truce brought forth new difficulties. Without the discipline imposed by war, morale declined, a trend hastened by the influx of 'trucileers' attracted to the prestige of ceasefire service. The Monaghan officer who greeted news of the truce with disappointment conceded that had it been broken 'we would have been in a worse position as men who had under orders been total abstainers, both from liquor and ladies, were now being feted and treated in the pubs and were talking to gossipy girls . . . morale was lowered, the men had gone soft and to many the resumption of hostilities would have come as an anti-climax. These facts influenced many when finally the treaty was signed.'[18] The truce presented an even greater, if yet unacknowledged, problem. Britain's decision to negotiate with Sinn Féin implied recognition of the Dáil and its army—a remarkable achievement—but it also implied that a compromise between the demands of both sides would have to be agreed. Returning from the United States shortly after the truce, the staunchly republican Mary MacSwiney was alarmed by the 'atmosphere of what I can only call compromise. I was told to the right and left of me that we could not possibly get a Republic.'[19] There were widely divergent expectations of what republicans could get. Monaghan's county inspector reported that opinion was 'generally in favour of a settlement even at the cost of cherished party shibboleths—not too much sacrifice but even the red hot party men are willing to go some way to meet the opposition and get peace'.[20] Those outside the republican movement were willing to accept far less. After de Valera rejected Lloyd George's initial offer of dominion status, British intelligence reported that the 'public are in favour of accepting the terms, but have not got enough spirit to insist openly that the "Dail" should close with the offer.'[21] During the next months, O'Duffy would play an important role in managing republican expectations and selling the leadership's inevitable compromise to a disappointed and suspicious rank and file.

Give them the lead

He had first to contend with a more pressing problem. On 11 July 1921 O'Duffy was appointed chief liaison officer in Ulster where the truce had been accompanied by a resurgence of sectarian violence. He was by now an influential voice on northern policy. Michael Hopkinson has observed that the GHQ triumvirate of Mulcahy, O'Duffy, and Collins 'attached a much greater importance to the North than that which generally applied in Southern Sinn Féin circles', but, according to Mulcahy, it was actually the latter two who were more preoccupied with the six counties: 'O'Duffy was very exercised as regards the position in the North and his mentality might be cut away a bit from mine... Collins and himself might have found themselves in more agreement dealing with the north.'[22] O'Duffy was tasked with liasing with the RIC and British army to ensure that the truce was observed and, more urgently, to defend Belfast's beleaguered Catholic population. Following the communal violence of 1920, Belfast's Catholics, enclosed in vulnerable enclaves throughout the city, 'presented a frightened and resentful picture'.[23] The shooting of three Belfast policemen by the IRA in June 1921 provoked more rioting in which fourteen people were killed. Further attacks on policemen and Specials on 6 and 10 July triggered another round of violence, resulting in twenty-six deaths that month. On 'Bloody Sunday', on the very eve of the truce, fifteen people were killed and a hundred houses burned down by Protestant mobs.

This violence was partly related to the unsettling impact of the truce. Dublin Castle, keen to secure peace in the south, enforced the terms of the truce throughout the thirty-two counties, suspending the 1920 Government of Ireland act, which had granted home rule to the six counties, and demobilizing the Specials. A largely powerless Unionist government looked on while Sinn Féin negotiated Ireland's future in London.[24] Both Protestants and Catholics regarded the truce as a victory for republicanism. Unionists were particularly appalled by the sight of policemen and soldiers meeting IRA officers on a semi-official basis. But although Protestant insecurity lay behind much of the violence of the summer of 1921, Belfast's Catholics were not passive bystanders. The day after O'Duffy's appointment, the IRA's Belfast commandant reported that 'the Catholic mob is almost beyond control'.[25]

O'Duffy arrived in Belfast amidst this chaos: 'I found the city in a veritable stage of war. The peal of the rifles could be heard on all sides, frenzied mobs at every street corner, terror-stricken people rushing for their lives, and ambulances carrying the dead and dying to the hospitals.'[26] He set up headquarters in St Mary's Hall in the city centre, establishing contact with the British army, RIC, and the press. With the tacit consent of the RIC, he organized IRA foot-patrols to restore order in areas where the police remained unwelcome.[27] O'Duffy's arrival, and his announcement that IRA sniping would cease except in self-defence, contributed to a spell of uneasy quiet lasting until 22 August.[28] Renewed rioting, triggered by an attack on Catholic homes in York Street, killed seven people on 31 August.[29]

Convinced 'that the police were conniving with the Orange mob', O'Duffy retaliated with characteristic determination, ordering the IRA back on to the streets: 'We'll give them the lead', he told one journalist.[30] His snipers, the *Manchester Guardian* reported, retaliated as effectively as the loyalist gunmen—their victims included Protestant workers making their way to the shipyards. By the third day of rioting, they had evened the fatalities to ten Protestants and ten Catholics.[31] As the RIC's grip on events loosened, General Tudor, chief of the RIC, and Alfred Cope, assistant under secretary, travelled to Belfast to meet both sides. Sir Dawson Bates, Northern Ireland's egregious minister for home affairs, demanded the immediate intervention of the British army, the deployment of 1,000 A Specials, remobilization of the B Specials, and the introduction of internment. In contrast, even some B Special commanders advised Cope against the force's mobilization—as did O'Duffy, who threatened a retaliatory escalation of violence. Cope's decision to place British troops back on the streets, and O'Duffy's willingness to take his men off them, temporarily restored order.[32]

O'Duffy's decision to deploy snipers has been credited for forcing the British military to act. The army responded not 'when the streets were red with Catholic blood', he claimed, only when 'things got hot for the loyalists'.[33] Army officers, however, insisted that their decision was taken several hours before they learned of the IRA's intentions.[34] Despite the lull in violence, O'Duffy was enraged by the rioting. He ordered his intelligence officers to interview eye-witnesses to every act of violence against Catholics.[35] On 2 September, in the first of several intemperate statements, he accused Unionists of attempting to destroy the truce: 'Practically every day since the beginning of the truce witnessed some act of provocation . . . There is nothing manly in 25 armed 'B' Specials (we are supposed to believe this class are disarmed and demobilised) ordering a defenceless man of 50 down off a crane, striking him with an iron bar on the head, asking him his religion, and because he refused to deny his faith, emptying a revolver into his almost lifeless body.'[36] He related further atrocities for which he blamed the B Specials, RIC collusion, and the reluctance of the British military to intervene. He accused the notorious District Inspector Nixon, several members of the northern parliament, and the judiciary of inciting loyalist violence.[37] He claimed also that there had been several attempts to assassinate him which 'would not deter him from acting in defence of his fellow Catholics'.[38]

It was against this unsettled background that O'Duffy travelled to Armagh on 4 September where Michael Collins, the deputy for south Armagh, and a delegation of leading brethren, addressed seven thousand supporters.[39] The meeting was intended to reassure northern Catholics that their plight would not be neglected by Sinn Féin. Collins combined a conciliatory tone towards Unionists with a firm declaration of his intention to achieve unity in the forth-coming negotiations. Describing himself as 'fresh from Sandy Row', where 'he had escaped the bullets and bombs' of loyalism, O'Duffy was characteristically less conciliatory. Threatening to intensify the boycott if 'Belfast continued to ally themselves with the enemy', he predicted 'a deserted city in three months' time'. But it was his subsequent remarks which created uproar in the north:

They were told it was not right to use force against the people of the North. That was so. They did not like to use force against them; they did not want to give medicine to other people that they would not like to have themselves. Ireland was a nation. Nobody ever said Ulster was a nation. He would be the last in the world to recommend force against the people of Belfast . . . If they were for Ireland then they would extend the hand of welcome to them as they had done in the past, but if they decided they were against Ireland and against their fellow countrymen, they would have to take suitable action . . . if necessary they would have to use the lead against them.[40]

Despite his recent desperate appeals for British army intervention in Belfast, he concluded by declaring that when the crown forces left Ireland 'the Ulster ques-tion would settle itself in a month's time without the shedding of a drop of blood'.

The speech earned O'Duffy a notorious reputation and nickname ('Give 'em the lead') among local Unionists, who immortalized it in song:

> When the rebel hordes paraded, on that peaceful Sabbath day,
> With flags and banners waving, and band in grand array,
> They thought to scare the Loyalists, who lived in Armagh town,
> But the fear was with the other side, before the night closed down.
> There were murderers from Maghery, and tramps from Crossmaglen
> Hooligans from Keady and rogues from moor and fen;
> There were cut throats from Killeavy and others from the bogs
> All gathered in our city, like mangy mongrel dogs . . .

Now Owen O'Duffy made a speech 'was marvellous it was said
To hear him tell the Rebels, the way to use the lead,
Against the loyal Ulstermen, who won't acknowledge Rome
And who only want the privilege of supporting Britain's Throne.[41]

His speech was notable not merely for its belligerence but for specifically advocating a united Ireland by force. Significantly, as Seán Ó Murthuile noted, it did so shortly after de Valera had publicly ruled out the use of coercion: 'Eoin O'Duffy was quite explicit in his disapproval of De Valera's statement in the matter in a speech at Armagh... This speech caused indignation, but when one comes to think of it, it was the speech of an Ulster Catholic, who had grown up among the scenes of the bigoted fury of anti-Catholicism, and again one ought not to be too mercilessly criticised for maintaining that majorities have a right to use force against rebellious minorities.'[42]

The speech was almost certainly a response to de Valera's recent suggestion that counties with Unionist majorities should be allowed to opt out of a unified Ireland if Britain agreed to a republic in the south. Speaking in the Dáil on that occasion, O'Duffy had made his position clear: 'as far as they in Ulster were concerned they thought force should be used... He had dealt with them by force in Monaghan, Fermanagh and Tyrone, and those people were now silent.'[43] O'Duffy's attitude to partition contrasted with that of most southern republicans, who, while aspiring to unity, prioritized sovereignty for the south.[44] He would subsequently criticize the treatyite executive council, and southern nationalism generally, for treating northern nationalists 'with complete indifference... except at Election time, or when it served party purposes'.[45] His outburst in Armagh was unlikely to have surprised Collins. Both men had privately reassured IRA commanders of their willingness to use force to undo partition. For Collins it was politically astute—both in terms of strengthening his bargaining position in London and reassuring northern nationalists—to have someone of O'Duffy's views to the fore in Ulster. The following year he would play a similar but more vital role for Collins by keeping northern republicans loyal to the treatyite government. Both rhetoric and reputation rendered him a difficult figure to outflank on the national question.

The speech at Armagh did little to improve O'Duffy's relations with the RIC. Lieutenant-Colonel Sir Charles George Wickham, RIC divisional commissioner, complained to the inspector general that O'Duffy's press statements

have only the result of inflaming feeling already high enough on both sides. His continued propaganda against the Special Constabulary is unjustified and untrue. His speech at Armagh was direct provocation. I am firmly convinced that if he is permitted to remain in Belfast, and to continue to publish such statements...it will be extremely difficult, if not impossible, to restrain the Unionist population. I think that the time has come when representations should be made in Dublin as to the desirability of withdrawing him and replacing him by another liaison officer more discreet and more tactful.[46]

Another senior official agreed: 'Owen O'Duffy is a bitter Sinn Feiner and is probably acting on, or even improving on, instructions received from HQ IRA. He is also apparently suffering from swelled head.'[47] Interestingly, these complaints were not well received by Cope or the army command. When Cope received a report from Belfast's RIC commissioner which denied collusion by the Specials and claimed that his men had 'done their utmost to preserve order', his annotations made it clear that he accepted neither finding. Cope's views were shared by a senior British civil servant who investigated the violence and by General Macready, commander-in-chief of the British forces in Ireland, who described the Specials as 'indisciplined scallywags' and their belligerent ministerial supervisor, Dawson Bates, as a 'physical and moral coward'.[48]

O'Duffy was not, as has been claimed, dismissed because of his speech at Armagh.[49] He was still liaison officer in mid-October when he met the influential Dublin Castle fixer Mark Sturgis, who recorded the occasion in his indiscreet diaries: 'I was especially interested to meet the gentleman that "The Morning Post" describes as "the sweet O'Duffy"—Chief liaison officer in Ulster—a clean cut direct fellow, not a bad sort at all, but, I guess, stupid and rather truculent. He seemed business like and on the whole reasonable and when he agreed with any point of mine said so at once without any gêne.' However, Sturgis 'noticed particularly the sign of "nerves" in these young men—I sat on the end of the bed during the talk smoking a pipe and when I gave O'Duffy a cigarette left my match box on the table—both O'Duffy and McAlister quite unconsciously picked my matches to pieces by the dozen all the time they were speaking...they all look like shop assistants for all their high sounding titles.'[50]

Nonetheless, his performance at Armagh certainly undermined his credibility as Ulster liaison officer. Liam Walsh described the speech as 'interesting and honest', admitting that 'he may have wandered into vague warnings and not entirely approved generalisations', before conceding that 'practical politics was not in O'Duffy's line'.[51] The latter felt it necessary to clarify soon afterwards that he had 'never advocated the coercion of Ulster...I said something at Armagh about using the lead, but when a statement is removed from context it often has a different meaning.'[52] The following month Mulcahy informed Cathal Brugha, the minister for defence, that a substitute had been appointed for O'Duffy who was too busy at GHQ to visit Belfast.[53] But, despite being eased out of his role as liaison officer, O'Duffy remained an important influence on Ulster policy. Indeed, among republicans in Belfast and elsewhere, his militancy ensured that 'he emerged with his reputation appreciably enhanced'.[54]

Deputy chief of staff

Although the office of deputy chief of staff was the second highest in the Irish Republican Army, there was a remarkable degree of confusion as to when O'Duffy assumed the post. In a letter to Brugha (who insisted that no such position existed), O'Duffy claimed that he had been offered the commission on 1 August 1921. [55] It was only in September, however, that he began using the title in his correspondence. Mulcahy thought that O'Duffy had been appointed deputy chief of staff in March 1921 (when he was actually made director of organization).[56] One reason for the confusion was that Mulcahy and Collins had deliberately not informed the minister for defence of the appointment. Another was that the new position (not to be confused with assistant chief of staff) was essentially the same as director of organization but was intended to signal the authority of Collins's rising protégé. Notwithstanding the determination with which would he would later cling to the position, O'Duffy professed reluctance about accepting it: 'I would much prefer a place in the fighting line which I had been always accustomed to'.[57] The promotion reflected the importance of the role O'Duffy had carved out in the post-truce GHQ. The lines of demarcation between the functions and powers of the GHQ triumvirate of Mulcahy, Collins and O'Duffy were by now remarkably vague; Mulcahy, the 'dour, unclubbable and sober' chief of staff, technically commanded the IRA but it was the 'plain-speaking, hard drinking and very sociable' Collins, who, as minister for finance, IRB president, and IRA director of intelligence, effectively called the shots.[58] O'Duffy was Mulcahy's deputy at GHQ but, as a member of the IRB supreme council, had access to a powerful network of intelligence and influence unavailable to Mulcahy. The dominance of Collins prevented significant tensions despite the unorthodox arrangement.

As deputy chief of staff, O'Duffy promoted promising officers, dismissed inferior, uncooperative, or out of favour ones, resolved internal disputes, and generally enforced the authority of GHQ. The IRA's guerrilla origins made this a much more important role than in a professional army. For much of the war GHQ had encouraged rather than directed activity: in some regions it had merely asked for reports. Its influence over the elite Munster brigades was particularly weak. Many IRA officers were inexperienced and untrained, and few owed their commissions to GHQ. Some areas, such as Kerry, were disorganized and divided by internal rivalry. Rural fighters often held a negative view of the pen-pushers at GHQ who had supplied instructions and criticism but few weapons during the war. Liam Lynch, leader of the 1st southern division, complained that GHQ 'showed all-round inefficiency, and gave very little help to the country'.[59] IRA officers in strong fighting areas resented GHQ's attempts to assert its authority, while those in weaker areas resented its criticisms. These tensions, accompanied by the usual personal animosities, were of minor importance during the conflict but would later become entwined with political issues to devastating effect.

O'Duffy brought his considerable abilities to bear on the task of professionalizing the army. Despite reservations about his temperament, Mulcahy acknowledged him as a 'tireless, effective, distinguished' deputy chief of staff.[60] O'Duffy's reports demonstrate a methodical approach and a confidence in his ability to assess the strengths and weaknesses of officers. In Wicklow, for example, he retained the battalion commandant ('A good man, perhaps a little slow but has the confidence of his subordinate officers') and adjutant ('very keen and intelligent'), but forced the quartermaster's resignation, and replaced the vice commandant with an officer he judged a 'live wire but too young to be completely in charge'.[61] He developed his own method of rating officers, noting of one: 'He is a good officer. According to my system of marking—Organisation, Command, Initiative, Training, Test & Outlook, and experience in actual operations, I allowed him 80%.'[62] His stern demeanour was useful in enforcing GHQ's authority in areas where it remained largely theoretical, even if this did not always prove possible. In south Roscommon, he was unable to implement GHQ's decision to dismiss an ineffective brigade commandant who retained the support of his officers.[63] Other attempts were more successful: for example, he overruled Frank Barrett's objections to his brigade's inclusion in the 1st southern division.[64] GHQ's improved resources helped it to tighten its grip on rural commanders. O'Duffy ordered Ernie O'Malley, commandant of the 2nd southern division, to move his headquarters from a remote cottage into a large hotel and begin running a bill. When O'Malley declined a GHQ salary, O'Duffy pointedly informed him that he had no choice: 'You are our Officer and represent GHQ in No. 2 Division.'[65]

As the summer stretched into autumn, leading IRA officers became increasingly concerned by the length of the truce. Although it would have been damaging, both in terms of IRA morale and Sinn Féin's bargaining position in

London, to adopt any other stance, O'Duffy depicted the truce as a temporary respite before a probable return to war. In late July he urged Frank Aiken, commander of the 4th northern division, to prepare for a renewal of hostilities.[66] Ernie O'Malley recalled a divisional council meeting in August when O'Duffy 'suggested that we ourselves should break the truce, when negotiations were approaching a deadlock, by attacking the British posts without giving the agreed seventy-two hours' warning'. His colleagues disagreed, chivalrously insisting that 'If it was going to be a fight to the finish, let us begin the war honourably'.[67] O'Duffy was still assuring republicans that 'they were going to fight it out' in October.[68] Nonetheless, men like Aiken grew more concerned:

From the end of September it seemed to us that the Truce and negotiations were dragging out too long; it puzzled us greatly how our representatives could talk to the British so long without the vital points cropping up and causing a breach. O'Duffy told a few of us once that GHQ had asked the President to keep the negotiations going until the winter (which is the most favourable season for the weaker side in guerrilla war).[69]

Aiken's concerns were not alleviated by a 'peculiar' meeting of divisional officers in Vaughan's Hotel in late October. He recollected that 'none of us knew what we were there for until Mulcahy put to each of us in turn a question which was something like: "What would be your attitude if the British offered us something less than the Republic?" Each of us replied, in turn, that it was for a Republic, the complete freedom of Ireland, that we had fought.'[70] As a member of the IRB supreme council and one of Collins's advisers during the negotiations, O'Duffy knew that a compromise was a more likely outcome than a republic or a return to war. His comrades were clearly less well prepared.

During the autumn of 1921 O'Duffy became embroiled in more immediate difficulties as relations between GHQ and the Dáil cabinet reached breaking-point. The origins of the dispute were twofold, stemming from the ambiguous relationship between the military and political wings of the republican movement, as well as the personal animosity between Cathal Brugha and Michael Collins.[71] As with the uneasy relationship between GHQ and local IRA leaders, the dispute was initially unrelated to political differences but would become entangled with them during the treaty split. Although the IRA was theoretically subordinated to the authority of the Dáil in March 1921, GHQ exercised sufficient autonomy, as we have seen, to make senior appointments without informing the minister for defence. In mid-1921, following de Valera's return from the United States, Brugha began to take a keener, and largely unwelcome, interest in army affairs. The tensions which followed stemmed from Brugha's obsessive suspicion of Collins, and GHQ's resistance to his involvement in its affairs. GHQ resented the fact that Brugha, and his incompetent ministerial colleague Austin Stack (who had been appointed deputy chief of staff some years earlier but had never attended GHQ meetings or played any role in military matters), began to exert their authority only after the truce was declared.[72] Brugha began complaining about relatively trivial issues such as the mishandling of funds and IRA heavy-handedness which he blamed on Collins or, in his absence, Mulcahy. These tensions came to a head in September, when Brugha suggested that the IRA's officers be recommissioned into a 'new army'. Ostensibly, this was intended to formalize the Dáil's ambiguous authority over the army, which, it was optimistically argued, would compel Britain to treat the IRA as prisoners of war rather than criminals if a renewal of conflict occurred. Brugha proposed the idea in cabinet without consulting GHQ, which inevitably viewed it as another attempt to exert his authority.

That there were some grounds for this suspicion was confirmed by Brugha's attempt to influence the shape of the reconstituted GHQ. Outraged by his belated discovery of O'Duffy's promotion to deputy chief of staff, Brugha informed Mulcahy that he had never approved the appointment. It was at this point, Mulcahy recollected, 'when they wanted to get rid of Collins and get a grip over the army that they woke up to the fact that Stack was deputy chief of staff'.[73] Mulcahy, however, could also be accused of duplicity, as he had obviously appointed O'Duffy without informing Brugha in order to undermine Stack's latent claim to the position.[74] Mulcahy made it clear that he would only continue as chief of staff if he, rather than Brugha, determined the composition of GHQ. When Brugha continued to insist that Stack be appointed deputy chief of staff in place of O'Duffy (who was to be demoted to director of organization), Mulcahy threatened to resign.[75] So too did O'Duffy, who informed Stack that he was 'reluctantly compelled to interpret the reduction in rank as a personal slight and a grave dishonour which I submit I do not deserve'.[76] But, notwithstanding the principle of governmental authority, Mulcahy's hand remained strong as the cabinet could hardly sack the army leadership in the middle of the negotiations with Britain. After Mulcahy politely requested that GHQ be allowed to meet the cabinet to discuss the issue, Stack conceded the reappointment of the original general staff.[77]

At this point, a remarkable intervention by de Valera revived the controversy. The president had previously stayed out of the dispute: when Mulcahy complained about Brugha's 'devitalising and degrading' attitude, de Valera had lent him a sympathetic ear and he had also opposed his dismissal by Brugha.[78] However, as a political figure with little military influence, it was clearly in de Valera's interest that GHQ's independence be curbed. That this would also curb the influence of his most powerful cabinet rival, Collins, could hardly be ignored.[79] On 25 November de Valera summoned Mulcahy to meet the cabinet, informing him that O'Duffy could remain deputy chief of staff but that Stack would serve as 'Cathal's ghost on the Staff'.[80] Mulcahy refused this proposal, at which point, he recollected, the rest of the general staff were brought in:

> they sat around the walls of the drawing room in the Mansion House where de Valera sat at a small table near one end of the centre with his Ministers sitting around him. He explained that he wanted to reform the Staff, and having spoken shortly about it he asked their opinion. One after another, starting from the left, the members of the Staff gave their opinion against the contemplated changes. The general tone was expressed by Ginger O'Connell who said that 'the General Headquarters Staff had been a band of brothers'. And the objection went all round the room until it reached O'Duffy who was the second last on the right. O'Duffy stood up and his voice became a little bit shrill as he characterised this as being an insult and a criticism to himself. A slight touch of hysteria in O'Duffy's approach to the subject reacted on de Valera in the chair, and after a very short time Dev rose excitedly in his Chair, pushed the small table in front of him and declared in a half-scream, half-shout 'ye may mutiny if ye like, but Ireland will give me another Army,' and he dismissed the whole lot of us from his sight.[81]

This nasty row illustrated tensions which were dividing the leadership of the republican movement long before the signing of the treaty. Like the treaty split, the dispute involved personal animosities, rivalries, and issues of political principle for which both sides could make a reasonable case. Its impact on O'Duffy, a firm admirer of de Valera before his appointment to GHQ, must have been considerable. The incident highlighted O'Duffy's defensiveness, volatility, and egotism. Notwithstanding his considerable abilities, these shortcomings, central to his subsequent political downfall, rendered him a deeply flawed figure. Mulcahy, questioned by his son Risteárd in a fascinating series of interviews, was loathe to criticize 'the band of brothers' but his reservations about O'Duffy are evident from his evasive replies. Pressed on whether he thought O'Duffy obsessive, Mulcahy finally agreed: 'Oh, I always got on well with O'Duffy. He was very efficient, he had a great sense of organisation. He was a great man on paper, and he was a great man for going and doing a job . . . as I say he was slightly a nerve [sic] character or touch of, never mind, people would say there was a touch of insanity in the family. Some kind of hysteria, nervous history.'[82] Curiously, this assessment, which came to be shared by many of the General's colleagues, did not prevent his appointment to positions of enormous responsibility; if anything, his unbalanced personality served merely to render it extremely difficult to remove him from them.

    The army dispute threatened relations not only within the cabinet, and
between the cabinet and GHQ, but also among the IRA leadership. O'Duffy's
indiscreet comments alerted some regional commanders to these tensions. Joe
Sweeney, who arrived in Dublin under the impression that 'everyone was all
one happy family', was shocked to learn about the divisions from O'Duffy
(whom Sweeney regarded as 'a queer customer').[83] Another divisional officer,
Frank Aiken, recalled that Brugha's circular informing them of the new commissions was the first he ever received from the minister for defence: 'I was
speaking to O'Duffy some days afterwards and, when I asked him to explain
the idea of the new commissions, he said I might not bother with them and
gave me to understand by some remark that GHQ staff did not think a whole
lot of Cathal Brugha. This was the first I heard of that sort of thing at GHQ.'[84]
Significantly, O'Duffy's protégé, Dan Hogan, was prominent among the
divisional commanders whose protests led to the oath being dropped by the
government.[85]
    It was against this background that the Anglo-Irish treaty was signed on 6
December 1921. The terms of the treaty, and the controversial manner of its
signing, are well known. Collins, Griffith, and the other delegates chose not to
refer the final settlement to the cabinet for approval, instead exercising their
plenipotentiary powers to sign the agreement. This decision reflected the mis-
trust between the plenipotentiaries and the cabinet's more doctrinaire republicans. Collins returned to Dublin with a settlement substantial enough to win
political and public support and wrong-foot his cabinet rivals, who were presented with a *fait accompli* which they were forced to accept or reject. The treaty
offered the twenty-six counties dominion status within the British Empire but
not the Irish Republic which the IRA had sworn to uphold. Most opposition
focused on the role of the British monarch in the Irish Free State and the oath
of fidelity which deputies would swear to him. The status of Ulster was to be
resolved by a boundary commission which, treatyites optimistically argued,
would cede sufficient areas of the six counties to make unification inevitable.
    Like many republicans, O'Duffy's immediate response to the treaty may not
have been positive. The anti-treaty Dr Jim Ryan recalled: 'I was in 19 Ranelagh
Rd alone with Dick Mulcahy when the Treaty was signed ... In walked Eoin
O'Duffy and he was dead against it: "the army won't stand for this Dick", he
said. And Dick was in a fever trying to get O'Duffy quiet and prevent him from
talking too much.'[86] Mulcahy's mollifying response was 'Wait until you see
Collins'. The publication of the treaty's terms took many by surprise, and there
are numerous accounts of indecision and wavering (each side invariably recalling how their opponents had originally agreed with them before defecting

under some malign influence). However, O'Duffy cannot have been greatly surprised by its terms. The IRB supreme council had been regularly briefed by Collins throughout the negotiations, while O'Duffy had advised Collins in London and received detailed position papers.[87] Moreover, on 3 December, Collins had provided Seán Ó Murthuile with a draft of the document to put before 'the lads' in the Gresham Hotel. When the supreme council took exception to the wording of the oath of allegiance to the king, O'Duffy and two other Brothers amended it to express allegiance to the Irish Free State with a secondary reference to fidelity to the British monarch. The final published version, Ó Murthuile noted with satisfaction, incorporated 'the change suggested by the Supreme Council'.[88]

O'Duffy's reservations, which probably concerned Ulster rather than the oath, were evidently resolved by Collins. Indeed, O'Duffy's important role in winning support for the treaty would soon earn him the bitter enmity of the Irregulars (as the anti-treaty IRA became known). Shortly after it was signed, Frank Aiken attended a *ceilidhe* in Clones at which all the leading northern and midland officers were present:

I knew that Owen O'Duffy, Deputy Chief of Staff, would be present and I went to it glad of the opportunity of meeting some one from GHQ . . . hoping in a vague way that he might have some explanation to give . . . O'Duffy, Joe McKelvey, Sean McKeown and several other important officers were present. O'Duffy assured us, with great vehemence, that the signing of the Treaty was only a trick; that he would never take that oath and that no one would [be] asked to take it. He told us that it had been signed with the approval of GHQ in order to get arms to continue the fight.[89]

Could O'Duffy have believed this? Aiken was not the only one to whom he made such remarks. Other Volunteers recollected his similarly belligerent attitude to partition which the treaty appeared to legitimize: 'O'Duffy called a meeting of the company officers for Ballybay or Clones. I heard him say "I am for the Treaty, as an individual. When we get arms we will blow the shit out of them." I think that he intended to do so but the sensible element of Sinn Féin would not hear of it.'[90] Never unduly scrupulous about the truth, O'Duffy may have been cynically attempting to win support by any means necessary. However, his sentiments echoed those of Collins, who assured IRA leaders that he did not intend to honour the treaty.[91] In late December, for example, Collins and O'Duffy told Ernie O'Malley that the treaty would provide a breathing space for a new campaign.[92] Moreover, their subsequent support for IRA attacks in the six counties revealed a willingness to break the terms of the treaty. Collins also hoped to sideline the oath, possibly by excluding it from the constitution of the new state. An oblique comment by O'Duffy during the treaty debates suggests that he also believed that the IRA could circumvent the oath.[93] The opinion of Aiken, who disliked O'Duffy, is worth noting:

Looking back now, and knowing that O'Duffy since fought a bitter and dirty war to enforce the articles of the Treaty which he denounced so vigorously that night, and knowing that he since took the oath of allegiance to the British king and has sworn to be faithful to a constitution which included partition and that he was to a large extent responsible for the murder of Joe McKelvey who was listening to him, I am, nevertheless, still convinced that O'Duffy believed then that he would never take the oath to King George nor recognise partition.

Aiken, in contrast, believed 'instinctively that the Treaty was wrong and that if it were allowed to come into operation it would be, because of the type of men who would work it, an obstacle instead of an aid to independence. I told O'Duffy what I felt about it, and he again assured us that he would never dream of taking the oath to the British king or asking anyone to take it and that the sole object of signing the Treaty was to get arms.'[94] However, the speech that O'Duffy went on to make that same night left Aiken in no doubt of his determination to crush any dissent from the treatyite line:

[MacEoin] only said he was glad to see us but O'Duffy started the campaign for the Treaty. 'There are people' he said 'who are now calling Mick Collins a traitor, who were "under the bed" when there was fighting to be done.' It was the first time I remember hearing the 'under the bed' phrase; alas, it wasn't the last! From that night to the attack on the Four Courts he worked like a fiend for the success of the pro-Treaty party; he seemed gradually to forget the nation and to subordinate its interests to party interests, and, when talking of his opponents, he forgot all sense of justice and sometimes even truth. It was very bad for Ireland that his energy became so misdirected because he was a splendid organiser and one of the hardest workers in Ireland; without him and Mulcahy & MacNeill, the civil war, I believe, would never have occurred.

The split

Responsibility for the Civil War must be shared rather more widely than the treatyite leadership: the British government and anti-treatyites played their parts. But, aside from highlighting a bitter personal animosity, Aiken's comments reflected the importance of O'Duffy's role in establishing the Free State régime. The treaty divided every republican body in Ireland: the cabinet, Dáil, Sinn Féin, IRA, and IRB. After de Valera failed to persuade the cabinet to reject the treaty, it was left to the Dáil to decide its fate. Despite his modest claim, during the private session on 17 December, that he was 'not a speaker and this is the first time I am speaking', O'Duffy's initial contribution to the treaty debates was skilful. Claiming not to have studied the document closely, he declared himself 'unreservedly' in its favour for two reasons. First, 'the British soldier and British Peeler will never again be seen in Ireland'.[95] Second, the choice was not between the Republic—which the plenipotentiaries could never have achieved—and the treaty, but between the latter and the similar compromise proposed in de Valera's 'Document No. 2'. He dismissed the issue of the oath on the grounds that it swore allegiance first to Ireland and secondly to George V: 'I do not want to take an oath to any English king but I do say that the first part neutralises the second'. Given his reputation, his analysis of the military situation probably carried most weight. He combined characteristic bombast—'For me war has no horrors. I am not a bit afraid of war…The only pleasure in freedom is fighting for it'—with a realistic appraisal of the enemy's superiority. If the treaty were rejected he would recommend every company to 'strike within 24 hours', but he was pessimistic about the outcome. He concluded by emphasizing his republican orthodoxy: 'I am a Republican. I hold that the action I am taking in this case is towards the Republic…I recognise it as a stepping stone only.'

Like Collins, O'Duffy saw the treaty as the most effective path to the Republic. Had he to choose between the Free State and the Republic, 'he would without hesitation have booted for the latter', and he did not accept those 'who opposed the Treaty were any more patriotic than those who accepted it'.[96] O'Duffy's sensitivity to the charge of apostasy—which, along with his hatred of de Valera, would become central to his political outlook—was clear from the debate. In a speech remarkable for its intemperance, even by the standards of the most bitter debate in the Dáil's history, Mary MacSwiney condemned GHQ (for failing to arm the IRA during the truce), the IRB ('a refuge for weaklings'), and Irish-Americans ('90% of them of the slavemind type'), before rounding on O'Duffy for his betrayal of the Republic. O'Duffy, close to tears, refused to allow her to continue unless she retracted her accusation: 'I would rather be shot on the spot, and would to God I were shot an hour ago, rather than this last statement should be made against me now.'[97] MacSwiney—who had actually been impressed by O'Duffy's earlier speech—described what followed to Frank Aiken:

Several people came to me afterwards and told me what a good fellow he was and how heartbroken he was at the suggestion that he had betrayed the Republic…On Monday morning before the public debate opened I met him in the vestibule of the University and spoke to him, pointing out that though none of them really meant the act as traitorous the Treaty would involve the betrayal of the Republic. He seemed to be very straightforward, very frank and in earnest and he assured me that he would not have minded anybody else saying a thing like that so much as he minded me just because of the great reverence he had for my brother.

Now here comes the extraordinary part of it. He assured me that while Terry was in Brixton, he once heard one of his own men declare that Terry was committing suicide and that he should give up the hunger-strike, and he assured me that he had taken that man out, had given him half an hour and had him shot as a traitor . . . I was horrified and I took no pains to hide it. I told him I considered it a very wrong thing to shoot any man for a conscientious objection to hunger striking, and that while I did not agree with that man's point of view, I considered it most unjust to shoot him for it. O'Duffy seemed greatly surprised at my attitude . . . [98]

MacSwiney discussed this disturbing revelation with several people 'who knew O'Duffy well', and put it down to an attempt 'to curry favour with me or perhaps with a view to stopping my criticism of him'. Aiken assured her that the only volunteer executed in Monaghan had been shot for informing.[99] O'Duffy may, however, have been alluding to the execution of Arthur Treanor, who, among other transgressions, had criticized a council resolution of sympathy for Terence MacSwiney. If the intention was to impress MacSwiney, it was clearly counterproductive: 'In either event it shows him thoroughly unscrupulous. His Catholicity is of a very poor type if the story be true.' The incident highlighted a revealing aspect of O'Duffy's personality (which MacSwiney and Aiken agreed was 'a peculiar mixture'). The General was not merely, in the words of Oscar Traynor, 'a bloody liar': he told lies of such magnitude that his dishonesty was often discovered.[100] Underlying the cultivated image of the strong leader, was an insecure figure who courted popularity by telling people what he thought they wished to hear.

O'Duffy made his second and final speech on the treaty during the public session on 4 January 1922. On this occasion, his intention was to sway public opinion rather than wavering deputies. He began by declaring that neither side could claim 'the monopoly of patriotism', a skilful gambit against the anti-treatyite claim to the high moral ground. He based his support for the treaty on its overwhelming popularity: 'the will of a constituency should prevail against the will of any one individual who may happen to be their mouthpiece'. This was an allusion to the fact that the Sinn Féin *comhairli ceanntair* and county council had unanimously declared themselves in favour of the treaty in Monaghan, and the stance of his constituency colleague Seán MacEntee, who had disgusted many by announcing that he would vote against it despite admitting that his position lacked local support.[101] This conversion to majoritarianism, eagerly if belatedly stressed by pro-treaty deputies, was a response to the wave of public support expressed in favour of the treaty over Christmas.

Reflecting his broader audience, O'Duffy deployed a variety of sporting metaphors to good effect. The treaty would bring 'the ball inside the fourteen yards' line' and 'by keeping our eye on the goal the major score is assured'.[102] He conceded its limitations but emphasized its strengths: 'we have now our destinies in our own hands and if we do not secure freedom then it is our own fault'. He addressed the allegation that it sold out northern nationalists, an issue ignored by most deputies, by pointing out the opposition's lack of an alternative policy. (He added, with considerable inaccuracy, that 'no one in this House, I think, suggests now, or ever suggested, that Ulster should be coerced'). O'Duffy predicted that unity would be achieved through political and economic pressure, dismissing the opposition's claim that the boundary commission might cede Free State territory to the north in a rather sinister fashion: 'I know the Unionists of Monaghan. The non-Catholics there are not fools. We made it very clear to them that if they were prepared to join up with the enemy they would get the same treatment as the enemy. Nine or ten of them have got the treatment of the Black-and-Tans, and they admitted they did not get that because of their religious belief, but they got it because they were part and parcel of the enemy.'[103]

He emphasized the argument, a convincing one for many northern nationalists, that republican disunity would encourage further violence in Belfast, his overdoing of the 'lead' references suggesting a certain pride in the moniker earned in Armagh: 'I know Ulster better than any man or woman in this Dáil because I have faced Ulster's lead on more than one occasion with lead, and in those places where I was able to do it, I silenced them with lead. I would have silenced them in every case with lead if I had as much lead as they had.' In contrast to his earlier speech during the private sessions, O'Duffy made little effort to conciliate opposition deputies. Few of these, he declared, had offered him much help during the Tan War: 'If the fight should begin again I will have with me some of these men who are trying to make history for themselves—I will take good care that they take a little risk also.'

O'Duffy's rhetoric went down well with the treatyite press: 'His sharp, terse tones betrayed his Northern origin, and his was one of the most effective speeches of the day…With all the passion of his soul that young soldier-deputy declared his intention, should the fight begin again, to take his place in the firing line…His voice fell as he spoke respectfully of the dead… He thrilled one as he announced his preference of war to political chaos.'[104]

A more restrained account noted that he 'spoke without any attempt at eloquence whatever, but his words, clear, lucid, distinct and sincere, reached every corner of the assembly'.[105] His speech was received less favourably by anti-treaty deputies, particularly Cathal Brugha, who had discovered that O'Duffy had been surreptitiously maligning him to other Sinn Féin deputies. The tone of Brugha's letter to O'Duffy captures the bitterness of the time:

that one whom I believed to be a brave man and a real fighter should have stooped so low as to stab in the back one who has made, and is willing to make, at least as great a sacrifice as any others for our common country, is certainly the worst disillusion I have yet experienced. When I heard of the notice that was sent out to the members of the I.R.B. by the body which calls itself the Supreme Council I made up my mind that when fighting started again I would challenge those vile creatures, who thus prostituted the body that brought the Republic into existence, to follow a lead that I would give. Fighting has now been temporarily stayed, but only temporarily. I believe that in our time, sooner or later, it will again begin. When it does you may expect to hear from me. I will give you and the creatures referred to above an opportunity of showing your willingness to face certain death for Ireland. And you may be sure that I will not ask you to do anything that I am not prepared to do myself.[106]

O'Duffy was more successful in winning republican support behind the scenes, deploying a variety of methods ranging from bribery to the manipulation of local rivalries. He was foremost among those who, Mary MacSwiney complained, 'are trying to seduce the army loyal to the Republic by offers of good salaries and other good things'.[107] He offered Dr Conn Ward the post of medical general director of the army in return for supporting the treaty.[108] Oscar Traynor was promised 'the position of Chief of Police. This was just before the vote on the Treaty...This is the bait for me I said to myself.'[109] Paddy Ruttledge steered clear of any such temptation: 'I had my mind made up...General O'Duffy wanted to get some people to meet me at the train and bring me to his hotel. I refused.'[110] Although many anti-treatyites claimed that senior Brothers used the IRB to win support for the treaty, there is little evidence of this among senior republicans for whom the importance of the issue outweighed any fraternal loyalties. The supreme council voted in favour of the treaty's ratification, a fact which swayed some, but, like every other republican body, it split on the issue. Moreover, the IRB allowed deputies to vote according to their conscience. Joe Sweeney, for example, met 'Mick Collins and Eoin O'Duffy coming out of the Wicklow hotel on the occasion when I came to Dublin before the Treaty debates and I asked them what my position was. They said I was a free agent.'[111] But IRB networks were utilized to their full potential as figures like O'Duffy toured the country using persuasion and the enormous patronage which accompanied the creation of a new state to win support. Nor should the importance of hierarchical fraternal relationships be underestimated: O'Duffy's loyalty to Collins, which prevailed over his doubts, was matched by the loyalty owed to him by figures like Dan Hogan, 'yes-man always to O'Duffy', and others further down the line.[112]

The Dáil ratified the treaty on 7 January 1922 by the narrow margin of 64 votes to 57. Arthur Griffith succeeded de Valera as president of the republic, inaugurating a period of confusion in which the Dáil cabinet remained in existence while a provisional government established the Irish Free State. It soon became apparent that the minority were not going to accept the decision of the majority. They did not regard their actions as anti-democratic, believing that their opponents had no right to disestablish the Republic which they had sworn to uphold. Mulcahy declared that the IRA would remain the army of the Republic, in the first of many attempts to prevent the political division from leading to civil war. Nonetheless, a majority of the IRA, led by the most experienced Munster brigades, rejected the treaty. The ambivalence of many IRA men towards politicians and constitutional politics had been reinforced by the events of the past six months: many felt they had defeated the British on the field, only to see their politicians squander their victory in London.

The fragmentation of the army placed enormous responsibility on O'Duffy, who succeeded Richard Mulcahy, the newly appointed minister for defence, as chief of staff on 10 January 1922. The appointment of O'Duffy was shrewd. He was admired by the regional IRA leaders, who perceived him as a fighting man rather than a pen-pusher like Mulcahy (who had actually distinguished himself in the fighting of 1916). O'Duffy expressed an apparently genuine reluctance to take the post, suggesting that he would make a better police commissioner, but, given the circumstances, he could hardly refuse it. Throughout the first half of 1922, he remained committed to preserving IRA unity. He was prominent on the committee of ten Dáil deputies which in early January proposed that de Valera should remain as president, while the treaty was implemented.[113] Like most of the negotiations which followed, its failure was largely due to disagreement among the badly divided anti-treatyites (who ranged from relatively pragmatic figures to uncompromising doctrinaire republicans). But, despite the intensity with which both sides adhered to their views, neither sought violent confrontation.

On 10 January a majority of the IRA's divisional officers met to devise an anti-treaty army policy. Accusing the treatyites of subverting the Republic, they withdrew their allegiance from the Dáil and demanded a convention to elect an independent IRA executive. When GHQ met the disaffected officers on 18 January, Mulcahy reluctantly agreed to hold an army convention two months later, establishing a 'watching council' of four, which included O'Duffy, to preserve unity in the meantime.[114] The latter achieved little, the anti-treaty Ernie O'Malley not even bothering to attend. Had the Irregulars reacted promptly they could have seized the initiative, although what they could have achieved in the face of a divided army, the continued British military threat, and strong public support for the treaty was less evident. Mulcahy's willingness to approve an army convention and allow local units, regardless of their allegiance, to occupy barracks as they were vacated by British forces postponed confrontation. Meanwhile, negotiations with anti-treaty leaders (conducted by Collins, Mulcahy, and O'Duffy through IRB channels) continued with little input from the provisional government.[115]

O'Duffy's principal preoccupation was now the creation of a new army at Beggars' Bush barracks. The longer this continued, the stronger the treatyite position.[116] GHQ enjoyed some advantages, notably patronage, which helped to tip the scale. In March, for example, Joseph Dunne asked the anti-treaty James O'Donovan for permission to accept the latter's old job as GHQ director of chemicals:

Since the publication of the peace terms and the subsequent debates in An Dáil I . . . am absolutely devoid of any wish to sacrifice myself in any way whatsoever for this benighted country. I look upon the above matter now simply in the light of a job and while believing the Republican Party right I am too selfish to make any sacrifice on their behalf. As you, I am sure, know I have just been living from hand to mouth and cannot afford to be without a job . . . I don't suppose the Beggars' Bush crowd will last long but in the meantime it will be something to go on with . . . I could, I suppose, have given you many fine reasons for my proposed cause of action but I preferred to be absolutely candid and frank with you.[117]

This letter illustrated the ambivalence of some of the most senior officers whom O'Duffy would depend on. Mulcahy recalled that in June 1922 many of Collins's notorious squad (who viewed O'Duffy's appointment as chief of staff as a threat to their prestige) 'were caballing against the Treaty almost'. He added: 'It is very hard for the historians today to know the thin ice upon which the army was built up.'[118] Where possible, O'Duffy removed anti-treaty officers in strategic positions. In March he removed Charlie Daly, O/C of the 2nd northern division, for not exercising sufficient control over his area.[119] Daly had no doubts as to the real reason: 'you knew my attitude towards the Treaty and where I would be in the event of a Division at the Convention'.[120] Conversely, O'Duffy persuaded key officers to remain in place until they could be safely replaced.[121] He also continued to advocate a radical interpretation of the treaty, as one officer witnessed when O'Duffy addressed a group of wavering soldiers in March: 'They were not Free State Soldiers. They were only taking this step with the intention of getting arms. The men rushed back to Kilkenny for the scrap.'[122]

The first serious military confrontation occurred when rival units of the IRA clashed over control of the Limerick barracks vacated by British soldiers. This episode began on 18 February when Liam Forde, O/C of the mid-Limerick brigade, denounced O'Duffy as a traitor and repudiated GHQ's authority, raising the possibility of government forces losing control of the strategically vital city which separated anti-treaty Munster from the similarly inclined west of Ireland.[123] The treatyites responded by ordering troops from Michael Brennan's 1st western division into Limerick. The Irregular forces, led by Ernie O'Malley's 2nd southern division, followed them into the city, where a tense stand-off ensued. O'Malley sought to expel the government forces but was thwarted by the reluctance of his more moderate comrades. Finally, at a meeting in Beggars' Bush barracks on 10 March, Collins, Mulcahy, and O'Duffy negotiated a compromise with Liam Lynch whereby all external forces left Limerick and the barracks were placed under the control of a small party of Irregulars.

Due to disunity and a commendable reluctance to fight, the anti-treaty forces had squandered their military advantage. However, the provisional government had also failed its first major test of strength.[124] Griffith and several of his cabinet colleagues, who saw the crisis as a missed opportunity to assert the government's authority, resented the conciliatory position adopted by Collins and GHQ.[125] The compromise also alienated elements within the provisional government forces, including the assistant chief of staff, Ginger O'Connell, who formally protested against it. It is not clear where O'Duffy stood. Although devoted to Collins, by temperament he might be expected to be found among those advocating the less compromising position. He had, for example, opposed the conciliatory policy of allowing Irregular units to occupy local barracks.[126]

The long-awaited army convention, set for 26 March, triggered the next crisis. Unsurprisingly, given the IRA's anti-treaty majority, the government had reconsidered the wisdom of allowing the convention to proceed and, on 15 March, banned what it described as 'an attempt to establish a Military Dictatorship'. Undeterred, the Irregulars proceeded with the convention, while Mulcahy instructed O'Duffy that those who attended should be regarded as having left the army. The convention, which represented around 60 per cent of the army, affirmed the IRA's allegiance to the Republic, denounced the treaty, and elected an army executive which repudiated the authority of O'Duffy, Mulcahy, and Dáil Éireann. O'Duffy, in turn, released Volunteers from the obligation of following the orders of their anti-treaty officers. On 9 April Liam Lynch was elected chief of staff of the IRA executive while, five days later, anti-treaty forces occupied the Four Courts and other prominent buildings around the city. The parallels with 1916 were not lost on either side.

The northern offensive

Tensions escalated further on 22 April when O'Duffy publicly accused Lynch's 1st southern division of retaining Thompson machine-guns intended for the northern IRA.[127] Lynch responded by blaming O'Duffy for the arms not reaching the north.[128] That such indiscreet exchanges could occur while the treatyites were officially pursuing a peace policy in Ulster demonstrated the extent to which the north was becoming embroiled in the split. Despite partition, most northern nationalists supported the treaty. Those living close to the border believed that the boundary commission would cede their territory to the south, while Catholics in the north-east desired a southern state strong enough to pursue unification. Even most northern republicans, viewing the oath as small beer compared to partition, preferred the treaty to disunity. During the six months between January 1922 and the Civil War, a period of almost constant sectarian violence in Belfast, Collins and O'Duffy devoted much attention to the north. Whereas O'Duffy's rhetoric had often indicated a willingness to coerce Ulster, Collins was more ambiguous, sometimes assuring northern republicans of his determination to use force, on other occasions pursuing a conciliatory policy towards James Craig, the prime minister of Northern Ireland. On 21 January Craig and Collins agreed to tackle the violence in Belfast by resolving a number of key grievances, including the boundary commission, the shipyard expulsions, and the boycott. However, in the face of the intransigence of supporters on both sides and the ambivalence of both leaders, this proved impossible. At a cabinet meeting (attended by O'Duffy) only one week later, it was decided that northern nationalists should refuse to co-operate with the northern state.[129]

Events elsewhere were also contributing to the unsustainable pressures on cross-border relations. On 14 January Dan Hogan, O/C of the 5th northern division, was one of several footballers arrested by Specials on their way to a game in Derry City (where they had intended to rescue three IRA men under death sentence). Collins was unable to secure their release as he was unwilling to accept Craig's advice that they apply for bail, a step necessitating recognition of the northern courts.[130] Responding to pressure from border nationalists to retaliate to Hogan's detention, O'Duffy proposed a radical strategy to Collins on 30 January: 'I have arranged for the kidnapping of one hundred prominent Orangemen in Counties Fermanagh and Tyrone . . . failing to hear from you to the contrary the kidnapping will commence at 7 o'clock tomorrow evening.' He also informed Collins that Sinn Féin's local representatives demanded that the boycott remain in place until Hogan's release, noting pointedly that 'there are 54 affiliated Clubs in Co. Monaghan and each of them are sending two delegates to the Ard Fheis. This means 108 votes for Monaghan for the Treaty.'[131]

On the night of 7 February, IRA raiding parties crossed over the border into Derry, Tyrone, and Fermanagh, returning with over forty Protestant hostages, mainly Specials, Orangemen, and Unionist officials.[132] Rosslea was targeted by the Monaghan IRA, who kidnapped twenty Specials from the village. The raids, described by Craig to Lloyd George as a 'deliberate and organised attack on Ulster', caused uproar throughout Northern Ireland. Craig requested permission to send 5,000 Specials across the border to recover the hostages, and demanded that the British army reoccupy border territory within the south.[133] Winston Churchill, the colonial secretary, refused due to the danger of the collapse of the provisional government and civil war. He did, however, halt the withdrawal of British troops from the south and set up a border commission of IRA men, Specials, and British soldiers.[134] Lloyd George warned Collins that 'such acts are a breach of the Truce and gravely imperil the Treaty'.[135] Collins assured him (and Arthur Griffith, who, like most of the cabinet, was kept in the dark on military matters) that he had done his best to prevent the raids. A less emollient O'Duffy expressed himself unsurprised at this 'spontaneous and determined action', given the sectarian behaviour of the northern government and its intention to hang the Derry prisoners. He made little effort to veil his threat of further reprisals: 'There will be no peace while a number of our people there are held in custody.'[136]

As always, the reprisals led to further violence. The Specials flooded the border area, destroying border bridges, mining the roads, and exchanging shots across the border.[137] Three days after the raids, a dramatic shoot-out between the IRA and A Specials in Clones train station left four Specials and an IRA officer dead, and some twenty other people injured. When O'Duffy arrived in Clones two days later, he attributed the incident to Dan Hogan's continued detention, and warned of his 'gravest fears for what may happen'.[138] The British cabinet, whether due to ignorance or pragmatism, attributed the kidnappings to the Irregulars. At Westminster, Churchill read a letter from O'Duffy blaming the Specials for the deaths in Clones, and assuring the Commons that the provisional government was attempting to secure the return of the kidnapped Unionists. A better informed Unionist MP asked Churchill if he was not aware that it was O'Duffy who had orchestrated the raids.[139] In the meantime, the violence continued. The shoot-out in Clones triggered further rioting in Belfast, killing thirty-one people between 13 and 15 February. The worst incident occurred when a bomb was thrown into the yard of a Catholic school near York Road, killing six children, an outrage Winston Churchill described as 'the worst thing that has happened in Ireland in the past three years'.[140] The British authorities finally defused the violence by ordering the release of Hogan (against the wishes of Craig's government) on 21 February in return for the release of the hostages.

This appalling chain of events helps to illustrate the motives behind the IRA's northern policy and O'Duffy's influence upon it. Collins was willing to use peaceful methods to destabilize the north but, if unsuccessful, was also willing to deploy violence: most of the time he combined both strategies. O'Duffy's letter advocating cross-border reprisals indicates not merely that he shared Collins's belligerent attitude but that he was a radicalizing influence. O'Duffy had made it clear that failure to hit the north would undermine pro-treaty support along the border. The dynamics behind the violence resembled the previous year's reprisals in Rosslea. One Monaghan IRA officer recalled that Hogan's arrest had 'caused a feeling of tension on both sides of the Monaghan–Armagh, Monaghan–Tyrone and Monaghan–Fermanagh frontiers. On our side we carried out raids on Unionist houses and attacks on Special Constabulary patrols... They were not really official but were tolerated by GHQ.'[141] Another Volunteer stated that O'Duffy had given his unit permission to kill Specials following Hogan's arrest.[142]

O'Duffy could hardly oppose such violence and expect to retain the loyalty of his men, particularly as he had assured them that support for the treaty did not constitute acceptance of partition. Indeed, his willingness to sanction violence reassured republicans like Tom Carragher that the struggle would continue: 'After the Treaty we did a job at Cullaville (in the North). It seems that Collins, O'Duffy and the I.R.B. intended to have a go at the North as soon as we had enough arms. Dan Hogan and Frank Aiken planned the Cullaville ambush... We killed a few policemen.'[143] The knowledge that the Irregulars would exploit any perception of treatyite weakness on the north added to the pressure on O'Duffy to sanction such violence. As one Monaghan Volunteer explained:

After the boys going to the football match were arrested there was tension on the border. At this time Dev was out against the Treaty, and Dr McCarville was anxious to condemn O'Duffy and the Treaty, and tried to promote activity to break the Treaty. He was very anxious to arrest people from across the border and jail them. O'Duffy was asked to give permission to raid across the border and make arrests there, and was continually condemned for not giving permission. Of course he got sympathy from the Free Staters (that is McCarville). In fact we all were anxious to retaliate. At last word came giving permission . . . At about 4 a.m. the cars began to arrive with old grey men and some young ones.[144]

Collins and O'Duffy were outraged by the sectarian violence in the north, and genuinely sought to destabilize the northern state, but their militancy also stemmed from the necessity of retaining the support of northern and border Catholics who were politically divided and suspicious of southern intentions. Anti-treaty republicans could not be allowed the opportunity to exploit northern grievances for their own ends: 'The key to Collins' involvement in a coercive Northern policy up to the outbreak of the civil war in the South in June was not the destabilisation of the Northern regime but the neutralisation of the Northern IRA and along with it the issue of partition.'[145] Another advantage of covert action in the north was that it offered both IRA factions an issue on which common ground could be found: the spectre of civil war in the north was invoked to avoid it in the south. Such factors explain the importance of the north in the months before the civil war and its insignificance once that conflict began. The British authorities, dependent on the provisional government to impose the treaty settlement, were equally concerned that sectarian attacks on northern Catholics would wreck the treaty by uniting both IRA factions, a fear which explains London's toleration of the flagrant breaches of the treaty which the northern incursions represented.[146]

This co-operation between both IRA factions remains one of the murkier episodes of the period. In early February GHQ established a shadowy body known as the Ulster council or joint Ulster command controlled by Aiken, O'Duffy, and Collins. It was located in Clones, the headquarters of the 5th northern division, within easy reach of Aiken's and MacEoin's Armagh and Longford divisions, and only miles from the Tyrone and Fermanagh borders.[147] It was this body which co-ordinated the mass kidnappings, sent reinforcements to the border, and armed the northern IRA. The latter was achieved by swapping the easily identifiable British-issued provisional government arms for

Irregular rifles from Munster which O'Duffy then sent north via Frank Aiken's 4th northern division.[148] The renewal of what republicans regarded as a pogrom in Belfast added impetus to this unlikely co-operation: although Catholics formed only 25 per cent of Belfast's population, they comprised over 60 per cent of the 200 fatalities between March and June.[149] The actions of Craig's government, which rejected nationalist calls for the introduction of martial law under British military authority, expanded the Specials to 32,000 men, and introduced the draconian Special Powers act provoking further concern.

However, the effectiveness of the latter measures also highlighted the obvious limitations of the IRA's northern policy. A GHQ-sanctioned offensive in west Ulster, which killed six policemen and Specials in March, merely provoked further retaliation against Belfast Catholics, including the notorious killing of five members of the McMahon household. This violence was followed by more peace talks in April, and a new consensus in favour of nationalist co-operation with the northern state. O'Duffy strongly supported the suggestion that Catholics take up the places set aside for them in the Specials, arguing that 'the cream of the flying column' should enlist. However, the proposal failed because northern republicans refused to take the required declaration of allegiance to the northern state, a principled but self-defeating stance which weakened the Catholic community's ability to defend itself.

Following the failure of this second Craig–Collins pact, GHQ reverted to a war policy. At a meeting of northern divisional officers on 5 May, O'Duffy agreed to set a date for a northern offensive which GHQ would arm, finance, and organize. The offensive, which began on 19 May, was directed by O'Duffy with the knowledge of Collins but not the cabinet. It was an unmitigated disaster, due to a lack of co-ordination, and its unrealistic objectives. The 2nd northern division began fighting before the other divisions were ready; the 4th northern division failed to participate; and the 2nd and 3rd divisions collapsed within weeks.[150] The hitherto effective Belfast IRA lost the support of a Catholic population unwilling to endure further reprisals for no apparent purpose. The failed offensive left the IRA a broken force in the north. Its defeated Volunteers drifted south to the Curragh over the summer, where many sat out the Civil War as non-combatant members of the Free State army.

The offensive was partly a product of the northern IRA's militancy, but the motives underlying GHQ's support were possibly more cynical. While many northern officers believed the offensive was intended to overthrow the northern government, GHQ clearly viewed it as a continuation of its strategy of low-intensity violence intended to pressure the Unionist government.[151] O'Duffy's failure to order the (southern-based) 1st midland and 5th northern divisions to support the offensive demonstrated that it was never intended as a serious attack on partition, although it has also been suggested that O'Duffy deliberately misled the northern IRA about the level of support it could expect. Although the offensive resulted in the collapse of the northern IRA, its containment within the north served to limit southern complicity in the offensive. At the same time, GHQ's measured support for it ensured the loyalty of the northern IRA during the critical period leading up to civil war in the south.[152]

It was by now increasingly evident that the cabinet resented GHQ's aggressive northern strategy, and the fact that it was formulated without its approval. Like GHQ's attempts to conciliate the anti-treaty IRA, this could be overlooked in the months leading up to the Civil War when the provisional government's survival hung in the balance, but there was no longer any incentive to do so once conflict appeared inevitable. Kevin O'Shiel, an influential adviser on northern policy, complained to the cabinet that while he 'was urging a policy of peaceful do-nothingness in Northern Committees', both IRA factions were conspiring to invade the north. He blamed Collins, who came 'to quick decisions without consulting many', for the collapse of the offensive.[153] Ernest Blythe's memo to the North East Ulster committee, established by the cabinet in August 1922 to tighten its control over northern policy, ruled out both the continued use of force against the six counties and further co-operation with republicans who refused to recognize the northern state.[154] The cabinet sanctioned this new strategy, subject to the approval of the absent Collins, who was unlikely to have overturned what was clearly a consensus among the cabinet. Had he managed to do so, it is difficult to envisage to what practical end. Collins was killed the day after receiving the cabinet's resolution.[155]

An exchange of letters between Séamus Woods and Richard Mulcahy the following October illustrated the consequences of this shift in policy. Woods, one of the officers who travelled south after the collapse of the northern offensive, had kept over 90 per cent of his division loyal to GHQ on the basis of O'Duffy's assurance that the army would 'try to overcome the Treaty position with regard to Ulster'.[156] However, rather than organizing the northerners in the Curragh into a new northern force as Collins and O'Duffy had promised, a hostile GHQ now insisted that 'these gentlemen' should 'join the Army or go back to their homes'.[157] When Woods brought up the earlier assurances from O'Duffy, Mulcahy curtly informed him that 'the policy of our Government here with respect to the North is the policy of the Treaty', adding, 'I don't presume to place any detailed interpretations on what are called "assurances that the GHQ would stand to the North".'[158] O'Duffy was not to blame for the shoddy treatment of the northern IRA. His views had not changed, but the death of Collins had removed the most powerful advocate of the idea of the treaty as a stepping-stone to unification. O'Duffy's resentment of the government's passive northern policy, shared by more than a few treatyite officers, would remain a source of grievance throughout the next decade.

Civil war

As the northern offensive foundered, so too did attempts to stave off conflict in the south.[159] Following the failure of the IRB's attempts to reach an agreement in April, Collins noted that O'Duffy was 'without hope of unity'.[160] A truce agreed by O'Duffy and his opposite number, Liam Lynch, in early May to allow further talks collapsed on the provisional government's insistence on acceptance of the treaty as a minimum requirement. However, negotiations between de Valera and Collins continued, culminating in agreement that a panel of Sinn Féin candidates, reflecting the Dáil strengths of both sides would contest an election to return a coalition government. The pact, which made no reference to the treaty, illustrated the lengths to which Collins was willing to go to achieve unity: he shocked London (and his cabinet colleagues) by declaring that 'if unity could only be got at the expense of the Treaty—the Treaty would have to go'.[161] Despite Collins's insistence that non-republicans be allowed to contest the election, the pact appeared to prevent the electorate from exercising a meaningful opinion on the treaty. It did, however, allow the provisional government to hold an election which could not otherwise have taken place and postponed violence for a further month. It was not followed by army unity despite agreement on a unified army council on which O'Duffy would continue as chief of staff, to be later replaced by Liam Lynch. O'Duffy, as he informed Mulcahy, did not wish to remain chief of staff:

Now that there is a good prospect of army unification, I consider I should retire. You understand I had strong objections to accepting the position of C.S. at the time I did, & I would have definitely refused only I felt it was incumbent on me to do what I could to secure unity in the army & that my accepting the position temporarily would prevent a split, the majority of the Div & Bde C'dants over the Country having confidence in me. The split came, however, & I made up my mind I would not resign during a troubled time.[162]

Given his ambition, O'Duffy's decision to relinquish the highest office in the army seems curious. He explained that it was 'not a hasty decision on my part. I consider that some other officers—with a much wider military knowledge than I can profess to have should hold the responsible position of Chief of Staff. I would stick it alright in time of war, but in peace!—well it's not the same.' He appeared sincere enough. Indeed, the one characteristic note of false modesty suggested that he simply wanted a different position: 'The Monaghan Co. Council have very kindly kept my position as Surveyor open for me, but I would be prepared to accept any minor position in the civil (or police) admin-istration.' The post was a challenging one, particularly for someone whose mil-itary experience did not extend beyond small-scale rural guerrilla war. Given his temperament it was also a frustrating one, as is demonstrated by a letter which he sent to Mulcahy on the same day, complaining that Ginger O'Con-nell had appointed ex-British officers to positions in the Curragh camp with-out seeking his permission: 'To avoid "scenes" I let things pass, but there is a limit . . . I entertained high hopes of the Irish army . . . The placing of such men where they will be in a position to mould the whole future of the army, puts me in a very rotten position now—it is very rough.'[163] But, whatever his motives, the anti-treaty executive's rejection of the proposals for army unity on 14 June ensured that he remained in place for a while longer.

Hopes for peace now rested on the electoral pact, and Collins's attempt to devise a constitution of sufficiently republican character to win anti-treaty acquiescence to the Irish Free State. Both the Irregulars and the British govern-ment insisted on seeing the constitution before its publication. London rejected the first draft, which contained little that republicans could object to. Forced to choose between the Free State and the Republic—appeasing Britain or the anti-treatyites—Collins could only make the same decision as the previ-ous December. His revised constitution incorporated references to the oath, monarch, and commonwealth, thereby estranging anti-treatyites from the new state. The apparently cynical timing of its publication on 16 June, the morning of the election, and the disintegration of the electoral pact increased tensions. Two days before the election, Collins had urged an audience to vote for the best candidates regardless of whether they were on the panel. In Monaghan, O'Duffy and Blythe went further, urging the electorate to transfer their votes to independents rather than anti-treatyites.[164] O'Duffy comfortably topped the poll in Monaghan, 75 per cent of which was cast in favour of pro-treaty candidates.[165]

Failure to achieve unity through northern aggression, a republican constitution, and an electoral pact left little alternative to conflict. The dramatic assassination of Sir Henry Wilson in London the following week gave Britain the opportunity to demand that the provisional government confront the anti-treaty IRA.

Events began to slip out of control. On 27 June Ginger O'Connell was kidnapped in retaliation for the arrest of an anti-treatyite; Ernie O'Malley courteously phoned a startled O'Duffy to let him know. The bombardment of the Four Courts began the following morning. The artillery, as General Macready recorded in his memoirs, was supplied by the British army after frantic telephone calls from O'Duffy—a claim which republicans endlessly publicized and O'Duffy bitterly denied throughout his life.[166] After three nights of shelling, the poorly directed artillery of the inexperienced government troops prevailed. Cathal Brugha died before getting an opportunity to test O'Duffy's willingness to die for Ireland. Having ordered the last of his men to surrender, Brugha, with a revolver in each hand, ran out of a burning hotel on Sackville Street into a hail of Free State bullets. The Irregulars were soon routed in Dublin, but the outcome of the Civil War remained in the balance. The Munster IRA was solidly anti-treaty and its forces were more committed, experienced, and numerous than those of the provisional government. In the long run, however, British financial and military support, a massively expanded army, and the lack of public support for the anti-treaty cause would prevail.

The Civil War necessitated a restructuring of the treatyite military leadership. Collins relieved himself of his government duties to become commander-in-chief. Mulcahy, who remained minister for defence, reverted to his former role as chief of staff in place of O'Duffy, who was given control of the newly formed south-western command where the serious fighting was expected. O'Duffy's demotion was offset by the unchanged hierarchy of the GHQ triumvirate now, rather grandiosely, known as the War Council of Three. Harry Boland sardonically noted in his diary: 'Mick, Dick and Eoin "the big three". What a change!'[167] Republicans like Boland depicted the war council, a little richly, as a dictatorial clique rather than a convenient rationalization of treatyite military authority.[168] The decision by Collins and Mulcahy to return to uniform reflected the gravity of the military situation as well as the fragility of their forces. Mulcahy's characteristically convoluted reply to his son's query as to why he replaced O'Duffy as chief of staff revealed a certain uneasiness about leaving the latter in place: 'I was the person that the army was responsive to ... I did not feel that O'Duffy was ... that ... I was holding on to one old loyalty, to an old contact, to an old state of organisation, and it was probably something the same reason that I asked Collins to come in, to strengthen the prestige and the command of the Army on top. It was very vital.'[169] Later, he awkwardly elaborated on this: 'to some extent all that feeling for prestige on top might have made it necessary for me to bring in Collins too ... it was ... is possible you see that ... and it's only just because you raise it now, it's possible that I might have had difficulties with O'Duffy.'[170] He was unsure whether O'Duffy resented the reshuffle: 'Well, I, it would be very hard to interpret O'Duffy . . . O'Duffy was a real primadonna, O'Duffy was a bit excitable and he had a bit of a streak in him that tended towards excitability.'[171]

Although O'Duffy had pursued army unity for six months, once the war began his attitude was more hawkish than that of Collins or Mulcahy. His intransigence was instrumental in ending the neutrality of Frank Aiken's 4th northern division.[172] O'Duffy had a 'testy relationship' with Aiken, which had not been improved by the former's attempts to arrange for pro-treaty troops to occupy barracks in Aiken's division.[173] In July O'Duffy ordered Aiken to suspend peace talks with Liam Lynch and occupy the anti-treaty barracks in his area.[174] After Aiken, with the support of his officers, refused to renounce his policy of neutrality, he found himself under arrest following a surprise attack on Dundalk barracks by soldiers under Dan Hogan's command. Aiken, subsequently freed when the barracks changed hands again the following month, led his men against the government, blaming O'Duffy for forcing his hand.[175]

O'Duffy adopted a similar policy in the strategically important city of Limerick, where both sides were observing an uneasy truce despite the fighting in Dublin. When O'Duffy heard rumours of negotiations between the heavily outnumbered treatyite force (led by Michael Brennan and Donnchadh O'Hannigan) and Liam Lynch, he criticized his officers 'for going soft' and sent Diarmuid MacManus to Limerick to quash the talks.[176] His instructions were ignored by O'Hannigan and Brennan, who signed a truce despite O'Duffy's insistence that he would repudiate any such agreement. When MacManus returned to Portobello barracks, O'Duffy was given the south-west command.[177] Although, as in March, Liam Lynch claimed the outcome as a major success, the truce enabled the weaker provisional government forces to remain in Limerick where they continued to consolidate their position. Lynch's unwillingness to fight his former comrades was a weakness which the more decisive O'Duffy would exploit. When O'Duffy, accompanied by reinforcements, arrived in Ennis in mid-July, he ordered O'Hannigan and Brennan to break the truce by reoccupying their old positions. Lynch responded in kind, and fighting resumed several hours later after a treatyite soldier was shot. On 19 July O'Duffy began a major offensive, bringing artillery to bear with lethal effect on the anti-treaty forces which were routed after two days of what O'Duffy described to Collins as 'the finest operation in the present war'.[178]

The fall of Limerick isolated the republican stronghold of Munster from the Irregular forces in the west and midlands.[179] Blaming 'the bitterness O'Duffy bred and nurtured wherever it was possible', Frank Aiken—who witnessed the events in Limerick at first hand—claimed that 'O'Duffy forced the fighting in Limerick. Brennan and Hannigan, of course, were immediately responsible, but only for O'Duffy they would not have started, as Brennan said, "I don't see how serious fighting can take place here, our men have nothing against the other lads".'[180] But although O'Duffy did force the pace of fighting, there is no evidence that he was not supported by Collins or Mulcahy. By not seizing Limerick in early July—as many republicans had urged—it was Lynch who had miscalculated: his strategy of attempting to consolidate control of Munster without extensive fighting, in the hope of winning a strong negotiating position, had failed.[181] While hardly a tactical masterstroke, O'Duffy's determination to fight was far more effective than Lynch's indecision.

O'Duffy issued a characteristically ebullient statement after the fall of Limerick, which he distributed in a news-sheet titled *Limerick War News*. Seizing on Lynch's unfortunate description of the people as 'a flock of sheep to be driven any way you choose', O'Duffy depicted his opponents as a minority of misled (if dictatorial) patriots, backed by a criminal mob 'out for loot'. He contrasted the heroism of his troops with alleged Irregular atrocities such as the mining of a hospital. Those who 'terrorise lonely women and children in the dead of the night' and 'murder your brave and fearless young Irish soldiers under protection of the Red Cross flag', he thundered, should 'be treated as they deserve'.[182] He overstepped the mark, however, by issuing a proclamation declaring his intention to try offenders by court martial.[183] One of his first measures on assuming the south-west command was to establish a publicity department to collect information and disseminate propaganda.[184] He issued frequent press statements and made himself widely available to journalists, a policy which reflected an astute awareness of the value of propaganda as well as his love of attention.

In an emotional report, composed in his new headquarters in the Anglican bishop's palace, O'Duffy informed Collins that the 'civil population are jubilant, and at all the Masses to-day thanksgivings were said for the success of the National troops, who saved the City from destruction'.[185] Highlighting law and order as the key issue in the propaganda war, he suggested that it would be 'a good stroke' if civic guards could be drafted in to Limerick, a recommendation which Collins duly forwarded to the cabinet.[186] Optimistically predicting 'that we will have Limerick County completely in our hands in a week's time', he concluded:

The 3rd Seige [*sic*] of Limerick has been a success. History has repeated itself. First we had the artillery arriving by train to Nenagh ... Sean Moylan made a desperate effort to repeat the Sarsfield stunt and left with 400 men to attack the artillery, but unlike Sarsfield he failed; then we had the attack on the self same Castle Saint John's. It was prophesied that the 3rd Seige [*sic*] of Limerick would render the City in ashes, and the Citizens had sad forebodings. I do not think that Sarsfield and his troops were as popular as the present victors. I will say no more, I am rambling. Goodbye now and good luck.[187]

In fact, the fall of Limerick proved the high point of his campaign in the south-west, which became bogged down in 'the heaviest continuous fighting of the civil war' as anti-treatyites fought desperately to hold the east Limerick road and rail routes necessary to defend Munster from an advance from the north.[188]

In late July O'Duffy informed the press that he was 'well pleased with the progress made by the troops in this command. The best fighting material the Irregulars can muster is ranged against us . . . they have the advantage in quantity but in quality the advantage is very much with us.'[189] The truth was rather different. O'Duffy, who complained that he was facing 'practically the entire force of the Irregulars', had encountered serious set-backs.[190] The capture of 30 government soldiers on 22 July, followed by the surrender of Commandant Ned Cronin and 47 of his men the following day, halted the advance into east Limerick. The entire mid-Limerick brigade staff had been captured ten days earlier. O'Duffy complained to Mulcahy that 'No officer in the South Western Command Area has the remotest idea of what number of Regulars, Machine Guns, Rifles, Ammunition or Transport they control. If 100 Rifles were handed over to the Irregulars by a treacherous soldier, it would not be detected.'[191] He broke up the 4th southern division in order to tackle the poor morale, drunkenness, and 'absolute inefficiency' of its officers, and banned all soldiers in his command from public houses.[192] Adding to his difficulties, 300 reserves sent to reinforce his command proved 'absolutely worthless. At least 200 of them never handed a rifle before, were never in the Volunteers nor in the British Army. They got no training in the Curragh.'[193] He attempted, without success, to return these 'indisciplined, cowardly and drunken men', some of whom had deserted at the first shot.[194] Although O'Duffy was prone to exaggeration, it is clear that the calibre of his soldiers was very poor.[195]

Nonetheless, treatyite superiority in numbers and weapons began to tell. In early August O'Duffy received substantial reinforcements in Limerick, while sea landings in Cork and Kerry forced an anti-treaty withdrawal into Munster's remote republican heartlands. Despite more desertions, O'Duffy's men took Kilmallock, Patrickswell, Adare, and Rathkeale in one weekend, pushing south into Munster.[196] Given the material he had to work with, O'Duffy appears to have handled his first experience of large-scale fighting competently. Mulcahy commended his performance in 'the tough division...facing the south'.[197] Frank Aiken, perhaps unaware of the poor quality of the government soldiers, was less complementary: 'The Free State leaders preen themselves on the result of O'Duffy's campaign. From a military point of view the strategy of the whole Free State campaign was good, but their commanders in the field did not handle men in action as well as ours...they relied on sheer weight of lead rather than O'Duffy's or W. R. E. Murphy's tactics.'[198] In fact, tactics remained largely the preserve of Mulcahy and Collins: O'Duffy's task was to instil discipline and purpose into the novices under his command, driving them forward against an enemy which, for a variety of reasons, they were reluctant to engage.

Inevitably, O'Duffy's self-important style of leadership created some problems. Calton Younger noted his propensity for delivering 'pompous little homilies' to his subordinates. On one occasion, furious about the truce which had preceded ten days of tough fighting in Limerick, he harangued his weary officers who 'listened unbelievingly as O'Duffy urged them to make up their minds which side they were on'. It reportedly took the intervention of two of the Brennan brothers from Clare to prevent a minor mutiny.[199] His relationship with officers in adjoining commands, particularly Emmet Dalton, the Cork GOC, was poor. In September, for example, he complained: 'So far as I can see, other Commands are not engaging the Irregulars as they might, and the latter have perfect freedom to move about as they wish. We engage them everywhere, and although we have suffered heavily, we have taught them a salutary lesson.'[200] Whether these complaints were well grounded is difficult to assess, but the resulting tensions certainly hindered co-operation.[201]

O'Duffy proved more popular with war correspondents, who welcomed his flamboyant interviews and press statements. Characteristically, the subject of the latter was often himself. In August, for example, his publicity department issued a dramatic account describing three attempted ambushes on him between Killarney and Limerick: 'General O'Duffy personally directed the operations of the troops, who sustained no casualties.' The second attack 'was much more vigorous...The detachment of troops accompanying the General, which was very small, but consisted of picked men, succeeded in beating off the attackers, who operated from the hills overlooking the road...The car in which the G.O.C. was travelling was struck by bullets.'[202]

Whether O'Duffy played an active role in the fighting, as he claimed, is difficult to ascertain. Frank Aiken, who rated O'Duffy's abilities but not his courage, heard a different version of this ambush: 'O'Duffy was ambushed a few times and once at least was in a serious engagement with our friend Fionan

Lynch. Fionan, as you know, left the fight and found safety under a table in a farm house. Our men say that O'Duffy left his men, accompanied Fionan to the safe place, and stayed there until the fight was over.'[203] Whatever the truth, O'Duffy enjoyed a favourable profile among the establishment press, eager for heroic figures to build up the Free State cause. A gushing profile by one English journalist enthused about the

sparsely built keen faced young man who is for ever pouring over maps of Ireland... He is full of brains and determination...under a shy and unassuming manner. You forget when you are talking to this kindly man, he is very little over thirty and that you are in the presence of one who as practically military dictator has power over life and death in a very wide area in Ireland. As a matter of fact you are apt to forget everything except wonder at the extraordinary brightness of his eyes; and the quiet humour with which he makes a jest or parries a question... That the men love the Chief is not to be wondered at; he is one of them and is never above sharing their risks and perils.[204]

The progress made by provisional government forces revived the issue of peace negotiations in August. A letter which O'Duffy sent to Collins, in response to a peace initiative by Dan Breen, reveals his firm opposition to a negotiated resolution. O'Duffy reported that Breen, who was in contact with the Irregular chief of staff, Liam Lynch, had asked for permission to meet Collins in Dublin. O'Duffy had refused to grant Breen safe conduct to Dublin, however, and urged Collins not to meet him on the grounds that peace talks would destroy the morale of his men, who were finally making good progress. He argued, not unreasonably, that it made more sense to negotiate from a position of strength after his forces met up with those of Dalton and Prout. His description of Lynch as a 'tool of de Valera', and his suggestion that Erskine Childers was really the Irregular commander-in-chief, reveals his lack of understanding of the balance of power within the anti-treaty leadership. Like many of the fighting men, O'Duffy was inclined to blame the Civil War on the malign influence of the politicians rather than his former comrades. The letter revealed an interesting underlying reason for his hawkish stance:

I believe the Labour element and Red Flaggers are at the back of all moves towards 'Peace', not for the sake of the country, but in their own interests. They realise that, if the Government can break the back of this revolt, any attempts at revolt, by labour, in future will be futile. When the National Army have entered this conflict with such vigour, Labour realises that they would be much more vigorous to crush any Red Flag or Bolshevik troubles. Naturally Labour does not desire a Military decision in the present conflict, but it is absolutely necessary that the Government should have such a decision.[205]

Besides misreading the forces behind the peace initiatives (which included treatyite comrades like Emmet Dalton), O'Duffy's assessment provides an early example of the reactionary and conspiratorial outlook which would become such an important aspect of his world-view.

In August, as the last anti-treaty towns fell, republicans reverted to a strategy of sabotage and guerrilla warfare to prolong the conflict. On 12 August, the same day that he advised Collins against peace talks (and the day on which Arthur Griffith died from a brain haemorrhage), O'Duffy began a series of sweeps to root out the remaining opposition in the south-west.[206] Collins, however, continued to believe in the possibility of a settlement. Indeed, one treatyite officer claimed that he disapproved of O'Duffy's tactics: 'Collins didn't want them steamrollered.'[207] On 20 August Collins left Dublin for the south-west, determined to negotiate an honourable peace. On the evening of 22 August, following a reckless foray into republican territory, he was ambushed and killed at Béal na mBláth. O'Duffy, who had arranged to meet Collins that night, stayed up until three in the morning. Two hours later, he was awoken to the devastating news.

The death of Collins threatened to destabilize the Free State, and heralded a vicious final phase in the Civil War, culminating in the infamous execution of 77 anti-treaty prisoners. For O'Duffy, it represented a personal tragedy and a serious blow to his ambitions. According to one much-quoted account, Collins had morbidly identified O'Duffy as his successor should he fall in battle: 'There is a coming man. He will take my place.'[208] However, it was Mulcahy who took over as commander-in-chief, ordering O'Duffy and other senior officers to remain at their posts to prevent reprisals and ensure calm. O'Duffy's eulogy to his men on the day that Collins was buried illustrated sorrow, bitterness, and a determination 'to finish the work that Michael Collins brought so near to conclusion':

Here in the shadow of death I am not going to say anything hard, but I feel this tragedy of the Irish nation in my very soul within. They who murdered Mick Collins say they were Republicans. Republicans! My God! He was the best Republican of them all, said Gen. O'Duffy, amid tremendous applause. He was the only man that England feared. He was the only man that could and would secure the absolute independence of Ireland ... Will the Irish people ever place their trust and the destinies of the future Irish nation in the hands of those who are responsible for the murder of Mick Collins? No, never. Do the leaders on the other side see this? They do, but they see they cannot rule Ireland now, and their policy is to ruin her ... There is no-one more anxious for peace than I am. I consider this an unnatural and unreal, and heart-breaking fight, but the will of the Irish people must prevail ... We don't want peace now and in two months to have another outbreak . . . It is quite possible before this struggle for freedom—and it is a struggle for freedom—is over, probably more of our bravest and best will die, but others will take their place, and please God, the Irish Nation will live.[209]

Collins's death marked the end of O'Duffy's military role in the Civil War. On 1 September Kevin O'Higgins, the minister for home affairs, presented Mulcahy with what he described as an 'astonishing' request, asking him to release the man he considered the army's 'right arm' to take command of the Civic Guard. Only a figure of O'Duffy's stature, O'Higgins claimed, could redeem the force which had been paralysed by indiscipline since its formation: 'The new commissioner's army service must be such as to dwarf that of any man or Officer in the Force. He must be a man of commanding personality, a disciplinarian, and himself a model to the men of efficiency and self-restraint.' Pointing out that major military operations had come to an end, O'Higgins argued that the conflict was 'less and less a question of war and more and more a question of armed crime':

At present, foundations are crumbling on the civil side, decrees cannot be executed, debts cannot be collected, credit is therefore at an end, all commercial enterprise is at a standstill because there is no security . . . If the situation is not boldly faced, we may have a social crisis in the winter which will shatter all hopes of founding a democrat- ically governed Irish State . . . You can do best work against Childers and de Valera now by giving the man who by general agreement is the only one capable of retrieving the Civic Guard mess, and on the doing of that depends whether we shall succeed or fail in laying the foundations of a State.[210]

Despite the charm offensive, O'Duffy begrudgingly pointed out that he had previously made it clear that he was 'better suited for the position now offered': 'that Force now stands very low in the estimation of the people. It would be difficult to retrieve its position.' (This response, one historian noted, 'was absolutely characteristic of O'Duffy in its combination of self-glorification, denunciation of others, reproach, and mock humility').[211] However, following discussions with his command staff ('very much upset over my leaving'), O'Duffy agreed to accept the post, recommending W. R. E. Murphy and Dan Hogan as his replacements in the south-west.

Curiously, despite leaving the army before the policy of executions was introduced (and over half a year before the infamous atrocity at Ballyseedy when Free State soldiers murdered eight republican prisoners by tying them to a landmine), O'Duffy was destined to become one of the most vilified figures of the Civil War—the man who made 'Kerry a graveyard in 1922'. But although 'the Butcher of Ballyseedy' was actually not involved in the conflict's most vicious phase, the bitter legacy of the Civil War would exert a profound influence. The final, tragic, phase of the Irish revolution had been shaped more by its violent means than its idealistic aims. The politics of the Irish Free State, in which O'Duffy would play a central role, would become disfigured by the hatreds, betrayals, and disillusionment of the Civil War. Reflecting on the impact of the conflict on the morale, and morals, of the nation, as opportunistic criminality coalesced with anti-treaty violence, and the Free State fought republican terror with greater counter-terror, Ernest Blythe observed that 'a kind of rot proceeded in the country'.[212] During the next decade O'Duffy would make it his mission to save the state from the republican threat, and the moral shortcomings of the population from which it derived.

5

The flower of the young manhood of Ireland

The Garda is the soldier of peace. His war against the criminal never comes to an end. He can never be a 'quitter'; he has to win or fail, to defeat or be defeated.[1]

DESPITE his churlish reply, O'Duffy's acceptance of the commissionership which, in characteristically unsubtle fashion, he had canvassed for was unsurprising.[2] O'Higgins's, letter to Mulcahy, clearly intended for O'Duffy's eyes, reveals his awareness of the latter's susceptibility to flattery. Its craven tone was an attempt to mollify O'Duffy, who was the cabinet's third choice for the job (after the unsuccessful Michael Staines and the unwilling Seán Ó Murthuile). Why was he offered the position? Informing him of the request, Mulcahy tried to appear non-committal: 'There could be very voluminous argument for and against . . . in making up your mind on the matter you may be quite free to do so on the merits of the case.'[3] However, Mulcahy's appointment of Seán MacMahon as chief of staff when he succeeded Collins as commander-in-chief made it clear that he found O'Duffy less indispensable than his predecessor. Mulcahy conceded that there 'was a kind of feeling, I think, on O'Duffy's part . . . that I deliberately got rid of' him but attributed this to the General's neurotic personality.[4] There is little reason to disbelieve Mulcahy, but the appointment did remove an influential and difficult colleague.[5] There may have been other pressures involved. By late 1922 divisions had emerged between the military and ministers such as Kevin O'Higgins, and it would take little foresight to see that O'Duffy might prove a formidable

obstacle to any attempt to clip the army's wings, particularly given his clash
with de Valera the previous autumn.[6] Given the unfashionable nature of his
views on the north following the death of Collins, it may also have been felt
prudent to remove such a potentially unsuitable candidate for senior military
office.[7]

Conspiracy theories aside, however, O'Duffy was appointed because his
leadership abilities and republican credentials were urgently required to restore
order to the Civic Guard. Blythe insisted that 'the opinion of O'Duffy amongst
Ministers was very high at the time. His excessive vanity had not manifested
itself, and he was thought of as a strict, thoroughgoing, enterprising man, who
could tackle such a job as the restoration and maintenance of discipline
amongst the Civic Guards very well. In fact, I am satisfied that O'Duffy did do
a very good job in his earlier days.'[8] Frank Aiken agreed: 'it was believed by
some of our men, who did not know his capabilities, that this meant he was
fired from the Army. I believe he was appointed Commissioner because he was
the best man the Staters had for the job.'[9]

The Civic Guard (soon renamed the Garda Síochána) had struggled since its
formation in early 1922. Eamon Duggan, a weak minister for home affairs with
a drink problem, and his ineffective commissioner, Michael Staines, had failed
to impose their authority over the force.[10] Many of its initial recruits were
ex-IRA men who resented Collins's insistence that former RIC officers who
had co-operated during the War of Independence be retained in senior positions. Insubordination, factionalism, and anti-treaty sentiment stoked this
resentment, culminating in a revolt led by assistant commissioner Paddy Brennan
which forced Staines to flee the Civic Guard's Kildare camp on 15 May. An
uneasy stand-off between the provisional government and its armed police
force ensued, made all the more precarious by the slide towards Civil War.
When Blythe replaced Duggan (who, he recalled, was 'so cut up about the
whole business that he simply disappeared down to Greystones') as acting minister, he was shocked by the mutinous condition of the force.[11] In June the
more formidable Kevin O'Higgins took over at home affairs, announcing the
appointment of an inquiry into the mutiny.

Its report, written by Kevin O'Shiel, proved an important turning-point for
the Civic Guard. The recommendation that the force be disarmed in order
to win public confidence ensured that it would not be deployed against
anti-treatyites in the impending Civil War. Attributing the mutiny to political
tensions, it suggested that elected deputies be excluded from the force, a sensible recommendation which offered a pretext for the dismissal of both Staines
and Brennan (one of the three Brennan brothers who had led the IRA in East

Clare). The inquiry also called for the appointment of ex-IRA men to top posts to counteract the damaging impression that the force was led by ex-RIC officers.[12] One of the first victims of this policy was O'Duffy's cousin, Patrick Walsh, who was forced to resign as deputy commissioner but employed as a civilian adviser.[13] However, due to the urgent need for a commissioner with impeccable republican credentials, O'Duffy became one of its first beneficiaries. Paddy Brennan, whose removal was proving 'more sticky' than that of Staines, finally agreed to accept a new sinecure as superintendent of the Dáil because he approved of O'Duffy's appointment.[14]

Recruitment, training, and deployment

Appointed commissioner on 11 September 1922, O'Duffy threw himself into his new role with characteristic vigour. Kevin O'Higgins, who received a great deal of latitude on policing from his cabinet colleagues, in turn allowed his dynamic commissioner considerable administrative autonomy. Both men agreed that the immediate objective was to restore order throughout the state, parts of which had been lawless since 1919. The most pressing problem was the restoration of discipline within the force, a task for which O'Duffy's experience and abilities equipped him well. Blythe described the transformation which ensued:

O'Duffy, once he had taken charge of the Guards and assured them that, as far as he was concerned, the past was past and that nobody was going to suffer for any part he may have had in the mutiny, began to enforce discipline with a stern hand. I was told that the first night that he was on duty in the Castle he heard a Guard quarrelling with another and using obscene language. O'Duffy dismissed him instantly, though in ordinary circumstances, the offence would not have called for dismissal . . . he established supremacy over the Guards very quickly, and after a little time no doubt remained as to their discipline and loyalty.[15]

He quickly weeded out the unsuitable elements most responsible for the earlier difficulties. Others were taken aside, informed of the new disciplinary régime, and told to take it or leave it. Forming a low opinion of many of his superintendents, O'Duffy dismissed, demoted, or forced out the most inadequate.[16] He halted the recruitment of Clare men after discovering that Paddy Brennan, TD, assistant commissioner, and former IRA commander, had packed a third of the first wave of recruits with loyal subordinates from the banner county.[17]

Raising the calibre of recruits and officers remained a priority as the force expanded from 1,150 in 1922 to 4,500 in the following year. O'Duffy discouraged politicians from seeking places for friends, relatives, and constituents (although he remains popular in some parts of Monaghan due to his generous recruitment policy there).[18] Despite the recommendation of the inquiry, and his tendency to extol the republican composition of the new force, O'Duffy adopted a pragmatic attitude towards the ex-RIC veterans. At least 6 of the 20 superintendents he promoted to chief superintendent in 1923 had belonged to the old force, while he persuaded O'Higgins to reappoint his cousin, Patrick Walsh, as assistant commissioner.[19] He also surmounted cabinet opposition to appoint his former National Army subordinate, the ex-British army officer W.R.E. Murphy, commissioner of the Dublin Metropolitan Police.[20] He actively sought out experienced ex-RIC men for civilian positions at headquarters, provided they had not shown an excess of zeal during the Tan War.[21] These men, one garda recalled, 'were all highly qualified in police duties... They were a necessity at headquarters. Financially, they were cheap as the salary paid by our Government was the difference between their RIC pension and their rank in the Garda... they were invaluable at the time they offered their services and while serving were faithful, zealous workers.'[22]

It was a testimony to O'Duffy's success in instilling discipline that there was no recurrence of dissension on this sensitive issue. He was also careful to balance these appointments by recruiting men of the right background to key positions.[23] Over 1,300 of the early recruits, including 50 of his officers, were ex-National Army men with Volunteer backgrounds. IRA men, O'Duffy enthused, were 'hardy and healthy... all that was best and manliest of the youth of Ireland. The vast majority of them had magnificent brains and brawn, and, what was even better, they were imbued with a spirit of patriotic devotion and selflessness.'[24] A GAA background was an equally valuable asset for recruitment: 'A candidate's best recommendation, in my eyes... was athletic fitness and keenness such as a GAA record shows.'[25] Describing 'the son of the peasant' as 'the backbone of the force', O'Duffy encouraged recruitment from rural areas 'where the standards of health, physical excellence and morals are the highest'.[26] Gaelic speakers were also encouraged: 'No Irish-speaking candidate was finally rejected on any grounds without my special authority and rejection was decided upon only where the candidate was clearly unfit'.[27] By 1928, O'Duffy reflected, there were 'hundreds of men in the guards today who would not have the remotest chance of admission were it not for their knowledge of Irish'.[28] The ideal recruit was an upstanding, rural, Gael with a sound national record: that many fell short of this ideal was ignored by the General who depicted the force as he envisioned it.

With the exception of his initial reliance on ex-RIC men, recruitment of the officer corps reflected similar nationalist criteria. O'Duffy was allowed a relatively free hand in making appointments, which were invariably confined to treaty supporters.[29] To remedy the shortage of middle- and high-ranking officers, he introduced a cadet system to promote promising internal candidates.[30] Cadetship was open to single, educated, men aged between 21 and 26 who stood over 5 feet 9 inches in height, possessed 24 teeth, and could demonstrate their sound moral and national outlook with references from their former IRA officer and local priest. The entrance examination, which set aside more marks for Gaelic than law of evidence, reflected a similar ethos.[31] Candidates required 'a fair knowledge of Irish History from 1172 to the present time', and O'Duffy reserved the right to award additional 'service marks' on the basis of an IRA or GAA record.[32]

After occupying temporary offices in Ship Street and Collinstown aerodrome, O'Duffy set up headquarters in the Phoenix Park. Despite the force's unarmed status, the depot was run on military lines with a chain of command running from O'Duffy down to the depot barber. Recruits lived and drilled like soldiers, reflecting (like so many aspects of the force) continuity with the RIC, as well as O'Duffy's belief in the necessity of inculcating 'habits of implicit obedience and discipline' among men who would work in remote areas with little supervision.[33] Recruits spent two hours a day studying Gaelic, the same amount of time as was allotted for policing duties, while voluntary Irish classes were held nightly. Gardaí had to pass a Gaelic examination personally conducted by O'Duffy before receiving their posting while, by 1923, some knowledge of the language had become a prerequisite for promotion.[34] O'Duffy also encouraged his recruits to participate in sports during their basic training as a means of inculcating the virtues of 'self-reliance, manliness, high courage, [and] abstinence' required by gardaí.[35]

This induction was intended to instil responsibility and deter vice. Young recruits, O'Duffy observed, entered the depot 'immature and unseasoned' but left as 'men in all senses of the word with a proper and adequate knowledge of life—real life; for that phrase "knowledge of life" is often misquoted to refer to a knowledge of an unsuitable and degenerate kind. But, yes, the Garda know of such "knowledge" ... They must be aware of it in order that they may be fully armed to combat it when the need arises.'[36] Many of his early General Orders focused on moral issues. General Order No. 2 warned guards they would be dismissed for failure to pay debts and for borrowing money from lower ranks.[37] General Order No. 14 made it clear that alcoholics had no future in policing:

Ireland requires and deserves a sober Police Force . . . a member of a police force who has developed a taste for spirituous liquors is always a corrupt official . . . The stolen visits to public houses are noted with an even greater care than the open violation and if any man of any rank thinks he is deceiving any person except himself, he is labouring under a fatal delusion. Of one fact the delinquent may rest assured, he is not deceiving me.[38]

In response to a clerical request, he allowed the gardaí to display the Pioneer pin on their uniform (along with the Irish speakers' *fáinne*, the only unofficial symbol which was permitted).[39] He exhorted his young charges to take the only measure which would 'prevent even the attempt to undermine your character as a public servant, or your manhood as one of Ireland's sons. Become a Pioneer.'[40] Articles in *Iris an Gharda* with headlines such as 'Poteen! Poison! Insanity! Death!' reinforced his temperance drive.[41] By 1924 1,000 guards had become full members of the Pioneers of the Sacred Heart Total Abstinence Society, while another thousand had taken the temporary pledge.[42] O'Duffy devoted his first public address to his men to the theme of abstinence. Calling for an all-party alliance against the drunkenness rife throughout rural Ireland, he contrasted such scenes with a recent station inspection, where he had found every guard sporting the pin and 'clear, open and happy expression' of the temperance member.[43] This impressive sight may not have been entirely fortuitous as ambitious guards were rumoured to procure the pin in the knowledge that it 'would impress him and help their promotion'.[44] This preoccupation reflected not only O'Duffy's personal views but also the real temptations for young and inexperienced guards living in isolated and difficult circumstances, and the expansion of the *poitín* trade during the Civil War which had become an issue of serious concern to government and clergy.[45] Indeed, it has been suggested that it was the crackdown on alcohol which first won the police widespread respect in rural Ireland.[46]

The most striking aspect of the depot's curriculum, the early general orders, the content of *Iris an Gharda*, and the commissioner's speeches was his determination to impart a moral and national outlook to his young recruits. As O'Duffy later observed:

The care taken in the selection of the recruits, the ideals of service placed before them during the period of training in the Depot, their inherently clean, moral outlook and temperate habits, the earnestness and zeal of the men themselves, their pride in their calling, their quickness to respond to the trust imposed on them by the Government on the one hand, and the people on the other . . . the opportunities provided for sport and recreation which brought them into contact with clean and healthy-minded people, the spontaneous desire of the Force to cultivate self-respect, a strong aspiration to stand well in the eyes of the people, their own individual efforts to raise themselves in the social scale—all contributed to the general efficiency, discipline, and conduct of the force.[47]

This was true, but it would later become evident that the reasons for this ideologically driven induction were not only pragmatic. O'Duffy, as one of the first historians of the force noted, was striving to create 'a force which would be a model reflection of his ideals, a perfect microcosm of the healthy, free and Catholic nation'.[48] Physically, culturally, and morally, O'Duffy regarded his men as 'the flower of the young manhood of Ireland'.[49] There was a striking similarity between this ethos, his earlier aspirations for young Gaels, and the values O'Duffy would advocate as leader of the Blueshirts. Throughout his life, the General preached a gospel of improvement which emphasized the importance of respectability, temperance, disciplined service, patriotism, and virility: values which he summarized as manliness. These ideals had been central to cultural nationalist organizations such as the GAA and, during the Irish revolution, had come to inform the ideology of Sinn Féin more profoundly than republicanism.[50] *The Ethics of Sinn Féin*, a pamphlet published in 1917, provides one example:

Independence is first and foremost a personal matter. The Sinn Féiner's moral obligations are many and restrictive. His conduct must be above reproach, his personality stainless. He must learn the Irish language, write on Irish paper, abstain from alcohol and tobacco . . . make examples of your life, your virtues, your courage, your temperance, your manliness, which will attract your fellow countrymen to the national cause.[51]

More than many of his idealistic generation, O'Duffy took these sentiments to heart. He not merely aspired to Irish Ireland values, he made them central to his own self-image, becoming one of a long line of patriots to identify his country's history and culture with his own identity, in much the same way as another republican pamphlet, *Mé Féin*, had urged: 'Each of us is the Irish nation in miniature. Therefore we ought to make ourselves as like as possible to what we think the Irish nation to be.'[52] O'Duffy's idealism appears extreme in retrospect, but seemed less so to his contemporaries who were striving to build a state which would measure up to the expectations and sacrifices of the revolution. Like many of the state's institutions, the Garda Síochána mimicked the British model but sought to express its distinctiveness through a self-conscious enunciation of its superior moral purpose.

Equally fundamental to the Garda Síochána's sense of moral purpose was its status as an unarmed and ostensibly non-political force. Kevin O'Higgins, the minister for home affairs, was primarily responsible for these innovations, shared by few other police forces, but was enthusiastically backed by his commissioner. O'Duffy's first address to his recruits exemplified this ethos, which represented a radical divergence from its discredited predecessor:

The Civic Guard is to be strictly non-political. It is a Police Force for all the people, and not for any section of the people ... It is not their business how the people think politically, everyone is entitled to their opinions—be these what they may. They are prohibited from taking part in politics, or from associating with one side more than another. They will serve whatever Government the people of Ireland put into office, and, as far as they can, they will protect the lives and property of all the people ... The Civic Guard is to be an unarmed force ... I take a certain responsibility for this step, and I do not regret it. An unarmed Force depends entirely for its success on the moral support of the people.[53]

This was a remarkable speech considering that those being addressed were to be despatched to areas where a significant proportion of the population supported the anti-treaty military campaign. Inevitably, given that anti-treatyites opposed not only the government but the state itself, the police failed to achieve universal support or, indeed, to live up to these high standards: in fact, it was this issue which ultimately undermined O'Duffy's position. In the short term, however, the successful depiction of the Garda Síochána as a non-political force proved vital to its widespread acceptance.

The government's admirable policy was not entirely selfless. O'Higgins and his advisers believed that the anti-treaty campaign derived its strength from the lawlessness which prevailed throughout the state. Republican violence, O'Higgins notoriously argued, was rooted in psychological rather than political grievances:

Only a very small proportion of it is due to genuine dissatisfaction with the Treaty. Only a very small proportion of it is a struggle to secure a particular form of Government, as against another form. A good deal of it is due to reaction from the high standards and selflessness which prevailed rather generally during the conflict with the British, and to an idea that anyone who helped, either militarily or politically in that conflict, is entitled to a parasitical millennium. Leavened in with some small amount of idealism and fanaticism, there is a great deal of greed and envy and lust and drunkenness and irresponsibility. All this is fostered by the idea that there is a breakdown of law and the sanctions of law, that the existing Government is unable to function effectively, and that the sun is shining for the law breaker. We are dealing with anarchy under cover of a political banner.[54]

O'Duffy did not share his minister's politics—the ambitious lawyer who had risen to the executive council without an Irish Ireland or military record of note was considered a reactionary imperialist by treatyite republican-militarists— but he did share his zealous outlook on 'the disingenuousness of de Valera', 'the weakness and the corruptibility of the people', and 'the impending threat of anarchy'.[55]

The support of both men for an unarmed force was, therefore, a pragmatic rather than a liberal or conciliatory stance (while supporting this measure O'Higgins also demanded military 'executions in every County').[56] Given the circumstances, the only way to ensure the widespread acceptance of the gardaí was to exempt them from responsibility for political crime. According to Blythe, the cabinet balanced the possibility of unarmed guards being thrown out of their stations against the certainty of IRA attacks on an armed force: 'we finally came to the conclusion that the only thing that would get real sympathy for the Guards was to have them, for the time being, defenceless'.[57]

Although some guards (including allegedly O'Duffy) were attacked, the IRA did not launch a concerted campaign against the force—a tactical error given the police's important role in legitimizing the state.[58] Interestingly, documents dating to autumn 1922 reveal that the IRA had been informed of this. A republican spy, 'Pro-Patria', told the IRA of the government's dependence on the police and courts to establish its authority. However, the IRA's director of intelligence casually dismissed the threat: 'If the Civic Guard are properly managed, they should not cause much trouble, as fifty per cent of the Force are more Republican than Free State—25% are useless to either side and may be disregarded, and the remainder . . . will be in no way dangerous.'[59]

Nonetheless, the violence which did occur was terrifying for those involved. As the first wave of police was deployed between September 1922 and the following summer, over 200 stations were attacked, bombed, or burned; 400 guards were assaulted, stripped, or robbed, and one was murdered. The latter, Harry Phelan, had entered a shop to buy hurleys for a local team set up by the guards when he was set upon by three men who held him to the floor and shot him in the head.[60] In November 1922 the Kerry 1st brigade O/C offered the local police, who he described as the new RIC, an opportunity to resign before being killed. Although deputy commissioner Coogan feared a general attack, O'Duffy held his nerve, arguing that the assaults were not 'part of a settled policy'.[61] The General exerted an important steadying influence during this crucial period: his ability to stand firm in a crisis accounted for many of his successes.

The commissioner's advice to gardaí as they departed for hostile regions has been described as 'utterly impracticable and supremely idealistic.'[62] It was certainly the latter, but it formed part of a shrewd strategy based on the exploitation of his men's unarmed status. O'Duffy exhorted them to resist the gunmen by placing their faith in the goodwill of the people and their own IRA records in what he described as a renewed struggle 'for the existence of their motherland':

Don't open your doors, let them be smashed in: don't surrender your property or that entrusted to your charge; defend it with your lives . . . Far better the grave than dishonour. Don't be alarmed by the sound of a shot. You heard it before and you were not subdued because you had right on your side and the gunman had only might . . . I know the stuff you are made of, and I know you would not allow me, if I wanted to, retain in the Civic Guard a weakling who would take off his uniform and hand it over to any coward who had never fought before . . . [63]

Those who surrendered without struggle were chastised. General Order No. 9 , issued after a series of raids on police stations and the murder of Phelan, exemplified O'Duffy's remarkable attempts to inspire his men to almost impossible standards of bravery through his brilliant use of propaganda and psychology:

The Civic Guard is largely composed of 'Column Men' whose name for bravery and resource has become household words. If they were nothing more, they are Irishmen, and the Gael is not by nature a coward or a Poltroon . . . Let there be no compliance with the demands of cowards, for only cowards come armed to unarmed people—they dare not walk without their guns. The reign of the gun in the hands of the coward is nearly over. Let there be no compliance—resist passively—actively—resist all the time—for you are right all the time.[64]

In these well-publicized speeches, O'Duffy highlighted the cowardice of the 'enemies of Ireland' who attacked the unarmed servants of the people, attempting to shame the IRA into a policy of non-belligerence: 'If these acts are authorised, the leaders should hang their heads in shame—the days of Irish chivalry are gone.' For example, he drew attention to the heroic resistance of a station party in Baltinglass, which had refused to open its door to its assailants. When the armed raiders finally broke in, Garda O'Halloran produced a picture of his former IRA commander, saying 'I fought with that man in the west for three years, and some curs like you murdered him. What do we care for you, a lot of contemptible robbers. I often looked down a rifle barrel.' Revealing his scars from the Tan War, O'Halloran taunted his assailants to do the same. The raiders robbed the station box, set the building alight, and departed to the jeers of the guards. O'Duffy circulated the report to his men, assuring them that he felt such injuries 'no less than if the cruelties were practised personally on myself'.[65] Naturally, he rarely publicized those occasions when guards chose loss of face over a bullet. Moreover, as one admirer conceded, he could be ruthless in 'his determination to make heroes', harshly denouncing or dismissing those who, he considered, fell short of his standards.[66]

He orchestrated elaborate funerals to win public sympathy and stiffen morale, deploying the emotive tradition of the graveside oration to depict his fallen guards as national martyrs. His speech by the graveside of Garda O'Halloran (the defender of Baltinglass who was later shot by bank raiders) provides one example:

Why did he risk his life? He gave up his young life on the altar of freedom to secure the happiness and prosperity of the Nation. He died for the people and for the people's rights . . . If I asked for volunteers to take the same risk as Guard O'Halloran took, every man, too, would step out. Do the Irish people realise all that this means? Do they realise that it was a martyr's blood flowed on the streets of Baltinglass? I know they appreciate the chivalry of the Garda, but I would like to see better co-operation on the part of the people.[67]

Soldiers and gardaí escorted the hearse through Gort, where a guard of honour kept vigil at the church through the night. O'Duffy led a mile-long cortege to the graveyard where the Garda band played Chopin's 'Funeral March' and the 'Last Post', and the army fired volleys over the grave. Grieving family members were interviewed, and the condemnations and condolences of politicians and clergy publicized. Such murders became publicity disasters for the IRA (even when it later transpired, as in O'Halloran's case, that it had not been involved). O'Duffy also used these ceremonies to reinforce his vision of the force as a civic élite. Murdered guards, he claimed in typically extravagant rhetoric, were martyrs 'whose unselfish patriotism sprang from ideals of an order too sublime and exalted, too celestial, elusive and detached to lend themselves to comprehension by those of us whose souls in the hour of danger have not been ennobled by an inspiration which, conscious not of material things, soars with angelic aloofness in a region to which none but the very great may aspire.'[68]

The need to raise morale and mobilize public support also underpinned O'Duffy's initial efforts to emphasize the Garda's nationalist ethos. In April 1923, as attacks on stations mounted, O'Duffy organized an elaborate ceremony in the depot consecrating the Civic Guard to the Sacred Heart of Jesus.[69] 'In a spontaneous movement', one guard recalled, 'the men already on duty in the scattered towns and villages invited local clergy to consecrate their stations and bless the Sacred Heart pictures that were still to be seen in some Garda stations up to recent times. Morale in the Civic Guard, and confidence in the

State struggling to be born, were restored through the faith of the young gardaí, reinforced in a simple religious service at Easter, 1923.'[70] Such ceremonies helped the police to win acceptance in rural Ireland where the power of the pulpit remained immense.[71]

O'Duffy used sports for much the same purposes. The Garda's first Gaelic sports day was described as 'a historic day for Ireland...one more proof of Ireland's victory'. Whereas the RIC had been banned from participating in Gaelic sports, it was now the guards who were urged to boycott foreign games.[72] Participation in sports eased the integration of guards into close-knit rural communities where, as outsiders, they were often regarded with suspicion. The commissioner's appeal to his men to 'play their way into the hearts of the people' was well received:

The Guards brought their sporting skill to the youth of towns and villages which had never heard the clash of hurleys, seen the speed and flash of Gaelic football or watched the fascinating dexterity of a good handballer. Hundreds of new local teams were raised under the coaching of Garda sportsmen, and the Guards themselves attained the status of local celebrities as selections for county teams. Particular encouragement was given by O'Duffy for the construction of handball alleys against the back walls of suitable police stations. These were usually built by joint efforts of police and people and then became meeting places for the guards and young people of the neighbourhood.[73]

There was another, more practical, reason for a sturdy force. O'Duffy urged his men to show more flexibility than the RIC (which had earned a reputation for petty officiousness) in the manner they dispensed justice. He emphasized the need for discretion, advising that 'it is not necessary that every trifling offence should be followed by a prosecution'.[74] Such pragmatism helped the guards to win public acceptance: 'In small rural communities the local family feud or land agitation could often be settled by a young agile guard taking the village tough down a laneway for a good thrashing, and respect for the law was often attained through the heavy hand of a Garda boxing or athletics champion.' The issuing of the occasional dig in the head in preference to the humiliation and expense of a jail sentence became 'an accepted part of the relationship between police and people' in a rural country long conditioned to be 'agin the law'.[75]

Leadership

O'Duffy encouraged, chastised, and inspired his inexperienced force through the difficult period of deployment. His efforts to recruit an athletic, teetotal, and devout Gael-force may appear naïve, but his emphasis on discipline and moral integrity contributed to the high standards within the new force, and served a vital propaganda role among the public. The Garda's genuinely impressive transition from a mutinous to an efficient and well-disciplined body of men, particularly in comparison to the standards in the National Army, demands further consideration of the General's leadership abilities.

Central to O'Duffy's effective leadership was his ability to forge a bond with his men. He closely identified with them in their struggles in an astute attempt to harness the camaraderie of the Volunteers to the guards: 'we were all comrades a very short time ago, and I wish you to look upon me still as a comrade, irrespective of what position in this little Force we may have been called upon to fill.'[76] Even his General Orders were issued in the same folksy, intimate, style: 'I wish each man to think I am speaking personally to himself— which is really what I am doing; for I feel I am very much one of the Civic Guard and I think they will understand me, and I think further that they are thinking of exactly the same things themselves.'[77] However, O'Duffy's talent was for addressing crowds rather than individuals; in person, his conversations with subordinates were formal and stilted.[78]

In reality, O'Duffy's leadership was more paternal than fraternal. If it was sometimes necessary to be stern or critical, his pride in his men was always evident. He wanted only what was best for them, and exulted in their achievements: 'He had heard the Civic Guard sarcastically spoken of as gentlemen. That was what he wanted them to be. He wanted every member to raise his head high and feel as good as any man in the land, to get rid of the slave mind, but to respect their officers . . . he was prouder than ever of the Civic Guard.'[79] He constantly praised his men, awarding them certificates for efficiency and fitness which he personally designed, and writing to politicians and bishops for letters of praise to publish in the Garda journal. He introduced the Scott medal for bravery in the same spirit. *Iris an Gharda* contains countless photographs of O'Duffy dispensing awards to young guards from the country, ill at ease in their first suit, at the depot's many functions and formal dinners.

His disciplinarian rhetoric—exemplified in his address to the first wave of cadets—also struck a paternal rather than tyrannical tone: 'They were setting out on the battle of life; they were beginning a new career . . . A great deal was expected of them, and to ensure that there would be no disappointment, discipline would be firm and rigid. For the slightest breach of discipline they would be instantly dismissed, and, having been warned at the beginning of their journey, they would only have themselves to blame if they placed themselves in difficulty.'[80] His paternalism even extended to forbidding his men to purchase motorcycles or cars without his approval: 'Such things tend to extravagance'.[81]

This paternalism was genuine, but also formed part of a deliberate style of leadership. The Garda journal made it clear that 'the higher interests of the Force are jealously watched and championed by the Chief'.[82] In return, gardaí were expected to be worthy of their commissioner's trust, and those who fell below his exacting standards could expect harsh treatment. Even admiring subordinates remembered him as an intimidating figure:

> Outside of the missing index finger, lost in the fight of 1920, perhaps the most striking physical characteristic was the piercing blueness of his eyes. Without endowing these with any mesmerising quality, they undoubtedly had a disturbing effect on the individual on whom they concentrated their gaze. Instances were not unknown where members collapsed in face of their concentration. The General was privately not a little vain of his ability to floor with a look . . . even for the most self-complacent, a summons to the aforesaid office was a journey if not into fear, at any rate into uneasiness.[83]

The General's ability 'to pass swiftly from the combination of hot temper, severe look and biting phrase to the other combination of gracious manner, infectious smile and merry laugh' inspired the strangely 'contradictory senti-ments of fear and affection'.[84] Such was his authority, he prevented strikes on more than one occasion simply by issuing emotive appeals reminding his men of his efforts on their behalf and his 'sternest opposition' to their intentions.[85] The contrast with Michael Staines, his uncharismatic predecessor, was striking.

O'Duffy's achievements, as he regularly pointed out to the press, were a consequence of his single-minded dedication to his job. He claimed to work a 17-hour day, seven days a week.[86] A depot officer recalled his gruelling schedule: 'Repeatedly we returned to Dublin with him late at night, after a day long of inspections of the remote stations in the west or south. We went to bed, he went to his office. Next morning, or should we say that same morning, he was sitting at his desk, "speck and span", awaiting to give interviews to each member of the GHQ Staff.'[87] Another officer remembered his endless 'reserves of health and stamina', and his habit of teasing ill subordinates by remarking 'Look at me! I have never taken a drop of medicine in my life.' While his exhausted officers had wilted by the end of his marathon meetings which ran into the small hours, O'Duffy remained alert to the end.[88]

For eleven years his life was almost entirely devoted to the force: he worked, slept, and socialized in the depot. No Garda society was too insignificant for him to decline the position of honorary president, attend its functions, and hand out its prizes. His solemn expression—'the set face which forbade any attempt at closer intimacy'—stares out from the centre of countless group photographs. In the latter years, his lengthy working days were followed by long nights of cards and drinking with an inner circle of senior officers.[89] Although 'he lived as a bachelor in the Officers' quarters', one of these officers recalled, 'he achieved a considerable private life of his own. He admitted but few to his more intimate circle but the junior officer who found himself there by chance was invited to remain and then put thoroughly at his ease. Here he was to be seen at his best, or rather his most likeable. The official aloofness of manner disappeared.'[90] More often, his vain and overbearing demeanour— exemplified by his habit of referring to himself as 'the commissioner' in conversation—made it difficult for him to relate to people beyond a formal capacity. Most of those he socialized with were his subordinates, and many did not like him. As one (sympathetic) depot officer conceded, he was 'a man one could not socially love'.[91] When he was not in the depot, or patronizing a vast range of voluntary and sporting societies, he socialized with former army comrades like Dan Hogan, Seán MacEoin, and Hugo MacNeill, with whom he was often photographed at horse-racing events in Punchestown and Fairyhouse, GAA matches at Croke Park, and other sporting occasions. Yet, for all this, he cuts rather a lonely figure: he was a man who holidayed alone and, despite sending over 300 Christmas cards, had few real friends.[92]

O'Duffy's commitment to his force, and to raising its profile (a deliberate leadership strategy) reinforced his celebrity, in Ireland and abroad. He was a keen student of policing methods in other countries, although this was also due to the welcome opportunity to strut the international stage. A conference in Berlin in 1926, for example, was followed by an epic tour through Germany, Austria, Czechoslovakia, Yugoslavia, Bulgaria, and Hungary. His foreign visits, involving receptions, parades, banquets, and endless speeches, did much to raise the profile of the Irish Free State as well as its police force. O'Duffy was often the first state official to visit many countries, meeting presidents, prime ministers, mayors, and bishops, and generating much favourable press coverage. In Germany, for example, he was greeted by the Reich chancellor, Dr Marx, in Berlin and flown by private plane to Bremen, Potsdam, Dresden, and Hamburg. He returned with a deep admiration for German efficiency and its police force's devotion to athletic training. He invited foreign police commissioners to visit Ireland to inspect its new force, and recognize its achievements by bestowing him with awards and honours.

He regarded himself as a roving ambassador for the Free State: he described his visit to a police conference in New York in 1923 as 'on onward step in the progress of Ireland on her way to Nationhood'.[93] To his credit, it was a role in which he excelled. During his visits to the United States, he missed no opportunity to extol 'the remarkable achievements of the Free State' and correct the 'false impressions' disseminated by anti-treaty propagandists.[94] He described a peaceful and potentially prosperous state, deserving of a peace dividend: 'the Killarney resorts and the places on the Connemara coast are as lovely as ever. We expect many of you this summer . . . We're getting ready to tell America some of the virtues of Irish cloth.'[95] The press reports reveal a deft popular touch. During a visit to a New York school, he compared the Free State to a character in a popular western movie: 'the Irish are on the road to freedom, and are only stopping to take refreshments, as did the pioneers on their way in search of gold'.[96]

The Garda Síochána was a success story for a state which did not have too many, one which reflected well on himself, his men, his country, and Irish-America (if not its republican die-hards who occasionally surfaced to hurl eggs at Ireland's Benedict Arnold).[97] He adeptly pulled on the heartstrings of Irish-Americans, thrilled by the achievement of Irish independence. Presenting the New York Police Department with a tricolour donated by his men, he reminded his audience that he had fought with them on the hillsides of Ireland: 'when the men who suffered, and whose comrades' blood ran red for that flag, asked me to present the Police Commissioner with it then they were giving of their best indeed'.[98] Even seasoned police chiefs were impressed by an audience with the General:

'I've shaken hands with Presidents and most of the great, but I want to tell you this handshake means more to me than all of them . . . God bless you, me bhoy!' And there was just a hint of a choke in his old voice as he said it. Outside in the corridor a hard bitten New York cop, one Capt. James Gegan, of the bomb squad, blustered and talked loud to cover something that the suspecting might have called emotion . . . [O'Duffy] is slim and straight and speaking with a cheery, clipped precision . . . a clear thinking, quick acting bunch of tight wire efficiency . . . for all the chilly glint his blue eyes can assume . . . Gen. O'Duffy is no stranger to emotion. He is an expert in emotion.[99]

As ever, O'Duffy was a hit with the press. Journalists revelled in the romance of his rebel background, as a *New York Evening Post* profile demonstrates:

This man who carried a price on his head of $5000 for three years, never has lost the smile in his blue eyes; nor the lightning power of his right arm. He has a laugh for a foe, and looks the world straight in the eye. Standing straight as an arrow, lean and strong and looking remarkably well set-up in his blue tunic and slacks, black Sam Browne belt and scarlet insignia of rank, General O'Duffy inspires confidence in his ability to keep turbulent Ireland in the palm of his hand . . . His words stream out in a sharp crackle, like a machine gun burst. When his thin lips are unsmiling, they make a firm, hard line at right angles to a thin hawk nose. His Irish blue eyes freeze suddenly into twin points of ice.[100]

Such reports allowed the gardaí to bask in their commissioner's reflected glory, instilling pride in their collective achievements, and a sense of being part of an important and successful experiment.

The army mutiny

By 1924, the Garda Síochána had proved itself a success. Armed crime in the capital had plummeted between 1923 and 1925. Outside Dublin, the fall in crime was less dramatic but substantial.[101] O'Duffy was credited for much of this, and his importance to the state was further emphasized when the government turned to him to subdue another mutinous body in the spring of 1924. The army mutiny was a complex and murky affair, partly rooted in internal army problems, and partly in the long-standing tensions between the civil and military treatyite wings personified by the rivalry between Kevin O'Higgins and Richard Mulcahy, the minister for defence. The ill-feeling between both men originated in O'Higgins's belief that the army had not prosecuted the Civil War with sufficient determination. Ernest Blythe was one of several ministers who agreed with O'Higgins, citing an occasion in September 1922 when Mulcahy secretly met de Valera despite the cabinet's decision to suspend negotiations until the anti-treaty IRA surrendered. In a revealing admission, Blythe stated that the only reason Mulcahy's resignation had not been demanded was because 'the Government was cut off from the army'.[102] Following the Civil War, O'Higgins continued to hold Mulcahy responsible for military indiscipline and the failure to suppress armed crime. Indeed, he complained that serving soldiers were responsible for much of the crime.[103] His prejudices were buttressed by O'Duffy's colourful monthly reports which presented a bleak picture of a nation 'under the shadow of the anarchist', its slums ruled by 'city scum', and its countryside wracked by 'wild and insane orgies of crime'. Moreover, the commissioner invariably stressed that the key factor was the military situation: 'where this is right all else is right, and where it is otherwise, the converse is the case'.[104]

   These tensions were exacerbated by a scandal which erupted in the summer of 1923, when three officers (including Major-General Paddy Daly, the controversial GOC of the Kerry command) were accused of assaulting the daughters of a Kenmare doctor. O'Higgins was infuriated by Mulcahy's decision not to court-martial the officers, whose dismissal had long been sought by a number of cabinet ministers due to their involvement in previous atrocities in Kerry.[105] O'Higgins, Blythe recalled, was 'frantic about Army misbehaviour, and he made up his mind to bring it to a test in the Kenmare case'. Blythe, who 'did not agree with O'Higgins in feeling particularly revolted at what seemed to be merely a case of a couple of tarts getting a few lashes that did them no harm', recalled an 'almost hysterical' O'Higgins storming out of a cabinet meeting after threatening to resign. He added, with some understatement, that 'the whole incident left Kevin with somewhat stronger feelings against General Mulcahy'.[106]

The ill-feeling between both ministers was aggravated by demarcation disputes between their respective forces. At a high-powered meeting in September 1923, attended by Cosgrave, Mulcahy, and O'Duffy, O'Higgins demanded that the army do more to reduce armed crime and improve military discipline. He forcefully insisted that the army, rather than the police, should continue to take the lead in tackling subversion: 'we must kill the active Irregular, tackle the passive Irregular, make friends with the rest'.[107] Although his damning reports were used by O'Higgins against Mulcahy, O'Duffy characteristically tried to keep on the right side of both men. In December 1923, for example, he warned Mulcahy that the Kerry command had lost the support of the local population due to its behaviour, but told him that he would omit the details of its latest transgressions from his confidential reports to O'Higgins in order to allow him to resolve the issue.[108] Within several months, however, a minor mutiny within the army would combine with the military's longstanding problems and the tensions between both ministers to render Mulcahy's position untenable.

The immediate causes of the mutiny included the opposition of a number of officers to demobilization, the army council's decision to revive the IRB to help impose its authority within the army, and the resentment of the army council by rival factions competing for influence in the diminishing force. The convoluted chain of events began on 6 March 1924, when a delegation of officers presented the government with an ultimatum on behalf of the 'IRA Organisation' demanding the removal of Mulcahy and his army council, the suspension of demobilization, and a more 'republican form of government'. The government's response to this potent combination of self-interest and patriotism was surprisingly ambivalent. It ordered the arrest of the mutineers but appointed O'Duffy as general officer commanding the forces over the army council, a measure signalling its lack of faith in Mulcahy and his senior officers. Conversely, the concentration of power over the military and police in the hands of one individual suggested a remarkable faith in O'Duffy. Cosgrave's willingness to assure Joe McGrath, the minister for industry and commerce (who had resigned from the cabinet in sympathy with the mutineers), that an investigation into the army command would follow, further demonstrated the government's ambivalence. Assured that their grievances would be addressed, the mutineers withdrew their ultimatum on the under-standing that the charges against them would be dropped if they returned to service by 20 March.

The crisis, it appeared, had been defused. On 18 March, however, a group of mutineers who had gathered in a Dublin pub were arrested on the orders of the adjutant general, Gearóid O'Sullivan, and Richard Mulcahy, who believed that they were still conspiring against the government. The following day O'Higgins demanded the dismissal of Mulcahy and the army council for breaking the government-brokered truce and acting without O'Duffy's authorization. He was pre-empted by Mulcahy, who resigned in protest at the government's conciliation of the mutineers.[109]

The significance of this dramatic chain of events remains disputed. Contemporary public opinion was largely sympathetic to O'Higgins, who depicted his actions as a principled defence of democratic government against an unaccountable army command. In contrast, historians have observed that O'Higgins (Cosgrave having taken to his sick bed for the duration of the crisis) adopted a conciliatory attitude to the outrageous demands of the mutineers, while sacking the army leadership for taking a firm line against them.[110] It seems likely that O'Higgins cynically exploited the mutiny to remove a power-ful cabinet rival. However, neither side could fully claim the moral high ground. Mulcahy's willingness to allow his subordinates to revive the IRB to advance the process of demobilization allowed O'Higgins to present his position as a principled stand against a conspiratorial élite. Moreover, the unsatisfactory state of the army had already lost Mulcahy the support of his cabinet colleagues.

O'Duffy was closely involved in these events but more as a proxy for O'Higgins than a player in his own right. Some observers regarded his initial appointment as the placing of a safe pair of hands at the helm during a moment of crisis. More knowledgeable insiders regarded it as an attempt by O'Higgins to reign in Mulcahy's army council.[111] O'Duffy was placed at the head of the army because he was trusted by O'Higgins and, as a former chief of staff with hard-line credentials, he was acceptable to the powerful regional GOCs.[112] Many years later, one such GOC, Peadar McMahon, recalled that O'Duffy had tried to sound him out in the event of a power struggle within the army:

McMahon—O'Duffy said the Government was asking him to become GOC and he didn't know quite what to do about it . . . I didn't know what it was about and he said he didn't know either, that he wasn't very keen on it, but I could see that he was keen on it. I said I was afraid I knew nothing about it and that it was a matter for himself and he would have to make up his own mind.

Mulcahy—How many others do you think O'Duffy sent for like yourself at that time?

McMahon—I would say MacEoin and Mick Brennan.[113]

Had the GOCs refused to accept the dismissal of the well-respected army council, a real mutiny might have followed. Ironically, it was the loyalty of Mulcahy and the army leadership which allowed O'Higgins to fire them.[114] Nonetheless, the appointment of O'Duffy was not an entirely risk-free strategy. O'Duffy had ideological and personal ties to Mulcahy and the army leadership, most importantly through the IRB (as O'Higgins would have known), and O'Duffy later claimed to have also been sympathetic to the mutineers' demands.[115] Forced to choose between old loyalties and obedience to O'Higgins (combined with a prestigious appointment), O'Duffy chose the latter.

If his appointment was merely intended as a reassuring gesture, this was not apparent to O'Duffy, who expressed himself dissatisfied with his 'obscure' powers and threatened to resign unless he was given 'full authority' over Mulcahy's army council: 'if I have not executive authority I cannot visualise success . . . I have no personal desires in the matter, my highest ambition being to return to the more tranquil position—control of the little Force under the Minister of Home Affairs'.[116] On 18 March O'Higgins persuaded the cabinet to create a new combined commission for O'Duffy as general officer commanding the forces and inspector general, which would enable him to 'exact absolute discipline, absolute loyalty and obedience from every Officer and Man in the Army'. In retrospect, the arrests at Devlin's pub, which occurred several hours after this appointment, appeared a deliberate snubbing of the cabinet by Mulcahy (particularly as Cosgrave had summoned him and O'Duffy to his bedside to instruct them to ensure an amicable resolution of the crisis). However, Mulcahy disagreed with this interpretation, insisting that O'Duffy had refused to assume responsibilities or issue any orders until his position was clarified.[117] Moreover, when asked why the minister for defence should need the permission of a military subordinate, albeit one with such an exalted rank, to sanction the arrests, Mulcahy retorted: 'I hadn't and I didn't ... And I would have to get him up at Monaghan that night if I wanted him.' Nevertheless, Mulcahy's insistence that O'Duffy 'wasn't Commander in Chief ... It was an ad-hoc thing, a gesture by the Government to show that light had been thrown on the situation' was not an accurate reflection of the cabinet's intentions.[118]

The circumstances behind the raid remain as confused as the mutiny itself. On learning of the mutineers' presence in Devlin's pub, Colonel Hugo MacNeill and Colonel Felix Cronin had sought permission to raid the premises from the adjutant-general, Gearóid O'Sullivan, who in turn received authorization from Mulcahy. Yet it appears that MacNeill had also asked his direct superior, Dan Hogan, who was in Clones with O'Duffy that night, for authorization to make the arrests. Crucially, this means that, contrary to the official record and general belief, O'Duffy was aware of the arrests.[119] Another army council member, Seán Ó Murthuile, the quartermaster-general, also claimed that 'General O'Duffy and the General Officer Commanding the Dublin Command [Hogan], who were absent from Dublin at the time, had been communicated with by telephone from Command Headquarters, and that they too, had authorised the Officer on duty to proceed with the arrests.' He added: 'It was argued that he [O'Duffy] was not in actual control of the Army on the night of the 18th, but, of course, he was and there was no doubt, in my mind at any rate, about the matter. I was satisfied that the arrests were in order when I became aware that he, as well as General Mulcahy had authorised the action that had been taken.'[120] Peadar McMahon, GOC the Curragh, gave a similar account, blaming the hapless Hugo MacNeill for the affair: 'It was just like him—half completing a job ... It seems that O'Duffy and Dan Hogan were up in Clones. Dan Hogan was O/C at the time and MacNeill phoned him to say that there was a rumour that these fellows were in Devlin's and they were going to attack the army or attack some barracks.'[121]

These accounts raise intriguing questions about O'Duffy's involvement. Did he secretly orchestrate the arrests in order to discredit the army council?[122] Shortly after the mutiny, O'Duffy promoted the two arresting officers, Cronin and MacNeill, to replace the resigned army council members (without asking Cosgrave's permission).[123] MacNeill, who was close to O'Duffy, had a well-earned reputation for unreliability. Moreover, O'Higgins and O'Duffy, both highly ambitious individuals, were working together during this chaotic period: at one point, having secured Mulcahy's resignation, O'Higgins even visited Cosgrave's home to pressure him to resign as president.[124] Or, less sinisterly, did O'Duffy know that the arrests were going to occur but decided to stay out of it? He probably would not yet have received the official papers confirming the powers of his new appointment that afternoon. Fortunately, or conveniently, the presence of O'Duffy and Hogan in Monaghan effectively relieved them of responsibility for the raid. O'Duffy would later dishonestly claim to have known nothing about it.

Whatever his motives, O'Duffy's appointment was resented by Mulcahy and the army council. On 20 March the beleaguered chief of the general staff, Seán MacMahon, refused the government's request that he resign, instead demanding that O'Duffy 'whose exact position I have not up to the present learned except through the newspapers, be withdrawn from the army'.[125] MacMahon was then dismissed by O'Higgins, and the resignations of Mulcahy and the other army council members were accepted. Later that year, Mulcahy criticized O'Duffy in the Dáil after he had appeared to suggest that Mulcahy and the army council had acted disloyally. O'Duffy's letter to Mulcahy disputing this inference illustrated a characteristic desire to present himself as a wronged and neutral party:

Your remarks in the Dail last evening annoyed me very much, & will I fear annoy many in the army & in the Guard who know the facts . . . I never assailed the C/S, A.G., QMG or yourself with the others [the mutineers]. Moreover you four resigned before my duties were definitely defined by the Executive Council & certainly I was not in charge of the Army at the time, nor had I any responsibility whatever for the resigna-tions . . . It was generally assumed by the Army, the Garda & indeed by the man in the street that there was no strained relations between yourself & the old Staff & me, but last evening would go to show that we were deadly enemies, watching for an opening to stab one another in the back. Some people are quite jubilant over it . . . [126]

Mulcahy accepted O'Duffy's explanation, naively harking back to their days as a 'band of brothers' and graciously overlooking the fact that O'Duffy's authority over the army was precisely why his resignation had been demanded by the cabinet. Mollified, O'Duffy told Mulcahy he was 'quite satisfied that there was no intention to injure me in any way', informing him of his resentment at the meddling of civilian politicians in matters best left to soldiers such as themselves: 'I intended to write under my name, & tell those people some home truths, whatever the consequences might be—but it is better as it is.'[127] The mutiny offers a good example of O'Duffy's *modus operandi*. He was a more determined figure than the buffoon of later repute, not particularly intelligent perhaps, but certainly cunning, duplicitous, and ambitious.

Forgetfulness of self and love of unit

O'Duffy spent the next six months striving to restore order within the army. He identified demobilization, low pay, factional rivalry, and meddlesome TDs as his main concerns. As with the Garda, his personality, administrative ability, and disciplinarian qualities made him the right man for the job. He told the government he would suspend 'any officer, of whatever rank' he suspected of fomenting disaffection. He was particularly concerned by fraternization between senior officers and mutineers, warning of a conspiracy 'of peaceful penetration to get control in every Department of the State Forces'.[128] However, his fears proved unfounded and the threat of further unrest receded. Indeed, his reports suggested that military discipline was reasonably satisfactory, the single case of disgraceful conduct within the first two months being an ex-British soldier charged with sodomy.[129]

Deciding that Mulcahy's scheme of army organization was unworkable, O'Duffy implemented his own scheme (devised by Dan Hogan). Its main innovation was to weaken the authority of the chief of staff and GHQ in favour of the regional GOCs.[130] O'Duffy characteristically approached the broader issue of army morale on a pragmatic and ideological level. In terms of the former, he sought to improve the army's employment conditions (which had been deliberately run down to hasten demobilization). Noting that 'practically the entire Army is on a 6 months contract', he persuaded the government to renew the recruitment of other ranks, and demanded better pay and longer contracts. He urged that all officers deemed worthy be commissioned: 'They will then look to the Army as a career, and efficiency, good conduct, and respect for their uniform will, I have no doubt, be the order.'[131] He promised his officers that they would receive commissions, later informing the parsimonious government that he could not 'without sacrificing my personal honour, leave the Army until my obligations in this respect are fulfilled'. He complained about the shoddy treatment meted out to officers who, when invited to state functions, were lucky to get a seat in the back row:

In every country in the world the Army Officer is looked up to and respected by all grades of society, but here a feeling is developing among our Officers that they are looked upon as armed mercenaries, unfit and improper persons to associate with, except when the safety of the State is threatened . . . it has already given rise to rather bitter feeling, which might tend to a certain extent, to undo our efforts to stabilise the Army and bring it to its rightful place in the Nation.[132]

Many of his initiatives focused on morals and morale. He promoted sports to counter the high level of venereal disease within the army.[133] He was much concerned with the lack of patriotism and—'that most essential of military virtues'—*esprit de corps*—within the National Army, which he described as a 'mercenary army', Irish in name only. The only tales that young recruits were likely to hear about the past deeds of Irish soldiers, he complained, were accounts of 'the "Dublins" in Gallipoli from the lips of some ex-British N.C.O.'. He argued that the army should exploit the nation's rich military tra-dition: 'we have listened to the Irregulars declaring that they are the rightful successors to every Irish soldier that fought in the Nation's cause, to every military force that ever battled for Irish freedom; while the first Irish Regular Army since the days of Sarsfield or indeed of Eoin Ruadh, remain silent, apparently admitting the fact'. He suggested that each battalion select a notable patriot whose portrait would be hung in the mess, and whose history the soldiers would study. The result would provide 'something more than a third rate imitation of the British Army dressed in green uniforms' and a 'higher ideal to fight for than the Pay Envelope. And some day we might be very thankful that we did cultivate such a spirit.'[134] O'Duffy's addresses to his men, such as at the unveiling of a memorial cross to Collins at Béal na mBláth in 1924 (an early example of his exploitation of Collins's legacy) illustrated this approach:

General Collins was a member of the National Army. What a boast for the Irish Army of to-day!... He did not know if there was any man that day who was more in General Collins' confidence than himself... The best way they could do honour to his memory was to do the work that was at their hand faithfully and well, to have respect for themselves and the uniforms they wore, and to give unqualified loyalty to the State for which he died. He was very pleased to see the esprit de corps that was developing in the army. It was nothing more than forgetfulness of self and love of unit.[135]

One interesting aspect of O'Duffy's military role was how his reports to the executive council broadened in scope, taking the form of extensive critiques of a government lacking in 'constructive and positive policies'.[136] His remarkably frank reports painted a bleak picture of the government's achievements which reflected a growing disillusionment with the régime which he had done so much to establish. In September, he reported:

Again it is being stated...that the country is now more than ever in the grip of Freemasonry, and it is becoming an established belief that the country generally is being controlled by the old gang in the interests of England. This is not all Irregular propaganda, it is the convinced opinion of hard-thinking people who supported the Treaty and helped the Government through, but who are absolutely disgusted with the way the affairs of the country are being run ... Trade is bad, Agriculture is worse ... It is doubtful whether Cumann na nGaedheal would be able to secure a sufficient majority at a General Election to form a Government.[137]

He urged the government to promote fisheries, lower taxes, reduce unemployment, tackle poverty, and discriminate in favour of ex-National Army men in public employment. He contrasted Cumann na nGaedheal's lacklustre electoral machine with that of Sinn Féin:

There are no meetings, no speakers, no explanations, no correction of false rumours, no political machinery of any kind, and, to make matters worse, the expenses of the last Election are not yet paid. Government supporters are quite apathetic, while the Irregulars have already completed a house to house canvas. It is bad policy for any political party, at any time, to rely entirely on past achievements, but it is especially bad when a country is steeped in economic misery and political uncertainty.[138]

He predicted the revival of republican and socialist unrest: 'Half starving men will lend a willing ear to Larkin & Co., and anything that weakens the prestige of the Government will be hailed with delight by the Irregular Organisation.'[139] He recommended the release of the remaining Civil War internees before the government's hand was forced by the courts, but warned against a policy of conciliation: 'a second Army or a second Government will not be tolerated ... very firm—even severe—government may be necessary.'[140]

While these reports indicate some confusion about the appropriate role of the military in a democratic state, it must be remembered that Sinn Féin remained committed to the overthrow of the state. His fears of a republican revival proved exaggerated, as a series of by-elections in 1925 revealed, but this was due to Sinn Féin's refusal to recognize the state rather than popular enthusiasm for Cumann na nGaedheal. These reports also offer some insights into O'Duffy's mindset in this period. His references to the growth of freemasonry and Larkinism demonstrated an intensification of his tendency to attribute political setbacks to the malign influence of conspiratorial forces. Their critical tone revealed that he shared the disenchantment of those treatyites who had expected the government to advance republican objectives as Michael Collins had promised, a disillusionment hastened by the decline of republican influence in Cumann na nGaedheal. Before the army mutiny, he privately claimed that Mulcahy was the only member of the cabinet who he admired.[141] The humiliating boundary commission crisis, which exposed the hollowness of the belief that the treaty would bring the freedom to achieve freedom, represented another blow. He confided to General Seán MacEoin: 'I am not very happy over the Boundary business & many good friends in Monaghan & across the

Border think I should resign as a protest—but I do not see where that would leave us.'[142] O'Duffy was, at the same time, sufficiently realistic to accept that 'the average citizen is sublimely indifferent to the Boundary Question'.[143]

The claim that O'Duffy was reluctant to step down from his army command is inaccurate.[144] As early as May 1924, he reminded the cabinet that he had accepted the position for only three months: 'All contentious matters arising in the Army or Garda are referred to me . . . This strain is too heavy to bear, particularly as I have worked a sixteen hour day—Sunday and Monday— for the past three years without a holiday.'[145] He also resented the government's failure to increase his salary: 'I am receiving my salary as Commissioner of the Garda—a salary altogether inadequate for the responsibilities attached to that position, and which compares very unfavourably with the salaries of a list of other Government officials whose names I have before me.'[146] In September 1924 O'Duffy filed the last of his lengthy, despairing, state of the nation reports; his successor's brief reports on mundane military matters must have come as a welcome relief to the cabinet. He formally resigned in February 1925 but, unusually, was permitted to retain his commission as an army general.[147] Despite his forthright views on the state of the army, and his energetic approach to its reorganization, his impact was minor. Conditions of service for officers improved following the granting of the commissions which O'Duffy pushed hard for, but his suggestions for raising the prestige of the military fell on deaf ears. Starved of funding, and apathetically regarded by politicians, civil servants, and the public, National Army officers would continue to observe state functions from the cheap seats.[148] Nonetheless, O'Duffy had completed the difficult task of demobilization, introduced a new scheme of organization, and defused a potential mutiny, while continuing to run the police. By any standards, it was an impressive performance.

6

Preaching the gospel of national virility

Without a clean, vigorous and healthy race the wealthiest nation is poor indeed.[1]

B Y the time the General returned to full-time policing, he had reason to be pleased with the Garda Síochána's progress. He had proved himself an effective and, in many respects, a progressive commissioner. He was an enthusiastic advocate of such innovations as the use of fingerprinting, photography, and forensic science.[2] Demonstrating an admiration of British achievements common to many anglophobic republicans, he was a keen admirer of Scotland Yard, which he hoped would assist in the training of his detectives.[3] (His admiration of Britain's security forces even extended to the Royal Ulster Constabulary, which he considered 'as near perfection as it is humanly possible'.)[4] Many would have agreed with the view, expressed by one newspaper, that there was 'no greater or more successful organiser holding office under the Free State Government'.[5] He was still thought of in some quarters as the coming man: the ever-vigilant Mary MacSwiney had heard 'that he is playing a very deep game; that he is idolised by his men; that he is considered a model Catholic and a model everything that he touches; and that he is far more likely to be a popular candidate for President than either McGrath or Mulcahy. I believe he is extremely unscrupulous.'[6] There was, however, a darker side to O'Duffy's success and celebrity, which this chapter seeks to explore.

Cult of personality

From his earliest days as commissioner, he promoted a cult of personality within the force.[7] The main vehicle for this was the Garda journal. In September 1923, a single issue of *Iris an Gharda* included thirteen pictures of O'Duffy—three of them full-page portraits. A preceding issue contained a lengthy account of his revolutionary record, another reprinted his entry in *Hue and Cry*, while others rehearsed his achievements in the GAA. An editorial in another issue of the same month (which reprinted his oration on the death of Collins) observed:

It was not uncommon, in districts where the Gardai were appearing for the first time, to hear a Garda referred to as 'Mr O'Duffy'. 'There is General O'Duffy, look; isn't he a fine fellow?' And again, 'Isn't his uniform lovely' . . . We smile! Yes, but the people who made these remarks were unconsciously right. Each Garda, once he dons the uniform and takes up duty, is 'General O'Duffy' inasmuch as he is acting on behalf of the Chief Commissioner.[8]

The more excessive of the pieces which he encouraged his men to contribute to the journal illustrated this burgeoning cult of personality. The following poem, described by O'Duffy as a work of 'singular beauty and appeal' and published on more than one occasion, provides one example:

> The Chief of the Force is not sleeping to-night, He's awake!
> A phone's at his side and a map's on the wall,
> And his look is intense as he answers a call—
> The General's awake, yes awake!
>
> He's working out plans for the good of the Force, He's awake!
> The wires keep hot as his messages speed.
> And he'll never slack off till he's met Erin's need—
> He's awake, awake, *wide* awake!
>
> The Chief is the brains of the wide-scattered Guard. He's alert!
> He holds all the lines that control Ireland's life,
> Yet he's perfectly cool in the midst of the strife,
> So calm, so collected and cool.[9]

O'Duffy's foreign trips, reported in sycophantic detail, provide further evidence of a disturbing egotism. Favourable press coverage (which O'Duffy collected in scrapbooks, no matter how trivial the reference) was recycled in the Garda journal for months afterwards. Even a casual walkabout in Bronx

Zoo during his visit to New York in 1923 was reprinted in all its intriguing detail:

When the antlers of moose who died in combat, horns locked, were pointed out, the general's military mind was intrigued. He studied the stuffed specimens with certain interest. At the lion house, Dr. Blair escorted Gen. O'Duffy into the enclosure within reach of the beast's sharp claws. The general went boldly toward 'Jennie', the largest lion, who was eating. Dr. Blair started to draw the general away, fearful of his safety, but 'Jennie', for the first time in her life, dropped her meat and retreated in her cage. Attendants expressed their astonishment . . . Gen. O'Duffy, although only 30 years old, is grey haired. The index finger of his left hand was lost in a battle five years ago. He has been wounded 12 times.[10]

On his return to Cork, he was received as a conquering hero by the depot staff who had travelled from Dublin to receive him, and honoured at a reception by the Cork chamber of commerce. He was welcomed back to the depot by a parade of 1,600 guards, complete with buglers and the Garda band's rendition of 'Welcome Home', in a ceremony breathlessly reported by *Iris an Gharda*:

General O'Duffy walked briskly to the dais from which he was to deliver his address. There was an intense silence as he rose to speak. Those of us who were present will never forget the opening words of his address. 'Comrade', he began. The word sent a thrill of love through us, for we knew it was not the catch word of a politician. It was not a word uttered in a haphazard way. No; it came direct from the heart of a chief, who loves his men, and is beloved by them . . . Privileges had been conferred on him that had not been conferred on others. He had the privilege of being conveyed by a destroyer from New York to West Point. He had been received by the Mayor of New York and the Archbishop of New York . . . One thousand members of the New York Police Force, with the heads of the Army and Navy, and other representative bodies were present on the dock while his vessel was leaving . . . He thought it right to let them know of this demonstration, which was intended for them, and was accorded to him as their Chief.[11]

Given that his egomania became much more pronounced during the latter stages of his tenure as commissioner, the fact that these examples occurred in 1923 is striking. By the time O'Duffy entered politics, his narcissism—stoked by a decade of flattery and power—had become his greatest weakness.

Irish in thought and in feeling and in action

Megalomania was only one aspect of the commissioner's extravagant behaviour to become a cause of concern for the government. O'Duffy's early attempts to impart the ideals of the revolution to the gardaí and, through them, to society were viewed positively. Indeed, his ability to cast the Garda as guardians of moral values was one of the reasons for the success of the force and his popularity as a public figure. By the late 1920s, however, his strident intensification of the cultural, religious, and moral ethos of the gardaí would begin to raise doubts about his behaviour among his own men and the government (if not the wider public, which displayed great enthusiasm for ostentatious piety during this period).

O'Duffy's attempts to promote Gaelic provide one example. After the failure of his efforts to gaelicize the force by voluntary means (setting aside 500 places for Gaelic speakers, for example, met with 'practically no response'), he became convinced of the need for compulsory measures.[12] Concerned that the teaching of Irish in schools would render it impossible for non-bilingual guards to perform their jobs, he urged the government to back an ambitious scheme to gaelicize the force in 1928.[13] To his dismay, he received no response. The following year he requested permission to announce that the entire force would become Gaelic-speaking within seven years (a declaration intended to deliver 'a death blow to the self-assurance of those opponents of the Language whose pet argument is that Irish will never come to anything').[14]

His scheme hinged on transferring gardaí to the Gaeltacht until they became sufficiently proficient to graduate to linguaphone classes in their former stations. The unpopularity of the 'bog stations' (due to the lack of promotion prospects) would provide an additional incentive. Those too 'sub-average in intelligence' to master Gaelic within five years would be dismissed. He proposed completely to gaelicize Galway City by populating it with Irish-speaking police, teachers, and other public servants. However, with the exception of Ernest Blythe, both civil servants and the cabinet (despite its rhetorical commitment to gaelicization) responded without enthusiasm. Taking a less optimistic view of the impact of compulsory Gaelic within the schools, they did not see the high proportion of English-speaking guards as a crisis in waiting, and were reluctant to add to discontent within the force. Responding to the suggestion that most guards would fail to master Gaelic, O'Duffy retorted: 'I should indeed be sorry to agree with this for if I thought the assertion correct, I would not have the slightest doubt that 75% of the Force will ultimately lose their jobs.' Although deeply discouraged, he continued to push for permission, securing approval for a diluted scheme in 1930 which allowed him to inform his men that 'the acquisition of Irish is no longer a matter of patriotic choice but one of stern necessity for those who intend to remain in the Garda.'[15] It was an approach which provoked resentment: 'some individuals were certainly annoyed with being compelled to pay for it, forced to study it, and threatened with dismissal if they failed to master it. The enthusiasm and idealism of early youth began to wane.'[16]

As with his advocacy of athletics, O'Duffy's enthusiasm for compulsory gaelicization was not accompanied by a personal commitment to using the language. Aside from names, titles, and salutations, his correspondence, even to other supposed *gaelgoirs*, was written in English. It would appear that he failed to master the language despite his Gaelic League background. He was coy on the subject, noting only that his Irish was 'not so strong as I would like it' due to the interruption of 'other national studies'.[17] One of the rare occasions when he publicly spoke Irish was at his trial during the Tan War, when he refused to recognize the court *as gaelige*, an apposite example of his symbolic attitude towards the language. (Another occurred when he exchanged *cúpla focail* with a dazed constable after blowing up his barracks).

However, O'Duffy's desire for a Gaelic-speaking nation was shared by the revolutionary generation, and his reasons were those of his peers: 'without the language I do not think we would be qualified for full independence'.[18] He regarded Irish as 'a means of distinguishing this nation, as a vehicle of our national pride of race and tradition, of our belief in the national future'. He viewed the peasants of the west, who had succeeded in retaining 'their language and their characteristics in face of the most appalling persecution', as the embodiment of a more authentic national spirit. For nationalists like O'Duffy, the survival of the Gaelic language, embodying the essentialist notion of the nation and its culture as an unchanging 'self-contained, homogenous entity', provided a powerful sense of historical legitimacy (notwithstanding the fact that this way of thinking about nationality was itself a nineteenth-century European import).[19]

His outlook reflected the anti-modern sentiments which infused the post-revolutionary language movement with 'the pervasive, puritanical ethos of the period, hostile to difference and pluralism'.[20] He viewed the Gaelic language as a cultural prophylactic against malign foreign influences: 'English is the most impure of all living languages, the most hybrid. Irish as it is to-day is the purest.' Like other languages, Irish had to develop new words to keep pace with modern life, but they were at least formed 'on the basis of traditional good style. They are not, as so many English words are, the product of eccentric writers, comedians, film directors, negro jazz musicians, or others who care nothing for tradition.'[21] His zeal provided an internal enemy, the *seonín*, to rail against and highlight his own purity. As Vincent Comerford has noted, the 'criteria of nationality advanced by nationalists are frequently directed not against the outside world but against internal opponents'; those, like O'Duffy, who succeeded in combining 'linguistic and religious correctness rose to the ultimate heights of judgmental self-righteousness in Catholic nationalist Ireland.'[22] Like most of his struggles, though, compulsory gaelicization proved a lost cause. Towards the end of his life, he complained that the hatred of Irish politics had destroyed the idealism of the revolution, producing 'a people constantly raging against England and at the same time becoming English in every detail'.[23]

Similar frustrations were evidenced in the cultural, as well as linguistic, sphere. In 1923 O'Duffy established Connradh Gaolach an Gharda to promote indigenous sports and pastimes within the force. Its annual *aerideacht*, he recalled, were permeated by 'the spirit of Gaelic culture, Gaelic fun, and clean, wholesome Gaelic recreation'.[24] Initially, he instructed his men not to play foreign sports. Subsequently, however, he relented, permitting them to play any game they chose but warning that no 'facilities would be given for such games as Rugby and Soccer, and any man playing these would . . . become automatically debarred from membership of the organisation'. In keeping with his selective definition of foreign sports, the society proscribed cricket, golf, and rugby while sponsoring swimming, boxing, and Ju Jitsu.[25] Whist-drives and dances were permitted but jazz, the fox-trot, and other dances 'which originated in doubtful haunts in London' were banned on the grounds that they would compromise the force's reputation for 'being thoroughly Irish'.[26] Although he never took to the floor, O'Duffy preferred the 'clean and charming atmosphere of the ceilidhthe' to the 'stiff formality of the garden party' and 'too-loose informality of the modern jazz-dance'.[27] Subsequently, however, he became 'so startled and ashamed at the statistics gathered throughout the country of the dancing evils and the consequent effects accruing to the purity of our Irish girls and to infant life that I stopped dancing at the Depot'.[28] He threw his support, and that of his force, into campaigns against 'filthy literature', the 'Jazz mania', and other threats to 'cleanliness and purity in the Children of Rosin Dubh'.[29] O'Duffy believed that his men should not only set impeccable personal standards but also combat immorality in society, particularly in rural Ireland where he urged them to act 'as guides and counsellors of the people'.[30]

O'Duffy's dedication to sports brought increasing success on the field. In 1927 a Garda team won the all-Ireland hurling club championship. Such achievements reflected well on O'Duffy. The capture of the British amateur heavyweight title by a garda boxer was attributed to the commissioner's 'vision and courage'.[31] However, his influence within Irish sports also led to resentment.[32] His tendency to transfer his best Gaelic players to Monaghan stations symbolized his willingness to use the gardaí to advance personal agendas, while the lavish resources granted to police athletes led opposing fans to greet the appearance of their teams with sarcastic cheers of 'Come on the professionals'.[33]

Tellingly, his attempts to regulate his men's sporting lives met with as little success as his efforts to create an Irish-speaking force. By 1928 rowing, tennis, and golf (a pursuit previously reviled by Gaels due to its association with the Anglo-Irish ascendancy) had infiltrated the Garda Coiste Siamsa's list of approved national games. Despite failing to master golf, O'Duffy even became president of the police club, arguing that all sport, regardless of provenance, was beneficial. This uncharacteristic drift from purism reflected several factors, including the *embourgeoisement* of the army and police officer class. Cultural boycotts made more sense when the only prospect of entering a golf club was as a caddy for the Big House gentry. It also reflected O'Duffy's power-base in the National Athletic and Cycling Association (which, unlike the GAA, could aspire to international competition), and his declining influence in the republican-dominated GAA.[34] However, like his failure to gaelicize a force which was intended to represent a microcosm of the ideal nation-state, it also reflected a more fundamental problem: the limits of cultural indoctrination in a society where individuals were relatively free to choose how they spent their own leisure time.

Similar tensions arose in the religious sphere, notwithstanding the fact that O'Duffy's piety was shared by many gardaí. As early as 1923, three priests were required to hear confession at the depot on Saturdays, and over 80 per cent of the force belonged to St Joseph's Young Priests Society, which provided financial support to seminarians.[35] Guards were expected to participate in the retreats, missions, sodalities, pilgrimages, and other religious ceremonies which O'Duffy organized, and were not permitted to absent themselves from the weekly church parade without reason.[36] The week-long annual mission conducted by the Passionist Fathers dominated depot life.[37]

Such ostentatious devotion, as we have seen, had its practical side. O'Duffy claimed that nothing distinguished his men from their predecessors more than the opening of the depot's chapel: 'No wonder the Garda made good, and are to-day respected and backed up by the people for whose protection they so well prepared themselves.'[38] So successful was the consecration to the Sacred Heart in 1923, O'Duffy organized the Garda Síochána's consecration to the Blessed Virgin:

nothing more impressive has ever been seen in the religious life of Dublin or elsewhere. Close on 500 Officers and men, with lighted candles held aloft, repeated aloud the Act of Consecration. This was followed by the singing of the famous Lourdes Hymn, 'Ave

Maria,' and each time these beautiful words were sung the men raised their lighted candles high over their heads. It was a soul-stirring spectacle . . . the closing ceremony was attended by the Commissioner, Officers and men in full uniform. A special Guard of Honour under the command of the Adjutant presented arms at the Elevation and Benediction, while the Colour Party of two officers dipped the National Flag and the Garda colours in honour of the coming of the King of Kings.[39]

In 1928 he decided to organize a pilgrimage to the Vatican. He did so without consulting the minister for justice, who, on raising the issue, was pointedly informed that the Pope was already 'very enthusiastic' about the 'first National Pilgrimage of an Irish Police Force since the introduction of Christianity in Ireland'.[40] The *Garda Review* went into overdrive, transforming itself into a religious periodical whose rhetoric reflected O'Duffy's distinctly non-secular view of his organization. The laws of the state, it observed, were 'simply the local application of divine commandments', and the gardaí 'fulfilling the law of Christ'. That two hundred and fifty guards sacrificed nine weeks' pay and half their annual leave to follow O'Duffy to Rome was a testament to the force's piety.[41]

Securing a private audience with Pius XI, the General informed the Pope of his men's 'work for religion, the respect in which they are held by the bishops and priests of Ireland, the number of daily and weekly communicants in the Force, the consecration of Police Headquarters to the Sacred Heart, the annual Police Retreats in the Depot and cities, the percentage of Pioneers in the Force, [and] the sacrifices made by the pilgrims'. According to O'Duffy, the delighted pontiff 'in ecstasy exclaimed "Ireland, my beloved Ireland"'. The citizens of Rome were no less impressed by the sight of hundreds of gardaí scouring shops for rosary beads, medals, statues, and engagement rings for the Pope's blessing: 'the student guides and the chaplains were questioned about the nationality of these fine young men, saluting priests and nuns at every turn, silent and reverent in every holy place, hearing Mass at daybreak.'[42] Newspapers, movie cameras, and large crowds witnessed remarkable scenes as the gardaí ascended the steps of St Peter's basilica to sing *Faith of Our Fathers* and *The Song for the Pope*, before spontaneously kneeling as the *angelus* rang out. After several days of intense religious ritual, O'Duffy was granted an audience with Benito Mussolini, to whom he passed on news of the Pope's good health, and related the history and evolution of the Free State. It was not to be their last conversation about politics in Ireland.

A brief stop in France, where a boxing tournament had been arranged with the Parisian police, provided another highlight. His willingness to please outweighing traditional republican attitudes to the Great War, O'Duffy even participated in a ceremony of remembrance. Laying a wreath on the Tomb of the Unknown Soldier, he informed his French audience that Ireland had sent 400,000 men 'to fight for France side by side', enduring proportionately more fatalities than every country but France.[43]

The General's commitment to the ostentatious demonstration of sporting excellence, cultural purity, and religious piety was driven by a desire for public approval and a love of ceremonies in which he formed one of the objects of adulation. For example, the success of the pilgrimage to Rome, like that of the force itself, was presented as proof of the greatness of O'Duffy as well as God:

This pilgrimage was led and organised by our police chief, General O'Duffy, whose genius has made the Garda Siochana the miracle that it is. No competent and impartial observer will deny that the Garda is the nearest approach to a miracle that cold and scientific analysis can discover. A completely unarmed force distributed over Ireland, at a time when terror reigned . . . What was behind this tremendous experiment? There can be one only answer—the faith of our fathers.[44]

O'Duffy's subsequent political career, in many respects, reflected a continuation of his role as a powerful and visionary leader of a devoted legion of manly followers who represented the cultural and moral élite of the new Ireland.

To what extent did this extravagant piety undermine his credibility? The Irish Free State was culturally defined by the influence of Catholicism and, as with most issues, O'Duffy merely exaggerated popular sentiment. Indeed, as chief marshal of the Catholic Emancipation Centenary Celebrations in 1929 and the International Eucharistic Congress in 1932, he played a central role in the most elaborate expressions of Catholic nationalist triumph in the history of Ireland.[45] He regarded his involvement in the latter as the crowning achievement of his public life (notwithstanding his resentment of de Valera's failure to advise the Pope to confer him with an honorary papal title).[46] However, some guards resented the pressure to conform to such high standards which O'Duffy applied, for example by giving hectoring lectures warning that he knew the identity of those who did not attend his religious services.[47] The department of justice was also uneasy about his pious excesses.[48] There were obvious tensions between O'Duffy's rhetoric and his depiction of his 98.6 per cent Catholic force as non-sectarian: like the Ulster Specials, 'there was no snug niche in O'Duffy's force for religious minorities'.[49] More importantly, though, it formed part of a broader pattern of extreme behaviour, extending to 'his obsession with the evils of drink and his insatiable appetite for self adulation', which increasingly did trouble the government.[50] Tellingly, the force's ostentatious Catholicism would disappear after his departure. As the disappointed parish priest of the

Holy Family Church (the unofficial depot chaplaincy) on Aughrim Street noted: 'the spiritual fabric, built up so patiently for many years, collapsed and the Guards vanished'.[51] None of his successors as commissioner would strive to make the Garda capture the imagination of the public by reflecting the values and aspirations of the nation.

Preaching the gospel of national virility

O'Duffy's views on cultural issues are of particular interest because they reflected concerns about modernization, immorality, and masculinity which subsequently manifested themselves in overtly political terms. Sport provides the best illustration of this. Outside of work, most of O'Duffy's time was devoted to the promotion of sport, whether lecturing on the subject, opening new grounds, throwing the ball in at matches, attending committee meetings, presenting awards, or writing a column ('Among the Gaels') for the *Gaelic Athlete*. His influence in Irish sports was immense. He was treasurer of the GAA Ulster council between 1921 and 1934, a unique honorary position which entailed no duties but provided him with a seat on the central council. In return, he provided the GAA with an influential voice, for example leading the negotiations with the department of finance which secured the exemption of the GAA (unlike the rugby and soccer organizations) from taxation in the 1927 Finance act. He held, among other offices, the presidencies of the Irish Amateur Handball Association (1926–34), National Athletic and Cycling Association (1931–4), and Irish Olympic Council (1931–2). He was one of the principal organizers of the Tailteann Games, an event which encapsulated the ideological impulses behind the Free State's sporting and religious spectacles.[52] He was, to list but some of his minor offices, vice-president of the Dublin Trout Anglers Association, a promoter of the Irish Motor Racing Club, a judge of the Dun Laoghaire Dog Show, a patron of the Neptune Rowing Club, a sponsor of the Irish Free State Bowling League ('a very ancient sport'), and president of the Metropolitan Marine Lake Conference standing committee (formed to build a water-sports centre in Dollymount). He was rightly described by the press as 'the leading spirit of Irish athletics' and 'the father of the athletic revival campaign'.[53]

This influence was underpinned by his power base in the army and gardaí which he used to promote a narrow ideological agenda. In 1923, for example, he spoke strongly in favour of maintaining the ban on those who played, or had ever played, foreign sports, despite the end of British rule which had provided its historic justification: 'it was not good for the country to bring about blending too rapidly. The National Army desired the rule to stand ... the same applied to the National police.'[54] Enraged that both candidates for the presidency of the GAA opposed the ban, O'Duffy demanded that they recant, declaring it 'an outrage on the living and the dead'.[55] His stance—which more accurately reflected grassroots (and anti-treaty) opinion than that of the presidential candidates—was successful. It also irritated the government: 'I was accused at Congress of using undue influence in the Army and Garda in this regard. I was told even by certain Ministers that from the "social" viewpoint I should seek union of all sportsmen—Gaelic, rugby and soccer. They could not convince me, however, that deviation from the Gaelic way would be genuinely beneficial to Ireland.'[56]

Like many Gaels, O'Duffy saw no contradiction between such exclusivism and his aspirations for unity.[57] He combined a staunch defence of the ban and a determination to prevent any dilution of the GAA's Catholic ethos with a belief that 'when they had all within the GAA there would be no partition'. In 1927, at a game which marked a new 'epoch in the history of the GAA' because the ball had been thrown in by 'a Prince of the Church', he declared: 'Every country in the world has its political and sometimes sectarian differences; but when it comes to a question of national tradition people are all one.'[58] His attitude to anti-treaty republicans was more flexible: he believed that the 'GAA did more to minimise bitterness in and after the fratricide than any other organisation in Ireland'.[59] During the Civil War, he had attended GAA central council meetings alongside anti-treaty combatants. He was the first leading treatyite to share a platform with an anti-treaty politician, at the opening of Breffni Park in Cavan in 1923 where he urged the GAA to 'bring together all sections of the Irish people' to 'save the youth of Ireland from the sea of moral degradation into which they were travelling'.[60]

His speech at Breffni Park encapsulated the ideological motives underlying his propagation of sports: national unity and moral improvement. Having failed to prevent the partition of the nation, O'Duffy embarked on a rearguard action against the partition of its sporting organizations, a campaign he described in his pamphlet *The Struggle for Irish Athletic Unity*. He was determined to reverse the fragmentation which had occurred among sporting bodies during the Irish revolution. As president of the Irish Amateur Handball Association, he met the Irish Amateur Handball Union in an attempt to form a unified body. However, the talks collapsed due to O'Duffy's insistence on the irrevocability of the ban, which would have entailed the expulsion of Union members who played soccer or rugby.[61] He fought expensive, lengthy, and often unsuccessful jurisdictional disputes on behalf of the Irish cycling and swimming bodies to establish their right to represent their codes in international competition.

It was his presidency of the National Athletic and Cycling Association (NACA), however, which offered him his most important power base in Irish sports. The NACA was established in 1922 when it was ceded authority by both the GAA and its anglophile rival, the Irish Amateur Athletics Association (IAAA), to regulate domestic and international athletics. However, the NACA's attempts to enforce amateur values (by prohibiting events where betting occurred, such as pony and whippet racing, and refusing to affiliate professional soccer clubs) led to schism in 1925, when discontent northern members seceded, forming the Northern Ireland Amateur Athletics, Cycling and Cross-Country Association. The latter successfully applied to return to the fold of the United Kingdom's Amateur Athletics Association (AAA), the IAAA's former governing body. The AAA, much despised by republicans like O'Duffy who had attempted to suppress its Irish section during the War of Independence, appealed successfully for international recognition as the Amateur Athletics Association of Great Britain and Northern Ireland, initiating a bitter dispute with the NACA which continued to assert its right to represent the entire country at international events.[62]

On his election as NACA president in 1931, O'Duffy launched a determined offensive against the AAA, winning the right to reopen the dispute at a meeting of the International Amateur Athletics Federation (IAAAF) at the Olympic Games in 1932. In the meantime, the AAA and NACA were directed to appoint a joint commission to select the Irish Olympic team (both organizations having banned the other's members from attending its sports meetings). After initially rejecting every proposal suggested by this commission (O'Duffy observing that 'we must have seemed very unreasonable'), the General accepted a compromise that would allow an Irish team to compete in Los Angeles. During the course of these disputes, O'Duffy played a leading, and often constructive, role in the negotiations to reunify Irish athletics. His suggested compromise entailed internal autonomy for the northern body, a compromise flag rather than the tricolour or union jack to be flown at competitions, and a unified body to regulate international participation. Much criticized by republicans for these compromises, O'Duffy (who, at one point, resigned over the issue) declared that he was 'prepared to go very far to ensure the appearance of Ireland as an individual unit in national and international affairs'.[63]

Despite initial progress, the attempts to unify Irish athletics foundered due to disagreements about the flying of the tricolour, with the IAAAF subsequently backing the AAA's position against the NACA.[64] The latter's refusal to accept this ruling ensured the Free State's disqualification from the 1936 Olympics. The parallels between these sporting disputes and the political relationship between the two Irish states (even down to O'Duffy's dubious claim that were it not for 'England's intrusion in this domestic difference the case would be settled long since') are obvious: what was perhaps more surprising was O'Duffy's flexibility as his pragmatic anti-partitionism prevailed over the southern tendency to prioritize sovereignty over unity.

O'Duffy achieved more success on the field than in the committee rooms, most notably as team manager at the Los Angeles Olympic Games in 1932—'One of the greatest and grandest experiences of my life'—which he described in his pamphlet *Ireland at an Olympiad.*[65] Elected president of the Irish Olympic Council in 1931, O'Duffy raised sufficient funds to enter a modest team of four athletes and four boxers. The delegation arrived in New York, where it was well looked after by the General's friends on the NYPD, before embarking on a week-long train journey across America. Coming from 'a tiny though well-beloved green island', O'Duffy enjoyed the experience of 'watching a whole vast continent slide past our train-windows—immensely broad rivers, apparently infinite plains glowing golden with corn, the towering peaks and terrifying chasms of the Continental Divide, the dark forests, the desert wastes of Nevada'.

Los Angeles during the golden age of Hollywood proved equally fascinating. The delegation visited the Metro-Goldwyn-Mayer studios, where O'Duffy met Louis B. Mayer and his stable of stars, including Maureen O'Sullivan ('Maureen remains her real self—a charming Irish colleen; very popular with everyone and very successful'). Invited to Beverly Hills to meet Douglas Fairbanks and Mary Pickford, 'the world's sweetheart', he took a wrong turn, mistakenly calling on Charlie Chaplin's house. O'Duffy was delighted by the warm reception from Fairbanks: 'I am from Kilkenny, and my wife Mary Pickford is a Hennessy from Waterford. He held up the reception of the 2,000 athletes assembled in the hall of his private house, and brought us up to see Mary who was in her chambers, temporarily indisposed. The representatives of all the other countries had to wait.' Indeed, the welcome accorded O'Duffy by so many glamorous and wealthy Irish-Americans at 'banquets, sports gatherings, picnics, ceilidhes, hurling matches, receptions, parties, amusements on private beaches and in private swimming pools' prompted him temporarily to revise his views on the iniquity of Hollywood: 'This is really a city in itself, it took over an hour to drive through the streets which represent every country in the world. Many of the film stars are of Irish descent, and all are courteous and decent—not at all the type they are sometimes represented to be. This struck me very forcibly.' O'Duffy received much favourable press coverage, regaling journalists with his views on prohibition (against), lengthy sentences without parole (for), armed police (against), gun control (for), and other issues of the day.[66]

The Games proved no less exciting. O'Duffy marvelled at the magnificent new stadium and the first ever custom-built Olympic Village. He also succeeded in repelling an underhand attempt, inspired by his athletic nemesis the AAA, to force the Irish delegation to compromise its national principles at the opening ceremony:

I discovered at the last moment that the U.S.A. athletic authorities had arranged that the Irish athletes should march behind a banner inscribed 'The Irish Free State' representing, of course, twenty-six counties. I protested and threatened to withdraw the Irish competitors from the Games. I hurriedly got them together, and it should never be forgotten that without a moment's hesitation they declared 'We refuse to compete as representatives of a truncated Ireland'. I asked for permission to announce on the loud speakers this unanimous decision to the assembled 100,000 people of Irish descent...

Faced by such a daunting opponent, and the possibility of an embarrassing international incident, the Olympic officials wilted, handing O'Duffy a previously prepared banner inscribed 'Ireland'. To his immense satisfaction, the athletes paraded behind the tricolour at the opening ceremony. Even better, the national flag was raised in victory twice, Bob Tisdall winning gold in the 400-metre hurdles and Dr Pat O'Callaghan taking first place at the hammer-throw.

Reflecting the cultural insecurity underlying his nationalism, O'Duffy regarded this remarkable performance ('the happiest moment of my life') as vindication more than success: it 'dispelled any false impressions which propagandists may have made against the character of our race', and provided 'an answer to the vilifications that have been levelled against us in the past'. The Olympic Games provide a good example of the inherently political concerns of sporting ideologues like O'Duffy. It was not until the inter-war years, as Hobsbawm noted, that international sport became unmistakably 'an expression of national struggle, and sportsmen representing their nation or state, primary expressions of their imagined communities'.[67] 'The importance of sport to cultural unity', it has been observed, 'lies not only within the game as it was played but in the sporting occasion as national spectacle. Sport as physical activity and collective ritual became part of the language of nationalism, as spectator and participator shared equally in the concepts of leadership, heroism and physical strength, all within a national sporting context.'[68]

In his celebration of the physical, and his conflation of sporting and national prowess, O'Duffy reflected the exciting spirit of his times:

Bodies were on display between the wars as never before, parading in what a previous generation would have regarded as underwear or scandalous near-nudity . . . Open-air public swimming pools were available for recreation and pleasure; new stadia were built—in Wembley, Vienna, Berlin—for grander sporting and political events. Massed together in ranks and rows, these bodies projected collective unity and political might.[69]

The political importance of sports became increasingly apparent during the 1930s. At its most extreme, the preoccupation with national fitness and physical superiority took a more sinister turn, resulting in the exaltation of masculine virility to the detriment of the moral and religious virtues previously associated with the concept of manliness.[70]

It was not difficult to see why sport appealed so strongly to nationalists like O'Duffy. The remarkable achievement at Los Angeles provoked the most spontaneous display of genuine national unity since independence. An estimated quarter of a million people greeted the team on its return to Dublin. At the celebratory banquet in the Gresham Hotel, the team was honoured by the newly elected president of the executive council, Eamon de Valera, the leader of the opposition, W. T. Cosgrave, and telegrams from Lord Craigavon, the prime minister of Northern Ireland, and the papal nuncio. Never one to miss an opportunity, O'Duffy took advantage of 'the greatest weekend they had in the athletics history of the country' to stun the audience by announcing the possibility of Ireland hosting the 1940 games, a proposal, he claimed, that would win approval from Olympic officials if the government stumped up the half million pounds necessary for a stadium.[71]

Undeterred by de Valera's cool response, O'Duffy suggested privately raising the finance necessary to convert the Phoenix Park into a vast national stadium and Olympic Village complex. 'It is not merely a question of holding the Games in Dublin', he enthused, 'I want to see our competitors sweep the board' (a proposal enthusiastically backed by one newspaper under the headline 'HE PLANS NATION OF SUPER-MEN').[72] However, as would increasingly occur in the latter part of his life, his proposal slipped into megalomaniacal fantasy. He was soon advocating a grandiose stadium comprising two pitches, a swimming pool, a car and motor-cycle track, a cinder track, tennis courts, a cricket pitch, baths, sports library, boardroom, concert hall, gymnasium, tea rooms, restaurants, and other facilities. A leaflet of unidentified provenance suggested that the 100,000 capacity stadium be run by a sporting council, representative of the government, civil service, security forces, schools, NACA, GAA, and other sporting bodies, but directed by one individual:

That man may or may not be General O'Duffy, though we contend that he is the only man for such an undertaking. He is a genuine enthusiast, diplomatic, a tireless worker, and he seems to be honestly concerned about the physical development of the youth of the country. He is also something of an athletic Mussolini. It is such a man that is wanted for this job, and it is imperative that he be a member of the government—the Minister for Sport. Whether General O'Duffy would consent is another matter. Mussolini has reincarnated the cult of 'Sport for Health' in Italy; physical culture is compulsory in Germany . . . other European nations have their own movements.[73]

It was an interesting early example of O'Duffy's admiration of at least one aspect of fascist régimes. He often compared Irish governmental apathy with the more serious attitudes to sport on the continent. By 1932, O'Duffy was openly advocating an Irish Olympic Federation which would unify all Irish sporting bodies under a permanent central organization. Little enthusiasm, however, was shown by the government or sporting bodies other than the NACA. O'Duffy's dreams of hosting the games and building a grandiose national stadium proved as elusive as those of politicians in more recent times.[74]

Morality and masculinity

That O'Duffy's interest in sport was not merely motivated by the opportunity for empire-building is illustrated by his remarkable campaign to revive the NACA. When O'Duffy assumed its presidency in 1931, the NACA was in serious financial and organizational difficulties. Athletics, once a greater draw than team games, was struggling to win an audience. Deploying characteristic zeal and energy, O'Duffy organized a fund-raising drive which cleared the NACA's debts and raised thousands of pounds. He overhauled the NACA's structure, modelling it on the GAA, the most successful amateur organization in the country. 'Pot-hunters' (athletes who competed for trophies to sell) were discouraged, as were competitors who claimed expenses 'bordering on profes-sionalism'. He shifted the NACA's emphasis from national and international meets to inter-parish and inter-provincial competition. He toured Ireland extensively throughout 1931 speaking at meetings of sports officials, school-teachers, clerics, politicians, and other leading citizens in an attempt to get 'the whole able-bodied youth of Ireland running or jumping, pole-vaulting, cycling, putting the shot, throwing the hammer, the weight, the javelin, the discus, walking, weight-lifting or tug o'warring. It was a grand idea.'[75]

And, in the short term, it was a brilliant success. The number of affiliated clubs in Munster mushroomed from 40 to 200, a revival continued by the spectacular triumph in Los Angeles.[76] O'Duffy was later criticized, however, when it transpired that the NACA had quickly spent the funds with little left to show for it. But what lay behind his efforts to preach 'the gospel of national virility', as O'Duffy described his campaign? A variety of personal, pragmatic, and political motives for his preoccupation with sport have been noted, but the overarching motive emphasized by O'Duffy was his desire to stem the moral and physical degeneration of the population. His reports as commissioner had revealed an increasing concern about immorality and the decline of civic spirit. Nor was he alone in expressing such anxiety. The idea that Ireland was verging on a catastrophic social and moral collapse, whether attributed to the experiences of the revolution or the remorseless infiltration of foreign influences, was shared by many cultural nationalists, civil servants, politicians, and Catholic clergy in the inter-war period.[77]

These concerns were most clearly demonstrated in his submission to the Carrigan committee, which was appointed by the minister for justice in 1930 to recommend legislation to regulate sexual offences. Although its subsequent report has been criticized as a product of inter-war Ireland's prurient preoccupation with dance-halls, picture-houses, and mixed company-keeping, O'Duffy's *in camera* submission detailed the relatively widespread existence of serious sexual offences such as rape, incest, and child abuse. He pointed out that in Ireland, far more than Britain, impoverished parents were compelled to leave vulnerable children alone in tenements or, in rural areas, to send young girls out to service.[78] Warning that 'the moral outlook of the country had changed for the worse in recent years', he drew attention to an alarming increase in recorded sexual abuse, notably against 'girls and children from 16 years downwards, including many cases of children under 10 years'. Between 1927 and 1929, sexual offences (a category which included indecent assault, rape, incest, and carnal knowledge) against girls under the age of 18 had increased by 63 per cent from the preceding three year period. Recorded sexual offences against boys had risen by 43 per cent during the same period. Moreover, O'Duffy's estimate that such offences represented only 15 per cent of the actual level of sexual crime indicated that he believed up to 6,000 children had been abused during this three-year period.

The committee's unpublished report, which treated O'Duffy's submission so seriously that it formed 'the framework around which the report was built', was buried after consultation between the department of justice, the executive council, and church leaders.[79] This was partly because some of its recommendations were impractical, and because many of the submissions confused the

supposed evils of dance-halls and other trivial issues relating to a fear of
increasing permissiveness (which O'Duffy shared) with more serious sexual
offences, but it was also due to a reluctance by church and state to confront the
implications stemming from the possibility that independent Ireland was less
virtuous than it had been under British rule.[80] The department of justice
rejected the committee's findings partly because of the appalling vista that their
veracity would present: 'that the ordinary feelings of decency and the influence
of religion have failed in this country and that the only remedy is by way of
police action. It is clearly undesirable that such a view of conditions in the
Saorstat should be given wide circulation.'[81] Significantly, even the committee
itself appeared reluctant to explore the implications of the extensive child
sex abuse which O'Duffy outlined.[82] His frankness can be attributed to his
characteristic diligence in compiling comprehensive statistics on sexual crime
(the shocking scale of which lay behind the official reluctance to publish the
report) as well as his deeply pessimistic outlook. O'Duffy's willingness to tackle
this problem was also in line with his view that the Garda could, and should,
play a central role in the shaping of a new moral order in independent Ireland.[83]

In contrast to church and state, which could only view an increase in
immorality as a reflection of failure, O'Duffy's apocalyptic world-view predis-
posed him to a bleak view of Irish society. Interestingly, his concerns were
voiced by others outside the political mainstream. In 1929 an editorial in the
Irish Times (which was still viewed as the voice of the ex-Unionist minority) had
noted the 'irony in the fact that, at this very time, when the Free State government has declared war on English newspapers, the Irish newspapers are forced
almost daily to touch matters which are both wicked and disgusting. The
standards of sexual morality are lamentably low. The abominable crime of rape
figures often in the police reports. Infanticide is common—one judge has
described it as a national industry.'[84] However, for most politicians, clergy, and
ordinary people, a strategy of denial which regarded immorality as a foreign
import was preferable to engaging with such distasteful and unsettling realities.
As the scandals of recent years have demonstrated, the consequences of this
culture of silence, insecurity, and defensiveness were profound.

It is within this context that O'Duffy's evangelical efforts to preach the
gospel of sport must be evaluated. At the Garda summer party in 1928 he
complained to his audience, which included the minister for justice and the
judiciary, of 'a revulsion from manual work, and a craze for excitement,
pleasure and leisure; the excitement of the dance hall and the music hall. The
farms are left deserted for life in the city.'[85] At a dinner in honour of the Irish
Olympic team during the same year, he warned that:

Neglect of athletics . . . is a sure sign of national decay. All countries are now alive to the importance of preventing race deterioration and physical decadence to keep the youth away from modern temptation, and it is accepted that the only sure way to do this is by a proper appreciation by Governments and citizens of the national importance of physical culture and athletic training . . . the greatest asset a country can have is a healthy, clean-living young manhood.[86]

The purpose of his nationwide tour in 1931 was to win support for the NACA by publicizing these dangers: only athletics could save 'our youth from the abyss of deterioration'. He confided to a teachers' conference that he possessed evidence of the decadence of Irish youth, 'though by virtue of my position, I am not permitted to say so publicly'.[87] He criticized the popularity of modern forms of entertainment—'the bus to the picture centres has not led to improvement in physique'—which he contrasted with the wholesome pleasures of his own childhood. He spoke of the dangers of dance-halls (which he had described in his submission to the Carrigan committee as 'orgies of dissipation'): 'Let us remember the characteristics of our forefathers. They were not loungers at the street corners. They did not go into dance halls and jazz until morning.' He told the people of Listowel that he had evidence that Ireland was 'gripped in this lure of modernisation'. In Balbriggan, he warned of the need to 'counteract the wave of immorality that seems to be sweeping over the world'. Young men, he complained, were 'ahead of the athletes of Continental countries, not in manliness, but in characteristics that were foreign and alien'.

This message won enthusiastic approval from press, clergy, and politicians. The *Sligo Champion* noted that O'Duffy (who described his campaign as a crusade and his athletes as soldiers) possessed 'the zeal and enthusiasm of the missionary'. A Clare newspaper echoed the praise of Bishop Fogarty:

It is regrettable that there should be need of such a crusade. But unrest of various types, the loss of the best material by emigration, the spread of alien fashions and habits, have done much to undermine native manliness. The stalwart youth of twenty or thirty years ago, who found their recreating in weight-throwing, running, jumping, hurling, ball playing, and so on, have unfortunately been replaced to a large extent by a race of lounge lizards, anaemic cigarette smokers and pallid jazz experts . . . General O'Duffy is the ideal leader for the movement to restore athletics to pride of place. The athlete is invariably a good citizen.

Throwing its weight behind his campaign, another newspaper warned that the 'physical development of our adolescent population is a matter of the greatest importance and greatest urgency today when the backwash of filthy living predominant in other countries threatens to ruin the physique of our people,

when the foul representations of American excesses have taken almost
complete possession of our picture houses, and when the tendency to indulge
in savage and indecent dancing is rife'. According to Monsignor Cummins,
only the vigilance of the hierarchy, repressive legislation, and healthy exercise
could protect young men from the 'orgy of artificial amusement' which led to
'wrecked souls and wrecked constitutions'. Identifying O'Duffy's mission as
part of a broader movement to create 'a better, healthier and a holier race',
Canon Masterson described his role as 'second only to that of the priest and
teacher'.

O'Duffy believed that the temptations of modern society were contributing
to the physical, as well as moral, degeneration of the population. In 1928 he
warned a government committee on gambling that the decline of participation
in sports would have 'very serious results so far as the physical development of
our race is concerned'.[88] 'Young men', he informed the Connaught NACA,
'are going down the ladder. They are not taking a manly interest in manly
sport... if the race was to be in existence at all in 50 years' time, the present
generation must face a very big responsibility... we are going to be wiped off
the map as a nation.' Although the rhetoric of moral and racial degeneration
dated back to the GAA's late nineteenth-century origins, such fears took on
added significance in the context of inter-war Europe.[89] The popularity of
pseudo-scientific notions such as racialism and Social Darwinism, coupled
with the profound social consequences of modernization and the Great War
(manifested in such alarming phenomena as the blurring of traditional gender
roles and the decline of birth rates), provoked widespread concern in most
countries: 'the idea that family health concerned society more generally, that
the nation needed racially sound progeny, that the state should therefore intervene in private life to show people how to live—all this ran right across the
political spectrum of inter-war Europe, reflecting the tensions and stresses of
an insecure world in which nation-states existed in rivalry with one another,
their populations decimated by one war and threatened by the prospect of
another.'[90]

The political implications of such thinking were obvious. In the same way
that politics was increasingly viewed in terms of military struggle and national
survival, physical fitness became a matter of national duty rather than personal
choice.[91] Despite the ostensibly apolitical nature of his campaign—'There is
no such thing as politics in this movement'—O'Duffy deployed the rhetoric of
the patriotic crusade which would become so central to Blueshirt propaganda.
He chided the government for 'talking politics' rather than fulfilling its 'duty
towards athletics as other countries have done'. The NACA would 'create the

athletic atmosphere in the home, the Dail, and the Senate'. His crusade was dedicated to nothing less than 'the redemption of our country from the national, moral and religious point of view'. For O'Duffy, sport symbolized the possibility of national regeneration. Privately, as we shall see in the following chapter, his campaign was also influenced by more conventional political concerns. His revival of the NACA occurred during a period when his alarm about the growth of communism and militant republicanism, forms of deviancy which he attributed to the moral degeneration of the populace, was giving way to despair. Having failed to redeem the nation through athletics, O'Duffy would turn to more direct means in 1933.

A close reading of the General's rhetoric offers further insight into his motives. The central theme of his lectures was the need to promote the ideal of 'clean manliness'. Sport, he repeatedly asserted, created 'clean manly youths', 'cultivates in a boy habits of self control [and] self denial', and promotes 'the cleanest and most wholesome of the instincts of youth'. The motif of cleanliness, in a literal and metaphorical sense, is ever-present in O'Duffy's rhetoric. Consider, for example, his remarks on inspecting military recruits at West Point: 'That is my idea of a perfect uniform, the finest support for authority is cleanliness. If I could dress my boys like that I'd be happy. Just imagine one of them trying to pass inspection with anything that looked like a spot on those white straps or gay trousers!'[92] Like manliness, the notion of cleanliness had specific connotations in this period, encompassing physical and moral qualities: 'impeccable dress symbolised moral virtue and a "clean" soul, or, in the case of a soldier, an impressively appointed uniform suggested courage, honour, self-sacrifice and, again, loyalty. The aesthetic and the moral—form and content—were inextricably fused.'[93]

The rhetoric of manliness also featured in Irish Ireland circles. Attention has recently been drawn to Patrick Pearse's 'ability to appropriate cultural discourses on history, masculinity and citizenship from imperial sources and to reinvent them as national traditions'.[94] Irish Ireland activists such as D.P. Moran, who championed the masculinity of the Gael, regarded the British imperialist depiction of Celts as a 'feminized' race as an insidious attempt to emasculate the Irish, presenting them as unworthy or incapable of self-government.[95]

The commissioner's anxieties about virility also formed part of a much broader contemporary discourse, rooted in the impact of the Great War, the 'greatest sexual catastrophe ever suffered by civilised Man', on gender roles.[96] Manliness, and masculinity, became increasingly admired post-war values. The *Evening Herald*, for example, backed O'Duffy's campaign precisely because it would combat the 'effeminacy so characteristic of the present-world'.[97]

A senior Garda advocated boxing on the grounds that the boxer 'learns to abhor vice, to love cleanliness, and to take an honest pride in the development of his body'.[98] This pervasive rhetoric, more readily associated with imperial Britain's muscular Christianity than Irish Ireland, can be found in the journals of the Irish Volunteers and National Army.[99] The increasing emphasis placed on the physical rather than moral aspects of manliness in the inter-war years was reflected by the growing popularity of physical fitness among civil populations. Much of the *Garda Review*'s content—its body-building tips, photographs of naked athletes, and illustrations of men in Grecian poses—which, to contemporary eyes, would suggest a fetishization of masculinity and the male body appeared normal to contemporaries. Underlying this concern with the male physique was not only the fear of physical degeneration, but the belief that physical training was essential for military strength, social cohesion, and national pride.[100]

But although the General's campaign reflected ideas which had a broader currency in contemporary society, it was also driven by more personal concerns. It is not so much O'Duffy's interest in the promotion of manliness as the intensity of his preoccupation with it and, by implication, with deterring those vices which undermined this ideal, which appears most striking. He invariably spoke of the threat to boys rather than girls, and described the problem in gendered terms, worrying that 'the effeminacy so characteristic of the present world [was] finding a way to our shores'. Too many boys, he complained, 'failed to keep their athleticism, but became weedy youths, smoking too soon, drinking too soon'.[101]

Sexuality

Given these concerns, what should be made of the fact that O'Duffy never exercised, smoked eighty Sweet Aftons a day, and had developed a serious alcohol problem? Arguably, more than hypocrisy lay behind the obsessive nature of his crusades. Psychoanalysts attribute a strong compulsion to tell other people how to resist particular vices with a disposition on the part of the person giving the advice to succumb to them.[102] Illegitimate desires which cannot be acknowledged, and therefore must be denied, are projected onto others. Freudians suggest that this phenomenon also stems from the fact that the guilt felt as a result of transgression can 'be assuaged by reparation through a sublimated activity such as reforming others. The worse the personal struggle against instinctual feelings, the more intense will be the desire to save potential sinners.'[103] Whether consciously or not, O'Duffy identified his own shortcomings as lacking in the general population, a process of transference which may have been reinforced by the gulf between his idealized and real identities. The fact that his concerns centred on the threat to the virility, manliness, and morality of young men raises questions about his own sexuality. Considered in the context of the inconsistencies between O'Duffy's prescriptive strictures on a wide range of issues and his actual behaviour, his preoccupation with the loss of the nation's 'great tradition of manliness' indicates a degree of anxiety about his own sexuality.

In many respects, O'Duffy's dedication to the moral and physical welfare of adolescent males resembled that of his contemporary, Robert Baden-Powell, with whom he shared many similarities.[104] The founder of the world's greatest youth movement also dedicated himself to the propagation of 'clean manliness'.[105] For Baden-Powell, the purpose of scouting was the attainment of manliness, an attribute closely bound up with patriotism and physical fitness. There can be little doubt that the influential rhetoric of Baden-Powell influenced O'Duffy: 'We badly need some training in our race instead of lapsing into a nation of soft, sloppy cigarette smokers'.[106] While acknowledging the broader discourses which existed in British society at the time, Baden-Powell's biographer persuasively attributed this obsession with promoting discipline and self-control among adolescent males to the sublimation of his own repressed homosexuality. His preoccupation with preventing 'self-abuse' was motivated by the fear that the 'clean young man' who succumbed to masturbation, 'the most dangerous of all vices', would turn his thoughts to 'beastliness' with women or, worse, 'the love that dare not speak its name'.[107] Such intriguing similarities suggest that the significance of O'Duffy's sexuality, and its influence on his career, requires further consideration, particularly in light of his recent posthumous outing as a homosexual.

A (minor) national debate on O'Duffy's sexuality was sparked by the broadcasting of *Dear Boy*, a television documentary on the life of Micheál Mac Liammóir, in 1999.[108] Born in London in 1899, Alfred Willmore, a charismatic actor, designer, artist, and writer arrived in Dublin—having invented a spurious Gaelic identity in the process—transforming Irish drama by founding the innovative Gate Theatre at a time when the Abbey Theatre's folksy productions were earning a reputation for stodgy nationalism. (Dublin wits had soon dubbed the two theatres 'sodom and begorrah'.) A remarkable figure of Irish theatre, Mac Liammóir was

temperamental, brilliant, exceptionally intelligent and intuitive, socially adroit, histrionic, multilingual and multi-gifted, with a genuine visual flair; he was also, of course—in his youth at least—exceptionally handsome, and as much a primadonna as a Leading Man. From the start, a personal mythology grew up around him, which he did nothing to discourage, and the press and public could never have enough of him ... of all the many roles Alfred Willmore played in his long, memorable career, perhaps the most brilliant and sustained was that of Micheál MacLiammóir.[109]

He was also unusual in making little attempt to disguise his homosexuality, wearing make-up in public and living openly with his partner Hilton Edwards, with whom he founded the Gate Theatre in 1928. Although the evidence attesting to a sexual relationship between O'Duffy and Mac Liammóir—consisting of the recollection of a minor literary figure, Mary Manning, that the actor had told her of O'Duffy's homosexuality—was insubstantial, the revelation provoked extensive media discussion and even debate in the Seanad.[110] O'Duffy, rather than Mac Liammóir, was the subject of considerable ridicule. Despite the scepticism of many of the historians contacted by journalists, much of the press coverage was characterized by a surprisingly uncritical acceptance of the claim. (Mac Liammóir was, after all, an obviously unreliable source, being— rather like O'Duffy—a flamboyant, self-invented, figure prone to flights of fantasy.) Admittedly, this may also have reflected the conflicting arguments advanced by historians. Tom Garvin spoke of 'constant rumours about O'Duffy's sexuality', while Gregory Allen, who had 'never picked up a breath of it', appealed for the 'witch-hunt' to end. Another historian dismissed the claim on the basis that the General 'had a strong Monaghan accent'.[111] However, the popular response owed much to O'Duffy's assigned role in Irish history. Thoroughly discredited by his fascist career, he had long become a figure of ridicule. The image of O'Duffy's official car waiting outside the Gate to speed Mac Liammóir to the depot for a night of romance provided welcome evidence of the absurd nature of Ireland's would-be *Duce* and his Blueshirt movement.

In striking contrast was the reluctance of many commentators, and some historians, to acknowledge the homosexuality of Roger Casement, whose infamous 'black diaries' were finally proven authentic by forensic tests around the same time. Aside from the important point that Casement's homosexuality was used to smear his reputation, thereby facilitating his execution in 1916, the underlying rationale behind this response was the assumption that Casement's enjoyment of sex with adolescent boys was incompatible with his status as a republican martyr.[112] Hence, a strain of homophobia must be disentangled from the controversy surrounding O'Duffy's sexuality. For example, the late Gregory Allen, the former curator of the Garda Museum and the only figure publicly to refute the documentary, described its claims as 'an outrageous calumny'. Apart from pointing out the lack of evidence to support the claim, Allen's counter-argument was unconvincing, relying as it did on an expression of regret by O'Duffy at not having married, and the insistence of O'Duffy (disconcertingly described as 'the prophet') that manliness was the one characteristic that he had consistently sought to develop in the force. Nor was the case for the defence strengthened by Allen's assertion that the commissioner's love 'for his men knew no bounds'.[113] His comments provoked a more politically correct response from a distant relation of O'Duffy, criticizing the General's political rather than sexual orientation.

The controversy raises two important questions. Was O'Duffy a homosexual? And, if so, how does this add to our understanding of his life? These proved difficult questions to answer. Little relevant written evidence exists, and potential sources, of whom there were few, were reluctant to discuss the issue. Despite the existence of a lively gay culture in inter-war Dublin, homosexuality in Ireland—which remained illegal until 1993—was rarely acknowledged until recent years. Certainly, there is no evidence that O'Duffy ever formed a close relationship with a woman, aside from his intense devotion to his mother; indeed it has been suggested that he was scared of women.[114] Although neither celibacy nor a fear of the opposite sex were remarkable characteristics among rural Irishmen of this period, O'Duffy's zealous championing of masculinity was more unusual. Also, despite *Dear Boy*'s impact, O'Duffy's sexuality had long been a subject of rumour.[115] Their friendship, an unlikely one given their contrasting social circles, was a matter of record. In his autobiography, Mac Liammóir related how the commissioner once provided himself and Hilton Edwards with a letter of introduction to the chief of the Athenian police force, who treated both men to 'a wild nocturnal drive through lashing rain to eat shellfish in a tavern on a cliff that hung over the Gulf of Corinth'.[116] Prior to *Dear Boy*, there were two occasions when O'Duffy's homosexuality was alleged in print. Reviewing a history of the Blueshirts, the writer Anthony Cronin asserted that O'Duffy 'was a habitué of Hilton and Michael's notorious parties in Dawson Street', and that 'when he was a Commissioner of the Garda Síochána he had friendships with young guards which may have been platonic but may also have been something more'.[117] Less coyly, Uinseann MacEoin described O'Duffy as a 'closet homosexual' in *The IRA in the Twilight Years*.[118]

Cronin had learned of O'Duffy's attendance at Mac Liammóir's parties from several literary figures, including the critic John Jordan and the writer Paul Smith.[119] However, his account merely confirms that Mac Liammóir claimed that O'Duffy was a homosexual. Significantly, the source of Uinseann

MacEoin's claim was different. While inspecting a house on South Anne Street, which had belonged to the minor Gate actor and tweed and tie shop owner Maurice O'Brien, for the prominent architect Michael Scott, MacEoin was told by Scott that O'Brien had told him that he was O'Duffy's lover. O'Brien had even told Scott that on the 'occasions going upstairs, the former General of the 5th Northern would turn the religious pictures to face the wall'.[120] The personalities involved support the plausibility of this account. As the talented young designer of the Gate Theatre, Scott was well acquainted with bohemian Dublin. Moreover, Cronin confirmed that Maurice O'Brien, whom he described as 'a spear-carrier' at the Gate, was a camp homosexual.[121] In this light, the Mac Liammóir claim seems credible, particularly given his reputation as 'a man with a very very substantial and lively appetite . . . he tended to have a number of sexual contacts everyday and a lot of these people he had sex with were soldiers who became friends'.[122]

A remaining doubt about these third-hand accounts concerns the fact that they originate from one social circle. If O'Duffy attended notorious parties thrown by bohemian homosexuals, surely there would be some hint of his sexuality in the other spheres of his life? In the wake of *Dear Boy*, additional uncorroborated accounts did come to light. It was alleged, for example, that O'Duffy was over-interested in 'the physical prowess of the young boxers under the aegis of the Irish Amateur Boxing Association, of which he was a patron'. A Waterford Gael alleged that O'Duffy had made an unwelcome advance on a Mount Sion hurler and naval petty officer named Willie O'Regan on *The Great Western* ferry en route to Fishguard: 'Shortly after the vessel debarked from the quayside at Waterford, and slipped its way along the silent waters of the River Suir, a scuffle broke out on deck, and a man was seen to fell the portly General O'Duffy with a single punch. Most of the onlookers assumed the row was over a political difference.'[123] Similar rumours predated *Dear Boy*. A Holy Ghost priest, who shared O'Duffy's anti-communist politics, warned Maurice Manning about O'Duffy's immoral practices, while the wife of deputy commissioner Coogan told another historian of O'Duffy's attraction to men.[124]

The existence of rumours, particularly relating to sexual scandal, does not prove their veracity. Moreover, there are no recorded contemporaneous references to O'Duffy's homosexuality by his many enemies or among the numerous police and intelligence reports in which he features. This may, however, be due to the taboos of the time and the secretive nature of Dublin's homosexual sub-culture. There is, after all, practically no written evidence of homosexuality in inter-war Ireland, despite the fact that there were reportedly seven public lavatories where cottaging was practicable between Mac Liammóir's

Harcourt Terrace home and the Gate Theatre. Sex between middle-class men was readily available on the right dinner-party circuits, while working-class men who mastered the esoteric dress code—red socks, for example, or a green tie on a Friday night—had little difficulty meeting partners in the right pubs.[125] The existence of a number of claims from sources pertaining to discrete spheres of O'Duffy's life, coupled with the unlikelihood of a literary circle inventing a story which remained private for six decades, would seem to confirm that O'Duffy was homosexual.

But how relevant is this to our understanding of the life? One consequence of the revelation was to facilitate the further tarnishing—were it deemed necessary—of O'Duffy's reputation. Even if it seems unrealistic to expect homosexuals not to have concealed their criminal behaviour, his behaviour was hypocritical given his self-appointed role as a guardian of public morality. However, this seems a relatively trivial point (if not for the victims of the repressive morality which O'Duffy played his part in reinforcing). In retrospect, it is the incongruity of his dual existence as a crusading moralist and a cruising homosexual which appears most striking. That his lifestyle combined such a prominent position of public respectability, epitomized by his role as chief marshal of the Eucharistic Congress, with such an unconventional secret life emphasizes his remarkable capacity for simultaneously leading radically different lives. Like Mac Liammóir, O'Duffy's public persona was possibly his most brilliant creation.

O'Duffy's sexuality offers other potential insights. One need not be a fully signed-up Freudian to posit a connection between his alarm about moral degeneracy in society and his anxieties about his own sexuality.[126] Desire, repression, guilt, and delusion are recurrent themes in the General's life. It seems likely that his homosexuality influenced the course of his career, an obvious aspect of which was that it was entirely devoted to the leadership of overtly masculine organizations: the GAA, the IRA, the Garda Síochána, and the Blueshirts. Like many men, heterosexual and homosexual, O'Duffy was drawn to organizations which embodied masculine values. Just as emotional intimacy between adolescent boys was central to the appeal of the Boy Scouts, the identification of volunteering with manliness, and the opportunities for male bonding, were central to the attraction of the Irish Volunteers.[127] There is a substantial literature which argues that participation in military organizations allows men to sublimate their homoerotic desires in a more socially acceptable form. By the early twentieth century, following the greater public awareness and criminalization of homosexuality, the Victorian ideals of manly love and boy love had come to be regarded with suspicion. The army remained one of the few places where the expression of love for one's fellow-man, even in homoerotic language, was not merely tolerated but encouraged.[128] It was, for example, only through their shared comradeship that O'Duffy could openly express his manly love for Dan Hogan.[129]

Manliness, camaraderie, loyalty, devotion, and love between men were not merely celebrated but idealized in O'Duffy's masculine organizations. The General expressed his admiration of the gardaí in physical as well as moral terms: they were 'splendid types of perfect manhood', 'a beauty of soul and a beauty of body'.[130] There are similarities here with Patrick Pearse's celebration of the physical, as well as moral, beauty of adolescent boys. Pearse's school, St Enda's, also dedicated itself to the celebration of 'bodily vigour', 'purity', 'cleanliness', 'discipline', and 'manly-self-reliance', values which formed part of a militaristic ethos which Pearse regarded as necessary for the regeneration of an effeminate Ireland: 'every day I feel more certain that the hardening of her boys and young men is the work of the movement for Ireland'. And, whilst Pearse's motives were complex, even the most cautious and nuanced of cultural readings has concluded that a sublimated sexuality, characterized by an eroticization of athleticism and boys' culture, was 'inextricably linked to Pearse's reworkings of history, tradition and physical culture'.[131]

Membership of masculine organizations met emotional as well as sexual needs, offering a sense of belonging which O'Duffy had strived for since childhood—the camaraderie which he once described as 'nothing more than forgetfulness of self and love of unit'. On a more practical level, it also facilitated proximity to young men, and there is little reason to believe that homosexuality was less widespread in the Irish military than other armies.[132] Membership of the IRA also provided opportunities for physical intimacy with other men (a subject for which there is not a substantial literature). One veteran of the flying columns, for example, claimed to have been propositioned by his comrades on at least four occasions.[133] O'Duffy's papers include many photographs of semi-clothed, muscular, young athletes (as does his collection of Italian and German fascist propaganda) and glossy portraits of handsome policemen and IRA Volunteers. It seems likely that O'Duffy's lifelong dedication to masculine organizations stemmed from a complex combination of ideological, emotional, and erotic impulses.

While O'Duffy's homosexuality should not necessarily be seen as the most essential aspect of his identity, a revelation which provides a key to understanding his life to the exclusion of the complex range of psychological, social, cultural and political influences which shape the behaviour of any individual, it forms a significant part of a broader theme of this study: the dissonance between his public and private selves. In certain respects, O'Duffy was an audacious fraud, an achievement which required an ability to shift seamlessly between his real and idealized personae. He responded to the crisis of his sexuality by projecting himself as a leading advocate of clean-living masculinity, a dissimulation which formed part of a wider process of self-invention.

Of course, everyone alters aspects of their identity and past, whether deliberately or as part of the unconscious process that is the construction of memory. Reinvention and mythopoeia are not unusual among public figures, particularly politicians for whom credibility and a favourable public image form prerequisites of success: what was unusual about O'Duffy's self-invention was its epic scale, a product of his mythomania.[134] He altered such fundamental aspects of his identity as his name, age, family history, and career, endlessly reshaping himself and the past in search of a more heroic self-image.[135] By the late 1920s he had constructed a public identity which evoked widespread public admiration, but was sharply at odds with his real self. Projection, sublimation, and self-deception contributed to his remarkable drive and determination, but there was a price to pay for his success. It was during this period that his extreme views and volatile behaviour became a serious concern for his colleagues.[136] The centre was no longer holding.

7

Red terror

The people must be saved, almost in spite of themselves.[1]

By the early 1930s, O'Duffy's optimistic belief in the Garda Síochána's ability to shape a new moral order had given way to bitter frustration. He was far from alone in thinking that independence had failed to create the nation for which his generation had fought. Indeed, many reactionary treatyites attributed this malaise to the experience of revolution and Civil War. In his classic polemic, *The Victory of Sinn Féin*, the treatyite politician P. S. O'Hegarty observed: 'We adopted political assassination as a principle; we devised the ambush; we encouraged women to forget their sex and play at gunmen; we turned the whole thoughts and passions of a generation upon blood and revenge and death . . . We derided the Moral Law, and said there was no other Law but force.'[2] Those who had opposed the treaty were held most to blame for this state of affairs: 'The Irregulars drove patriotism and honesty and morality out of Ireland. They fouled the wells which had kept us clean, and made the task of saving Ireland tenfold harder.'[3] As another treatyite politician mournfully noted in his diary, 'it was the actions of the Irregular-republicans which killed idealism in my own soul; idealism that is, in connection with this country and its people. And I *know* they killed it in many others as well.'[4] An important aspect of this mindset of despair was the way in which the moral decline of society and the political degeneration of the nation were seen as interconnected. O'Duffy's pessimism about his country's future, and his growing belief that only radical measures could redeem its people, was bound up with his struggle against anti-treaty republicanism. The experience of fighting a losing battle against republicans, hampered by liberal judges, ungrateful politicians, and an increasingly critical public did much to shape his trajectory towards the political extremism he embraced in the 1930s.

The revival of the IRA

It was not until 1925, when responsibility for political crime was transferred from the National Army to the Garda Síochána, that the suppression of republicanism became the most important aspect of O'Duffy's role as commissioner. Prior to this, relations between gardaí and republicans had been tolerable. In some areas armed republicans attacked gardaí to demonstrate the impotence of the state but, more often, both sides arrived at discreet understandings. During the Civil War, one guard recalled, 'we used to meet the IRA with arms in Elton and we said good night to them and they said good night to us'.[5] Yet, even in this early period, there were tensions between O'Duffy's depiction of the gardaí as a non-political force and its crucial role as an arm of the government. In 1923, the first of a series of public safety acts had allowed for the internment of subversives on the recommendation of the police and, increasingly, it was the gardaí rather than the army which acted as the eyes and ears of the government. Moreover, O'Higgins decided that it would be the police rather than a secret service, O'Duffy's preferred option, which should assume responsibility for monitoring subversives.[6] In 1925, by which time the decline of armed crime no longer justified the policing role of the National Army, the Garda Síochána was pushed forward as the state's first line of defence. The implications of this new role were never publicly acknowledged by O'Duffy or the government, which continued to refer to the IRA as criminals and depict the police as a non-political force. No issue would do more to undermine the Garda's hard-won public acceptance than its responsibility for the suppression of militant republicanism.

This new role necessitated a reconsideration of the Garda's unarmed status and its relationship with the detective division of the Dublin Metropolitan Police (DMP). The latter was the haphazard result of the amalgamation of a series of disreputable forces, including the DMP's despised G Division, Michael Collins's notorious squad, and the infamous 'Oriel House' Criminal Investigation Department, which enjoyed well-earned reputations for ill-discipline and murder.[7] Kevin O'Higgins had pushed for the expansion of the DMP's detective division into a national armed force in 1924 but had been opposed by O'Duffy, who feared the Garda Síochána's subordination to a rival force.[8] However, the problems associated with maintaining separate administrative structures and the need to strengthen the police to cope with its new responsibilities prompted a further reorganization. In December 1924, as the army withdrew from its policing function and armed crime began to rise, O'Duffy told O'Higgins that he could no longer guarantee law and order without strengthening the Garda.[9]

Consequently, two important measures were introduced in 1925. The Treasonable Offences act replaced the emergency measure of internment with habeas corpus and trial by jury, but allowed for the prohibition of anti-state organizations and the use of the death sentence for political crime. O'Duffy would later complain that this legislation, an attempt to move towards a more conventional law and order régime, had been 'disembowelled' by politicians before its enactment.[10] The Amalgamation of Police Forces act merged the DMP and Garda into a single force which included a special armed detective branch under the authority of David Neligan (who had been one of Collins's most important informers in the DMP's G division during the War of Independence). Despite reservations, O'Duffy agreed to the latter body (soon known as Special Branch) as the most acceptable alternative to retaining the National Army's policing function.[11] The decision—partly O'Duffy's—to organize the Special Branch as a distinct body, with its own officers, stations, and chain of command, was intended to preserve the apolitical image of the Garda Síochána. Uniformed guards continued to focus on conventional crime, ignoring republicans unless provoked, while Special Branch tackled political crime. Although an initially successful arrangement, Special Branch's subsequent reputation would soon undermine O'Duffy and the government.

The year 1925 was also a period of reorganization for republicanism. The rumour that de Valera intended to lead Sinn Féin into the Dáil prompted a parting of the ways between armed and political republicanism, leading to the establishment of Fianna Fáil the following year. Despite his rhetorical denunciations of the Free State's legitimacy, de Valera had come to believe that violence no longer served any useful function. Nonetheless, O'Duffy, like many Free Staters, would persist in seeing the political and military wings of republicanism as inextricably linked. The IRA, which had been under the authority of the notional republican government established by de Valera during the Civil War, now vested governmental authority in its own army council, restructuring itself into a secret army committed to physical force to achieve its objectives. Its primary enemy was not Britain or Northern Ireland but the Free State government, which, as Britain's garrison in Ireland, was most responsible for maintaining the humiliation of the treaty settlement.

The first dramatic evidence of the threat posed by the new IRA was its co-ordinated assault on twelve police stations in November 1926 which resulted in the death of two unarmed gardaí. Equally significantly, this incident highlighted the potential for tension between the government and O'Duffy on security policy. The cabinet was outraged when it was revealed that gardaí in Waterford had retaliated by beating republican prisoners in their custody. O'Duffy, summoned to O'Higgins's office, refused to dismiss the men involved: ' "Resign then", said O'Higgins, white with indignation.'[12] Blythe recalled it as the first of several serious clashes between the government and its commissioner:

The Cabinet felt that if Civic Guards were to be allowed to beat up anybody, the results would be serious. O'Duffy had to admit misbehaviour by the Guards, but he pleaded a measure of justification. He pleaded also the good record of the Guards concerned, and alleged that anything that they did was not for personal advantage or from personal motives, but was for the repression of a certain type of crime for which it was difficult to obtain conviction in Court. In spite of all he could say, the Cabinet decided that the Guards in question . . . should be dismissed. O'Duffy thereupon stated that the Cabinet had no power to dismiss members of the Guards, as the Act laid it down that Guards should be appointed and dismissed by the Commissioner. O'Duffy was asked to retire from the room, and the members of the Cabinet agreed that they would not tolerate such an attitude on his part. When he returned, he was told by Mr. Cosgrave, on behalf of the Cabinet, that if he did not dismiss the Guards in question . . . the Government would provide itself with a new Commissioner who would dismiss them. O'Duffy went away without making any promise, but next day he dismissed the offending Guards.[13]

In fact, Blythe was mistaken: what followed was far more interesting. O'Duffy continued to refuse to allow the prosecution of his 'young and zealous' charges. While he made it clear that he did not condone the torture of prisoners (on the grounds that it was unjust, counter-productive in terms of public confidence, and a tacit admission of inefficiency), he argued that the public interest was not served by prosecuting 'loyal servants of the state' for paying back 'armed desperadoes . . . a debt which the natural law recognises to be long overdue'. He was not, he informed the government, a believer in turning the other cheek. O'Duffy demanded that he be allowed to deal with the issue as an internal disciplinary matter. If he found that they had tortured the men for 'mere satisfaction' he would dismiss them, but if he was satisfied that they had done so 'in the interests of the state', they would be cautioned and a strong circular would be issued to the force.[14] Faced by O'Duffy's intransigence, it was the minister for justice and not the commissioner who backed down, after his colleagues persuaded him to accept an inquiry into the incident. O'Higgins promised the Dáil that it would be the last occasion that a plea of extenuating circumstances would be accepted for such behaviour.[15]

It was a significant incident, and not merely because of what it revealed about O'Duffy's insubordinate streak. The dispute highlighted an important distinction between O'Duffy's attitude to state violence and that of the government. O'Higgins did not lack the stomach for brutal methods, but he believed that coercion should be measured and legal. This principle had underpinned his unremitting opposition to indiscipline within the National Army: 'When we joined issue with the Irregulars we went out not simply to catch or kill a particular combination of individuals but to defeat and suppress and utterly smash a mentality which menaced the political and economic life of the nation. If the mentality manifests itself in our ranks we must recognise it as being not less but more fatal to the body politic than when it masqueraded under the banner of the Republic.'[16] In reality, the government's position (as its willingness to turn a blind eye to its Oriel House murder gang had demonstrated) was rather more ambiguous. O'Duffy, moreover, made no secret of the fact that Special Branch operated a policy of counter-repression, a policy generally tolerated by the cabinet. But although the issue of when such coercion crossed the bounds to unlawful violence remained a matter for ministerial opinion rather than specific guidelines, the important point for O'Higgins was that this was a decision made by the executive rather than the initiative of unruly elements of the security forces. The controversy also illustrated just how quickly relations between O'Duffy and the government had soured. According to one well-informed source: 'There was a barely concealed joy in the cabinet when O'Duffy tendered his resignation, for the vain, self-centred Commissioner had long lost most of his friends in the government, the only exception being O'Higgins himself.'[17]

The Irish public is rotten

The government was provided with further grounds for concern about its commissioner's authoritarian proclivities when, three weeks later, O'Duffy set out his views on coercion in a remarkably frank report. Observing that centuries of British rule had instilled a destructive antipathy to civilized government in the Irish psyche, O'Duffy argued that the War of Independence (in which Britain pragmatically chose to withdraw rather than pursue a serious military campaign) and the Civil War ('as a result of the manner in which the conflict terminated') had reinforced the notion that armed violence was an effective and relatively safe policy. Church and state were also to blame for this mentality: 'civics is not taught in the school, citizenship is rarely, if ever preached in the Church, as in other countries'. Consequently, it was up to the police to teach those who did not practise 'the duties of citizenship' that violence does not pay. This, O'Duffy argued, would necessitate the creation of a force

capable, not alone of its own defence, but of aggression, real aggression ... To this body could be entrusted the task of demanding and insisting on respect for the law of the land, and the extermination of the type that is incapable, or unwilling to assume the responsibilities of citizenship, with the express purpose of ensuring that the child of to-day may attain to maturity in an atmosphere free from traditional fallacies and false standards, and with reasonable hopes and even assurance of a future free from periodical attacks upon the stability of the State.[18]

O'Duffy wanted emergency powers to pacify the state and enforce the values of citizenship upon its recalcitrant population, 'the vast majority of whom know or care little about such principles'. His extremism was, in part, a consequence of his concern about the effects of IRA violence. A police force without the ability to protect itself or its citizens could not prevent the collapse of central authority itself. In a revealing admission, he questioned his men's loyalty in the face of republican violence, given that they considered themselves servants not of the state but a government which 'has not been as generous as it should have been in its treatment of the force'. The culmination of this dramatic report was his request that the Garda be armed. While conceding that the force's popularity was partly due to its unarmed status, O'Duffy argued that this had been necessitated by the circumstances of the Civil War. An armed force in normal conditions would win public support in Ireland as in other countries: 'The Police Officers and others interested in law and order whom I met in the various European countries recently, could not understand an unarmed, and at the same time, effective Police Force. I tried to explain, but they were incredulous.'

O'Higgins, backed by the department of justice and the cabinet, rejected the proposal which must have raised doubts about O'Duffy's suitability for office.[19] By seeking to overturn four years of successful policing, O'Duffy's over-reaction to the IRA raids was as illogical as it was volatile: his argument for arming the guards, the opposition of a substantial minority to the state, was precisely why an unarmed force had initially been deemed necessary. His proposal was also opposed by some of his officers—at least one chief superintendent had threatened to resign if the force was armed.[20] Despite claiming the credit for the idea of an unarmed force, O'Duffy had always been ambiguous on the issue. During his oration over the grave of a murdered guard in 1924, he declared: 'If it is your wish that the Garda should be armed with revolvers for a time to cope with this robber menace, we are at attention to obey the people's will', a characteristically indiscreet utterance which prompted the government to rule out the suggestion.[21] O'Duffy's report also highlighted his pessimistic view of the national character: his very first report as commissioner had observed that the 'people must be saved, almost in spite of themselves'.[22]

The November raids marked the beginning of a low-intensity campaign of violence by the IRA, initially directed at the police but later extended to the more vulnerable court system. Within two days of the raids, the government had accepted the need for coercive legislation. A new Public Safety act was introduced as a permanent measure, to be used in times of emergency following a formal proclamation by the cabinet. It was a response not so much to the raids as to the knowledge that the IRA had broken free of political control in order to pursue a campaign of violence, a development described by the government as 'a minor state of war . . . a challenge to the very institutions of the State'.[23] This violence, sometimes dismissed as purposeless, was effective. The government's reliance on ever more illiberal coercion measures to fight an increasingly dirty war gradually eroded public confidence in the government and gardaí.[24]

The shocking assassination of Kevin O'Higgins as he walked, alone and unarmed, to mass on 10 July 1927 appeared to confirm this bleak assessment. Upon hearing the news, O'Duffy rushed to Blackrock, where the minister lay dying. He described their last meeting to the *Garda Review*:

Looking into my eyes as I was kneeling by his side, the Minister said: 'Is that you, Owen? I am dying, Good-bye, Owen. You were very good. We have done good work. Continue on the same lines.'. . . Mr. Hogan, the Minister for Agriculture, came into the room, and knelt on the other side of our Chief. Looking at Mr. Hogan, the Minister said: 'Hogan! My two best friends, Hogan and Owen—Owen and Hogan, good bye . . .[25]

Lest the significance of O'Higgins's final request be missed, O'Duffy added: 'I think it is right that I should tell the Garda these things, and that the man who was ever a guide and an inspiration to us had in his last moments . . . added—a helpful word of advice—"Continue on the same lines." Please God, the Garda will not forget the last message of Kevin O'Higgins.'

Notwithstanding this emotional account, O'Higgins was neither a close friend nor mentor, and his assassination—in contrast to that of Collins—did not weaken O'Duffy. Indeed, it was rumoured that high-ranking guards had killed O'Higgins to prevent disciplinary measures against Special Branch.[26] Whatever his personal feelings, and there is little reason to doubt that he was appalled by the assassination, O'Duffy used it to strengthen his position, for example by passing on O'Higgins's reassuring, if uncorroborated, final message to the press on the night of his death.[27] The phrase attributed to O'Higgins—'Continue on the same lines'—was one often used by O'Duffy in his speeches.[28] More suspiciously, there is evidence that O'Higgins had actually resolved to dismiss his commissioner. A subsequent memo by a senior civil servant, detailing a conversation with a well-placed member of army intelligence, claimed that O'Duffy 'had been all but dismissed from the Commissionership . . . when Mr. O'Higgins was murdered'.[29] Within the force, moreover, it was believed that O'Higgins had already selected his replacement.[30]

The assassination also strengthened O'Duffy's hand by justifying his calls for more extreme measures. He attributed the murder to a new 'secret society' within the IRA, like 'the old I.R.B., but much more select and dangerous':

I believe that other desperadoes of a bad type from extreme labour and communist elements are being enrolled . . . two out of the three members of the Supreme Council can meet and decree that certain things should be done—the lives of Ministers or important officers of the State are declared forfeit, the order is given to willing subordinates, and when opportunity offers the decree is executed . . . It is more dangerous to the State than Civil War—the National Army could deal with that. It is much more difficult to deal with a Secret Society composed of carefully selected desperadoes filled with vengeance against the administration, and who are prepared to stop at nothing, the object being the overthrow of the State by assassination and other violent methods.[31]

Predicting that the assassination of more politicians and police officers would follow, he demanded 'the extension of the Detective Branch, armament and transport, and a substantial increase in the Secret Service vote'.

This alarmist memo—which combined factual if exaggerated elements (the IRA's readiness to use violence and its links with the far left) with unfounded allegations—was characteristic of the distorted reports O'Duffy would present to the government in later years. O'Higgins's assassination, while not inconsistent with *An Phoblacht*'s murderous rhetoric—was an opportunistic action, carried out without the authorization of the army council.[32] There was no plan to assassinate political leaders and no secret society within the IRA, whose structures remained surprisingly democratic despite its élitist contempt for the Free State. Aside from his paranoid fear of conspiracy (a characteristic of many conspirators), O'Duffy's alarmist response was conditioned by his awareness of the relative ease with which republicans like himself had undermined law and order during the revolution, as judges and policemen accommodated themselves to the coming men rather than risking their lives for a potentially lost cause. In light of the public outrage at the killing of O'Higgins, and the clear challenge to democracy which it represented, O'Duffy's call for firm measures met with approval.

The Public Safety act (1927) provided the draconian powers he demanded, including the suspension of habeas corpus, the reintroduction of internment, and the replacement of jury trials with special courts empowered with the death penalty. It was essentially a return to the emergency measures of the Civil War, the government's declaration that it was necessary for the preservation of peace removing it from the provisions of the constitution which it otherwise infringed.[33] A second act, obliging deputies to take their seats in the Dáil or forfeit them, represented an attempt to end Fianna Fáil's abstentionism, which, treatyites believed, encouraged IRA violence by undermining the legitimacy of the state. The response of de Valera, who had been nudging his deputies in the direction of Leinster House for some time, was never in doubt. On 12 August 1927 de Valera led his party into the Dáil. Far from destabilizing the state, the assassination of O'Higgins had reinforced its legitimacy, an irony the minister would have been pleased to accept as his legacy.

After the narrow failure of a no confidence motion against the government, Cumann na nGaedheal won a slim electoral victory in September 1927. Despite de Valera's condemnation of the assassination and his belated acceptance of the principle of representative government, the republican threat would intensify during Cosgrave's final term. With its references to 'the so-called minister for defence' and 'de facto government', Fianna Fáil continued to question the government's legitimacy, and retained a cordial relationship with the IRA despite its violence. In certain respects, the emergence of a 'slightly constitutional' Fianna Fáil increased O'Duffy's difficulties as the party utilized the Dáil, Senate, and local government to undermine coercion while depicting republican violence in the best possible light. Given the importance of public support for the Garda's earlier achievements, this proved an effective policy. Conversely, however, O'Duffy benefited from the increased republican threat which strengthened the government's dependence on him. He was also strengthened by the appointment of James FitzGerald-Kenney as minister for justice, who, in contrast to his predecessor, would exercise little restraint over his commissioner.

Red terror

Despite O'Duffy's fears, the assassination of O'Higgins was not followed by a murder campaign. The IRA went to ground, leading the government—much to his annoyance—to suspend its constitutionally dubious emergency legislation without consulting him. The government's decision, which inevitably restored the initiative in the cycle of violence to the IRA, represented an attempt to conciliate republicans by building on Fianna Fáil's decision to enter the Dáil. A divergence in outlook between O'Duffy and the government became increasingly apparent in this period. At one reception, the commissioner complained about the constant accusations of police brutality by 'judges, juries, and councils, and from the public', while the minister for justice explained that the decision of 'a large body of our fellow-countrymen' to recognize the state had created 'a transition period': 'It must always be a difficulty to the Gardai to recognise this change has taken place, but the Gardai must do it ... persons who were regarded as enemies of the State must now be regarded as enemies no longer.'[34] Although treatyite security policy has been caricatured as 'a narrow and ruthless consolidation of its military and political victory in 1923', the generally underestimated Cumann na nGaedheal administration was actually 'prepared to sacrifice its own party interests in its attempts to construct political life on the foundations of the Treaty'.[35] O'Duffy, for all his patriotic rhetoric, was not.

Gathering his senior officers together after the suspension of the Public Safety act in late 1928, O'Duffy warned them to expect renewed violence. The IRA, an extremist body which regarded conciliation as weakness, widened its campaign of violence to include jurors in political trials in an effort to break the courts, demoralize the police, and demonstrate its power. As IRA violence mounted, so too did O'Duffy's extremism. The judiciary and the public were the most frequent targets of his invective, but an underlying disillusionment with the government and democracy itself became evident, a process which can be traced through his surviving quarterly reports. In March 1929, following the collapse of the trial of a prominent republican who had told the court that he had no desire to prove himself innocent, O'Duffy warned of the police's inability to secure convictions for political crime. He blamed the judge, whom he described as an 'ex Black and Tan prosecutor', for criticizing the gardaí and refusing to convict on the sole basis of incriminating documents.[36] 'Weak benches', he thundered, 'have brought down States before and they will bring this State down if they persist in their weak-kneed attitude'.[37] He began using the *Garda Review* to admonish judges who criticized the police.[38]

After the murder of a witness in another political trial, state solicitors began automatically to request a change of venue to Dublin for all rural political cases. Describing this as 'an admission of failure', O'Duffy warned that if this practice extended to the agrarian trials arising from Peadar O'Donnell's anti-annuity campaign it would bring about 'a red terror'.[39] Accusing the state of going soft, O'Duffy angrily denounced 'the nonchalance and weakness of the Judiciary, the almost contemptuous attitude of people in official positions and the filling of official and semi-official positions with persons who had devoted years—several years—to the destruction of the institutions of the State.'[40] The steady rise in support for Fianna Fáil, a party which tacitly encouraged the IRA's campaign against the courts, was particularly galling:

It is a comparatively easy matter to upset the jury system; it is a comparatively easy matter to murder a citizen. Possessed of sufficient weapons, funds and the necessary human material sworn in a secret cabal, and given a public cowardly or apathetic enough, it is indeed easy. Let us make no mistake about it, from the point of view of their outlook on so-called political crime, the Irish public is rotten. Their sense of citizenship is negligible . . . We have the spectacle, following so quickly on murder and attempted murder at their very door, of twenty eight thousand citizens voting for [Oscar] Traynor, the personification of subterranean crime, when this State was fighting for its very existence.[41]

FitzGerald-Kenney's cows

Although O'Duffy's reports were exaggerated, the police were struggling to contain the IRA without emergency powers, and the resulting problems were corroding morale and public support. This was particularly prevalent in Clare, the most incorrigibly republican county in the state. Special Branch's 'cat and mouse' policy of harassment (the continual arrest, detention, and re-arrest of suspects) had been particularly marked in west Clare, which was never fully pacified after the Civil War. Republicans ambushed guards and intimidated their families, while the gardaí often responded in kind. In 1925 an unarmed guard was murdered. Three years later an informer disappeared without trace. In the same year O'Duffy dismissed William Geary, a diligent superintendent in Kilrush, for bribery after he was successfully framed by the IRA.[42] A detective was murdered in 1929 while, later that year, David Neligan uncovered a plot by his own officers to drown T. J. Ryan, a leading republican. In the course of denying one of Special Branch's numerous assaults on Ryan, the minister for justice suggested that his injuries had been caused by a cow, resulting in the force becoming widely ridiculed as 'FitzGerald-Kenney's cows'.

Public bodies, including several county councils, called for the disbanding of Special Branch: one senator pointedly observed that the last minister had at least managed to keep the police in check.[43] O'Duffy's response was uncompromising. Attributing the criticism to the 'actively or passively hostile' attitude of Clare's inhabitants ('this rabble'), and the police's successes rather than its excesses, he urged the government to hold its nerve: 'We have to ask ourselves whether we will abandon the country to these men and their methods, or rule it; whether we will allow an illegal army to flourish [or] destroy it.' Describing the county council as 'a body of irresponsible blackguards', he accused its chairman of bank-robbery. He dismissed the calls for a public inquiry into the events in Clare as a propaganda stunt by gunmen, unscrupulous lawyers, 'unfortunate women like Maud Gonne McBride and other apostles of evil'.[44]

Having decided that harassment was a necessary policing method, O'Duffy was unwilling to undermine his men's efforts. Special Branch, as O'Duffy understood, was in an impossible position. Political crime could never be suppressed while republicans enjoyed the support or acquiescence of much of the community. But although republican violence was as much a political as a policing problem, the government appeared willing to follow its commissioner's belligerent lead in the absence of a political solution. O'Duffy, for his part, could hardly allow the IRA to challenge the legitimacy of the police, even if the intensification of coercion merely provoked ever more extreme responses. After the IRA stepped up its campaign, killing a juror, witness, and guard in the first half of 1929, O'Duffy warned that 'the system of trial by jury of political offences has broken down'.[45] In July he reported that thirty treason prosecutions had been dropped, describing the IRA's campaign against jurors as 'a complete success'.

The government's response was the Juries Protection act, which allowed for the secret empanelling of juries, majority rather than unanimous verdicts, and imprisonment for non-recognition of the courts. Jury intimidation, however, continued to rise. When a case against a republican found in possession of a land mine collapsed after several jurors had refused to convict on the grounds 'that they would have a policeman standing outside their door guarding them for the rest of their lives', O'Duffy blamed the cowardice of Dublin's Protestant jurors: 'It is now useless to put unionists or loyalists on such juries as these classes are notoriously "gun shy", and have moreover, been struck at directly by the murder of Armstrong, and the attempted murder of White. There can be no doubt that some of them also would be glad to see chaos here and the return of the British.'[46] These criticisms were unreasonable, but they illustrated O'Duffy's growing disgust at the lack of civic virtue among the public: 'one or two attacks...has thrown them back into the abyss of moral cowardice'.[47] The state's legal system, a legacy of British rule, had been intended for a people with 'a highly developed civic sense and moral courage which is entirely lacking here'.[48]

The strategy of harassment suffered a further setback when the judiciary began ruling that Special Branch's 'cat and mouse' policy was unconstitutional.[49] O'Duffy naturally blamed the judiciary: 'If those latter learned gentlemen persist in treating this menace lightly it will wreck the State. If, further, by a pretended air of detachment they give every aid and encouragement to those malefactors and conversely throw slurs on the police it will wreck the State. Maintaining the strict letter of the law is commendable but there is no use worrying over the varnish if the wall is undermined.'[50] He made clear his detestation of those judges who 'sneered openly' at police evidence. Obsessed by 'the theory of the liberty of the subject', they too often proved 'the straw bending before the storm of violence and terrorism'. In contrast, the department of justice, having reviewed the evidence, concluded that the judges and juries had acted properly in each case.[51]

His frustration was compounded by the knowledge that the IRA's ability to murder informers, witnesses, and over-diligent gardaí rendered it 'almost impossible' to convict republicans.[52] Increasingly resentful of judicial concern for the civil rights of IRA members, O'Duffy began to question the need for a conventional judicial system: 'It is impossible to even surmise what these Juries and Judges are aiming at; it is certainly an object lesson on the weakness of democratic rule.'[53] He pressed for a restoration of emergency powers: 'Temporary legislation and periodic panicky Acts will not serve the purpose. What is required is a well-considered comprehensive measure, scrapping all the existing Acts, prepared in consultation with this Headquarters, and made the permanent law of the land.'[54]

His demands were strengthened by the continuing spiral of violence. In January 1931 an IRA informer was shot twice in the head and then blown up: the police collected fragments of his skull ten yards away from his body. In March, Superintendent John Curtin was murdered for taking too close an interest in republicans in Tipperary, while a witness to his murder was killed three months

later. The openness of the republican challenge—particularly the revival of
public drilling—unnerved the police:

> when a political crime is now committed they are helpless; there is no hope whatever
> under the existing law to bring the perpetrators to justice ... Members of the Irregular
> Organisation and their followers treat the Gardai with absolute contempt; criminal
> suspects refuse to answer any questions and the ordinary citizen in the affected areas
> who, under normal conditions, would assist the Gardai to the utmost of his ability is
> through fear driven into silence.[55]

Submitting a sixty-page report in June 1931, O'Duffy claimed that the IRA
was on the verge of open insurrection, and the police close to breaking-point.[56]
For once, his claims were not greatly exaggerated. The IRA's reviving confidence
was demonstrated by its mass defiance of the government's ban on attending
Bodenstown that month, and its chief of staff's belief that the authorities were
'undoubtedly losing their grip'.[57] Moreover, the discovery of sensitive documents the following month, demonstrating the IRA's decision to align itself
with revolutionary socialism by establishing a socialist front organization
known as Saor Éire, allowed O'Duffy to assert 'a concrete link' between the IRA
and communism. Given that O'Duffy had always believed that communism
was one of the guiding hands behind anti-treaty republicanism, his alarm at this
discovery was palpable: 'If the Soviet comrades are not dealt with more deter-
minedly at once the State will perish'. At the same time, the existence of a red
threat strengthened his demand for legislation which would remove republicans
from the protection of the constitution and allow him to crush the IRA.[58]

Influenced by political and security considerations, and a certain degree of
shared pessimism concerning the flawed character of the population, the government agreed to the request, arguing that the link between republicanism
and communism confirmed O'Duffy's prediction of imminent revolution.[59] A
government report drew on the exaggerated memoranda of the commissioner
and Special Branch to depict the IRA as a front for Soviet infiltration. This
impressively detailed report—which included the names of IRA men who
belonged to such dubious organizations as the Friends of Soviet Russia, outlined republican attempts to get support from the USSR, and identified republicans known to have visited Russia, attended Soviet-backed international
congresses, or enrolled in Moscow's Lenin College—presented a superficially
persuasive case. In reality, relatively few rank-and-file or leading republicans
admired communism, but the radicals among the leadership had capitalized on
the success of the anti-annuities campaign and the social unrest of the time to
win support for Saor Éire's socialist programme.[60]

Although the red scare of 1931 reflected genuine concerns, particularly in light of the well-publicized growth of anti-clerical socialism in Catholic republics such as Mexico and Spain, and the militant anti-communism of Pope Pius XI, O'Duffy and the government exaggerated the communist aspect of the threat to the state in order to win ecclesiastical approval for coercion.[61] While the hierarchy abhorred republican violence, it did not view it as a threat to Catholic morality as the IRA was not particularly anti-clerical, while Fianna Fáil and Sinn Féin were clericalist in outlook. The Catholic Church's reluctance to denounce the IRA also stemmed from the knowledge that their support for the treatyite régime in 1922 had permanently alienated many Catholics. As recently as 1929, Archbishop Byrne had refused a government appeal to condemn the murder of witnesses on the grounds that 'it would come badly from the Bishops'.[62]

The spectre of communism changed matters. In August 1931 Cosgrave wrote to Cardinal MacRory seeking a clandestine meeting to discuss 'a situation which threatens the whole fabric of both Church and State'. Forwarding a dossier on the conspiracy to the hierarchy which emphasized the threat to ecclesiastical as well as governmental authority, Cosgrave requested a pastoral in support of the government's stance.[63] In the meantime, O'Duffy and department of justice officials drafted a coercion bill to be introduced when the Dáil resumed on 14 October. The decision to rush the legislation through the Dáil heightened the atmosphere of crisis, as did the publication of the hierarchy's first joint pastoral since the Civil War. The bishops warned of 'a campaign of Revolution and Communism, which, if allowed to run its course unchecked, must end in the ruin of Ireland, both soul and body'.[64] Although its timing strengthened the credibility of the red scare, O'Duffy and the cabinet were disappointed by its content, which drew a distinction between the moral dangers posed by Saor Éire's 'blasphemous denial of God' and the lesser evils constituted by the IRA's unlawful violence.

Article 2A, as the Public Safety (1931) act became known, contained most of the measures which O'Duffy had demanded. The establishment of military tribunals with the power of the death penalty removed the weak links of judge and jury. The act allowed the government to proclaim organizations, censor propaganda, and intern subversives. Although heartened by the measure, O'Duffy demanded more powers to enforce the act in a disturbing memo which demonstrated his increasing extremism. He asked for the arming of all Garda station parties. He suggested doubling Special Branch's personnel, and deploying the force in self-contained heavily armed mobile units capable of an 'offensive campaign against an organization which refuses to take the field as an

Army'.[65] He recommended that Colonel Michael Hogan, a serving army officer, lead the reorganized force, which would recruit 'men who are, on the one hand efficient in the use of lethal weapons and who, on the other hand, would have their heart in such work'. (Having acquired a notorious reputation for torture in Kerry during the Civil War, Hogan would have met both criteria.)[66] Most disturbingly, O'Duffy urged the deployment of paramilitary units composed of army veterans and civilians in the most troubled areas: 'such local organisations would be a great asset to the recognized forces of the State, as they undoubtedly have been in Northern Ireland'. He also demanded a free hand to crush the IRA without regard to public criticism:

While I am prepared now, as I always was, to accept any responsibility however heavy, I could not bear this additional burden unless I can count on the absolute support of the Government, individually and collectively against all attacks whether from the enemies of the State or from some of its so-called backers . . . It may be said that these proposals are somewhat extreme. Their justification lies in the fact that the purpose is to deal with extremists—murder gangs—that these people are not entitled to the protection afforded by the Constitution'.[67]

The government did not assent to O'Duffy's proposals, which, at their most extreme, evoked images of death squads hunting down republicans in troubled areas like Leitrim and Clare. Such units might have proved effective, but would have done little for the stability of the state. Moreover, O'Duffy had only recently been given permission to increase Special Branch by 300 men and to arm all garda officers.[68] The executive council was only too aware of the need to keep its commissioner on a tight leash. A number of sensitive issues relating to the use of special powers—such as who could be brought before the Military Tribunal—remained under political rather than police control, and O'Duffy was warned that any 'unnecessary act of violence by the police or any unnecessary discourtesy will be visited with most severe punishment. The police now have ample powers within the law to deal with political crime.'[69]

Twelve republican and socialist organizations were banned when Article 2A was enacted on 20 October. (Sinn Féin, to the embarrassment of its ageing die-hards, was deemed unworthy of inclusion.) The fact that it was the IRA rather than communist organizations that bore the brunt of the crackdown provided further evidence of the opportunistic aspect of the red scare. In a narrow operational sense, Article 2A was effective. The IRA went to ground, some republicans fleeing the state, and political violence declined rapidly. In addition, clerical condemnation of Saor Éire marginalized the socialists within the IRA leadership.[70] Politically, however, the measure was regarded as a failure, one which almost certainly contributed to Cumann na nGaedheal's subsequent electoral defeat in 1932. After the air of panic surrounding Article 2A's implementation had subsided, its measures appeared heavy-handed and its very success added to public concerns about the government's authoritarianism.

Disillusionment and dejection

Security was not the only issue where serious tensions between O'Duffy and the government had arisen; indeed, co-operation on the red scare masked a serious deterioration in their relationship. From his earliest days as commissioner, O'Duffy had resented interference in his force by civil servants and cabinet ministers. Claiming that he had originally been offered full control over the force, he struggled to come to terms with the civil service's authority over financial expenditure, and often acted as if it did not exist.[71] As early as 1922 he had made the first of many threats to resign following a bitter row with the department of finance. While Kevin O'Higgins, who was never slow to let the commissioner know when he overstepped the mark, was at home affairs, the government had few difficulties keeping him in line, but FitzGerald-Kenney failed to restrain his excesses.

His annual report of 1929, which drew attention to unrest in the force resulting from cutbacks and complained about a lack of public support, provides one example. After it was officially suppressed, O'Duffy simply published the offending material in the *Garda Review*.[72] His response to the mounting criticism of the Garda was one of complacency, as was illustrated by his publication in 1929 of a triumphalist account of its establishment: 'There are times when in the quiet of the night I rest awhile in my office in the Depot and sense the smooth efficiency all around me and hear the rhythmic step of the faithful sentry outside my window. Then my mind wanders back over the years that have gone since then, and I am satisfied.'[73] This complacency was shared by the *Garda Review*, which attributed public criticism of the force to the theory that 'the more closely a social unit is brought to the enviable state of complete immunity from crime, the more leisure and liberty are its members afforded for finding fault with the methods by which its security and general well-being are maintained'.[74] In reality, relations between the police and the people had never been worse: 'There were no-go areas in a number of towns in Cork and Kerry— districts where the Guards could not enter and where their very appearance resulted in violence... The wheel had nearly come full circle since the first idealistic venture of the unarmed guard among the people ten years before.'[75]

By the end of the decade, the General's behaviour was verging on insubordination. He publicly stated his opposition to government decisions on staffing
and station levels. He backed the demands of the Garda representative bodies
for increased pay, and made no effort to restrain the *Garda Review*'s attacks on
the government.[76] He accused the state of treating the dependants of murdered
guards 'in a most heartless way, unprecedented in the history of any Police
Force'.[77] He harangued the government about its 'ingratitude and lack of
appreciation', warned of the 'disillusionment and dejection' in the force, and
endlessly reminded it that the loyalty of the police to the state was conditional
on its treatment.[78]

Against this background of growing unrest, the government would have
viewed O'Duffy's involvement in a new organization, the National Defence
Association (NDA), with alarm. The NDA was established in August 1929 with
the support of the recently resigned chief of staff, General Seán MacEoin, to
voice discontent within the National Army. Its membership included several
Dáil deputies, most serving and retired officers, and many senior gardaí, rendering it a potentially far greater threat than the 'IRA Organisation' of 1924.
O'Duffy's old crony, the mercurial Major-General Hugo MacNeill, was one of
the main movers behind the organization, leading the talks which persuaded the
minister for defence, Desmond FitzGerald, to sanction its establishment. By
1930 the NDA's powerful membership—which united both sections of the
security forces in common grievance against the government's cut-backs—and
belligerent rhetoric had prompted the government to order serving officers to
leave the organization. Fortunately for the government, the organization's inept
leadership, reflected by the misunderstandings between O'Duffy and MacEoin,
limited its threat. At one point, MacEoin warned O'Duffy that the government
intended to dismiss him as commissioner because of his membership, an allegation denied by the secretary of the department of justice. O'Duffy, in turn,
denied MacEoin's accusation that he had issued a warrant for his arrest.[79] The
NDA had dissolved itself by late 1930, but many of its members and grievances
would reappear in the form of the Army Comrades Association.[80]

Coup d'état

O'Duffy had used the NDA as 'an alternative means of applying pressure on
the Executive Council', allowing him to remind the government 'that his influence still spanned both arms of the state's defence forces'.[81] Given the events

which would soon follow, as Cumann na nGaedheal faced a general election
which it looked set to lose, it was a reminder which ought to have been taken
more seriously. It was during this period that relations between O'Duffy and
the government reached breaking-point. The trigger was the cabinet's decision
to reduce police pay as part of a remarkably ill-timed austerity budget in the
run-up to the election. When the minister for finance, Ernest Blythe, informed
him of this decision, O'Duffy refused to accept it. In a memo, which verged on
political blackmail, the General reminded Blythe that it was the support of 'the
local Sergeant, not the local clergy as in the past' which had swung previous
elections for Cumann na nGaedheal.[82] The General noted that his men had
considered themselves 'servants of the Government Party rather than of the
State' but, due to the government's ingratitude, this was no longer the case.
This candid admission illustrated the extent to which O'Duffy had fallen away
from the ideal—or, at least, rhetoric—of a non-political force. His attitude—
which was shared by senior officers, particularly in Special Branch, rather than
the rank and file—was an inevitable consequence of the politicization of the
police by its role in combating republican violence. The General, once the
strongest arm in the defence of the state, had become a loose cannon: it was
almost certainly in this period that the government decided to dismiss him if it
won re-election.[83]

However, O'Duffy's insubordination was not the most worrying aspect of
his behaviour during this critical period. Despite presenting a brave face to the
government, O'Duffy was deeply worried about the possible election of a party
which he regarded as the thin end of a republican wedge dedicated to the
destruction of the state which he had done so much to defend. His well-developed
instinct for self-preservation and loyalty to his men reinforced his concerns.
The opposition frequently complained about over-employment and excessive
rates of pay within the Garda. Seán T. O'Kelly, for example, spoke of tiny
villages policed by 'a sergeant and four or five men with nothing to do, simply
lolling about the roads and lying about the ditches half their time'.[84] Describing 'the general air of inactivity that prevails around a police barrack which is
disturbed only when the sergeant and one of his men play handball against the
gable end', Seán Lemass claimed that 'the Guards themselves will tell you that
they are killed with boredom.'[85] Underlying these criticisms was republican
resentment of police harassment. When elected, Seán MacEntee threatened,
his party would 'punish the responsible parties for their illegal acts'.[86] Fianna
Fáil politicians were careful to emphasize that they blamed O'Duffy and
Special Branch rather than the police in general and, as the election approached,
they grew even more circumspect, reassuring public servants that there would

be no reprisals. Nonetheless, the government was expected to disband Special Branch, and O'Duffy can have been under no illusions about his future under the new régime.

It was against this background that O'Duffy began to canvass support for a *coup d'état*. It is not difficult to see how he could rationalize such a move. He had little faith in the government, indeed numerous reasons to resent it, and he regarded the opposition as unfit for power. His reports revealed his lack of respect for the constitution, and an underlying belief that the public lacked the civic virtues necessary for democratic rule. In other words, Fianna Fáil's success was 'the last straw rather than the original cause of his disenchantment with the conventional political system'.[87] The conspiracy to overthrow the government— drawing together a shadowy alliance of disgruntled army officers, gardaí, and treatyite politicians—remains a murky affair. The evidence indicates a number of inept attempts to sound out support, rather than one abortive effort to over-throw the government, which failed due to the opposition of responsible figures who remained loyal to the state rather than the treatyite cause.

The crucial role in any coup would have been played by the army. Peadar McMahon, a senior officer and former chief of staff, reported Hugo MacNeill and several other officers to Ernest Blythe when he learned of their plans for a coup in late 1931. Blythe, in the presence of the chief of staff, Michael Brennan, summoned MacNeill to account for himself but did not dismiss him.[88] This appears to have had little effect. The following spring, shortly after Fianna Fáil's election, an appalled Richard Mulcahy was asked by MacNeill and Michael Hogan for his support in overthrowing the new government: 'I told Hugo not to be an ass. But that was the idea—casually there at the entry to a civil service Patrick's Day episode in the Mansion House.' The calibre of the conspirators may explain why insiders like Mulcahy dismissed the possibility of a coup: 'He would be talking like that and he wouldn't have any force behind him'.[89] O'Duffy was, nonetheless, a central figure in this inept conspiracy, which ulti-mately involved more wishful thinking and barrack-room bluster than serious planning. MacNeill, an Ulster man, was a less successful version of O'Duffy, sharing his flamboyant personality, alcoholism, irredentism, fascist sympathies, and loose grasp of political realities.

The main evidence for O'Duffy's involvement in these intrigues comes from David Neligan, the head of Special Branch, who claimed that in late 1931 the commissioner urged senior police and army officers to support a coup if Fianna Fáil won election. Michael Brennan, the chief of staff, reportedly responded by transferring several senior army officers of questionable loyalty from sensitive commands and warning O'Duffy that he would be arrested at the first sign of impropriety. One evening, several weeks before the election, Neligan alleged that O'Duffy showed him a proclamation declaring a military dictatorship under his authority which he had printed at the Ordnance Survey Office in the Phoenix Park:

O'Duffy indicated it with a gesture and said: 'Well Dave, what do you think? Neligan read it and quickly replied: 'You don't expect me to have anything to do with this?' and walked towards the door. O'Duffy followed him as Neligan went down the steps towards the front door of the mess and said: 'You know, Dave, 'you'll be the first one to go under de Valera'.[90]

Neligan claimed that he immediately reported this incident to the University College Cork historian, James Hogan, who drove to the depot where, after a long night of argument, he persuaded O'Duffy of the necessity of preserving the state's democratic institutions. Ten days later, Neligan was summoned to see Cosgrave, who demanded to know what O'Duffy was up to. Without denying the rumours, Neligan assured the president that everything was under control.[91]

The accuracy of Neligan's uncorroborated and possibly self-serving account has been questioned, while other security force sources have dismissed the rumours as hot air.[92] As with previous treatyite tilts against the state, the threat was probably more inept than insignificant. The idea of a coup enjoyed some political support. In 1930 an article in Cumann na nGaedheal's newspaper attributed to Ernest Blythe, the vice-president of the executive council, had speculated that 'It might happen that the Army would be bound to subdue a political people for the welfare of the people in general'.[93] The success of dictatorships elsewhere had led Blythe to question whether 'the gods of democracy have not feet of clay ... the franchise in the hands of an ignorant and foolish populace is a menace to any country'.[94] The following year Blythe's parliamentary secretary, James Burke, indiscreetly declared: 'Rather than that we should go down in futility ... I would say a hundred times, let us have a Dictatorship.'[95] Even moderate cabinet ministers such as Patrick McGilligan had considered the suspension of parliament during the autumn of 1931 in light of 'the Irregular and Bolshie situation'.[96] Although it is unlikely that Cosgrave seriously contemplated such measures, the government would have borne some responsibility had a coup occurred, given its decision to revive the red scare during the election campaign. Its sensational propaganda portrayed de Valera as a second Kerensky, while the minister for justice irresponsibly warned of a second Civil War if Fianna Fáil was elected. Ironically, such rhetoric would pave the way for a far greater threat to democracy than de Valera in the form of the Blueshirt movement.

Fianna Fáil in power

On 16 February 1932 Fianna Fáil narrowly won the general election. De Valera's election as president on 9 March confirmed many of O'Duffy's fears. The cabinet's first decision was to release all political prisoners. Article 2A was suspended, the ban on republican newspapers was lifted, and, by the end of the week, the IRA was no longer an illegal organization. Although *An Phoblacht* bayed for O'Duffy's dismissal, de Valera moved cautiously. There was certainly no love lost between both men. The last occasion they had spoken was when de Valera had screamed across a table a decade earlier, accusing him of mutiny, while O'Duffy held de Valera personally responsible for the Civil War. However, the president was in no position to sack his commissioner, given his promise that there would be no retribution against public servants, the untested loyalty of the security forces, and his reliance on the parliamentary support of the Labour Party, which had also guaranteed that there would be no political dismissals. Much to *An Phoblacht*'s disapproval, de Valera appointed James Geoghegan, a former Cumann na nGaedheal TD, as minister for justice in a deliberately conciliatory gesture.[97]

During this period of transition, rumours of a possible coup continued to circulate. They deserve to be taken seriously in light of O'Duffy's influence among those with reason to fear the new régime.[98] The uncertain atmosphere—illustrated by a pep talk by one Garda superintendent to his men two days after the formation of the new government—must also be kept in mind: 'You see how things are going. These [IRA] prisoners are after being let out and we may have a *coup d'état* or a military dictatorship or maybe in a few days no government at all, and it is up to every man to mind himself. There may be big changes in the guards. Some of us may not be kept on at all.'[99] What made O'Duffy a particularly dangerous figure was his position at the centre of an influential network of disgruntled treatyites bound together by their Civil War experiences, fear of retribution, and membership of fraternal organizations such as the NDA and a shadowy new body known as the Army Comrades Association. O'Duffy was, for example, a close friend of Hugo MacNeill, whose leadership of the NDA he had backed. Colonel Michael Hogan, another figure linked to the rumours was a brother of the UCC academic James and the government minister Paddy, and had been O'Duffy's choice as commander of his paramilitary Special Branch. It was fortunate for de Valera that O'Duffy's closest crony, Dan Hogan, had unexpectedly resigned his post as National Army chief of staff in 1929.[100]

Ultimately, it seems that O'Duffy considered the idea of a coup, identified potential supporters, but, and not for the last time in his career, pulled back from the brink, presumably due to lack of support. As O'Halpin noted: 'Whatever their fears...the prospect of forcibly putting O'Duffy in charge of the nation's destinies cannot have been very attractive for anyone with previous experience of his distinctive and capricious style of command.'[101] Internationally, the transition of power from the victors of a Civil War to the vanquished within a decade was regarded as a remarkable achievement, one which historians have attributed to the strength of democratic values among both sides. These values were not shared by O'Duffy, whose actions indicated an alternative course the state could have taken, one which proved the rule more than the exception throughout most of inter-war Europe. De Valera's election marked the consolidation of democracy in southern Ireland and the final phase of the Irish revolution. If O'Duffy aspired to dictatorship, he had missed an opportune moment. For the time being, however, he remained close to the centre of power.

Removal

Nonetheless, it was hardly business as usual at the depot. IRA membership was no longer an offence, while republicans who committed crimes could only be prosecuted with the unlikely approval of the attorney-general, a political appointee. Fianna Fáil's victory led to a sharp rise in IRA recruitment and activism but also, for reasons of pragmatism, a decline in violence against the state. Republican agitation was now directed at the Cumann na nGaedheal 'traitors' rather than the forces of the state: Richard Mulcahy's public meeting in Dublin was broken up by a barrage of sticks and bottles, as the police looked on without interfering.[102] The government's response to the opposition's complaint that such attacks represented a denial of free speech was ambivalent, de Valera observing that it was not the government's duty to make the opposition popular. As a minority government elected with IRA support, Fianna Fáil could not afford to alienate its republican base. Instead, de Valera hoped to wean the IRA from violence through an ambitious policy of reform and conciliation. The alternative, he argued, was a return to the counter-productive era of coercion. Such logic afforded little comfort to those being attacked on the streets, and it was partly in response to the policing vacuum which was allowed to develop that the Army Comrades Association (ACA) emerged.[103]

De Valera's conciliatory policy placed the gardaí, many of whom feared for their future, under immense strain. Their powerlessness in the face of IRA agitation sapped morale. After the election, some guards were approached by republicans with instructions on how policing should now be conducted. The gardaí in Listowel were ordered to pack their bags before their anticipated republican replacements arrived. Others were jostled off the footpath and spat on. Nor were the official signals encouraging: de Valera snubbed a police guard of honour in Skibbereen, crossing the road to receive the salute from the local IRA.[104] Superficially, the relationship between O'Duffy and the new government appeared cordial. Geoghegan was featured on the cover of *Garda Review*, and welcomed on his first visit to the depot. In reality, though, the government was gradually but purposefully moving to emasculate Special Branch and isolate O'Duffy. In April, Geoghegan disbanded an armed unit in line with the government's decision that Special Branch be 'greatly reduced'.[105] An ominously heavy-weight committee, consisting of de Valera, MacEntee (finance), Geoghegan, and Aiken (defence), was formed to consider the division of functions between the police and army, the future of Special Branch, and the general direction and control of the Garda.[106]

The pressures of managing a declining Special Branch in the face of growing republican agitation began to tell. In June O'Duffy complained to Geoghegan about the widespread drilling throughout the country and *An Phoblacht*'s persistent campaign of vilification against Special Branch. He told Geoghegan that his officers had requested unambiguous instructions on how to deal with the IRA, and that he proposed to order them to arrest republicans who openly broke the law, a move which 'will certainly lead to an increased campaign against the Commissioner and the Detective Branch, if not to something more serious'. Moving on to even more sensitive territory, O'Duffy complained about the IRA's efforts to persuade Fianna Fáil *cumainn* to pass resolutions calling for the disbandment of Special Branch:

I submit, Sir, it is the duty of the Government to protect the members of the Detective Branch who were prepared, and who are still prepared to risk even life itself so that the Government writ may run. These decent, self-respecting members (the majority of the Detective Branch are Pioneers of the Total Abstinence Association) have their feelings like all of us. Many of them have wives, and families, which they are trying to bring up respectably, and it is painful to recall the recent incident in Leitrim where the young wife (only a few months married) of a D.O. was subjected to the treatment, by a large body of *men* (?) which I have already reported. Again the *great majority* of the members of the Detective Branch were admitted thereto because of their service in the Volunteer movement.[107]

O'Duffy was requesting an end to the policy of ambiguity, a return to law and order, and, inevitably, coercion. The cabinet was unlikely to have been swayed by O'Duffy's emotional appeal on behalf of the most despised element within the former régime, but his reasonable request had to be handled carefully. Concerned that the resolutions from party *cumainn* might compel the government to declare its policy on Special Branch, Geoghegan suggested that an inquiry into its past misdeeds might allay the growing clamour.[108]

It was during this period that an eruption of violence in west Clare offered the government a pretext to move against Special Branch.[109] On 15 August, following a period of renewed IRA militancy which appeared to meet with the tacit approval of the local government deputies, two IRA men, T. J. Ryan and George Gilmore, were shot by two Special Branch officers in the town of Kilrush. Detectives Muldowney and Carroll brought their prisoners to hospital after first charging them with attempted murder. Two days later, the charges were dropped by the state and the detectives suspended pending a public inquiry. The subsequent inquiry did not reflect well on either side, but was particularly damning for the police. Although the Special Branch officers claimed that they had shot Gilmore and Ryan in self-defence after being fired on by a large crowd, the inquiry found that the officers had shot the republicans without provocation, framed them for attempted murder, pistol-whipped them in their hospital beds, and lied to their superiors.[110] To the disgust of Special Branch, Muldowney and Carroll were dismissed.

Kilrush had two important consequences. By exposing the fact that its officers were effectively out of control, it allowed de Valera to move against Special Branch. The barrister who presided over the inquiry privately informed Geoghegan that Special Branch was 'in a very anomalous position. They have no written or printed rules to guide them or regulate discipline'. He felt its officers were 'the victims of circumstances, of a system established without proper safeguards for discipline and conduct'.[111] Geoghegan told the cabinet that he had not informed O'Duffy of these findings but pointedly observed that the commissioner had insisted that 'the Branch has been organised in no loose or haphazard fashion, either from the point of view of discipline or efficiency'.[112] The government swiftly announced its intention to reorganize and reduce the force.

The second consequence was to provide the government with its first scalp among the police leadership. In early November O'Duffy authorized David Neligan, the head of Special Branch who had been infuriated by the dismissals, to organize a collection for the sacked detectives. When Geoghegan learned of this, he immediately suspended Neligan and summoned O'Duffy before the executive council to explain his actions. O'Duffy claimed that he had seen no reason to prohibit the collection which was 'not unusual in other services'. The cabinet formed another heavyweight committee to consider this explanation. Shortly before Christmas, he was informed that his action would be recorded as 'a grave indiscretion'.[113]

The noose was tightening but, as his letter to the department of justice demonstrated, O'Duffy had no intention of going without a fight:

For the past ten years I have worked from 14 to 18 hours every day of the week in building up a Police establishment for this country under most difficult and trying circumstances. I believe no other man in Saorstat Eireann to-day has laboured more zealously or more conscientiously since I accepted a position which I never sought, and I trust that your minute ... does not indicate lack of appreciation ... I would wish to feel that my work was fully appreciated by the members of the Government individually and collectively.[114]

Neligan was exiled to a well-paid sinecure in the Land Commission for the next thirty years, where he claimed never to have learned 'what he was supposed to be doing in an office all to himself'. Some officers urged a mass resignation but O'Duffy cautioned that such a protest would simply free up hundreds of positions for Fianna Fáil supporters.[115] In the meantime, Inspector Edward O'Connell inherited the poisoned chalice that was the day-to-day running of Special Branch, under the authority of Chief Superintendent Ned Broy, who had won favour with the new government. Broy, like Neligan, had been one of Collins's most important Dublin Castle informers during the War of Independence. Unlike Neligan, he found it less difficult to repeat the process of accommodating himself to serving his former enemies.

In January 1933 de Valera, buoyed by the success of his first year in office, called a snap election which returned him to power with an overall majority. After Geoghegan congratulated his commissioner for the Garda's conduct during the election, a particularly stormy one due to street-fighting between the ACA and IRA, O'Duffy cannily requested a letter of appreciation for publication in the *Garda Review*:

I do not think any Government can boast of a more loyal police force than ours. Although I may not get credit for it always, it has been my aim and ambition to organise and maintain for the State a police force the members of which would consider no sacrifice too great in the honest and fearless execution of their duty as interpreted by the Government chosen by the people. How far I have succeeded in this is not for me to say. All I will say is that I am becoming every day prouder of the Garda Siochana and I do not regret my own labour and self sacrifice ...[116]

The letter's craven tone suggests that, despite his earlier intrigues, O'Duffy would have been willing to subordinate principle to ambition in the service of the government. However, he was not to be allowed the opportunity as de Valera was no longer reliant on Labour's parliamentary support. Significantly, his only change to his new cabinet was to replace Geoghegan with P. J. Ruttledge, a republican hardliner whose IRA sympathies were well known.

On 19 February Inspector O'Connell, the acting head of Special Branch, and Colonel Michael Hogan were arrested in dramatic midnight raids under the Official Secrets act. As both men languished in Mountjoy Jail, rumours of a foiled coup swept the city. The reality was more mundane, but significant in terms of O'Duffy's loosening grip on power. In 1930 O'Duffy had been asked by the government for his opinion as to whether it should publish a number of documents on communism. Special Branch—concerned about exposing the identity of its agents—advised against, but many of the documents found their way into the dodgy dossier which the government subsequently compiled for the hierarchy. Two years later, when Professor James Hogan approached Neligan for some 'dope' on communism for a lurid exposé of the IRA that he was writing, Neligan began passing him bundles of these files from the registry. Following Neligan's suspension, O'Connell had naïvely continued the arrangement, forwarding the documents to the professor's brother, Colonel Michael Hogan. When Broy stumbled upon this arrangement, he moved swiftly, ordering the searching of Neligan's house and the immediate arrest of O'Connell and Hogan.[117]

The casual distribution of sensitive documents was clearly unprofessional, but it was evident that Broy, encouraged by the cabinet, had made the most of it. O'Connell, a diligent apolitical officer, and Hogan, a more partisan figure, were subsequently found not guilty of breaching the Official Secrets Act in a rather farcical trial (one highlight was O'Connell's questioning of the need for his midnight arrest, given that he could have been taken into custody when he arrived at Special Branch headquarters as he did every morning).[118] However, the government had reason to be concerned about some of the individuals involved—Colonel Hogan had been involved in the *coup d'état* intrigues of the previous year—and the disturbingly informal co-operation between its security forces and treatyite propagandists.[119] The arrests were also a means of exacting revenge on some of those responsible for the 1931 red scare which had also attempted to smear Fianna Fáil. The drama also provided a pretext to move against O'Duffy. Reviewing the trial transcripts some time later, the attorney-general was most interested in the fact that Neligan had claimed that he had been authorized to distribute the files by O'Duffy: 'the question to be considered is, whether the blame for what happened does not rest on the Commissioner rather than on Colonel Neligan'.[120]

At 3 p.m. on 22 February, three days after the arrest of O'Connell and Hogan, O'Duffy was summoned to de Valera's office. Patrick Ruttledge was also present. The president bluntly told O'Duffy that he had made an irrevocable decision to remove him from his post. O'Duffy, shocked, mentioned his successful handling of the Eucharistic Congress and the general election, demanding to know what offence he had committed. De Valera told him that there was no charge but that owing to the duties the police would soon be called to perform his position would become a difficult one. He pressed him to accept an alternative post at the same generous salary, suggesting a position as director of natural resources. O'Duffy refused, returning to the depot to put his papers in order.[121] Later that night, at around 10 p.m., he was summoned back to de Valera's office. Dressed in plain clothes, O'Duffy must have presented a forlorn sight as he trudged through the empty streets amidst a heavy snowfall. He later described the meeting to his acolyte Liam Walsh:

Looking far from happy the President and again Mr Ruttledge met him in the former's room, but as he noticed and remarked at the time they looked sincere. A long talk ensued; for over an hour Mr de Valera endeavoured to persuade O'Duffy to accept an alternative post—his youth, the desirability, what he (de Valera) would do in a similar position, his unquestionable ability as an organiser . . . O'Duffy sat and listened, not being helpful one might say. He could remain aggravatingly silent, reserved and cold, and not in any way encouraging one to talk, as I found out so often myself. Eventually he was asked to name a position himself.[122]

The General refused to accept an alternative position. His career as a public servant was over.

O'Duffy's removal provoked consternation and jubilation. He was widely regarded as having performed efficiently since 1932, particularly during the recent election. While the government had not suggested any link between the arrests of O'Connell and Hogan and O'Duffy's dismissal, its timing suggested as much.[123] Although many people believed that the General had been ruthlessly sacrificed to appease the IRA, there was more to his dismissal than retribution. De Valera chose not to play to the republican gallery. He offered the commissioner alternative employment, was restrained in his criticism of him, and faced down his own party to award him a generous pension.[124]

His removal was harsh but hardly unjustified or inexplicable. Always a man of great strengths and weaknesses, the longer his tenure the more the scale had tipped towards the latter. Given his neurotic behaviour, flawed political judgement, obsession with communism, rumoured involvement in a coup, and the problems within Special Branch, de Valera's decision seems justified. His removal was also in the broader public interest. O'Duffy had been commissioner since the foundation of the state, a lengthy tenure in comparison to the three-year terms served by army chiefs of staff. Indeed, one reason why he had not been fired earlier by either government was the unhealthy degree of power which he had accumulated. Ultimately, however, it was the broader political context that explained his removal. The claim that O'Duffy was sacrificed to militant republicanism misses the fact that his dismissal was necessary to allow de Valera to tackle political radicalism on both sides. De Valera had understandable concerns about Special Branch's appetite for suppressing the militantly treatyite ACA, while the IRA presented an even greater challenge. Given the growing public and police disquiet over the policy of conciliation, the government had reached the point where it had to win over or repress the remaining IRA die-hards: neither option was politically viable with O'Duffy as commissioner.

In a single afternoon O'Duffy had lost his job, home, car, driver, personal staff, and a public role which had meant everything to him for over a decade. It was the greatest setback of his life, and one from which he would never fully recover. His performance as commissioner was controversial, but his inspirational efforts in the early years deserve some recognition alongside the later shortcomings. O'Duffy rightly regarded this period as the most successful of his life. Just over a decade of failure later, as he lay slowly dying from alcoholism, heart disease, and disillusionment, Liam Walsh poignantly noted that it was only then that he realized how much O'Duffy had 'loved every moment spent with the Garda Siochana. He never seemed to tire, even far into the night . . . of telling me some of his experiences, pleasures and trials, joys and sufferings, as Commissioner.'[125]

The personal toll exacted by the job—reflected by his striking physical decline—should not be overlooked. O'Duffy was a wiry, energetic, and youthful figure in 1922. A decade of seven-day working weeks, stress, disillusionment, and—in the latter years—chain-smoking and serious drinking had transformed him into an overweight and prematurely aged man with his best years behind him. The decline was not merely physical, as one of his officers noted: 'Physically and mentally, his energy seemed inexhaustible. But time wears down the most energetic, and by the time he vacated office, he was, at least mentally, a spent force.'[126] On the other hand, he had at least mellowed, the pompous formality of the early years softened by an 'approachable and even genial' demeanour.[127]

O'Duffy, one of the great hate figures of Irish republicanism, has been widely criticized for his illiberal tenure as commissioner but it seems only fair to note that he had been set an impossible task by the treatyite government, and that his men had struggled against a real threat to law and order and democracy itself. He had behaved in an unacceptably heavy-handed manner, occasionally dirtying his hands more than the government would have liked, but he had essentially done its bidding. De Valera, when he later deemed it necessary, would treat republicans with similar ruthlessness. Having become disillusioned by service under Cumann na nGaedheal, O'Duffy left office disgusted by his victimization by Fianna Fáil and the hypocrisy and corruption of politics. His reports during his final years as commissioner had revealed an authoritarian contempt for constitutional rights and liberal democracy. He was a much less mentally stable and competent figure than the ambitious and idealistic young man who had resigned his Dáil seat a decade earlier. All in all, then, it was not the ideal apprenticeship for the next step of his career: a return to politics as the saviour of the treatyite cause.

8

The Irish Mussolini

As sure as we are here we shall be Masters of Ireland in three years. We do not want party politics and politicians; we want a disciplined and well governed country. This evolution is inevitable.[1]

D E VALERA's dramatic move placed O'Duffy at the centre of an intense political storm. The opposition depicted it as 'the most sinister and alarming occurrence' since his election, and further evidence of the success of the subversive forces behind de Valera's rise to power: 'The Government's surrender to the Irish "Reds" on this matter will bring joy to the hearts of their Communist masters in Moscow, for it is an essential part of the Bolshevik revolutionary technique'.[2] Privately, Cosgrave was more concerned that it would mark the beginning of a purge of the civil service and security forces, a fear shared by a broad spectrum of non-republican political opinion. The *Irish Times* regarded it as a serious assault on the integrity of the state: 'If a public servant is liable to lose his office at the desire of a minority, it is time that President de Valera should abandon his pretence of democracy.'[3] The *Connacht Tribune* suggested that O'Duffy 'has been the victim of unworthy clamour finding a repercussion in high places.'[4] The *Southern Star* described his dismissal as both 'a stupid blunder and an unpardonable crime', while the influential Irish Ireland journal *The Leader* predicted that de Valera's dictatorial behaviour had brought his successor into the political arena.[5]

O'Duffy's dismissal was debated in the Dáil on 14 March, when Cumann na nGaedheal moved a resolution condemning the government's action. The former commissioner's shortcomings were forgotten as opposition deputies lined up to sing his praises. W. T. Cosgrave described his services to the police, army, Irish language, athletics, and Catholicism, quoting from the Holy Father's address to O'Duffy for good measure.[6] Dr O'Higgins described O'Duffy as 'the best Commissioner in the whole world'.[7] FitzGerald-Kenney enquired: 'What living man has served the State better?'[8] Noting that his successor, Broy, had been appointed above more senior officers, Cosgrave declared that no one was safe from de Valera's politicization of the state. Underlying the vehemence of this response was the memory of the Civil War and the fear of retribution. As Desmond FitzGerald put it: 'General O'Duffy, the greatest Irishman this generation could produce, was dismissed from his post because he was not persona grata with the gun bullies and Communists. The decent people of this country were only sheep to be driven as they had been in 1922.'[9]

The Labour Party also criticized the government for removing O'Duffy without producing any evidence of wrong-doing. Praising his role during 'the dark days from 1917 to 1921', William Norton believed nothing should 'besmirch the name or reputation of one who, in other days, rendered to this nation services which ought always entitle him to the gratitude of the Irish nation.'[10] Even Fianna Fáil's former justice minister, James Geoghegan—despite insisting on the government's right to appoint whoever they regarded as the best candidate and pointing out the dangers of such a powerful position being regarded as a position for life—appeared ambivalent, conceding that O'Duffy 'was a competent and able man, so far as I could judge in 1932'.[11] Interestingly, the *United Irishman* noted: 'We do not think there has ever been a parallel to the atmosphere which prevailed during the time when Mr. Geoghegan, the ex-Minister for Justice was speaking . . . it was plain to be seen that his Party were on tenterhooks, fearful for what he might say next . . . When the ex-Minister for Justice finished his half-hearted washing of hands an almost perceptible sigh of relief passed over the ranks of Fianna Fáil.'[12] In contrast, a more bullish de Valera insisted that O'Duffy had been dismissed because of his record of condoning police indiscipline: 'We want a chief of police of whom no section of the community can say that man is deliberately and politically opposed to us, and is likely to be biased in his attitude because of past political affiliations.'[13]

O'Duffy remained uncharacteristically quiet throughout the furore. He moved out of the depot into a city-centre flat in early March, but remained silent except to issue a statement protesting his impartial record. He postponed making any decisions on his future until his return from a holiday.[14] In early April he departed on a cruise to the Middle East. He sailed from England to Port Said, via Gibraltar, arriving in Egypt for the religious ceremonies on Good Friday. He continued overland to Alexandria, where he observed the Greek Orthodox Church services on Easter Sunday. He travelled on to Cairo, staying with a former colleague on the Egyptian police force, before touring Jerusalem, the Holy Lands, Jordan, and Cyprus. He returned to Europe the following month, travelling through Trieste, Venice, and Paris, where he spent a week, before arriving home on 15 May.[15]

The rise of Irish fascism

Within weeks of his return, O'Duffy's decision to lead the Blueshirt movement would make him the central figure in the most turbulent period of the Irish Free State's history. The Blueshirts originated in the Army Comrades Association (ACA), formed by Colonel Austin Brennan and Commandant Ned Cronin in February 1932. Its initial aims of upholding the state and honouring War of Independence Volunteers appeared uncontroversial, although the fact that it originated from a more secretive organization founded after the murder of Superintendent Curtin in 1931 suggested a more partisan agenda.[16] In contrast to the National Defence Association, it was open only to retired soldiers. In August 1932 Brennan was replaced by Dr T. F. O'Higgins, a Cumann na nGaedheal deputy and brother of the assassinated minister for justice. He was accompanied by an influx of treatyite politicians, including Richard Mulcahy, Seán MacEoin, and Ernest Blythe, a trend which reflected growing concerns about de Valera's agenda. Many treatyites feared discrimination in public service appointments and state patronage (an understandable concern given their own previous discrimination against republicans). It was also believed that Fianna Fáil's commitment to protectionism and land redistribution would undermine the export-oriented farming and business interests represented by Cumann na nGaedheal, another well-founded fear. The government's retention of land annuity payments to Britain in June 1932 triggered an economic war with disastrous consequences for cattle farmers. De Valera's efforts to impose his authority over the police and military, combined with his conciliation of an unrepentant IRA, also heightened treatyite insecurity.[17] These fears, reinforced by the Civil War's legacy of hatred, provided the context for the emergence of the Blueshirts.

During O'Duffy's final year as commissioner, the opposition had depicted de Valera as an Irish Kerensky, who would pave the way for the triumph of extremism. In October 1932 the Cumann na nGaedheal newspaper, *United Irishman*, had warned: 'Communism is coming and unless the people want it foisted on them they will have to take steps to defeat it.'[18] Fianna Fáil's policies were described as 'half-baked Bolshevism', 'Trotskyism', and 'State Socialism', while dramatic headlines warned of 'THE MENACE OF CIVIL WAR . . . A

BOLSHEVIK GOVERNMENT NEXT'.[19] Cumann na nGaedheal even
presented the government's modest land redistribution bill as the 'first step in
an Irish anti-Kulak campaign'.[20] To what extent such rhetoric represented
political opportunism rather than genuine fear is not clear. The sheer volume
of anti-communist rhetoric in the treatyite press and private correspondence of
politicians suggests that they took the threat seriously, as did the influential
farming interests which stood to lose if Fianna Fáil implemented its radical
programme of land redistribution.[21] However, the 1933 election results demonstrated that these fears were not widely shared. After a year of mild reform,
voters were unimpressed by opposition posters warning that 'Your Country,
Your Family, Your Livelihood, Your Title to your Holding, all you possess or
Hold Dear, stand at this moment in DEADLY PERIL.'

However, Cumann na nGaedheal's extremist rhetoric had important
consequences which help to explain why the party would turn to O'Duffy as its
saviour in 1933. First, it deepened concern about the rise of communism and,
more realistically, the IRA. In mid-April 1933, as O'Duffy contemplated his
future from the Middle East, the *United Irishman* reported that anti-communist
riots were 'almost nightly events last week. It seems that disorder is to become
the rule of life in Ireland.'[22] Second, treatyite propaganda created a climate in
which the government's legitimacy was called into question. In August 1932,
for example, the *United Irishman* claimed that de Valera was encouraging the
IRA's revival in order to establish a dictatorship.[23] Readers were constantly
reminded of 'the blind unceasing hatred which burns in this man's breast
against all, whether living or dead, who opposed his attempt to strangle the
new-born Irish State in 1922'.[24] Fianna Fáil's electoral victory in 1933 was
credited to the unscrupulous nature of its campaign, its mass bribery of the
poor through policies of cheap food and subsidies, and its electoral personation
and intimidation.[25] Months after the election, the *United Irishman* continued
to complain that

the Government have not a record of respect for the national will or for the democratic
rights of the people. They tried to fight themselves into power in 1922 and 1923; they
deliberately lied themselves into power in 1932; they kept themselves in power in 1933
by a judicious mixture of misrepresentation and impersonation. Now they are preparing
to prolong their disastrous tenure of office by shameless vote-stealing aided by
organised terrorism.[26]

There were clear parallels between such rhetoric and the political discourse
of other failing democracies. In Spain, for example, the election of a republican
government which challenged the vested interests of the establishment

provoked similar attempts to undermine the legitimacy of the new régime. Indeed, treatyite propagandists often compared both régimes. In Spain, as in Ireland, these criticisms served to justify the anti-democratic rhetoric of the electoral losers. In both countries, the new governments had reason to suspect the loyalty of the police and army. Another worrying similarity with continental politics was the rise of private armies, and the conservative right's willingness to form alliances with such groups for the purpose of self-preservation. From the summer of 1932, Cumann na nGaedheal looked to the ACA as the guardians of 'the people and every threat to their freedom, whether it takes the form of mob-rule, Communist tyranny, or a Valerian dictatorship'.[27] Opening its membership to the public, the ACA took on a new, more politicized, role protecting opposition meetings from the IRA.

Its first test of strength occurred in October 1932, when a meeting in Kilmallock came under attack from hundreds of hurley-wielding republicans. With the gardaí unable to maintain control, some fifty Blueshirts under the command of Ned Cronin rushed to their assistance. A pitched battle ensued, broken up by Cronin's shots over the heads of the crowd.[28] A triumphant report in Cumann na nGaedheal's newspaper noted that 'Patriotic citizens no longer feel that the country is drifting into an abyss of Balkanisation or Mexicanism'.[29] Its belligerent columnist, 'Onlooker', predicted that democracy would be preserved 'only by the strong hands and stout sticks of the citizens enrolled in the ACA'.[30] After Kilmallock, the *United Irishman* took to describing the ACA as the 'the hope of the future' and 'the greatest regenerative force in the political life of the country'.[31] It declared that the movement would change 'the tenor of Irish political thought as profoundly as it was changed by the Young Irelanders or the Gaelic League' by making 'the spirit of discipline and perseverance pervade our whole national life'.[32]

Such fascistic rhetoric became increasingly commonplace, an influence confirmed by the ACA's decision to adopt the blue shirt and raised arm salute. Although denied when necessary, admiration for fascism was barely concealed in treatyite propaganda. The adoption of the shirt, for example, was described in unambiguously militant terms: 'It obliges members of the Youth Movement to have the courage of their convictions and it will keep out wobblers and faint-hearts who might corrupt their comrades. It exposes members not only to the verbal or economic attack of the enemies of the movement, but also ... to physical attack ... The blue shirt, therefore, spells the end of laissez faire and all the shibboleths of liberalism.'[33]

Before turning to O'Duffy's emergence as leader of the Blueshirts in July 1933, it is important to consider how the movement's fascist traits pre-dated his arrival. Although the ACA's extremists were not representative of the opposition as a whole, they formed a vocal minority who persuaded O'Duffy to lead their movement and subsequently backed his leadership of Fine Gael. Foremost among this group was Ernest Blythe, the Presbyterian Ulster *gaelgoir* with a penchant for rhetorical extremism. Although it has been argued that Blythe's political vision derived more from the papal encyclicals than fascism, close analysis of his writings suggests otherwise.[34] Under the pseudonym 'M. G. Quinn', Blythe urged replacing parliamentary democracy with 'a diast' involving 'a drastic limitation of the powers of parliament, and the creation of a voluntary disciplined public-service organisation, with fifty thousand to a hundred thousand members' to stand between the electorate and government: 'demagogic agitation and mob auctioneering will cease and Government will be conducted on non-party lines'. The unemployed would be put to work in labour units, strikes banned, 'corruptionists and mountebanks' excluded from politics, 'discordant political propaganda' permitted only 'within narrow limits', and a spirit of discipline would pervade the nation.[35] Writing under the pseudonym 'Onlooker' in the *United Irishman*, Blythe promoted his ideas in a more crude fashion. The role of youth was endlessly eulogized, the raised hand salute was encouraged, and the ACA depicted as the saviour of the state.[36] Complaining that 'all parliaments gabble too much', 'Onlooker' contrasted the ineffectiveness of politicians with Blueshirts, who relied 'not on persuasion but on combat'.[37]

The most ideologically committed fascist within the Blueshirt leadership was Thomas Gunning, a sinister figure who would come to exercise considerable influence on O'Duffy. Born in rural Roscommon, Gunning, the son of an RIC man, was educated at a junior diocesan seminary in Ballaghaderreen, Co. Roscommon. He trained as a seminarian in Fribourg, where his admiration for fascism may have originated, before turning to a career in journalism, writing for the *Irish Independent* and editing the *Catholic Standard*. He became O'Duffy's personal secretary and publicity agent (or, in contemporary terms, spin doctor) in October 1933, and remained his close political adviser until they later fell out in Spain.[38] Gunning's ideological strengths were recognized by an Italian official in Ireland who described him as 'an expert fascist, well versed in the doctrines and practices of corporatism'. O'Duffy, in contrast, was dismissed as a 'second rater'.[39]

Two prominent academics, James Hogan and Michael Tierney, were also central to the promotion of authoritarian ideas within the Blueshirts. Hogan, a professor of history at University College Cork, who had served under O'Duffy in the Civil War, was an outspoken opponent of republicanism and socialism. Like Tierney, a classics professor at University College Dublin, he joined the ACA in its early days. Both men shared an authoritarian outlook characterized by strident anti-communism and a belief that liberal democracy was inadequate to the challenges of modern society. Although Tierney and Hogan advocated the curtailment of parliamentary democracy, neither embraced the principle of dictatorship. They proposed instead a corporate state, similar to that which existed in Italy, but influenced more by the teachings of Pius XI's recent encyclical *Quadragesimo Anno* than Mussolini's fascism. Like Blythe, they envisaged the Blueshirts playing a central role in the corporate state. Both men acknowledged the ideological influence of fascism, but looked to the authoritarian régime of Engelbert Dollfuss (which had suspended parliamentary democracy) in Austria rather than Nazism as a political model.[40] Their outlook was typical of many right-wing Catholic intellectuals in inter-war Europe.[41]

Hogan and Tierney's influence extended beyond the Blueshirt movement. Both contributed articles to intellectual Catholic periodicals such as *Studies* and cruder fare to newspapers such as *United Ireland*. Hogan was the author of *Could Ireland Become Communist?*, a populist exposé of communism in the IRA. Their academic credentials, the lack of alternative political ideas within Cumann na nGaedheal, as well as their family and social background made them influential figures within treatyite circles. Tierney, a former Cumann na nGaedheal TD, was a son-in-law of Eoin MacNeill. Hogan also belonged to a wealthy and well-connected family. One of his brothers, Patrick, had been Cumann na nGaedheal's minister for agriculture, while another, Michael, was the senior army officer arrested for passing on state documents to James Hogan. In other words, they were highly placed members of the conservative élite which had run the state for the last decade.

The reactionary agenda pioneered by these ideologues won the support of treatyites such as the former cabinet minister and University College Dublin professor John Marcus O'Sullivan. It met with the approval of a wide circle of intellectual priests, including Fr Edward Cahill and Fr Edward Coyne. Reactionary Catholicism was a more important ideological influence than was fascism in 1930s Ireland, even if the distinction was often difficult to discern.[42] Another example of the radicalization of the treatyite élite is provided by Desmond FitzGerald. The former minister was close to Kevin O'Higgins in the 1920s, but his élitist, artistic, and intellectual inclinations had limited his political influence. (During the Civil War, O'Duffy had complained to Collins that FitzGerald acted as if 'there was a lot of the "mob" about the people of Ireland'.)[43] Although described as a champion of Catholic social teaching and a defender of the democratic role of the Blueshirts, his writings indicate that his political views lay significantly further to the right.[44] Like many of his colleagues, FitzGerald had become disillusioned with parliamentary democracy since de Valera's election.[45] Following the 1933 election, he warned the French Thomist philosopher Jacques Maritain that 'the country may go Bolshevist'.[46] His pessimism was underpinned by his belief that state intervention, by raising public expectations which the state could not meet, would inexorably lead to communism.[47] He was one of a circle of intellectuals interested in formulating what the poet W. B. Yeats described as a 'philosophy of action' based on 'fascism modified by religion'.[48] Despite his dislike of totalitarianism, FitzGerald had, like many Catholic intellectuals, come to regard fascism as a necessary bulwark against communism, and was one of a number of TDs who would embarrass Cosgrave by wearing his blue shirt in parliament.[49] While incapable of practical application, his ideas illustrate the deeply reactionary and pessimistic thinking among the treatyite élite.

The extremist ideas of these figures were not representative of the opposition, but recent events had created an opening for them. The disillusionment arising from two electoral defeats within twelve months to a party which it regarded as uncommitted to democratic values, unchecked IRA violence, the disruption of the economic war, and the lack of any obvious alternative allowed the treatyite right to seize the initiative. As in many other European countries in this period, the atmosphere of crisis which had characterized the final years of the treatyite government provided the ideal backdrop for the rise of right-wing extremism: even ministers such as Patrick McGilligan who showed little interest in fascism or the Blueshirts had felt that 'the Irregular and Bolshie situation' might require the suspension of parliament and rule by governmental decree in 1931.[50] In Ireland, as elsewhere in Europe, the principal threat to democracy came not from the left but from the opposing alliance formed by traditional conservatives and the radical right.[51] All that was missing was 'another Collins' to lead the way.[52] It was at this propitious moment that the uncharismatic T. F. O'Higgins announced that he was no longer willing to lead the ACA.

Director General of the National Guard

O'Duffy, who had come to personify the vindictiveness of de Valera's régime, was the obvious choice to replace O'Higgins. In contrast to many of the treatyite élite, he had an exemplary national record. He was a dynamic and charismatic figure with proven organizational abilities. He was identified with the treatyite tradition but not tainted by its failures, an important point for both the fascistic and corporatist elements within the ACA who wished to establish a new form of politics rather than simply restore Cumann na nGaedheal to power. Within days of his return to Ireland in mid-May, Blythe had urged O'Duffy to lead the Blueshirts. During the next weeks, most of the ACA's leadership, including O'Higgins, Tierney, and Cronin, followed suit.[53]

Although in need of a new public role, O'Duffy hesitated before acceding to these flattering appeals. Liam Walsh claimed that it was because he was reluctant to become drawn into the world of politics of which he had such a low opinion.[54] There was some truth to this—even if O'Duffy would subsequently milk the reluctant leader pose for all it was worth—but his hesitation was also based on his awareness of the competing agendas within the movement:

> I met some of the heads of the ACA one night to talk things over with them...A conversation started on what the work of the National Guard would be and I sat back and listened. There was a long argument between Dr O'Higgins and Mr Gunning from which it was evident to me that Dr O'Higgins had no idea of an independent future for the Blueshirts; in fact he was quite satisfied with Cumann na nGaedheal and the old system and only wanted the Blueshirts to be a sort of breakdown gang to clear the rails for Cumann na nGaedheal. Mr Blythe as usual tried to take all sides and keep in with everybody, and while Commandant Cronin was not of the opinion that the Blueshirts should bend the knee to Cumann na nGaedheal, he was not very interested in a new policy or in getting away from the existing system. In the end after the discussion had gone on for hours without any contribution from me, I said 'it is evident to me that you don't know your own minds, but I will have nothing to do with any organisation which is under the thumb of any political party'.[55]

O'Duffy's recollection, while unreliable, accurately encapsulated the tensions within the movement which would later lead to his rancorous departure. The most radical section of the Blueshirts, fascists like Gunning (and, for a period, Blythe), envisaged a radical movement dedicated to establishing an authoritarian régime. The loyalties of Ned Cronin and his followers lay primarily with the Blueshirts rather than Cumann na nGaedheal, but this less politicized faction did not envisage any political role for the movement other than as a treatyite bulwark against the IRA. Another influential section, led by T. F. O'Higgins, viewed the Blueshirts merely as a useful means of restoring Cumann na nGaedheal to power. O'Duffy instinctively adhered to the outlook of the first group but had no desire to accept a mere figurehead position. He agreed to lead the ACA only if it maintained its independence and he was given a position of real authority.[56] It was only when these demands were conceded that he agreed to lead the movement.

. Pulling the strings: the first known photograph of O'Duffy (far right), with Monaghan's tri-
mphant 1914 hurling team

O'Duffy (centre), flanked by Tom Ennis (left) and Emmet Dalton (right), salutes as the Free
ate forces enter Portobello Barracks in 1922

3. An intense-looking Commissioner O'Duffy (centre) with Garda headquarters staff including his cousin Patrick Walsh (in plain clothes), *c.*1922

4. The blessing of the force, *c.*1922

5. Cruising: the General, looking dapper in customised formal wear, c.mid-1920s

6. One of the many portraits to appear in the Garda periodical, c.mid-1920s

O'Duffy, with minister for justice Kevin O'Higgins, at the Phoenix Park depot, *c.*mid-1920s

The General, surrounded by fellow Gaels, enjoys a GAA match, *c.*early 1930s

9. A sketch by the celebrated artist Seán Keating. Another Keating portrait of the General resides in McKee Barracks

10. O'Duffy, miscellaneous actors, and the Irish Olympic delegation at MGM studios in Hollywood, 1932

11. The General toured the Middle East shortly after his removal by de Valera in 1933

12.   O'Duffy and followers give the raised-arm salute, c.1933

13. The General addresses a Blueshirt meeting in County Cork, c.1934

14. O'Duffy addresses an audience from the balcony, c.1934

15. A Blueshirt parade in rural Cork, *c*.1934

16. O'Duffy poses with members of CAUR's 'fascist international' (including leaders of the Austrian Heimwehr, Norwegian Nasjonal Samling, Romanian Iron Guard, and Spanish Falange)

17 (*above*). On the circuit: O'Duffy, and other aspiring demagogues, sign autographs for admirers at a Blackshirt rally in the Netherlands, 1935

18 (*left*). The General poses in the uniform of the Irish Brigade, *c*.1937

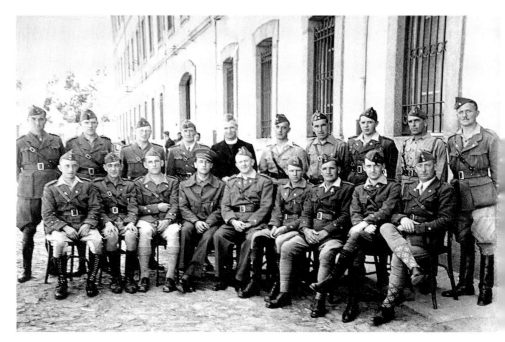

19. Putting on a brave face: the Irish Brigade leadership, 1937. The General is seated between his sec
ond in command, NCP stalwart Dermot O'Sullivan (on his right) and prominent Blueshirt Padraig
Quinn. The sinister Tom Gunning is seated second from far left

20. An ailing O'Duffy addresses the NACA, c.1943

The convention to approve O'Duffy's election, held in the Hibernian Hotel in Dublin on 20 July, was described by the *Irish Independent* as 'one of the most remarkable meetings ever held in the city. Blue-shirted delegates acclaimed the National Guard and General O'Duffy by springing to their feet, with hands upraised in the Fascist Salute, amidst a thunder of cheers.'[57] O'Duffy had taken his first steps towards becoming Ireland's *Duce*. Although partly scripted by Blythe, O'Duffy's address provides some insight into his ambitions. He told his enthusiastic audience that after twenty years of service he was reluctant to return to public life but, given the spontaneous nature of their appeal, he had felt compelled to lead them. (Even in this first speech, 'the quasi-messianic note' was already evident.)[58] He was not a politician. He hoped, rather, to 'raise the youth of this country above the bitterness and confusion of mere party politics'. He emphasized the need for national unity, pointing out that National Guard members could join any party whose aims were not opposed to its constitution.

He stressed the importance of the North: 'As one who risked his life daily over a number of years in the heart of Ulster when I could have volunteered for active service in less dangerous areas, as one who suffered with our nationals in the North, and shared their sorrows, I must confess that I have been sorely disappointed at the lack of interest in the Northern position taken in the Free State.' Partition, he predicted, would not survive the 'rotten foundation' on which it rested. (His observation that 'many so-called Unionists in the North appreciate this fact, and secretly hope that something will soon turn up to remove what they realise is only a temporary construction' shows that, while he attached more importance to the north than most southern nationalists, he did not have any better understanding of its political realities.) There was little in the way of explicitly fascist rhetoric, but the tenor of his speech was mildly anti-democratic. He spoke of the need for 'a national spiritual awakening', and the necessity of 'changes in the parliamentary system which will bring the constitution of the State into closer harmony with national needs'. His movement would inculcate 'patriotic enthusiasm', 'zeal for disciplined voluntary public service', and 'readiness for self-sacrifice'. It would attract those 'who think that the debates in the Dail are undignified and barren of good results', although he conceded that 'we may appeal to the Electorate on our own policy'.

O'Duffy was careful to avoid giving the government grounds to ban the organization. The National Guard would stay within the law, and physical drill would be practised only 'as a means of promoting good health, character and discipline'. The blue shirt would be worn for the same reasons, 'just as Sports Clubs adopt a distinctive blazer'. Indeed, the National Guard would assist the police to maintain order, and strengthen the state by promoting the Irish language, physical fitness, and civic values. The only issue on which O'Duffy would brook no compromise was communism: 'We do not accept the view that Communists should be free to organise; or to preach the subversion of Christianity and individual liberty. We do not believe that the establishment of a Communist regime could be validated by any constitutional process or by any majority of votes. In short the attitude of the National Guard towards Communism and all it stands for is aggressive. We will not have it.' Of course, such rhetoric must be considered in the context of opposition propaganda which relentlessly depicted Fianna Fáil as the thin end of the red threat.[59]

O'Duffy's career as leader of the National Guard was short, dynamic, and dramatic. Within a fortnight he had established a weekly newspaper, *The Blueshirt* (thereby emphasizing the movement's independence from Cumann na nGaedheal, whose organ it had previously depended on), embarked on a national organizational tour, and published a new constitution. The latter's objectives included anti-communism, opposition to alien control and influence, the upholding of Christian principles, the maintenance of social order, the promotion of disciplined voluntary public service, the formation of corporatist organizations of employers and workers, the prevention of corruption, and the inculcation of discipline, zeal, and patriotism among the Irish people.[60] It combined traditional aspects of Irish political organizations, such as the aspiration for unification, with less familiar ideas such as corporatism. It also reflected the treatyite concerns which had led to the formation of the Blueshirts. More novel—and authoritarian—were the references to discipline and the exclusion of non-Christian citizens. The term 'alien control' signified foreign (and, most obviously, British) influence, but it was also a common euphemism among right-wing Catholics for Jewish influence, particularly when juxtaposed with communism.

The General's extensive organizational tour provides further insights into his political ambitions. He denied that his movement was fascist—it was 'purely the product of Irish needs and conditions'—but conceded that it was open to ideas from abroad. He denied any dictatorial ambitions, claiming that he had accepted the leadership of the Blueshirts to prevent a dictatorship, but described corporatism as a potential alternative to liberal democracy.[61] The corporate state, he explained, would entail the formation of a parliament composed of representatives of every social and economic sector in the country, thereby eliminating the need for political parties.[62] O'Duffy was not particularly interested in political theory, and saw no need to consider the complexities of the corporate state beyond outlining a utopian vision of cross-class national harmony. The fact, for example, that the agricultural sector comprised graziers, arable farmers, and agricultural labourers with conflicting interests did not trouble him. He could, in any case, rely on his Blueshirt intellectuals and the fashionable reputation of corporatism abroad for political credibility.

O'Duffy and fascism

More interesting than O'Duffy's simplistic advocacy of the corporate state were the reasons for his admiration of it. As commissioner, O'Duffy had visited Italy, where he had met Mussolini and been impressed by his great experiment. He was attracted to Mussolini's political agenda of fierce opposition to communism and the dramatic nature of his movement. According to Liam Walsh, however, O'Duffy's admiration of fascist Italy also stemmed from his belief that corporatism represented 'a historical progression of the Old Gaelic State to the modern ideal'. Gaelic society, he believed, shared many similarities with other corporatist societies, particularly those of ancient Rome and the medieval guild system, which he described as 'the most perfect thing ever conceived by man'. Fascism, as envisioned by O'Duffy, represented a return to a lost spiritual perfection. Reminiscent of his belief in the Gaelic provenance of rugby, O'Duffy believed that the roots of the 'new fangled, continental idea generally misnamed Fascism' were actually Irish: 'it was from the impetus the Corporate Gaelic mind gave to the European intellect of the Middle Ages that evolved logically and naturally the Corporate Guilds of that time'.[63]

Had it not been for the waves of invasion by lesser civilizations, corporatism would have been perfected in Ireland. Now, O'Duffy argued, as the world desperately sought an alternative between the evils of communism and the corruption of party politics, Ireland had the perfect system 'ready to hand'. One of the few European countries 'with a national State', and 'racially the most compact nation in Europe', Ireland had preserved much continuity with its glorious past. The memories of its lost golden age lay dormant among the Irish people. Underlying these ideas was an essentially spiritual view of politics based on a mythical conception of Ireland's history and destiny: 'The Irish being the sons and heirs of an ancient civilisation, whose mission it has always been to preach and to teach peoples to embrace a higher ideal of life, it was but natural therefore when civilisation was scientifically returning to barbarism that O'Duffy should urge the Irish people to be irremissibly sundered by the spirituality which is the source—the very soul and life of Irish history.'[64]

These views—while not publicly expressed by O'Duffy and possibly not fully formed by 1933—help to clarify O'Duffy's attitude to fascism. As with his ideas on most subjects, they were idiosyncratic but unoriginal distortions of prevailing currents. The championing of medieval guilds was a fashionable aspect of Catholic thought since Leo XIII's *Rerum Novarum* (1891). More recently, Pope Pius XI's influential *Quadragesimo Anno* (1931) had sought to revive the guild as a corporatist third way between liberal individualism and communism, and similar ideas formed part of the neo-Thomist outlook of right-wing Catholic intellectuals like FitzGerald.[65] O'Duffy's core theme—the need for national regeneration through rejection of democracy—was central to all varieties of inter-war fascism. His banal belief that European fascism originated from Ireland's corporate past, while possibly a self-conscious product of wishful thinking, nonetheless elucidates his many contradictory references to fascism. Although he clearly admired and imitated European fascism, his claim to have discovered Ireland's unique corporatist past enabled him to deny the charge of mimicking international fascism. For reasons of chauvinism, egotism, and political expediency, European fascists invariably portrayed fascism as a product of their own country's specific history, culture, and destiny: the achievements of the Gaelic era fulfilled the same mythical functions as those of ancient Rome for Italian fascism or the Teutonic age for Nazism.

There is no consensus on whether the Blueshirts constituted a fascist movement, nor is there ever likely to be. This is partly due to the politicized nature of the question, but also to the fact that both the Blueshirt movement and Fine Gael comprised elements with conflicting views on fascism. Moreover, as the Blueshirts never came to power, it is impossible to know whether the democratic, authoritarian, or fascist elements within the movement would have prevailed. Certainly, ordinary Blueshirts knew little about fascism. They were motivated by the legacy of the Civil War and their concerns about the IRA and the economic war. Although some figures within the treatyite political leadership admired fascism, most remained committed to democracy. Maurice Manning's influential study concluded that the 'Blueshirts had much of the appearance but little enough of the substance of Fascism'.[66] Mike Cronin, drawing on a more complex historiography, argues that the question is not whether the Blueshirts were fascist but where they belonged on the spectrum between authoritarian conservatism and radical fascism. He concluded that a Blueshirt régime would have resembled the authoritarianism of Salazar's Portugal or Franco's Spain, states which adopted aspects of fascism to defend the established élites such as the church and army but regarded radical fascism as a threat.[67]

Whether or not the movement was fascist, most historians have accepted that O'Duffy was the genuine article.[68] However, analysis of O'Duffy's fascism is complicated by his opportunism. Although some aspects of his ideological outlook remained consistent, his fickle politics reflected the fashions and opportunities of his times. In the mid-1930s, he was an admirer of Mussolini. By the late 1930s, he had jumped on the Nazi bandwagon. A second complication was his ideological incoherence—a consequence of his genuine lack of interest in political theory. That the General considered action and spectacle more important than ideology has been widely noted. O'Duffy, as one historian observed, 'saw himself as a man of destiny, but so long as he was in unchallenged command he was relatively indifferent to the direction pursued ... some of the more cerebral Cumann na nGaedheal politicians may have grasped the intricacies of corporatist ideology, but O'Duffy was not one of them.'[69] This was also apparent to contemporaries. W. B. Yeats's naïve hope that Irish fascism might take the form of the enlightened despotism of the educated classes did not survive a brief meeting with the General, whom he described as 'an uneducated lunatic' after he failed to comprehend the poet's challenging treatise on the historical dialectic.[70] But, although his knowledge of fascist political theory appeared to have been acquired 'during a fortnight's cruise on the Mediterranean', as Seán Lemass sarcastically observed in the Dáil, it was clear that 'Fascism of some kind is the type of political association he wants to establish'.[71]

That O'Duffy's fascism was, as Manning observed, 'emotional and instinctive rather than intellectual' suggests—as is often argued by historians of fascism—that the cultural, moral, aesthetic, and psychological attractions of the ideology were in some respects more important than the theoretical or political ones.[72] Robert Paxton, for example, has recently argued that fascism can be defined 'as a form of political behaviour marked by obsessive preoccupation with community decline, humiliation, or victimhood and by compensatory cults of unity, energy, and purity'.[73] Although the psychological attraction is the most difficult to understand, it is perhaps the most important. The reasons why any individual is drawn to a particular belief system are never entirely explicable, but our knowledge of O'Duffy's mentality over a long period, coupled with the insights provided by scholarly research on the psychological dynamics of fascism, provide strong clues. The most important issue was arguably the link between his (unacknowledged) existential crisis and the public one so vociferously identified by him. Not only did fascism offer a way of combating the corruption and decadence of modern society which O'Duffy had become preoccupied by; it met a vital psychological need by offering a way of tackling the internal disorder which he projected on to society.[74]

In his authoritative study, *The Nature of Fascism*, Roger Griffin has argued that 'the psychological precondition for the ideology of fascism to be espoused with a degree of genuine affective commitment is an individual's need for self-transcendent myth which, in the "right" historical circumstances, is satisfied by one centred on the reborn nation'. Paramount among these circumstances, Griffin suggests, is the notion that 'the life of the nation can be subjectively perceived as undergoing a profound crisis'. The promise of national regeneration held out by fascism functions as a 'mythic panacea', offering an explanation for the failure of society (or in reality, the self) and a renewed sense of hope and meaning for the world (or the individual):

The committed fascist is thus someone who has resolved his 'sense-making crisis', whether objective or subjective, by projecting the experience of chaos and longing for a feeling of wholeness and meaning on to external reality so that it is the nation which he experiences as sick and the nation which is to be healed. Were he psychically healthy he would surmount the crisis by creating a new *psychological* order for himself in which he would become the hero of his inner life and achieve spiritual self-control, self-knowledge and freedom. . . . Instead he wants to play a heroic role in public life by participating in the foundation of a new *social and political* order under the aegis of a national leader-figure, one who has total certainty of the mission history has assigned 'his' people . . . that is if he does not, like Mussolini and Hitler, arrogate the historical role of leader to himself and thus find an even more radical solution to his crisis of identity.[75]

More prosaically, we can explore the attractions of fascism for O'Duffy by examining his thoughts on the role of the Blueshirts, which offer far more clues than his banal policy documents which were usually written by his advisers.[76] Interestingly, he first considered the movement's potential some months before he assumed its leadership, possibly even while serving as commissioner, when he penned a number of suggestions in the margins of a draft ACA policy document which he passed on to Ernest Blythe. The most revealing aspect of his suggestions was how they revealed his view of the ACA as a movement dedicated to physical and moral improvement rather than conventional political activity. Indeed, he explicitly objected to the proposal that the ACA contest elections, instead emphasizing the necessity of voluntary service (suggesting as a motto: 'Ireland, we serve!') and independence from the state: 'If you aim at something similar to the position in the life of England . . . of the Baden-Powell Scouts, I agree . . . a body which should be a spontaneous product of instructed enthusiasm [should] not be deprived of its life force by the almost soulless thing called *State Control*.'

He recommended that the ACA form athletic and mountaineering clubs emulate similar German movements by planting trees rather than erecting expensive stone crosses to memorialize their fallen comrades, develop 'a taste for the German & Austrian habit of long walking trips', establish sections for women, girls, and boys, introduce compulsory physical training for all male members between the ages of 15 and 35, and generally seek to instil discipline and habits of healthy living through mass physical training. He concluded, rather enigmatically, by noting: ' "Comrades" is a word with fine meaning and a good full sound. It should be used [as] often as possible, above all for the purpose of striking the eye (and at the same time indicating the actual mouth formation). I should like to see it spelled with a "K" that is "Komrades". That spelling will give you the easily made and striking initials AKA.'[77]

The Irish Mussolini

Now, as leader of the movement, O'Duffy could translate his ideas into action. He announced the formation of a section for boys aged between 10 and 17. They would be taught not politics but 'discipline, perseverance, self-control, self-denial, a sense of fair play and a spirit of sportsmanship and physical and moral courage. In short, we shall help them to become good citizens.' They would receive the 'opportunity of rendering active and manly national service' by participating in the responsibilities of national leadership and military training.[78] This fascistic ethos of active citizenship was emphasized by the new movement's motto: 'Service, discipline, country'. The formation of the Young Comrades was followed by a women's division and an auxiliary for less committed associate members. Drawing on past experiences, O'Duffy instructed his followers to infiltrate and seize control of rival social, political, and sporting organizations (although this directive did not prevent him from attacking the GAA for becoming 'the tool of a political party').[79]

Aside from the commitment to corporatism, the ideological aspects of the National Guard most emphasized by O'Duffy were anti-communism and nationalism. He drew on his own record to inspire supporters and shame opponents. He told a meeting in Tipperary:

I don't like parading records but I challenge any man in Ireland to-day to come along who has a better national record, or who suffered more or worked harder or more conscientiously, or took more risks for Ireland's sake than I did . . . They had people very prominent to-day, when he was organising the Volunteers in Ulster against the Specials, when he was lying on the plank bed, or was leading the hunger-strikers of Munster, though then able-bodied, were not in the fight. Some of them he knew well only escaped the traitor's death by accident. As director of the organisation . . . he

knew the record of every man in Ireland to-day. If he was driven to it he would
make some very awkward revelations with regard to individuals who had much to
say now.[80]

The limitations of his agenda would later become apparent, but his first
weeks of leadership were successful. On 23 July he announced that the National
Guard had recruited 25,000 members, a figure which rose to 30,000 three days
later.[81] By mid-August, he claimed a membership of 40,000, predicting that it
would ultimately rise to 200,000.[82] The real figure was much lower, around
20,000 in this period rising to a peak of between 30,000 and 40,000, but there
was little doubt that O'Duffy's leadership had resulted in a flurry of activity and
excitement.[83] As always, he enjoyed favourable press coverage, particularly
from deferential foreign journalists on the lookout for a dramatic story. Even
his unremarkable physical appearance attracted admiration. The *Boston
Sunday Post* noted that 'he had broadened and put on weight but has lost little
of his physical fitness...his appearance has become more impressive and
commanding'. A Danish article on 'the Irish Mussolini' gushed that 'Ireland
has got a new heroic figure...He has an athletic figure, and sharp strong lively
eyes. He carries himself like a man who has always lived among men.'[84]

A movement which glorified action required spectacle as well as speeches. In
late July, O'Duffy announced that 20,000 of his Blueshirts would march to the
cenotaph outside the Dáil to mark the annual commemoration of the deaths of
Griffith, Collins, and O'Higgins. Observers immediately drew parallels with
Mussolini's march on Rome. O'Duffy's announcement provided the government with an opportunity to move against the National Guard, and events
began moving rapidly. On 29 July, Special Branch raided the houses of prominent treatyites, demanding the surrender of their legally held firearms. Fearing
assassination, O'Duffy initially refused to part with his automatic pistol and
Webley revolver. In an effort to compromise, however, he announced that he
would reduce the scale of the parade, denying the rumours that he intended
'seizing the seat of government and the military barracks in Dublin'.[85] This
failed to reassure de Valera, who reiterated his determination to stamp out private armies. However, the president's failure to move against the IRA (on the
lame grounds of its 'roots in the past'), and his recruitment of several hundred
republicans into a new Special Police Auxiliary, reinforced treatyite fears that it
was de Valera who was the menace to democracy.[86] The recruitment of these
'Broy Harriers', who were provided with 'guns, police powers, and a ten-
minute lecture on the law', indicated the government's concerns about the
state's security forces (whose loyalty Broy felt unable to guarantee) as much as
the Blueshirts.[87] O'Duffy, who was kept informed of these moves by his former

colleagues on the force, denounced the arming of this militia with '300 rifles, 8 Thompson guns, a Lewis gun, two machine gun instructors, 3 whippet armoured cars and a hooded terror'.[88]

Tensions continued to rise in the days before the parade. On 8 August, a National Guard dance ended in street-fighting and baton-charges on O'Connell Street when republicans clashed with Blueshirts. In a stormy Dáil debate the following day, the minister for justice, P. J. Ruttledge, quoted a police report in which O'Duffy, as commissioner, had described the Blueshirts as 'a very formidable insurrectionary force, and a source of extreme danger to the peace and stability of the country'. He also quoted from the *United Irishman* to demonstrate the Blueshirts' admiration for European fascism.[89] Unperturbed, O'Duffy chose this moment to declare that political parties had outlived their usefulness and to outline his plans to replace the 'present bad system' of English parliamentary democracy with a corporate state. Asked if his proposals were modelled on Italy, he replied: 'Yes, but it is the only part of our movement which is Fascist'—a reply which ignored the rather obvious provenance of his movement's shirt and salute.[90]

On 11 August, de Valera, alarmed by the prospect of thousands of Blueshirts descending on government offices, revived Article 2A, proclaimed the parade, and placed hundreds of armed gardaí outside key buildings. He justified these measures on the grounds that it was 'the avowed aim of the association to destroy the existing parliamentary institutions, and the military character of its organisation and the symbols it has adopted are evidence that its leaders are prepared, in favourable circumstances, to resort to violent means to attain this end.'[91] The department of justice judged it 'a threat to the government of the most serious kind', and it is now clear that de Valera believed the threat was genuine.[92] Although O'Duffy would later compare the parade to Mussolini's march on Rome, it was unlikely that the event, planned before he became leader, was intended to trigger a *coup d'état*. However, it would have led to serious violence, and it could not be ruled out that O'Duffy, whose unpredictability knew few bounds, would have exploited any opportunities arising from this disorder.

The ban placed O'Duffy in a difficult position, as he had not only repeatedly declared that the Blueshirts would abide by the law but also insisted that it was his 'sacred duty' to lead the march come what may.[93] O'Duffy cancelled the parade, announcing a series of smaller gatherings in church grounds the following week (which he was also forced to cancel when the bishop of Galway informed him that they contravened church law).[94] The march on Dublin was significant for a number of reasons. It offered de Valera the opportunity to resurrect the last government's hated emergency legislation in circumstances which militant republicans would otherwise have opposed. It also indicated the limits of O'Duffy's radicalism and political ability. Faced by his first test of strength, he chose capitulation over confrontation. But although commentators drew comparisons with Daniel O'Connell's submission at Clontarf, O'Duffy's reputation remained intact. This was due not to his inept handling of events but rather to the widespread excitement resulting from the ban and the dramatic sequence of developments it provoked.

The ban, and the rumours of the government's intention to prohibit the Blueshirts, allowed O'Duffy to tap into a long-established tradition of public admiration for outlaw movements, particularly as the Blueshirts had merely attempted to stage a peaceful march. Better suited to the role of wronged patriot than statesman, O'Duffy was quick to turn the rhetorical tables after years of abuse from republicans:

The National Guard will probably be banned. If so every man and woman who remains a member must be arrested. There can be no discrimination. They must be tried under martial law conditions and huge internment camps will have to be erected capable of accommodating tens of thousands of Irish citizens... The unfortunate Government, acting on bad and prejudiced advice, now finds itself in the position of Balfour and Hamar Greenwood—they will be confronted with the problem of putting half the Irish nation in jail and still posing as a popular administration at home and abroad.[95]

The first part of his prediction was correct. The National Guard was proclaimed on 22 August and the military tribunals were reconstituted. Ruttledge justified the government's actions on the dubious grounds that the Blueshirts were involved in gun-running; while de Valera, now supported by Labour, highlighted the fascist threat: 'they knew when people were reading the English newspaper versions of happenings on the Continent, that some nincompoop would think he had some divine commission to become a dictator; but when that gentleman tried to organise ex-soldiers, to give them uniforms, then the government thought it was time to call a halt'.[96] O'Duffy continued to tour Ireland, dodging the police and addressing meetings, which were increasingly broken up. De Valera's decision, which inadvertently confirmed O'Duffy as the leading opposition figure, was to herald the most turbulent period of political unrest since the Civil War.

President of Fine Gael

Another unintended consequence of the ban was to add impetus to the political negotiations between Cumann na nGaedheal and the smaller Centre Party (which represented farming and neo-Redmondite interests) that would ultimately unite the opposition. O'Duffy—keen to preserve the independence of the National Guard—was not involved in these talks and later insisted that relations between the National Guard and Cumann na nGaedheal had been poor: 'the T.D.'s kept away from our Headquarters at 5 Parnell Square. The relationship could not be more strained...because I refused to allow the National Guard to become the soulless thugs of a political party.'[97]

On 24 August, while in Waterford to speak at yet another proclaimed meeting, O'Duffy was met by a deputation from Dublin which informed him that the Centre Party and Cumann na nGaedheal wished the Blueshirts to join their ranks under his leadership.[98] Despite claiming to have been unaware of these talks and unenthusiastic about the proposal, he agreed to put it before the National Guard executive. Although he exaggerated his opposition to the proposal, O'Duffy did have genuine concerns which were shared by rank-and-file Blueshirts. On 3 September Special Branch learned of a secret meeting between Cumann na nGaedheal supporters and Blueshirts in Ennis which had been organized by Bishop Fogarty (a fervent opponent of de Valera since the Civil War): 'The rank and file of the National Guard (as far as Co. Clare is concerned) are opposed to the merger, preferring to maintain the National Guard as a separate organisation'. The police enquired if they should arrest O'Duffy or whether the government might prefer the negotiations to continue on the grounds that they might result in the formation of a democratic party.[99] On 8 September the National Guard's executive approved the merger, although not without debate, on the understanding that the National Guard would continue as a distinct body in the new organization.[100]

Why, given O'Duffy's opinion of democratic politics, did he agree to a merger which he would later describe as 'one of the greatest mistakes and sincerest regrets of his life'? O'Duffy would depict himself as a naïve victim of wily politicians, who only belatedly realized that his popularity was being exploited.[101] There was some truth to this, but O'Duffy had long known that Cumann na nGaedheal wished to use the Blueshirts for its own ends. Aside from his ambition, the most pressing motive was the new political context brought about by coercion which would result in either the suppression or marginalization of the National Guard. The Italian minister in Dublin, who kept a close eye on the rising star of Irish fascism, noted that the merger came at just the right moment to save O'Duffy from an embarrassing loss of face.[102] It also made it difficult for de Valera to ban the Blueshirts without also suppressing the opposition. In explaining his volte-face, O'Duffy claimed that he considered it 'a high tribute to an outlawed organisation' that the opposition had turned to the Blueshirts.[103] That after only seven weeks in politics O'Duffy had been offered the leadership of the opposition—and thus a genuine opportunity of leading the next government—can only have reinforced his sense of messianic destiny: 'he was not joining two small and defeated political parties: they were joining the most dynamic and exciting political movement ever to manifest itself in treatyite politics'.[104] This belief was reinforced by the terms of the merger. O'Duffy would be president, appoint one-third of the executive, and the party would adopt the corporatist agenda of the Blueshirts, who would comprise the vanguard of the new movement.

Perhaps the more pertinent question is why the opposition was willing to unite under O'Duffy. There were, after all, many reasons why it should not. Cumann na nGaedheal's front bench knew how erratic his behaviour could be, while O'Duffy's final years as commissioner had provided evidence of his neurotic tendencies. He was also drinking heavily, although this may not have been so widely known. (Tellingly, the Italian consul, while enthusiastic about the apparent fascistization of the opposition, was under no illusions about O'Duffy's drinking and political limitations.)[105] It was certainly known to treatyite insiders that the General was an extreme nationalist, an admirer of fascism, and had been connected with the rumours of a coup against Fianna Fáil. Considering these factors, the decision to support his leadership must rank not merely as 'an act of catastrophic ill-judgement in every respect' but as one of the most opportunistic decisions in the history of Irish politics.[106] As Robert Fisk observed: 'they had given the General a cloak of constitutional propriety that overnight made the Blueshirts far more formidable in the politics of Ireland than Oswald Mosley's Blackshirts ever became in Britain'.[107]

Why? The key factor, present wherever the far right advanced in 1930s Europe, was the prevailing sense of crisis. Reflecting many years later on this disastrous decision, Mulcahy ruefully recalled:

I had no heart in that particular type of thing and the way in which it was developing at the time. Maybe it was only after O'Duffy got going... Oh, I hated wearing the Blueshirt, you see, and all that and I hated ... see O'Duffy replacing Cosgrave. But in the circumstances in which O'Duffy replaced Cosgrave you were running into an absolute clash with the Government at that time.[108]

There is a hint of special pleading here—Blueshirt extremism did not originate with O'Duffy and no one forced Mulcahy to wear his shirt—but the atmosphere of crisis is evident. The survival of democracy in any state depends on a consensus that all the parties are playing by the rules. The coercion of the National Guard confirmed the opposition's doubts about de Valera. Despite the flags, shirts, and provocative rhetoric, the National Guard was an unarmed body which had vowed to work within the constitution. From the treatyite perspective, Fine Gael represented a defensive merger against a government which was assaulting its political and economic liberties. In retrospect, of course, the opposition was wrong. Even Blythe would later concede that 'the intention of Fianna Fail, from the beginning, was to preserve freedom of speech and democratic institutions'.[109] Crucially, however, this was not how it appeared at the time.

There were other motives. It was also a response to Cumann na nGaedheal's electoral decline. Having lost two elections within twelve months, it might have been expected that W. T. Cosgrave would have resigned or been ousted: one reason why this had not occurred was that it was far from clear who might do a better job. As one party official bleakly informed Cosgrave: 'There is a very general and growing belief that Cumann na nGaedheal is finished.'[110] The press was not slow to highlight the glaring contrast between the coming man and the has-been of treatyite politics: 'General O'Duffy is a gay debonair edition of the old Michael Collins. Fearless, a joke on his lips, this new stormy petrel of Irish politics, whose movement is a movement of youth, clad in his blue shirt, rushes through Ireland like his prototype. Mr. Cosgrave is, at the moment, a spent force.' 'Reckless and slashing', the *Western Mail* observed, the General was 'a more romantic figurehead than the ex-President could ever be'.[111] The temptation to harness the opposition's declining fortunes to this vibrant movement was irresistible. O'Duffy's subsequent failures should not overshadow his stature at this time. For all his faults, he was a figure whom the treatyite élite had previously turned to in times of crisis. And, as elsewhere in Europe, the conservative right believed that it could benefit from an alliance with a more dynamic and radical junior partner, while remaining in control of its destinies.

O'Duffy's leadership also suited a number of interests within the opposition, none of which would later admit to backing him. The National Guard extremists viewed the merger as an opportunity to advance their radical agenda and standing. Blythe had urged Cumann na nGaedheal and the ACA to merge since 1932, arguing that only an infusion of Blueshirts into the ageing party membership could challenge Fianna Fáil's dominance of grassroots politics.[112] Similar factors appealed to Hogan and Tierney, who, despite their political inexperience, were appointed vice-presidents and saw corporatism adopted as the centrepiece of the new party's programme.[113] The moderate Centre Party leadership of Frank MacDermot and James Dillon—although favouring Patrick Hogan as the new leader—preferred O'Duffy's leadership to that of

Cosgrave, which would have made the merger appear more like a take-over.[114]
Given the Centre Party's doubts about O'Duffy's suitability, Cumann na
nGaedheal's leadership bears most responsibility for the General's appointment. Although they had reservations, Cosgrave and Patrick Hogan accepted
the need for political unity. In contrast, many others within the party were
more enthusiastic about the idea of replacing Cosgrave with a more charismatic
leader.[115]

Such was the atmosphere of crisis in which it emerged, the United Ireland
Party (soon better known as Fine Gael) was launched before a coherent set of
policies had been agreed, and it was not until the following year that its constitution was published. O'Duffy became president, chairing an unwieldy executive of eighteen members and six vice-presidents, but Cosgrave continued to
lead the party within the Dáil. Three of the vice-presidents, Cosgrave, Dillon,
and MacDermot, were leaders of the former parties but the other three (Peter
Nugent, Hogan, and Tierney) lacked political experience, as did much of the
executive. By mid-November Fine Gael had formulated a policy document
reflecting the divergent views within the party. The party sought reunification
within the British Commonwealth, a position reflecting the moderate nationalism of Cumann na nGaedheal and the Centre Party. It sought to abolish proportional representation, reform local government, and tackle unemployment
through public works. The Blueshirt agenda was most evident in the proposal
to establish statutory industrial and agricultural corporations. But what was
missing from the new programme was also revealing. There was no mention of
a corporatist parliament—let alone a fascist agenda—and the party explicitly
committed itself to democracy and unconditional opposition to dictatorship.
This was the price demanded by the constitutional parties for supporting
O'Duffy's leadership.[116]

The Young Ireland Association

The continued existence of the Blueshirts, renamed the Young Ireland Association (YIA) to circumvent de Valera's ban, continued to provide O'Duffy with
an outlet for radicalism. Although he toned down his anti-democratic rhetoric,
he never fully embraced a conventional political role. As he informed supporters
in Cavan shortly after the merger: 'he was never in a political organization in
his life, and he did not regard himself as a political leader, or that the United
Ireland Party was a political organization in the sense understood in this country.
"I have no politics".'[117] He continued to profess his admiration of Mussolini,

while denying any desire to emulate fascism. The wearing of shirts was sometimes described as a practical measure to distinguish members from enemies, but on other occasions explicitly identified with order, discipline, strength, youth, and combativeness.[118] What the press routinely described as the 'fascist salute' was described by the leadership as the 'Victory Salute'. A number of innocent explanations were also offered to explain this phenomenon, O'Duffy coming up with the most ludicrous: 'It is not a fascist salute, it is an Irish salute. In former times when duels were fought with sword or bayonet in this country, it was customary for opponents after the duel had been fought to greet each other with extended arm. In other words our salute is one of friendship.'[119]

The YIA remained an autonomous section within Fine Gael, subject to party discipline only in matters of constitutional and political policy.[120] 'Onlooker' continued to advocate a corporate state under Blueshirt control.[121] Hogan and Tierney continued to promote their authoritarian agenda without concealing their low opinion of parliamentary democracy. Hogan, for example, insisted that it was 'the growing menace of the Communist-IRA that called forth the Blueshirts as inevitably as Communist anarchy called forth the Blackshirts'.[122] He continued to advocate the corporate state, noting that 'revolutionary proposals are in the air in every country'.[123] Tierney's propaganda sailed equally close to the wind. Italian fascism was not a crude dictatorship but a development certain 'to be adapted to the needs of every civilised country'.[124] 'Parliament', he observed, 'is just as un-Irish as the Republic... If the Whigs throw Hitler at us, we have a very solid and heavy missile with which to reply.'[125]

The Blueshirt organ continued to encourage violence on the streets. It devoted little attention to Fine Gael's politicians, instead instructing Blueshirts to 'pay the closest attention to this great Italian experiment, and learn from it whatever they can which may be of use when the Blueshirt Government comes into power'.[126] The reading list for its study groups included such titles as *The Universal Aspects of Fascism*.[127] Articles praised the 'new democracy' pioneered by Mussolini, who was considered 'not so much a dictator as the instrument of the will of the vast majority of his countrymen and the supreme expression of the spirit of a resurgent nation'.[128] James Burke, a deputy and former minister, opposed the abolition of proportional representation on the basis that it would be more honest to adopt 'minority rule through Fascism or restriction of the franchise'.[129] County directors were told not to put themselves forward for the next general election on the grounds that the 'higher officers of the organisation ought to show their faith in its future and in its policy by displaying no particular anxiety to enter the Dáil'.[130]

There is no evidence that these views permeated the party rank and file, but they demonstrate the continued existence of a fascistic agenda despite the merger. From its inception, Fine Gael consisted of two overlapping and potentially conflicting elements, a conventional political party—centred on the parliamentary party and its executive committee—and O'Duffy's Blueshirts, who participated in mass rallies, street-fighting, and illegal agitation. The hierarchically structured YIA, organized around appointed county directors who controlled thousands of activists, was a potentially far more powerful organization than the political party. O'Duffy was certainly more at home directing operations from the Blueshirts' northside headquarters on Parnell Square, an area with strong associations with Collins's Brotherhood, than his office in Fine Gael's headquarters on Merrion Square. He described his movement as the most important section of Fine Gael, dismissing Cumann na nGaedheal as a party which had 'served its period of usefulness', and criticizing its deputies for their lack of effort in building the new party.[131] In the sense that the enormous public interest in Fine Gael during the next twelve months focused on the Blueshirts rather than the parliamentary party, he was right.

Defiance

From the outset, O'Duffy's leadership of the opposition was defined by conflict. Blueshirts clashed with Fianna Fáil supporters, IRA activists, gardaí, and even soldiers. Although fatalities were rare, police reports attest to widespread violence: 'Perhaps never before, and certainly never since, has Irish politics been so thoroughly a politics of hatred, as it was at this time.'[132] Much of the impetus behind this disorder, which would deepen in 1934, stemmed from the impact of the economic war. There was an important class dimension to this conflict: it was middling and large farmers who were most affected by the collapse of the cattle export trade; whereas small farmers and rural labourers benefited from free beef and the prospect of land redistribution. The government's decision to impound the cattle of hitherto prosperous farmers who could not—or would not—pay land annuities provoked fury. Their resistance manifested itself in various ways, often reminiscent of the violence of the Land War and earlier traditions of faction fighting. Violence was particularly marked in the prosperous Munster and midland farming counties and areas where Civil War hatreds continued to run deep. Republicans and Blueshirts painted slogans on roads and walls. Dance-halls, handball courts, and other public spaces were fought over, blown up, or burned down. Beatings and even shootings were meted out. There was often a ritualistic aspect to the violence. Blueshirts would arrive in town for a parade or dance, their very uniformed appearance a provocation. Slanging matches with republican youths would follow. A typical exchange after a dance in Ballyporeen was recorded by the police: ' "Up Dev.'. . . "By the neck". . . "Up Dev". "Up Duffy". "F——Dev". "F——Duffy". "Up Tom Barry". "F——him and you too".[133] Insults were followed by blows which, depending on the result, met with enthusiastic headlines in *An Phoblacht* or *United Ireland*. Competing versions of which side had come off best were commemorated in IRA and Blueshirt songs.[134]

O'Duffy's decision to embark on a national organizational tour placed him at the heart of this wave of violence. News of an impending visit was guaranteed to raise tension in a rural town for weeks. The following scene, which occurred in Kilkenny, unfolded on numerous occasions in late 1933:

As the scattered crowd sauntered in expectation near the towers of the Norman castle a lorry rushed past, from which we heard the words: 'Up Dev! Up Dev!' . . . Shortly after more than a hundred men in everyday clothes marched past resolutely, in perfect time and discipline. It was a demonstration of the Irish Republican Army, a gesture of defiance against their enemies, the Blue Shirts, and a warning that trouble was to come. Soon, guarded by police, a tall, well-built man like an ex-Rugby International, with sparse fair hair, wearing a blue suit and a blue cornflower in his buttonhole walked towards the platform and stretched his right arm out as a salute to the thousands who greeted him.

It was Gen. O'Duffy. From one end of the town square came savage shouts and crowds began running hither and thither. 'The IRA are starting all right', remarked someone. Catcalls resounded from one section of the audience, while heads bobbed up and down to see what has happening. Stones flew through the air and bottles crashed until the police attacked the Republicans with sticks and drove them, up the street. But the rioters were not suppressed, and before long a band of scattered soldiers, wearing steel helmets to protect their heads against bricks . . . ran into the square and order reigned again.[135]

O'Duffy revelled in the excitement and disorder which accompanied his meetings, his response to Blueshirt violence ranging from studied ambivalence to encouragement. In republican areas, Blueshirts often came off worst. One of the most violent meetings occurred when O'Duffy visited Tralee on 6 October. While making his way to a local hall, he was attacked by a republican mob and struck in the head with a hammer: 'the whole street', one observer recalled, 'was involved in a mêlée'.[136] He finally reached the hall, where he remained besieged for seven hours despite the presence of 200 policemen who were unable to disperse the crowd. At one point a Mills bomb was thrown through the skylight but failed to explode after it was caught in the netting. Another unexploded bomb was discovered at the back of the hall the following morning. O'Duffy, whose car had been torched, escaped only after the arrival of soldiers whose tear gas and fixed bayonets finally restored order. His head swathed in bandages but unbowed, O'Duffy addressed another meeting in Castlebar two days later.[137] Two weeks later the army was required to restore order at a meeting at which O'Duffy accused his hecklers of being communists. The following week two prominent Blueshirts from Bandon were taken from their homes in a midnight raid and brutally beaten, one of them dying two months later.[138]

This violence, although often provoked by the IRA, was used by the government to justify further coercion of the Blueshirts. A police raid on the latter's headquarters on 30 November provided evidence that the YIA was merely the National Guard under another name.[139] On 8 December the government proclaimed it as an unlawful association, closing its offices throughout the country.[140] On the same day, the police visited several shirt manufacturers, ordering them to cease production of blue shirts.[141] The government made little effort to explain the rationale behind its actions, which many considered undemocratic. The *Irish Times* accused it of acting 'as ruthlessly as the Nazi government in Germany'.[142] O'Duffy's response was defiance. Blueshirt meetings, and the wearing of shirts, continued. Despite the rumours of his imminent arrest, he commenced a tour of the north-west. On Friday 8 October he spoke at Ballybofey. The meeting was held on a fair day, resulting in the attendance of many drunken supporters and opponents, but although 'things looked ugly at the time', there was no violence.[143] Later that evening, he informed a crowd in Glenties that de Valera 'had actually gone mad, and it was because of that he had proclaimed half the people of the country'. He attributed the coercion to 'His Britannic Majesty's Ministers in this country', adding (somewhat contradictorily) that it was 'the policy of Communist Russia'.[144]

The following day O'Duffy spoke in Ballyshannon at an extraordinary meeting which illustrated both the incendiary atmosphere of the time and O'Duffy's volatility. The arrest of Ned Cronin for wearing a blue shirt in nearby Bundoran earlier in the day added to the excitement among the thousands of Blueshirts and republicans who had been gathering since early morning. O'Duffy arrived without mishap, having sent a decoy Blueshirt procession trailed by a hostile crowd to enter one end of the town while arriving from the other. After ascending the platform without the usual formalities, he was confronted by the local chief superintendent, who warned him not to speak while attired in a blue shirt. O'Duffy retorted: 'I will address the meeting, you do your own duty.' As soon as he began speaking, an irate crowd attempted to rush the platform but were held back by a police cordon. A rambling and incoherent speech followed. The government of de Valera (repeatedly denounced as a 'bloody foreigner') had 'divided the children at school, and shot down their people. They had murdered Kevin O'Higgins and Michael Collins because they said in 1922 and 1927 what Fianna Fáil were saying now.' Exploiting recent government criticism of the IRA, O'Duffy appealed to the die-hards in the crowd:

I say as a Republican myself . . . that he is a damned liar. You are not in the pay of John Bull, and whenever Mr de Valera runs away from the Republic and arrests you Republicans, and puts you on board beds in Mountjoy, he is entitled to the fate he gave Mick Collins and Kevin O'Higgins. He does not understand the people of this country, because he is a half-breed . . . the policy of the Government was to assassinate him. Should every one of the 62,000 members of the U.I.P. have a gun or a revolver and drill every night with arms, should they fire into the people's houses, take out aged people and kick them and beat them with revolvers, fire into dance halls and shoot down innocent little girls there trying to amuse themselves: should they refuse to recognise the courts of the country, and disregard the law, for all these things they would be spoon-fed by the present Government.[145]

As his intemperate diatribe rose to a crescendo, O'Duffy dramatically removed his overcoat, revealing the illicit blue shirt underneath. This gesture, the *Derry Journal* reported, 'created a tense atmosphere, all eyes turned in the direction of where a few Gardaí officers were standing, but none of them made any attempt to approach the speaker'.[146] This was probably prudent as the cheering, baying, crowd was ready to erupt at the slightest provocation. O'Duffy pressed on:

I am not doing this for stage effect . . . I want to be free, but I have never asked any to do what I would not do myself. Therefore, I appeal to you to get some kind of blue colour. This movement is the only hope for this country. We want you to come out and say that you will not sell your souls for bribes, hairy bacon, or anything else. It is not to your credit that there are not more blue shirts here tonight. Any man not prepared to wear a blue shirt is unworthy of being an Irishman. This may be the last opportunity I will have for a long time of addressing an Irish audience.

Before gardaí or republicans could react, O'Duffy leapt off the back of the platform, pushing his way to the safety of a local priest, who shepherded him back to his hotel. He was not yet safe, as the police recorded: 'In a moment a shouting, yelling, mob was rushing up the street to a hotel . . . when the Superintendent and his men arrived at the hotel it was surrounded by a furious mob trying to gain admission . . . as it was getting out of hand he ordered a baton charge'. By the time his decoy car was spotted emerging from the hotel yard, O'Duffy had already escaped.

Although scheduled to speak elsewhere in Donegal, O'Duffy abruptly disappeared from sight for two days, reappearing on 12 December to chair an emergency meeting of Fine Gael's national executive. He denied that he had been on the run, but offered no explanation for his lost weekend. Ballyshannon was significant for several reasons. It was the first striking example of O'Duffy's unpredictability when provoked. The scurrilous tone of his speech, possibly alcohol-fuelled, was unparalleled for a leader of the opposition: the accusation that the government wished to assassinate him indicated a considerable degree of paranoia, while the suggestion that de Valera deserved the same fate was clearly seditious. The press reports of this meeting, particularly O'Duffy's description of himself as a republican, must have set alarm bells ringing among Fine Gael's leadership.

Any concerns about O'Duffy's behaviour, however, took second place to the need to respond to de Valera's proscription of the YIA. Indeed, one of the unintended consequences of de Valera's coercion was to prolong the unity between the disparate elements within Fine Gael. Hogan warned fellow vice-president Michael Tierney that whatever decision was 'taken should be and must be taken by the leaders as a whole. It will not do to have Gen. O'Duffy left to handle the situation alone', a comment which indicated early reservations about the president's leadership.[147] Hogan suggested 'that it would be a mistake to resist the ban—gross outrage and tyranny as it may be', as any such resistance would allow de Valera to ban the entire opposition, a view which highlights the extent to which the president's commitment to democracy was doubted.[148] The professor's colleagues showed more mettle. On 15 December the party announced the dissolution of the YIA and the establishment of an identical organization, the League of Youth, serving a writ on the High Court to establish its legality. The ploy evoked popular memories of Daniel O'Connell's outwitting of the British government.

Undeterred, indeed buoyed, by the government's actions, O'Duffy issued a rousing call to his supporters:

No persecution can stop our onward march; no sacrifice will be too great for us. Some of us may fall by the wayside, but there will be many to grasp the flag as it falls from our hands and to carry it on to the glorious victory that awaits us. Where every other tyrant, from Cromwell to Hamar Greenwood, failed, de Valera, too, will fail. Our cause is just, and with us is the unconquerable spirit of the youth of Ireland—a rampart against which despotism will dash itself in vain. Courage, comrades![149]

He announced his intention to attend his next scheduled meeting, in Westport on 17 December, come what may. While approaching the town, however, he was spotted by gardaí and arrested. While being escorted to the local station, he was recognized by the crowd, who surged forward, liberating him from the police, and triumphantly bearing him shoulder-high to the platform. As soon as he began speaking, however, he was re-arrested and brought to the nearest barracks, while a chaotic meeting continued in his absence. O'Duffy indignantly recalled how unpleasant an experience it was to see 'the force which I created alone and unaided against terrible odds, and under most difficult circumstances, that force for every member of which I was prepared to make any sacrifice, even life itself—drag their former Commissioner ignominiously through the streets'.[150]

When news of his arrest reached Dublin, O'Duffy's legal team rushed to the Supreme Court to petition for his release. In the meantime, he was moved under heavy guard to Arbour Hill military prison, where many of his republican enemies had been detained since 1922. He was released two days into his appeal, when a High Court judge ruled that he had not been arrested under an offence specified under Article 2A (the sort of technical decision that had infuriated O'Duffy when commissioner). His release was a tremendous propaganda coup, and a rare own goal for de Valera. O'Duffy released a jubilant statement expressing his hope that 'the decision of the Court will teach the Government to keep within the law. The law has been vindicated today.'[151] The perception of a triumph over oppression was reinforced by a telegram from the fanatically anti-de Valera Bishop Morrisroe: 'Congratulations on victory of justice over shameless partisanship and contemptible tyranny'.[152] Noting that 'it is a bad for a government to be laughed at in Ireland', the *New York Times* described the General's release as the worst blow to de Valera since he had assumed office.[153]

Two days later, however, he was summoned to appear before the Military Tribunal. O'Duffy, who had been celebrating in the smoke room of the Dolphin Hotel, did not take the news well, as the report of the detective inspector detailed to deliver the summons makes clear:

Eventually at 12.45 a.m. he came from the room and addressed me by saying 'Good Night, young fellow' and shook me by the hand. I then gave him the document which he read and having done so addressing me he asked 'What is next? What follows this? What is next?' I replied that the last paragraph explained. He then read the last paragraph again and said 'I suppose you will be Commissioner some day'. I replied 'I will try to perform the duties allotted to me'. He then said 'I suppose you would assassinate if directed, you would assassinate if directed'. I said 'It is a very unfair remark, General, especially coming from you . . . He said 'The Irish People will pronounce their opinion of you. This is assassination.' I might add that in my opinion the General was under the influence of alcohol.

O'Duffy was charged with membership of an illegal organization and incitement to murder the president of the executive council. On 1 January, the day before the trial was due to begin, his lawyers applied to the High Court for a conditional order of prohibition, allowing the Military Tribunal ten days to show why it should hear the charges. The Military Tribunal suspended its trial to avoid a complex dispute between the military and civil courts. The High Court case to test whether the tribunal could try O'Duffy was not resolved until three months later, when it ruled that O'Duffy could only be charged with membership of an illegal organization. A further appeal to the Supreme Court postponed the hearing until late into 1934.[154]

Like O'Duffy before him, de Valera was discovering the ineffectiveness of conventional legislation against organized political opposition. The department of justice complained that 'O'Duffy could have snapped his fingers at any court in the land except the Military Tribunal'.[155] The attorney-general discovered that even the draconian Article 2A did not permit a ban on Blueshirts parading in uniform: 'It is a very unwieldy instrument save for the one purpose it was designed viz: to deal with the IRA'.[156] Fine Gael's leadership, which was not exactly short on barristers, proved as effective as republicans in exploiting legal loopholes. Much to the disgust of the department of justice, the former attorney-general, John A. Costello, who had been Cumann na nGaedheal's legal adviser when Article 2A was first introduced, challenged the government's use of the legislation on the grounds that it was 'wholly subversive of many vital and fundamental principles of the Constitution'![157] O'Duffy, meanwhile, did not miss the opportunity to indulge in the nostalgic rhetoric of the Tan War. On 13 January, for example, he thanked 'the Boys of the Wexford for their very cordial Irish welcome to a jailbird. I have begun to measure my freedom in hours rather than in days or weeks ... it would appear his Majesty's law officers in the Free State are in a muddle ... The anti-coercionist Government are in a fair way towards breaking the jail-filling record of Hamar Greenwood.'[158]

His organizational tour continued, as did the violence between Blueshirts and republicans. The inconvenience and expense to the state was considerable. Over 200 guards, 21 Special Branch officers, and 20 soldiers were required to police a single Blueshirt meeting in Clonmel on 31 December.[159] On 4 January, a Cork vintner died from injuries after a beating by republicans, producing the movement's second martyr. In January, meetings in Wexford, Fethard, Athlone, and Skibbereen were marred by serious violence. Despite republicans firing over the heads of Blueshirts, attempting to burn down the town's platform, and mounting road blocks, O'Duffy entered Skibbereen at the head of a procession of mounted Blueshirts. A meeting in Dundalk on 11 February was accompanied by baton-rounds and the bombing of the house of a Military Tribunal witness in a case against local Blueshirts which resulted in the death of an elderly woman. O'Duffy addressed violent meetings in Balbriggan and Galway later in the month. In the Dáil, each side was accusing the other of murder and dictatorial ambitions. The debate on the murdered Cork vintner resulted in some of the most savage exchanges in the Dáil's history. At one point, 'nearly half the members were on their feet shouting angry comments and personal abuse across the floor of the House. Epithets such as "murderer" and "traitor" were used with abandon.'[160] These scenes—like the sight of shirted representatives—had become familiar in the last days of parliaments throughout continental Europe as liberal democracy struggled to contain the politics of hatred.

O'Duffy continued to focus his energies on grassroots organization, pursuing a punishing schedule of meetings: 'It was organisation, and not policy, which won for Fianna Fáil, and United Ireland must get a superior organisation to win'.[161] A natural demagogue, O'Duffy was much more comfortable addressing the masses than involving himself in the minutiae of policy formulation and political intrigue. By the end of his first six months in charge, 1,200 Fine Gael branches had reportedly been established and the League of Youth claimed a membership of 124,000.[162] The figures may have been vastly exaggerated, but the opposition had strengthened in numbers, purpose, and confidence.[163] For the former Cumann na nGaedheal politicians who had shown neither ability nor appetite for enthusing the grassroots, O'Duffy's energy initially appeared impressive. Subsequently, however, colleagues like James Hogan would question the cost and purpose of 'enormous activity without any reflection'.[164]

Fine Gael's first *ard-fheis* on 8 February offered an impressive demonstration of the new movement's strength. O'Duffy's relatively restrained address ranged across the now familiar subjects: the IRA's 'armed terrorism', the government's 'watery, diluted Communism', the hardship of the economic war, the need for 'the friendly re-conquest of the North', and the importance of inculcating 'a spirit of voluntary disciplined service' among the youth. Parliamentary democracy and 'the corrupt character of party politics' were critiqued in restrained terms: 'There is no reason why we should make an idol of Parliament. It is a human institution.' Corporatism, credited to the Pope rather than to Mussolini, was outlined in moderate terms, O'Duffy reassuring the party faithful that 'United Ireland stands unequivocally for the principles of democracy, majority rule and the absolute rule of Parliament'. Corporatism was presented, much as Hogan and Tierney envisioned it, as a check on the state's power rather than a means of extending it. It was de Valera who was accused of dictatorial ambitions: 'the present Government is using the Public Safety Act as a stepping stone to a dictatorship . . . It has ambushed democracy for the second time.'[165] This spirited performance met with a positive response from the non-republican press. D. P. Moran's *Leader* enthused: 'O'Duffy is the word and O'Duffy is the man . . . It seems to us that de Valera gets out of mental control when he contemplates O'Duffy. O'Duffy is going to beat him in the political arena.'[166]

With few real alternatives, the government continued to coerce the Blueshirts. Its attention switched to the movement's paramilitary trappings. The introduction of the Wearing of Uniforms bill on 23 February, intended to prohibit the public wearing of uniforms, the use of military titles in political organizations, and the carrying of weapons at meetings, heralded three weeks of vicious Dáil debate. The following press report illustrates the incendiary atmosphere:

'This Bill was a political measure to bring under the lash of the law people who had the courage to oppose Mr. de Valera.' 'It is,' said Dr O'Higgins, 'a Spanish vendetta against opponents.' At this observation there was loud cries from the Government back benches; and Mr. Lemass, jumping to his feet excitedly, cried out 'If you make a statement like that, inside or outside, I will stop you.' Dr O'Higgins repeated the phrase and the House was in turmoil, with the Minister for Finance shouting 'Murderers! The man who murdered Kahn . . . There were some remarks which could only be answered by a slap in the teeth.'[167]

Government speakers pointed to Blueshirt violence and the movement's similarities with European fascism to justify their actions. Fine Gael's deputies accused the government of dictatorial intentions, illegal coercion, abandoning the rights to assembly and free speech, and allowing the growth of communism and IRA violence. FitzGerald-Kenney was appalled by the notion that gardaí could 'tear the clothing off a respectable, decent Irish girl'. Many, but not all, opposition deputies insisted on the constitutional nature of the movement. One of the most infamous speeches was made by future taoiseach John A. Costello, who declared that just as 'the Hitler shirts were victorious in Germany', the Blueshirts would 'be victorious in the Irish Free State'.[168]

Although the bill was passed by the Dáil on 14 March, the Senate refused to approve the legislation, ensuring an eighteen-month delay before the measure became law. De Valera's response to yet another embarrassing setback was significant. The day after its rejection of the legislation, he introduced a bill to abolish the Senate. The peremptory nature of this response illustrated why de Valera's commitment to democracy was genuinely doubted by the opposition. De Valera's actions may appear more defensible in hindsight, but to many contemporary observers it provided further evidence of his willingness to contravene the spirit of the constitution.

Six months into his presidency, O'Duffy's leadership appeared successful. The Blueshirts had made considerable organizational progress, introduced new ideas into Irish politics, stimulated massive activism, and attracted massive publicity at home and abroad. Despite the occasional wobble, O'Duffy appeared a plausible leader, inflicting a series of setbacks on Fianna Fáil for the first time since its election. Coercion, as previous treatyite and British administrations had discovered, was a double-edged weapon in Irish politics. There were, admittedly, shadows on the horizon. The growth of the Blueshirts had provoked widespread violence. As long as this was attributed to the IRA or the government O'Duffy's leadership remained credible, but there was little appetite for illegal agitation among Fine Gael's senior leaders. The General's occasional moments of madness also offered the government some encouragement, as Fianna Fáil deputies began to notice the discrepancies between O'Duffy's extravagant rhetoric and his party's policies. Nonetheless, it was Fianna Fáil which was most on the defensive in early 1934.

9
Hoch O'Duffy!

The spirit of Michael Collins is abroad today, the nation is once more upon the march, who dares cry 'Halt' to us?[1]

THE General's carefully scripted performance at his first *ard-fheis* offered few hints of the extent to which his own ideas deviated from the party line cobbled together between Fine Gael's disparate parts. Although O'Duffy's politics are often dismissed as an incoherent imitation of continental fascism, there was clearly much continuity between his political outlook and the concerns which had characterized his earlier years in public life. Irish fascism, like other variants, was an indigenous product of the political, social, and cultural discontinuities produced by modernity, the Great War, and the crises that followed. It did not represent the creation of a new set of political ideas so much as the drawing together of old ideas in a dramatic new form. This chapter will examine how O'Duffy's eclectic ideology combined aspects of European fascist ideology with domestic political traditions. It will also explore how the incompatibility between the General's radical instincts and his party's conservatism led to his inevitable political demise.

Custodians of the national tradition

O'Duffy's treatyite background, and the IRA's hatred of his movement, has obscured the importance of nationalism in his leadership of the Blueshirts.[2] His dissatisfaction with Cumann na nGaedheal had stemmed from the party's drift from its republican roots following the death of Collins, and its resolute commitment to a defence of the treaty settlement within the Commonwealth. His frustration was shared not only by Cumann na nGaedheal's declining electorate but much of its parliamentary party.[3] In many respects, O'Duffy's leadership of Fine Gael represented an attempt to remobilize treatyite republicanism. The General, who had long resented the way treatyite politicians had conceded the superior patriotic credentials of their opponents, insisted that Fine Gael would 'not play second fiddle to anybody in the matter of Nationality'. The party would not contest elections 'for monetary or economic reasons...the prevailing motive will be nationalism'.[4] This ethos was not shared by Fine Gael's senior politicians, who despised de Valera's ability to exploit nationalism to win support for policies which were opposed to the national interest as they saw it.

Like the Garda Síochána, the Blueshirts laid claim to the legacy of the Irish Volunteers. Blythe explicitly described the movement as 'the authentic successors of the volunteers', while its republican credentials were celebrated in marching songs:

> Free and faithful sons of Erin are those dauntless men in blue,
> And their fighting strength and courage well the Saxon soldier knew.[5]

Central to this image was O'Duffy's depiction of the Blueshirts as the inheritors of Michael Collins's legacy. The fallen hero of the Irish revolution provided inspiration and legitimacy. The cult of Collins was celebrated by mass rallies at Béal na mBláth, parades to the cenotaph, and endless reiteration of the movement's imagined links with the Big Fella.[6] The Blueshirts, O'Duffy declared,

are doing the work for which Collins and O'Higgins gave their lives. While we uphold the ideas of these great leaders we remain, under God, the only true custodians of the national tradition of our people, the only true guardians of Ireland's historic cause. Death saw the work of our leaders unfinished. It is for us to continue that work and to be daunted by nothing, not even by death. If we die, it will be as guardians of the cause for which Collins was a martyr.[7]

The obvious corollary of the cult of Collins was the depiction of O'Duffy as his successor. Shortly before he took over the movement, *Hymn of the Comrades* had prophesied that God would raise 'another Collins...One whom men will follow far.'[8] The General lost no opportunity to lay claim to the legacy of Collins (although much less was said about O'Higgins and Griffith). A notice for the Béal na mBláth commemoration exhorted Blueshirts to 'Remember the words of Collins—"If I fall, you have O'Duffy".'[9] A typically sycophantic article noted 'that though the great heart of the Cúchalain of our day is stilled in death and his giant frame is mouldering in the cold grave, we have with us the legacy that Collins left us—we have O'Duffy.'[10] Although Collins was the patron saint, O'Duffy was willing to lay claim to other members of the national pantheon without undue concerns about inconsistency. The Blueshirts also posed as the inheritors of the Land League tradition: 'If Parnell or Davitt were alive today they would lash those who are driving the Irish farmers into a destitution greater than slavery.'[11] Sharing a platform with John Redmond's daughter-in-law in Co. Waterford, O'Duffy declared that if Redmond were alive, he too 'would be on the platform of United Ireland'.[12]

The return to nationalism mobilized a treatyite constituency which had been neglected by Cumann na nGaedheal. It appealed to the movement's regional leadership of disgruntled ex-army officers such as Colonel Jerry Ryan, Colonel Paddy Coughlan, Colonel Tom Carew, Major Dalton, Captain John Sullivan, Captain Padraig Quinn, Captain Denis Quish, Captain Sean Keane, and Lieutenant Pa Quinlan, whose disillusionment in some cases dated back to 1924 when they had absconded with their weapons. It attracted the National Defence Association veterans, the men whom O'Duffy had considered as candidates for his armed militias, and the Civil War veterans who resented the transition of 1932. At the higher echelon of the movement, O'Duffy attempted to broaden its nationalist base by inviting General MacEoin and General Mulcahy into his inner circle. Although Fianna Fail's rise to power had demonstrated the importance of nationalism, it was the first time since the Civil War that a treatyite leader had challenged republicans on patriotic grounds.

O'Duffy drew attention to the incompatibility between Fianna Fáil's constitutional strategy and the IRA's anti-state politics in an attempt to divide republicans. Cultural nationalism provided another line of attack for O'Duffy, who rehearsed his Irish Ireland credentials, while pointing out that de Valera, a Blackrock College old boy, was 'a Rugby enthusiast'.[13] *United Ireland* attacked Seán MacEntee—'the Minister for Jazz'—for allowing the national broadcasting station to 'ooze sponsored jazz'. Nor was MacEntee the sole jiver in the cabinet: 'MacEntee and Ruttledge, apparently for sheer joie de vivre, danced in the New Year at the Gresham Hotel ... on Monday the full team of MacEntee, Ruttledge and Lemass, augmented on this occasion by Mr. O'Kelly (who announced at Ottawa that he did not dance owing to a bullet in his knee) took the floor again at the Metropole.'[14] Such juvenile taunts illustrated the Blueshirts' attempts to embrace a more populist nationalism than Cumann na nGaedheal, which republican propaganda had successfully associated with formal dances, top hats, and indifference to the patriotism of the plain people of Ireland. Fine Gael pledged itself to the Pearsean ideal of a Gaelic Ireland: 'We want Ireland not only to be free, but to be Gaelic as well, and not only to be Gaelic, but to be free from sea to sea.'[15]

However, O'Duffy's use of nationalism was problematic on a number of levels. Despite his rhetoric of national unity, treatyite republicanism necessitated a return to Civil War politics. Blueshirt activities frequently centred on commemoration of the Civil War dead.[16] Whereas Cumann na nGaedheal, wary of identifying loyalty to the state with treatyite politics, had neglected such commemoration, O'Duffy had no reservations in stoking Civil War hatreds. Many of the counties where the Blueshirts were strongest were those where the IRA was most militant; memories of the Civil War, and violence between republicans and Blueshirts, reinforced support for both movements.[17] This Civil War agenda was most crudely expressed whenever O'Duffy returned to Monaghan (where Cumann na nGaedheal had humiliatingly lost its only seat in 1933). At a meeting in February 1934, he unleashed an onslaught on his long-standing local nemesis, the parliamentary deputy Dr Conn Ward:

Conn of the hundred battles. (Laughter). Conn who made the Black and Tans shiver in their skins in that county, and before whom the British auxiliaries cowered in their Glengarrys. Fianna Fail asserted that it was the Republican Party, but the great majority of the leaders in this county only became Republicans when the Black and Tans left Ireland. (Loud applause). When they satisfied themselves that they could safely shout 'Up the Republic' and escape with their whole skins, and at the same time hold their comfortable jobs, they became Republicans.[18]

In May 1934 he returned to Ballytrain, scene of his greatest triumph, to launch another broadside against his local enemies:

When he brought a party to Ballytrain to risk their lives in the famous barrack attack they were poorly armed, and their strongest weapon was, perhaps, an old revolver that hadn't fired a shot for over 100 years. But they took the barracks. I would be reluctant to boast had blackguards and cowards not belittled my efforts then, but when we blew a hole in the wall it was I who entered that breach in face of rifles, and we took that barracks—the first barracks taken in Ireland. He would go so far as say that 99 per cent of the people in that attack 'funked' it. He knew them and could place his hand on them. There were cousins of his own who denied him the drink of water but God save Ireland from such creatures.[19]

Such speeches illustrated a glaring contradiction within Blueshirt rhetoric. O'Duffy's willingness to revive Civil War hatred conflicted with his fascistic pleas for Irish youth to turn against the 'old gang' and embrace 'a national spiritual awakening' that would 'substitute unity for sectionalism'. This contradiction might be seen as an aspect of O'Duffy's tendency to project his own shortcomings onto others. Despite doing more than any other individual to embitter Irish politics in the 1930s, he genuinely regarded himself as a victim of base partisanship, a 'noble spirit' who never said 'an unkind word' against those who slandered and persecuted him.[20] In reality, his dismissal of his rivals as 'sham patriots' who use 'their avowed profession of super patriotism as a convenient cloak to garb their own selfishness and dishonesty' mirrored their view of him. Just as O'Duffy accused de Valera of aiming to 'consolidate alien control of Ireland', republicans depicted the General as the willing servant of British interests.[21]

O'Duffy's attempt to exploit populist nationalism was doomed to failure, but not because of its lack of appeal. In contrast to Britain, where Oswald Mosley's political aspirations were constrained by the absence of a populist nationalist tradition, Irish politics offered much more promising ground.[22] Separatism, an élitist militant tradition, dedicated to the achievement of the national will, even when it conflicted with the democratic expression of the people, was more than susceptible of mobilization to fascist ends.[23] Anti-enlightenment thought—including opposition to rationalism, liberalism, socialism, materialism, and individualism—was well established in the political culture of Catholic Ireland. The idea of mobilizing a mythic past to serve as the basis of a resurrected Irish nation was not seen as exotic fantasy by a generation of activists which had come to power due to the cultural nationalist revival and Pearse's sacrifice in 1916.[24] The legacy of a humiliating treaty which limited national sovereignty was as capable of winning political support in Ireland as in Germany. Interestingly, a close reading of Blueshirt propaganda suggests that the movement's zealous nationalism was influenced by fascist ideology. Patriotism occupied a specific function in the fascistic rhetoric of O'Duffy and his inner circle which was not apparent in the propaganda of Fianna Fáil. It was identified with 'a complete change in the spirit of politics', one which would transcend the selfishness, dishonesty, and bitterness of party politics, replacing it with 'a strong and all-pervading love of country'.[25]

However, as the personification of the treatyite cause, O'Duffy was never in a realistic position to manipulate such forces, no matter how extreme his rhetoric. His militant rhetoric appealed to a limited political constituency and was often counter-productive. After a poor electoral showing in Leinster, for example, he declared: 'We know what Wicklow and Kildare did from 1916 to 1921. I met an old lady over there with an apron and if she shook that apron she would beat what I.R.A. they had in these counties.'[26] On another occasion, he claimed that 'Kerry's entire record in the Black and Tan struggle consisted in shooting an unfortunate soldier the day of the truce'.[27] Such outbursts prompted the *Irish Press* to assign a reporter to follow him around the country.[28]

O'Duffy's republicanism irritated many ex-Unionists who had supported the treatyite party since the Civil War and undermined his standing among

Fine Gael's moderate leaders. During the first months of his presidency, he supported his party's policy of unification through conciliation and cross-border co-operation as 'plain common-sense', adding regretfully that its 'only defect is that it is unbellicose and unromantic'. He criticized de Valera for 'sparring with the British and directing waves of hot air against the North. Does he expect us to believe that the boundary can be removed without negotiation with the people of the North?'[29] He described Fine Gael's Commonwealth policy as 'a matter of good business' rather than 'fidelity to forms of symbols', criticizing de Valera's ambivalence: 'they have not the courage to go out decently or to stay in decently, and the country is suffering as a result.'[30]

However, such sentiments did not reflect his own republicanism, which quickly surfaced when provoked. On one occasion he declared it 'mere childishness...to demand from us frank and open allegiance to the Commonwealth—whatever that may mean—while we know, and everybody knows, how our fellow-Irishmen are being governed, under the shadow of the British Commonwealth, in Northern Ireland'.[31] The Blueshirts, he claimed, would be delighted to support de Valera in declaring a Republic 'if we believed he meant what he said'.[32] This tendency grew more pronounced in the final months of his presidency. At a meeting in Cavan, he responded to reports that Britain was fortifying its defences in Northern Ireland by declaring: 'If that is for war against this country, please God I will be in that war. I am one of those who think the only pleasure in freedom is fighting for it. I believe that 95 per cent of the Blueshirts, against whom stones are being thrown by corner-boys, would be with me in that war if it was declared.'[33] Far from building bridges to the north, as Fine Gael had hoped, O'Duffy was made the subject of an exclusion order by the Stormont government.[34]

The General's refusal to apologize for these outbursts was a major reason why the moderates eventually moved against him.[35] MacDermot observed that O'Duffy spent an increasingly 'large part of every speech by unsaying or explaining away something that he had said before'.[36] *United Ireland* would also complain about 'the absurdities and contradictions which had so often embarrassed and shaken the confidence of supporters'.[37] But although O'Duffy's rhetoric demonstrated that his political tact had not improved since his 'Give them lead' speech, his populist instincts held more public appeal than his colleagues' pro-Commonwealth position. O'Duffy's simple nationalism—'My ambition in life is to see my country enjoy the greatest possible measure of her independence'—reflected that of Collins and the pro-treaty republicans who had defended the state since the Civil War. Soon after his resignation, O'Duffy would denounce Fine Gael as 'the pan-British party of the Free State'.[38] He resigned, he claimed, 'because he was not prepared to lead the League of Youth with the Union Jack tied to his neck'.[39] Despite the overblown rhetoric, many treatyites would have agreed with his critique of Fine Gael's position on the national question:

Fine Gael say they are the Treaty party. May I ask which Treaty? You could hardly recognise it now. Many of its main provisions are already gone, and I do not think any party will ever attempt to restore them. If acceptance of the Treaty position means renunciation of the teachings of Parnell and Pearse, of Griffith and Collins, then away with it ... We have worked the Treaty, recognising it as an advance, and we put up with Commonwealth status for almost 14 years ... The epithet 'Free State' is now regarded as an insult by our youth. Our Army desires to be known as the 'National' rather than the 'Free State' Army, and our Cabinet Ministers would not wish to be referred to as His Majesty's Ministers for that portion of the Empire known as the Free State. Indeed few in the Free State are enthusiastic over the status the Treaty gives us.[40]

These were harsh truths which his colleagues had failed to recognize. The political logic imposed by the Civil War had bound the opposition to an anachronistic position that increasingly lacked popular support, one which Fianna Fáil's advances made ever more redundant.

A self-respecting nation

O'Duffy's deviations from the party line on economic issues, while irritating to his colleagues, also reflected a firmer grasp of popular sentiment than the treatyite party had traditionally demonstrated. Fine Gael's agricultural policy sought a return to the dependency on cattle exports which had enriched a minority of the rural population but frustrated many land-hungry farmers. O'Duffy, who had experienced smallholder poverty, was never comfortable with his party's association with the grazier élite. 'The U.I.P.', he declared, 'was not a Ranchers' Party. They did not give a damn about the ranchers, and if the U.I.P. were a rich man's party he would not be in that party.'[41] Such rhetoric intensified after the disappointing local election results in July 1934, when he accused large farmers of deserting Fine Gael. In the course of a rambling speech, he declared: 'If this were a ranchers' platform I would not be on it. They had the poor behind them. What country in the world to-day had stood by the parliamentary system?'[42] The outburst suggests that his reservations about his party's rural policy stemmed from his populist instincts: 'O'Duffy, for all his demagogic faults, recognised the need to forge a wider coalition of malcontents.'[43] There was also a broader ideological impulse at work. O'Duffy believed that he represented the interests of the ordinary man: 'The movement was depending on the shilling or the half-crown of the Blueshirts'.[44] He led a movement which represented the best of the nation, rather than a mere party which exploited sectional interests. Such an outlook reflected a well-established discourse in nationalist politics, but it also complemented the rhetoric of inter-war fascists who exulted in subordinating the interests of the individual to the nation.

His opponents were quick to exploit the contradictions in his populist stance on the land question: 'If the statements of the Director-General of the party may be taken seriously, the Farmers' Party, the Centre Party and Cumann na nGaedheal, out of which his movement was largely built, are definitely pushed to one side.'[45] But, although he resented his party's pro-grazier image, O'Duffy did not advocate radical change in land ownership or rural policy. He supported de-rating, a measure which benefited wealthy farmers. He agreed that tillage should be encouraged but disapproved of de Valera's autarchy, seeing no reason why the government should subsidize goods which could be produced more efficiently elsewhere.[46] He opposed Fianna Fáil's redistributive policies: 'They went back to the famine for their policy. They preached a doctrine of doles and soups. Instead of appealing to the national pride and self-respect of the Irish people they appealed to their weakness.'[47] O'Duffy, in contrast, advocated a 'self-respecting nation'. He criticized the conservatism of Cumann na nGaedheal but offered no alternative to a return to dependency on the British market: 'When the O'Duffy fairs come along they would be some fairs, and we will see the happy smile on the farmers' faces again. (Applause).'[48] Such rhetoric has led to O'Duffy being described as 'a fascist, albeit one capable of striking a very traditional, rural conservative note that was almost bucolic in its simplicity'. The future he envisioned was a simple one: 'It will be a great time again when farmers can go to the fairs and come home again whistling and singing—and having a little drink if you like. (Applause). We intend bringing back that time. (Applause) I deny that I am a Dictator.'[49]

Ultimately, O'Duffy's views on the land question were inconsistent. At Fine Gael's *ard-fheis* in February 1934, he defended graziers, inquiring why 'the man who followed the calling which nature best fitted the country for, and who incidentally helped to keep our export and trade balance solvent, was regarded as an enemy of the country'.[50] Cattle farmers, after all, provided the *raison d'être* of the Blueshirt movement, which was strongest in the south-west and midlands but weaker in non-pastoral counties, even those with a strong treatyite tradition.[51] There was an important class dimension to the spectre of Irish fascism:

It appeared that the nationalist leadership was going to go beyond the traditional pieties about the need for more tillage and breaking up the ranches; above all, it seemed that the wealthy farmers were going to lose their direct access to the British market, which had been the foundation of their prosperity. The Blueshirt movement represents their revolt against this possibility, ironically employing many of the methods—resistance to cattle seizures, etc.—which had previously been employed...in the Land League struggle. Many of the wealthy farmers were prepared to break with parliamentary democracy and legality—to adopt, in short, fascist styles and rhetoric to safeguard their economic position.[52]

In this sense, at least, O'Duffy's claim to the legacy of the Land League was a valid one: 'From the boycott to Blueshirtism, the Irish agrarian revolution reached its unromantic terminus.'[53]

Coexisting with this conservative impulse, O'Duffy's awareness of the need to tap into the widespread resentment against graziers—the 8 per cent (or 33,000) of farmers who owned half the agricultural land valuation—resulted in ambivalence. It was not possible to claim popular support while defending the interests of a wealthy minority. Hence, while O'Duffy might concede that 'the few [ranchers] there are, are entitled to justice and fair play', he opposed 'a few men holding huge tracts of land and using it in an unproductive way'.[54] The purpose of such rhetoric was clear. As the *New York Times* observed, O'Duffy 'carried the Blueshirt organisation into the peasantry, Mr de Valera's own country, and planted it there whenever the economic war with England was engendering poverty and despair'.[55] In reality, this was precisely what he failed to do as small farmer interests were less directly affected by the economic war. His attempts to balance two conflicting constituencies merely resulted in a contradictory policy. He backed the violent campaign of cattle farmers against the payment of rates, while also calling for the abolition of annuities and rents on labourers' cottages—a more radical position than Fianna Fáil—in an unconvincing effort to woo the rural poor.

The General's deviation from his party's economic policies reflected similar pressures. While Fine Gael urged a return to free trade, O'Duffy believed that the protectionist experiment deserved encouragement.[56] Fianna Fáil's policy of encouraging industrialization by imposing tariffs was popular with workers and indigenous capitalists. It was also in accordance with Sinn Féin policy dating back to Arthur Griffith. Indeed, the treatyite government's refusal to adopt its own parliamentary party's protectionist policies during the 1920s had strengthened Fianna Fail's claim to the legacy of Sinn Féin, resulting in protectionism becoming 'the litmus test for differentiating between the reconstructed-revolutionary and the unwashed' elements within treatyite politics.[57] The conservative élite's political and economic drift from treatyite republicanism had created an ideological void which eased O'Duffy's emergence at the head of Fine Gael.[58] Conveniently, there was little inconsistency between the economic thinking of Irish republicans and O'Duffy's European role models. Fascism also sought to harness 'all classes to the national purpose, and to the struggle for economic self-sufficiency within a national sphere of influence'.[59] Many of O'Duffy's policies, such as his call for the creation of a labour corps of unemployed men to drain bogs, reclaim land, and reforest the nation echoed both traditional Sinn Féin ideas and the much admired example of Mussolini's Italy.

O'Duffy's speeches on social and economic policy permit some counter-factual speculation as to the likely nature of a Blueshirt régime. Like the dictatorships of Franco's Spain and Dollfuss's Austria, Irish authoritarianism would have 'defended the primacy of a constellation of conservative interests: property, church, family, the military, the administration'.[60] There would have been little attempt to control private initiative, religious freedom, civil society, or the family. With the exception of corporatism, his policies would not have differed greatly from those of Fianna Fáil. Indeed, the similarities illustrate the common ground between both sides of the Irish political divide. Although some political scientists have argued that the divisions over the treaty were based on distinctive ideological traditions, O'Duffy's agenda supports the contention that Free State politics 'were conducted on a narrowly defined nationalist consensus within which great hates grew over small divisions'.[61] However, even had he been able to establish his authority over Fine Gael, it is unlikely that O'Duffy could have mounted a serious electoral challenge to Fianna Fáil. The problem, which left- as well as right-wing republicans wrestled with, was how to challenge a party which so successfully dominated the centre ground of Irish politics and society.

The cause of discipline

A Blueshirt régime would have been distinguished not by innovative policies but by its repudiation of the democratic consensus which underpinned Irish politics, and its willingness to incorporate certain features of the fascist state such as the suppression of its enemies. (At the extreme end of this spectrum O'Duffy's adviser, Gunning, believed that the execution of 500 people would sort out the country.)[62] What follows is an attempt to analyse the extent to which O'Duffy's movement pursued a fascist agenda, despite its integration within Fine Gael. It will focus first on the liturgical elements of the movement—which historians acknowledge as the movement's most obvious debt to fascism—before examining other aspects of Blueshirt ideology which appeared to emulate fascist movements elsewhere. The intention is not to revisit the question of whether the Blueshirts were fascists but to identify how, and with what degree of success, O'Duffy's inner circle presented fascist ideas to the rank and file.

Much of the debate on the fascist nature of the Blueshirts has focused on the movement's aesthetic. The liturgical aspects of fascism (the uniforms, salutes, parades, and mass rallies) were important because they symbolized the populist ultranationalism at the core of the ideology, the notion of mobilizing the national community to resurrect the nation to greatness.[63] While most historians agree that the Blueshirts lacked the characteristics of radical fascism, their argument has been undermined (at least in popular terms) by the visual evidence provided by images of mass rallies of shirted supporters indulging in raised arm salutes and shouts of 'Hoch O'Duffy'. The Blueshirts, like other authoritarian movements, adopted some of the trappings of fascism while rejecting others: the liturgical element was enthusiastically embraced. Blueshirt meetings were elaborately choreographed affairs. O'Duffy was often met at the edge of town by a horse-back detachment, followed by long lines of shirted men, women, and children. In Newcastlewest, for example, the procession included 41 horsemen, 1,700 Blueshirts, 900 Blue blouses, and 3 bands.

Did such rallies constitute pale imitations of Nuremberg, or did they owe more to Ireland's tradition of parades and monster meetings? O'Duffy's 'fondness for outrageous rhetoric and elaborate uniforms' has been described as 'more O'Connellite than Hitlerian'.[64] The General's love of ceremonial processions, uniforms, parades, funerals, flags, and organizations pre-dated his political career, and in part reflected the popularity of liturgical processions and orchestrated ceremonies like the Eucharistic Congress. Nor was such activism unique to the Blueshirts: de Valera's rallies were also accompanied by horse-back escorts, blazing tar barrels, and torchlight processions. Contemporaries viewed Blueshirt activism in both contexts. O'Duffy's abortive march on Dublin was compared both to O'Connell's capitulation at Clontarf and Mussolini's march on Rome. Blueshirt parades, like those of the Orange Order and Hibernians, represented a show of strength and a territorial claim (which is why they were so often accompanied by violence). But socialist republicans also regarded them as fascist rallies 'intended primarily to terrorise. Blueshirts are gathered in from faraway centres, equipped with batons, knuckle-dusters and stray revolvers. The assembly is then to spread terror through the district so that the local Fascist branch may appear a formidable force, backed by an irresistible might.'[65]

A close reading of Blueshirt propaganda suggests that the movement's emphasis on mobilization in the public sphere was primarily influenced by

European fascism. In contrast to republican propagandists, Blueshirts drew inordinate attention to the emotional force of their rallies, highlighting their highly organized, disciplined, and dynamic nature, and how their atmosphere transcended sectional differences:

There was nothing like this since the Eucharistic Congress... Something unique in the history of Irish politics occurred when during the singing of the National Anthem, the whole gathering stood with arms upraised in the victory salute—not the only inspiration that Fine Gael has got from its Youth Movement... Young and old, the townsman and the farmer, the professional man and the labourer, all were there, and all felt equally happy and at home. The deeply-lined face of the sturdy, home-spun clad Connemara man, in his sixties, lighted up with joy at sight of the Blueshirts, who are the symbol of all that is best in Irish life.[66]

While the emphasis on spectacle was fascist in tone and scale, the movement drew upon established nationalist traditions such as the commemoration of fallen martyrs (as did fascist movements elsewhere). Its highly orchestrated ceremonies—such as the annual pilgrimage to Béal na mBláth (the site 'made sacred by the blood of Michael Collins')—combined Catholic nationalist and fascist traits:

General O'Duffy, accompanied by Commandant Cronin, reviewed the contingents prior to their march. He subsequently walked at the head of the procession to the Memorial, where he ascended the raised platform that fronts the monument, and from there gave the Organisation salute as the long parade passed by... the Last Post was sounded by a bugler, while the vast throng stood in silence with upraised hands. General O'Duffy then recited a decade of the Rosary in Irish, to which the responses were given by all present. This over he delivered a striking oration, which was frequently punctuated by enthusiastic cheering.[67]

But although such propaganda consciously presented Blueshirt meetings as fascistic spectacle, it does not follow that their participants experienced them in this light. A visit by O'Duffy to a rural town was an exciting event, but so too was a travelling circus or a market. Like the latter, the Blueshirt meetings were boisterous affairs, characterized by drunkenness and casual violence, often extending into the small hours. The recollections of rank-and-file Blueshirts who participated in them evoke images not so much of Weimar Germany as the Irish Civil War and earlier traditions of faction fighting. Andrew Forrest, one of the young men packed into lorries and driven long distances to riotous meetings, recalled the period with excitement but insisted that his friends had 'no love for Hitler or Mussolini'.[68] Patrick Lindsay, 'an unrepentant Blueshirt', dismissed the charge of fascism as 'total nonsense. Most of us did not know what it was and had we known we would have been totally opposed to it.'[69] While the Blueshirt press, like socialist republican propagandists, depicted the violence of this period as an ideological clash between left and right, there is little evidence that the actual participants viewed it in such exotic terms.[70]

Evidence that the rank and file remained largely oblivious to the ideological significance of such mobilization is provided by the Blueshirt leadership's unsuccessful attempts to educate their followers in the etiquette of fascist spectacle. Letters purportedly written by local activists (but authored by one of the inner circle) were published in *United Ireland* urging the adoption of the 'Victory Salute' or 'Front Line Shout'.[71] 'Onlooker' advised Blueshirts as to when it was appropriate to salute or break into song. After *The March of Youth* was designated the official rallying song, Blueshirts were informed that in 'other countries where there are powerful Youth Movements, enthusiasm is generated not merely by marching in uniform under a distinctive flag and by giving mass salutes to distinguished national leaders, but also by community singing.'[72] With the exception of the salute, these initiatives met with little enthusiasm from self-conscious Blueshirts who resisted the pleasures of submerging the ego to the collective. They were regularly chastised for not singing the *March of Youth* loud enough and for not bothering to learn the words.[73] In mitigation, Blueshirt songs were notoriously difficult to sing. Even *United Ireland* greeted the publication of three obscure songs by its short-lived Poet Laureate, W. B. Yeats, with an air of bemusement: 'One of them seems to be a poetical restatement of the central doctrine of Fascism.'[74] Moreover, the injustices of the economic war did not provide quite the same emotional register as the Tan War:

> Every Tipperary cow is shedding tears of woe;
> nevermore the milking-bane will hear a happy low.
> Pound apiece! What dacint baste could bear that bitter blow?[75]

Another aspect of Blueshirt propaganda which drew on republican and fascist inspiration was the attempt to exploit a pantheon of martyrs. Although Michael Collins and the Civil War dead were posthumously claimed as the movement's first martyrs, the violent clashes between Blueshirts and the IRA soon produced more authentic Horst Wessels. The first of these was Hugh O'Reilly, who died on 30 December 1933, two months after his night-time abduction from his Bandon home and brutal beating. His funeral was an elaborately choreographed affair, presided over by the redoubtable Bishop Cohalan: 'General O'Duffy occupied a priedieu before the High Altar while the county Deputies of Dáil Eireann were accommodated in the Sanctuary. Around the catafalque on which rested the coffin draped with the colours of the League of Youth stood a guard of honour of six comrades of the deceased. Over 1,000 members of the League of Youth all wearing Blueshirts, and several hundred women members in blue blouses occupied the nave of the church.'[76] Fifteen hundred Blueshirts marched in the 2-mile-long funeral procession.[77] During the highly politicized ceremony, Cohalan warned that governments should not become 'more anxious for the interests of the faction than for the interests of the country'. A rash of Hugh O'Reilly songs, adapting the rhetoric and themes of established republican classics, followed:

> Soldiers of the Vanguard, Youth must take the lead!
> Hugh O'Reilly watches on you—do no evil deed.
> Onward! Never falter, lads, tho' the way be hard:
> Eoin O'Duffy leads you,
> Soldiers of the Legion of the Rearguard![78]

O'Reilly was acclaimed alongside Collins in the Blueshirt anthem, *March of Youth*, while, in true republican style, competing Blueshirt factions would later fight over which group had the right to parade to his grave. Speaking at his party's *ard-fheis*, O'Duffy encouraged his men to draw inspiration from O'Reilly's fate:

What do we offer to these young people?...Not material gain certainly, but hard work, sacrifice, even death at the hands of cowardly assassins—death for a principle, a hero's death such as our comrade, Hugh O'Reilly, died. The young men who wear the blue shirts of the League of Youth and the girls who are also its members are proud of Hugh O'Reilly. They look up to him as a martyr for our cause, and they will never cease to draw inspiration and fortitude from the memory of his sacrifice.[79]

Cornelius Daly, who died following a beating on Christmas morning, was added to the 'roll of heroic martyrs in the cause of discipline' in January 1934.[80] In June Patrick Kenny, a 21-year-old from rural Tipperary, died from injuries sustained at a Blueshirt meeting.[81] In his graveside oration, O'Duffy predicted that 'more sacrifices will have to be made in the Great Cause'.[82] And so they were, young Michael Lynch from Cork joining 'the pantheon of fascist heroism' in August 1934.[83]

Back to Tara

While not unique to fascism, the cult of the heroic leader played a central role in fascist movements. Historians have underestimated this aspect of the Blueshirts.

Joe Lee, for example, has claimed: 'The Hero did not feature prominently in the pantheon of Blueshirt man . . . Fianna Fáil extended its emotional sway over past as well as present, establishing a virtual monopoly on the historical mythology market'.[84] In contrast, Mike Cronin has argued that O'Duffy did inspire a cult of leadership among the faithful: 'To those men he did appear as a saviour of State, and despite his failings he was a hero in their minds'.[85] O'Duffy's indifferent oratory, lack of charisma, and intellectual limitations have facilitated his posthumous dismissal as a buffoon. Many dictators, however, were dismissed as absurdities until they harnessed the forces of the state behind their apparently ludicrous projects. And while the Blueshirts failed to mobilize the nation around the heroic, it was not due to want of effort. O'Duffy was often depicted by his propagandists and countless impressionable foreign journalists as the Irish Mussolini. Songs like *Marching to Freedom*, *Stand for Ireland*, and *Tho' the Way be Hard, Blueshirt* depicted him as a providential hero destined to rescue the nation in its hour of need.[86]

Following the merger with Cumann na nGaedheal, however, less emphasis was placed on O'Duffy's role as leader, something the General attributed to his colleagues' jealousy. It was not until the final chaotic months of his presidency, amidst the resurgence of rural violence, that the messianic tone reappeared in Blueshirt propaganda. A young Blue blouse was struck by a vision of O'Duffy as the reincarnation of Red Hugh O'Donnell, the Gaelic chieftain who had attempted to drive the English out of Ireland: 'His blue eyes were alight, and his outstretched hand pointed in the distance, I followed the direction of his hand, and the man he was pointing to was General Eoin O'Duffy. I gazed fascinated, and as I gazed I saw lines of blue clad figures marching by.'[87] Noting the 'admiration for heroism which is so striking a feature of the Fascist regime in Italy', another Blueshirt cautioned that 'Irish boys should not forget our own great heroes', offering the example of the raid on Ballytrain barracks.[88] Blueshirts who witnessed the General's mesmerizing effect on his audiences also testified to his heroic appeal:

When General O'Duffy established the Blue Shirts, he took Ireland clean out of the slime of monstrous politics, and at one bold, imaginative stroke that had in it the magic of genius, placed his unhappy country on a level with glorious Italy . . . thinking on the real meaning of the wonderful meeting, I was struck suddenly by a strange and pleasing, if terrible truth. It is this—and I write it with something like awe: General O'Duffy is now the most powerful individual leader that Ireland has known since Charles Stewart Parnell.[89]

In reality, the gap between the heroic depiction of O'Duffy and the more mundane reality strained credibility. The testimonials to his greatness were mostly invented, and there were less than might have been expected. O'Duffy was unable to assert his authority over the Blueshirt hierarchy, let alone Fine Gael. He was popular with the Blueshirt rank and file but, as the split would reveal, he did not even enjoy the obedience of its national or regional leadership. He was a poor judge of character, unable to dominate or marginalize rivals such as Cronin. In contrast to his earlier positions, he surrounded himself with sycophants of limited ability and integrity. His fickle allies, figures like Blythe, Gunning, and Paddy Belton, were political lightweights. He possessed the ego but not the calculating ruthlessness of a dictator. As *The Round Table*'s correspondent noted, he was 'much too genial to fill the role of a Mussolini, which his admirers thrust upon him'.[90] F. S. L. Lyons similarly observed that 'the real trouble with O'Duffy was not that he was cold-heartedly authoritarian, but that he was warm-heartedly incompetent'.[91] The younger, meaner, O'Duffy would have been a more formidable proposition. His inability to inspire loyalty, and the jealousy and infighting within the upper echelon of his movement, helps to explain his failure to dominate Fine Gael and the abruptness of his subsequent fall from power. It was not until after the split that O'Duffy would dominate his movement, by which time it had shrunk to insignificance.

The use of historical mythology, an important aspect of fascist ideology, featured strongly in Blueshirt propaganda. The blue shirt and red cross were selected as symbols of the movement because of their association with St Patrick, who fulfilled a similar role in Irish fascist iconography as Joan of Arc in the French version.[92] Although pre-Christian mythology had provided inspiration for cultural nationalists like Patrick Pearse, the inner circle's heavy-handed attempts to mobilize mythical figures like Cuchulain were more influenced by European fascism. 'Onlooker' suggested building a National Palace of Victory at Tara, the sacred coronation site of ancient Irish kings, after Fine Gael's victory, an idea enthusiastically promoted in another unsung anthem, *Back to Tara*.[93] Gunning urged replacing British statues with heroic figures like Brian Boru and Niall of the Nine Hostages:

Our whole outlook is still bounded by the confines of the Anglo-Irish struggle. Our best history lies outside that boundary...The salvation of this age must come mainly from the Heroic Ages...We must try to take up the spiritual threads and draw them together again. We must teach our children of their glorious and heroic heritage as freemen and of the valour and discipline and order and all the high nobility of that life which revolved around Royal Tara.[94]

Although the League of Youth's first congress called for the restoration of Tara as the national capital, there is little evidence that these exotic ideas attracted much interest among the rank and file, or that the attempts to exploit ancient mythology proved any more successful than the efforts to create a heroic leader.[95]

A great virile national organization

O'Duffy's ideas about the role of youth and women are of interest, given their importance within other authoritarian movements. Despite the masculine and aggressively anti-feminist nature of fascism, the far right proved successful in soliciting female support. This was also true of the Blueshirts: women comprised around a quarter of its membership.[96] The Blue blouses, many of them young and single, were attracted by the same factors which appealed to young men. As one member recalled, the movement enlivened rural life at a time when 'Sitting on a stile was considered amusement enough for teenage youngsters. Grown men could look forward to the occasional wake.'[97] Sporting competitions, whist-drives, picnics, hikes, dances, and other entertaining activities facilitated social interaction away from the prying eyes of priests and parents.[98] O'Duffy encouraged female participation in the movement, chastising an audience in Cavan because 'he did not see any ladies present; in other places the first four seats at the Conventions were occupied by girls wearing blue blouses, and he advised them to get in the ladies'.[99]

One of the ironies of the far right's success in recruiting females was that, rather than reinforcing the traditional role of women in the home, the mobilization of women in the public sphere constituted a very modern form of politicization. However, the role of Blue blouses was carefully demarcated: they were encouraged to confine their interests to the domestic sphere (for example, by taking classes on housewifery) rather than economic or public life.[100] Uniforms and parading were optional—although the pictorial evidence and the complaints about girls giggling on parade—suggest both were popular. As in the IRA's female auxiliary, women were organized in segregated units, but Cumann na mBan did not provide a model for Blue blouses. Denouncing that organization's assertiveness, O'Duffy curtly insisted: 'We want no chin straps'.[101] Blue blouses were expected to perform organisational roles appropriate to their gender. Aside from catering, their principal duties were canvassing and fund-raising. When the Blueshirts ran into financial difficulties in 1934, its Victory Fund was largely collected by women.[102] And, although women were prominent in terms of numbers and activism, they were absent from the leadership of the movement.

In contrast to the marginal position of women, O'Duffy believed that the role of youth was pivotal to the Blueshirts (which he often described as 'our Youth movement'). His decision to rename his movement the League of Youth signified his belief 'that there is a wisdom of youth which is no less valuable in public affairs than the wisdom of age'.[103] His speech at the *ard-fheis* was characteristic: 'As I have said a hundred times before, our strength is in our youth, in the young manhood of Ireland which is rising as it never rose before'.[104] As with his earlier efforts to recruit young people into sporting organizations, the focus of his rhetoric was adolescent boys rather than girls: 'It is significant that our membership should be drawn largely from those who have barely reached the age of manhood'.[105] Despite railing against the politicization of children by his opponents, O'Duffy urged his followers to organize children's clubs in every parish to inculcate the values of disciplined public service. In some towns fighting between the children of republicans and shirted boys broke out in schools.[106]

His motives reflected those of his earlier sporting crusade, in particular his desire to build character and disseminate the citizenship ideal. He used sport to mobilize support among the youth, and demonstrate the strength and vitality of his movement. Such events formed a vital aspect of the movement's appeal in rural Ireland.[107] After failing to gain control of the GAA, O'Duffy established the Blueshirt Athletic Association in June 1934 to foster 'a love for manly outdoor sport and indoor recreation'.[108] (It was decided that the GAA would come under his movement's formal control after Fine Gael's election.) Despite his transparently political exploitation of sports, Mike Cronin suggests that the rank and file failed to detect any ideological purpose behind such activities: 'As with many other areas of Blueshirt policy, the activities of the members seemed to be a million miles removed from the expectations of the movement's hierarchy. The motivation for the member was pure self-indulgent enjoyment.'[109]

The General's preoccupation with youth and sport formed part of a broader attempt to depict his movement, despite its core of middle-aged veterans, as a 'great virile national organisation'.[110] This manly élite was favourably compared to the effete old guard of Irish politics, including the former Cumann na nGaedheal politicians who were criticized for wearing the blue shirts intended to distinguish those pledged 'to do personal service and to face any special risks that are going'.[111] It was 'the spirit and enthusiasm' of the Blueshirts which would ultimately 'dominate the organisation as a whole'.[112] The cult of the physical body (evidenced by the body building and exercise tips in Blueshirt newspapers, the movement's objective of promoting physical fitness, and its devotion to sport) reflected a prioritizing of masculinity common to all forms of fascism.[113] This exaltation of virility was an exaggerated distortion of the traditional belief that manliness could ameliorate the social and national problems which were responsible for the physical and moral decline of the individual and society.[114]

Recent research has highlighted the importance of such thought within fascism. It has been argued that the 'reassertion of masculinity and the violent rooting out of all vestiges of effeminacy was at the heart of British fascist politics in the 1930s'.[115] Moreover, these ideas were not simply borrowed from Europe but rooted in the militaristic masculinity of Victorian and Edwardian Britain. The politics of the BUF have been described 'as the ethos of public school masculinity as a political programme'.[116] Given the similarities between the imperialist and Gaelic sporting ethos previously highlighted, it is not surprising that much of the rhetoric of British fascism should seem so familiar. The BUF championed 'virile government', 'the spirit of British manhood', 'manliness, courage, thought and discipline', 'hardness', 'the full beauty of our manhood', 'our ordered athleticism of life', 'the virility of its manhood', and the 'masculine spirit' while denigrating 'pale, weak, bespectacled youths', 'the Pink and the Pansy', 'middle-aged softies', and the 'softness' of liberal democracy. In Ireland, as in Britain, the fascistic exaltation of hard-bodied virility exaggerated an ethos which was embedded in the popular culture, tapping into the widely shared anxiety that the nation was being undermined by decadence and modernism.

In contrast to many variants of fascism, racism and anti-Semitism did not play an important role in Blueshirt ideology. Nonetheless, Irish Jews were sufficiently alarmed by the National Guard's exclusion of non-Christians to seek a meeting with O'Duffy 'who assured them that he was not against Jews generally'.[117] Long before O'Duffy joined the Blueshirts, there had been an undercurrent of anti-Semitism in treatyite rhetoric which was much less evident in republican propaganda. Robert Briscoe, the most prominent Jew in Fianna Fáil, had been a frequent target of Cumann na nGaedheal's invective. Among other transgressions, 'Bobski Briski' was accused of importing Russian aliens and liaising between Russia and the Irish left.[118] When de Valera responded to persistent anti-Semitic abuse by pointing out that his paternal background was Spanish rather than Jewish, sceptical Blueshirts drew attention to the high level of Jewish immigration to Spain during the Moorish occupation.[119] Although such rhetoric intensified in the Blueshirt era, it reflected Catholic traditions of anti-Semitism more than the influence of fascism. Anti-Semitism remained more prevalent in periodicals such as the *Catholic Bulletin* than Blueshirt propaganda and did not form a central aspect of Blueshirt ideology or activity.[120]

Although racism was not an essential prerequisite of fascism (as the example of Italy demonstrates), fascist movements were invariably characterized by a xenophobic mentality. Irish anti-Semitism, whether in the Blueshirts or society generally, formed part of a broader xenophobia characteristic of an extreme Irish Ireland mentality. Much of it was opportunistically aimed at the American-born de Valera. One of 'Onlooker's preoccupations, shared by O'Duffy, concerned the danger of foreigners exercising influence in Irish affairs. Blythe, a descendent of Planter stock, believed 'that no question can be raised about any man whose people have been in the country even for two or three generations. The difficulties come when we have to decide about people who though born in Ireland were born of foreign parents, about people who were born abroad of Irish parents, about people of mixed parentage whether born in Ireland or abroad.'[121] Lest anyone miss his point, Blythe elaborated: 'if the parents have become, say, American citizens, their child, born in America, is clearly an American and not Irish . . . If the birthplace is foreign and the domicile of the parents is foreign, and one of the parents, particularly the father, is foreign, then the child can be by no stretch regarded as Irish.' Also excluded from Blythe's national community were voluntary emigrants, emigrants who chose not to return, and involuntary emigrants who posed as superior patriots. The problem with foreigners like de Valera, even if they mastered Ireland's language and history, was that because they understood Irish nationality only as an abstract ideal they were willing to sacrifice the true interests of the people in favour of their 'own ideal conception of what they ought to be'. Motions at Fine Gael's *ard-fheis* advocated that the presidency be restricted to 'a true born son of Ireland' and that cabinet ministers 'be the children of Irish parents on both sides'.[122]

There are countless examples of Blueshirt xenophobia. Denis Quish insisted that the Blueshirts did not owe allegiance to a government 'of Spaniards, Jews and Englishmen'.[123] Ned Cronin (unlike O'Duffy an outspoken anti-Semite) did not object to people 'with foreign blood in their veins' like de Valera and Briscoe residing in Ireland but felt that 'if they were going to live here and be tolerated they must become decent citizens'.[124] A less liberal Blueshirt urged the repatriation of 'foreign-born or unassimilated' agitators like 'the de Valeras, the Larkins, the Madam Gonnes, the Hugo Flinns, and so forth'.[125] Blueshirts derived great pleasure from alluding to de Valera's exotic origins in songs which referred to 'the Spaniard's cruel laws', the 'Spaniard's thrall', the 'Spanish vendetta', and the 'Mexican Dictatorship'.[126]

O'Duffy occasionally indulged in this sort of rhetoric, urging Blueshirts to 'stand by your own, against the de Valeras, the Briscoes, the Lemasses, the Hugo Flinns, the Aikens and the Ruttledges'.[127] Like many Irish Catholics, he associated Jews with communism and viewed white supremacy as a given, but there is little evidence to support the assertion that racism or anti-Semitism formed 'an integral feature of his Fascist philosophy'.[128] This charge stems from O'Duffy's alleged support for an anti-Semitic resolution at a fascist conference in Switzerland in late 1934. However, the Montreux resolution had actually opposed racial persecution, merely condemning those Jews who exercised 'an influence harmful to the material and moral interests of the nation which shelters them'.[129] O'Duffy, moreover, had sided with the Italian sponsors of the conference for whom Mussolini's 'universalism' represented an important ideological distinction from Nazi racism against an anti-Semitic motion proposed by the Romanian Iron Guard. O'Duffy had told the conference that 'they had no Jewish problem in Ireland' and that he 'could not subscribe to the principle of the persecution of any race'.[130] The following year, O'Duffy's newspaper attacked the anti-Semitic Aontas Gaedheal: 'we do not admire anti-Semitism as a panacea for all or any national ills; there is no justification, to our mind, for singling out Jews for persecution just because they are Jews'.[131] It also attacked 'chief Jewbaiter' Julius Streicher and 'the intolerant and tyrannical persecution of religion which Hitler stands over'.[132]

As with many issues, O'Duffy's personal views are not very clear. During the same period that his movement was denouncing anti-Semitism, he complained about the opposition to his party from ranchers, gombeen-men, Freemasons, and Jews. He had no hesitation in aligning himself with rabid anti-Semites such as Paddy Belton and some of his most fanatical supporters in later years were extreme anti-Semites. His criticism of anti-Semitism may simply have been intended to curry favour with Mussolini. By 1936 O'Duffy was complaining about Jewish influence in the Irish Free State, and the more anti-Semitism dominated international fascism the more this was reflected by his rhetoric.[133] The evidence would suggest that like Mussolini he was an unprincipled opportunist rather than a dedicated anti-Semite—a conclusion which hardly renders him a more endearing figure.[134]

Anti-communism, a vital element of far-right politics, appeared to offer more domestic potential than anti-Semitism. Blueshirt preoccupation with this issue preceded O'Duffy, but under his leadership it took precedence over the more popular commitment to free speech.[135] The establishment of the National Guard had coincided with a resurgence of popular anti-communism triggered by the formation of the Communist Party of Ireland, and a campaign by church and state to deport Jim Gralton (a Leitrim-born communist proselytizer with American citizenship). Blueshirts had been among the hymn-singing mob which burned down the communist-owned Connolly House, but the main impetus had come from the clerical press and militant Catholic organizations.[136] The fear of communism, which O'Duffy had successfully exploited as commissioner, provided a useful mobilizing cause and a rationale for his apocalyptic predictions. While touring the country, he cited the reports which he had seen as commissioner as evidence of the communist threat. In Castlecomer he warned of the existence of a heavily armed 'Communist anti-God cell' while, much to the irritation of its county council, he claimed that Sligo was infiltrated by red cells.[137]

In contrast to most of his extreme views, O'Duffy's rabid anti-communism was widely shared by his colleagues. The normally level-headed James Dillon urged the residents of Boyle to drag communism 'and its agents into the open, expose it, and destroy it'.[138] Cosgrave accused Fianna Fáil of paving the way for communism.[139] T. F. O'Higgins described de Valera as an 'arch-Communist agent'.[140] FitzGerald-Kenney believed that the government was 'leading young men along the path that led to the burning of the churches in Spain'.[141] But, despite the political and popular constituency for anti-communism, there were limits to its effectiveness. O'Duffy's campaign against the deranged Irish-American John Barry provides one example. In 1933 Barry's implausibly titled organization—the Irish Workers' Republican, Atheist, Birth Control, Civil and Industrial Emancipation Alliance—announced its intention to host an international anti-God congress in Galway. The objectives of the alliance, presumably a one-man band, included the building of longitudinal, transverse, diagonal, and coastal concrete highways, the eradication of 'priestcraft and skypilot manipulation of education', the planting of fruit trees along roads, and the architectural remodelling of villages to supply them with astronomical observatories, electric yachts, and dirigible airships. Despite the lunacy of Barry's manifesto, Leitrim county council and some local priests joined the campaign against the congress.[142] Although a raft of resolutions at Fine Gael's *ard-fheis* blamed the government for the decision to locate the congress in Ireland and called for the banning of communism, the failure of the congress to materialize left O'Duffy looking foolish.[143] The General was taken in again several months later, when it was revealed that another fantastic conspiracy which he and the *Standard* had publicized was the invention of a disgruntled ex-communist whom they had paid for the information.[144]

Despite the public enthusiasm for red scares, the decision to make anti-communism such a central policy in a country where few communists existed was questionable. As with many aspects of the leadership's agenda, it was an issue of little concern to the rank and file. Few Blueshirts cited anti-communism as a motive for joining the movement and many 'positively scorned the idea', dismissing it 'as an attempt by the Blueshirt hierarchy and the Church to drum up support'.[145] By late 1934, de Valera's success in curbing IRA violence and the collapse of Republican Congress rendered anti-communism a redundant force: 'the Red Scare proved to be a flimsy base on which to build a political career, and as the spectre of the communist menace receded from Irish minds, so did O'Duffy'.[146]

Regardless of how serious the General considered the red threat, the underlying purpose of his anti-communist rhetoric was to undermine the legitimacy of the government. 'Everything that was now happening in Ireland happened in Soviet Russia before Communism got a grip on that country. The seizure by the State of the property of one section of the people, and the jailing of the owners if they made a fight for their own, the wholesale distribution of doles and bribes, the outlawing of the most law abiding section of the community, the banning of peaceful organisations like the League of Youth, the toleration of an Irregular Army, the attacks on the clergy.'[147] The fact that Fine Gael's politicians also believed that the government harboured dictatorial ambitions which could only be opposed by the Blueshirts raises interesting questions about the relationship between the party and its shirted auxiliary which would come to a head in the summer of 1934.

What sort of role did Fine Gael envisage for the Blueshirts after its election? Did O'Duffy intend to use Fine Gael's mandate to introduce a corporate state? O'Duffy and the inner circle expected the Blueshirts to be integrated into the state after Fine Gael's electoral victory.[148] Blueshirt documents proposed that the movement would detach itself from the party to establish the corporations which would exercise power on behalf of the most conscientious elements of the community: 'This may be attacked as undemocratic and Fascist, but it is necessary.' The parish councils which would form the basis of the corporations would recruit 'the most intelligent, most industrious and most patriotic', while excluding 'the very old, those who had any ill-reputation, the wind-bags, the notoriously lazy, the drunkards', and 'bad farmers'.[149] Cumann na nGaedheal, however, had spent the last decade creating a constitutional democracy in which the functions of the governing party were carefully demarcated from the powers of the state. Given the fundamental divisions within the party, it was not surprising that the future of the Blueshirt movement under a Fine Gael government remained a thorny question.[150]

Such proposals, along with his unguarded outbursts, left no doubt that O'Duffy's ultimate ambition was dictatorship: 'What country in the world to-day had stood by the parliamentary system? Not one country except John Bull. It is gone all over Europe.'[151] This was widely understood by his admirers and enemies. Dino Grandi, the Italian ambassador in London, informed Mussolini 'that there exists today in Ireland a man and a movement who take their inspiration from the doctrine of fascism. That man and that movement appear to be destined for a very vital and very important role in the life of the country.'[152] Boasting of his support among the army and police, O'Duffy had told one fascist official that the next time he visited Rome it would be as 'leader of *Fascismo Irlandese* or as head of government'.[153] Blythe had also declared that it was the army which would decide whether the government was acting properly, and that it might prove necessary to oust Fianna Fáil with 'sword and rifle'.[154] Other reports by Italian officials in Ireland support Frank Aiken's claim that 'Ernie Blythe and a lot of Fine Gael TDs eulogized the dictatorial *principe*'. Driving from Donegal to Dublin, Aiken had been alarmed by the sight of 'Blueshirts standing at every cross-roads along the 150-mile journey, patrols of them every few hundred yards'.[155]

Aiken's fears, which may sound far-fetched, were shared by the government. A secret report described O'Duffy as a Jekyll and Hyde figure: 'Without his blue shirt he poses as the President of a political party and with it he struts about as the *Generalissimo* of a revolutionary army.'[156] Outlining his attempts to establish a 'highly developed Intelligence Organisation' involving postmasters, bus conductors, and van drivers, it noted: 'General O'Duffy is still attempting to form the youth of this country into a skeleton revolutionary army to be trained by ex-military officers—a potential insurrectionary force'. It believed that his 'inner circle' sought to capture control of Fine Gael to advance its revolutionary aims: 'Instead of the National Guard being swallowed by the U.I.P., as we were all led to believe, the U.I.P. is eventually to be swallowed by the National Guard'. Given O'Duffy's limitations, it is clear that there was little chance of this happening, but it seems reasonable to assume that it was his intention.

Revealingly, the General's colleagues had also become alarmed by his ambitions. Frank MacDermot, the party's urbane vice-president, resented the idea of the Blueshirts as 'a sort of military ascendancy . . . to prevent their political opponents getting back into power'. He regularly criticized the movement's propaganda at the national executive meetings: 'I hate scurrility'.[157] He wrote to the General in July, formally criticizing him for advocating 'a Blue Shirt ascendancy modelled on Fascism' when only 'a small fraction of our Party desire to discard Parliamentary Democracy'. O'Duffy replied that he merely wanted to improve Irish democracy, adding that it was 'aiming very high to get every member of a heterogeneous party like ours to voice exactly the same views all the time'. MacDermot's request for permission to publish the exchange was ignored by O'Duffy, who went on to declare at his next meeting that 'Hitler had done more for Germany than any other leader in the world'.[158]

MacDermot was not the only one to express such concerns. Standing behind O'Duffy as he addressed an audience of thousands in west Cork, James Dillon experienced a moment of revelation:

He was speaking very rapidly. It dawned on me that they were hanging on his words in a kind of obsessed way and I suddenly realized that he was speaking without any verbs. It had no discernible meaning. It dawned on me that if this fellah told them to go and burn the town, they'd do it. I thought: 'We've got to get rid of this man—he could be dangerous'. I remembered Hitler.[159]

Dillon's recollection raises a final aspect of the Blueshirt agenda which requires analysis before turning to the split: the role of violence. Dillon's belief that 'something dangerous was getting loose' reflected the increasing level of rural violence throughout the country. This violence was partly due to the intensification of conflict between Blueshirts and republicans, but it was primarily a consequence of growing anger about the economic war. Blueshirts were increasingly coming into direct conflict with the forces of the state as they attempted to enforce the payment of annuities by protesting farmers. 'Onlooker' even offered guidelines on the measured use of violence, advising 'every Blueshirt officer to keep a little list of those who have been misbehaving', particularly schoolteachers and gardaí, so that those who did the government's dirty work could later be 'ruthlessly thrown out'.[160] His approval of the beating meted out to 'a band of scoundrels' who trailed the Blueshirt flag in the mud was revealing: 'In a flash six or eight Blueshirts had broken from the ranks and were laying into the blackguards with boots, fists and batons . . . That such an insult should be offered to the flag of the League of Youth in the presence of a large number of Blueshirts would seem to show that our men have been too tolerant and long suffering in the past.'[161]

O'Duffy's rhetoric also grew more intemperate in the final months of his presidency. Blueshirts, if attacked, should 'make it such for them that they'll never be able to attack you again'.[162] He urged his followers in Cavan to give 'ten times more than they gave'.[163] In Mullingar he chastised gardaí and Blueshirts for failing to suppress the disorder caused by a few 'cornerboys', warning that interrupters would be dealt with at his next meeting.[164] At the following meeting, he recommended that 'whenever they felt in danger they should carry a baton or stick, and that if any member of the Garda took action, they should take an action.'[165] In Ballina, a week later, he delivered a rambling and incoherent oration through a hail of stones:

I say here that we can mop up the whole damn lot of them in 24 minutes . . . You see that mob. That's the kind sheltering behind Paddy Ruttledge, the present Minister for Justice . . . I was Police Commissioner for eleven years and I charge Chief Supt. O'Meara

with wilful neglect of duty. Where is he now? He knew this was going to happen...
they may put 120,000 of them in jail, there will be 120,000 more to take their place.
They will never be able to get concentration camps big enough to hold them. There's
not, he said, a man in their organisation with a drop of Imperial blood in his veins.
I believe if an English gun boat came up the Liffey it would, he said, be a blue shirt that
would fire the first shot... If any Guard left a hand on any of that mob over there
Paddy Ruttledge would know in the morning and the poor devil would be sent to
Ballinahob within 24 hours.

He concluded by instructing his followers 'to give it to them and not spare
them'. Much to their disgust, he then asked the gardaí to escort him from the
county.[166]

While Irish politics was characterized by militaristic rhetoric and a certain
degree of rough and tumble, Blueshirt rhetoric went well beyond this tradition
by presenting violence as a necessary aspect of achieving the movement's
objectives.[167] There were clear echoes of the fascist concept of national regeneration through violent struggle in O'Duffy's rhetoric: 'Some of our members
have been murdered, some are now in hospitals as a result of wounds received
from gun bullies, but these sufferings are only the birth pains of the new Irish
Nation which the Blueshirts are going to bring into being.'[168]

O'Duffy's robust attitude towards conflict was shared by the inner circle.
'Onlooker' declared that the movement was 'organised for combat and it wants
members who will not shrink from combat'.[169] Embellishing his leader's
injunction that Blueshirts should 'break the skull of anyone who said they were
traitors', Cronin urged them to 'break gobs if necessary'.[170] A police report
described a revealing incident when Cronin, Blythe, and Patrick Quinn were
heckled on their way to an all-night dance. Cronin 'jumped out of the car...
pulled a baton and challenged the crowd to come on now and shout if they
were able'. When one of the hecklers retorted, he was 'struck with batons and
wounded in the face. Both Cronin and Quinn displayed unusual bad temper
and made a shameful exhibition of themselves... Quinn remarked to the
Chief Superintendent "Do you think we are going to leave this town like mice".'
'Onlooker', who revelled in violent rhetoric, showed less mettle when put to the
test: 'Senator Blythe, although being in the centre of the scene, did nothing'.[171]
However, many other prominent Blueshirts did not shirk from violence. Sean
MacNamara, county director for Clare, received two years for the manslaugh-
ter of a republican.[172] Colonel Jerry Ryan, a member of the party's national
executive, was charged with attempted murder after shooting a rate collector.[173]
Captain Denis Quish, Limerick divisional director, was jailed for violent
misconduct. Captain Hughes and Captain Quinn were incarcerated for

lengthy sentences. Another county director torched a TD's house, after first turning his wife and children onto the road.[174] Violence and intimidation became commonplace as Blueshirt extremists placed themselves at the head of the anti-annuities campaign. It was the issue which ultimately brought O'Duffy down.

Decline and fall

Blueshirt violence, particularly attacks on the police, undermined the movement's credibility as defenders of public order and appalled those treatyite politicians who prided themselves on their law-abiding tradition. Despite the continued appearance of unity, it was not surprising that a series of self-inflicted setbacks quickly resulted in O'Duffy's swift and unceremonious fall from grace. The first of these was the local election of July 1934, the party's first test of strength. O'Duffy, swept away by the enthusiasm of his audiences, had rashly announced 'good news to give to the people . . . they were going to win every County Council in the election'.[175] Fine Gael won 7 to Fianna Fáil's 15, a solid result which was viewed as a disappointment in light of O'Duffy's prediction and the circumstances of the economic war. O'Duffy declared himself 'delighted, and particularly delighted with the result in the towns', denouncing those counties which had not supported him.[176] In contrast, *United Ireland* conceded that 'people are slow to change sides and that a good deal of additional hard work' was needed.[177] The Italian minister gave the movement just one more year of life.[178]

The following month O'Duffy announced that Fine Gael had dispensed with its organizers. Almost 50 party workers, many of them leading Blueshirts, were dropped from the payroll.[179] This was the first indication of the financial strain which Blueshirt activism, particularly the bussing of followers to meetings, had placed on the party: James Dillon described the party's debt of £8,000 as appalling.[180] The announcement was exacerbated by rumours that O'Duffy's minion, Liam Walsh, had absconded with party funds.[181] The reason O'Duffy had been appointed president, and his behaviour tolerated, was because it was believed that a charismatic leader could restore treatyite fortunes. The General's failure to do so ensured that his leadership came under pressure. It appeared, moreover, that Blueshirt membership had finally begun to decline.[182] A new note of desperation became apparent in O'Duffy's public speeches in the final messy weeks of his presidency. James Dillon later speculated that the local election had confirmed O'Duffy's belief in the futility of constitutionalism, prompting him to ease the way towards a split from Fine Gael.[183]

Another factor undermining O'Duffy's leadership, albeit one hidden from public view, was the remarkable level of animosity within the party. It was becoming increasingly obvious that Fine Gael—unkindly dubbed the 'cripple alliance' by republicans—was the product of three organizations with little in common aside from their hostility to de Valera. Most problems stemmed from the relationship between the party and the Blueshirts, and the infighting within the latter. O'Duffy, who would later relate these disputes with relish, complained that the vice-presidents (riddled with 'envy and animosity') had kept running to him with their grievances. He believed that Cronin, who had envied his leadership from the outset (and supported him only to prevent Cumann na nGaedheal from gaining control of the movement), had betrayed him by colluding with the politicians.[184] The only unifying figure was Ernest Blythe, on the grounds that he was disliked both by senior Blueshirts and the politicians: 'He out-Blueshirted the most suspicious Blueshirts in suspicion of his former colleagues'.[185]

However, it was the issue of rural violence which finally split Fine Gael. The government's decision to slaughter 200,000 cattle and distribute free beef to the poor had intensified the outrage and polarization caused by the economic war.[186] By the summer of 1934 over 40 per cent of farmers in the south and midlands had withheld their rates. The government had dissolved four county councils for encouraging the protest. Vast numbers of police were drafted in to rural areas to protect bailiffs with orders to seize cattle and goods from non-paying farmers. The latter responded by hiding their property, blocking roads, and cutting trees and telegraph wires. In an emotive echo of the Land War, the auction of seized goods, purchased by government agents for resale elsewhere, became a focus for communal violence.[187] Officially, neither Fine Gael nor the Blueshirts supported the illegal campaign or its violence. In reality, an increasingly desperate O'Duffy had decided to hitch his fortunes to the campaign, although in doing so he was encouraged by Blythe, Cronin, and other leading Blueshirts. One indication of this stance was his promotion of Paddy Belton, a right-wing firebrand who had served time for riotous behaviour at a cattle market, to Fine Gael's front-bench.[188]

The Blueshirt's first congress brought the issue of rural violence to a head in mid-August. The atmosphere at the congress was influenced by an incident which had occurred five days earlier during a sale of seized cattle in Cork. A lorry driven by Blueshirts had broken through the police cordon surrounding the sales yard; it had been followed by a group of supporters intent on forcing the abandonment of the sale as had occurred on previous occasions. This time, however, the Broy Harriers (the force of untrained ex-IRA men hastily recruited into the police by de Valera) lay in wait. They opened fire, killing Michael Lynch and injuring seven others. (The police involved were later condemned by the High Court as 'an excrescence upon that respectable body'.)[189] O'Duffy's graveside oration seized on the death of the second martyr of the summer to heighten emotions on the eve of the congress:

Was it necessary to shoot these unarmed men? Everyone who was there, Pressmen and all, will say that deliberate aim was taken. I blame the Government . . . In days to come they [Lynch's parents] will be proud of having raised a son, a martyr, who willingly gave his life for his fellow-man. All Blueshirts, I say, should try to emulate his bravery and nobleness. This is a young and great organisation.[190]

The congress which followed reflected the ugly mood of the Blueshirts. Fine Gael's leadership was criticized for failing to support rural agitation, while other radical motions called for the corporatist agenda to be more vigorously pursued and the establishment of the Blueshirts in the six counties. The demand for the scrapping of Special Branch would not have been out of place at a republican convention. A motion by Colonel Carew calling for the League of Youth to split from Fine Gael was withdrawn, but the congress formally committed the Blueshirts to supporting the illegal agitation against the economic war if the government did not cease collecting annuities. O'Duffy scotched some of the more extreme motions but promised the protesting farmers 'the wholehearted and unqualified support of the Blueshirts'. He also placed his support behind violent activists such as Colonel Jerry Ryan: 'They may keep Jerry in gaol but they will never break his spirit. We are sorry, too, that Sean McNamara is not here . . . We know that he acted in self-defence.'[191]

The decision to support the anti-annuity agitation appalled the Fine Gael moderates. Dillon described it as morally and politically indefensible but, revealingly, believed it might win the support of the national executive when it met on 30 August. Tierney—who felt that 'no responsible politician would dream of standing over' the resolution—had also had enough: 'Personally, I should prefer to be off, and intend to try and drop out unobtrusively if I can as an alternative to resigning later on.'[192] Even the rank and file were becoming aware of the rifts within the party: a police report noted the 'feeling of certain delegates leaving the convention . . . that all is not well'.[193] The most startling demonstration of these internal tensions occurred on 14 August, when a party of Cork Blueshirts assaulted William Kent, a Fine Gael deputy, in his own home for not supporting the anti-annuities agitation. On 25 August, a week after the congress, O'Duffy told the press the rumours of a split were 'too ridiculous to deny', proceeding none the less to insist that there was 'no vestige of truth in them'.[194]

The national executive meeting on 30 August was dominated by the annuities issue. Backed by Cronin, the party moderates, led by Dillon and Tierney, had conceived a plan to force O'Duffy to back down on the controversial resolution without having to resign.[195] Tierney reported to the absent MacDermot that 'all the Fine Gael type of people' opposed the resolution, while the Blueshirts supported it: 'some very curious speeches were made. The General himself began mildly, but gradually an atmosphere developed with which I think you are familiar—a suggestion that any criticism was an attack on the Blueshirts or himself.' Tierney insisted it was time the party stopped 'sitting harmlessly in Dublin and letting every lunatic in the country decide their policy for them. Quinn of Galway and a new recruit, from Arklow, I think, were very hot in their desire for action. The latter even thought there was no reason why we should not derail trains.'[196] Cosgrave, however, made it clear there could be no justification for civil disobedience, a strategy which would place the party on a par with de Valera's Civil War stance: 'I will never hold the basin while he washes his guilty hands'. He drew on the legacy of the Civil War to urge a unified moderate position: 'We have to teach the people to understand if they vote wrong, the opposition cannot pull the chestnuts out of the fire for them. Fianna Fail is neither honest nor democratic, nor national. But we have not succeeded in getting that over to the people.' If the opposition did not obey the law, it would be banned and a 'Mexican' dictatorship would follow.[197]

After much disagreement, a compromise was reached the following day. The resolution urging the government to cease collecting annuities would remain, but it was agreed to limit support for the anti-annuities campaign to 'practical help and assistance, consistent with the Moral Law'.[198] This outcome, however, was undermined by a careless remark by Hogan about his respect for Cronin, which, Tierney reported, had the effect of a

red rag to a long-tortured bull. He [O'Duffy] sprang up, denounced Hogan as a villain who had always been trying to oust him, and after a torrent of painful vituperation refused to allow him to explain himself. When Hogan did at length get leave to speak, he did the only thing open to him—resigned there and then. The debate went on and was ultimately wound up by a long speech from O'D, in which he represented himself as foully ill-used and finally prepared to withdraw the obnoxious resolution altogether—exactly what most of us had wanted, except that we were prepared to try some plan for gilding the pill, which he forgot all about doing in his excitement.[199]

Dillon reported that O'Duffy, never at his best when cornered, had abused Hogan 'like a fishwife', resulting in a 'most disgusting scene'.[200] Tierney, who feared that 'the whole organisation is going to drift irremediably into violence', tendered his resignation after the meeting.[201]

The following day the national executive attempted to make the best of it, issuing an upbeat account of the meeting which attributed Hogan's resignation to personal reasons and declared its unanimous confidence in O'Duffy.[202] In response, however, Hogan announced that his resignation had been due to O'Duffy's 'destructive and hysterical leadership'. In a devastating attack, the professor declared that Fine Gael had 'no future so long as it retains at its head as leader General O'Duffy. Whatever his good qualities may be, in politics I have found him to be utterly impossible. It is about time the U.I.P. gave up its hopeless attempt of saving General O'Duffy from his own errors.'[203]

O'Duffy's response was unusually dignified: 'I have seen many such onslaughts emanating from various quarters—Communist, so-called IRA, Fianna Fail, and more recently in the Unionist Press of Northern Ireland—but these, like Prof. Hogan's remarks, only urge me to greater effort.'[204] Amazingly, it appeared that O'Duffy might weather the storm. Flanked by Dillon and Cronin at Béal na mBláth on 2 September, he declared 'there is no split and never shall be'.[205] The *Cork Examiner* agreed that 'there was no question of a split', while *United Ireland* argued that Hogan's 'solitary exit' had demonstrated 'the unshaken solidarity of the movement'.[206] Tierney, who believed that O'Duffy's prestige had been irreparably damaged, was less certain: 'it is just on the cards there may be a split'.[207]

The General's self-destructive behaviour ensured it. On 3 September, he declared that de Valera 'had a perfect right to declare a Republic', reminding his followers that he had been 'sentenced to death for the Republic, and I have not changed since'.[208] The revelation, during the same week, that O'Duffy was in contact with foreign fascist organizations also caused embarrassment. The press reported that he was involved in secret negotiations with the Ulster Blackshirts, a fascist organization committed to 'King and Empire and the building of the greater Britain'.[209] It had also recently been alleged that he had been in contact with Oswald Mosley, the leader of the British Union of Fascists, and Terje Ballsrud, the head of the Norwegian Greyshirts.[210]

O'Duffy was now contemplating resignation. On 4 September he spoke to the League of Youth's central council about the difficult position which the politicians had placed him in but, as he later recalled, he 'was unanimously requested to carry on'. On 5 and 7 September, Cosgrave, Cronin, and Dillon met O'Duffy in a series of secret meetings intended to clarify party policy and prevent any further embarrassing outbursts. The resulting agreement called for greater co-operation and weekly meetings between the president and vice-presidents. Humiliatingly, however, it stipulated that O'Duffy could 'deliver only carefully prepared and concise speeches from manuscripts' and give press interviews 'only after consultation and in writing'.[211] This agreement—which any party leader would have found unacceptable—demonstrated his colleagues' utter lack of confidence in his leadership.[212] Nonetheless, by the end of the final meeting, on 7 September, the vice-presidents believed that they had secured an agreement, but only until O'Duffy threatened to resign later that night. He was persuaded to defer his decision until he met Cronin and Blythe four days later. By 11 September, as he confided to Seán MacEoin, he remained unsure of his intentions:

I have been trying to make up my mind what is best to do in the interests of the organization—to get out quietly, or to try to carry on for another while. I am still undecided. I was brought into politics against my own judgement—you know what I thought about politics for the years 1919 to 1932 and now being in for twelve months I am confirmed in my former beliefs. I saw hope for Ireland in the National Guard provided they maintained their independence & esprit de corps—and a National ideal—the urge & driving spirit behind Fine Gael—but the last meeting of the National Executive shattered all my beliefs in this regard. All the talk we had about the moral law was—you know what Dan Hogan would call it.[213]

O'Duffy was torn in several directions. He could remain on as a weak leader of the opposition (albeit with a real possibility of winning power in the future), quit politics, or, as his closest advisers urged, lead the Blueshirts back out of Fine Gael. He appeared unable to make up his mind. Following a lengthy discussion with Cronin and Blythe on 11 September, he agreed to remain.[214] By 15 September, however, Dillon remained unsure whether O'Duffy would accept the new terms of his leadership: 'though he has provisionally accepted it Paddy Belton is now trying to engineer a split, and I had to attack him pretty savagely at the Standing Committee, when it met yesterday. As I told you two years ago, he is a dirty dog.'[215]

Finally, on 18 September, O'Duffy arrived at party headquarters with a letter of resignation. He refused what appeared to be genuine pleas for him to reconsider but agreed not to publicize his resignation until it was considered by the Blueshirt central council and Fine Gael's national executive three days later. At the first of these meetings, he read out an uncharacteristically conciliatory valediction:

Circumstances compel me to sever my connection with the organisation . . . I cannot go into details here; but the only alternative could result in a split in the Fine Gael organisation. I believe this would be disastrous just now, and in order to avoid any such eventuality . . . I have decided to stand down. I appeal to the Blueshirts who have given me such unqualified loyalty while I was your leader not to be disheartened now, but to give to the new leader that loyalty and obedience you so cheerfully gave to me . . . Every time I see the blue shirt or the blue blouse I will be reminded of the happy though anxious time we worked and strove together, doing our little best for the land we love. I wish you well.[216]

Having concluded this prepared statement, O'Duffy then made the extraordinary announcement that he was willing to continue as leader of the Blueshirts, leaving the room to allow the central council to decide whether to re-elect him or accept his resignation. It appeared that O'Duffy's offer of resignation was merely tactical, a ploy he had used on countless occasions throughout his career.[217] Dillon believed that O'Duffy had originally planned to split the Blueshirts from Fine Gael but, when it became clear that this would be opposed by Cronin and Blythe, he had offered his resignation to strengthen his hand by confirming his leadership of the League of Youth. (Cronin had never fully supported O'Duffy's leadership while Blythe, a career politician, had apparently realized which way the wind was blowing.) Cronin, stunned by O'Duffy's unexpected manoeuvre, turned on one of the General's acolytes: 'Cronin challenged Gunning in the presence of other members of the Central Council with having urged him after his release from Arbour Hill to murder O'Duffy. Gunning was unable to deny this, and shortly afterwards the Central Council unanimously accepted the resignation.'[218] By this stage many of the delegates were utterly disoriented, having known little about the difficulties which preceded O'Duffy's resignation. Taking advantage of the confusion, O'Duffy's opponents moved quickly, nominating Cronin as the new director general to the agreement of the bemused council members.

The central council meeting was immediately followed by a meeting of the party's national executive. O'Duffy did not attend but, as Dillon reported, his supporters did: 'Belton addressed himself vigorously to the task of splitting the organisation, and while we were in session we discovered that Gunning . . . was telephoning to O'Duffy, every quarter of an hour for instructions, and that Belton had been twice out at his house'.[219] In what was either an attempt to secure O'Duffy's return or lay the groundwork for splitting the party, Belton told the executive that O'Duffy would withdraw his resignation if given the opportunity to explain his position on a number of issues.[220] This offer was refused by the national executive, who endorsed the General's resignation with unsurprising alacrity. O'Duffy's disastrous leadership of Fine Gael was at an end.

What conclusions can be drawn from O'Duffy's brief tenure as Fine Gael's first president, a position which destroyed his credibility and historical reputation? Arguably, Irish historiography has underestimated the potential for Irish fascism. The Blueshirts have generally been seen as the 'final instalment of the

Civil War saga' rather than a fascist movement.[221] Manning's influential account argued that although the movement 'drew some of its inspiration and some of its practices from the continent . . . essentially it was an Irish phenomenon, for most of the factors which influenced its growth and origin were the products of conditions peculiar to Ireland'.[222] However, this misses the point that similar European movements, while drawing on foreign influences, were the products of the conditions within their own countries. In contrast, Cronin's recent study has argued 'that there existed in Ireland during the 1930s a situation which was favourable to the growth of fascism, and that the Blueshirts, although not a fascist movement comparable to those of Hitler and Mussolini, were fascistised in a way analogous to other movements and regimes in Europe'.[223]

Ironically, O'Duffy's commitment to fascism has led some historians to dismiss the potential for Irish fascism. He may have been a fascist, it is argued, but once discovered he was quickly ejected from the political mainstream. However, this interpretation does not adequately address how it was that O'Duffy, for all his obvious shortcomings and extremism, came to lead the opposition; a less charitable view from the left is that 'Irish conservatives did not abandon fascism because of its authoritarianism . . . but because it failed to deliver the goods.'[224] It seems clear that the atmosphere of crisis resulting from Fianna Fáil's election led to a willingness among the conservative right to consider authoritarian alternatives. It was this sense of crisis, reinforced by doubts about de Valera's attitude to the IRA, the economic war, and democracy itself which saw O'Duffy emerge as leader of the opposition.

The argument that the Blueshirts merely adopted the superficial trappings of fascism 'underestimates the admiration for fascist forms within Ireland's political class'.[225] Over a year before O'Duffy entered politics, influential treatyite politicians were denying the legitimacy of the elected government, criticizing parliamentary democracy, and looking to countries like Italy to legitimize their views. The role played by establishment figures in legitimizing anti-democratic views has not been sufficiently acknowledged by the many historians who draw a clear distinction between the support of Blueshirt intellectuals for the corporatist ideas associated with the Vatican and fascist ideology.[226] Although the position of figures like Blythe was far more ambiguous, O'Duffy proved an ideal scapegoat by allowing them to attribute the violence and anti-democratic rhetoric of this period to his leadership.[227] One year after O'Duffy's resignation, Hogan complained to Desmond FitzGerald about Cosgrave (whose commitment to parliamentary democracy, in contrast to both intellectuals, had never wavered): 'He was so sure O'Duffy was a great man that he sat still and let him run amok for a whole year, while I was a crank and a lot worse because even in council I dared to oppose the mad mullah in some of his most outlandish suggestions. I wonder what does Mr. Cosgrave think of his choice for the role of national saviour now?'[228]

Consideration of this period within the broader context of inter-war Europe strengthens the view that the potential for Irish fascism existed. It should be borne in mind that the survival of democracy was the exception rather than the rule in 1930s Europe, and that the Irish Free State was the only state which won its independence in the aftermath of the Great War to remain fully democratic by the Second World War.[229] In most countries, the greater threat to democracy came not from communism or (as in Ireland and Spain) republicanism, but rather the opposing 'coalitions of conservatives, military officers, and nationalists, often emphasising the threat to the nation or traditional society'.[230] The crisis of Irish politics in the 1930s was, in large part, a consequence of the Civil War, but it also formed part of a broader trend of political upheaval as democratic states struggled to overcome economic problems and the rise of political radicalism. The large numbers enrolled in the ranks of the IRA and Blueshirts, and the influence which both organizations exerted on the mainstream parties, constituted a clear threat to Irish democracy. In per capita terms, the membership of the National Guard represented one of the largest non-governing fascistic organizations in the world.[231] The fact that Irish democracy did not succumb to authoritarianism does not mean that the threat should be discounted as negligible.

What part did O'Duffy play in the failure of Irish fascism? Viewed in the context of inter-war Europe, O'Duffy was an archetypal candidate for dictatorship: a dynamic figure with strong ties to the military and police; the leader of a militant movement of army veterans that a desperate establishment had turned to in order to defeat an apparently revolutionary threat to their interests. O'Duffy's leadership is often identified as an important factor in the collapse of the Blueshirts and, by extension, the threat to democracy. From the bungled march on Dublin to his farcical resignation, the General played his hand consistently poorly. But, although it was fortunate that the leadership of the far right remained in such inept hands, the failure of Irish fascism was due to a lack of suitable raw materials rather than the shortcomings of one individual.

Certain elements favourable to the emergence of authoritarianism existed in Ireland: a well-established tradition of populist nationalism, a deeply conservative ethos influenced by Catholic rural values, a resentment of the limited sovereignty imposed by the treaty, and a strong tradition of élitist anti-state violence. However, the absence of other important factors—a genuine communist threat, a destabilizing ethnic question, class hatred, or economic discontent on a scale which existed in countries like Spain or Germany—combined with a democratic consensus among most of the political élite and population ensured the survival of democracy. The role of the security forces, which—despite the experience of the Civil War and years of republican violence—had much less difficulty than O'Duffy in differentiating between party and state, was also important. The comparison between the marches on Rome and Dublin are instructive; whereas Mussolini, supported by the public and encouraged by the establishment, pushed at the open door of an enfeebled state, de Valera's government would not have capitulated to a Blueshirt putsch.

The Blueshirts remain the skeleton in Fine Gael's cupboard, as is demonstrated by the frequency with which the term is hurled across the floor of the Dáil. Recent years have also seen a revisionist tendency to present the Blueshirts in a more positive light, emphasizing their role as protectors of free speech.[232] But although O'Duffy's extremism was not fully embraced by Fine Gael, its brief flirtation with fascism blemished an otherwise impressive commitment to democratic values dating back to 1922. Despite much hysterical propaganda, and some wishful thinking, Ireland was not Weimar Germany or post-war Italy: in retrospect, it is difficult to see how intelligent politicians persuaded themselves otherwise.

O'Duffy's short-lived cameo on the Irish political stage undermines the interpretation of the Civil War as a conflict between a rational constitutional tradition within nationalist politics and élitist republicanism.[233] In reality, both sides of the divide were influenced by these traditions. If republicans behaved in an undemocratic fashion in 1922, so too did treatyites when power slipped from their grasp a decade later. Fianna Fáil must also accept some responsibility for the violence of 1933–4. The double standard epitomized by coercion of the Blueshirts and toleration of the IRA strained the democratic consensus, alienating much liberal as well as right-wing opinion. Nonetheless, it is de Valera who emerges as the real winner from this period. Ironically, the most important legacy of O'Duffy's involvement in Irish politics was to enable Fianna Fáil to shed its slightly constitutional image and turn the forces of the state against the more long-standing threat to democracy represented by the IRA.[234] For O'Duffy, as we shall see, his resignation left him free to follow his instincts towards undisguised fascism.

10

The third greatest man in Europe

We must make life intolerable for those who will not yield to our demands.[1]

O'DUFFY appeared to accept the abrupt demise of his political career with uncharacteristic good grace, informing the press that he was 'glad to be out of politics'.[2] But, as it became apparent that he retained some support, he began to reconsider his options. On 24 September he declared that he had resigned from Fine Gael rather than the League of Youth, but made it clear that he was not claiming the leadership of the Blueshirts. Several days later, he described his letter of resignation as 'an unsigned and undated draft' which he had intended to issue only if his resignation was accepted: 'Before leaving the meeting of the Council I said very clearly and deliberately that I was prepared to continue as Director General'.[3] On 1 October, he attended a Blueshirt dance in Carrickmacross, declaring: 'I am still your leader. Anybody who stands in our way will be sent back in a very short time to the obscurity in which I found them twelve months ago.'[4] Finally, some days later, O'Duffy announced his intention to lead the League of Youth as an independent movement, challenging his followers to decide whether they wished 'to stand by the Blueshirt leadership or hand themselves over to political adventurers'.[5] The response was one of utter confusion. After several branches appealed for a congress to clear the air, both factions began expelling the other's members. O'Duffy attributed the split to the jealousy and conservatism of the politicians and the treachery of Cronin, Blythe, and O'Higgins. Cronin, unwilling to concede that policy differences played a part, blamed it on O'Duffy's refusal to accept the conditions imposed by his vice-presidents.

The split

Attempting to seize the moral high ground, both factions debated the split in exhaustive detail throughout the next months; O'Duffy even published a lengthy pamphlet titled *Why I Resigned from Fine Gael*. Both he and Cronin frantically toured the movement's rural strongholds attempting to win local branches over. In early October, Dillon described O'Duffy as 'on the rampage, but...showing signs of self-destruction'.[6] His diagnosis appeared to be confirmed by the General's desperate appeals to erstwhile supporters like Captain Quinn, which suggested that his campaign was motivated by little more than a sense of betrayal:

I am very sorry indeed that you above all others have deserted your leader, and that you are even going into outside Divisions to induce others to do likewise. No one was more opposed to political interference than you...I hope that in the action you are taking that you are satisfied in your own conscience that you are doing good work for Ireland, that you believe these people are more patriotic than I am, that Cronin and Blythe are serving Ireland in going from County to County making shocking falsehoods and vile slanders against me...I am not going to remain silent now when the minds of the League of Youth are being poisoned against me. After all, I have to live in this country, and I have a little pride left, and I am proud of the part I played for my country and I must make my prestige clear with the League of Youth for whom I worked harder for the last year than ever I worked in the Volunteers, Army or Garda...I will never lead a faction, and if I thought that the majority of the Blueshirts still desire to stay under Fine Gael I will stand down for ever, but I do not think this. I believe that you will be back with me again, and the majority of those who left me will return to their pre-merger allegiance. I am not going to stampede the Blueshirts, I am not going to rush matters at all. Time is on my side...These meetings of Cronin and these engineered snow ball resolutions of confidence are absurd. Conviction is better than hash.[7]

Despite the bluster, and an appetite for infighting honed by two decades of GAA service, O'Duffy was shaken by the split. Colonel Coughlan, one of the few senior Blueshirts to remain loyal to the General, recalled that 'he came down to Bandon to see me. He cried in the room & I told him dry up—that I for one was not & would not let him down—come what may'.[8] Although the split damaged both factions, Cronin's position was much the stronger due to his retention of Fine Gael's offices and newspaper and the support of most of the central council.

Undeterred, O'Duffy set up his own newspaper, *The Blueshirt*, financed by his own savings and whatever share of the Victory Fund his supporters could commandeer. His initial strategy was to present himself as an advocate of reconciliation, while also exploiting his ability to appeal to the movement's wilder constituency. Claiming that he had been forced out of Fine Gael because he 'did not venerate the Moneybags or trim his national policy to suit them', he insisted that there was no more difference between Fine Gael and Fianna Fáil than Tweedledum and Tweedledee.[9] He exploited the opposition's ambiguity on annuities, pointing out that it condemned the agitation as illegal while supporting the imprisoned activists in Arbour Hill.

Police reports reveal that this tactic met with mixed results. At a meeting in Newcastlewest on 19 October, O'Duffy attacked the local leadership for disloyalty and urged Blueshirts 'to cut down trees and telegraph wires and poles at every favourable opportunity' to disrupt the state's attempts to collect outstanding annuities. However, the assembled delegates backed Cronin by a majority of 2 to 1, informing the General that 'he would not get any support from the League of Youth of West Limerick on the occasion of his next visit'.[10] At a meeting in Cavan a fortnight later (where he encouraged further tree-felling), he claimed

that the Fine Gael Executive had been jealous of his popularity in the country. They saw 'Up O'Duffy' on every wall in the country, they saw the crowds carrying him shoulder high, they saw him received everywhere with the Victory Salute and they were jealous of him . . . Every time he returned to Headquarters they said 'You should not have said this, it will offend the English people. You should not have said this about the Six Counties, it embarrasses us'.

Again, however, he met with hostility from his audience, who demanded to know why it had taken him so long to refute the reports of his resignation. Although he had spent the previous six weeks denying that he had ever resigned, he conceded that he had been 'quite happy to return to civil life' but had changed his mind after a deluge of calls 'clamouring for my return'.[11]

The demand for unity was a transparent ploy to regain control of his movement. Fine Gael responded to a call for conciliation by Paddy Belton, O'Duffy's most prominent remaining ally within the party, by expelling him: O'Higgins remarked that 'Belton as a peacemaker was as realistic as an olive branch in the beak of a vulture'.[12] Belton, worn down by the 'vile rottenness of politics', contemplated retiring from the Dáil before throwing his weight behind O'Duffy's wrecking campaign against his former party.[13] Fortified by the support of his 'old and trusted friend', O'Duffy set about placing his faction on a more permanent footing, opening headquarters on Middle Abbey Street, and appointing Thomas Gunning and Colonel Coughlan as general secretary and deputy director general. In early November, he confronted Cronin for the first time since the split when both men vied for the loyalty of east Limerick's Blueshirts. O'Duffy lost the vote.[14] Another meeting in Limerick ended in violence when Denis Quish, an ally of Cronin, arrived with his supporters. Both factions clashed again in Donegal, although on this occasion it was O'Duffy who won control of the local organization.[15] An appearance in Roscommon, where O'Duffy compared the campaign against him to the Irish Party's treatment of Parnell, provoked further violence.[16]

In mid-November Belton announced the formation of a new political party known as the National Association, although it was not clear who would lead it. The proposal received support from some Blueshirts but O'Duffy remained silent.[17] An anti-Semitic bigot, Belton was an obvious ally but for the problem that there was room for only one *Duce* in Irish fascism. Despite the disunity which characterized many of his public appearances, O'Duffy seemed upbeat when he addressed a rally of 1,000 Blueshirts at Hugh O'Reilly's grave in an end-of-year speech which rather laboured the nautical metaphors:

Eighteen months ago I was entrusted by the Blueshirts of Ireland to steer their new ship. They were not satisfied with the old ship. I have tried to steer a straight course and to avoid the whirlpools. Recently I found it necessary to take a certain line to save the ship from foundering. Some of the crew did not agree with me, and went back to their old ship again. It braved many storms, but we believe it is no longer seaworthy . . . Hugh O'Reilly did not die so that the old ship might float again; he joined the crew of the new ship and he met his death at his post . . . Stand faithfully by your posts, put your trust in God, be loyal to the captain on the bridge . . . Hugh! We will never lower the flag of blue.[18]

The General had not won control of the good ship *Blueshirt* but he was doing an impressive job of scuttling it. Several weeks after predicting O'Duffy's self-destruction, Dillon confided to MacDermot: 'We are still afloat, but little more. O'Duffy is on the rampage with a vengeance. The Blueshirts are split from stern to stern, and the morale of Fine Gael is shattered'. Dillon considered Cronin 'a decent man' but doubted whether he had 'the leadership necessary to hold the Blueshirts together'.[19] Tierney regarded the General's return to politics as 'grotesque' but felt he would win sufficient support 'to cripple the whole movement as an effective opposition'.[20] An equally pessimistic MacDermot complained that 'the chief asset of the Government was the

Opposition ... The spectacle of former colleagues attacking each other every day was one that was profoundly discouraging and disgusting', an observation which did not deter him from publicly savaging O'Duffy:

> I am not able to make out what policy he has got, and I am driven to the conclusion that there is nothing more or less in it than personal pique. At a time when unity is so essential General O'Duffy forgets what honours were conferred on him in the past—all the attempts we made to popularise him with the public, to lift him up and make him an idol of the Irish people ... I would implore him for the sake of his own reputation, if not for the sake of the Irish people, to desist.[21]

Although O'Duffy's attempts to win the support of the Blueshirt movement have been dismissed, he initially presented more of a threat than has been acknowledged. The police cautioned that his success would 'be commensurate with the amount of funds he can lay his hands on. If he can get plenty of funds he is capable of making spectacular but spasmodic efforts at real organisation work; without funds he suffers very severely indeed.'[22] By late 1934 O'Duffy was still speaking to meetings of several thousand and had embarked on a new fund-raising campaign: 'If we can get cash now success is absolutely assured ... we have put our hands to the plough now, and we must win out. Nothing less than a complete victory should satisfy us.'[23] His Christmas message was equally optimistic:

> The year which is closing has been a great year in the history of our movement, a great year in the history of our land ... a year of glory and of triumph for Blueshirt ideals. Let us remember 1934 as a year consecrated by the blood of three Blueshirt martyrs ... Let us resolve that the cause for which they died will never be deserted by us, and that, come what may, we shall go forward steadily and fearlessly to our goal.[24]

Having broken with Fine Gael, it was now necessary for O'Duffy to clarify what that goal was. A meeting in the Mansion House in early November raked over the split but offered no new policies. He criticized Cosgrave's abandonment of Collins's nationalism and de Valera's posturing on the north, but offered no alternative: 'I want no foolish spectacular gestures towards the north and I want no cynical abandonment, but I want the Blueshirts to keep the thought of the North warm in their hearts and I believe that the hearts of the North will be warm to them.'[25] When it came to partition, the main parties did not have policies so much as rhetorical stances: O'Duffy's merely oscillated between de Valera's hostility and Cosgrave's conciliation. He called for an all-party conference to mandate the government to resolve the economic war, but emphasized his support for the campaign against annuities. A twelve-point policy statement in early December proved equally thin, merely reiterating the well-worn corporatist rhetoric of the movement's previous incarnations.[26]

The principal distinction between O'Duffy and his former colleagues was his freedom to strike a more radical pose by reviving the militant rhetoric of the National Guard. He edged closer to undisguised fascism, preaching the necessity of bringing 'the State into harmony with the more personal elements of the national will' and praising the principles of social inequality, hierarchy, and dictatorship.[27] The clearest indication of this new direction was his decision to forge contacts with international fascism. In December 1934 he rubbed shoulders with Oswald Mosley at the Nazi-sponsored International Action of Nationalisms conference in Zurich. He attended a conference in Montreux organized by a newly formed Italian organization, the Committee of Action for the Universality of Rome (CAUR), which brought together the most important fascist organizations outside Germany including the Austrian Heimwehr, Norwegian Nasjonal Samling, Romanian Iron Guard, and Spanish Falange. Ever the networker, O'Duffy was appointed to CAUR's international secretariat, which was tasked with establishing a fascist international whose functions would include propaganda, policy development, promoting co-operation between national fascist movements, and—most importantly— eulogizing the genius of its corporate sponsor, Benito Mussolini.[28] In early 1935 he accepted an invitation to meet the great man in Rome, where they discussed, among other issues, agriculture, the physical training of the nation, and the *Duce*'s dislike of 'urbanism'.[29] Here, O'Duffy glimpsed the future: 'What I saw in Italy, although it was a great rush, convinced me that the Corporate System, from the point of view of the plain working farmer, simply cannot be beaten. Mussolini expressed regret that I could not remain longer, and urged me to return . . . I am going back as soon as ever I can to learn from the experience of the men who have built a new Italy on the ruins of the old.'[30]

O'Duffy attended further meetings of CAUR's international secretariat in Paris, Geneva, and Amsterdam in 1935. These occasions provided a welcome opportunity to strut the foreign stage among the convivial company of like-minded megalomaniacs and a flattering international profile at odds with his leadership of a tiny faction. Thomas Gunning snidely recalled an occasion when, returning by express train from Holland, 'O'Duffy thumped his chest and said "I'm the third greatest man in Europe".'[31] O'Duffy was not alone in milking CAUR for all it was worth. The organization was soon wound up by Count Ciano, the Italian foreign minister, after he received a report condemning its delegates as opportunistic nonentities bent on eliciting funds for their own diversion and advancement.[32] Nonetheless, the Italian legation in Dublin noted with satisfaction that O'Duffy's visit to Rome had placed him firmly within the ideological orbit of Italian rather than German fascism.[33]

On the home front, however, O'Duffy was wary of leaving himself open to the charge of subordination to a foreign ideology by unambiguously identifying himself as a fascist. He occasionally conceded that the shirt, salute, and corporatist policy had been inspired by Italy—'If Sinn Féin from Hungary was a good inspiration, then the Corporative State from Italy was not necessarily bad'—but generally described himself as a corporatist rather than a fascist.[34] In the course of eulogizing Mussolini at a Trinity College debate, for example, he declared that he did not 'know anyone in this country who advocates Fascism', a remarkable claim considering the circles he moved in. His stance fooled few observers; Dillon observed that 'O'Duffy has returned from his interview with Mussolini definitely Fascist . . . He will strengthen himself by declaring categorically for Fascism, but he will also strengthen us.'[35]

Like other fascist leaders outside Germany and Italy, O'Duffy mimicked most aspects of fascist ideology, liturgy, and rhetoric, while simultaneously claiming to pursue a political destiny uniquely rooted in his own country's traditions.[36] His speeches, policy documents, and propaganda only thinly disguised his new direction.[37] His Mansion House speech, for example, combined the palingenetic rhetoric of authentic fascism with the not entirely discordant notes of Catholic nationalism:

Discipline is that quality which makes a person responsive to orders; to subordinate his own ideas and opinions to those of his superiors, to fit himself into that part of the organisation allotted to him, and to control himself under the most trying conditions . . . It was that spirit that led the Volunteers to victory . . . our country's chief hope of national salvation lies in the increasing strength, manly resolve and maturing discipline of our movement. The young Blueshirt is the expression of the new Ireland. He must temper his enthusiasm with discipline; he must strengthen his body and his spirit; he must spurn danger and love daring: he must serve the Blueshirt cause with loyalty and carry out his duties cheerfully and with pleasure. In all ranks we must have affectionate comradeship . . . They will serve to promote the greatness of Ireland; they will endeavour to bring our country back to her ancient place as one of the foremost Nations in Christendom. They will wipe out the signs of the conquest, and they will teach the people that in the New Ireland there is no place for the slave mind, no place for apes to dance to any tune that comes over the water; they will make Ireland a country fit for Irish people to live in. Our first work will be to educate the rising generations in good citizenship. We have a glorious tradition as a Christian land, and the fight against modern paganism must find us in the van.[38]

A similar radicalism was evident in his attitude to the annuities campaign which he identified as the basis for his political resurrection. At the time of the split this remained a viable strategy: the police estimated that there were over 10,000 farmers with outstanding annuities in rural Cork alone.[39] In January 1935 O'Duffy and Belton threw their weight behind a new organization, the New Land League, to unite farmers against the annuities.[40] Belton and another radical Blueshirt also formed a 'Demolition Squad' to block roads in an unsuccessful attempt to pressure O'Duffy to follow suit.[41] Although balking at such hands-on participation, O'Duffy did incite farmers to further violence (in a series of seditious speeches recorded by the police with a view to prosecution). At a meeting in Bandon he 'said that any man who went out and cut a tree should be prepared to take his medicine if caught . . . any Blueshirt who goes out and does what his people thinks he should do, who feels he is carrying on the Land League like Michael Davitt and who then goes into Court and says he is sorry for doing what he did will never wear a blueshirt again.'[42]

However, O'Duffy had misjudged the potential of the anti-annuities agitation. By 1935 the government's determined application of coercion, which had resulted in the conviction of 349 Blueshirts during the previous year, was taking effect, as was its resolve in building secure sale yards and employing sufficient sheriffs, court officials, and police to enforce the collection of annuities. The Anglo-Irish coal–cattle pact of December 1934 had also signalled the beginning of a return to the economic status quo.[43] Moreover, by allowing Fine Gael to place clear ground between itself and the rural agitation—now denounced by Cosgrave as 'deplorable breaches of the law'—O'Duffy's campaign reinforced his marginalization.[44] As the Garda noted: 'the Press and some prominent public men have come out against this form of lawlessness . . . the moral position of the police is much stronger'.[45] Blueshirts fell away from Cronin's organization, which lacked purpose once it disassociated itself from the agitation, but chose not to follow O'Duffy.[46] By mid-1935 the police confidently predicted 'smashing the "No Annuity" conspiracy now showing signs of disintegration'.[47] O'Duffy had hitched his fortunes to the campaign just as it had run its course.

The National Corporate Party

By the spring of 1935 it appeared that O'Duffy's political career had also run its course. He maintained his hectic schedule but attracted ever decreasing audiences and press attention, except from his own newspaper. One of the few advantages of the split was that he was again the unrivalled centre of attention of his movement, appearing in dance-halls decked with such gratifying slogans as 'O'Duffy Leads, We Follow' and 'Remember O'Duffy Stood by Collins and We Stand by Him'.[48] But, despite the endless rehashing of his past heroic deeds, *The Blueshirt*'s overwrought propaganda betrayed hints of a struggling organization. 'The Message of 1935' urged Blueshirts to

Stand beneath the blue flag and perhaps you too will hear the message in the whispering breezes that stir our flag, the breezes that sigh over Beal na Blath away in the heart of old Munster. They bring a message from the dead; interpret it rightly—it is the immortal message 'Carry on.' Michael's message to the Blueshirts and all who love Ireland. Carry on for 1935. Carry on for always with O'Duffy and the Blueshirts.[49]

Aside from sycophantic biographical features, bitter accounts of the split, and the leader's repetitive speeches there was little of consequence in the newspaper. The movement existed as little more than a personal appreciation society. Descriptions of events such as the following 'At Home'—'one of the most enjoyable and successful social evenings held in Dublin this season'—inadvertently highlighted its status as a weird and purposeless sect:

The rooms were tastefully decorated and the whole place had an air of gaiety. The members of the committee, who left nothing undone to ensure that it would be a huge success, were rewarded by the praise and congratulations of the guests. A very nice tea—supplied gratis by members of the committee—was served during the evening. During the evening two members of the committee went to the Director-General's house to invite him to attend. Although it was a surprise invitation and although he had to leave early the next morning for a meeting, General O'Duffy readily agreed. On his arrival the General was accorded a rousing reception. He greatly enjoyed the concert, and when called on to make a speech he laughingly refused, and recited a humorous recitation instead. His contribution to the programme evoked round and round of applause . . . The party reluctantly broke up at midnight, all present standing to attention, with hands raised in salute during the singing of the Blueshirt Rallying Song and National Anthem.[50]

O'Duffy's interest in such activity is understandable but the appeal of Irish fascism to its hardcore following remains more difficult to fathom. However, the support of a loyalish network of supporters was an insufficient basis for a national movement: without the economic war, IRA violence, or a red threat the movement struggled to justify its existence.

O'Duffy responded by attempting to broaden his appeal. One such initiative was the 32 Club, launched in Wynn's Hotel in Dublin in February 1935, with the purported objective of promoting cross-border contacts.[51]

The 32 Club embraced the familiar, if idiosyncratic, elements of O'Duffy's organizations—such as the disavowal of political intentions and the identification of corporatism with medieval Gaelic guilds—except for its lack of republicanism. Instead, the club explicitly advocated reunification through 'the reinstitution of an independent Irish Monarchy linked by dynastic ties to the British Commonwealth of Nations'. Behind this curious policy lay an attempt to forge an alliance with the Ulster Fascists, one of Northern Ireland's tiny ultra-right organizations. It was led by Job Stott, a former B Special and director of the Ulster Centre of Fascist Studies.[52] Closely associated with Mosley's British Union of Fascists, the Ulster Fascists aspired to a united Irish dominion within a fascist British Empire.[53] (A previous attempt to forge links between both organizations had ended badly, heightening tensions within Fine Gael and splitting Stott's organisation.)[54] Despite describing itself as 'the most British Organisation in the Empire', its detection of the 'Grasping Hand of Communism and the Grabbing Fist of Party Government' behind the 'Red Hand of Ulster' revealed that it shared O'Duffy's hostility to the Stormont establishment and his conspiratorial world-view. A meeting between Blueshirts and Ulster Fascists in Belfast's Grand Central Hotel, however, ended in failure: RUC Special Branch dismissed it as 'a huge farce', describing one Ulster Fascist as a 'mental case' and the leader of the Blueshirt delegation as 'falling within the same category'.[55] O'Duffy optimistically continued to believe that the Ulster Fascists would be won round to green rather than orange fascism.[56]

O'Duffy, whose speeches often revealed a sneaking regard for the IRA's uncompromising nationalism, also attempted to woo militant republicanism during this period. Despite the IRA's contempt for his movement, the General had always regarded its rank and file as decent, if misled, lads who could be won round once the hypocrisy of de Valera was exposed, a view shared by other leading Blueshirts.[57] Observing his furtive attempts to contact republicans in Cashel, the police reported that he was 'most anxious to draw as many as possible of the extreme Republican element into the new Organisation, and the rank and file of his supporters are instructed to cultivate the utmost friendliness with the IRA'. O'Duffy advised his supporters to wear Easter lilies and desist from informing on republicans. The police noted, without undue concern, that 'this new pose will not have a very long life'.[58] By the following spring, however, O'Duffy continued to voice his support for the IRA, backing its new political initiative, Cumann Poblachta na h-Eireann.[59] There was a certain logic behind his attempts to draw republicans into an anti-state alliance: the IRA's left wing had recently seceded to form Republican Congress, strengthening the position of its conservative militarists, while both the Blueshirts and the IRA had borne the brunt of de Valera's coercion. Moreover, the ideological common ground between O'Duffy's party and the IRA's new political front included ultra-nationalism, anglophobia, sectarianism, a Gaelic ethos, and their mutual admiration of Italian aggression.[60] But while the IRA had something to offer, the General had little to bring to the table. Four years later, the circumstances (and O'Duffy's standing in republican eyes) would radically change. In 1935, the strategy—like his attempt to recruit the Ulster Fascists—smacked more of desperation than ambition.

These initiatives were followed by the establishment of a new political organization, the National Corporate Party (NCP), which, judging by its first congress on 8 June, represented little more than a rebranding exercise. O'Duffy cited Pearse's usefully vague Proclamation as the basis of its national policy: 'We will take our stand where the men of 1916 stood, and their goal will be our goal, and I can promise, too, that there will be no bluff about it'. There would be no more ambiguity about the Commonwealth either: 'We will establish a Republic de jure for thirty-two counties and de facto for twenty-six' (a pragmatic distinction between nation and state which would later feature in de Valera's constitution).[61] He appealed for support from the IRA, which had 'chosen the hard road all through', criticizing de Valera for his recent assurance that he would not allow Ireland to be used as a base for an attack on Britain by a foreign power: 'If we are sincere in striving for independence we must be prepared to use every means'. (Denounced as disgraceful by the *Irish Times*, the latter statement was transmitted to Rome by the Italian legation as further evidence of Mussolini's influence in Ireland.)[62]

The NCP's populist social policy advocated land redistribution, increased tillage, de-rating, a minimum wage, and profit-sharing. The blue shirt remained, but now accessorized by green tie and 'Volunteer hat' rather than black tie and beret.[63] It was an inauspicious debut. Much of the congress was taken up by unseemly wrangling between the executive committee and O'Duffy, who, at one point, had to threaten to resign to get his motions through. While *The Blueshirt* observed that 'rarely, if ever, has there been so enthusiastic and loyal a gathering behind any leader', Special Branch described it as 'little better than a huge farce' (a description increasingly applied to the General's political initiatives), concluding that there was 'little to fear from this Movement'.[64]

The next twelve months did little to disprove this prediction. Despite claiming to have shunned 'the scramble for Press publicity' in favour of a 'quiet but intensive system of organisation', O'Duffy established few branches.[65] His following continued to diminish, while several attempts to establish branches in rural Cork were broken up by Cronin's followers.[66] The party's membership was unlikely to have exceeded the 3,000 supporters who attended the annual Béal na mBláth commemoration.[67] In late 1935 the police noted that support for O'Duffy in the important west Cork region—which had rivalled Cronin's following the split—had sharply declined, while another report noted that he was unlikely to 'meet with any organising successes in Mayo'.[68] O'Duffy's arbitrary style of leadership did not help. He responded to organizational difficulties in Cork city by removing every divisional officer and replacing them with sixteen new officers, few of whom proved willing to accept their appointments.[69] Financial difficulties compelled him to suspend publication of *The Nation* and dispense with Gunning's services as general secretary.[70] Like its predecessor, the NCP appeared devoid of purpose aside from adulation of its leader; a characteristic venture, establishing a non-partisan committee to honour O'Duffy's cultural and sporting achievements, was dismissed by gardaí as 'a Blueshirt stunt of a most exaggerated nature'.[71]

Despite the NCP's decline, O'Duffy appeared unable to accept his political marginalization. Describing the west Cork NCP as the most perfect electoral machine in Ireland, he predicted a haul of twenty-five seats in the next election: 'a wonderful achievement'.[72] Fuelled by a confidence more delusional than optimistic, his plans grew increasingly ambitious. When his corporate state came into being, he declared, there would be 'no machinery to get rid of it. There would not be any more politics.'[73] The NCP would become a state auxiliary, with a role extending from the co-ordination of public services to the maintenance of law and order.

Significantly, the only burst of enthusiasm within the party resulted from international developments when O'Duffy's opposition to the League of Nation's campaign of sanctions against Mussolini's invasion of Abyssinia temporarily galvanized his movement into action. At a meeting in Geneva in September, O'Duffy informed the Fascist International's other aspiring dictators that his followers had volunteered to fight for Italy. Before returning to Ireland, he spent several days in Cologne and Dusseldorf visiting what he described as 'military camps for the Storm Troops' and 'labour camps for young people'. Finding that 'the workers in the camps worked together in harmony', he concluded that 'Hitler was very much misrepresented' abroad.[74] Enthusiasm for the Abyssinian venture declined in late 1935 when the NCP decided that Italy required moral rather than military support, but it had provided O'Duffy with his first popular issue since the economic war.[75] His opposition to de Valera's determined pro-League of Nations stance had been shared by many within Fine Gael and the Catholic Church who professed to regard Mussolini as a champion of Christian values. Even the *Duce* had reportedly expressed 'his profound appreciation of the brave stand taken by the National Corporate Party of Ireland on behalf of the Italian people'.[76] A realignment of similar reactionary forces on a far greater scale in the summer of 1936 would provide O'Duffy with a golden opportunity to seize the limelight.

During the first half of 1936 the NCP continued to decline. In March, it adopted a new uniform of green shirts: 'Blue is not our national colour no more than yellow or red. All over the world green is, and ever shall be, recognised as the national colour of the Emerald Isle'.[77] Such rhetoric only partially disguised O'Duffy's failure to win control of the Blueshirt movement. In the absence of significant domestic support, the NCP continued to forge links with foreign movements. Liam Walsh entered a correspondence with Alexander Raven Thomson, the British Union of Fascists' director of policy. Professing his 'utmost goodwill' towards the NCP, Thomson assured Walsh that a fascist Britain would not demand the payment of annuities ('a bitter hatred of usury is a vital part of our policy') and would 'welcome a Corporate Ireland into free and equal co-operation with ourselves and the other dominions in the development of Empire resources'.[78] However, Walsh's insistence that Commonwealth membership could never be regarded as a basis for Irish unity provoked the exasperation of the BUF's leading intellectual: 'I would regard it as a catastrophe for Ireland if she were to cut herself off from the Commonwealth of the British Empire merely for sentimental reasons, when the Free State already enjoys all the practical advantages of an independent nation . . . Is it still not possible for you people to look beyond the Parish Pump?'

Thomson held out the lure of full participation in imperial trade to an Irish dominion which would recognize 'the great part her own people have played in founding, building and protecting the great Empire which is the mutual heritage of Great Britain and Ireland'.[79] Unimpressed, Walsh retorted:

We do not and will not accept the Empire or Commonwealth idea, that idea only appeals to those who regard themselves as British Colonists. We are not a Colony, we never were a Colony and we never will be a Colony. We are a mother country with a proud tradition, greater and nobler than Britain. Yes! It is possible for us people in 'Southern Ireland' 'to look beyond the Parish Pump'. We look to 'Northern Ireland' which is part of our territory . . . General O'Duffy said, 'The Six Northern Counties are either part of Ireland or part of England. The coast of Antrim is either the Irish coast or the English coast' . . . The North is to us what Alsace was to France, what the Saar was to Germany.[80]

Commending this 'magnificent outburst of Irish feeling', Thomson politely concluded: 'What more can I say? Perhaps we may yet meet in a Fascist World Order, but I still grieve for the Irish elements in our widespread Empire, whom you leave entirely to our tender Anglo-Saxon mercies. I do not regard Ireland as a Colony, but as one of the Motherlands of Empire, and we offer her her rightful place ... I must admit that I shall never understand the Irish, North or South; and I feel that a further discussion of our differences can scarcely lead to any useful result.'[81] Contacts with the Scottish Fascists proved similarly unproductive, although the occasional exchanged greetings between Mosley and Walsh indicated a cordial, if distant, relationship with the BUF.

By mid-1936 the NCP was washed-up. A visit by O'Duffy to the formerly strong Rosscarbery area, an attempt to generate interest for his party's annual congress, attracted a single-figure audience and was described by police as 'a tame affair, devoid of any interest'.[82] The congress proved equally disappointing. Attendance had declined to 250 and, despite the elaborate pomp and ceremony of the occasion, the mood was subdued: 'Nothing of a revolutionary nature was proposed or discussed ... The proceedings did not occasion much public interest ... Even the presence of the delegates attired in green shirts did not excite attention on the part of the few onlookers.'[83] But although O'Duffy had not the slightest inkling, the apathy enveloping his party was about to be shattered by a dramatic event which had begun while the NCP's second and final congress was still in session.

We are going to Spain

The Spanish Civil War began on 17 July 1936, when a military cabal rose against the democratic Popular Front government. It divided those on the left (socialists, republicans, anarchists, and communists) from the right (conservatives, monarchists, and fascists), a political alignment which reflected deep-rooted social divisions between Nationalist Spain—comprising the army, the Catholic Church, landowners, and wealthy—and the landless labourers, workers, and liberal middle class of Republican Spain. Regional factors, such as the opposition of the Catalan and predominantly Catholic Basque provinces to the Nationalists, added to the complexity of these divisions. It soon became apparent that what many foreigners initially regarded as the collapse of yet another unstable Spanish régime would have wider implications. As Italy and Germany lent support to the Nationalists, and the Soviet Union backed the Republic, it became clear that the conflict had the potential to spark the wider European war which many observers expected. In response, Britain and France won international agreement for non-intervention—a policy of holding the ring while the Spanish settled their own affairs. In reality, non-intervention proved ineffective and morally questionable. The fascist powers and the Soviet Union continued to intervene, while the agreement placed the rebels on the same international footing as the legitimate Spanish government.

Throughout Europe and beyond, the Spanish Civil War polarized the bitter social and ideological divisions of the inter-war period into a compelling choice: Franco or the Republic; left or right. The most distinctive aspect of the Irish response was the enormous outpouring of public support for the Nationalists. As the trade-union movement, Labour Party, and IRA stood aside, Irish supporters of the Spanish Republic struggled to make their voice heard. Although de Valera adopted a neutral diplomatic stance, he voiced his sympathy for Franco's Nationalists, as did almost every politician in the Dáil. This near-unanimous response was reinforced by the reports of anti-clerical atrocities in Republican Spain during the summer of 1936. Although the lurid accounts of executed priests, raped nuns, and burned churches were often exaggerated, the shocking brutality of anti-clerical violence in Spain would have been sufficient to place Catholic Ireland squarely behind Franco, an emotional response best understood in the context of the militant Catholicism of the period. Within weeks of its outbreak, Cardinal MacRory, the primate of all Ireland, declared: 'There is no room any longer for any doubt as to the issues at stake in the Spanish conflict . . . It is a question of whether Spain will remain as she has been so long, a Christian and Catholic land, or a Bolshevist and anti-God land.'[84] Local bodies and branches of all the main parties declared their support for Franco, while a new mass movement—the Irish Christian Front—emerged to mobilize support for Nationalist Spain.

Ireland's previously impotent fascist sympathizers moved swiftly to exploit the ensuing anti-communist frenzy. Paddy Belton had soon seized control of the Irish Christian Front as a vehicle for his own political ambitions. The red scare provided a much needed fillip to the National Corporate Party, which, despite its shortcomings, had long staked its claim as the most anti-communist movement in the state. O'Duffy was offered an even better opportunity to capitalize on events in Spain when he was urged by Count Ramírez de Arellano, a London-based Carlist aristocrat, to raise a militia to help liberate Spain from the reds: 'What a glorious example Ireland could give the whole of Christendom!'[85] O'Duffy had been recommended to him by Cardinal MacRory who described the General as 'a chivalrous, courageous, upright man and a good Catholic, and above all a fine organiser'.[86]

On 10 August O'Duffy publicized the idea in the press, emphasizing the religious dimension of the conflict: 'In Madrid priests are battered to death on the altars, and their heads stuck on the railings outside the churches by howling mobs of women and youths armed by the Government.'[87] His proposal, offering a practical means of striking a blow for the faith, caught the mood of Catholic Ireland. Fr Alexander McCabe, the rector of the Irish College in Salamanca, who had recently returned to Ireland (and would later become embroiled in the controversies surrounding the Irish Brigade), observed that 'most people regarded him as a hero. They contrasted his attitude with that of the Irish Government which "sat on the fence" and "did not take sides".'[88] McCabe had attended a meeting of the Irish hierarchy, where he had been struck by the militant attitude of bishops like Dr Fogarty: 'a most striking man, with the white hair of an old chieftain, and the young heart and enthusiasm of a boy. At seventy, he would be prepared to take a rifle and go out and fight in Spain.'[89] Within days, the NCP and other organizations such as the Catholic Young Men's Society had expressed their support for an Irish brigade. Backed by the *Irish Independent* and the Catholic press, the revitalized NCP began processing a reported 7,000 applications to join what O'Duffy called the Irish Crusade against Communism.[90]

Why did O'Duffy decide to organize an Irish brigade? One reason which should not be discounted—on the grounds that it accounted for many of his decisions—was that he was encouraged to do so. Ramírez's flattering request was supported by Cardinal MacRory, who had secretly met O'Duffy; the General later claimed that it was the latter's intercession which 'settled the matter'.[91] The Italian minister in Dublin also claimed responsibility for the Irish Brigade. Under instructions from Rome—which regarded military support from a non-fascist state as politically valuable—the legation offered O'Duffy encouragement and financial support.[92] O'Duffy also had his own reasons. His autobiographical memoir, *Crusade in Spain*, attributed his decision to the historic links between Ireland and Spain, anti-communism, and, above all, his desire to defend the Catholic Church. His acknowledgement of the ties 'of friendship, of faith and of blood' between both countries referred not only to such episodes as the battle of Kinsale, the flight of the Wild Geese, and the training of priests in Salamanca during the penal years, which occupied a celebrated place in nationalist history, but also to the mythical descent of the Irish race from the Milesians of ancient Spain. 'The dark eyed Galway colleen, hiding her beauty beneath that coloured shawl, and the tall dark fisher lad from the Cladagh', O'Duffy poetically observed, 'are as Spanish as any Spaniard I met in journeying through Spain.'[93]

More pertinently, however, the conflict vindicated O'Duffy's lonely stance against the red menace and his oft-imagined destiny as national saviour. As early as 1934 the General had warned: 'Chaos seems again to be about to spread all over the world; let us resolve that once again Ireland, the last outpost of

Europe, will be ready to relive her heroic past and stem the tide of Communism and materialism.'[94] Spain offered O'Duffy, who had been much ridiculed since the split, not merely political rehabilitation but an opportunity to fulfil his heroic destiny. His supporters predicted that the Irish Brigade would 'go down in history and be recognised for its fidelity to the Christian religion, the bravery of its loyal volunteers, and the military genius of its leader'.[95] O'Duffy declared that 'the Irish nation would rally behind it, and Communism would never again raise its ugly head in Ireland'; his former crony and competitor for the leadership of Irish fascism, Paddy Belton, made much the same pitch to elicit mass support for the Christian Front.[96] As the name of the Irish Crusade against Communism indicated, O'Duffy depicted the conflict as a holy war: 'the opening action in the long expected clash of the new barbarism and the ancient Christian civilisation'.

Although it is generally accepted that O'Duffy was primarily motivated by anti-communism and militant Catholicism, it seems more likely that his principal considerations were self-interest, opportunism, and egotism.[97] For the first time since 1934 he found himself at the head of a popular movement, the focus of admiring press and public attention, and in a position to resume the pose of man of destiny. O'Duffy, who had never lacked a sense of the epic, viewed his crusade in grandiloquent terms. On the eve of his departure, he announced: 'We are leaving for a battlefield, and now words seem in a sense to have no great significance, for we have entered that phase when action will speak far louder...I am reminded of Lincoln's simple words at Gettysburg: "The world will little note nor long remember what we say here, but it can never forget what they did here." '[98] While he insisted that the Irish Brigade was a non-political crusade, his efforts to present his new movement in this light were unconvincing. The Nationalist political programme, as described by O'Duffy, resembled that of the NCP.[99] He depicted Franco not merely as an important ally but as a version of his own idealized self:

His strategy is brilliant, and his leadership perfect. Yet he has no dictatorial ambitions. He wants to see Spain powerful and happy, but he is not a politician, he is not attached to any 'ism', he makes no speeches, and he avoids a public demonstration like a plague. He is a genuinely devout Catholic. He makes no pretensions, he does not beat his breast piously in public, but his sense of duty to God and to the Church and to his country is complete.[100]

Nor did the General's concern about the politicization of the brigade prevent him from purchasing 1,000 green shirts, the uniform of the NCP, for his volunteers.[101] Despite his claim 'that there was not one political discussion' within the brigade, others reported 'that his speeches were "all politics" and that he was always assuring them about what they would do when they returned to Ireland. Mussolini's March on Rome would be nothing in comparison.'[102] In short, the Irish Brigade was yet another attempt to mobilize support by any means possible: by halting what had appeared an irreversible decline into obscurity, the Spanish Civil War had achieved the unlikely result of rehabilitating O'Duffy as a relevant political figure. Ned Cronin's concern that his rival might overshadow him was apparent from his initial snide prediction that the brigade was as likely to reach Spain as the moon, followed by his own scramble to organize a rival militia.[103] The motives which brought O'Duffy to Spain—from ideological compatibility to self-interest—also accounted for the presence of contingents from the Romanian Iron Guard, Action Française, and other minor fascist movements who believed that the gesture would pay dividends on the home front.[104]

He travelled to England in September to meet Nationalist officials. Despite some cloak-and-dagger antics involving clandestine rendezvous in public parks, train stations, and Westminster Abbey, Scotland Yard's Special Branch observed O'Duffy meeting Count de Arellano and Juan de la Cierva (one of the original conspirators behind the military coup) who would oversee the transport arrangements.[105] Reunited with Thomas Gunning, a Spanish speaker who had already picked up some propaganda work in Spain, O'Duffy travelled to Pamplona, where he was received like a war hero. After a celebratory mass in the cathedral, they drove to Burgos to meet General Cabanellas, the nominal head of the Nationalist junta, who reportedly rejected O'Duffy's offer of support. Although the Nationalists were eager for the assistance of regular German and Italian soldiers, not all foreigners were welcomed with the same enthusiasm due to well-founded suspicions about the ideological motives, political reliability, and military capabilities of the adventurers and opportunists making their way to Spain.[106]

Fortunately General Mola, whom O'Duffy met in Valladolid on 22 September, was more enthusiastic. While they were talking, news of the relief of the Alcázar in Toledo—the besieged Nationalist fortress which had become a symbol of heroic resistance—was phoned through to Mola, who, O'Duffy recalled, 'rushed towards me and embraced me in an ecstasy of joy'. Two days later, General Franco cabled his approval of the brigade. When the news was announced to the massed troops and Nationalist supporters gathered in Valladolid to celebrate the relief of the Alcázar, the crowd substituted '*Viva Irlanda*' for '*Viva Espana*' during the Falange hymn.[107] Like most people who had any dealings with O'Duffy in the 1930s, Franco would later come to regret his decision. O'Duffy would also experience some regrets but for the moment was thrilled by the flattering attention which he, like other foreigners deemed useful to the Nationalist cause, received in Spain.[108] On his return he proudly recounted the arrangements in hand to greet the Irish Brigade, which, he was led to believe, would be met on arrival in Vigo from its luxurious ship by a chartered train, a fleet of planes, and the cardinal primate of Spain.[109]

The terms under which the Irishmen would fight were generous:[110] 5,000 Irishmen would form eight *banderas* (battalions) of the *Tercio* (Foreign Legion), while O'Duffy optimistically informed Franco that there would be no difficulty in recruiting thousands more. Each *bandera* would function as a self-contained unit, commanded by Irish officers with its own drill, medical staff, chaplains, and cooks. The General even secured permission for St Mary's anti-communist pipe band to accompany his men. O'Duffy, who would be provided with a Spanish aide-de-camp, would undertake the duties of inspector general of the Irish *banderas* with the rank of brigadier-general. He would be directly responsible to General Franco, without prejudice to the position of the colonel-inspector of the *Tercio*, Juan Yagüe Blanco. The Spanish officers and legionaries who would join the Irish *bandera* in subordinate and liaison positions would 'be tactful and courteous in their relations with their new comrades, whose friendship and confidence they should seek'. Enlistment was for six months or, if shorter, the duration of the war. The Irishmen would receive the same rate of pay as the *Tercio's* élite legionaries—over twice that of the regular soldiers—but they would not qualify for compensation or pensions. O'Duffy initially insisted that his men should not be deployed against the Catholic Basques but later dropped this caveat, having decided that the Basques were 'no more entitled to partition from Spain than the six counties of Ulster are to partition from Ireland'.[111]

The 17,000 strong *Tercio* formed the élite of the Nationalist forces. Battle-hardened and brutalized by years of service as shock troops in the vicious Moroccan campaigns, the all-volunteer force lived by an austere code dominated by a belief in the virtue of honourable death on the battlefield. This remarkable cult of death was reflected by their fearsome reputation as 'the bridegrooms of death' (*los Novios de la Muerte*). Although better paid than regular soldiers, legionaries were forbidden to retreat in battle or abandon comrades on the field, and were whipped for minor infractions of discipline. They fought alongside Moroccan mercenary units which, like the *Tercio*, had earned a notorious reputation for the savagery of their atrocities as much as their ruthlessness in combat.[112] The Irishmen fought as part of the *Tercio* not, as has been suggested, due to high expectations of their military capabilities but because it was technically regarded as a foreign legion.[113] It would later become evident that the iron discipline and fanatic militarism of the *Tercio* did not provide a conducive environment for the Irishmen. None the less, the degree of autonomy which Franco granted to O'Duffy's men ensured that they were treated more leniently than other foreign legionaries.

O'Duffy returned to Ireland to oversee the recruitment and transport of his militia. Despite press reports that his force would contravene the non-intervention agreement, O'Duffy correctly predicted that the government could not legally prevent unarmed men from leaving the country. He continued to promise the Nationalists a 5,000 strong force (including an Irish-American cavalry squadron) to be led by a senior serving Irish army officer, General Hugo MacNeill.[114] Notwithstanding the immense public enthusiasm for Franco, O'Duffy grossly exaggerated the resources at his disposal. Ultimately, less than 700 Irishmen would make it over, although this was also due to organizational shortcomings on Franco's side. The Irish-American cavalry failed to arrive—as did MacNeill, whose absence would prove a more serious setback.

Hundreds of young men, however, did heed the call. They came predominantly from rural Ireland, particularly the south-west and midland counties where the Blueshirts had been strongest. In contrast to the 200 mainly working-class Irishmen who joined the International Brigades, they came from a wide variety of backgrounds ranging from business-owners and professionals to seminarians and unskilled workers. A substantial minority had some military experience. Several, including Major Patrick Dalton, Colonel Carew, and Brigadier-General Eamon Horan, had held senior ranks in the National Army—although the extent to which this corresponded to military expertise was questionable. The brigade also recruited a significant contingent of former soldiers and guards due to O'Duffy's background, the large numbers of demobilized soldiers in Ireland, and the existence of embittered members of the security forces who had faced career setbacks after Fianna Fáil's accession to power. The Irish Brigade, like the Blueshirts, attracted many who were unhappy with their lot in de Valera's Ireland.

Most of the brigade officers were NCP members. Many of the ordinary volunteers were not but those with political affiliations were generally Greenshirts or Blueshirts. Even those without political backgrounds came from strong Blueshirt areas as they were recruited by a clandestine network of NCP officials. Recruitment—described by one west Cork organizer as 'a mess'—was not a slick operation. Even where the NCP did have some local support, it was often badly organized and its leaders made divisive efforts to exclude 'Ned's pets' (pro-Fine Gael Blueshirts) and other suspect elements.

NCP recruiters lacked funds for such basic expenses as transport costs, were distrusted by mainstream politicians, and often received little support from local priests.[115]

Mirroring the anti-fascist motives of their left-wing compatriots, O'Duffy's followers viewed Spain as the frontline in the struggle against the relentless expansion of communism. However, anti-communism formed only one aspect of the militant Catholicism central to the appeal of the brigade and skil-fully exploited by O'Duffy. The Irish Brigade was depicted as the most recent of a long tradition of brigades to fight for faith and fatherland in Europe. Press reports of the scenes at Dublin's North Wall described the pious atmosphere as departing recruits were presented with miraculous medals, scapulars, rosary beads, Sacred Heart badges, and prayer books. They were blessed by priests while cheering supporters and weeping girls sang 'Faith of Our Fathers' which would become the unofficial anthem of the crusade.[116]

Casting a concerned eye over proceedings, the department of external affairs noted that the 'general character of the volunteers . . . does not appear to be very high, but we have information that some of them are very young men who have been enticed from their families through the impression that they are going to fight for Christianity'.[117] Certainly not all the volunteers were motivated by religious zeal. Fr Alex McCabe believed many 'were idealists, who came out to fight for religion and Spain. Some were of the adventurous type who, in the old days, would take the English "bob" and join the British Army to see the world. It was a change from standing at the corner and staring at the pump.' Idealistic motives, combined with the lack of employment and emigration opportuni-ties, and the lure of travel and adventure made service in the Irish Brigade an enticing prospect for O'Duffy's naïve young followers.[118]

The most pressing difficulty faced by O'Duffy was transport. A ship intended to collect the first contingent of 500 men from Waterford on 16 October was postponed because Franco's diplomats feared that such a conspicu-ous breach of non-intervention would sour relations with the British foreign office.[119] To the consternation of Nationalist officials, an irate O'Duffy promptly returned to Spain to pressure Franco into action. The *generalísimo* apologetically explained that he could not allow the Soviet Union a pretext to break with the non-intervention committee but asked O'Duffy to remain in Salamanca's Grand Hotel as a guest of the nation. He was showered with flattering attention over the next few days. Franco placed a driver and car at his disposal, and arranged for the Duke of Algeciras from his own staff to accom-pany him on a tour of the front. He was brought to meet the cardinal primate of Spain, who showed him around his cathedral in Toledo.[120] In O'Duffy's absence, a debate on the brigade's viability ensued between Franco's diplomatic advisers and several influential aristocratic descendants of the Wild Geese (including the Duchess of Tetuan—a descendant of the O'Donnells—and the head of the Nationalist air force, General Kindelán), who were more susceptible to the romantic aspect of the venture.[121] The latter successfully argued that the support of the Irish volunteers, in contrast to that of the fascist powers, would enhance the Nationalists' image as defenders of Catholicism. O'Duffy was instructed to continue his preparations.

The logistical problems nonetheless continued. Reluctant to authorize large contingents, Franco's headquarters instructed the Irishmen to make their own way over in small groups. O'Duffy, pointing out that hundreds of his followers who had quit their jobs had no means of support, was furious but sent some key personnel ahead. In late November he demanded another meeting with Franco, which appeared to galvanize the Nationalists into action until news of the cancellation of another ship arrived. At this point, Captain Liam Walsh flew to Berlin to see if the Nazis would supply a ship.[122] Having sent less than 250 men to Spain, O'Duffy finally received word that a German steamer would collect 500 volunteers off the Galway coast on 13 December. One Blueshirt recalled the colourful scenes in Eyre Square as the volunteers arrived through the night: 'It was an atmosphere which is etched in my mind and makes me understand the reasons why people join armies. There were bands, musical instruments, and the singing of "Faith of Our Fathers".'[123]

In the early hours of the morning, the men began boarding the *Dun Aengus*, which was to ferry them out to the steamer; three adventurous locals spontaneously jumped aboard as it disembarked. The ship's departure, however, coincided with a terrible storm. By the time the *S. S. Urundi* appeared several hours later—its Swastika ensign visible from the shore—many of those on the ferry had succumbed to seasickness. The mid-sea transfer to the *Urundi* necessitated a terrifying ascent of a 30-foot rope-ladder in high winds. Some 50 men refused to leave the *Dun Aengus*, the remainder completing the manoeuvre without accident.[124] But their ordeal, as one officer recalled, was only beginning: 'The men were crammed like cattle into the stinking holds of an ancient, unseaworthy ship, with bad and inadequate food and barely enough water to drink.'[125] Some strapped themselves to girders to prevent injury on the wildly pitching vessel. The diary of one passenger recorded: 'Sunday: slept on top of one another and slept on coal bed...very sick...weather very bad...a lot sick, one man broke leg, others scared when ship swayed'.[126] The foul weather persisted until the ship's arrival in Galicia, where the hungry and shaken men were transferred to the *S. S. Domino* for the final stretch.

In contrast, O'Duffy and a small coterie of favoured officers travelled to Lisbon by commercial liner, their 'very happy journey' enlivened by Spanish classes, military lectures, deck games, and the occasional *ceilidhe*.[127] The differing fortunes of leaders and led would become an increasingly obvious aspect of the brigade's sojourn in Spain.

Much to O'Duffy's chagrin, the *Urundi* was the only ship to reach Irish waters despite Nationalist assurances that it would be followed by weekly rendezvous. Over the next month, several more ships were cancelled at short notice, while both Germany and Italy refused further requests for assistance. The introduction of non-intervention legislation by the Irish government on 22 February precluded the possibility of another large-scale shipment. Nationalist indecisiveness, the sensitivities surrounding non-intervention, and communication difficulties meant that a force of 700 rather than several thousand arrived in Spain. This had two important consequences. Relations between Franco and O'Duffy were strained from the outset; and the under-strength *bandera*'s ability to function as an autonomous unit was greatly restricted.

To the glory of God and honour of Ireland

O'Duffy's recently discovered Spanish diary provides an intriguing, if succinct, record of his time in Spain. Perhaps the most striking revelation is the contrast between how much time he spent lounging around Cáceres, sightseeing, and travelling between Ireland and Spain and how little he spent preparing his men for combat. The diary begins with his departure from the North Wall on 20 November 1936. He left Liverpool on the *S. S. Avoceta* the following day: 'Very pleasant. Journey most enjoyable. Calm sea, well looked after'.[128] After his arrival in Lisbon, where he was received by a delegation of Irish priests and nuns, he travelled to Salamanca to meet the Nationalist command. He then returned to Dublin, via London and Paris, to finalize arrangements on the Irish side. He stayed several nights in the Gresham Hotel, meeting organizers and well-wishers before returning to London, where he put up at the Grosvenor. There, he met 'La Cervia' [*sic*] who had already formed a low opinion of the General. He travelled on to Paris, crossing the Spanish border on 9 December where he learned of Juan de la Cierva's death in an air accident. O'Duffy would later describe this as the first of several close brushes with death (the Spaniard having asked him to accompany him on his flight).[129] He spent the next weeks in the Hotel Álvarez in Cáceres, awaiting the arrival of his men and sightseeing.

On 13 December he attended a bull-fight in Seville ('not impressed'). The following day he explored the vineyards and sherry factory of the Duke of Algeciras ('most interesting'). On 15 December he inspected the Falange headquarters in Seville and the city's famous cathedral ('wonderful structure'). The arrival of the main contingent of volunteers, on 20 December, precipitated a day of parades, receptions, and over-boisterous celebration (a terse entry the following day recorded his address to a 'full parade... following complaints').

Despite his men's arrival, this leisurely pace of life continued. On 22 December he motored out to the country. The following day was devoted to lectures, presentations, and getting measured for his uniform. Christmas Day was celebrated by a 'parade to St. Domingo Church, 3 masses & Benediction'. The afternoon was spent 'meeting and greeting local officials' and addressing his men after dinner ('remarkable reception. remained for 2 hours'). The entry for 29 December merely records: 'Fit on uniform'. On New Year's Eve, he hosted a party attended by the austere commander of the Foreign Legion, Colonel Yagüe. New Year's Day proved equally agreeable: 'First parade of Irish Bde in uniform & carrying arms... Looked very smart. My own first public appearance in uniform'. On 3 January he set out on what he described as an official tour of the province in search of a well-known Irish monastery:

Reception & ovation at every village en route... Tricolour everywhere in evidence— parades of thousands of school children... received by Rector Franciscans' outside church by cheering crowds... spent 4 hours viewing... church & cloisters—with £50,000 vestments, chalice, speeches by Rector, Judges, Mil[itary] Gov[ernor] & reply by me. Return journey—most edifying. Road lined with troops all the way from Guadalupe to Caceres.

The next two days were spent recovering: 'In bed, sore throat'. The following morning he set off on a 'drive to [the] mountains'. On 7 January, accompanied by his entourage and the Duke of Algeciras, he drove to Salamanca ('in uniform'), where he spent an hour in discussion with Franco. He stayed overnight at Burgos, before crossing the border ('in mufti', alas) to Paris, and on to the Grosvenor. The next week was spent at the Gresham, liaising with Irish Brigade recruiters, Christian Front organizers, and General MacNeill (his old friend, who was evidently experiencing second thoughts about service in Spain). O'Duffy returned to Burgos on 23 January, where he spent the next two days in bed with the flu. He made it back to Cáceres on 26 January but spent the next week confined to bed. It took the prospect of a full day of religious and

social festivities, marking the brigade's completion of basic training, to lure
him from his sick bed on 31 January:

Church. Parade. Mass. Ceremonial & military parade of Irish Brigade & all arms of the
Service in Cacere [*sic*] . . . Unveiling of memorial Tablet by me . . . Procession to Plaque.
Solemn. Led by me. Blessing by Bishop. My address . . . March past through Plaza. Irish
Bde & all arms of the service in Cacere [*sic*]. Salute taken by me supported by all above.
Band. Very Solemn.
    Concert in B[arrac]ks, very good . . . My address to troops. Reception in Hotel . . . 80
Guests present. Mil[itary] Governor Guest of honour. Wine & cake. My address.
Mil[itary] Gov[ernor] replies. 6 to 10. a very pleasant ev[enin]g.[130]

Much of the final week before the *bandera*'s departure for the front was devoted
to sightseeing. He spent two days in Seville with the Duke: 'Shopping. Great
coat etc. Drive through city'. On Sunday, he drove to Trajillo, receiving a
gratifying 'Ovation by people of train'. The day of the brigade's departure was
spent addressing the bishop and other provincial worthies. A rare reference to
his men noted: 'Troops in great form'.
    Despite its brevity the diary—presumably intended as an *aide-mémoire* for
his subsequent memoir—is a revealing document, conveying a deeply
unflattering impression of his priorities in Spain. Aside from recording his daily
movements, its entries primarily concern sightseeing trips, public appearances,
honours bestowed, and social engagements. O'Duffy clearly basked in the
attention which Nationalist Spain lavished upon him. Notwithstanding his
frequent and expensive travel between Cáceres, Salamanca, Paris, London, and
Dublin, there is scant evidence of the organizational drive for which he was
known. Instead, the days in bed, nights of socializing, and sightseeing trips
suggest a dilettantish existence. The entries are also revealing for what is not
mentioned. There are few references to training or other military preparations
which were evidently conducted with little input from O'Duffy. Much of the
time which he did devote to work was spent on trivial tasks such as censoring
mail, designing a company pennant (a red cross on a field of emerald green
inscribed with the motto, *In Hoc Signo Vinces*, recalling earlier Irish brigades) and
bandera standard (a saffron-shaded Irish wolfhound against a green background),
both of which—flanked by a guard of honour—were displayed during church
services.[131] His diary contains few references to any difficulties within the brigade.
    In contrast, other sources present a different picture of the brigade's basic
training. Fr McCabe, the rector of the Irish College in Salamanca, visited the
Irishmen on several occasions. On his first visit on 6 January he described the
brigade as 'an inspiring sight, linking up the present with the historic past'.

O'Duffy had 'the simple, friendly, hospitable way of all Irishmen with one another, and especially, of the Irish lay folk with their priests'. The volunteers 'looked athletic, clean, and muscular and seemed to be a crowd that will give a tough account of themselves'. The officers were 'manly, cheery, and refined...good companions, like school-boys going home for a holiday.'[132] By the next day, however, he had discovered the tensions lurking beneath the surface. Much of the trouble centred on two difficult personalities: Captain Tom Gunning, 'the brains of the Brigade'; and Fr Mulrean, the 'physically huge, fanatically puritanical and tactless' chaplain from Westmeath.[133] Mulrean, McCabe noted, 'looks very mysterious and serious, pouts, picks his nose, and keeps on scratching himself, and plucking at his thigh. He's not unlike Falstaff, without the charm.'[134] He was resented by many of the soldiers: 'In the pulpit, he doesn't preach. He growls at them, worries them in canine fashion, and is always denouncing them. He does this when the Spanish officers are present in the Church, and it humiliates the Irish officers.' According to McCabe, the latter 'regarded him as a "bully" addicted to gossip, a sneak and mischief maker'. Alarmed by his inquiries into 'intimate and even feminine affairs' during confession, 'They feel that he sits down in the box and listens eagerly just to satisfy his morbid curiosity'. McCabe was also taken aback by Mulrean's practice of issuing attendance slips to the soldiers, allowing him to identify the unpenitent: 'It's quite obvious that the Irish Brigade isn't going well, and the Chaplain is probably to blame.'[135]

McCabe discovered other tensions between the officers who 'live too closely together and have got on one another's nerves'. In particular, Mulrean and Gunning despised one another. The chaplain said 'awful things...really indecent' about Gunning and his wife (who was also staying in Cáceres), while Gunning insisted that he 'would like to shoot Mulrean'.[136] But it was the rift between O'Duffy and Gunning which would prove most serious. O'Duffy was dependent on Gunning as his 'right-hand man and factotum' and one of his few Spanish speakers.[137] Peter Kemp, an English officer in the Carlist Requetés, noted that Gunning had turned several Irish and Spanish officers against O'Duffy: 'A skilful intriguer, he contrived, so long as he remained O'Duffy's secretary, to keep the Irish Brigade divided against itself'.[138]

McCabe also formed a low opinion of the Irish doctors attached to the *bandera*. He discovered one in bed with a hangover and described the other as a mystic: 'very cultured and refined and an excellent talker. But he is regarded as a bit crazy, and he is probably a drug addict.'[139] The transfer of two Anglo-Irish officers, Lieutenant Noel Fitzpatrick and Lieutenant Bill Nangle, from another battalion of the *Tercio* created further difficulties.

The Sandhurst-educated ex-British army officers resented serving under O'Duffy, who described them as his 'Protestant Englishmen' but was compelled to appoint them to senior positions.[140] Given their background, friction was inevitable. Fitzpatrick was a big-game hunter, Kipling devotee, and Freemason with a tendency to act the stage Irishman; Nangle, who had served in the Indian army and the French Foreign Legion, suffered from bouts of manic paranoia 'which made him an awkward, sometimes dangerous companion'.[141]

Ned Cronin's appearance at the Spanish border led to more problems. Cronin had travelled to Portugal on the *S. S. Aguila*, where, one Irish Brigade volunteer recalled, he had 'created a measure of uneasiness by suggesting that we were being enlisted in a foreign legion with no hope of return'.[142] Promising to 'lay aside all political differences so as to help Spain to fight the common danger from Russia', Cronin sought Franco's permission to raise a militia from his own, more numerous, Blueshirt movement. However, O'Duffy's second-in-command, Major Dalton, informed the Nationalists that his men would never fight alongside Cronin.[143] Gunning was despatched to Lisbon where, according to Cronin, he arranged for the Portuguese secret police to seize his passport and instructed the Spanish border police to shoot him on sight.[144] What Franco made of all this can only be imagined, but one journalist reported that his archives were 'simply bursting with letters from Irishmen denouncing other Irishmen'.[145] Cronin's treatment, as an NCP recruiter from Cork complained, also went down badly on the home front: 'I am told by sound people that it looks damn bad for the General—it looks as if he blocked him from fighting for his God—and the argument put up is—what would Franco know about Cronin only for O'Duffy telling him.'[146]

McCabe detected a degree of scepticism about Franco's Spain among the Irish volunteers. The brutality of Nationalist Spain concerned some: even O'Duffy had objected to the sight of *Tercio* officers whipping their own men.[147] From the vantage-point of a tree inside his barracks, Jim Kavanagh witnessed Civil Guards execute prisoners who had been pulled from covered lorries. Two other Irishmen stumbled across the execution of a group of republicans by firing squad. Another witnessed executions 'in scores'.[148] McCabe also observed that some of the men were disappointed by the Spanish Catholic Church, due to its low mass attendance and identification with the rich and powerful, 'even though that's what the whole row is supposed to be about'.[149]

The Spanish, for their part, were not impressed by the behaviour of some of the Irishmen: when they 'see these idealists, and frequent church-goers drinking and "having one too many" they are profoundly shocked'.[150] Public drunkenness, common enough in Ireland, was taboo in Spanish society.

McCabe—who learned that Irishmen had smashed up the local café 'on more than one occasion and the Police had to be called'—preached ineffectually on 'the drink problem'.[151] Other sources confirm that drunkenness was a problem from the outset. The war correspondent Francis McCullagh accompanied one officer to Lisbon to meet a contingent of Irishmen in late December. Moved by the sight of row after row of ruddy Irish faces at the bulwark, singing 'Faith of our Fathers' as the ship entered the harbour, he recalled 'the many ship-loads of my countrymen who had come in this way to France, Spain, and Portugal during the last four hundred years, all of them swordsmen, destined to fight, under foreign leaders, in quarrels not theirs, and to die for causes of which they knew nothing.' This romantic reverie was ruined, however, when some of the volunteers 'jumped ashore, got drunk, fought the police, and caused an awful scandal along the whole water-front'.[152] Lieutenant Pete Lawler witnessed equally embarrassing scenes when the main contingent broke their journey in Salamanca for a *vin d'honneur* hosted by Nationalist officials:

I knew it was going to be sheer bloody murder with the boys drinking all that wine on empty stomachs... Sure enough, when the time came to get back into the train the boys were so drunk it was all we could do to push them into it. And even that wasn't the end of our troubles... all the time the band was playing, there was one of our lads—as drunk as a coot he was—leaning out of the carriage window being sick all the down the neck of an old General. And the old boy—I was watching him—stood there like a rock at the salute through it all.[153]

Although an over-zealous guardian of his charges' morals, Fr Mulrean's decision to launch a crusade against immorality suggests that there was little improvement in Cáceres: 'I preached against drunkenness and the Kips [brothels]... The attendance at the Kips has increased to my knowledge from 5 the 1st fortnight to over 40 a week now. O my work gets more difficult every day. Drunkenness is a curse, I told them they were trying to make a national virtue out of it, and the language vile.'[154]

O'Duffy later denied these allegations—'We have heard of drunkenness in the Brigade. I did not see it'—but conceded that 'a few doubtful characters' had been recruited. (Mulrean, escorting yet another disgraced officer to the border, put it more harshly: 'Strike me pink, if I know where the old man managed to pick up all the scum he has collected.'[155]) Matt Beckett recalled that most of his comrades were 'honest sincere men' but described the contingents from Dublin and Clonmel as 'liabilities and blackguards' whose 'idea was more to escape things at home than to help the national cause in Spain'.[156] One of the more extreme examples of this phenomenon was the *bandera* armoury sergeant, Sam McCaughey, who enlisted to extricate himself from bigamous marriages in Wexford and Portlaoise; he was later exposed when one of his penniless wives discovered a third marriage after his return.[157]

Following a second visit to the barracks, McCabe registered more reservations about the *bandera*. The Irishmen looked 'soft' compared to the Spaniards: several 'have a crazy look', others were 'limp, spineless and worthless'. One volunteer, who enlisted in the hope that the climate would improve his tuberculosis, died within several months. Another convalescent, also hospitalized on arrival, had been twice operated on in Ireland. McCabe discovered two deserters from Liverpool 'in a wretched hole of a cell'. In the next cell, he came upon two insane men, 'one stripped naked to the waist, was up in the window, and clinging to the bars . . . having a sun-bath on a frosty day in January'. Nonetheless, he concluded that when the men were on duty discipline was strict and that the training, conducted by ex-British army veterans, appeared to be progressing. However, even this optimism faltered when he discovered that two volunteers had been badly beaten by their officers in what he suspected was a political dispute: 'It was so serious that there was a military inquiry over it. If these incidents spread, they would ruin the Brigade.' He concluded that the 'sooner they are sent to the front, the better for themselves, and for the town of Cáceres'.[158] His reference to an inquiry, and Mulrean's claim that the brigade's departure for the front had been delayed because 'the Spanish Authorities would not take the responsibility of sending so many men with officers unfit to lead them', suggested that his reservations were shared by the Nationalists.[159]

O'Duffy's diary sheds little light on these problems which he appears to have ignored. His memoir, *Crusade in Spain*, resolutely focused on the positive aspects of the *bandera*'s stay in Cáceres. The piety, strength, and discipline of his men, O'Duffy claimed, astonished the Spaniards. The General's complaints concerned more minor cultural differences. Bacon and ham, although purportedly smoked, were served raw. Disconcertingly, boiled eggs were served without their shells in bowls of hot water. The sickly sweet deserts were indigestible. Weak green tea was served cold in glasses without sugar or milk—although O'Duffy did eventually warm to Spanish coffee. Fortunately, the *bandera* had brought its own cooks: 'I was quartered in the principal hotel in Caceres, but the only meals I really enjoyed were those cooked and served by our own volunteers—splendid soup, real Irish stew, nicely-boiled potatoes, and all free from olive oil. It is not possible to get a meal in any hotel in Spain without the meat, fish, fowl, vegetables, in fact everything, swimming in olive oil.'[160] (McCabe would later complain about O'Duffy's 'horror of eggs cooked in olive oil. It is little trifles and "fads" like this, to which the Irishmen should be quite accustomed by this time that are helping to create mountainous troubles in the Brigade.')[161] O'Duffy's men admired but failed to emulate the Spanish custom of spending hours over a glass of beer: 'Whatever the drink our lads consumed it without delay, and left the café, a custom the inhabitants could not understand at all.'

Like many visitors to Spain, O'Duffy frowned on the traditional six course lunch and siesta: 'Personally I considered this a great waste of time, for it is no exaggeration to say that nearly half the day is usually spent between eating and the mid-day *siesta* that follows a long and heavy meal.' He was irritated by the country's many minor inefficiencies. The mail—containing such welcome commodities as cigarettes, newspapers, razor-blades, and news from home—was frequently delayed or lost. On one occasion following a six-week delay, O'Duffy drove to Lisbon, retrieving two lorry-loads of mail. Aside from the arrival of the mail, trips to the cinema, mass, and the Sunday evening concerts—which featured singing, dancing, recitations, and music—provided the highlights of the week. A specially arranged bullfight at which green-robed toreadors threw darts decked in the Irish national colours proved less successful. Although the matador dedicated his prey to Ireland, presenting one of its ears to a bemused legionary, O'Duffy observed that the sport's cruelty 'did not appeal to the Irishmen's sense of sportsmanship'. On their return to barracks, 'a unanimous wish was expressed that Franco would abolish bull-fighting as a pastime in the new Spain'.[162]

Whether reviewing the troops or mixing with celebrities like Colonel José Moscardó, the hero of the Alcázar, O'Duffy revelled in the social side of the war. Press reports filed by Gunning, who was moonlighting as the *Independent*'s 'Special Representative', kept the brigade in the public eye at home. The impressive celebrations marking the *bandera*'s departure for the front proved the highlight of the stay in Cáceres. An elaborately choreographed mass concluded with a procession to the Lady Chapel:

a sharp order rang out, and the entire bandera, which had been facing towards the High Altar, turned right as one man. Amid a breathless silence, General O'Duffy saluted the Bishop and stepped forward to unveil the tablet, saying: 'On behalf of the officers and men of the First Bandera of the Irish Brigade, I unveil this tablet to the glory of God and the honour of Ireland.' The flags fluttered apart, a steel helmeted guard of honour of non-commissioned officers presented arms, and the band played the Irish National Anthem.[163]

The presentation of a silver casket, engraved with a Celtic cross and bearing 2,000 pesetas collected by the *bandera*, was followed by orations from

O'Duffy, the bishop, and the military governor. Afterwards, the Irishmen marched to the town square, where O'Duffy, watched by thousands of cheering locals who packed the surrounding streets, took the salute from his *bandera* and columns representing the army, air force, civil guards, assault guards, Falange, and Carlists. 'Never, even at home,' he recalled, 'have I seen that tricolour given a more enthusiastic reception'.

The parade was followed by lunch and a concert: 'General O'Duffy himself contributed "The Top of the Morning", and the cries of "Arís" were only stilled when he commenced a short address to the men—an intimate, fatherly address congratulating them on their fine appearance'.[164] A telegram conveying Franco's gratitude was read to the men. The festivities concluded with a reception hosted by O'Duffy for local dignitaries and further rounds of presentations, speeches, and drinks. Back on top, after two years in the political wilderness, O'Duffy found these ceremonies immensely gratifying:

These were the moments when he relished his role to the full, when he was fêted by grandees of Spain and princes of the Church, when the conversation was dominated by talk of crusade and duty, of Spain and Ireland and their joint historic destiny. It was then that the general could imagine himself a paladin of Charlemagne, standing shoulder to shoulder with Franco, Hitler and Mussolini against the infidel Red Horde—and putting Eamon de Valera to shame.[165]

Like other Catholic visitors, O'Duffy must have been impressed by the combination of piety and order which characterized Franco's Spain: 'Flags flew everywhere, carrying the image of the Virgin superimposed on the red and yellow of traditional Spain. Pictures of Nationalist leaders, Franco most commonly, were on windows and hoardings, often with the image of the Sacred Heart above and the words 'I will reign in Spain' in a scroll underneath. Carlist Requetés marched to the front with medals and rosaries around their necks, the badges of the Sacred Heart sewn to their tunics, and their cloaks embroidered with large white crosses. Church dignitaries were prominent at all official events and public celebrations of Mass were common.'[166] The glamour of life behind the lines in wartime Spain was equally appealing. O'Duffy was a regular in Salamanca's 'packed and deafeningly noisy' Grand Hotel where 'high-spirited young officers from the Foreign Legion, with their collars turned back to reveal their smooth brown throats, jostled for tables with Falangists, whose blue shirts sported the insignia of the yoke and the red-tipped five black arrows. Fair-haired German aviators, the backs of their necks bright red from the sun, sat earnestly drinking cocktails.'[167] O'Duffy's lavish lifestyle, which contrasted with his relatively minor status, was the subject of much comment.

One journalist was struck by the dramatic impression made by the arrival of his cortege of motor-cars containing his large entourage of Irish officers, Spanish aristocrats, and personal bodyguard of 'the tallest and lustiest men in his bandera'.[168] The *Daily Mail*'s correspondent observed 'O'Duffy taking tea in the Grand Hotel at Salamanca, with a couple of his volunteers on guard at the door of the room carrying sub-machine guns somewhat ostentatiously', while an amused Nationalist diplomat reported that he had 'a dozen aides-de-camp' and lived in 'great style... like a Marshal'.[169] Unfortunately for O'Duffy, and his increasingly divided officers, the war could not be put off forever.

Death to O'Duffy

On 16 February the brigade received orders for the Madrid front, which had become a focus of intense fighting when General Orgaz launched a major assault to take control of the Valencia road.[170] The following morning, as his men entrained for the front, the General set off separately by car. The war correspondent Francis McCullagh, to whom O'Duffy was generally rude, observed that he was 'in the best of health and humour, and as pleased as getting to the Front as a schoolboy at getting home for the holidays. For the first time in our acquaintance he greeted me without a shade of suspicion lurking in the corners of his eyes or a wrinkle of private worry corrugating his rubicund brow.'[171] After a lengthy delay, while a train driver was sought to replace the one who had inexplicably disappeared, the *bandera*'s train pulled off at a startling speed, hurtling out of control and slamming to an abrupt halt within minutes. The Irishmen later learned that a communist driver had attempted to plunge the train into a lethal crash.[172] The train resumed its journey as far as Plasencia, where it was forced to halt while the recently bombed track was repaired. It was not until the evening of 18 February that they reached Torrejón de la Calzada, marching the remaining 12 miles to Valdemoro where—long overdue—they arrived around midnight. Despite their hunger and exhaustion, they received orders to relieve a battalion at nearby Ciempozuelos before dawn. Considering this an unreasonable request, O'Duffy drove to the divisional headquarters of General Orgaz at Navalcarnero to insist on a later start. Having secured the agreement of Orgaz, O'Duffy returned to Valdemoro to notify his officers of the change of plan, before leaving to introduce himself to the regional military governor in Toledo. By the time he returned, his men had set off on the 7 mile journey to Ciempozuelos.

The *bandera*'s short route lay behind their own lines in territory which the Nationalists had swept through with great force in early February but which had since witnessed several counter-attacks. As the *bandera* marched to Ciempozuelos, the surrounding Nationalist units—unsure of the precise location of their own lines—remained on high alert.[173] These circumstances partly explain why, on coming upon an English-speaking unit in unfamiliar uniforms, a Nationalist *bandera* from the Canary Islands opened fire without warning. The Irish men—marching in attack formation due to their own uncertainty about the terrain—had been mistaken for a unit of the International Brigades. Two Spanish officers from the Irish Brigade who had stepped forward to greet the officers of the advancing unit were killed almost instantly. Both sides exchanged fire for an hour, neither willing to advance. Two Irishmen, Tom Hyde, a popular cinema proprietor, and Dan Chute, the son of a publican from Tralee, were killed. O'Duffy claimed that his men exacted a much higher toll on the enemy, who eventually withdrew from the field.

The revelation that their first engagement had been against their own side came as a setback. The only consolation, according to O'Duffy, was that it was deemed the fault of the other *bandera,* whose officers had failed to follow the correct procedure.[174] Although several disgruntled Irish officers would later criticize Dalton's decision to march in battle formation, the evidence supports O'Duffy's interpretation.[175] Much was subsequently made of this incident by the brigade's detractors, but it does not appear to have destroyed the *bandera*'s credibility with the Nationalist command. When O'Duffy met Franco on 22 February, the *generalísimo* 'expressed his high appreciation ... & sympathy'.[176]

O'Duffy arranged for the bodies to be brought to Cáceres for an elaborate military funeral—'the largest ever seen in Cáceres'—attended by the mayor, military governor, and local bishop.[177] Not only did O'Duffy enjoy a good funeral, he was skilled at exploiting their value for self-aggrandizement. A telegram to the Irish press, shrewdly omitting the fact that the men had been shot by Franco's forces, declared: 'As true Irish soldiers and followers of Christ, they have made the supreme sacrifice.'[178] A memorial mass at the Pro-Cathedral in Dublin organized by the Irish Crusade against Communism attracted opposition politicians, Christian Front supporters, NCP activists, and Blueshirts in a display of political unity which emphasized O'Duffy's leadership of the pro-Franco cause.[179] The public was urged to demonstrate its support for the two martyrs—and its opposition to the government's non-intervention policy—by wearing harp badges and becoming associate members of the brigade: 'show those brave men that in your hearts you know they are not criminals, but glorious Crusaders who, undeterred by the Gates of

Hell, are resolved to replace on His throne Christ the King for Whom their ancestors suffered and died'. Chute's stricken mother told the press: 'My boy is an only son who went to fight for Christ. Although there is a load on my heart, I offer him to Christ for Whom he fought.'[180]

While O'Duffy arranged the funerals, his men continued to Ciempozuelos where they would spend the next five weeks. The small town, 40 miles south of Madrid, had been the scene of vicious fighting on 5 February, when a battalion of Moroccan soldiers overwhelmed a larger Republican force. As was customary, the Moors had taken no prisoners: 1,300 Republicans were killed, many by the knife, and the town had been looted.[181] Any relief the Irishmen felt on reaching their destination must have been countered by their first sight of this 'town of the dead'.[182] Sergeant-Major Timlin described their arrival, only hours after the fight with the Canary Islands *bandera*:

'A' Company entered the town under cover of shell-racked buildings, finding desolation on all sides...Suddenly the air was rent with a terrific explosion, made greater by the previous quiet, and followed by another, and still another. Shells were coming screeching through the air, ploughing up the roads and knocking the sides and tops from already partly demolished buildings. A halt was called in sight of a railway station, where we first caught sight of humans apart from ourselves. These were Moors arrayed in long multi-coloured robes and holding rifles cradled in their arms. They were tall and dark-skinned, adorned with beards and moustaches; turbans enveloped the tops of the heads. . . . I entered several houses on a tour of inspection. It required no great stretch of imagination to visualise the haste and terror in which some of these houses were vacated. Children's toys were trampled on, babies' shawls and bottles strewn about—one could almost hear the wailing of the mothers.

On reaching Ciempozeulos, Moss Fennell had dived into a shell-hole to seek cover from the bombardment: 'after the dirt and stones cleared away, a new and sickening sensation gripped me. It was the stench of rotting human flesh. I opened my eyes, there were three dead and decaying bodies, partially covered, one only inches away and seemingly looking straight at me with glazed and sightless eyes.'[183] The Moors had slaughtered 'troops wherever they had found them—on duty and in their beds—the whole place was covered in blood, and dead bodies were to be seen piled in the cellars'.[184] One of the brigade's first unsettling duties was to bury the hundreds of decomposing corpses scattered throughout the town.[185]

It was a stark introduction to the Spanish Civil War, whose savagery appalled the idealistic crusaders. The involvement of Muslims in Franco's crusade must also have come as a shock (even if volunteers recalled getting on better with the Moors than the Falangist extremists).[186] O'Duffy deemed it necessary to devote four pages of his memoir to justifying the involvement of the Islamic soldiers, who, he came to realize, were not 'savages, without culture of civilisation' but 'Spanish citizens . . . fighting in defence of God and their religion'. He was concerned that the Moors—whose cultural achievements in literature, music, art, and architecture were renowned—should not be confused with negroes: 'the shape of the head, nose, and mouth, their hair and eyes, are more characteristic of the European'. They were also 'splendid soldiers, brave, loyal, reliable and well-disciplined . . . not given to the torturing of prisoners, or to the other inhuman acts imputed to them'. Indeed, given a choice, O'Duffy would have preferred imprisonment by the Moors than the Russian OGPU. These favourable impressions were confirmed by a subsequent meeting with the Grand Vizier of Spanish Morocco who was reportedly much impressed by O'Duffy's pipers and his men's piety.[187]

The Irish *bandera*'s section of the front, running just below the crest of a range of low hills overlooking the Jarama valley, was not excessively exposed, but it was shelled daily and sniped at by International Brigade soldiers from the opposing lines. Some of the latter claimed to have communicated with their compatriots across the trenches. One recalled that 'Frank Ryan [the leading Irish officer among the Republican forces] used to speak on the speaker, he says: "Irishmen go home! Your fathers would turn in their graves if they knew that you'd come to fight for imperialism." '[188] Aside from such taunts, the brigade endured freezing nights and inadequate uniforms which soon led to an epidemic of rheumatism, pleurisy, and colds. At one point, over 150 men were hospitalized.[189] The shallow, poorly constructed trenches provided little protection from the torrential rain and the men also suffered from the normal privations of the front: lice, filth, bad food, and shortages of water. O'Duffy did not expose himself to these conditions; during the five weeks his men were stationed in Ciempozuelos, he made only six briefs visits to the front.[190]

Life at the front was harsh. Each company alternated between four days in the trenches and two days in the cheerless town of Ciempozuelos, which provided little respite from the privations of the trenches. Its four churches and convents had been ransacked. The altars and fixtures had been smashed to fragments, the hammer and sickle and obscene inscriptions had been daubed on the walls, and the corpses of nuns were reportedly discovered in the convent cellars. The Irishmen posted scraps of burned vestments home 'as silent witnesses to the reality of the Red terror'. One of their first duties was to assist in the reconsecration of the parish church.

The only building left unscathed by the fighting was the massive and overcrowded women's mental hospital. One volunteer recalled 'the eerie sound of their screams mingling with those of shells during the regular bombardment from enemy batteries'.[191] Others remembered the sound of the wild dogs which feasted on the corpses littering the landscape. After a time, a trickle of locals began to return: 'They had heartbreaking stories to tell of the days of terror in the town, and of the horrible ways in which their husbands and sons had been butchered, or compelled to join the Red forces; of the fate of wives and daughters they did not care to speak.'[192] O'Duffy ensured that his men, who had witnessed the vicious behaviour of Franco's Moors, were exposed to a steady diet of red atrocities. A graphic homily by an Irish priest who had preached to the *bandera* in Portugal was circulated in leaflet form:

You are fighting in God's holy name . . . to save the world from the fiendish atrocities which have been perpetrated in Russia, in Mexico, and now in Spain . . . Never before were sweet young girls stripped in the public streets, flogged and beaten, inhumanly violated and mutilated and subjected to such unspeakable torments . . . You are going to fight those monsters, who are more like demons let loose from Hell than mortal men . . . Why wait to see our churches burned, our priests and nuns butchered, our women—your mothers and wives and sisters—violated and mutilated . . . ?[193]

Notwithstanding such propaganda, morale declined amidst the harsh conditions of Ciempozuelos although there is little indication of this in O'Duffy's diary, which contains only occasional references to his men such as 'All troops in great fighting form & cheerful'.[194] In contrast, the Irish minister in Spain, Leopold Kerney, had been informed by Dublin that they were 'discontent with their lot. They complain of the bad food, poor clothing and of their treatment generally.'[195] He was instructed to keep an eye on the men, both from the point of view of their welfare and the unappealing prospect of O'Duffy's triumphant return to Ireland with a battle-hardened militia in tow. In mid-March, while meeting Nationalist officials in Salamanca, Kerney discovered that relations between O'Duffy's *bandera* and the Nationalists were poor. He had caught sight of a letter by a Spanish general which referred to the Irishmen in a disparaging fashion. Fr McCabe, who was with him, had also noticed its contemptuous tone: 'a full translation would be, "And those damn, good-for-nothing Irish?" '[196]

The Nationalists had discovered the alarming divisions within the Irish *bandera*. By early March even O'Duffy had begun to record cryptic references to shootings and other incidents in his diary.[197] On 3 March he ordered the self-medicating Dr Freeman from the front. Mulrean claimed that after overhearing 'O'Duffy and others, drunk at the time, discuss plans for assassinating . . . Dr. Freeman, he spirited latter away to safety in an ambulance.'[198] Freeman departed Spain, leaving only a large hotel bill. On 6 March a second chaplain arrived, much to the irritation of the *Tercio* command which refused to accredit him. Fr O'Daly quickly acclimatized himself to life in the *bandera*, falling out with his confrère, Fr Mulrean, and having his faculty for confession revoked by the local bishop after a drunken scene. Among other petty disputes, the quarter-master was accused of 'making a good thing' from his position.[199]

More seriously, the brigade O/C, Patrick Dalton, had abruptly returned home. Although the *Irish Press* was informed that he was injured during an engagement, O'Duffy recorded in his diary that Dalton had hospitalized himself on 6 March, deciding ten days later to return home. Dalton—who blamed himself for the deaths of Hyde and Chute—was unable to handle the stress of command.[200] Describing him as 'a thin, worn man of about forty years . . . badly wounded by a British bullet which had traversed his stomach', McCullagh noted that although 'full of pluck and energy, he was not so young in 1936 as he had been in 1921, and the strain of the Spanish war proved too much'.[201] To the disgust of most of the other officers, O'Duffy chose the NCP's assistant director general, Dermot O'Sullivan, as his replacement.[202] The General's tendency to assign commands to his political favourites had created discontent from the outset, particularly among those with their own ambitions of leadership. On 12 March T. F. Smith, captain of B company and one of the few Irish officers respected by the Spanish, abruptly followed Dalton home.[203]

It was against this background that the brigade's first military test—against the enemy, at least—arrived on 13 March, when it was ordered to capture the village of Titulcia, located 2 kilometres east of Ciempozuelos on the opposite side of the Jarama river. O'Duffy had to be summoned to the front to supervise the operation. In the face of heavy artillery, difficult terrain, and torrential rain, the brigade failed to cross the river or engage any enemy troops in combat by nightfall. Three Irishmen were killed, while a fourth, Sergeant Gabriel Lee, died soon afterwards. As his exhausted men regrouped, O'Duffy received orders to repeat the advance at dawn. Convinced that there was no chance of success, he ordered his men to stand-to while he sought out General Saliquet at field head-quarters to request that his order be set aside. Saliquet, he recalled, appeared surprised, but assented. O'Duffy claimed that Franco, whom he met shortly afterwards at Navalcarnero, also approved of the decision: 'I felt very happy after this interview, inasmuch as while I had succeeded in saving the lives of those who had shown so much loyalty and trust in my leadership, I had at the same time now received a renewal of the confidence of the Generalissimo.'[204] Having staved off the threat of further combat, he returned to Cáceres to supervise the funerals of his fallen comrades: 'Bishop, Mayor etc. Army band, troops etc. St. Mary's Pipers Band appeared for first time, looked well. Sympathy from all'.[205]

O'Duffy's account of the anticlimactic battle for Titulcia was full of holes. While local commanders cannot arbitrarily disobey divisional orders in any professional army, it was almost inconceivable in the *Tercio*. Although Titulcia—located on the crest of a cliff overlooking marshy open terrain and supported by well-positioned artillery batteries—may well have been impregnable, the small number of Irish casualties suggests that relatively little effort was expended in ascertaining this. *Tercio* units, renowned for their bravery, regularly absorbed casualty rates of higher than 50 per cent during offensives.[206] It was also unlikely that Franco should support O'Duffy's decision to appeal the orders of Saliquet, commander of the assault on Madrid, particularly as the purpose of the advance was not necessarily to capture Titulcia but to relieve pressure on Mussolini's beleaguered forces at Guadalajara.[207] Moreover, other sources suggest that it was not O'Duffy but his officers who refused to advance on Titulcia. One account, written by a soldier loyal to the General, blamed Tom Cahill, the captain of A company.[208] Franco's subsequent insistence that O'Duffy execute his orders without consulting his subordinates supports this account, as does Cahill's ignominious repatriation. It can have been no coincidence either that Franco decided to inspect personally what was fast becoming the most troublesome battalion in his army. O'Duffy's absence from the front on this occasion, while predictable, was unfortunate given that the date of Franco's surprise inspection—17 March—found some of the Irishmen in a more relaxed state than was considered appropriate. According to Mulrean, when Franco met O'Duffy at Navalcarnero two days later he took him 'to task and also asked for an explanation of shooting incidents and indiscipline'.[209]

Undeterred by his men's unconvincing performance, O'Duffy seized on the propaganda opportunities offered by this first engagement with the enemy. Throughout the past months, Gunning's jingoistic reports had kept Irish readers abreast of the brigade's progress. 'General O'Duffy', the *Independent* reported, 'spends almost his entire time at the front—suffering the same joys and the same hardships as his men'.[210] 'The Brigade is doing heroic work', another report noted, 'and the Irishmen are numbered among the best and bravest men in Spain . . . General O'Duffy spends his entire time at the front with the men, and is within earshot of the Red battle cry in that part—"Death to O'Duffy"'.[211] The battle for Titulcia—described as 'the greatest offensive of the war'—was reported under the headline: 'Irish Brigade Wins Madrid Battle'.[212] O'Duffy was, however, frustrated by the combined efforts of Spanish military censorship and hostile English journalists which kept any mention of the Irish presence in Spain out of the British press.[213]

A press release marking the casualties at Titulcia, in the style of an oration from the graveside, also made for good copy: 'The cause for which John McSweeney and Bernard Horan died is our cause, and it is a cause that we shall never betray. Faithful unto death as they were, so shall we here be faithful to them, and if dying at the foot of the Hill of Angels has helped to lessen the load of sacrilege and blasphemy showered on their Redeemer, they shall not have died in vain.'[214] The Redeemer referred to was God rather than the leader of his Irish crusade but, by helping to lessen the load of past calumnies showered on O'Duffy, his followers had also done the General an important service. On the home front, O'Duffy was now regarded by many as a hero rather than a failed politician. Gabriel Lee's memorial mass permitted another show of strength in Dublin although the attendance of his Fine Gael comrades, nostalgically attired in blue, provoked a sharp statement accusing the opposition of political opportunism. O'Duffy, Captain Walsh reminded the press, 'is the leader, and he alone was the first public man in Ireland to offer support and sympathy to the Christian forces of Spain'.[215] The General, concerned lest any political capital accruing from Lee's death be appropriated by the opposition, let it be known that Lee's final request was for his burial in a green shirt 'in respect to my leader'.[216]

The legion of the lost

The loss of nerve at Titulcia proved pivotal, confirming Nationalist doubts about their Irish allies. On 23 March, shortly after the failed assault, the *bandera* was transferred north of Madrid to the less exposed village of La Marañosa. Despite being stationed among the more convivial company of the Requetés—the military wing of the Catholic Carlist movement which had originally invited O'Duffy to Spain—the disintegration of the brigade continued apace. Life at the front remained harsh. McCullagh, the only journalist to visit the Irishmen at La Marañosa, found them 'unhappy, owing to the isolation, the intense monotony of trench warfare, ignorance of the language, the difficulty of communicating with Ireland . . . the austere Spanish landscape, wrecked houses and burned villages'.[217] The most common complaints were ill-health, inaction, boredom, the diet (watery coffee and black bread), and the lack of alcohol.[218] McCullagh reported that the hatred between the Spaniards and the number of executions they witnessed 'shook the nerve of the toughest'. As one Kerryman complained: 'It is a fine thing to be shot and done with the job. But in Spain no Russian prisoner is shot outright. He is absolutely tattooed with bullets from the firing squad. They start at his legs and arms and finish up by practically covering his whole body with bullets.'[219] McCullagh also formed a low opinion of the brigade leadership: O'Duffy and his officers knew little of 'modern mechanized war'.[220] According to Fr McCabe, the Spanish had assumed that the Irish officers would have been trained at a military academy but discovered that their combat experience was limited to 'cross-road ambushes'.[221]

However, it was indiscipline rather than inexperience which accounted for the brigade's plight. Gunning became the next senior officer to leave, absconding with a large number of passports and a sum of cash embezzled from the brigade paymaster. The mysterious lack of post from home was also solved when thousands of unposted letters—for which Gunning had collected money for stamps each week—were discovered after his departure.[222] Gunning remained in Spain, ingratiating himself within Nationalist circles in Salamanca, where he delighted in blackening his former leader's reputation. Kerney reported that both men had attempted to get the other shot: 'Gunning thinks O'Duffy is mad and that this Spanish business has actually unbalanced his mind. He threatens to show up O'Duffy and to spare no effort to put an end to his political career.'[223]

After the opportunities in Spain dried up, Gunning moved on to wartime Berlin, securing a job in Joseph Goebbels's ministry of propaganda. He was replaced by Captain O'Ferrall, a Canadian of Hispanic-Irish descent, who claimed to be a veteran of the British, Chilean, and Spanish armies. McCabe described him as having 'glassy, fishy eyes, and a bulldog face and expression . . . a bumptious bounder full of himself. He would seem to be an agent and I am surprised that O'Duffy took him into the Brigade, much less into his confidence.'[224] O'Duffy's reliance on O'Ferrall—who worked for Franco's secret service—further diminished his authority.[225] O'Ferrall, like Gunning, would later skip town leaving months of unpaid debts.

O'Duffy's relations with his Spanish officers were also poor. These men, many of them drawn from aristocratic backgrounds as a gesture of respect, were appalled by the *bandera*'s lack of professionalism.[226] Following the incident with the Canary Islands *bandera*, additional Spanish officers had been drafted in, much to the irritation of O'Duffy and his officers who regarded them as spies.[227] O'Duffy had also fallen out with the commander of the *Tercio*: 'A ruthless perfectionist, obsessed with the reputation of his regiment and uncompromising in its defence, Yagüe had been uneasy about the Irish from the start.'[228] O'Duffy was not entirely to blame for this breakdown, as the experience of the Irishmen was much the same as that of other nationalities in the *Tercio* which 'did not welcome foreigners with open arms'.[229] Nonetheless, O'Duffy's complaints about conditions on the front and his requests for more salubrious postings, had not endeared him to either Yagüe or Franco.

Yagüe had clearly resolved not to tolerate any further trouble from his Irish *bandera*. Following an inspection on 24 March, he complained of widespread drunkenness, insubordination, and low morale, claiming that the Irish unit would endanger any front on which it was stationed. Like other observors, he attributed these deficiencies to the officers rather than the rank and file. He recommended the *bandera*'s dissolution and its redistribution throughout the *Tercio*.[230] The following week, a second report claimed that O'Duffy— described as an 'Operetta General'—was exploiting the Nationalists for his own purposes and that his men were setting a dangerous example for the rest of the *Tercio*. It referred to violence between men and officers, unexplained shootings, and drunkenness in the trenches. Yagüe also refused to accept the appointment of O'Sullivan as commander, insisting that a Spaniard be placed in charge (a demand which he probably suspected O'Duffy would not accept).[231] These reports—although hostile—did not exaggerate the extent of the crisis. Several Irish officers had also refused to serve under O'Sullivan, while on 4 April O'Duffy had ordered two more officers from Spain.[232] Two days later Seán Cunningham, captain of D company, tendered his resignation after a fracas with another officer. O'Duffy also relieved his 'English' officers (Fitzpatrick and Nangle) of their commands due to disloyalty.[233] A bleak entry in one legionary's diary recorded: 'everybody resigning... bandera is becoming smaller and weaker every day'.[234]

On 9 April O'Duffy wrote to the *generalísimo* in response to Yagüe's demands. He accused his Spanish and Irish officers of undermining his authority but assured Franco of his loyalty. The letter was a characteristic combination of his recriminatory, obsequious, self-pitying, and obstinate style: 'I have not seen beggars so badly dressed, but there is a loyal heart behind these rags and, thanks be to God, their loyalty is as great today as on the day they embarked from Ireland to fight for the faith of their ancestors, although their lives have not been very happy lately... I left behind what I cared for most in order to help the cause that Your Excellency has been leading so proudly'. He was clearly set on returning home:

I am forced to believe, unfortunately, that Your Excellency does not trust the battalion any longer and I feel we cannot stay here unless we enjoy Your Excellency's total confidence... I have no alternative but to ask Your Excellency to order the proper transportation in order to send the battalion to its own country. It will be a sad journey but it has to be done. We came here full of sincere wishes to help Spain and also to be able to have the honour of raising our flag beside yours when Your Excellency takes Madrid. We leave Spain, unfortunately, with pain and sadness.[235]

He asked Franco to allow those who wished to stay on to form an Irish company within another *bandera*, assuring him that 'as long as one decent Irishman remained' he would also stay to fight for Spain (albeit as a military attaché at the well-appointed Grand Hotel). Franco declined the offer and, on 16 April, disbanded the Irish *bandera*. The following day O'Duffy visited La Marañosa to hold a plebiscite which recorded near unanimity in favour of returning home.[236] After less than two months in action, the Irish Brigade had collapsed.

Going home

Clearly, much of the blame for the shambles belonged to O'Duffy, who displayed few of the abilities which had previously served him so well. As an officer in the Requetés remarked: 'Few Generals can have had so little responsibility in proportion to their rank, or so little sense of it'.[237] Although he was the only Irish officer with experience of commanding large numbers, he did not involve himself in the day-to-day command of his *bandera*. Despite mustering less than a single battalion, he played the part of an inspector general, directing operations from a well-staffed headquarters behind Nationalist lines. While his men endured squalid conditions, he resided in comfortable surroundings in Cáceres and Salamanca where, among the convivial company of Nationalist high society and like-minded fascist opportunists, he could act out his role as a man of destiny.[238] It was a pose which fooled few well-informed observers. McCullagh reported that the foreign journalists who addressed O'Duffy 'with such adroit flattery that I almost expected him to emit a loud purr' ridiculed him behind his back as 'a bum politician who, having become extinguished in Ireland, had come out to light up again at the flames of the Spanish Civil War'.[239] On his short and infrequent trips to the front, he showed little inclination to expose himself to danger. He visited La Marañosa, where his men were stationed for over five weeks, on only four brief occasions.[240] Fr McCabe recalled O'Duffy describing how on one such visit 'a shell burst beside him. It did him no harm "but I risked my life", he said boastfully.' McCabe believed that O'Duffy 'never intended to die in Spain or for Spain'.[241] It did not seem to occur to O'Duffy—who described this incident in his diary as 'My miraculous escape'—that his men were routinely subjected to bombardment.[242]

The scale of O'Duffy's incompetence in Spain was striking: whatever his previous shortcomings, he had always been able to lead, motivate, and discipline those under his command. One possible explanation is that he cynically decided to exploit the war for optimum personal advantage in return for the least possible risk and effort. Peter Kemp claimed: 'Whatever the ostensible purpose of the Irish Brigade, he never lost sight of its real object, which was to strengthen his own political position.'[243] O'Duffy—like most observers in late 1936—had anticipated a swift Nationalist victory to be followed, presumably, by a triumphant return to Irish politics.[244] Despite the rhetoric of martyrdom, it seems unlikely that O'Duffy had intended his role or that of his men to be a particularly active one. According to McCabe and several Irish officers, 'O'Duffy believed that, instead of fighting, the Brigade would do more good if it had a Band and went round on a Propaganda tour of Spain. O'Duffy wanted to avoid casualties and liabilities, and to give his men what they wanted—a holiday in Spain!'[245] It seems unlikely that he had been prepared for the rigours of frontline service with the bridegrooms of death.

The deterioration of the General's mental faculties—exacerbated by heavy drinking—was also a factor. Only in his consumption of alcohol did he lead by example. McCullagh recalled drinking three double pegs of Irish whiskey during a short conversation with him. Fr Mulrean claimed that 'O'Duffy and his officers were rarely sober'.[246] McCabe identified a more general lack of commitment, noting for example how little effort he made to acclimatize to his surroundings: 'The Germans have all been learning Spanish . . .[O'Duffy] who has been in Spain for over six months has not learnt a word of Spanish. His pronunciation of some Spanish towns, like "Kem-po-zu-los" (Ciempozuelos) creates great hilarity.'[247] His diary reveals that he was unable to spell the towns where his men were stationed for long periods or even the names of the Spanish officers whom he worked alongside, one consequence of which was to increase his dependence on his unreliable subordinates. His erratic behaviour attracted much comment. He was regarded by habitués of the Grand Hotel as 'flippant', 'fantasque', and 'a queer fellow'.[248] Describing him as a 'big, benevolent-looking man with a red, clean-shaven face like that of a parish priest', an American journalist identified his shortcomings as 'bad judgement of men, extreme irascibility, and an absolute incapacity for working with anybody at all'. McCullagh noted that his 'mentality was an especially interesting study—his vanity, the generosity with which he threw himself into his work, his incompetence, his irritability, and the unevenness of his temper'. Fr McCabe similarly observed that he 'seems to have two separate halves in his brain. One of them belongs to a genial capable man, and the other to a plunging obstinate mule'.[249]

The brigade descended into farce during its final weeks. A damning report on 22 April outlined the collapse of discipline. An Irish officer had intervened in a fight between a drunken cook and another officer, wounding the latter. Spanish officers had been fired on by an Irish officer. Shots were fired at the unpopular chaplain after a badly received sermon on drunkenness. Overhearing one Irish officer threatening to shoot another in a café in Cáceres, McCabe referred to the brigade's 'murderous spirit'.[250] This litany of incidents culminated in a spectacular row between a senior Nationalist officer and Dermot O'Sullivan, the *bandera* commander, in which the latter declared that he would lead his men—representing '*la gran democracia Irlandesa*'—to fight for the Spanish Republic. Officers had been shot for much less in the *Tercio*. When Yagüe learned of the incident, he ordered O'Sullivan's arrest and the disarming of the *bandera*.[251] By late April, as one of the unfortunate legionaries recorded in his diary, rank-and-file morale had collapsed: 'Bandera cracking up—all men are getting very sick & weak, dozens going to hospital each day... men sticking it out, thin, worn, pale, half gone crazy on co[g]nac and having sleepless nights... Great rumours about going home.'[252]

O'Duffy, who had some experience in depicting events which others would regard as failure in positive terms, accepted the brigade's demise with apparent equanimity, turning his thoughts to his political future. He established the Irish Brigade Association to perpetuate the brigade's name and repatriate its martyred dead. He became the first president of the association, which incorporated the usual panoply of complex rules, elaborate voting structures, and non-political ambitions that characterized his organizations.[253] Its first meetings were preoccupied with deciding which volunteers to expel.[254] Relieved of the burdens of active service, O'Duffy divided his time between socializing in Cáceres—where his men were stationed until their return (still a somewhat sticky issue) was arranged—and sightseeing. He spent a week touring Portugal in May, visiting the picturesque university towns of Coimbra ('interesting') and Evora ('very interesting'). He resumed the tour in early June: 'North Portugal, fishing villages—casino tonight'.[255]

He was also kept busy fending off the determined attempts of numerous well-wishers—including two bishops, the head of the Nationalist air force, and the Duchess of Tetuan—to patch up relations with Franco; McCabe cunningly tried to tempt him with the suggestion that he would be remembered as a second Sarsfield if he remained until the end. The priest, however, believed that, despite encouraging the brigade's patrons to think that he might reconsider his departure, O'Duffy had already resolved to return: 'One sometimes despairs of this world and the people running it. Most of them seem to be irrational, fanatical or half-mad'.[256] He finally confronted the General in May:

As we walked in the sun, on the upper gallery, I came to the point, and asked O'Duffy if he would drop Capt. O'Sullivan and, for the sake of the Brigade, have a Spanish Major instead. O'Duffy got quite thick and obstinate, and began to splutter something about O'Sullivan's merits, and then he shouted out violently, 'No, I'll take the Brigade home. I wouldn't stop here for the Duchess of Tetuan or all the O'Donnells in Ireland and we'll close the Irish College, too . . .' He almost jumped about in his rage, and he looked a coarse, rough type that reminded me of a 'pub' on Saturday night.[257]

O'Duffy's determination to return was strengthened by the news that a general election had been called in Ireland. He had already paved the way for a triumphant homecoming by issuing press statements attributing his early return to high casualties and other insurmountable difficulties.[258] On 18 May he wrote to a sceptical Nicolás Franco outlining the urgency of a speedy return in order to enable him to place the Nationalist cause before the Irish electorate. Fortunately for O'Duffy, the Nationalists had no desire to hinder his departure. Rejecting an offer of mediation from the Duchess of Tetuan, Yagüe told her that he would rather 'pack them all into aeroplanes and send them over to the "Reds"'.[259] The Franco brothers, according to Kerney, were of a similar mind: 'they realise now that O'Duffy's venture in Spain is a political one . . . General Franco now refuses to see O'Duffy and is anxious to liquidate the whole affair as smoothly as possible.'[260] O'Duffy's interpreter, Captain Meade, reported that at their final meeting Franco 'told O'Duffy he must either do what he was told or clear out. It appears that Franco is usually a mild-mannered man, but that, when he does get into a temper, he can be very stern and energetic.'[261] Gunning reported similar scenes with Yagüe, who was 'a man of violent disposition'.[262]

During the next weeks O'Duffy and Franco haggled over the terms of the brigade's return. O'Duffy claimed that Franco ordered 'one of the best ships on the sea', laden with 'first class fare', to repatriate the *bandera*.[263] It was actually O'Duffy who demanded this, ostensibly to counter any 'pernicious propaganda' resulting from their early departure but in reality (as he told the Italian legation in Dublin) to ensure that he was 'saluted as a defender of the Catholic faith' on his return.[264] He urged Franco to announce that the brigade was leaving because of its casualty rate and its successful completion of its tour of service. He even asked the appalled *generalísimo* for permission to deliver a live radio speech to mark his departure. Franco—keen to see the back of him—agreed to all but the last of these requests.[265] Although the Irish *bandera* had cost Franco a small fortune—and killed more of his own soldiers than the enemy—it made sense for the Nationalists to present its departure in as positive a light as possible.[266] On 17 June 1937 the Irish Brigade, along with three British deserters from Franco's army whom they agreed to smuggle out of the country, sailed out of Lisbon on the *S. S. Mozambique*. They left behind them fifteen dead compatriots, six hospitalized legionaries, and a badly tarnished reputation. But for the General, an eternal optimist when it came to his career, the voyage left ample time to plot his triumphant return to Irish politics.

11
Ireland's Quisling

> There never was a time like the present in the world's history of exalting
> the youth ... Surely we can now cherish the hope that we may be destined
> to play an important part in the future of Christian civilisation?[1]

THE return voyage was not all smooth sailing. O'Duffy, appalled by the
'gossiping' and 'misleading stories' sweeping the ship, was forced to expel
several mutinous volunteers from his new organization. The Irish Brigade
Association's determination to avoid politics proved another casualty of the trip
when it was decided to invite a number of public figures to contest the general
election as 'standard bearers of the Volunteers'.[2] None took up the offer. O'Duffy
had hoped to depict his men as returning heroes and, at least in his own mind, this
proved to be the case: a triumphant final diary entry described the 'immense
crowds' and 'splendid reception' that greeted his arrival on 21 June. In *Crusade in
Spain* he recalled that over 10,000 supporters assembled at the quays, while
thousands more lined the streets to the Mansion House where he was received by
the Lord Mayor, Alfie Byrne, and other dignitaries. Liam Walsh presented
O'Duffy, who was addressed in Spanish fashion as 'His Excellency', with an ornate
certificate in recognition of the glory won fighting for Christianity.[3]

In reality, the homecoming was a more muted affair, accompanied by the
almost inevitable element of farce. A malicious telegram from Fr Mulrean
alleging that the volunteers had been infected with contagious diseases ensured
that they were quarantined on the *Mozambique* until cleared by a medical
officer. The *Irish Times* described the police's intrusive search of the irate
General as the only excitement in 'a long and dreary performance'. The
volunteers, clothed in ragged uniforms, ill-fitting civilian attire, cheap tennis
shoes, and broken boots, presented a striking contrast to their smartly turned-
out leader. Nine of them were arrested for possession of guns, smuggled home

as mementoes from the war. Good humoured cries of 'What about a pint?' and 'We want Frank Ryan' echoed around the Alexandra Basin, but the enthusiasm 'seemed to be entirely on the part of those on board the ship. Crowds, shut out from the landing dock, stood silently along the other quays, and only an odd wave of the hand revealed someone who was greeting a returning "veteran".'[4] O'Duffy, one reporter noted, 'looked as if he has been through a period of very great strain . . . the men also looked very tired and worn out'.[5] As soon as they were allowed to disembark, discrete contingents of Kerrymen and northerners split from the main body. The remainder tramped in silence to the Mansion House, interrupted only by the occasional jeer and cries of 'Remember Ballyseedy' and 'Up the Republic'. A French diplomat attributed the silence of the watching crowds to their disapproval of the brigade's early return and suspicions about O'Duffy's political opportunism.[6]

Worse was to follow when the infighting which wrecked the brigade was revealed for all to see. Disgruntled officers informed the press that the *bandera* had refused to fight at Titulcia, that its only real battle had been against one of Franco's units, and that it had been ordered out of Spain. Some volunteers admitted that they had seen little evidence of massacres aside from those conducted by the Nationalists. Brigadier-General Horan accused O'Duffy of exploiting their martyred dead for his own self-aggrandizement. He declared that the brigade, rather than adding 'one of the most glorious chapters to the pages of Irish history', had returned 'humiliated and disgraced'. Colonel Carew attributed its failure to O'Duffy's leadership.[7] Gunning—suffering from what would prove a terminal case of tuberculosis—continued his vendetta from Spain:

O'Duffy and his entourage of bosthoons have given us a black eye here that will last for generations . . . We have insulted, swindled and hurt the grandest people on earth who thought of us as the finest soldiers and the most self-sacrificing Christians in the world. I should have known O'Duffy well enough to realise that he could and would make a mess even of this affair, which seemed so foolproof. I was very stupid, and I did a poor day's work for both Spain and Ireland when I helped the insane, uncultured lout to put his flat and smelly feet across the frontier last October.[8]

The brigade's failure prevented O'Duffy from capitalizing on the Spanish adventure at home or abroad. In Nationalist Spain, where the brigade's early departure had 'destroyed the popularity of the Irish', there was little sympathy for subsequent attempts by Franco's Irish supporters to bask in his victory.[9] Franco's allies proved no more grateful. An anonymous letter to the Italian legation complained about its lack of recognition:

You are no doubt, Excellency, personally aware of General O'Duffy's [record], may I add that Captain Walsh who was his secretary was equally . . . untiring in his efforts on their behalf and at all times keeping the Fascist cause before the people. Today he still is quietly spreading the light of Fascism . . . Ireland has many Fascist friends. Give them a chance, Excellency, of coming out. Show that your Government recognise them and appreciate the work of those who have led . . . in the cause, Excellency, of 'Fascism'.[10]

The *Irish Catholic* declared itself 'a little ashamed' of the brigade's early return.[11] Volunteers returning to Kerry were dubbed 'the Rosary Brigade' by sarcastic locals. (In time, these men would learn not to mention their service in Spain, some dying decades later without having told their wives or children about their youthful adventure.) Following a public spat between O'Duffy and Belton about missing Christian Front funds, the *Church of Ireland Gazette* summed up the widespread feeling of cynicism: 'As so often happens in Ireland—a country where anything in the grand manner seems doomed from the start to an inglorious con-clusion—the homecoming of these men was marred in every way by anti-climax . . . It has been a sorry business.'[12] The reactionary figures who did so much to send them to Spain remained silent, careful to avoid identification with the discredited brigade if not Franco's cause, which remained popular. Only in Kilkenny, where he managed to prise the freedom of the city from its reluctant corporation, did O'Duffy receive any recognition for his efforts. Moreover, this was achieved only after he pressured some Blueshirt supporters into bribing the corporation's Labour Party's representatives with patronage over a number of sought-after jobs. The police reported that there was 'little public interest' in the ceremony.[13] At home and abroad, the brigade had been judged a failure.

The resulting public ridicule deeply affected O'Duffy, who had expected derision from the left but not from those who had encouraged his departure. The publication of *In Franco's Spain* by Francis McCullagh shed yet more damaging light on the brigade. One pro-Franco reviewer commented that the journalist could be 'excused for lashing out at the ignorant self-seekers who parodied the whole military history of Ireland by their clowning on the sacrificial altar of a great Christian people . . . For the first time in history Ireland is brack-eted with England as a state of no principle, and Irishmen have been talked of as cowards.' O'Duffy angrily retorted:

It would have been better perhaps if the shells of the Communists, which exploded in our trenches and dug-outs every day and every hour of the day, for eleven weeks on the Jarama front, had effectively found their mark, rather than we should be subjected to such vilifying attacks . . . on our return to the country for the honour of which we risked everything that held life dear to us.[14]

Whether due to the decline in his health or his credibility, O'Duffy maintained an uncharacteristically low profile after his return. He began writing a memoir of his time in Spain to set the record straight. One year after his return, he was described by a social columnist as living 'quietly at his fine bachelor house at Mount Merrion, Dublin, enjoying the pleasures of his garden, said to be one of the best furnished and best kept in the country, writing his book, visiting his friends, helping the returned volunteers and their dependants'.[15] His only public role was as president of the struggling Irish Brigade Association, which he devoted to denouncing the ingratitude of Catholic Ireland and revising the brigade's history. The association's lacklustre meetings were enlivened only by its numerous splits and arguments about its finances. By late 1937 it had raised almost 2,000 pounds, but O'Duffy's expenditure of around 3,000 pounds had left the association unable to maintain its office or cover the costs of the funerals of the small number of veterans who died following their return. Its dispiriting meetings were preoccupied with preventing the association from being sued by its debtors and contemplating libel actions against Fr Mulrean and Paddy Belton (who accused O'Duffy of receiving, but not accounting for, 'fabulous sums' from the Christian Front). It disintegrated during the summer of 1938 following an anniversary service for the dead in the Pro-Cathedral.[16]

Crusade in Spain, published in 1938, bore all the usual hallmarks of O'Duffy's crude propaganda. The tone throughout was one of false modesty; the minor role played by the brigade was blamed on the obstacles imposed by de Valera but offset by lengthy testimonials of O'Duffy's bravery at the front. The near-miss by republican artillery was depicted as one of many close shaves with death. The war itself was attributed to an international communist conspiracy against Christianity. The depiction of Nationalist Spain—where Civil Guards were admired by the people for their impartial devotion to duty and Franco lauded for his generous treatment of vanquished enemies—was unconvincing even by the prevailing standards of anti-communist propaganda. O'Duffy's treatment of Spain's recent history revealed more about his own political agenda than events in Spain. He praised the post-war dictator Primo de Rivera, but observed that he lacked 'the forcefulness of a Mussolini'. Gil Robles, the authoritarian leader of the Catholic right in the early 1930s, was 'a great Catholic and a great Statesman' but had failed to defend Spain from communism due to his misplaced faith in democracy. The Falange was dedicated to 'sound Catholic and national principles', and the 'anti-Liberal, anti-capitalist' Carlists were valiant 'knights of Christ and Faith', but it was Franco's corporatism which would forge the 'ideal State—Catholic not merely in name, but in spirit'.[17]

The book's undercurrent of anti-Semitism marked something of an ideological departure for O'Duffy. From the outset, the brigade organizers had indulged in anti-Semitic rhetoric. Justifying the brigade's mobilization, Liam Walsh had declared that there was 'no greater evil than Communism, unless, perhaps Freemasonry and Jewry' and blamed the non-intervention agreement on the French prime minister, Leon Blum, who he described as a 'freemason, Jew and Socialist'.[18] After his return from Spain, O'Duffy took to referring to the Irish Brigade as a crusade 'against Communism, Jewry and Freemasonry'.[19] His book made much of the purported role of Russian Jews within the Republican army, and described the anti-clerical socialist and anarchist trade unions as 'powerful political Jewish-Masonic organisations, directed and focussed by the Communist International'.[20] The notion of communism as the Satanic product of a Judeo-Masonic conspiracy was surprisingly widespread among anti-communist clericalist circles in Ireland.[21] It was also an idea increasingly expressed by European fascists who were aligning their ideologies to Nazi racialism. Jewish involvement in the French Popular Front and other anti-fascist movements had revived the myth of communism as an international Jewish conspiracy.[22] Other writings by O'Duffy in 1938 confirm this ideological shift. In an *Irish Independent* article celebrating Nazi Germany's seizure of the Sudetenland, O'Duffy urged anti-partitionists to draw inspiration from Hitler's victory over 'that queer coalition of International Jewry, the International Secret Societies, International Finance and the Comintern', adding that it was time for the south's Protestant minority to 'show whether they have or have not gratitude'.[23]

   Crusade in Spain, generously described by Liam Walsh as 'one of the best books in the English language', was favourably reviewed in the Irish and international Catholic press. Republicans and socialists were less impressed. The *Irish Press* noted that it revealed just how little time O'Duffy had spent at the front.[24] George Orwell, despite finding pro-Franco propaganda 'less irritating than the rather subtler type of lie that has been evolved by the other side', dismissed it as 'badly written and uninteresting', observing that O'Duffy's 'adventures in Spain do seem in one way to have resembled a crusade in that they were a frightful muddle and led to nothing in particular'.[25] Most importantly, *Crusade in Spain* failed to alter the public perception of his crusade as a failure or create an opportunity for his political rehabilitation. The General's reputation as a politician had been destroyed by his leadership of Fine Gael. By destroying what remained of his reputation as a man of action, Spain left him humiliatingly exposed in the eyes of the Irish public. Even Walsh's hagiography noted the toll:

In mind and body General O'Duffy was now a tired man. Although he never complained of strain following the campaign when his energies were taxed to the limit fighting endless disappointments, still the sustained mental excitement and physical effort must naturally have resulted in a breakdown, as yet more apparent than real. He was not a 'sick man', but his new timidity and indifference towards affairs was so unusual as to set one thinking.[26]

Flirting with the IRA

Despite the Spanish disaster the storm clouds over Europe ensured that
O'Duffy—who remained the undisputed figurehead of Irish fascism—
retained a modicum of political relevancy. Lacking a power base of his own and
in increasingly uncertain health, his occasional forays onto the political stage
took the form of occasional contacts with other extremists, republicans, and
representatives of the fascist states. Liam Walsh now began to play a more independent role, partly intended to shield his leader from unwanted police
scrutiny. Corrupt and treacherous, Walsh exemplified the calibre of many of
those who attached themselves to the cause of Irish fascism. He was widely disliked within the Irish Brigade Association due to what Special Branch charit-
ably described as his 'laxity in control of funds'. Even O'Duffy had accused him
of embezzling 2,300 pounds intended to cover the cost of transporting volunteers to Spain and pocketing another 1,000 pounds for sabotaging the arrival of
a troop ship.[27] His behaviour was at least consistent: he had a track-record of
fraud dating back to 1923, when he was drummed out of the National Army for
embezzlement.[28] After the association's demise, O'Duffy—who remained
inexplicably loyal to Walsh—found him employment with the *Sunday Independent* and the Italian legation. Neither job worked out. The *Independent* fired
him for selling the keys to its prize crosswords, while the Italian legation sacked
him for theft. Walsh then began blackmailing his former employers at the
legation by threatening to expose their subversive activities.[29]

It was the latter appointment which brought Walsh to the attention of G2,
the branch of Irish military intelligence formed to counter the threat of foreign
subversion as war in Europe loomed. Walsh had become a central figure in the
seedy subculture of cranks, opportunists, and anti-Semites which emerged in
response to the rise of fascism in Europe, and his lack of discretion (on one
occasion he cabled birthday greetings to Hitler) ensured that he and the General remained under surveillance. By 1939 Walsh was distributing fascist propaganda on behalf of the Italian legation and the Deutscher Fichte-Bund, a Nazi
propaganda organization based in Hamburg. He had also established a secret
fascist organization—known variously as the International Fascist Movement,
the Celtic Professional Societies, and the All-Purposes Guilds—which had
been penetrated by the authorities.[30] A Special Branch report of one of its
meetings in August illustrated its sinister, if bizarre, nature. Walsh urged the
establishment of a fascist Ireland to 'line up with Germany, Italy, Spain and
Portugal and others who have the Totalitarian ideal in view', while another

speaker denounced Irish culture as 'Jewish and Freemason interest dressed up in green clothing'. The organization established a short-lived paper, *The Irish World Review*, which soon ran into financial problems (partly due to Walsh's sticky fingers).[31] Prior to September 1939, G2 did not take Walsh very seriously, describing him as a 'chancer' with 'a considerable sense of his own importance' and 'a failing for living beyond his means'.[32]

G2 remained more concerned about O'Duffy. In February 1939 they observed him meeting German agent Oskar Pfaus during his clandestine mission to Ireland.[33] Pfaus—who had led an adventurous life as a soldier, lumberjack, cowboy, and Chicago cop before turning his hand to espionage as head of the Fichte-Bund's Irish and American departments—had aroused suspicions due to his contradictory statements to immigration officials and curious luggage ('a change of clothing, an expensive camera and £30'). His mission, G2 surmised, was to establish contact with the IRA—which had just begun a bombing campaign in Britain—in order to facilitate its co-operation with Nazi Germany when the war broke out. During their meeting Pfaus asked O'Duffy whether Germany could expect support from his fascist organization but was rebuffed by the cautious General on the grounds that the 'time was not yet ripe'. O'Duffy did, however, put Pfaus in contact with the IRA, thereby facilitating what would later prove an important link between Germany and the IRA. However, the fact that Abwehr (German military intelligence) could think of no one better placed to put it in touch with the IRA highlighted its limited understanding of Irish politics. With one exception, Germany's subsequent spy missions to Ireland were characterized by ineptitude.[34]

After Pfaus returned to Hamburg, G2 noticed that his efforts to contact potential Irish sympathizers intensified. Military intelligence regarded his letters as

the last word in diplomacy. Their general tenor was calculated to encourage friendly and intimate correspondence. He studied each letter he received very carefully with the result that to some of his correspondents he sent Catholic religious pictures, while others who seemed more strongly in favour of Germany's cause, were invited to send him press cuttings or reports on such matters as the Jewish situation in Ireland, the attitude of the Irish people to Germany or the reaction in Ireland to his propaganda campaign.[35]

His main contact remained Walsh who (for a price) supplied him with press cuttings and useful information. Walsh also tapped Pfaus for funds to establish a pro-Nazi newspaper and press bureau, visiting Hamburg in July 1939 to secure financial backing for the Celtic Confederation of Occupation Guilds.

G2 were concerned but not overly alarmed by Walsh's activities, describing him to MI5 as an individual 'of poor calibre who would do anything for money'.[36]

Dependent on overheard gossip and intercepted communications, G2 remained uncertain but more wary about O'Duffy's activities. In August 1939 it reported 'that at present he is doing nothing except writing his autobiography which is to cause fireworks all round. He looks well (is probably not drinking much).' However, G2 was more concerned that the General had 'stated that he is in touch with both Hitler and Mussolini and made some other statements which would indicate he is both interested in and possibly in touch with German and Italian activities'.[37] O'Duffy also boasted that he was a political adviser to the Spanish ambassador in Dublin, but G2 was much more impressed by the fact that he had reportedly 'forecast the German-Russian pact (which was described as a political bombshell) well in advance' of its announcement.[38] It suspected that O'Duffy was casting around for an organization such as the National Anti-Partition Council to commandeer 'for his own use'.[39] It concluded that although he 'scrupulously avoided Press publicity he is nevertheless very active in the political sphere'.[40]

A speech on international affairs delivered by O'Duffy to a meeting of the Celtic Confederation of Occupational Guilds offers an insight into his thinking in this period. His admiration of Mussolini had predictably paled in line with the *Duce*'s fading reputation: 'Events in Europe move swiftly. Yesterday it was Mussolini and Fascism; today it is Hitler and Nazism.' The struggle against Bolshevism had divided Europe into two camps: O'Duffy believed that Ireland, as a Christian nation, belonged among the states ranged against 'subversive and materialistic Bolshevism' rather than those 'governed by grasping and greedy capitalistic masters'. Ireland owed Britain nothing for seven centuries of oppression but, he reminded his minions, had yet to repay Germany's 'moral and material support during the hour of the present Irish generation's trials— 1916'. Comparing Britain's propaganda 'regarding the alleged persecution of religion, and of course the Jews' to its discredited accounts of German atrocities in Belgium during the Great War, O'Duffy outlined the case for German expansion into the territory which Britain had 'filched from her under the Versailles Treaty' and those other areas 'where she has interests and majorities or large numbers of her own people'. For obvious reasons, this was not a terribly difficult case to make in Ireland: even de Valera had sympathized with Hitler's claims to the Sudetenland.[41]

Germany's reasonable demands were opposed only by British and French 'war mongers' and 'Jews, Marxists and Freemasons' who preached destruction and anarchy. The rise of fascism presented a historic opportunity rather than

a crisis: 'Europe is decadent, hesitating and undermined by the corrosive germs
of senile decay due to corrupt politicians, and the unchristian and antiquated
system of political party government... Surely we can now cherish the hope
that we may be destined to play an important part in the future of Christian
civilisation.'[42] Ireland should emulate rather than criticize the 'energy and
patriotism' of the 'old nations with young minds' and act as a moderating influence in world affairs: 'Pious platitudes and hysterical hypocrisy against the
virility of Fascist, Nazi or Corporate States issued under the cover of a smoke
cloud by the Democratic States, can but result in a cataclysmic revolution ending
in world-wide Bolshevism.'

   G2's concerns—and those of MI5 which had belatedly realized the potential
security threat arising from Nazi infiltration of Ireland—were heightened by a
reported meeting between O'Duffy, the German diplomat Dr Eduard Hempel,
and several leading IRA men in a remote corner of Donegal. G2 suspected
O'Duffy was 'flirting with the IRA' by acting as a 'negotiator between the
Germans and the IRA'.[43] MI5, which had learned of a recent meeting between
Admiral Canaris (the head of Abwehr) and James O'Donovan, the IRA's envoy
in Berlin, also suspected that O'Duffy had facilitated this alliance.[44] G2's suspicion that O'Duffy saw himself as the guiding hand behind a conspiracy to
unite Irish fascism, the IRA, and Nazi Germany was confirmed by an intercepted letter from another fascist, Commandant Brennan-Whitmore, to Liam
Walsh, which revealed tensions over the General's strategy:

I am, frankly, disturbed about O'D...I have latterly come to the conviction that he
is 'slightly' touched. No man in normal balance would have went on the way he did
the Meeting night: & made the statements which he did in front of us both. I am now
satisfied that, despite what certain people say, so far as the ordinary citizen is
concerned O'D cuts no ice. And his flirting with the IRA will be fatal. No one can get
under way in this country with that bunch: & even if they work him in now: it would
only be to ditch him later on. His claim that the IRA is purged of communism is pure
bunk.[45]

   Evidence from the Italian archives sheds further light on the General's
scheming in 1939. In February O'Duffy had requested a meeting with Vincenzo
Berardis, the recently appointed Italian minister whom MI5 rightly considered
'an ardent fascist'.[46] Although aware of O'Duffy's disastrous record in Spain,
Berardis agreed to meet him given his previous services to fascism. He assessed
him as a man bitterly disappointed by the past but an enthusiastic and
committed fascist, noting in particular his approval of the republican bombing
campaign in Britain and his opposition to de Valera's coercion of the IRA.

O'Duffy, with characteristic exaggeration, had claimed the credit for the IRA's new strategy. Berardis formed a mixed impression of O'Duffy, viewing him as a generous 'man of faith and actions with a deep knowledge of his country' but lacking in 'cultural and political conscience' and popular support. He was also aware that O'Duffy's ambition of Irish unification through violence lacked political credibility.[47]

Accompanied by Brennan-Whitmore, O'Duffy met Berardis again three months later to solicit his support for a new corporatist party. The General told him of his plans to unite Ireland's fascists and militant republicans and form a 10,000 strong militia composed of Spanish Civil War veterans and IRA supporters. It was clear to Berardis, however, that not only would such a movement attract little political support but that O'Duffy and Brennan-Whitmore (who claimed to represent a separate nucleus of corporatists) did not even trust one another.[48] Brennan-Whitmore—Whit to his friends—exemplified the eccentric nature of many Irish fascists. A veteran of 1916 and an anti-Semite of long standing, Whit had fought in the War of Independence and Civil War before serving in Irish military intelligence. He made his living as a farmer, sometime press correspondent, and publisher. G2 considered him a 'vain, superficially brilliant' figure with 'a "glib" pen, and tongue which considerably impress the inexperienced. Owing to his vanity he would be greatly influenced by attentions from foreign organisations'.[49] He had first come to G2's attention in the summer of 1939 as a writer of pro-Nazi letters to the press and the founder of the All Purposes Guild (which would later merge with O'Duffy's tiny fascist movement). His ideological outlook—hinging on the notion that Nazism, Fascism, and Falangism were variations of medieval corporatism originally stemming from Gaelic Ireland—resembled that of the General.[50]

Although O'Duffy's political strategy in 1939 had changed little from the mid-1930s, the prospects for co-operation between the far right and republican extremists had improved. The departure of the IRA's left wing and state coercion had left the once formidable IRA a shadow of its former self by 1939. Its leadership—an apolitical and extremist faction led by chief of staff Seán Russell, who had ordered the futile bombing campaign in Britain—was enthusiastic about the possibility of securing finance, weapons, and even military reinforcements from Germany (for which, of course, there was a recent historical precedent). Following the meeting with Pfaus which O'Duffy had facilitated, Jim O'Donovan—GHQ's director of chemical warfare—had travelled to Germany to establish contact with the Nazi régime.[51] While O'Duffy's claim to have fostered the alliance between the IRA and Germany was an exaggeration, he was now considered a useful figure by both sides.

The impetus behind the growing convergence between Irish fascism and republicanism stemmed from ideology as well as *realpolitik*. O'Duffy's belief that the IRA had been purged of socialism was broadly correct, as was demonstrated by the increasingly anti-Semitic and fascistic content of the IRA's *War News*. The growing importance of young northern republicans such as Seán McCaughey and Charlie McGlade was also relevant. These men represented militarist and clericalist tendencies, preoccupied with partition but relatively indifferent to the faultlines of Civil War politics, which were much more receptive to O'Duffy than the Twomey-era leadership. It was not, however, until 3 September 1939 that the most important prerequisite for the political realignment desired by O'Duffy fell into the place.

The representative of the Axis powers in Ireland

The Second World War—or the Emergency as it became known in Ireland— elevated O'Duffy's status from political crank to potential enemy of the state. As in 1936, international events had invested his extremist politics with a certain relevancy. Although the return of the Treaty ports in 1938 had enabled de Valera to declare Irish neutrality, the government's position remained relatively vulnerable. Most of the very small number of European states which successfully protected their wartime neutrality did so either because they were well defended or strategically unimportant. Southern Ireland, in contrast, was poorly defended and of considerable strategic significance to both Britain and Germany, particularly between the fall of France, in May 1940, and the invasion of the Soviet Union, in June 1941. Moreover, influential British figures such as Winston Churchill (who regarded Irish neutrality as nothing less than treachery) urged the occupation of southern Ireland on defensive grounds.[52]

Although there was little de Valera could do to prevent a German or British invasion, he could deny either side a pretext for such aggression. Within this context, the most obvious danger to the state lay in the contacts between Nazi Germany and its potential fifth column, the IRA. Nor was the threat necessarily a military one: MI5 believed that the 'most potentially dangerous consequence' of Irish neutrality 'was to provide the enemy intelligence services with a very favourable situation for operating against this country and Northern Ireland'.[53] Moreover, for the marginalized but resilient republican tradition which de Valera had failed to suppress, the principle that England's difficulty represented Ireland's opportunity was axiomatic. There remained also the problem of public opinion, given recent Irish history and the widespread resentment of partition. While many Irish people militarily, economically, and ideologically supported the British war effort, a deep vein of ambiguity ran through nationalist opinion.[54] For all these reasons the threat to Irish security posed by an alliance of fascists and republicans was taken extremely seriously in Ireland and Britain.

It is also worth noting that accounts by foreign visitors to Ireland between 1939 and 1941 suggest that public opinion on the war was more fluid and finely balanced in the early stages of the conflict (when most observers expected Germany to win) than would later be admitted. A report filed by a Czech diplomat (and subsequently intercepted by G2) offered a perceptive insight into popular sentiment at the height of German success in May 1940.

The majority of the Irish people have had from the beginning their own special relationship to the war. They have regarded the war as an English enterprise, something which generally speaking has nothing to do with Ireland. The plain man and the educated man look upon the ideological background of the European struggle as bluff, as invention thought out in order to justify the war. The Irish, in accordance with their traditions have considered this war only from the standpoint of their relations with Great Britain, from the standpoint of old wrongs and from the standpoint of Irish political aims. For the ordinary Irish person who does not know Germany it is sufficient that Germany is striking the English. Of anything further he does not meditate and does not wish to meditate. Even the educated man finds it difficult to free himself from the logic of the ideas which arise from an anti-British complex consciously maintained by the Irish after a decade . . . The Irish were and are in these circumstances very easily accessible to the arguments which flow on the ether from Hamburg and Bremen in an intonation familiar to them. The Irish voice of Lord Haw Haw gains thus very many and willing hearers.[55]

Outraged by Irish public sympathy for two republicans who had been sentenced to death for their involvement in a bungled IRA bombing which killed five civilians in Coventry, Sir John Maffey, the British representative in Ireland, made much the same point: 'In this country if any agitation can be based on an anti-English motif that agitation, however unreasonable, is bound to succeed . . . I am surprised to find that hatred is a bigger factor here than it was 25 years ago . . . England is now an abstraction. It has been a state industry to indoctrinate the younger generation with antagonism and the results are not surprising.'[56] A visiting Polish Catholic aristocrat, writing in early 1941, was troubled by the lack of interest 'in what is going on in Europe, even as regards the Church', a moral neutrality he attributed to censorship: 'Nothing is allowed to appear in the Irish press on the subject of the ruthlessness of the Germans or even of the Soviets . . . Nothing is published which contains an appreciation of the magnificent spirit shown by the British people.'[57] He felt, nonetheless, that public opinion was shifting towards the allies. However, by mid-1941, a Dutch official could still report that most Irish Catholics were 'inclined to be pro-German. This means that they are anti-British rather than pro-German . . . This tendency is to be noticed especially amongst the large group that support Mr. De Valera's policy and admire the German people as being efficient and industrious.'[58]

Although most of these sources accepted that Fine Gael was 'entirely devoted to the Allied cause', a number of senior Irish officials—including the minister for the co-ordination of defensive measures, Frank Aiken, and the secretary of the department of foreign affairs Joe Walshe—were regarded as German sympathizers.[59] Even de Valera—whose discreet policy of 'friendly neutrality' favoured Britain—publicly affected to regard the war as a clash between unsavoury imperialist powers. These assessments by allied supporters, which often confused the popularity of neutrality (a policy which necessitated the censorship of criticism of all the belligerents) with opposition to England, were probably over-pessimistic. In the more measured opinion of MI5—which described neutrality as Ireland's 'own private war'—the Irish attitude was not 'one of goodwill, but rather of indifference to either side, except in so far as the acts of either belligerent might affect his own or Irish interests generally'.[60] Even Hempel qualified his claim of popular Irish sympathy for Nazi Germany by noting that it was 'not so much the product of direct understanding of the German nation as the reaction of anti-British feeling. Even the readiness of IRA circles to appeal for German help in their fight against England does not imply that they are willing to subordinate themselves to German leadership.'[61] None the less, it was the fertile ground offered by this widespread public ambiguity about the war and the very real possibility of a German victory which the IRA and Irish fascists sought to exploit during the early years of the Emergency.

This was done in various ways, none particularly successfully. Propaganda was the most obvious strategy. Pro-Nazi leaflets—which combined fascist and Irish prejudices—were discreetly distributed in public places:

WHO let loose the scum of England—the Jew Greenwood's Black and Tans—to murder, burn and loot in our country? WHO is flooding Ireland with Jewish-Masonic drivel and filth insulting to our national aspirations and the Christian religion . . . England's foes are Ireland's friends—May they increase and multiply! Moladh go deo leo![62]

Walsh and O'Duffy helped to devise such propaganda. Among their papers are badly written anti-Semitic tracts, which originated from the Fichte-Bund, amended with corrections to improve their language and appeal. A typical piece—again devoted to Sir Hamar Greenwood, the (non-Jewish) former chief secretary of Ireland—stated: 'We need not dwell upon how this Jew and his heavily armed hordes in the uniforms of the English despots ran riot . . . today one can still see the horrible traces of the English-Jewish terror in the Irish Free State'.[63]

O'Duffy and Walsh—the latter playing the more risky public role—formed a series of secret organizations intended to facilitate the German war effort and place themselves in a favourable position when the widely anticipated invasion occurred. The earliest reported meeting of the Irish Friends of Germany (IFG), also known as Cumann Náisiunta, occurred in O'Duffy's home in February 1940. Its attendance included two ex-Cumann na nGaedheal TDs (the Christian Front leader, Alexander McCabe, and a former minister, James Burke), several prominent republicans, and a priest.[64] The next occurred in April when Walsh organized an 'At Home' for ex-Blueshirts, former Christian Front activists, and other unsavoury elements of the Catholic right.[65] The following month Special Branch observed O'Duffy attending a small meeting in Wynn's Hotel, where Cumann Náisiunta was formally established. Its members were told that the new movement would be dedicated to 'counteracting propaganda' and 'general cultural and informative studies'. G2, however, intercepted a more indiscreet reference to the movement's purpose by Walsh: 'It is well to let Irish Friends or whatever name they may choose to call themselves think that propaganda is their function—other work can be carried on behind the scenes and without their knowledge'.[66] In late May a series of public meetings—which O'Duffy did not attend—followed in the Red Bank Restaurant, a popular haunt for Dublin fascists. A garda who infiltrated the organisation by posing as a member of the Society of St Vincent de Paul described its insidious nature. At one meeting in the Red Bank the principal speaker, George Griffin, attempted to rouse the audience by claiming

that the propaganda regarding the German cruelties and the persecution of the Catholics were nothing but a fabrication of lies and that it was the Jews that were responsible for the circulation of such stories, the time had now come when this organisation must take definite action. He stated that there were at present 27,000 Jews in the country . . . and before the termination of the war a further 27,000 would be here if action was not taken . . . from what he knew Hitler was the only man whose policy in the extermination of the Jews lead to the Success of National Socialism.[67]

Another member denied that the IFG represented a fifth column, insisting that 'it was the Jews they were after and everything must be done to make their lot

330 EOIN O'DUFFY: A SELF-MADE HERO

miserable and to get rid of them out of the country'. The meeting ended with
raised-hand salutes and the playing of the Irish and German national anthems.
At another meeting in the Swiss Chalet restaurant, Griffin claimed that the
organization was directly in touch with Germany: 'he had information that the
German army would be inside England by 14th July, 1940, and that they would
be here by 15th July, 1940; also that they had groups ready to facilitate the
German army in every respect. They would then come out into the open... he
had been checking on all firms in town which were run by Jews or Freemasons.'[68]

These meetings attracted a lower middle-class attendance of public servants,
gaelgoirs, journalists, political has-beens, German expatriates, and intelligentsia (reports noted the attendance of a struggling artist and the rather better
known poet Patrick Kavanagh). Nazi Germany's Irish friends were insignificant figures. Some were anti-Semites and fascists, others were cranks, motivated
by vanity or grievance, while some—lured by the singing, dancing, and free
drinks on offer at the Red Bank—were only there for the beer. A police informant noted the generous provisions doled out at one meeting: 'we were given
tea, Sardines and egg sandwitches [*sic*], buscuits [*sic*] and cigarettes... in boxes
of 50s and 20s'.[69] G2's character profiles suggested that the movement's prominent figures were—rather like their leader—psychologically flawed malcontents.
The anti-Semite propagandist Dr O'Sullivan, an inspector at the department
of education, was described as 'shrewd, disgruntled, extremely egotistical and
very ambitious and discontented... Very keen on all Gaelic activities, to [the]
extent of being called something of a crank. But some indication that he
regards Gaelic movement cynically.'[70] The deranged ex-Blueshirt George
Griffin was diagnosed as 'slightly abnormal', 'easily led', and 'suffering from
anti-Jewish mania'.[71] Among the more bizarre fellow travellers who fell under
G2's gaze were Pat O'Connor 'the Bearded Artist' and 'Ellen Purser known
as Madame Riviere'.[72]

These reports reveal the squalid underbelly of wartime Dublin but also a
movement which, in the absence of a German invasion, would not seem to
have presented a grave threat to the state. As one historian of Nazi espionage
speculated: 'In the event of an actual German invasion, these cranks would
have been a ready, if not altogether valuable, asset to occupying German
figures'.[73] They certainly would have assisted in identifying Ireland's small
Jewish population for extermination. In the meantime, they added to the
growing level of anti-Semitism in wartime Ireland. A government memo noted
'that the Germans have had some success in spreading the virus of anti-Semitism
in Ireland with the help of such elements as General O'Duffy's Irish Fascist
Party which has adopted a Nazi-inspired "Jewish peril" line'.[74]

The existence of an active circle of Nazi sympathizers would have done nothing to raise morale during a period when rumours of invasion were circulating wildly, and there was always the risk of its exposure by a hostile British press which revelled in depicting neutral Ireland as a hotbed of Nazi intrigue. G2 were also concerned that the IFG might pose a greater threat than its amateurish membership suggested. The fact that a number of the Abwehr spies who arrived between 1940 and 1941 had been given Walsh's name as a contact led the authorities to believe that O'Duffy was using the IFG as a cover for more sinister activities.[75] O'Duffy, moreover, had told one police informant that his well-placed contacts within the security forces provided him with sensitive information on police activities and military movements. The potential threat represented by the IFG was also difficult to estimate due to its strategy of compiling secret lists of potential sympathizers to be approached at the right moment. As late as 1944, Hempel claimed that Germany's propaganda bulletin was read by over 12,000 people.[76] One police informant reported that 'many civil servants, members of the Army and Police Forces, and Government pensioners were sympathetic...but they could not be expected to come out openly and say so. He said there were also two Secretaries of Government Departments who were definitely pro-Nazi.'[77] G2's more sober assessment conceded that the IFG had influenced 'certain members of the Defence Forces' who 'would require careful attention' if circumstances changed.[78]

Describing O'Duffy as a bombastic individual with a tendency to exaggerate his own importance, G2 adopted a measured attitude to the threat that he posed:

It can be accepted as certain that he is anxious to cultivate the legations of certain belligerents and that he has already probably transferred certain unimportant information to them. It is quite probable that he would act in the same manner but in a more discreet way in connection with information of importance and in this connection his friendship with and the obvious influence he exercises over persons holding some important State positions is of some significance.[79]

It was not surprising that the General's wide circle of dubious acquaintances caused concern. It included politicians, government officials, republicans, senior police, and army officers such as Hugo MacNeill (with whom he spent boozy weekends in Bundoran), the diplomatic and intelligence staff of the Spanish, Italian, and German legations, and 'a variety of people whose antecedents are not known'.[80] Although he was primarily viewed as a security risk, O'Duffy was also one of four figures identified by G2 as potential Quislings if Germany were to invade: the others (all former members of Cumann na nGaedheal) were J. J. Walsh, Cecil Lavery, and Ernest Blythe.[81] O'Duffy was not alarmed by his notoriety. Although he avoided compromising meetings with his IFG minions, he made no effort to hide his German connections, inviting the SS officer and diplomat Henning Thomsen to accompany him to the GAA all-Ireland final, corresponding with Oskar Pfaus, and dining with the Hempels. In some circles, the police noted, he was even described as the 'representative of the Axis Powers in Ireland'.[82]

As well as adding to his social cachet, another welcome consequence of the triumph of fascism in Europe was to bring about his rehabilitation within republican circles. Following the anglophobic logic of the IRA, O'Duffy—or more to the point his powerful friends—were now allies: 'The enemies of England are, by that fact, the friends of Ireland. We are no more Nazi or Fascist than Connolly or Pearse were Imperialistic by seeking the aid of Imperialist-Germany in 1916.'[83] Despite such rhetoric, however, the ascendancy of apolitical militarists and right-wing clericalists within the new leadership had contributed to an ugly pro-Nazi stance. This was clearly demonstrated by the IRA's principal wartime periodical, *War News*, which after 1939 espoused not merely pro-German but anti-Semitic and fascist sentiments. One issue declared that the 'cleansing fire' of German militarism had forced Jewish 'parasites' to Ireland, where they were tolerated by de Valera's 'Jew-ridden' government. 'Yidds', it claimed, were now the 'new owners of Ireland'.[84] Such rhetoric reflected the views of the average IRA man no more than *An Phoblacht*'s Marxism in the early 1930s but illustrated the insidious ideological convergence between the IRA's leadership and Irish fascism in this period.[85] One tangible manifestation of this was the establishment of Córas na Poblachta in March 1940. Remarkably, for an IRA-sponsored front, its inaugural meeting included O'Duffy and former Christian Front leaders. Nor did it escape G2's attention that Córas had attracted 'a miscellaneous collection of people whose political associations in the past varied considerably' including prominent figures from the Irish Friends of Germany who 'hoped for a German victory and were preparing the ground for their own selection as leaders in Irish politics following such victory'.[86]

It was perhaps this convergence which finally prompted the government to act. In June 1940—at the height of official alarm about the possibility of invasion—G2 arrested fifteen IFG members, interning Liam Walsh and several other fascists. O'Duffy's instinct for self-preservation and public profile appears to have prevented his arrest, but a perceptive memo (written after the fear of invasion had subsided) suggests that it was carefully considered by G2:

O'Duffy is unquestionably regarded as the leader of the political school of thought that draws its inspiration from what is now termed 'the Axis Powers'. He is in the position of a man who has had 'greatness thrust upon him' and whether he is wholly convinced of the wisdom of his political activities or not he is looked upon as a leader and must play up to that role . . . he is aware or at least suspects that his movements etc. are subjected to surveillance and he is consequently behaving with increasing discretion in recent times. He actually denied on one occasion that he had any knowledge of the organisation known as the 'Irish Friends of Germany' though there is no doubt whatever that he is in close touch with all the members of this group. His friendship with Major Genl. Mac-Neill appears to be intimate. He addresses that Officer as 'Hugo'. . . a reasonable conclusion is that O'Duffy and his friend were convinced that following the collapse of France, Germany would invade both England and Ireland. Following such an invasion a new form of Government would be set up here with O'Duffy and his satellites replacing the existing Government . . . Owing to the failure of the anticipated invasion to materialise the activities of O'Duffy in relation to foreign powers are circumscribed—but taking the long view it seems desirable that we should not lose sight of his former associates who are now in the Defence Forces or of O'Duffy's potential capacity for intrigue in the inevitable post war reconstruction of existing systems of government.[87]

Following the arrests—Special Branch presumably leaving its most useful informants on the loose—the IFG went the way of most of O'Duffy's organizations, splitting into mutually hostile factions of little importance. O'Duffy, who feared that Walsh had forged documents to incriminate him as the leader of an Irish fifth column in order to secure his own release from internment, became even more cautious. In late July he risked a brief meeting in the Broadway Soda Fountain and Café on O'Connell Street to warn his followers that the government would smash the IFG if its members were found together under any guise. He told them that he had insufficient time to organize a fascist party but that they should 'get as many people as possible together as the military situation might change overnight'. He would send two of his most trusted men to monitor their meetings but would not attend in case he brought them to the attention of the police.[88]

In early September he told another follower that 'no organisation could be formed without its being treasonable and that in any case this step was hardly worth while at the present moment as the German Minister was fully aware of all those who supported him'.[89] Such behaviour supports G2's assumption that O'Duffy felt it necessary to pose as a Quisling in waiting, while being careful to deny the authorities a reason to intern him (the harsh environment of the Curragh camp being no place for an ailing alcoholic): 'in the event of a German-Italian victory he hopes to be able to associate with the victors, while if this eventuality does not ensue he can resume an ordinary Irish political career when opportunity offers'.[90] The General's caution did not appear to bother his naïve followers, who, G2 noted, continued to speak of him 'as the leader who will appear at the right moment'.[91]

Spies in Ireland

Fortunately for Ireland—if not for O'Duffy's political aspirations—the right moment failed to arrive. Following Germany's failure to win control of the skies over Britain in the summer of 1940, the threat of invasion receded, as did the potential threat posed by the IFG, which collapsed in 1942.[92] However, O'Duffy's contacts with the IRA and Nazi Germany continued to cause security problems. Between 1939 and 1943 Abwehr despatched twelve spies to Ireland tasked with a variety of missions ranging from sabotage to anti-British agitation. Hindered by poor intelligence and unrealistic objectives, their efforts were often farcical. A drunken Walter Simon was arrested only one day after his arrival in rural Kerry, following some ill-advised banter with a group of detectives on the Dublin train. Henry Obed, an Indian, and two German-South Africans, Dieter Gaertner and Herbert Tributh, were arrested on the day of their arrival after failing to pass themselves off as native Corkonians. Wilhelm Preetz lasted two months, albeit much of it 'in dissipation', transmitting only a few weather reports before his arrest. Ernest Weber Drohl—described by MI5 as 'slightly mental'—remained at liberty for two years but only because G2 believed his bizarre but partially true cover story that he had come to Ireland to find his two sons conceived during a previous tour of the country as 'Atlas the Strong' in 1907. He was eventually interned on 'moral grounds' after producing more illegitimate progeny.[93]

Despite its ineptitude, German espionage was taken seriously by G2 and MI5 in light of the potential threat to Irish neutrality and British security posed by co-operation between Germany and the IRA. The presence of the IRA chief of staff, Seán Russell, and the Spanish Civil War veteran, Frank Ryan, in Berlin (whom Abwehr intended to play a leading role in the event of a German invasion of Ireland) added to these concerns, as did the activities of the only German agent to create genuine problems in Ireland, Herman Goertz, who parachuted into Ireland in May 1940 and remained at liberty for almost two years.[94] Goertz's ambitious mission was to facilitate an understanding between the IRA and the Irish government that would undermine Britain's occupation of Northern Ireland. Following a series of mishaps, including a narrow escape from a police raid on an IRA safe house which resulted in the loss of 20,000 dollars and valuable documents, Goertz realized that the IRA was no longer a formidable organization. Despairing of its poor leadership, penetration by the police, hostility to de Valera, and reluctance to fight a northern campaign, the enterprising spy decided to pursue his objectives independently by forging links with influential political and military officials.[95] The most alarming and, in hindsight, suspicious aspect of Goertz's mission was not his success but rather the fact that he was able to move freely around Ireland for eighteen months despite his supposed status as the most wanted man in the country. Goertz, as Eunan O'Halpin noted, 'acquired almost mythic status in Ireland, being rumoured to enjoy the protection of powerful government figures, and to be an unofficial ambassador. The failure for so long to catch him raised questions about both the efficiency of the security services and the instructions they were under, while the enthusiasm with which he pursued his aims marked him out as a serious figure.'[96]

Goertz's predictable strategy was to harness Irish irredentism to German interests. He dismissed Fine Gael's policy of peaceful unification within the British Empire as of 'no interest' to Germany, while perceptively observing that de Valera's strategy of 'negotiation while maintaining the complete independence of Ireland—is out of the question. Even de Valera himself is surely convinced of that. It amounts to a perpetuation of the border'. In his subsequent and comprehensive mission report, Goertz claimed to have received a largely positive reception from the 500 or so influential people with whom he discussed the issue of unification: 'I was received into that high-standing circle of nationalist and loyal Irishmen only because reliance was placed on me that I wished to fight England, that I wished to support the national fight of the Irish for their independence from easily understood German interest, that I wished to avail of the circumstance that in Ireland there existed an organisation whose one goal was the fighting of England for nationalist Irish interests.'[97]

Given his mission, it was unsurprising that Goertz sought a meeting with O'Duffy, which he arranged through Jim O'Donovan in early November 1940:

We spoke for over two hours alone. I first thanked him for having taken on himself the risk of seeing me. I said I was a soldier and only what was soldierly interested me; it was doubtless known to him through my friends who had arranged the meeting that I was striving to study the possibilities of an open or secret fight of the Irish in Northern Ireland against England . . . It needed only this short introduction to get the General to speak. He spoke with Irish power of expression. I could not do much, he said, in this direction with the IRA; I had probably seen that already myself. He had started his Blue Shirt movement unfortunately too early; Ireland was not yet ripe . . . He had fought his whole life long for a Christian free Ireland. This goal could be reached only by means of a military dictatorship . . . it was with the Army that Germany should get in touch— this was realised by leading heads within the Army.

O'Duffy made an uncharacteristically good impression on Goertz, who was much impressed by his 'flaming' hatred for de Valera. Had it not been for the Civil War, Goertz mused, a 'man of such high organising capabilities would doubtless have succeeded otherwise in uniting [with] the IRA . . . to the advantage of both, for his movement lacked the storm-man who conquers the street when it is disputed to him, whilst the IRA lacked political [skill]'. His admiration may also have stemmed from the fact that O'Duffy, in contrast to most of the IRA men whom Goertz disliked dealing with, was motivated more by fascism than nationalism.

Goertz wanted to know why the government was creating such a large army when it was obvious that it would be unable to resist a British invasion for more than a few days. He speculated that its real purpose was to function as an auxiliary force for—rather than against—Britain. O'Duffy denied this, insisting that the Irish army would defend the state against any aggressor. Finally, arriving at the nub of the issue, Goertz enquired 'Why had the Irish army not made, without being in any way politically bound, at least some kind of general staff agreements?', pointing out that in the case of a British invasion, German planes would not even be able to refuel in Ireland. This was a legitimate query, given that the Irish government had reached a similar secret understanding with Britain in the event of a German invasion.[98] According to Goertz: 'The General replied that De Valera would hinder that at any price. Then he asked whether I had full powers. I said no, that I was not sent to Ireland to direct negotiations with the Irish army. The further result of this discussion and another talk was that I reported to Berlin that I would probably come round about the 15 November by aeroplane to report.'

Goertz's report revealed O'Duffy's willingness to put him in touch with officers of sufficient seniority to draw up a bilateral military understanding—presumably without the knowledge of the Irish government—in the event of a British invasion. Even the normally cautious Hempel agreed that this was a possibility as the army's 'chief officers are in principle in favour of an incursion into Northern Ireland'.[99] Goertz did not identify the officers he subsequently met in his enciphered report—which was written after his arrest and intended only for the eyes of his Abwehr superiors—but G2 believed that they included Major Niall MacNeill, an intelligence officer in the second (northern) division. Niall—Hugo's cousin—was a chip off the family block, being a self-proclaimed Nazi supporter with a tendency for rash behaviour.[100] The subject of military co-operation was also pursued at another meeting between O'Duffy, Hugo MacNeill (the northern division O/C who had long advocated a first strike policy against the occupied six), and the Nazi diplomat Henning Thomsen in early December 1940.[101]

The potentially serious implications of these contacts in terms of diplomatic relations with Britain were greatly heightened by the fact that MI5 suspected that a far greater conspiracy was afoot. At one point, MI5—which had cracked Germany's encryption and was thus able to read its diplomatic traffic from Dublin—erroneously believed that two cabinet ministers, Thomas Derrig and Dr James Ryan, had authorized O'Duffy's attempt to negotiate a secret military agreement with Germany:

We have always known that O'DUFFY and [Hugo] McNEILL were firm friends and that McNEILL was an admirer of German methods and efficiency. If one accepts for Eire the principle of collective Cabinet responsibility, and the story of [James] RYAN's activities is (as I believe it is) true, then the De VALERA Government have been guilty of the basest treachery. On the other hand, I have the feeling that this was an intrigue of RYAN and McNEILL behind the back of De VALERA . . . GOERTZ had blamed his arrest on the loose talk of McNEILL and O'DUFFY. It may well be that the story of this intrigue got to the ears of De VALERA . . . and that De VALERA promptly put a stop to the whole business.[102]

However, the unreliable source of much of the information in Hempel's telegrams to Berlin—a version of a discredited confession extracted by force from the IRA chief of staff, Stephen Hayes, by his mutinous subordinates—led MI5 to conclude that the conspiracy was an invention. Although there is no evidence to suggest that de Valera or any of his ministers formally authorized (as opposed to contemplated) a military understanding with Germany, what made O'Duffy's attempts to forge an understanding between Germany and pro-Axis elements of the National Army particularly dangerous was that they overlapped with tentative high-risk contacts between the Irish military and the German legation on the same subject.[103] Fortunately, Goertz never managed to return to Berlin and his capture—followed by the internment of Jim O'Donovan—eliminated a potentially serious threat to Irish neutrality.

Goertz's arrest produced one interesting postscript. Although the spy had met hundreds of figures—quite a few of them embarrassingly close to the centre of power within the state—his G2 interrogators focused their efforts on forcing him to implicate O'Duffy. While they accepted Goertz's refusal to identify the many republicans he had contacted, they insisted that he name his 'other much more dangerous' collaborators. They presented him with a list containing three names headed by that of O'Duffy. Goertz recalled that when he refused to admit meeting O'Duffy, his interrogator 'stepped for the first and only time out of his distinguished demeanour, which he had otherwise always preserved: "We want to get at these arch-traitors; if you are really the man who wanted to fight only England, then give us these names." ' Goertz stood firm—a lucky break for O'Duffy—taking his incriminating evidence to the grave when he committed suicide rather than face deportation to Germany in 1947.

The arrest of Goertz and O'Donovan represented a severe setback for the prospect of republican collaboration with Nazi Germany. G2 none the less continued to pay close attention to O'Duffy, who remained in contact with the German legation and his well-placed friends in the National Army. Gratifyingly, O'Duffy remained welcome in the republican circles from which he had previously been ostracized. Such was his rehabilitation that he was even offered a position as an IRA intelligence officer and, on another occasion, invited to join Moss Twomey and Andy Cooney, former chiefs of staff of impeccable republican credentials, in a protest against 'the Yankee invasion of the Six Counties' in the summer of 1941.[104] However, the popularity of de Valera's policy of neutrality and Germany's opening of a second front in Russia consigned this realignment of the marginalized to insignificance. The government continued its suppression of the IRA—effectively breaking the organization by 1943—leaving militant nationalist and fascist opinion represented by such toothless concerns as Córas na Poblachta and Ailtirí na hAiséirghe (led by a former member of the Irish Friends of Germany). Fortunately, the question of how Ireland would have responded to German occupation remains a counter-factual one.[105] For reasons beyond his control, O'Duffy had once again missed his moment for greatness. Although the war allowed him to create considerable mischief, it had not enabled him to join the illustrious company of his former colleague on the Fascist International, Vidkun Quisling, as a mediator of Nazi power in his own country. There can be little doubt that, had the opportunity arose, he would have been happy to oblige.

The final years

Politically, O'Duffy was finished by 1942. The IRA was on the ropes and the Irish public—no longer fearful of invasion—viewed the war with relative apathy.[106] In light of events on the eastern front, there was no longer any German enthusiasm for espionage in Ireland. O'Duffy, who rather belatedly in life appeared to have developed an ability to spot lost causes, detached himself from the crumbling netherworld of Nazi collaboration. So too did Ireland's other potential Quislings, returning—just as G2 had predicted—to their former careers, eventually eliding the embarrassing memories of their wartime flirtation with fascism. Ernest Blythe, for example, sublimated his unhealthy political tendencies into a new fascist project, Ailtírí na hAiséirghe, and his role as managing director of the Abbey theatre. O'Duffy's final contacts with the Axis powers were characteristically unproductive. Inside Athlone's gloomy prison, Goertz received word that the General was willing to assist his escape but nothing came of his efforts—if any were made.[107] O'Duffy's last reported gesture typified the impractical and bizarre notions which emanated from Germany's Irish friends. In early 1943 he asked to be flown to Berlin to discuss the organization of a 'Green Division' to fight communism on the Russian front. Germany offered some encouragement but only to 'utilize, for propaganda purposes, the fact that Irishmen have declared themselves willing to fight against Bolshevism'.[108] In light of his experiences in Spain and the inhospitable climate of the region, it was unlikely that he would have found many willing recruits. Given the impracticality of the venture and his deteriorating health, the rumours were more likely the product of alcohol or self-delusion than any real intent.

One serendipitous consequence of the surveillance of O'Duffy by G2 and MI5—which included phone-taps, the recording of his conversations, and the monitoring of his correspondence (and even his off-licence tab)—was to leave an intimate record of the General's unusual day-to-day life in his final years.[109] Much of his time was spent writing his (unpublished) memoir, which, despite his threats, proved curiously unrevealing. A weekly column in the British *Sunday Chronicle* provided another outlet for his opinions on sport, culture, history, and politics (which varied remarkably little throughout his life). His first column—a critique of the Irish government's strict censorship—provoked the very same censors to warn the *Chronicle* that its Irish edition would be banned if further offending material was published.[110] The censors, nonetheless, found it necessary to remove O'Duffy's subsequent references to evacuation schemes, the mining of coastal waters, the type of weapons used by the army, and military complaints about shortages of funding and armaments.[111]

He spent much of his time involved in eccentric schemes, meeting or corresponding with advocates of obscure causes like monetary reform. He wrote to his German friends, exchanging books, praising Lord Haw-Haw's broadcasts, and generally offering encouragement in the struggle against 'Bolshevism and so-called Democracy'.[112] He stayed in touch with many of those who had served under him in the police or army, occasionally pulling strings to secure an appointment or promotion within the defence forces. He socialized in clerical, sporting, and Axis diplomatic circles. A typically sarcastic G2 report described his attendance at a reception in the German consul:

O'Duffy as usual was quite at ease when talking about himself, his theories, and his predictions...He talked about his health; he should be in hospital having some bronchial tube swept; he shouldn't have come to the party; he shouldn't be drinking; in fact, he was doing everything he shouldn't be doing that night in order that he might grace the party with his presence.[113]

He drank heavily and engaged in mysterious activities which G2 found difficult to explain. On one occasion, for example, G2 asked local police to investigate P. V. Hoey, a district court clerk in Carrickmacross, with whom O'Duffy was conducting a 'rather peculiar' correspondence. G2 believed he was attempting to embroil Hoey into a plan for 'some new political coup'. The local gardaí, however, dismissed Hoey as 'going "bats", family failing, & drink & can be written off', adding that sightings of O'Duffy in Monaghan were rare but when seen 'he'd knock you down for a bottle of Brandy... [he] had no other interest in life but to get hold of brandy'.[114] His health, poor for some time, began to fail. In late 1941 he was hospitalized, reportedly for appendicitis. Although only in his early fifties, he looked twenty years older.

In need of a public outlet for his declining energies, O'Duffy muscled his way back into the National Athletic and Cycling Association, which had fallen on hard times since his departure. He resumed its presidency in Easter 1942, an office he would hold until his death in 1944. His agenda—fund-raising, grass-roots revival, and the rescuing of adolescents from moral depravity—remained familiar. He took to the airwaves to campaign for a national stadium, the unification of sporting bodies, and the imprisonment of bicycle thieves. As in earlier years, he received favourable press coverage for his zealous championing of sport but ill-health and the constraints of the Emergency limited his impact on the flagging NACA. The government could at least be relieved that his return to sports administration offered a less troubling forum for his ambitions.

O'Duffy's final years were marred by ill-health. He was too ill to attend the NACA's conferences in 1943 and 1944. In September 1943 MI5 reported that the 'potential Quisling, General O'Duffy, is ill in a Cork Nursing home, suffering it is said, from acute alcoholic poisoning'.[115] Two months later, a sympathetic Hempel asked Whit whether 'nothing could be done for him'.[116] According to Walsh, O'Duffy was not a good patient:

he found inactivity and confinement irksome, but he was resigned to the will of God that his illness was fatal and his end approaching. Never actually in pain he suffered much discomfort and distress and his friends who called to see him may not always have understood his desire at times to be left alone and at others to be surrounded by company. But they came nevertheless and he did appreciate the kind consideration of the thoughtful few as he deprecated the ungratefulness of the thoughtless many.[117]

O'Duffy and Walsh had by now reconciled despite the mutual suspicions which had followed the latter's internment. Although a married man, Walsh moved in to O'Duffy's home as his paid employee and left an interesting account of the General's final years. Although deprived of a public role, O'Duffy continued to regiment his days in the methodical fashion devised in earlier life:

His day began with the morning post, and even for a man virtually out of public life it was always heavy—enquires about Volunteer pensions, recommendations for jobs, appeals for help or subscriptions, invitations, reports from Sports bodies etc. His morning paper then arrived. With a pencil at hand to mark items of interest he read it through—nothing was missed. After a frugal breakfast he rose. It was not until he had finished dressing he lit his first cigarette . . . he was in later years a very heavy chain smoker—seventy to eighty a day—but he never smoked in bed and seldom in his bedroom. With a scissors he made short work of the newspaper; every marked item was cut out, dated and put away for filing or a note recorded of its contents. Even the radio announcements were noted, and for such items only as he wished to hear did he 'switch on'. My share of the 'Irish Independent' when I was staying with him was small by the time he had finished.[118]

He lived unostentatiously, eating three simple meals and rarely after six o' clock. Walsh denied the rumours of the General's drinking, claiming that his 'unforgivable sin among a self-satisfied hypocritical element' was to drink 'openly—when and where he liked. He never drank beer and but seldom drank wines; he preferred Irish whiskey which, in his last years, he had made into punch. Unlike so many of his contemporaries his domestic life was one of happiness; the gross indulgences and debaucheries indulged in by so many of his time and his class had no appeal for him—his morals were pure and his life stainless.'[119]

O'Duffy had a life-long abhorrence of debt—possibly as a result of his impoverished childhood—and lived frugally: 'the first of each month was a day of reckoning when the expenditure of the previous month was recorded and outstanding accounts paid. It was a day to be dreaded; without a moment's hesitation he would sanction expenditure of a "fiver", but would "skin" you for spending a penny unwisely or unnecessarily.'[120] According to Walsh:

He had no hobbies other than the garden, and even that was largely denied him in the last years. He was not a great reader although surrounded by books and literature of every possible kind, for he had a mind of such extraordinary activity that he found it impossible to concentrate on the literature of the modern-day world. He disdained ordinary comforts and seldom sat in an easy chair except when entertaining visitors, and those he frequently received in his Study where a really comfortable chair was taboo.[121]

Lacking a public role, his final years were lonely ones: 'only those intimately associated with General O'Duffy can realise how much he kept to himself and how reserved was his life notwithstanding that he was a public figure whom neither jealousy or ridicule could efface'. Even as his health faded he retained his love of spectacle, organizing parades but with local children taking the place of loyal followers. Long after his death, his neighbours in the comfortable southside suburb of Mount Merrion recollected a kindly gentleman who 'was not above organising small parish functions' and 'took pride in turning out well-dressed processions for the summer festivals'.[122] His few visitors discovered a mellow, even genial, figure who had lost his 'asperity of speech, or tendencies to dogmatism in utterance' and discussed his 'approaching dissolution with calm and resignation.'[123] Few of these, however, were intimate friends or relatives. Walsh claimed that although always considerate to his family—to whom he 'contributed generously during his life time'—O'Duffy was 'never closely attached' to them. After his death, Walsh recalled with a note of bitterness, there were 'no close relatives to say good-bye and God bless you. No one to claim the Rosary which he clasped or his mother's ring which he always wore.'[124]

Perhaps all political lives end in failure, but few Irish careers have ended as ignominiously as that of O'Duffy, who lived long enough to become a figure of ridicule and then an increasingly forgotten one.[125] The shadow of failure hung heavily over his final years of broken health and tarnished reputation: 'he was really a pathetic and lonely figure at the end; a recluse in the midst of society, an organising genius who grew irritable as neglectfulness and inactivity increased with each passing day'.[126] He took some consolation from religion, remaining pious to the end: 'Many a night I placed the Beads in his hand when he was scarce able to hold it, and it was too almost the last service I did for him on this earth, and when death set him free still twined around his fingers was his Rosary.'[127] During his final illness he was moved to Pembroke Nursing Home. On 30 November 1944, in the presence of a nurse and his semi-faithful companion, General Eoin O'Duffy passed away.

Epilogue

O'Duffy's life-story, worth telling in its own right, sheds light on diverse aspects of modern Ireland. It helps us to understand the mindset of some of those swept up in the remarkable cultural nationalist revival of the late nine-teenth century which did so much to shape revolutionary and independent Ireland. Vincent Comerford has noted that 'O'Duffy is the classic example of a politician who worked his way to public prominence through involvement in the organisational activities of the GAA'. He is also a classic example of the puritanical ethos which played such an important role in the invention of modern Ireland, a process which Comerford outlines in his valuable study and, without taking account of which, 'one cannot understand twentieth-century develop-ments in language policy, literature, sport, music or politics'.[1] This ethos, exhibited by the self-appointed fundamentalists of Gaeldom rather than the great majority of those drawn to cultural nationalism, was deeply unattractive:

It was highly prescriptive and dogmatic, promoting the assumption that everything was either obligatory or forbidden, and so did not place a high value on individual free-dom of choice. Intolerance was epitomised in a readiness to demonise dissidents and opponents and to brand people and institutions as untouchable, without concern for the human dignity or rights of individuals, including the right of reply. Such a censori-ous system depended on vigilantes ready to discover and, if necessary, to root out departures from prescribed behaviour or ideas. Not all the vigilantes were clerics, and not all clerics were vigilantes.[2]

For James Joyce, the claims of religion and nationalism represented the nightmare of history from which he sought to awaken. For the Free State's cultural zealots, manipulation of these forces—through imposing their own standards of purity, acting as national guardians of propriety, and excluding or condemning those who failed to conform to their standards—provided prestige and influence. To contemporary eyes, O'Duffy may appear a ludicrous figure, but the status and power which he enjoyed during his lifetime tells us something about the nature of the society in which he lived. Gifted with a talent for self-invention, O'Duffy was fortunate to live through a remarkable period of nation-invention. He personified the worst excesses of the narrow nationalism, religious bigotry, and repressive hypocrisy which have become a cliché of contemporary representations of this period of history.[3]

O'Duffy represented an extreme manifestation of a mindset which existed more broadly in inter-war Ireland, and is often found among other post-revolutionary élites. His generation of idealists sought to create a spiritual society that would reflect the moral values which had motivated them since the emergence of the Irish Ireland movement and the bloody sacrifice of Easter 1916. The inevitable failure to achieve a united, Gaelic and devout nation led to frustration, confusion, and disillusionment.[4] Having failed to unite the nation, and having never intended to transform its social structure, the cultural dimension of the revolution became its only radical legacy: it was only in the cultural sphere that the imagined Ireland could be created. But the cultural nationalism which strengthened republicanism during the struggle against British rule proved more limiting in the post-revolutionary era, as nationalists failed to create the desired utopia in spite of the attainment of independence.

Many of the evasions, contradictions, and hypocrisies evident in O'Duffy's life were those of his society writ large. O'Duffy was willing to enforce gaelicization despite being unable to speak the language, but so too was Professor Timothy Corcoran, the ideologue responsible for compulsory Irish in the schools system.[5] Nor did the fact that few people could speak Irish prevent de Valera from designating it the first official language in the 1937 Constitution. As Hobsbawm has noted, nationalism requires considerable 'belief in what is patently not so'.[6] Where O'Duffy differed from his peers, therefore, was in his extremism, by responding to the failure to create the ideal nation by indulging in ever more zealous purism and self-deception rather than retreating into the platitudes which contented most of his contemporaries. In many respects, this response provides the key to his subsequent career: O'Duffy succumbed to cultural extremism long before fascism.

O'Duffy's mindset is explicable not only by puritanism but also its first cousin, paranoia. Throughout his life, the General was an exponent of the politics of fear. His life was dominated by struggles against apocalyptic conspiratorial forces, whether creeping anglicization, anti-treaty republicanism, communism, freemasonry, or world Jewry—a mode of existence which undermined his judgement and credibility. Like many ideologues, he exaggerated and distorted an imperfect reality to reinforce his radical world-view. That his warnings went unheeded by a liberal state and the indifferent masses served only to reinforce his concerns. His life provides a case study in the paranoid style of politics, a mentality which found expression among an extreme Catholic fringe in inter-war Ireland struggling to come to terms with modernity and its culture of reason but also, as Richard Hofstadter has argued, in many societies throughout history, from the millennial sects of medieval Europe to 1950s McCarthyite America:

The paranoid spokesman sees the fate of conspiracy in apocalyptic terms—he traffics in the birth and death of whole words, whole political orders, whole systems of human values. He is always manning the barricades of civilization. He constantly lives at a turning point. Like religious millennialists he expresses the anxieties of those who are living through the last days...As a member of the avant-garde who is capable of perceiving the conspiracy before it is fully obvious to an as yet unaroused public, the paranoid is a militant leader. He does not see social conflict as something to be mediated and compromised, in the manner of the working politician. Since what is at stake is always a conflict between absolute good and absolute evil, what is necessary is not compromise but the will to fight things to a finish.[7]

His enemy, Hofstadter suggests, represents 'a perfect model of malice, a kind of amoral superman—sinister, ubiquitous, powerful, cruel, sensual, luxury-loving', responsible for subverting everything from morality to the proper course of history. In the light of how this biography has argued that O'Duffy's extremism stemmed from a personal struggle against his own compulsions, the similarities between the mindset of the General and that outlined by Hofstadter appear striking: 'It is hard to resist the conclusion that this enemy is on many counts the projection of the self; both the ideal and the unacceptable aspects of the self are attributed to him.'[8]

There are indeed numerous intriguing parallels between O'Duffy and such leading figures of American anti-communism as Senator Joseph McCarthy, Roy Cohn, and, perhaps most pertinently, J. Edgar Hoover. Like the General, the legendary founder of the Federal Bureau of Investigation was a brilliant and dedicated administrator whose inspired leadership created a loyal, independent, and efficient force. Both men interpreted their role as not merely one of law enforcement but the defence of morality, religion, authority, and patriotism, which they saw as the only real safeguards against crime and subversion. Both viewed human nature and moral failure rather than social conditions or historical forces as the root cause of criminal and political evil. Most obviously, there was a darker side to both men's vigilance, which included an obsessive preoccupation with conspiracy, the promotion of a cult of personality, an eagerness to resort to suppression and intimidation, the manipulation of public anxiety for the accumulation of institutional and personal power, and a willingness to vilify others for moral shortcomings despite their own unconventional private lives.[9]

The life of Eoin O'Duffy illustrates the extraordinary circumstances of the era in which he was born. His was the first generation in which the children of peasant farmers could attain the highest positions in the state. This revolutionary possibility, unthinkable before the turmoil which followed the Easter Rising, owed much to the broader upheaval of the Great War. Had O'Duffy been born a couple of decades earlier—or later—he would probably have lived an uneventful life as a prosperous, if not entirely scrupulous, provincial business-man and GAA stalwart. Instead, his revolutionary talents earned him a place among the national élite which could only be reached by more conventional routes in other periods. As one correspondent observed after the spectacular implosion of his career, he was one of those figures 'who so often come to the top in a revolutionary struggle but who are unable to adjust themselves to the more prosaic requirements of ordinary political life'.[10] Had Irish politics been a little less prosaic, his political career might have prospered. Similar forces, albeit on a more profound scale, such as the social, economic, and political dislocation caused by the Great War, the collapse of a more deferential social order, and the rise of political radicalism created the opportunities seized by the same generation of extremists in Europe. O'Duffy's career, despite its obvious limitations, demonstrates how Irish politics were buffeted by the forces which shaped inter-war Europe.

In many respects, O'Duffy remains a unique political figure. Despite super-ficial comparisons with Daniel O'Connell, and his fondness for posturing as the new Michael Collins, there are few domestic parallels for the style and personality of the General's politics. He remains the only flamboyant leader to emerge from the respectable and uncharismatic ranks of treatyite politics. Comparison with de Valera merely highlights the unflattering differences. Ironically, the only politician of modern Ireland whose political style bears any meaningful comparison with O'Duffy is the present-day leader of Irish Union-ism, the Revd Ian Paisley, a far more formidable and politically astute figure, whose demagogic intertwining of religious, moral, and political certainties, are more than a little reminiscent of the General.[11]

More useful comparisons can be drawn with the political figures whom O'Duffy consciously emulated. In terms of personality and politics, there are obvious parallels with Mussolini, whom he was often compared to by admiring and hostile contemporaries. The less flattering comparisons are probably most pertinent. Historians have struggled to detect the substance behind Mussolini. A. J. P. Taylor famously dismissed him as 'a vain, blundering boaster without either ideas or aims', a façade hiding nothing 'but show and empty rhetoric'.[12] Denis Mack Smith's biography of the *Duce* depicted a shallow opportunist, a posturing actor rather than a statesman, who combined monumental vanity with extraordinary incompetence.[13] Historians invariably emphasize the extent to which Mussolini relied on opportunism and action over ideology, and his good fortune in living through 'a period in which outrageous bluff had a better than usual chance of success'.[14] Mussolini's rise and fall, moreover, has been attributed to his own powers of self-invention, which allowed him to create a brilliant but unsustainable edifice that collapsed into self-delusion and failure. His most recent biographer depicts him as a hollow and accommodating figure, who came under increasing pressure to live up to his popular image.[15]

Comparisons can also be drawn with another of O'Duffy's allies, General Franco, another deeply flawed figure who combined a deep sense of inadequacy, a desperate hunger for adulation, and innate deceitfulness with 'a startling intellectual mediocrity which led him to believe in the most banal ideas'. Raised by a deeply pious mother to whom he was deeply attached, and a father whose love he never won, Franco's lonely childhood helped to motivate his drive for power. According to his biographer Paul Preston, Franco endlessly rewrote his own life story, altering reality in order to create ever more successful public personae.[16] O'Duffy, it would seem, embodied many of the shortcomings of the dictators while lacking most of their strengths.

Nonetheless, the points of similarity between O'Duffy and those in the premier division of demagogues should remind us that a deeply flawed personality and an irrational outlook were not insurmountable barriers to power under the right circumstances. It should alert us, also, to the danger of interpreting O'Duffy's life through the prism of his final decade of failure, as most of his contemporaries naturally did, or of exaggerating the significance of his personal shortcomings in explaining a fall from power which was by no means inevitable. Had events taken a different turn in the 1930s, he would have been remembered very differently. Had he managed to avoid being removed by de Valera in 1933, in the way that J. Edgar Hoover succeeded in outmanoeuvring successive hostile presidents, he would have remained, and been remembered as, a much more formidable figure, the man who steered the Garda through a difficult political transition. Or had he, as some of his friends advised, spurned the political career for which he was so unsuited, he would have secured a sympathetic legacy as a dutiful servant of the nation who was harshly sacrificed in the greater interest of the state.

Memory

What, then, of the legacy? On 2 December 1944 O'Duffy was buried, as he requested, close to the grave of Michael Collins. He was granted a state funeral by the government, a surprising gesture which may have reflected his contribution to the struggle for independence, the conciliatory atmosphere of the Emergency, or de Valera's regret that a life which had promised so much potential had ended in such ignominy. The taoiseach, and most of his cabinet, attended the requiem mass in the Pro-Cathedral, afterwards following the military cortege to Glasnevin. Funerals had played an important role in the life of the General. He would have appreciated the elaborate formality of his own ceremony, a final opportunity to take centre stage:

Every phase of the national life—Government, Oireachtas, Judiciary, Army, Garda and Diplomatic Corps joined in as the cortege headed by the No. 1 Army Band wended its way through streets interrupted of traffic and lined with people. As the coffin draped with the Tricolour, with six Army Colonels as pall bearers and a battalion of Infantry as Guard of Honour, was borne on a gun-carriage to Glasnevin Cemetery, it was followed by old comrades... The Garda Siochana which he loved and served so well, were a striking body as led by their Commissioner, the Officers, and men drawn from all over the country marched in the funeral procession.[17]

But the turnout, respectable and respectful as it was, did not, as the *Standard* claimed, signify a 'nation united to do him honour'. Indeed, its obituary proceeded to complain that the 'public jibes flung after that coffin, folded in the Tricolour, were cast by the known enemies of everything Irish and Catholic'.[18] The diplomats present represented only the fascist powers which O'Duffy had served. The absentees were also noteworthy. Many of his former political allies were missing, as were the bishops with whom he had been so closely associated during his life. Only a handful of veterans from Spain made an appearance. He was buried in a grave which lay unmarked by a gravestone for several years, and remained overgrown until its recent weeding by the author of a revisionist account of O'Duffy's crusade in Spain.[19] In contrast to the generous tributes from the Catholic press, the *Irish Times* noted that 'the name of General O'Duffy had ceased to mean much to the public'.[20] While tactless, it was more accurate than the *Irish Independent*'s assertion that he would be remembered by a grateful Irish nation as a 'champion of liberty'.[21]

Any reckoning must take into account the General's positive contributions to Irish life. He was an important figure in the organizational history of the GAA, and in the history of Irish sports generally. The O'Duffy Cup, awarded to the All-Ireland Senior Camogie champions, remains a much sought-after prize and Gaels, although not those from republican South Armagh, still view matches from the O'Duffy Stand in Clones. He remains the pre-eminent figure in the history of the independence movement in Co. Monaghan, a role honoured by Monaghan County Museum and the naming of O'Duffy Street in Clones. His contribution to the survival of the Irish Free State in its early years is still remembered within the Garda Síochána.

The General's political career, however, has ensured that his legacy will remain tarnished and controversial. In the course of a recent, not entirely convincing, attempt to revise perceptions about the General's involvement in Spain, one historian described the air of official embarrassment and public-house ridicule which has surrounded his reputation, and the ease with which his detractors have resorted to the vocabulary of six decades of hostile comment: 'In the unanimous verdict of Irish and non-Irish historians alike, O'Duffy was not only a fascist, but an incompetent, and a drunkard. Others argue that he was a coward. Others still discern a covert homosexual.'[22] This biography has attempted to explain rather than condemn his life, but has uncovered little to warrant revision of negative assessments of his character and influence. O'Duffy represented some of the darker shades of the Irish revolution and its aftermath, a period of history which, like all others, was shaped by the opportunistic, the cynical, and the intolerant, as well as the sincere, the brave, and the patriotic.

R. A. Stradling has argued that national embarrassment about 'what was—in relative terms—the largest non-governing fascist organisation in the world' has resulted in O'Duffy's displacement 'from the mainstream of public memory':

Neither in 1992, centenary of his birth, nor in 1994, fiftieth anniversary of his death, was any mark of recognition given to O'Duffy as one of the founding fathers of the Irish state. Not even a commemorative article in a national history has come to my attention. In between these dates, a new history of Fine Gael appeared from the main party publisher. Here, although O'Duffy was acknowledged *en passant* as its first leader, he did not figure among fifty-odd vignette biographies of party personnel, and whilst all the other leaders from Collins to Bruton were given photographic portraits, he appears only on the platform (background) whilst Kevin O'Higgins is making a speech (foreground). It is as though Keir Hardie were to have been deliberately and systematically ignored by historians of the Labour Party.[23]

Due to Fine Gael's understandable reluctance to identify itself with its first president, O'Duffy has never been regarded as a figure of relevance by the treatyite tradition. The only organizations to have displayed any interest in his political legacy are a number of racist and fascist fringe movements with little presence beyond the Internet.[24]

O'Duffy has been vilified for having fought on the wrong side, not only in Spain but in Ireland, where Civil War commemoration has remained a republican tradition. Indeed, by linking his involvement in both conflicts, republican propagandists since Somhairle Macalastair have sought to transfer the emotional force and legitimacy from one conflict to the other:

> O'Duffy's dupes are killing as their Fascist masters bid.
> Gas bombs are falling on the Mothers of Madrid.
> The birds at Ballyseedy picked flesh from off the stones
> And Spanish suns at Badajoz are bleaching baby bones.[25]

Another of Macalastair's ballads, recorded by Ronnie Drew of The Dubliners, links Franco's atrocities with Blueshirt violence against Irish workers, the *Irish Independent*'s infamous support for the execution of James Connolly, and O'Duffy's role in the Irish Civil War.[26] Christy Moore's powerful ballad, *Vive la Quinte Brigada*, juxtaposes the Irish Brigade who 'sailed beneath the swastika to Spain' with Frank Ryan's comradeship of heroes who matched 'truth and love against the force of evil', linking the Irish and Spanish civil wars through reference to the anti-republican stance adopted by the Irish hierarchy on each:

> The word came from Maynooth, 'support the Nazis'
> The men of cloth failed again.[27]

Such songs highlight that far from being displaced from the collective memory, O'Duffy's legacy has retained a prominent place in the national discourse: 'few modern leaders can have had such a collective mauling from commentators of almost every shade of political opinion'.[28] From the pragmatic, post-nationalist, perspective of twenty-first century Ireland, it is clear that O'Duffy, the epitome of irredentist Catholic nationalism, fought not only on the wrong side of the Spanish Civil War but on the wrong side of Irish history. For radical republicans and socialists, vilification of O'Duffy has served useful functions, not the least being to impugn the treatyite tradition and reinforce a progressive anti-fascist self-image. For others, ridicule of O'Duffy has served a useful purpose by allowing the troubling and embarrassing phenomenon of the Blueshirts to be dismissed.

Despite the serious historical treatment accorded the movement, the Blueshirts are still more readily thought of as an Irish farce than a manifestation of Civil War hatred or fascist ideology: 'In this way "Irish fascism" is shuffled off as a ritual joke, empty of meaning, sanitised and unthreatening'.[29] Perhaps the cruellest fate for a man who devoted his life to self-aggrandizement was that he should be remembered as a figure of ridicule. Having failed to come to power—whether at the head of a coup in 1931, a putsch in 1933, or a Vichy Ireland in 1940—O'Duffy will remain a national joke. His life might be better remembered as a cautionary tale.

Notes

Chapter 1

1 Eoin O'Duffy (hereafter: EOD), 'Reminiscences', ch. II (hereafter *II*), 1, National Library of Ireland (hereafter: NLI) Accession 5694, unsorted O'Duffy papers (hereafter: ODP).

2 District electoral division, 23/3, National Archives of Ireland (hereafter: NAI), 1901 Census; EOD, 'Reminiscences', *I*, 1.

3 Records for Cargaghdoo townland, Castleblayney rural district, Land Valuation Office, Dublin.

4 Peadar Livingstone, *The Monaghan Story* (Enniskillen, 1980), 365–6.

5 Theodore Hoppen, *Ireland Since 1800: Conflict and Conformity* (London, 1989 edn.), 10–11.

6 Livingstone, *Monaghan Story*, 364.

7 Major Madden, quoted in Livingstone, *Monaghan Story*, 366.

8 David Fitzpatrick, 'The Geography of Irish Nationalism 1910–1921', *Past and Present* (Feb. 1978), 78.

9 Monaghan county inspector's 'State of County in 1916' report (hereafter: 'State of County'), 24 Jan. 1917, Public Record Office, London (hereafter: PRO), CO 904/120; Fitzpatrick, 'Geography of Irish Nationalism', 78.

10 'State of County'.

11 Livingstone, *Monaghan Story*, 362.

12 Ibid., 363; Cumann Seanchais Chlochair [Fr Lorcan Ó Mearáin, Fr Joseph Duffy and Fr Peadar Livingstone], *The War of Independence in Monaghan* (n.p., 1966), 8; Jim Sullivan, Military Archives, Dublin (hereafter: MA), Bureau of Military History witness statement (hereafter: BMH WS) 518.

13 Tom Carragher, Monaghan County Museum (hereafter: MCM), Marron papers, folder 7 (hereafter: 7).

14 EOD, 'Reminiscences', *I*, 9.

15 *Dundalk Democrat* (hereafter *DD*), 17 Feb. 1934. O'Duffy was, however, defending himself from accusations of murdering Hibernians at the time.

16 EOD, 'Reminiscences', *I*, 1.

17 Ibid., *I*, 4.

18 Antoinette Quinn (ed.), Patrick Kavanagh, *Selected Poems* (London, 2000), p. xviii. See Kavanagh's *The Green Fool* (London, 1938) and Quinn's *Patrick Kavanagh: A Biography* (Dublin, 2001), 14–30, for accounts of a harsh but probably not untypical childhood in rural Monaghan.

19 EOD, 'Reminiscences', *I*, 8, 13, 7–8.

20 Ibid., *I*, 9.

21 Ibid., *I*, 10.

22 Ibid., *I*, 11.

23 Ibid., *I*, 12.

24 Ibid., *I*, 11–12.

25 District Electoral Division (DED) 23/3, NAI, Census of Ireland report 1901.

26 EOD, 'Reminiscences', *II*, 1.

27 Ibid., *II*, 3–4. The *Dundalk Democrat* (despite its title) and the *Anglo-Celt* were the most important newspapers for the Monaghan area.

28 EOD, 'Reminiscences', *II*, 4.

29 Ibid., *I*, 3.

30 Records for Cargaghdoo townland, Castleblayney rural district, Land Valuation Office, Dublin.

31 EOD, 'Reminiscences', *I*, 3–4.

32 Bridget Duffy was 48 when she died in 1902 from liver cancer, diagnosed one year earlier (death certificate of Bridget Duffy, General Register Office, Dublin). O'Duffy records in 'Reminiscences' (*I*, 7) that he was 7 (rather than 12) when she died. He later (*III*, 9) recorded the date of his father's death as 1905 (rather than 1915). He also claimed he was born on 30 October 1892 rather than 28 January 1890. People often recall important dates inaccurately, sometimes as a function of memory construction, but it seems implausible that O'Duffy orphaned himself at the tender age of 13 (rather than 25) by mistake.

33 EOD, 'Reminiscences', *I*, 7. Patrick Duffy, a relative (and godson of O'Duffy's brother) informed me that despite his celebrity O'Duffy was seldom mentioned by his family. He recalled two exceptions: once, when after his appointment as police commissioner in 1922, O'Duffy instructed his family not to visit him in Dublin, meeting them in Dundalk instead; and a second, when he rejected a relative's request for a job in the gardaí.

34 Liam Walsh, 'General O'Duffy: His Life and Battles', unpublished manuscript (hereafter: Walsh memoir), 3, ODP.

35 EOD, 'Reminiscences', *II*, 1.

36 Walsh memoir, 4. Walsh claimed to have written his biography in response to O'Duffy's death-bed request: 'He repeated several times: "Poor fellow, poor fellow, you will have to write it, who else would know" . . . I said: "You will have to tell me what to write". Quite clearly he replied: "Oh I couldn't, you will have to do it yourself" ' (Walsh memoir, 159). In fact, O'Duffy had already written most of his autobiography, which Walsh passed off as his own by changing the first person to the third person, and adding some original material on the political career which O'Duffy could not bring himself to describe. A 'labour of love', outlining the 'true, unvarnished facts of the life of this really great man', Walsh's unreliable biography lacks literary merit but provides useful insights. Copies of both manuscripts can be compared in the O'Duffy papers.

37 EOD, 'Reminiscences', *II*, 7.

38 O'Duffy came first out of twenty candidates, earning 325 out of 400 marks. (Joe Murnane to John Duffy, 20 April 1991, O'Duffy file, Garda Síochána Museum, Dublin Castle).

39 EOD, 'Reminiscences', *II*, 7–8.

40 Ibid., *III*, 1.

41 Ibid., *III*, 2–6. For O'Duffy's application and testimonials, see Denis Carolan Rushe papers, St Macartan's College, Monaghan (information kindly provided by Al Connolly).

42 Eddie Kelly, MCM Marron papers, 7.

43 *DD*, 26 Feb. 1916.

44 EOD, 'Reminiscences', *III*, 6.

45 Walsh memoir, 7.

46 Livingstone, *Monaghan Story*, 546. Clones in the 1960s provided the setting for Patrick McCabe's powerful novel *The Butcher Boy* (London, 1992), subsequently filmed by Neil Jordan. Many of the themes which it (and McCabe's other Clones novel, *Carn*) evokes—a fervent but hysterical devotional Catholicism, a repressive preoccupation with small-town respectability coexisting with hypocrisy, frustration, and sudden outbreaks of violence, and a pervasive sectarian nationalism—are pertinent to O'Duffy's life story.

47 Livingstone, *Monaghan Story*, 359.

48 EOD, 'Reminiscences', *VI*, 6; *DD*, 2 Sept. 1905.

49 Account of Gaelic League activist, MCM Marron papers.

50 Livingstone, *Monaghan Story*, 360.

51 Ibid.

52 EOD, 'Reminiscences', *VI*, 6.

53 Ibid., *II*, 3, *VI*, 7.

54 Martin Waters, quoted in Charles Townshend, *Ireland: The 20th Century* (London, 1998), 41.

55 John Hutchinson, *The Dynamics of Cultural Nationalism: The Gaelic Revival and the Creation of the Irish Nation State* (London, 1987).

56 EOD, 'Days That are Gone', in Seamus O'Ceallaigh (ed.), *Gaelic Athletic Memories* (Limerick, 1945), 161.

57 EOD, 'Reminiscences', *III*, 9.

58 Quoted in Walsh memoir, 8.

59 *War of Independence in Monaghan*, 9. The GAA's 1972 congress charter noted that the GAA had helped to resurrect the 'pride of race . . . crushed out of most of our people by famine and armed oppression', creating 'a new spirit which was to influence and affect the subsequent history of Ireland'.

60 *War of Independence in Monaghan*, 9.

61 Patrick Maume, *The Long Gestation: Irish Nationalist Life 1891–1918* (Dublin, 1999); R. F. Foster, 'Thinking from Hand to Mouth: Anglo-Irish Literature,

Gaelic Nationalism and Irish Politics in the 1890s', in *Paddy and Mr Punch: Connections in Irish and English History* (London, 1993).

62 R. V. Comerford, *Ireland* (London, 2003), 212; W. F. Mandle, *The Gaelic Athletic Association and Irish Nationalist Politics, 1884–1924* (London, 1987), 142.

63 David Fitzpatrick, *The Two Irelands 1912–1939* (Oxford, 1998), 16; Mandle, *Gaelic Athletic Association*, 132, 142, 158.

64 R. F. Foster, *Modern Ireland, 1600–1972* (London, 1988), 448–54.

65 Fitzpatrick, *Two Irelands*, 17–18.

66 F. S. L. Lyons, *Ireland Since the Famine* (London, 1973 edn.), 226.

67 J. J. Lee, *Ireland, 1912–85: Politics and Society* (Cambridge, 1989), 81.

68 EOD, 'Days', 161.

69 *DD*, 16 Nov. 1912.

70 Quoted in *DD*, 10 Jan. 1914; *DD*, 8 April 1916.

71 *DD*, 23 Nov. 1912. See also Con Short, *The Ulster GAA Story* (Monaghan, 1984), and Seamus McCluskey, *The G.A.A. in Co. Monaghan . . . a History* (Monaghan, 1984), 111.

72 *DD*, 14 March 1914.

73 *DD*, 20 March 1915, 19 Nov. 1914.

74 Ibid., 19 Nov. 1914.

75 Ibid., 26 Nov. 1914.

76 Ibid., 19 Nov. 1914.

77 Ibid., 20 Feb. 1915.

78 Ibid., 8 April 1916.

79 Richard Mulcahy interview, UCDA p7/Cassette 136a; *DD*, 14 March 1914, 26 Jun. 1915.

80 *DD*, 7 Nov. 1914.

81 Walsh memoir, 4; Paddy McGlynn, 'Clontibret's Golden Era', in Seamus McCluskey (ed.), *The Monaghan Gael: Eighty Years a Growing 1887–1967* (Emyvale, 1967), 92.

82 *DD*, 28 Aug. 1915.

83 Ibid., 18 Sept. 1915. O'Duffy attempted a similar ploy against Antrim in 1913.

84 Short, *Ulster GAA Story*, 66–7. See McCluskey, *G.A.A. in Co. Monaghan*, 27–31, for the Cavan–Monaghan dispute.

85 EOD, 'Days', 164.

86 Ibid., 165; *Anglo-Celt*, 29 Nov. 1919.

87 EOD, 'Reminiscences', *IV*, 3.

88 Townshend, *Ireland*, 39. See also J. J. Walsh, *Recollections of a Rebel* (Tralee, 1944), 16.

89 Foster, *Modern Ireland*, 453.

90 *DD*, 6 Sept. 1913, 24 Feb. 1912.

91 EOD, 'Days', 181.

92 *DD*, 9 Dec. 1916.

93 Ibid., 13 Jan. 1917.

94 For examples of how sport helps to define moral and political communities, see Jeremy MacClancy (ed.), *Sport, Identity and Ethnicity* (Oxford, 1996).

95 Comerford, *Ireland*, 220.

96 *Anglo-Celt*, 29 Nov. 1919.

97 EOD, 'Days', 164; Walsh memoir, 11.

98 J. J. Lee, *The Modernisation of Irish Society 1848–1918* (Dublin, 1973).

99 EOD, 'Reminiscences', *IV*, 1–3; *Anglo-Celt*, 29 Nov. 1919.

100 *Anglo-Celt*, 29 Nov. 1919.

101 EOD, 'Days', 162. Until recently, such views were commonplace. The GAA's centenary yearbook (Cumann Lúthchleas Gael, *Irish leabhar an Chéid, a Century of Service 1884–1984*) traces handball to the pre-Christian era, claiming the credit for its introduction to countries as ancient and distant as Mexico. For a more nuanced view of the origins of Irish sports and their relationship to nationality, see Comerford, *Ireland*, 212–35.

102 *DD*, 16 Sept. 1916.

103 EOD, 'Days', 162. See also *DD*, 19 Nov. 1914.

104 Quoted in Mandle, *Gaelic Athletic Association*, 155.

105 Comerford, *Ireland*, 214.

106 See Mark Mazower, *Dark Continent: Europe's Twentieth Century* (London, 1998), 92–6; Elaine Sisson, *Pearse's Patriots: St Enda's and the Cult of Boyhood* (Cork, 2003), 119–23.

107 Mandle, *Gaelic Athletic Association*, 154.

108 *The Gaelic Athlete*, 7 Sept. 1912.

109 Mandle, *Gaelic Athletic Association*, 14.

110 Gerard J. DeGroot, *Blighty: British Society in the Era of the Great War* (Harlow, 1996), 32.

111 EOD, 'Days', 191.

112 Ibid., 176.

113 Tom Garvin, *Nationalist Revolutionaries in Ireland, 1858–1928* (Oxford, 1987), 67–8, 74–5.

114 Livingstone, *Monaghan Story*, 367.

115 *DD*, 24 Jan. 1914.

116 Fitzpatrick, *Two Irelands*, 49–50

117 Monthly report of the inspector general (hereafter: IG's report), Jan. 1914, CO 904/92.

118 *War of Independence in Monaghan*, 13.

119 IG's report, May 1914, CO 904/93.

120 Monthly report of the county inspector for Monaghan (hereafter: CI's report), May 1914, CO 904/93; *DD*, 18 July 1914; John McGahey, MA BMH WS 740.

121 IG's report, May 1914, CO 904/93.

122 IG's report, June 1914, CO 904/93; CI's report, Aug. 1914, CO 904/94.

123 CI's report, July 1914, CO 904/94.

124 IG's report, May 1914, CO 904/93.

125 IG's report, June 1914, Jan. 1915, CO 904/93.

126 IG's report, Oct. 1914, CO 904/95.

127 Lee, *Ireland*, 20.

128 *DD*, 15 April 1916.

129 Mandle, *Gaelic Athletic Association*, 169, 172, 177; Short, *Ulster GAA Story*, 64.

130 Livingstone, *Monaghan Story*, 370.

131 *DD*, 10 Oct. 1914, 9 Jan. 1915.

132 Ibid., 26 Sept. 1914, 14 Nov. 1914; 14 Aug. 1915.

133 Ibid., 12 June 1915. See also *DD*, 19 June 1915, 17 July 1915.

134 Ibid., 9 Oct. 1915.

135 Ibid., 13 Nov. 1915.

136 Ibid., 13 Nov. 1915. See P. V. Hoey, MA BMH WS 530, for the perspective of one of the assailants.

137 Ibid., 8 Jan. 1916.

138 *DD*, 13 Nov. 1915.

139 *DD*, 8 Jan. 1916.

140 *DD*, 15 Jan. 1916.

141 *DD*, 26 Feb. 1916. For Maguire, see Terence Dooley, *Inniskeen, 1912–1918: The Political Conversion of Bernard O'Rourke* (Dublin, 2004), 35–7.

142 'State of County'.

143 P. V. Hoey, MA BMH WS 530; Jim Sullivan, MA BMH WS 518.

144 'State of County'.

145 Livingstone, *Monaghan Story*, 371–2.

146 *DD*, 20, 6 May 1916.

147 Tom Carragher, MCM Marron papers, 7.

148 *DD*, 6 May 1916.

149 Dooley, *Inniskeen*; P. V. Hoey, MA BMH WS 530.

150 Account of Gaelic League activist, MCM Marron papers.

151 'State of County'.

Chapter 2

1 EOD, 'Days', 177.

2 *Iris an Gharda*, 10 Sept. 1923; EOD, 'Days', 176–7.

3 EOD to Brugha, 24 Nov. 1921, UCDA P7a/5.

4 *Iris an Gharda*, 10 Sept. 1923.

5 Collins to Stack, 19 Nov. 1918, Kilmainham Gaol collection, 18 LR Ib 13 04. I am grateful to Peter Hart for this reference.

6 *Nationality*, Feb. 1917–May 1918.

7 Castle file 3725, file 70, PRO WO 35/207.

8   Ó Murthuile memoir, 124, UCDA P7a/209.
9   EOD, 'Days', 177.
10 *DD*, 19, 26 Aug., 14 Oct. 1916; 21 July 1917; Mandle, *Gaelic Athletic Association*, 180.
11 *DD*, 3 June 1916.
12 Tom Carragher, MCM Marron papers, 7.
13 Tom Garvin's description of the Gaelic League as 'the central institution in the development of the revolutionary elite' could apply to the GAA in Monaghan. However, Peter Hart's research has questioned the link between IRA activism and levels of Gaelic League and GAA membership; the fact that cultural nationalist movements were also a negligible motivating factor for the Longford IRA suggests that their significance varied widely from county to county (Peter Hart, *The IRA at War 1916–1923* (Oxford, 2003), 55; Marie Coleman, *County Longford and the Irish Revolution 1910–1923* (Dublin, 2003), 177).
14 Joe Shevlin, MCM Marron papers, 2.
15 Francis Tummon, MA BMH WS 820.
16 CI's report, Feb. 1917, PRO CO 904.
17 CI's report, June 1917, PRO CO 904.
18 CI's report, June 1917, PRO CO 904.
19 See Séamus McCluskey, *Emyvale GAA Club, A History* (n.p., 1984), 3; Sean Hegarty, 'The GAA in Tydavnet Parish', in McCluskey (ed.), *Monaghan Gael*; Short, *Ulster GAA Story*, 79–80.
20 CI's report, June 1917, PRO CO 904.
21 *DD*, 6 Jan. 1934; 20 Aug. 1921.
22 CI's reports, June, July, Sept., Oct., Nov., Dec. 1917, PRO CO 904.
23 *DD*, 13 Oct. 1917.
24 *DD*, 13, 27 Oct. 1917.
25 *War of Independence in Monaghan*, 24; *DD*, 21 July 1917.
26 Tom Carragher, MCM Marron papers, 7.
27 *DD*, 20 Oct. 1917. Around one-sixth of the priests at Count Plunkett's convention in April 1917 came from the Clogher diocese (*DD*, 21 April 1917). See also Dooley, *Inniskeen*, 35.
28 *DD*, 5 May 1917.
29 Michael Laffan, *The Resurrection of Ireland: The Sinn Féin Party 1916–1923* (Cambridge, 1999), 191–3; Tom Garvin, *Nationalist Revolutionaries in Ireland 1858–1928* (Oxford, 1987).
30 Walsh memoir, 18.
31 EOD, 'Reminiscences', *III*, 9.
32 *The Police Gazette; or, Hue-And-Cry*, 5 Nov. 1920.
33 Walsh memoir, 19. Elsewhere (166) Walsh notes: 'His eyes missed nothing; indeed so searching and penetrating were they that to sit opposite him, as I have done so often, gave you the uncomfortable feeling he was cognisant of your every thought.'
34 Walsh memoir, 19.

35 There were exceptions. One disillusioned veteran commented: 'the meek shall possess the land but the hustlers will have the rents. All the Duffy faction attached themselves to the political junta that adopted this policy.' (F. J. N. to Fr Marron, 11 March 1971, MCM Marron papers, 5).

36 Joe McCarville, MCM Marron papers, 4.

37 Interview with Dr Conn Ward, Fr Duffy's notebook, MCM Marron papers, 4.

38 Walsh memoir, 19.

39 EOD, 'Reminiscences', III, 8.

40 K. Gilsenan, MCM Marron papers, 7.

41 Joe Shevlin, MCM Marron papers, 2.

42 Joe McCarville, MCM Marron papers, 4.

43 James McKenna, MCM, Marron papers, 1.

44 Packie Coyle, MCM, Marron papers, 5.

45 Jimmy Kirke, MCM, Marron papers, 7.

46 Tom Carragher, MCM Marron papers, 7.

47 Patrick Corrigan, MCM Marron papers, 7.

48 James McKenna, MCM Marron papers, 1; Harry Martin, MCM, Marron papers, 7.

49 Jim Sullivan, MCM Marron papers, 5.

50 Francis O'Duffy, MCM Marron papers, 11.

51 Dr Conn Ward, Fr Duffy notebook, MCM Marron papers, 4.

52 Patrick McGrory, MCM Marron papers, 2.

53 Fitzpatrick, *Two Irelands*, 86.

54 Brian MacMahon, 3, MCM Marron papers, 6. MacMahon's brother, Peadar, would become chief of staff of the National Army. Presumably O'Duffy's influence, like that of O'Daly, was partly due to the patronage available to him as assistant surveyor.

55 James McKenna, MCM Marron papers, 1.

56 Quoted in Walsh memoir, 19.

57 *DD*, 2 Feb. 1918.

58 Ibid., 16 Feb. 1918.

59 Ibid., 29 June 1918.

60 Ibid., 5 Oct. 1918.

61 Joost Augusteijn, *From Public Defiance to Guerrilla Warfare: The Experiences of Ordinary Volunteers in the Irish War of Independence, 1916–21* (Dublin, 1996).

62 Quoted in Michael Laffan, *Resurrection*, 211.

63 David Fitzpatrick, *Politics and Irish Life 1913–1921: Provincial Experience of War and Revolution* (Cork, 1998 edn.), 124.

64 CI's report, March 1918, PRO CO 904.

65 *War of Independence in Monaghan*, 24; *DD*, 13 April 1918.

66 *DD*, 13 July 1918.

67 CI's report, July, Aug., 1918, PRO CO 904/106.

68 Short, *Ulster GAA Story*, 71–2; *DD*, 20 July 1918; Mandle, *Gaelic Athletic Association*, 184.

69 Mandle, *Gaelic Athletic Association*, 185. For O'Duffy on Gaelic Sunday, see *DD*, 18 Jan. 1919.

70 *DD*, 10 Aug. 1918.

71 Ibid., 28 Sept. 1918.

72 EOD, Jail Diary, 14 Sept. 1918, ODP.

73 Ibid., 20 Sept. 1918, ODP.

74 *DD*, 28 Sept. 1918.

75 Walsh memoir, 25–6.

76 CI's report, Aug. 1918, PRO CO 904/106.

77 Walsh memoir, 25.

78 *DD*, 18 Jan. 1919; EOD, 'Days', 175; Walsh memoir, 25; McCluskey, *The G.A.A. in Co. Monaghan*, 35–7.

79 EOD, Jail Diary, 14 Sept. 1918, ODP.

80 EOD to Maggie Murray, 24 Oct. 1918, MCM Marron papers, *8*; 'Statement by Mr. Ernest Blythe' (hereafter: Blythe memoir), 96, UCDA P24/1783.

81 Blythe memoir, 90, UCDA P24/1783.

82 Blythe memoir, 92–3, UCDA P24/1783.

83 EOD, Jail Diary, 25 Sept. 1918, ODP.

84 Ibid., 10, 13 Oct. 1918, ODP.

85 Ibid., 12 Oct. 1918, ODP; EOD to Maggie Murray, 24 Oct. 1918, MCM Marron papers, *8*.

86 EOD to Mullen, 21 Oct. 1918, MCM Marron papers, *8*.

87 Blythe notebook, n.d. [1918], UCDA P24/2183.

88 EOD, Jail Diary, 28 Sept. 1918, ODP.

89 EOD to Mullen, 21 Oct. 1918, MCM Marron papers, *8*.

90 Collins to Stack, Nov. 1918, NLI MS 5, 848.

91 EOD, Jail Diary, 4 Oct. 1918, ODP.

92 Blythe memoir, 94, UCDA P24/1783. Another outsider, Seán MacEntee, was put up in the equally faction-ridden south Monaghan constituency.

93 Castle file 3725, enclosed in file 70, PRO WO 35/207; Walsh memoir, 26.

94 *DD*, 7 Sept. 1918.

95 Ibid., 4 Jan. 1919; see also CI's report, Nov. 1918, PRO CO 904/107.

96 *DD*, 21 Dec. 1918.

97 Ibid., 4 Jan. 1919.

98 Tom Carragher, MCM Marron papers, *7*.

99 CI's report, Dec. 1918, PRO CO 904/107.

100 Lyrics posted on Monaghan Online (www.thebluesboard.com), 6 Feb. 2000; see also CI's report, Dec. 1918, PRO CO 904/107.

101 *DD*, 27 Aug. 1921.

102 Livingstone, *Monaghan Story*, 377.

103 IG's report, July 1918, PRO CO 904/106; CI's report, July 1919, PRO CO 904/109.

104 CI's report, Aug. 1919, PRO CO 904/109.

105 CI's report, June 1920, PRO CO 904/112; *DD*, 14 Aug. 1920.

106 IG's report, April 1919, PRO CO 904/108.

107 IG's report, Aug. 1920, PRO CO 904/112; See also IG's report, July 1920, PRO CO 904/112.

108 *DD*, 28 June, 9 Aug. 1919.

109 IG's report, Aug. 1919, PRO CO 904/109.

110 Henry Murphy, crown solicitor for Co. Monaghan, to general headquarters, n.d. [*c.* July 1920], file 332, PRO CO 904/211.

111 Paddy Mohan, MCM Marron papers, *3*. Informal, and unpopular, understandings reportedly existed between senior IRA and RIC men, allegedly brokered by their wives (Brian MacMahon, 5, MCM Marron papers, *6*).

112 Brian MacMahon to Fr Ó Mearáin, 7 Jan. 1965, MCM Marron papers, *6*.

113 Dr Conn Ward, quoted in *War of Independence in Monaghan*, 164; see also Joe Shevlin, MCM Marron papers, *2*.

114 Dr Conn Ward, Fr Duffy notebook, MCM Marron papers, *4*; Paddy Mohan, MCM Marron papers, *3*.

115 Philip Marron, MA BMH WS 657.

116 Crime Special report, 30 June 1920, file no. 332, PRO CO 904/211. See also CI's report, Sept. 1919, PRO CO 904/110. Peadar O'Donnell, the socialist republican, left the weapons in O'Duffy's house shortly before the raid. Local Volunteers 'had no use for O'Donnell after this' (Tommy Donnelly, MCM Marron papers, *2*). O'Donnell's role in organizing the revolution's first 'Soviet', the take-over of a lunatic asylum in Monaghan in January 1919, would not have endeared him to O'Duffy.

117 *DD*, 12 Feb. 1921.

118 Ward's motion was passed, the three Unionists dissenting (*DD*, 12 March 1921).

119 *DD*, 6 March 1920.

120 Walsh memoir, 6.

121 Richard Mulcahy, UCDA P7/Cassette 6A.

122 P. V. Hoey, MA BMH WS 530.

123 Joe Shevlin, MCM Marron papers, *2*.

124 Padraig Puirséal, *The GAA in its Times* (Dublin, 1984), 179; Walsh memoir, 18.

125 *Anglo-Celt*, 18 Nov. 1919.

126 Ibid., 13 Dec. 1919.

127 Sisson, *Pearse's Patriots*, 116; Alan Bairner, 'Ireland, Sport and Empire', in Keith Jeffrey (ed.), *An Irish Empire? Aspects of Ireland and the British Empire* (Manchester, 1996).

128 *DD*, 18 Jan. 1919; Short, *Ulster GAA Story*, 75.

Chapter 3

1 T. P. O'Neill (ed.), *Private Sessions of the Second Dáil* (Dublin, 1972), 17 Dec. 1921, 240–2.

2 Phil Marron, MCM Marron papers, *2*; John Sullivan, MCM Marron papers, *5*.

3 *DD*, 21 Feb. 1920; see Phillip Marron, MA BMH WS 657, for an (illustrated) account of the attack.

4 Jim Sullivan, MCM Marron papers, *5*; Mrs Murtagh, MCM Marron papers, *5*.

5 *DD*, 21 Feb. 1920.

6 Mrs Murtagh, MCM Marron papers, *5*.

7 James McKenna, MCM Marron papers, *1*.

8 Ibid.

9 *War of Independence in Monaghan*, 54.

10 *DD*, 21 Feb. 1920.

11 James McKenna, MCM Marron papers, *1*.

12 Paddy Mohan, MCM Marron papers, *3*; Johnnie McKenna, MCM, Marron papers, *4*.

13 *War of Independence in Monaghan*, 47.

14 John McAnerney, MA BMH WS 528.

15 James McKenna, MCM Marron papers, *1*.

16 *War of Independence in Monaghan*, 48; Short, *Ulster GAA Story*, 78–9; James McKenna, MCM Marron papers, *1*; Francis Tummon, MA BMH WS 820.

17 *Irish News*, 4 May 1920.

18 NAI GPB/1920/6178 (I am grateful to William Murphy for this reference).

19 *Irish News*, 4 May 1920.

20 Phil Marron to Mrs Marron, n.d., MCM Marron papers, *2*.

21 Ibid.

22 *DD*, 15 May 1920. The pride taken by Gaels in their IRA activism was often accompanied by a curious sense of injustice when arrested. Short (*Ulster GAA Story*, 77) observed of O'Duffy's arrest that 'any prominent GAA man was liable to arrest on the flimsiest pretext'.

23 *DD*, 28 Feb. 1920.

24 IG's report, June 1920, PRO CO 904/112; *DD*, 8 May 1920.

25 *DD*, 15 May 1920.

26 Ibid., 31 July, 19 June 1920.

27 Anthony Daly, MCM Marron papers, *5*.

28 EOD to Mulcahy, 27 May 1921, UCDA P7/A22/239.

29 *DD*, 19 June 1920.

30 Ibid., 24 July 1920; CI's report, July 1920, PRO CO 904/112.

31 *DD*, 7, 21 Aug., 4 Sept. 1920.

32 Ibid., 10 July 1920.

33 Ibid., 7 Aug. 1920.

34 Ibid., 7 Aug. 1920; CI's report, Aug. 1920, PRO CO 904/112.

35 IG's report, Aug. 1920, PRO CO 904/112.

36 *War of Independence in Monaghan*, 34–5.

37 Francis O'Duffy, MCM Marron papers, *11*.

38 Police reports, Co. Monaghan, 1921, PRO CO 904/154; DD, 4 March 1922.

39 Tom Carragher, quoted in *War of Independence in Monaghan*, 35.

40 Police reports, 1921, Co. Monaghan, PRO CO 904/154.

41 IG's report, July 1920, Aug. 1920, PRO CO 904/112.

42 Harry Martin, MCM Marron papers, *7*.

43 Brian MacMahon, 5, MCM Marron papers, *6*.

44 *War of Independence in Monaghan*, 48; IG's report, June 1920, PRO CO 904/109; CI's report, July 1920, PRO CO 904/112.

45 CI's reports, May, July, August 1919, PRO, CO 904/109; *War of Independence in Monaghan*, 33–4.

46 *DD*, 10 July, 14 Aug., 18 Sept. 1920.

47 EOD to battalion O/Cs, Monaghan brigade, *c.* Dec. 1920, MCM Marron papers, *5*. Inevitably, his advice was not always heeded. The RIC arrested one IRA raider after discovering a quart of *poitín* in his home.

48 RIC summary of evidence, 18 July 1920, PRO CO 904/211. See also Francis Tummon, MA BMH WS 820.

49 RIC summary of evidence, 18 July 1920, PRO CO 904/211.

50 Col. Toppin, Irish command, to Andy Cope, 17 July 1920; CI, Fermanagh, to IG, 19 July 1920; note of deputy IG, 20 July 1920, file no. 332, PRO CO 904/211.

51 EOD to Brugha, 24 Nov. 1921, UCDA P7a/5.

52 CI's report, June 1920, PRO CO 904/112.

53 Outrage report, 10 June 1920, file no. 332, PRO CO 904/211.

54 Ibid.; for the RIC's loss of control in Monaghan see IG's reports, July, Aug. 1920, PRO CO 904/112.

55 Jim Sullivan, MCM Marron papers, *5*; *War of Independence in Monaghan*, 55.

56 *DD*, 4 Sept. 1920.

57 Peter Woods, MCM Marron papers, *2*; Francis O'Duffy, MCM Marron papers, *11*; Thomas Carragher, MA BMH WS 681.

58 John Sullivan, MCM Marron papers, *5*; Pat McDonnell, MCM Marron papers, *4*.

59 Patrick Corrigan, MCM Marron papers, *7*.

60 Jim Sullivan, MCM Marron papers, *5*.

61 James Mulligan, MCM Marron papers, *3*.

62 *War of Independence in Monaghan*, 56.

63 Jim Sullivan, MCM Marron papers, *5*.

64 *DD*, 25 Sept. 1920.

65 Ibid., 4 Sept. 1920.

66 Ibid., 4 Sept. 1920.

67 Ibid., 11 Sept. 1920.

68 Terence Dooley, *The Decline of Unionist Politics in Monaghan, 1911–23* (Maynooth, 1988), 42; *War of Independence in Monaghan*, 59.

69 Pat McDonnell, MCM Marron papers, *4*.

70 Francis O'Duffy, MA BMH WS 654; John McGahey, MA BMH WS 740.

71 *DD*, 25 Sept., 2 Oct. 1920.

72 *The War of Independence in Monaghan*, 57.

73 *DD*, 2 April 1921; CI's report, March 1921, PRO CO 904/114.

74 *DD*, 2 April 1921.

75 Ibid., 9 Oct. 1920, 13 Nov. 20; Edward Micheau, 'Sectarian Conflict in Monaghan', in David Fitzpatrick (ed.), *Ireland and the First World War* (Dublin, 1988).

76 Tom Carragher, MCM Marron papers, *7*.

77 *DD*, 16 Oct. 1920; P. V. Hoey, MA BMH WS 530.

78 Brian McMahon, 7, MCM Marron papers, *6*.

79 James Mulligan, MCM Marron papers, *3*.

80 Matt Ó Shoin, quoted in Fr Duffy to Fr Ó Mearáin, 19 Jan. 1966, MCM Marron papers, *4*.

81 EOD, 'Reminiscences', *III*, 9.

82 Townshend, *Ireland*, 151.

83 *DD*, 18 Sept. 1920. The board of guardians subsequently backed down.

84 Terence Dooley, 'From the Belfast Boycott to the Boundary Commission: Fears and Hopes in County Monaghan, 1920–26', *Clogher Record* (1994), 90–106.

85 Henry Macklin, MCM, Marron papers, *2*; Johnnie McKenna, MCM Marron papers, *4*; IG's report, March 1921, CO 904/114.

86 Blythe memoir, 119–20, UCDA P/24/1783.

87 Markievicz to FitzGerald, June 1921, UCDA P80/354.

88 CI's report, Dec. 1920, Jan. 1921, PRO CO 904/113–14.

89 CI's report, Feb. 1921, PRO CO 904/114.

90 P. V. Hoey, MA BMH WS 530.

91 *DD*, 8 Jan. 1921; CI's report, Jan. 1921, PRO CO 904/114.

92 *DD*, 29 Jan. 1921.

93 IG's report, May 1921, PRO CO 904/115.

94 Paddy Mohan, MCM Marron papers, *3*.

95 James Mulligan, MCM Marron papers, *3*. James McKenna (MCM Marron papers, *1*) noted: 'Willaghan was our number one enemy and his twelve men were young and active and very loyal to him'.

96 EOD to battalion O/Cs, Monaghan brigade, *c.* Dec. 1920, MCM Marron papers, *5*.

97 Dr Conn Ward, Fr Duffy notebook, MCM Marron papers, *4*.

98 Quoted in Peter Hart, *British Intelligence in Ireland 1920–21: The Final Reports* (Cork, 2002), 96.

99 *DD*, 26 Feb. 1921.

100 Paddy Mohan, MCM Marron papers, *3*; John McGonnell, MA BMH WS 574; James McKenna, MA BMH WS 1028.

101 James McKenna, MCM Marron papers, *1*.

102 *DD*, 26 Feb. 1921; CI's report, Feb. 1921, PRO CO 904/114.

103 Monaghan brigade, monthly report, February 1921, UCDA P7/A/39.

104 James McKenna, MCM Marron papers, *1*; John McKenna, MCM Marron papers, *7*.

105 James McKenna, MCM Marron papers, *1*.
106 Ibid.; *DD*, 26 March 1921. Unionists were attacked in Scotstown and Smithboro on the same night (Phillip Marron, MA BMH WS 657).
107 *DD*, 26 March 1921.
108 *DD*, 26 March 1921; Sir Arthur Hezlet, *The 'B' Specials: A History of the Ulster Special Constabulary* (London, 1972), 36.
109 CI's report, March 1921, PRO CO 904/114.
110 *DD*, 26 March 1921.
111 Harry Macklin, MCM Marron papers, *2*.
112 James McKenna, MA BMH WS 1028.
113 *DD*, 26 March 1921.
114 CI's report, March 1921, PRO CO 904/114.
115 EOD to Brugha, 24 Nov. 1921, UCDA P7a/5.
116 Cited in *Garda Review*, May 1926.
117 Castle file 3725, enclosed in file 70, PRO WO 35/207.
118 Francis Tummon, MA BMH WS 820.
119 Oscar Traynor, O'Malley notebook, 50, UCDA P17b/98.
120 Jimmy Ward, MCM Marron papers, *7*.
121 Peter Woods, MA BMH WS 578.
122 Patrick Woods, MCM Marron papers, *2*.
123 Jim Sullivan, MCM Marron papers, *5*.
124 IG's report, March 1921, CI's report, March 1921, PRO CO 904/114; Anthony Daly, MCM Marron papers, *5*.
125 John McGahey, MA BMH WS 740.
126 Jim Sullivan, MCM Marron papers, *5*.
127 Ibid.
128 Hart, *British Intelligence*, 12.
129 CI's report, March 1921.
130 Brian MacMahon, 25, MCM Marron papers, *6*.
131 Ibid.
132 James Mulligan, MCM Marron papers, *3*.
133 Patrick Corrigan, MCM Marron papers, *7*.
134 Peter Hart, *The IRA and its Enemies: Violence and Community in Cork 1916–23* (Oxford, 1998).
135 Patrick Corrigan, MCM Marron papers, *7*.
136 *DD*, 16 April 1921.
137 P. V. Hoey, MA BMH WS 530.
138 CI's report, April 1921, PRO CO 904/115.
139 *DD*, 2 April 1921.
140 CI's report, March 1921, PRO CO 904/114.
141 Jim Sullivan, MCM Marron papers, *5*.
142 *DD*, 23 April 1921.

143 Ibid., 7 May 1921.

144 Joe Shevlin, MCM Marron papers, *2*; Dr Conn Ward, Fr Duffy notebook, MCM Marron papers, *4*; *DD*, 7 May 1921.

145 CI's report, April 1921, PRO CO 904/115.

146 James McKenna, MA BMH WS 1028.

147 *DD*, 23 April 1921.

148 Dooley, *Unionist Politics*, 19.

149 Seamus McPhillips, 'The Ancient Order of Hibernians in County Monaghan with particular reference to the parish of Aghabog from 1900 to 1933', MA thesis (NUI Maynooth, 1999), 107; Jim Sullivan, MCM Marron papers, *5*.

150 EOD to Blythe, 10 Nov. 1926, UCDA P24/499. My thanks to Terence Dooley for this reference.

151 *DD*, 12 March 1921

152 Ibid., 16 April 1921

153 CI's report, March 1921, PRO CO 904/114.

154 McPhillips, 'Ancient Order of Hibernians', 107.

155 John McGonnell, MA BMH WS 574.

156 Quoted in McPhillips, 'Ancient Order of Hibernians', 111.

157 *DD*, 17 Feb. 1934.

158 Ibid., 24 Feb., 3, 10 March 1934.

159 McPhillips, 'Ancient Order of Hibernians', 111.

160 AOH Board of Eireann minutes, June 1922, cited in McPhillips, 'Ancient Order of Hibernians', 111.

161 *DD*, 2 July 1921.

162 Joseph McKenna, MCM Marron papers, *3*; John McGonnell, MA BMH WS 574.

163 James McKenna, MA BMH WS 1028.

164 Paddy Mohan, MCM Marron papers, *3*.

165 Dr Conn Ward, Fr Duffy notebook, MCM Marron papers, *4*. Ward was obviously not an impartial witness, and it was in his interest to pin the blame on O'Duffy. James McKenna stated that O'Duffy ordered both of the executions in his areas (Carroll and Treanor), but as a result of information received by Ward.

166 John McGahey, MA BMH WS 740; Jim Sullivan, MCM Marron papers, *5*.

167 CI's report, April 1921, PRO CO 904/115.

168 Hart, *The IRA*, 303–4.

169 *War of Independence in Monaghan*, 39.

170 Ibid., 65.

171 P. V. Hoey, MA BMH WS 530.

172 John McGahey, MA BMH WS 740.

173 Hart, *The IRA*, 293–315; Joanna Bourke, *An Intimate History of Killing: Face-to-face Killing in Twentieth-Century Warfare* (London, 1999), 188–9.

174 Garvin, *Nationalist Revolutionaries*, 151–2. As one British intelligence report noted: 'for the first time in history the Irishman has not succumbed to the temptation of

gold . . . a surfeit of terror has replaced an appetite for gain'. Ormonde Winter, 'Report on the Intelligence Branch of the Chief of Police from May 1920 to July 1921', 7–8, PRO CO 904/156B.

175 Richard English, *Ernie O'Malley: IRA Intellectual* (Oxford, 1998), 80.

176 Garvin, *Nationalist Revolutionaries*, 150–7, 120–1; English, *O'Malley*, 79–80.

177 Michael Hopkinson, *The Irish War of Independence* (Dublin, 2002), 147.

178 Peter Hart, *The IRA at War, 1916–1923* (Oxford, 2003), 79.

179 Ibid., 192.

180 Monaghan brigade, monthly report, March 1921, UCDA P7/A/39.

181 Hart, *The IRA at War*, 80.

182 Meda Ryan, *Tom Barry: IRA Freedom Fighter* (Cork, 2003).

183 Hart, *The IRA at War*, 78, 80.

184 For example, there was little evidence of a sectarian dimension to IRA violence in Longford, the most violent county outside Munster (Coleman, *County Longford*, 155–7).

185 *DD*, 31 Dec. 1921.

186 EOD to executive council, 30 Sept. 1924, UCDA, P24/222.

187 Ernie O'Malley, *On Another Man's Wound* (Dublin, 1936), 110.

188 Hart, *The IRA at War*, 39.

189 EOD to Brugha, 24 Nov. 1921, UCDA P7a/5.

190 Hart, *The IRA at War*, 44.

191 Richard Mulcahy, UCDA P7/Cassette 6b.

Chapter 4

1 O'Neill, *Second Dáil*, 17 Dec. 1921, 241–2.

2 Maryann Gialanella Valiulis, *Portrait of a Revolutionary: General Richard Mulcahy and the Founding of the Irish Free State* (Dublin, 1992), 70–3.

3 EOD, O/C 2nd northern division to director of organization, GHQ, *c.* 27 April 1921, UCDA P7/A/18/104.

4 EOD, O/C, 2nd northern division, to chief of staff, GHQ, 27 May 1921, UCDA P7/A/18/273.

5 EOD, O/C, 2nd northern division, to director of organization, GHQ, *c.* 27 April 1921, UCDA P7/A/18/104. O'Duffy's replacement, Charlie Daly, formed a similar opinion of the 2nd division's shortcomings.

6 EOD to minister for defence, 24 Nov. 1921, UCDA P7a/5.

7 EOD, O/C, 2nd northern division, to chief of staff, 27 May 1921, UCDA P7/A/18/273.

8 Richard Mulcahy interview, UCDA P7/Cassette 6b. For Price's alcoholism, see Oscar Traynor, O'Malley notebook, UCDA P17b/98.

9 Oscar Traynor, O'Malley notebook, UCDA P17b/98.

10 Tom Garvin, *1922: The Birth of Irish Democracy* (Dublin, 1996), 56–7.

11 Garvin, *Nationalist Revolutionaries*; John M. Regan, *The Irish Counter-Revolution 1921–1936* (Dublin, 1999), 247.

12 Seán Ó Murthuile memoir, 119–20, UCDA P7a/209.

13 Conversation between Joe Sweeney and Richard Mulcahy, 1962, UCDA P7/D/43.

14 Brian MacMahon, 24, MCM Marron papers, 6.

15 Tom Carragher, MCM Marron papers, 6.

16 Frank Aiken memoir (1925), UCDA P104/1308; Ernie O'Malley, *The Singing Flame* (Dublin, 1978), 13.

17 Ó Murthuile memoir, 157, UCDA P7a/209.

18 Brian MacMahon, 24, MCM Marron papers, 6. As Frank Aiken put it: 'We got too long a rest and became lazy; our muscles became flabby and our nerves & spirit lost their tone' (Aiken memoir, UCDA P104/1308).

19 O'Neill, *Second Dáil*, 17 Dec. 1921, 247.

20 CI's report, July 1921, PRO CO 904/116.

21 British army intelligence summary, *c.* late Aug. 1921, UCDA P7/A/23/10.

22 Michael Hopkinson, *Green against Green: The Irish Civil War* (Dublin, 1988), 88; Richard Mulcahy interview, UCDA P7/Cassette 136a.

23 Eamon Phoenix, *Northern Nationalism: Nationalist Politics, Partition and the Catholic Minority in Northern Ireland 1890–1940* (Belfast, 1994), 136.

24 Phoenix, *Northern Nationalism*, 139–40.

25 O/C, 3rd northern division, to chief of staff, 12 July 1921, UCDA P7/A/22/5.

26 EOD, 22 Sept. 1921, quoted in Walsh memoir, 34.

27 Michael Farrell, *Arming the Protestants: The Formation of the Ulster Special Constabulary and the Royal Ulster Constabulary 1920–27* (London, 1983), 63. See also Jim McDermott, *Northern Divisions: The Old IRA and the Belfast Pogroms 1920–22* (Belfast, 2001), 105–7.

28 Hezlet, *'B' Specials*, 46.

29 Phoenix, *Northern Nationalism*, 146.

30 EOD, 22 Sept. 1921, quoted in Walsh memoir, 36.

31 *Manchester Guardian*, quoted in Phoenix, *Northern Nationalism*, 147; Farrell, *Arming the Protestants*, 66.

32 Farrell, *Arming the Protestants*, 66–7.

33 EOD, 22 Sept. 1921, quoted in Walsh memoir, 36; McDermott, *Northern Divisions*, 109.

34 Colonel commandant, 15th infantry brigade, 3 Sept. 1921 to staff col., general staff, Irish command, GHQ, PRO WO 35/88.

35 McDermott, *Northern Divisions*, 107.

36 *Irish News*, 2 Sept. 1921.

37 Ibid., 3 Sept. 1921.

38 McDermott, *Northern Divisions*, 107–11.

39 David Fitzpatrick, *Harry Boland's Irish Revolution* (Cork, 2003), 229–31.

40 *Irish News*, 5 Sept. 1921; Walsh memoir, 32.

41 Walsh memoir, 33–4. The 'fear' may refer to the beatings and shootings (one fatal) by loyalists following the meeting, or the unsuccessful attack on the car in which Collins and O'Duffy travelled on to Clones.

42 Ó Murthuile memoir, 151, UCDA P7a/209. See also Arthur Mitchell, *Revolutionary Government in Ireland* (Dublin, 1995), 310.

43 O'Neill, *Private Sessions*, 22 Aug. 1921, 29.

44 Phoenix, *Northern Nationalism*, 145–6.

45 EOD, report to executive council, 22 Sept. 1924, UCDA P24/223.

46 Wickham to inspector general, 8 Sept. 1921, PRO CO 904/151. O'Duffy initially made a good impression on Wickham, who judged him 'very just and fair', notwithstanding that 'he was very much ill at ease, and referred to him more frequently than was necessary, as "Sir" '. His associate, Sir William Young Darling, found him 'a level headed fellow and apart from a certain wildness about his eyes, which characterises most of them…rather a tolerable fellow.' George Boyce, 'An Encounter with Michael Collins, 1921', *Journal of the Cork Historical and Archaeological Society* (July–Dec. 1975), 57. My thanks to Peter Hart for this reference.

47 Memo, 9 Sept. 1921, PRO CO 904/151.

48 RIC commissioner, Belfast, to RIC divisional commissioner (with annotations added by Cope), 6 Sept. 1921; miscellaneous reports by Stephen Tallents, PRO CO 906/26; General Neville Macready to Winston Churchill, 8 March 1922, PRO, CO 739/11. See also Michael Hopkinson (ed.), *The Last Days of Dublin Castle: The Diaries of Mark Sturgis* (Dublin, 1999), 217.

49 Hezlet, *'B' Specials*, 50; McDermott, *Northern Divisions*, 117.

50 Quoted in Hopkinson (ed.), *Mark Sturgis*, 218–19.

51 Walsh memoir, 32.

52 *Irish Bulletin*, 27 Oct. 1921.

53 Chief of staff to minister for defence, 1 Oct. 1921, UCDA P7/A/26/417.

54 *Irish Independent*, 21 Nov. 1936.

55 EOD to minister for defence, 24 Nov. 1921, UCDA P7a/5.

56 Richard Mulcahy, UCDA P7/D/102.

57 EOD to minister for defence, 24 Nov. 1921, UCDA P7a/5.

58 Hopkinson, *War of Independence*, 19–20.

59 Quoted in Hopkinson, *Green against Green*, 12.

60 Copy of letter by Mulcahy to *Irish Times*, *c.* 14 Oct. 1962, UCDA P7/D/1.

61 Director of organization to chief of staff, 6 Sept. 1921, UCDA P7/A/25/93.

62 Report on south Roscommon brigade, n.d. [*c.* Oct. 1921], UCDA P7/A/26/49.

63 Ibid.

64 Michael Brennan, *The War in Clare 1911–1921: personal memories of the Irish War of Independence* (Dublin, 1980), 106–7.

65 O'Malley, *Singing Flame*, 16; D/O to O/C, 2nd southern division, 7 July 1921, UCDA P7/A/22/53.

66 Aiken memoir, UCDA P104/1308.

67 O'Malley, *Singing Flame*, 23.
68 IG's report, Oct. 1921, PRO CO 904/117.
69 Aiken memoir, UCDA P104/1308.
70 Ibid.
71 Valiulis, *Portrait*, 101–10; Regan, *Counter-Revolution*, 7–10. Blythe noted that 'Brugha and Collins never seemed to hit if off'. Blythe regarded Brugha as a man of 'unlimited physical courage' but 'very limited intelligence', and viewed his proposals for 'machine-gunning the audiences in British picturehouses' and a suicide attack on the House of Commons as 'absolute lunacy' (Blythe memoir, 126–7, UCDA P24/1783).
72 W. T. Cosgrave observed that 'Stack was incompetent and just couldn't help it'. (Michael Hayes, note of conversation with Cosgrave, 20 April 1963, UCDA P53/324). Collins, who could be brutally rude, told Stack in front of the cabinet, 'Your department is a bloody joke' (Blythe memoir, 117, UCDA P24/1783).
73 Richard Mulcahy, 'Talk with Lieut. Gen. Costello', 23 May 1963, UCDA P7/D/3.
74 'Note on the differences between Cathal Brugha and Stack and other members of the Volunteer Executive and Cabinet', n.d., UCDA P7/D/96.
75 Chief of staff to minister for defence, 1, 11, 16 Nov. 1921, UCDA P7a/2.
76 EOD to minister for defence, 24 Nov. 1921, UCDA P7a/2.
77 Chief of staff to minister for defence, 22 Nov. 1921; minister for defence to chief of staff, 22 Nov. 1921, UCDA P7a/2.
78 Richard Mulcahy, 'Talk with Lieut. Gen. Costello', 23 May 1963, UCDA P7/D/3.
79 Laffan, *Resurrection*, 349. See also Regan, *Counter-Revolution*, 27–31.
80 Mulcahy, 'Note on the differences between Cathal Brugha and Stack and other members of the Volunteer Executive and Cabinet', UCDA P7/D/96.
81 Ibid.
82 Richard Mulcahy interview, UCDA P7/Cassette 6b.
83 Richard Mulcahy, talk with Joe Sweeney, 28 Jan. 1964, UCDA P7/D/43.
84 Aiken memoir, UCDA P104/1308.
85 Regan, *Counter-Revolution*, 28.
86 Ryan added that Mulcahy told O'Duffy 'you can build up your army . . . and then knock hell out of England' (Jim Ryan, O'Malley notebook, UCDA P17b/103).
87 Misc. treaty position papers, ODP.
88 Ó Murthuile memoir, 151, UCDA, P7a/209; Fitzpatrick, *Boland's Irish Revolution*, 261–2.
89 Aiken memoir, UCDA P104/1308.
90 Tom Carragher, MCM Marron papers, 6.
91 Tim Pat Coogan, *Michael Collins* (London, 1990), 339; Garvin, *Nationalist Revolutionaries*, 144.
92 O'Malley, *Singing Flame*, 46.
93 *Official Report: Debate on the Treaty between Great Britain and Ireland* (Dublin, n.d.), 4 Jan. 1922, 227.

94 Aiken memoir, UCDA P104/1308.

95 O'Neill, *Second Dáil*, 17 Dec. 1921, 240–2.

96 Walsh memoir, 45.

97 O'Neill, *Second Dáil*, 17 Dec. 1921, 253.

98 MacSwiney (director of publicity) to Aiken (chief of staff), 22 April 1924, UCDA P104/1317.

99 Aiken to MacSwiney, 29 April 1924, UCDA P104/1317.

100 Oscar Traynor, O'Malley notebook, 50, UCDA P17b/98.

101 *DD*, 7 Jan. 1922.

102 *Debate on the Treaty*, 4 Jan. 1922, 223–7; David Fitzpatrick, ' "Unofficial emissaries": British Army Boxers in the Irish Free State, 1926', *Irish Historical Studies* (Nov. 1996), 217.

103 *Debate on the Treaty*, 4 Jan. 1922, 225.

104 *Irish Freeman* (n.d.), quoted in *DD*, 7 Jan. 1922.

105 De Burca, *Free State or Republic?* (Dublin, 2002 edn.), 44–5.

106 Brugha to EOD, 12 Jan. 1922, ODP.

107 *Dail Debates*, 21 Dec. 1921, 112; Garvin, *Nationalist Revolutionaries*, 144.

108 Dr Conn Ward, Fr Duffy notebook, MCM Marron papers, 4.

109 Oscar Traynor, O'Malley notebook, UCDA P17b/98.

110 *Anglo-Celt*, 14 Oct. 1933.

111 Talk between Joe Sweeney and Richard Mulcahy, 1962, UCDA P7/D/43; see also Jim Ryan, O'Malley notebook, UCDA P17b/103.

112 Frank Aiken, O'Malley notebook, UCDA P17b/93.

113 C. Desmond Greaves, *Liam Mellows and the Irish Revolution* (London, 1971), 279.

114 NAI DT S1233.

115 Fitzpatrick, *Boland's Irish Revolution*, 264–85.

116 Hopkinson, *Green against Green*, 61–2.

117 Joseph Dunne to James O'Donovan, 28 March 1922, NLI MS 22, 301.

118 Richard Mulcahy, conversation with Vincent Byrne, n.d. [*c*.1963], UCDA P7/D/3.

119 EOD to C. O'Daly, 4 March 1922, UCDA P17a/184.

120 C. O'Daly to EOD, 8 March 1922, UCDA P17a/184.

121 Joseph McKenna, MCM Marron papers, 3.

122 Brogan, O'Malley notebook, UCDA P17b/98.

123 Greaves, *Mellows*, 296.

124 Hopkinson, *Green against Green*, 62–6; O'Malley, *Singing Flame*, 55–62.

125 Blythe memoir, 139, UCDA P24/1783.

126 Valiulis, *Portrait*, 148; EOD to Collins, 7 June 1922, UCDA P7/B/26.

127 *Irish Independent*, 26 April 1922.

128 Greaves, *Mellows*, 313.

129 Phoenix, *Northern Nationalists*, 177–8.

130 Coogan, *Collins*, 343.

131 EOD to Collins, 30 Jan. 1922, cited in Coogan, *Collins*, 344.

132   Farrell, *Arming the Protestants*, 92. The IRA claimed that it abducted seventy hostages (Phoenix, *Northern Nationalists*, 183).

133   Craig to Lloyd George, 8 Feb. 1922, cited in Coogan, *Collins*, 345.

134   The commission was not taken seriously by any of the parties involved. General Macready described it as a farce, while IRA men under O'Duffy's authority were given permission to disarm its members (Joseph McKenna, MCM Marron papers, *3*).

135   Lloyd George to Collins, 8 Feb. 1922, cited in Coogan, *Collins*, 345.

136   *Irish Independent*, 9 Feb. 1922.

137   Robert Lynch, 'The Clones Affray, 1922—Massacre or Invasion', *History Ireland* (Autumn 2004), 34.

138   Press cutting, *c.*13 Feb. 1922, ODP.

139   Press cutting, *c.*15 Feb. 1922, ODP.

140   Coogan, *Collins*, 346–7. Phoenix, *Northern Nationalists*, 183–4; Lynch, 'Clones Affray', 36.

141   Peter Woods, MCM Marron papers, *2*.

142   John McGonnell, MA BMH WS 574.

143   Tom Carragher, MCM Marron papers, *6*.

144   Patrick Murray, MCM Marron papers, *13*.

145   Regan, *Counter-Revolution*, 62.

146   Farrell, *Arming the Protestants*, 94.

147   Lynch, 'Clones Affray', 34.

148   John McCoy, 'Personal Narrative', UCDA P104/1413.

149   Regan, *Counter-Revolution*, 61; Phoenix, *Northern Nationalists*, 191–2.

150   Hopkinson, *Green against Green*, 84–5; Staunton, *The Nationalists of Northern Ireland 1918–1973* (Dublin, 2001), 66–7; Regan, *Counter-Revolution*, 63–5.

151   Hopkinson, *Green against Green*, 85; Phoenix, *Northern Nationalists*, 213.

152   Regan, *Counter-Revolution*, 65.

153   O'Shiel memo, 6 Oct. 1922, quoted in Hopkinson, *Green against Green*, 85.

154   Blythe, memo on north east, 9 Aug. 1922, UCDA P24/70.

155   Coogan, *Collins*, 384–5.

156   Woods to Mulcahy, 21 Sept. 1922, UCDA P7/B/287.

157   Diarmuid O'Hegarty, D/O, to minister for defence, 16 Sept. 1922, UCDA P7/B/287.

158   Mulcahy to Woods, 20 Oct. 1922, UCDA P7/B/287.

159   Hopkinson, *Green against Green*, 96.

160   Fitzpatrick, *Boland's Irish Revolution*, 285.

161   Hopkinson, *Green against Green*, 98.

162   EOD to Mulcahy, 22 May 1922, UCDA P7/B/192.

163   EOD to Mulcahy, n.d., UCDA P7/B/194.

164   Michael Gallagher, 'The Pact General Election of 1922', *Irish Historical Studies* (Sept. 1979), 412.

165 *DD*, 24 June 1922.

166 Sir Nevil Macready, *Annals of an Active Life* (London, 1924), 655.

167 Quoted in Jim Maher, *Harry Boland* (Dublin, 1998), 237.

168 Maher, *Harry Boland*, 192.

169 Richard Mulcahy interview, UCDA P7/Cassette 6b.

170 Ibid.

171 Richard Mulcahy interview, UCDA P7/Cassette 136a.

172 John McCoy, 'Personal Narrative', UCDA P104/1413.

173 Hopkinson, *Green against Green*, 170.

174 EOD to Aiken, 7 July 1922, UCDA P104/1241.

175 Aiken to MacSwiney, 29 April 1924, UCDA P104/1317; Hopkinson, *Green against
     Green*, 170.

176 Calton Younger, *Ireland's Civil War* (Glasgow, 1968), 373.

177 Younger, *Civil War*, 376.

178 EOD to Collins, 21 July 1922, UCDA P7/B/68.

179 EOD to Collins, 23 July 1922, UCDA P7/B/21.

180 Aiken to MacSwiney, 29 April 1924, UCDA P104/1317.

181 Hopkinson, *Green against Green*, 148–9.

182 *Limerick War News*, 25 July 1922, UCDA P7/B/68.

183 Collins to Mulcahy, 28 July 1922, UCDA P7/B/43.

184 EOD report, n.d. [late July], UCDA P7/B/68.

185 EOD to Collins, 23 July 1922, UCDA P7/B/70.

186 Collins to government, 28 July 1922, UCDA P7/B/38.

187 EOD to Collins, 23 July 1922, UCDA P7/B/21.

188 Hopkinson, *Green against Green*, 150.

189 *Irish Times*, 31 July 1922. See also 4 Aug. 1922.

190 EOD to Mulcahy, 26 July 1922, UCDA P7/B/68.

191 EOD memorandum, n.d. [late July], UCDA P7/B/39.

192 EOD to chief of the general staff (hereafter: CGS), 26 July 1922, UCDA P7/B/68;
     EOD report, 8 Aug. 1922, UCDA P7/B/113.

193 EOD to CGS, 4 Aug. 1922, UCDA P7/B/68.

194 EOD to CGS, 19 Aug. 1922, UCDA P7/B/113.

195 See also EOD to CGS, 6 Sept. 1922, UCDA P7/B/71. O'Duffy's view of the poor
     quality of treatyite troops was shared by other senior officers (Hopkinson, *Green
     against Green*, 136–7) and British intelligence (NAI DT S1784).

196 EOD to Mulcahy, 7 Aug. 1922, UCDA P7/B/68.

197 Richard Mulcahy interview, UCDA P7/Cassette 6b.

198 Aiken to MacSwiney, 29 April 1924, UCDA, P104/1317.

199 Younger, *Civil War*, 382–3, 258.

200 EOD to CGS, 6 Sept. 1922, UCDA P7/B/71.

201 Sheila Lawlor, *Britain and Ireland 1914–1923* (Dublin, 1983), 210; Hopkinson,
     Green against Green, 137.

202 *Irish Times, c.*23 Aug. 1922.

203 Aiken to MacSwiney, 29 April 1924, UCDA P104/1317.

204 Quoted in Walsh memoir, 55.

205 EOD to Collins, 12 Aug. 1922, UCDA P7/B/39.

206 EOD to Mulcahy, 12 Aug. 1922, UCDA P7/B/39.

207 Paddy O'Connor, O'Malley notebook, UCDA P17b/100.

208 Batt O'Connor, *With Michael Collins in the Fight for Irish Independence* (Dublin, 1929), 181–2.

209 *Iris an Gharda*, 10 Sept. 1923.

210 O'Higgins to Mulcahy, 1 Sept. 1922, UCDA P7/B/70.

211 Eunan O'Halpin, *Defending Ireland: The Irish State and its Enemies since 1922* (Oxford, 1999), 9.

212 Blythe memoir, 161, UCDA P24/1783.

Chapter 5

1 *Garda Review*, August 1926.

2 During a long drive to Monaghan, Ernest Blythe recalled O'Duffy speaking 'at great length about his interest in police work and about his belief in his own capacity to do it well' (Blythe memoir, 174, UCDA P24/1783).

3 Mulcahy to EOD, 2 Sept. 1922, UCDA P7/B/70.

4 Mulcahy added that O'Duffy was 'perfectly happy and had full scope for anything that he wanted to have in primadonnaism and control and displaying all that in the Guards' (Richard Mulcahy interviews, UCDA P7/Cassette 6B, 136A).

5 The recollections of Paddy O'Connor, who served under O'Duffy (and considered him 'as friendly as be damned, though he tried to sack me in the [Beggars] Bush') seem plausible: 'I rather liked him. Our friend [Collins] thought the world of him, but they counted him a failure in the South and Dick Mulcahy had no opinion of him. The police job was ideal.' Ernie O'Malley notebooks, UCDA P17B/100.

6 Richard Mulcahy, Note on conversation with Lieutenant General McMahon, 19 Aug. 1963, UCDA P7/D/3.

7 This is the view of Tim Pat Coogan. Cosgrave asked his father, Eamon, whom he appointed deputy commissioner, to keep O'Duffy in check (Author interview, 13 Feb. 2001).

8 Blythe memoir, UCDA P24/1783, 174; Conor Brady, *Guardians of the Peace* (London, 2000 edn.), 72–3; O'Halpin, *Defending Ireland*, 9.

9 Aiken to MacSwiney, 29 April 1924, UCDA P104/1317.

10 Conor Brady, 'Police and Government in the Irish Free State 1922–33' (UCD MA, 1977), ch. 4, 4.

11 Blythe memoir, 150–1, UCDA P24/1783.

12 Report by Kevin O'Shiel, 17 July 1922, NAI DT S9048.

13 NAI DT S6485a.

14 Blythe memoir, 175, UCDA P24/1783.

15 Ibid.

16 Brady, *Guardians*, 75; Liam McNiffe, *A History of the Garda Síochána: A Social History of the Force, 1922–52* (Dublin, 1997), 67.

17 Gregory Allen, 'The People's Guard', *Síocháin*, March 1994, 25.

18 EOD to Desmond FitzGerald, 24 May 1923, UCDA P80/433; McNiffe, *Garda Síochána*, 57.

19 McNiffe, *Garda Síochána*, 67; EOD to O'Higgins, 24 Aug. 1923, NAI DT S9050.

20 Murphy, who featured on the old IRA's list of 'objectionable' army officers, was appointed in April 1923 despite the opposition of Joe McGrath (NAI DT S9050).

21 EOD to MacEoin, 17 Nov. 1922, UCDA P151/177.

22 Denis O'Kelly, *Salute to the Gardai, 1922–1958* (Dublin, 1959), 23.

23 Richard Mulcahy, conversation with Lieut. Col. Tom Ryan, 7 Aug. 1963, UCDA P7/D/108a.

24 *Garda Review*, May 1929.

25 EOD, 'Reminiscences', V, 3.

26 *Garda Review*, May 1929.

27 Ibid., Dec. 1929; EOD, 'Reminiscences', VI, 11.

28 EOD, cited in McNiffe, *Garda Síochána*, 124.

29 McNiffe, *Garda Síochana*, 80.

30 O'Kelly, *Salute*, 23.

31 EOD, 'Reminiscences', VI, 11.

32 EOD to O'Higgins, 3 Feb. 1923, UCDA P7/B/293.

33 *Garda Review*, June 1929.

34 EOD, 'Reminiscences', VI, 9–18; *Garda Review*, Dec. 1929; McNiffe, *Garda Síochána*, 126.

35 *Garda Review*, Aug. 1927.

36 Ibid., June 1929.

37 EOD, General Order 2, *c.* Oct. 1922, UCDA P7/B/293.

38 EOD, General Order 14, *c.* Nov. 1922, UCDA P7/B/293.

39 John J. Dunne, *The Pioneers* (Dublin, 1981), 105.

40 *Iris an Gharda*, 16 April 1923.

41 Ibid., 9 April 1923.

42 McNiffe, *Garda Síochána*, 137.

43 EOD speech, 20 Nov. 1922, quoted in EOD, 'Chapter I: Early Days', *Garda Review*, March 1929. See also General Order 10, 21 Nov. 1922, UCDA P7/B/293.

44 Oscar Traynor, quoted in Ernie O'Malley notebooks, UCDA P17b/98.

45 Gregory Allen, *The Garda Síochána: Policing Independent Ireland 1922–82* (Dublin, 1999), 83–6.

46 Brady, *Guardians*, 109–10. In 1923, the police made close to 10,000 prosecutions outside Dublin for licensed trade and *poitín* offences, and over 12,000 the next year, banishing *poitín* to remote areas by 1925.

47 *Garda Review*, April 1930.

48 Brady, *Guardians*, 73.

49 EOD, 'The Nation's New Civic Guard' in William G. Fitz-Gerald (ed.), *The Voice of Ireland: A Survey of the Race and Nation from all Angles* (Dublin, 1924), 393.

50 Garvin, *Nationalist Revolutionaries*.

51 Riobard Ua Floinn, *The Ethics of Sinn Féin* (Limerick, n.d.), 5; Maurice Goldring, *Faith of Our Fathers* (Dublin, 1982), 21–9.

52 Quoted in Ben Novick, *Conceiving Revolution: Irish Nationalist Propaganda during the First World War* (Dublin, 2001), 138. O'Duffy was also an accomplished mé féiner in the more commonly understood sense of the expression.

53 EOD speech, 20 Nov. 1922, quoted in *Garda Review*, March 1929.

54 Kevin O'Higgins memo, n.d., *c.*1923, NAI DT S3306.

55 Regan, *Counter-Revolution*, 86; O'Halpin, *Defending Ireland*, 32–4.

56 Kevin O'Higgins memo, n.d., *c.* late 1922, NAI DT S3306.

57 Blythe memoir, 176, UCDA P24/1783.

58 O'Duffy claimed that he was ambushed while driving through Dublin in 1922, the bullet passing through the back of his cap (*The Western People* (n.d.), quoted in *Garda Review*, August 1926).

59 Report by IRA D/I, 11 Oct. 1922, 27 Oct. 1922, UCDA P7a/2/81.

60 Allen, *Garda Síochána*, 71–2.

61 Gregory Allen, 'The People's Guard', *Síocháin*, June 1994, 47–9.

62 Brady, *Guardians*, 80.

63 EOD speech, 20 Nov. 1922, quoted in *Garda Review*, March 1929, 334–6.

64 EOD, General Order 9, 21 Nov. 1922, UCDA P7/B/293.

65 Allen, *Garda Síochána*, 62–3.

66 Ibid., 64.

67 *Iris an Gharda*, 11 Feb. 1924.

68 EOD, quoted in Walsh memoir, 89–90.

69 *Iris an Gharda*, 1 April 1923.

70 Allen, 'The People's Guard', *Síocháin*, June 1994, 51.

71 O'Kelly, *Salute*, 20.

72 *Iris an Gharda*, 11 June 1923.

73 Brady, *Guardians*, 117–18.

74 EOD, General Order No. 6, 16 Oct. 1922, UCDA P7/B/293.

75 Brady, *Guardians*, 115–16.

76 EOD speech, 20 Nov. 1922, quoted in EOD, 'Chapter I: Early Days', *Garda Review*, March 1929, 334.

77 EOD, General Order No. 9, 21 Nov. 1922, UCDA P7/B/293.

78 Walsh memoir, 162.

79 ' "Comrades": Editorial Address by Chief Commissioner', *Iris an Gharda*, 28 May 1923.

80 *Iris an Gharda*, 9 July 1923.

81 Press cutting, ODP.

82 *Garda Review*, April 1928, Jan. 1930.

83 Quoted in Walsh memoir, 162. As a *Daily Express* (22 Oct. 1932) journalist admiringly noted: 'His penetrating light blue eyes miss nothing. As I sat facing him across the desk I had an uncomfortable feeling that he was cognisant of my lack of a back collar-stud.'

84 Senior Garda officer, quoted in Walsh memoir, 163.

85 EOD, General Order No. 29, 13 Feb. 1924, quoted in *Garda Review*, Jan. 1930.

86 *New York Evening Post* (n.d.), quoted in *Garda Review*, May 1926; *The Western People* (n.d.), quoted in *Garda Review*, Aug. 1926.

87 O'Kelly, *Salute*, 21; Allen, *Garda Síochána*, 91.

88 Quoted in Walsh memoir, 162–3.

89 Author interview with Tim Pat Coogan, 13 Feb. 2001.

90 Quoted in Walsh memoir, 163.

91 O'Kelly, *Salute*, 21.

92 O'Duffy's Christmas card list for 1943, ODP.

93 See, for example, *New York Times*, 5 May 1923.

94 *Iris an Gharda*, 28 May 1923.

95 Press cutting, ODP.

96 *Iris an Gharda*, 4 June 1923.

97 These Clan na Gael orchestrated attacks (by mainly female republicans) received short shrift from the American press as is indicated by headlines such as 'WOMEN LEAD EGG ATTACK ON IRISH POLICE CHIEF' and 'EX-ENGLISH SOLDIER HIDES BEHIND SKIRTS OF IGNORANT VIXENS'.

98 *Garda Review*, Oct. 1926.

99 Press cutting, ODP.

100 *New York Evening Post* (n.d.), quoted in *Garda Review*, May 1926.

101 Brady, *Guardians*, 114; Allen, *Garda Síochána*, 251, n. 81.

102 Blythe memoir, 177–8, UCDA P24/1783; For Mulcahy's perspective, see UCDA P7D/69, P7D/78.

103 O'Higgins to executive council, 10 Jan. 1924, UCDA P22/323; Fitzpatrick, *Two Irelands*, 174.

104 O'Higgins memo to executive council, 7 Feb. 1924, UCDA P24/153; EOD to O'Higgins, 14 April 1923, UCDA P80/725; Allen, *Garda Síochána*, 61.

105 Blythe memoir, 180, UCDA P24/1783; Regan, *Counter-Revolution*, 173–5.

106 Blythe memoir, 181–3, UCDA P24/1783.

107 NAI DT S3306.

108 EOD to Mulcahy, 23 Dec. 1923, UCDA P7A/134.

109 See Lee, *Ireland*, 96–105; Regan, *Counter-Revolution*, 182–7.

110 O'Halpin, *Defending Ireland*, 51.

111 Press cuttings, NAI DT S 3694; UCDA P7/B/196.

112 O'Halpin, *Defending Ireland*, 51.

113 Richard Mulcahy, conversation with Peadar McMahon, 19 Aug. 1963, UCDA P7/D/3.

114 Lee, *Ireland*, 102–5; Regan, *Counter-Revolution*, 191–2.

115 Walsh memoir, 73. A document among O'Duffy's papers, dated 5 Aug. 1924, recording his transfer of IRB funds of £3,809 to Martin Conlon and Seán Ó Murthuile, suggests that O'Duffy was still the IRB's treasurer when appointed head of the army by O'Higgins.

116 EOD to executive council, 18 March 1924, NAI DT S3677; Maryann Valiulis, *Almost a Rebellion: The Irish Army Mutiny of 1924* (Cork, 1985), 69–71.

117 Valiulis, *Army Mutiny*, 71, 78–9.

118 Richard Mulcahy interview, UCDA P7/Cassette 6A.

119 O'Halpin, *Defending Ireland*, 50; Fitzpatrick, *Two Irelands*, 171; Lee, *Ireland*, 96.

120 Seán Ó Murthuile memoir, 242, UCDA P7a/209.

121 Richard Mulcahy, Notes on conversation with Peadar McMahon, 19 Aug. 1963, UCDA P7/D/3.

122 A well-informed *Irish Times* (20 April 1966) article by 'Black Raven' blamed Hogan rather than the army council for the raid.

123 NAI DT S3678a.

124 Richard Mulcahy interview, UCDA P7/Cassette 6A.

125 MacMahon to minister for defence, 20 March 1924, P7/b/196.

126 EOD to 'Dick' [Mulcahy], 6 Nov. 1924, UCDA P7b/56.

127 Mulcahy to 'My dear Eoin', 7 Nov. 1924; EOD to 'A cara dil', 15 Nov. 1924, UCDA P7b/56.

128 EOD to executive council, 7 April 1924, UCDA P24/221.

129 EOD to executive council, 12 June 1924, UCDA/P24/222.

130 EOD to executive council, 29 May 1924, UCDA P24/222; NAI DT S3442/A-B.

131 EOD to executive council, 7 April. 1924, UCDA P24/221.

132 EOD to executive council, 8 Sept. 1924, UCDA P24/222.

133 EOD to executive council, 8 Sept. 1924, UCDA P24/222.

134 EOD to executive council, 30 Sept. 1924, UCDA P24/222.

135 Press cutting, ODP.

136 EOD to executive council, 29 May 1924, UCDA P24/222.

137 EOD, 22 Sept. 1924, UCDA P24/222.

138 EOD, 8 Sept. 1924, UCDA P24/222.

139 EOD, 22 Sept. 1924, UCDA P24/222.

140 EOD, 5 July 1924, UCDA P24/222.

141 This information is contained in an intriguing report by an unidentified anti-treaty writer, who, to his surprise, was befriended by O'Duffy on a cruise to America in May 1923: 'I really can't help liking him. He had such a boyish, quick-moving personality, and is so direct. Although I do not agree with him in his reasons for voting for the Treaty in the Dail, I think his love of Ireland is unimpeachable... He also knew poor Charlie Daly very intimately, has slept with him many a night,

and did all he could to prevent his execution. It is curious that we both should have known and loved the same two men; of course it has made our friend's acquaintance more intimate than it otherwise could have been. He wants to give me a revolver, with a permit to carry it in Ireland. I almost dropped dead at that proposition, having so carefully disposed of mine before leaving... He hates Mrs. Skeff. and admires Mrs. McSwiney, and agrees that he would like to get a pot shot at the ones who are blackening her character. In fine, we agree on most of the personalities of both sides—that there are sincere, fine people on both sides, and that there are politicians on both sides too'. Report to IRA, n.d., ODP.

142 EOD to MacEoin, 16 Dec. 1925, UCDA P151/279.
143 EOD to executive council, 8 Sept. 1924, P24/222.
144 Lee, *Ireland*, 105.
145 EOD to executive council, 29 May, 12 June 1924, UCDA P24/222.
146 EOD to executive council, 8 Sept. 1924, UCDA P24/222. He subsequently received a gratuity of £505 for 'exceptional services' (NAI DJ H235/46).
147 NAI DT S3677.
148 O'Halpin, *Defending Ireland*, 85–93.

Chapter 6

1 *Black and White*, June 1943.
2 *Garda Review*, Aug. 1926, Jan. 1930; EOD, 'The Camera—A New Eye for the Police', *The Irish Sketch* (Christmas, 1925).
3 Richard English, ' "The Inborn Hate of Things English": Ernie O'Malley and the Irish Revolution 1916–1923', *Past and Present* (May 1996); *Iris an Gharda*, 7 Jan. 1924.
4 EOD to executive council, 30 Sept. 1924, UCDA P24/222. He advocated cross-border co-operation on policing, sending guards to RUC sports days and dances as early as 1925, and dismissing his critics as singers of the 'Frothblowers Anthem'.
5 *The Western People*, cited in *Garda Review*, Aug. 1926.
6 MacSwiney to Aiken, 22 April 1924, UCDA P104/1317.
7 Michael Farrell, *Irish Times*, 1 March 1983; Brady, *Guardians*, 164–5.
8 *Iris an Gharda*, 3 Sept., 13 Aug., 16 April, 13 Aug., 10 Sept. 1923.
9 *Iris an Gharda*, 8 Oct. 1923; EOD, 'Chapter III: The Garda: How he is Recruited', *Garda Review*, May 1929.
10 Press cutting, ODP; *Iris an Gharda*, 4 June 1923.
11 Press cutting, ODP; *Iris an Gharda*, 28 May 1923.
12 EOD, 'Reminiscences', *VI*, 10–11; McNiffe, *Garda Síochána*, 123–39.
13 NAI DT S5975a; UCDA P24/477.
14 EOD to secretary, department of justice, 2 Dec. 1929, UCDA P24/427.
15 EOD, 'Reminiscences', *VI*, 18; *Garda Review*, Sept. 1930.
16 McNiffe, *Garda Síochána*, 128; Comerford, *Ireland*, 146.
17 EOD, 'Reminiscences', *VI*, 5–6.

18 *Dáil Debate*, 4 Jan. 1922, 3, 224.

19 Comerford, *Ireland*, 141.

20 Ibid., 144.

21 EOD, 'Reminiscences', *VI*, 3–5; EOD, 'Chapter X: The Garda and the Language', *Garda Review*, Dec. 1929, 6.

22 Comerford, *Ireland*, 220, 144.

23 Walsh memoir, 138.

24 EOD, 'Chapter X: The Garda and the Language', *Garda Review*, Dec. 1929.

25 *Iris an Gharda*, 12 Nov. 1923.

26 Ibid., 15 Oct. 1923.

27 EOD, 'Chapter X: The Garda and the Language', *Garda Review*, Dec. 1929; Walsh memoir, 163. O'Duffy, like many cultural nationalists, invested *céilí* dancing 'with an aura of constraint and decorum that supposedly distinguished it from other, morally hazardous dances' (Comerford, *Ireland*, 194).

28 Quoted in Walsh memoir, 120. The reference to infant life presumably refers to the danger of unwanted pregnancy, leading to infanticide (which was frequently reported in the press during this period).

29 *Iris an Gharda*, 15 Oct. 1923; Fr O'Farrell to Archbishop Byrne, 30 Sept. 1929, Dublin Diocesan Archive, Garda Síochána folder.

30 Gregory Allen, *The Garda Síochána: Policing Independent Ireland 1922–82* (Dublin, 1999), 69; EOD, 'Chapter XIV Discipline', *Garda Review*, April 1930, 420.

31 *Garda Review*, May 1928.

32 In May 1928 the *Garda Review* accused his 'carping critics, within and without the establishment' of being 'inspired by ideals [no] higher than those which distinguish the primitive negro'.

33 Information kindly provided by Brian Fallon.

34 For criticism of the insufficiently nationalist outlook of O'Duffy and the NACA, see *An Phoblacht*, 25 Jan. 1930, 16 April 1932, 18, 25 Feb. 1933.

35 McNiffe, *Garda Síochána*, 136–8.

36 EOD, 'Chapter XIII: Chaplains', *Garda Review*, March 1930, 322.

37 McNiffe, *Garda Síochána*, 135.

38 EOD, 'Chapter XIII—Chaplains', *Garda Review*, March 1930.

39 Ibid.

40 EOD to secretary, department of justice, 28 April 1928, NAI DJ H235/257.

41 McNiffe, *Garda Síochána*, 138. O'Duffy's expenses were covered by his men.

42 *Garda Review*, Feb. 1929.

43 Walsh memoir, 86; *Garda Review*, Dec. 1928.

44 *Garda Review*, Dec. 1928. It was followed by another pilgrimage of 340 guards to Lourdes in 1930.

45 Comerford, *Ireland*, 116.

46 Walsh memoir, 103.

47 *Garda Review*, March 1928, 301.

48 NAI DJ H235/257.

49 EOD, 'Chapter XIII: Chaplains', *Garda Review*, March 1930, 322. Fitzpatrick, *Two Irelands*, 167.

50 Brady, *Guardians*, 165.

51 *Records of the Parish of the Holy Family, Aughrim Street* (Dublin, 1941), 22.

52 Mike Cronin, 'Projecting the Nation through Sport and Culture: Ireland, Aonach Tailteann and the Irish Free State, 1924–32', *Journal of Contemporary History* (2003), 395–412.

53 See press cuttings, ODP.

54 *Iris an Gharda*, 1 April 1923.

55 Mandle, *Gaelic Athletic Association*, 210.

56 EOD, 'Reminiscences', *V*, 7–8. See Marcus de Búrca, *The GAA*, 132–4 for a sympathetic interpretation of pro-ban sentiment as a response to an outbreak of anglomania in GAA and official circles.

57 The GAA charter (adopted in 1972) reminds Gaels that 'until complete nationhood is achieved, the Association must continue to maintain an all-embracing patriotic spirit. To that end its creed represents a simple choice between qualities which are native and characteristic of our land and qualities which are foreign and imported.' The notion that the choice was not simple, or that exclusivism might retard national unity, has only gained ground recently, as a consequence of broader social and political developments.

58 EOD, 'Reminiscences', *V*, 17.

59 Ibid., *V*, 2.

60 *Anglo-Celt*, 23 July 1923.

61 EOD, 'Reminiscences', *V*, 6.

62 Padraig Griffin, *The Politics of Irish Athletics, 1850–1990* (Ballinamore, 1990).

63 *An Phoblacht*, 16 April, 27 Aug. 1932; EOD, *The Struggle for Irish Athletic Unity*.

64 *Partition in Irish Athletics* (n.p., 1946); Padraig Griffin, *Irish Athletics*, 103–16.

65 EOD, *Ireland at an Olympiad* (n.p., n.d.), ODP. Except where specified, the following account is taken from this source.

66 Press cuttings, ODP.

67 Eric Hobsbawm, *Nations and Nationalism since 1780* (Cambridge, 1992 edn.), 143.

68 Sisson, *Pearse's Patriots*, 119.

69 Mazower, *Dark Continent*, 96.

70 J. A. Mangan, 'Global Fascism and the Male Body', in J. A. Mangan (ed.), *Superman Supreme: Fascist Body as Political Icon—Global Fascism* (London, 2000), 1–26.

71 Griffith, *Irish Athletics*, 110–14.

72 Press cuttings, ODP.

73 'Build a Stadium like this', ODP. See also *Irish Press*, 4 Feb. 1933.

74 Then, as more recently, critics objected that the money might better be devoted to local needs, and that only Croke Park could serve as the national stadium.

75 EOD, 'Reminiscences', *VII*, 1.

76 Ibid., *VII*, 7.

77 J. H. Whyte, *Church and State in Modern Ireland 1923–1979* (Dublin, 1984 edn.), 24–34.

78 See NAI DT S5998 for O'Duffy's testimony. In contrast to the civil servants in Justice, he revealed an egalitarian streak by urging that not only prostitutes but their male patrons be penalized.

79 Mark Finnane, 'The Carrigan Committee of 1930–31 and the Moral Condition of the Saorstát', *Irish Historical Studies* (Nov. 2001), 531.

80 Finnane, 'Carrigan Committee', 533–6.

81 Memo, 2 Dec. 1931, NAI DT S5998. Cosgrave instructed O'Duffy to omit references to sexual crime from the Garda Síochána annual report (NAI DJ H235/302).

82 Finnane, 'Carrigan Committee', 534. Submissions were offered by organizations, such as the Magdalen Asylum, which were not merely aware but complicit in the abuse of children.

83 Finnane, 'Carrigan Committee', 521.

84 Quoted in Diarmaid Ferriter, *The Transformation of Ireland 1900–2000* (London, 2004), 9.

85 *Garda Review*, June 1928.

86 Ibid., Dec. 1928.

87 Press cutting, *c.*1931, ODP. Unless specified, the following quotations on sport derive from the same album.

88 EOD, 2 Nov. 1928, NAI DT S4233.

89 Séamus Ó Ceallaigh, *Story of the GAA: A History and Book of Reference for Gaels* (Limerick, 1977), 27.

90 Mazower, *Dark Continent*, 78; Joanna Bourke, *Dismembering the Male: Men's Bodies, Britain and the Great War* (London, 1996), 171–9.

91 Mazower, *Dark Continent*, 97.

92 *Iris an Gharda*, 28 May 1923.

93 DeGroot, *Blighty*, 35. It should also be borne in mind that before universal running water many of the poor were dirty. Touring rural Ireland to meet party activists during the 1940s, Erskine Childers was struck by the low standards of hygiene among the foot soldiers of destiny. Cleanliness, then, was an indication of respectability. I am grateful to Patrick Maume for this point.

94 Sisson, *Pearse's Patriots*, 2–3.

95 Ibid., 9–17. Sisson notes that Moran's 'analysis of the debilitating effects of imperialism on the psychology of masculinity predates, by almost eighty years, the now established post-colonial critiques of Albert Memmi, Frantz Fanon and Ashis Nandy.'

96 Magnus Hirschfeld, quoted in Mazower, *Dark Continent*, 80.

97 *Evening Herald*, 27 July 1931.

98 Cited in Fitzpatrick, 'British Army Boxers', 209.

99 Novick, *Conceiving Revolution*, 136.

100 Bourke, *Dismembering the Male*, 176.

101 EOD, 'Reminiscences', *VII*, 5.

102 Tim Jeal, *Baden-Powell* (London, 1989), 101.

103 Ibid.

104 Points of similarity include intense maternal and distant paternal relationships, dislike of female company, obsession with masculinity, hostility to urban life, enjoyment of cross-dressing, uniforms, and pranks, strong moral-religious and patriotic impulses, militarism, anti-communism, establishment of sporting and youth movements, anxiety about moral and racial degeneracy, preoccupation with the moral and physical welfare of adolescent males, and homosexual tendencies. One of O'Duffy's models for the Blueshirts, interestingly, was Baden-Powell's movement.

105 Jeal, *Baden-Powell*, 90.

106 Tony Collins, 'Return to Manhood: The Cult of Masculinity and the British Union of Fascists', in Mangan (ed.), *Superman Supreme*, 151.

107 Jeal, *Baden-Powell*, 100–9.

108 'Dear Boy—The Story of Micheál Mac Liammóir' (RTE documentary, 1999).

109 Brian Fallon, *An Age of Innocence: Irish Culture 1930–1960* (Dublin, 1998), 142.

110 See, for example, 'The Odd Couple: Leader of Irish Blueshirts and the Gay Actor', *Sunday Times*, 17 Oct. 1999, 'No Gay Days for Monaghan', *Irish Times*, 23 Oct. 1999, and the correspondence in the *Irish Times* on 29 Oct., 2, 3, 4, 15 Nov. 1999.

111 *Sunday Times*, 17 Oct. 1999. Considerable unease about the trend for historical outing was expressed two weeks later when the *Sunday Times* (31 Oct. 1999) published unsubstantiated allegations that Archbishop John Charles McQuaid was a paedophile.

112 Jeffrey Dudgeon, *Roger Casement: The Black Diaries* (Belfast, 2002); W. J. McCormack, *Roger Casement in Death; or, Haunting the Free State* (Dublin, 2002).

113 *Irish Examiner*, 5 Nov. 1999.

114 Mike Cronin, *The Blueshirts and Irish Politics* (Dublin, 1997), 48.

115 Adrian Frazier, 'McGuinness and the Boys', *Dublin Review* (Summer 2002). Christopher Fitzsimon, who alluded to the relationship without naming O'Duffy in his biography of Mac Liammóir, believed that it was well known among certain circles (*Sunday Times*, 17 Oct. 1999).

116 Micheál Mac Liammóir, *All for Hecuba: An Irish Theatrical Autobiography* (London, 1946), 247.

117 *Sunday Independent*, 7 Dec. 1997.

118 Uinseann MacEoin, *The IRA in the Twilight Years* (Dublin, 1997), 202.

119 Information kindly provided by Anthony Cronin, 18 May 2000.

120 Uinseann MacEoin, letter to the author, 27 April 2000.

121 Information kindly provided by Anthony Cronin, 27 June 2000.

122 Denis Staunton, quoted in *The Love that Dare not Speak its Name* (broadcast on RTE, 2000).

123 'General O'Duffy: A Soft Touch for Hurlers', *An Fear Rua* (www.anfearrua.com), n.d.

124 Information kindly provided by Maurice Manning and Liam McNiffe.

125 *Love that Dare.*
126 O'Duffy's childhood—the distant paternal relationship, the intense devotion to his mother, and her traumatic early death—would also give the Freudian much to muse over. For a recent psychoanalytical biographical approach, see Seán Farrell Moran, *Patrick Pearse and the Politics of Redemption* (Washington, 1997).
127 Novick, *Conceiving Revolution*, 135–6.
128 Bourke, *Intimate History of Killing*, 141–6; Bourke, *Dismembering the Male*, 24, 128–70.
129 O'Duffy's letter of introduction for Dan Hogan, ODP.
130 *Garda Review*, Jan. 1930; press cutting (*c.*1932), ODP.
131 Sisson, *Pearse's Patriots*, 115–52; Moran, *Pearse*, 174–202.
132 Tim Jeal, *Baden-Powell*, 98–9.
133 Diary of Rosamund Jacob, 31 Jan. 1928, NLI MS 32, 582/53.
134 Eamon de Valera and Gerry Adams provide two interesting examples: see Patrick Murray, 'Obsessive Historian: Eamon de Valera and the policing of his reputation', *Proceedings of the Royal Irish Academy*, 101C/2 (Dublin, 2001), R. F. Foster, *The Irish Story: Telling Tales and Making it up in Ireland* (London, 2001), 174–86.
135 The opening page of his autobiography contains two trivial but deliberate lies, a rate sustained throughout the text. He changes such details as his family name, and the date of both his parents' deaths. He altered the spelling of his name often: Duffy, O'Duffy, Ua Dubhthaigh, O'Dubtaig. A short entry which he wrote for a biographical dictionary (contained among his papers) gave his date of birth as 30 Oct. 1892 (the date used by historians), added architect to his list of qualifications, and altered the dates and importance of his public positions.
136 Brady, *Guardians*, 165.

Chapter 7

1 EOD, quoted in Allen, *Garda Síochána*, 62.
2 Quoted in Regan, *Counter-Revolution*, 180.
3 Ibid.
4 Diary of Liam de Róiste, 27 Aug. 1924, quoted in Regan, *Counter-Revolution*, 182.
5 Edward O'Loughlin, quoted in Garvin, *1922*, 110.
6 Scheme of organization, May 1924, NAI DT S3442B; O'Halpin, *Defending Ireland*, 59.
7 O'Halpin, *Defending Ireland*, 11–15.
8 O'Higgins, memo to executive council, 7 Feb. 1924, UCDA P24/153.
9 Brady, *Guardians*, 135.
10 EOD, report for period ended 31 March 1930, to secretary, department of justice, UCDA P80/856.
11 Brady, *Guardians*, 135; NAI DT S4185.
12 Terence de Vere White, *Kevin O'Higgins* (Tralee, 1966 edn.), 231.

13 Blythe memoir, 176–7, UCDA P24/1783. For the Waterford controversy, see
   Roche to Boland, 15 May 1931, UCDA P24/422 and department of justice memo,
   1930, UCDA P80/853.
14 EOD to department of justice, 8 Dec. 1926, UCDA P7b/68.
15 De Vere White, *O'Higgins*, 231.
16 O'Higgins speech, 29 Oct. 1923, UCDA P7/B/366.
17 Brady, *Guardians*, 146.
18 EOD to O'Higgins, 6 Dec. 1926, NAI DT S5260.
19 Allen, *Garda Síochána*, 67–8.
20 EOD to O'Higgins, 6 Dec. 1926, NAI DT S5260.
21 *Iris an Gharda*, 11 Feb. 1924; *Irish Independent*, 12 Feb. 1924.
22 Cited in Allen, *Garda Síochána*, 62.
23 Draft speech written by Henry O'Friel for W. T. Cosgrave, executive council meeting, 15 Nov. 1926, NAI DT S2257.
24 Brady, 'Police and Government', ch. 7:6.
25 *Garda Review*, Aug. 1927.
26 Gerry Boland and Seán T. O'Kelly, for example, claimed that Dave Neligan had
   ordered the shooting (UCDA P80/851).
27 *Irish Times*, 11 July 1927.
28 See, for example, press cutting, 28 July 1923, ODP.
29 Maurice Moynihan, 22 Dec. 1948, NAI DT S5478b.
30 Allen, *Garda Síochána*, 70. This claim was disputed by the biographer of O'Higgins (De Vere White, *O'Higgins*, 231) who, nevertheless, stated elsewhere (*Business
   and Finance*, 7 July 1967) that O'Higgins was disillusioned with O'Duffy and disturbed by the condition of the Garda.
31 EOD to secretary, department of justice, 25 July 1927, ODP.
32 NAI DT S5478b.
33 NAI DT S5486.
34 *Garda Review*, March 1928.
35 Alvin Jackson, *Ireland, 1798–1998* (Oxford, 1999), 276.
36 Fearghal McGarry, *Frank Ryan* (Dundalk, 2002), 20.
37 EOD, report for quarter ending 30 June 1929, to secretary, department of justice,
   UCDA P24/477.
38 *Garda Review*, August 1928; Brian Hanley, *The IRA, 1926–1936* (Dublin, 2002), 46.
39 EOD, report for period ending 31 March 1929, to secretary, department of justice,
   UCDA P80/856.
40 EOD, report for period ending 31 March 1929, to secretary, department of justice,
   UCDA P80/856.
41 EOD, report for period ending 31 March 1929, to secretary, department of justice,
   UCDA P80/856.
42 Geary spent the next seventy years protesting his innocence, finally winning an
   apology from the state in 1999.

43 *An Phoblacht*, 6 July, 3 Aug. 1929.
44 EOD to secretary, department of justice, 8 April 1929, UCDA P80/851.
45 EOD, report for period ending 31 March 1929, to secretary, department of justice, UCDA P80/856.
46 EOD, report for period ending 31 Dec. 1929, UCDA P80/856. See NAI DT S5838 for the Juries Protection act, 1929. John White had been the foreman of the jury in the trial of Con 'the One Eyed Gunner' Healy. Albert Armstrong, another Protestant, had given evidence against republicans who removed a Union Jack from the Royal Insurance Company offices in Dublin.
47 EOD, report for period ending 31 March 1929, UCDA P80/856.
48 EOD, reports for period ending 31 Dec. 1929, 31 May 1931, UCDA P80/856.
49 EOD, report for period ending 31 March 1929, UCDA P80/856; NAI DT S6017.
50 EOD, report for period ending 31 March 1930, UCDA P80/856. See also P24/167.
51 Department of justice memo, April 1930, UCDA P24/167.
52 EOD, report for period ending 31 March 1930, UCDA P80/856; EOD, report for period ending 30 June 1929, UCDA P24/477.
53 EOD, report for period ending 31 Dec. 1930, UCDA P80/856.
54 EOD, report for period ending 5 July 1929, UCDA P24/477.
55 EOD to secretary, department of justice, 27 July 1931, UCDA P80/857.
56 EOD, report for period ending 31 May 1931, UCDA P80/856.
57 Hanley, *The IRA*, 124; O'Halpin, *Defending Ireland*, 78–9.
58 EOD to secretary, department of justice, 27 July 1931, UCDA P80/857.
59 'Alliance between Irish Republican Army and Communists', NAI DT S5864B; 'Memo on Revolutionary Organisations', 4 April 1930, NAI DT S5864A; misc. police reports, ODP.
60 Richard English, *Radicals and the Republic: Socialist Republicanism in the Irish Free State 1925–1937* (Oxford, 1994); Henry Patterson, *The Politics of Illusion: A Political History of the IRA* (London, 1997).
61 Patrick Murray, *Oracles of God: The Roman Catholic Church and Irish Politics, 1922–37* (Dublin, 2000), 317–33; Regan, *Counter-Revolution*, 290.
62 FitzGerald-Kenney to Byrne, 17 June 1929, Dublin Diocesan Archives, Byrne papers, department of justice folder.
63 Cosgrave to MacRory, 13 Aug. 1931, NAI DT SS5864B.
64 NAI DT S5864.
65 EOD to minister for justice, 7 Oct. 1931, NAI DJ 8/306.
66 Regan, *Irish Counter-Revolution*, 295.
67 EOD to minister for justice, 7 Oct. 1931, NAI DJ 8/306.
68 Secretary, minister for justice to secretary, executive council, 9 June 1931; EOD to secretary, department of justice, 10 Aug. 1931, NAI DT S2207A.
69 'Notes for the Information of the Minister for Justice', 19 Oct. 1931; EOD, Memo re Constitution Act 1931, 20 Oct. 1931, Memo, 23 Oct. 1931, NAI DT S2449.
70 Hanley, *The IRA*, 179–80.

71 Allen, *Garda Síochána*, 90–4; McNiffe, *Garda Síochána*, 41.

72 NAI DT S6093; EOD, 'Chapter XVIII: Reductions in Strength of the Garda', *Garda Review*, Sept. 1930.

73 EOD, 'Chapter I: Early Days', *Garda Review*, March 1929.

74 Editorial, *Garda Review*, Jan. 1930.

75 Brady, *Guardians*, 159–60.

76 Allen, *Garda Síochána*, 105; Editorials, *Garda Review*, Jan. 1928, May 1929.

77 EOD to secretary, department of justice, 18 Oct. 1929, NAI DJ H235/166/1.

78 EOD to minister for justice, 28 Jan. 1930, NAI DJ H235/166/2; EOD to minister for justice, 5 May 1931, NAI DJ H235/166/4; EOD to secretary, department of justice, 19 Oct. 1929, NAI DJ H235/166/1.

79 EOD to MacEoin, 17 Sept. 1940, UCDA P151/177.

80 Fitzpatrick, *Two Irelands*, 173; O'Halpin, *Defending Ireland*, 101.

81 Regan, *Counter-Revolution*, 297–9.

82 EOD to Blythe, 22 Jan. 1932, UCDA P24/488.

83 Ernest Blythe, letter to editor, *Irish Times*, 2 Nov. 1970. The government decided to appoint him consul to the United States, a convivial post for which he would have been well suited.

84 Quoted in *Garda Review*, June 1930.

85 Ibid.

86 Report of meeting, 1 Nov. 1929, department of justice, 'Calendar of Events', UCDA P67/534.

87 O'Halpin, *Defending Ireland*, 80.

88 Richard Mulcahy, Note on conversation on 19 August 1963 with Lieut. General Peadar McMahon, UCDA P7/D/3.

89 Ibid.

90 Brady, *Guardians*, 167–8.

91 Ibid., 169.

92 O'Halpin, *Defending Ireland*, 80.

93 *The Star*, quoted in *An Phoblacht*, 5 April 1930.

94 *The Star*, quoted in *An Phoblacht*, 12 April 1930. See also *An Phoblacht*, 9 April 1932; Fitzpatrick, *Two Irelands*, 175–6.

95 Burke speech, 22 Nov. 1931, quoted in *An Phoblacht*, 5 Dec. 1931.

96 Regan, *Counter-Revolution*, 293; For the rumours of a coup, see also M. J. MacManus, *Eamon de Valera* (Dublin, 1962 edn.), 281–2; *Irish Press*, 26 Feb. 1932.

97 *An Phoblacht*, 7 May 1932; O'Halpin, *Defending Ireland*, 106–7.

98 O'Halpin, *Defending Ireland*, 80, 103–4.

99 Statement by unnamed Garda officer from Howth barracks to minister, 11 March 1932, extract from cabinet minutes, 22 March 1932, NAI DT S2204.

100 Hogan left for the United States under a cloud, financial or sexual. He was killed in a bar brawl there in the early 1940s.

101 O'Halpin, *Defending Ireland*, 80; Regan, *Counter-Revolution*, 294–5.

102 Brady, *Guardians*, 170–1; Regan, *Counter-Revolution*, 327.

103 O'Halpin, *Defending Ireland*, 108.

104 Brady, *Guardians*, 163–4.

105 Geoghegan, memo to executive council, 18 April 1932, NAI DT S2207A.

106 M. Moynihan, memo, 17 Aug. 1932, NAI DT S2206.

107 EOD to Geoghegan, 29 June 1932, NAI DT S2206.

108 Geoghegan, memo to executive council, 29 June 1932, NAI DT S2206.

109 Geoghegan to executive council, 31 May 1932, NAI DT S6292A.

110 Kilrush Enquiry report, 15 Sept. 1932, NAI DJ 8/376. The fact that both men were invited to apply for reinstatement by a Fianna Fáil government in 1944 suggests they were scapegoats for a wider problem (NAI DT S6292B).

111 Lynch to Geoghegan, 22 Sept. 1932, NAI DT S2206.

112 Geoghegan to executive council, 28 Sept. 1932, NAI DT S2206.

113 EOD to secretary, department of justice, 18 Nov. 1932; Extract from cabinet minutes, 16 Dec. 1932, NAI DT S2874.

114 EOD to secretary, department of justice, 29 Dec. 1932, NAI DT S2874.

115 Brady, *Guardians*, 176.

116 EOD to Geoghegan, 1 Feb. 1933, quoted in Walsh memoir, 113.

117 NAI DJ 8/712.

118 Brady, *Guardians*, 182, 177.

119 O'Halpin, *Defending Ireland*, 113.

120 Conor A. Maguire, attorney-general, to secretary, department of justice, 12 June 1933, NAI DJ 8/712.

121 Walsh memoir, 115.

122 Ibid., 116.

123 Brady, *Guardians*, 177.

124 Robert Brennan, *Allegiance* (Dublin, 1958), 130; Brady, *Guardians*, 180.

125 Walsh memoir, 122.

126 Denis O'Kelly, *Salute to the Gardai*, 21.

127 Quoted in Walsh memoir, 162, 164.

Chapter 8

1 EOD, 14 Aug. 1933, quoted in Cronin, *Blueshirts*, 51.

2 *United Irishman*, 4, 11 March 1933.

3 *Irish Times*, 16 March 1933.

4 *Connacht Tribune*, 25 Feb. 1933.

5 *Southern Star*, 25 Feb. 1933; Patrick Maume, *D. P. Moran* (Dundalk, 1995), 50.

6 *Dáil Debates*, 46, 765–8.

7 *Cork Examiner*, 6 March 1933.

8 *Dáil Debates*, 46, 785.

9 *Anglo-Celt*, 24 June 1933.

10 *Dáil Debates*, 46, 802–4.

11 Ibid., 46, 789–91.

12 *United Irishman*, 25 March 1933.

13 *Dáil Debates*, 46, 758–814.

14 Maurice Manning, *The Blueshirts* (Dublin, 1987 edn.), 69.

15 Walsh memoir, 125.

16 Regan, *Counter-Revolution*, 293.

17 O'Halpin, *Defending Ireland*, 107–12.

18 *United Irishman*, 29 Oct. 1932.

19 Ibid., 13 Aug., 24 Dec., 9 July 1932, 22 July 1933, 10 Dec. 1932.

20 *United Irishman*, 22 July 1933.

21 Terence Dooley, *The Land for the People: The Land Question in Independent Ireland* (Dublin, 2004), 206–7.

22 *United Irishman*, 8 April 1933.

23 Ibid., 27 Aug. 1932.

24 Ibid., 20 Aug. 1932.

25 Ibid., 4 Feb. 1933.

26 Ibid., 27 May 1933.

27 Ibid., 1 July 1933; see also 20 Aug., 3 Sept. 1932.

28 Manning, *Blueshirts*, 41.

29 *United Irishman*, 15 Oct. 1932.

30 Ibid., 20 May 1933.

31 Ibid., 11, 18 Feb. 1933.

32 Ibid., 25, Feb. 1933.

33 Ibid., 21 Oct. 1933.

34 Cronin, *Blueshirts*, 94–7.

35 Unsigned memo, n.d., UCDA P24/690; M. G. Quinn, 'NEW TYPE OF STATE NEEDED', in *United Irishman*, 15 April 1933. See also *The Diast (An Occasional Bulletin)* No. 1, May 1933, UCDA P24/691. For Blythe's numerous aliases, see *The Blueshirt*, 26 Jan. 1935.

36 *United Irishman*, 29 April, 13 May, 20 May, 17 June 1933.

37 *United Irishman*, 10 June 1933.

38 Regan, *Counter-Revolution*, 368; *An Phoblacht*, 28 Oct. 1933.

39 Dermot Keogh, *Ireland and Europe 1919–48* (Dublin, 1988), 47–8.

40 *United Ireland*, 24 March 1934.

41 Mazower, *Dark Continent*, 28–31.

42 Brian Girvin, 'Nationalism, Catholicism and Democracy: Hogan's Intellectual Evolution', in Donnchadh Ó Corráin (ed.), *James Hogan* (Dublin, 2001), 154–9.

43 Regan, *Counter-Revolution*, 91.

44 Cronin, *Blueshirts*, 99.

45 *United Irishman*, 10 Sept. 1932.

46 'Notes on Bolshevism', UCDA P80/1346; FitzGerald to Maritain, n.d., UCDA P80/1280.

47 'Review of Fr Cahill, *The Framework of a Christian State*', UCDA P80/1326; FitzGerald to Coyne, 17 Feb. 1937, UCDA P80/1286.

48 UCDA P80/1212; Cronin, *Blueshirts*, 103.

49 Mabel FitzGerald to Desmond FitzGerald, 14 Oct. 1938, UCDA P80/1416/15; Regan, *Counter-Revolution*, 280–2; Cronin, *Blueshirts*, 97–9.

50 Regan, *Counter-Revolution*, 293–4, 302–3.

51 Girvin, 'Nationalism', 144; O'Halpin, *Defending Ireland*, 112.

52 *United Irishman*, 17 June 1933.

53 Walsh memoir, 126; *The Blueshirt*, 6 Oct. 1934; Manning, *Blueshirts*, 70.

54 Walsh memoir, 126.

55 EOD, 19 Feb. 1935, NAI DJ 8/296.

56 *The Blueshirt*, 6 Oct. 1934.

57 *Irish Independent*, 16 July 1933.

58 Manning, *Blueshirts*, 73.

59 UCDA P24/659.

60 *United Ireland*, 29 July 1933.

61 *The Blueshirt*, 12 Aug. 1933.

62 Ibid.

63 Walsh memoir, 134.

64 Ibid., 132–4.

65 Regan, *Counter-Revolution*, 281.

66 Manning, *Blueshirts*, 244.

67 Cronin, *Blueshirts*, 62–8.

68 Manning, *Blueshirts*, 243; Paul Bew, Ellen Hazelkorn, and Henry Patterson, *The Dynamics of Irish Politics* (London, 1989), 62, 67; Cronin, *Blueshirts*, 49, 51.

69 O'Halpin, *Defending Ireland*, 118.

70 Elizabeth Cullingford, *Yeats, Ireland and Fascism* (London, 1981), 205; R. F. Foster, *W. B. Yeats–A Life: II–The Arch-Poet* (Oxford, 2003), 474.

71 Quoted in Manning, *Blueshirts*, 123.

72 Manning, *Blueshirts*, 229–30; see, for example, Juan Linz, 'Some Notes Towards a Comparative Study of Fascism', in Walter Laquer (ed.), *Fascism: A Readers Guide* (London, 1976), 7–8.

73 Robert O. Paxton, *The Anatomy of Fascism* (London, 2004), 218.

74 For another example of how a non-rational ideology could meet the specific cultural and political requirements of a period in history, as well as the deep-seated psychological needs of a particular individual arising out of emotional conflict, see Moran, *Pearse*, 176–7, 182.

75 Roger Griffin, *The Nature of Fascism* (London, 1993), 196.

76 Cronin, *Blueshirts*, 50–1.

77 Draft of suggestions ACA, n.d., UCDA P24/654.

78 *The Blueshirt*, 12 Aug. 1933.

79 Ibid., 14 Oct. 1933.

80 Ibid., 12 Aug. 1933.

81 Manning, *Blueshirts*, 78.

82 *The Blueshirt*, 19 Aug. 1933.

83 Regan, *Counter-Revolution*, 329–30; Cronin, *Blueshirts*, 118.

84 *Boston Sunday Post*, n.d., ODP; *Hjemmet*, n.d., ODP.

85 Manning, *Blueshirts*, 79.

86 Manning, *Blueshirts*, 81; Regan, *Counter-Revolution*, 337.

87 O'Halpin, *Defending Ireland*, 116–17; Brady, *Guardians*, 192–9.

88 *The Blueshirt*, 19 Aug. 1933.

89 Manning, *Blueshirts*, 83.

90 Ibid., 84.

91 Ibid., 85.

92 Secret memo, 25 Nov. 1935, NAI DJ 8/364; see also Terry de Valera, *A Memoir* (Dublin, 2004), 58–9. An elderly de Valera told one politician that, along with his 1937 constitution, he regarded his decision to ban the march as his greatest achievement (*Irish Times*, 5 March 2001).

93 *Cork Examiner*, 9 Aug. 1933.

94 *Irish Independent*, 16 Aug. 1933; EOD to Bishop O'Doherty, 16 Aug. 133, Galway Diocesan Archive. My thanks to Patrick Murray for this reference.

95 *The Blueshirt*, 19 Aug. 1933.

96 Manning, *Blueshirts*, 89.

97 Richard Mulcahy interview, UCDA P7/Cassette 6A; EOD speech, 19 Feb. 1935, NAI DJ 8/296.

98 EOD, 18 Aug. 1934, *United Ireland*, 25 Aug. 1934.

99 Garda report, 3 Sept. 1933, NAI DJ 8/722.

100 Walsh memoir, 127.

101 Ibid.

102 Alessandro Mariani to ministry of foreign affairs, 4 Sept. 1933, Archivio Storico Diplomatico del Ministero degli Affari Esteri (ASMAE), serie affari politici, B.2, Irlanda 1933, (1) rapporti politici.

103 *United Ireland*, 18 Aug. 1934.

104 Regan, *Counter-Revolution*, 343; Manning, *Blueshirts*, 92–7; Cronin, *Blueshirts*, 52.

105 Alessandro Mariani to ministry of foreign affairs, 25 Sept. 1933, ASMAE, serie affari politici, B.2, Irlanda 1933, (1) rapporti politici.

106 Maurice Manning, *James Dillon: A Biography* (Dublin, 1999), 79.

107 Robert Fisk, *In Time of War: Ireland, Ulster and the Price of Neutrality, 1939–1945* (Dublin, 1983), 426.

108 Richard Mulcahy interview, UCDA P7/Cassette 6A.

109 Blythe, 'Blueshirt memories', n.d., UCDA P24/1942.

110 Memo to Cosgrave, 23 May 1933, UCDA P7b/96.

111 Shaw Desmond, press cutting, ODP; *Western Mail*, 8 Nov. 1933.

112 Regan, *Counter-Revolution*, 339.

113 Manning, *Blueshirts*, 96.

114 Regan, *Counter-Revolution*, 343; Manning, *Blueshirts*, 96.

115 Manning, *Blueshirts*, 97; Manning, *Dillon*, 78–81.

116 Manning, *Blueshirts*, 100.

117 *Anglo-Celt*, 21 Oct. 1933.

118 *United Ireland*, 21 Oct. 1933.

119 EOD speech, 31 May 1934, NAI DJ 8/154.

120 For the origins of the YIA, see misc. documents, UCDA P24/664–7.

121 *United Ireland*, 30 Sept., 28 Oct., 18 Nov. 1933.

122 Ibid., 18 Nov. 1933.

123 Ibid., 26 May 1934.

124 Ibid., 16 Dec. 1933.

125 Ibid., 24 March 1934.

126 Ibid., 25 Aug. 1934.

127 Ibid., 15 Sept. 1934.

128 Ibid., 3 Feb. 1934.

129 Ibid., 23 Dec. 1933.

130 Ibid., 31 March 1934.

131 Statement announcing merger of National Guard with Fine Gael, UCDA P24/663; *Anglo-Celt*, 25 Nov. 1933.

132 Manning, *Blueshirts*, 110.

133 Garda report, 11 Nov. 1934, NAI DJ 8/161. See also NAI DJ 8/39.

134 *United Ireland*, 7 Oct. 1933; Cronin, *Blueshirts*, 179–80.

135 *The Western Mail*, 8 Nov. 1933.

136 Tomo Costelloe, quoted in MacEoin, *IRA in the Twilight Years*, 472. The IRA in Tralee had intended to assassinate O'Duffy (Manning, *Dillon*, 89).

137 MacEoin, *IRA in the Twilight Years*, 257. See also Manning, *Blueshirts*, 107–8.

138 Manning, *Blueshirts*, 108.

139 Ibid., 110.

140 NAI DJ 8/734, 735.

141 NAI DJ 8/261. See also NAI DJ 8/419.

142 *Irish Times*, 9 Dec. 1933.

143 The following references to the Donegal meetings are taken from press and police reports in NAI DJ 8/732.

144 *Derry Journal*, 11 Dec. 1933; *Anglo-Celt*, 16 Dec. 1933.

145 Garda report, 9 Dec. 1933, NAI DJ 8/732.

146 *Derry Journal*, 11 Dec. 1933.

147 Hogan to Tierney, n.d. [*c.* 8–9 Dec. 1933], quoted in Regan, *Counter-Revolution*, 346.

148 Hogan to Tierney, n.d. [*c.* 8–9 Dec. 1933], quoted in Regan, *Counter-Revolution*, 345.

149 *United Ireland*, 16 Dec. 1933.

150 *Anglo-Celt*, 13 Jan. 1933.

151 Walsh memoir, 129.

152 Manning, *Blueshirts*, 115–16.

153 A. A. Dudley to Leeper, 22 Dec. 1933, PRO FO 395/506.

154 Manning, *Blueshirts*, 116–17; *Irish Press*, 17 July 1934.

155 Secret memo, 25 Nov. 1935, NAI DJ 8/364.

156 NAI DJ 8/419.

157 NAI DJ 8/444.

158 *Anglo-Celt*, 13 Jan. 1933.

159 NAI DJ 8/419.

160 Manning, *Blueshirts*, 118–19.

161 *Anglo-Celt*, 25 Nov. 1933.

162 *The Blueshirt*, 6 Oct. 1934.

163 Manning, *Blueshirts*, 120.

164 Regan, *Counter-Revolution*, 350.

165 *United Ireland*, 17 Feb., 24 Feb, 1934.

166 *The Leader*, 5 Aug. 1933.

167 *DD*, 24 Feb. 1934. Nouky Kahn, a Jewish non-combatant, was murdered by treatyite forces during the Irish Civil War.

168 *Dáil Debates*, 50, 2237.

Chapter 9

1 *Cork Examiner*, 3 Sept. 1934.

2 The theme of nationalism receives little analysis in Cronin's study, while Manning (*Blueshirts*, 234) suggests that the 'nationalism of the Blueshirts was moderate'.

3 Regan, *Counter-Revolution*.

4 *Anglo-Celt*, 21 Oct. 1933.

5 *Irish Press*, 18 June 1934; *United Ireland*, 10 March 1934.

6 Anne Dolan, *Commemorating the Irish Civil War: History and Memory, 1923–2000* (Cambridge, 2003), 188–93.

7 EOD, 26 Aug. 1934, quoted in NAI DJ 8/276.

8 *United Ireland*, 17 June 1933.

9 *The Nation*, 3 Aug. 1935.

10 Ibid.

11 Quoted in Bew *et al.*, *Dynamics*, 50.

12 *Anglo-Celt*, 25 Nov. 1933.

13 EOD, 9 Sept. 1934, UCDA P7b/93.

14 *United Ireland*, 6 Jan. 1934.

15 EOD, *An Outline of the Political, Social and Economic Policy of Fine Gael* (Dublin, 1934), 23; Cronin, *Blueshirts*, 84–5.

16 Dolan, *Civil War*, 173.

17 Bew *et al.*, *Dynamics*, 53; Hanley, *The IRA*, 84–90.

18 *DD*, 24 Feb. 1934.

19 *Irish Press*, 29 May 1934.

20 Walsh memoir, 139.

21 Ibid., 138.

22 Richard Thurlow, *Fascism in Britain: A History 1918–85* (Oxford, 1987), 13.

23 See Garvin (*Nationalist Revolutionaries*, 122–4) for comparisons between separatist extremism and fascism.

24 Seán Farrell Moran (*Pearse*, 176–7, 182) and others have suggested that Pearse's revolt against reason, rejection of modernity, and embracing of violence was a manifestation of a broader trend in European thought and experiences in this period.

25 *United Ireland*, 21 April 1934.

26 *Irish Press*, 5 July 1934.

27 See, in response, T. Ryle Dwyer, *Tans, Terror and Troubles* (Cork, 1999).

28 For his recollections, see Brendan Malin, 'When the General went Marching', *Irish Press*, 5 Sept. 1981. My thanks to Michael MacEvilly for this reference.

29 *United Ireland*, 23 June 1934.

30 Ibid., 17 Feb. 1934.

31 *Anglo-Celt*, 28 Oct. 1933.

32 *The Blueshirt*, 15 June 1935.

33 *Irish Press*, 9 July 1934.

34 *Cork Examiner*, 28 Aug. 1934.

35 *The Blueshirt*, 15 June 1935.

36 *Irish Times*, 3 Dec. 1934.

37 *United Ireland*, 18 Oct. 1934.

38 *The Blueshirt*, 15 June 1935.

39 *Irish Press*, 2 Jan. 1935.

40 *The Blueshirt*, 15 June 1935.

41 *Irish Press*, 14 May 1934.

42 Ibid., 5 July 1934.

43 Bew *et al.*, *Dynamics*, 66.

44 *Irish Times*, 9 July 1934.

45 *Irish Press*, 11 July 1934.

46 EOD, 9 Sept. 1934, UCDA P7b/93.

47 *Anglo-Celt*, 13 Jan. 1934.

48 *Derry Journal*, 11 Dec. 1933.

49 Bew *et al.*, *Dynamics*, 62.

50 *United Ireland*, 17 Feb. 1934.

51 Fearghal McGarry, *Irish Politics and the Spanish Civil War* (Cork, 1999), 33.

52 Bew *et al.*, *Dynamics*, 66.

53 Ibid., 52.

54   Quoted in Bew *et al.*, *Dynamics*, 59.

55   Ibid., 67.

56   EOD speech, 9 Sept. 1934, UCDA P7b/93.

57   Regan, *Counter-Revolution*, 139, 261.

58   Ibid., 207, 249.

59   Kevin Passmore, *Fascism: A Very Short Introduction* (Oxford, 2002), 151.

60   Passmore, *Fascism*, 27–8; 77–82.

61   Regan, *Counter-Revolution*, 382.

62   Ibid., 434.

63   Griffin, *Nature of Fascism*, 32–7; Passmore, *Fascism*, 20–6.

64   Jackson, *Ireland*, 300.

65   Quoted in McGarry, *Frank Ryan*, 35.

66   *United Ireland*, 17 Feb. 1934; see also Cronin, *Blueshirts*, 48–9.

67   *United Ireland*, 8 Sept. 1934. The sombre atmosphere was punctured by shouts of 'Fuck Collins' from youths on the opposite hill. Blueshirts gave chase, and a mêlée ensued (NAI DJ 8/38).

68   Andrew Forrest, *Worse Could Have Happened* (Dublin, 1999), 195.

69   Patrick Lindsay, *Memories* (Dublin, 1993), 54.

70   McGarry, *Frank Ryan*, 36–7.

71   *United Ireland*, 24 Feb. 1934.

72   Ibid., 2 Dec. 1933.

73   Ibid., 10 March 1934, 19 May 1934.

74   Ibid., 3 March 1934; Foster, *Yeats*, 477–9.

75   *United Ireland*, 17 March 1934.

76   Ibid., 6 Jan. 1934. Cohalan was one of three outspokenly anti-de Valera bishops: the others were Bishop Morrisroe of Achonry and Bishop Fogarty of Killaloe.

77   *Anglo-Celt*, 6 Jan. 1933.

78   *United Ireland*, 2 June 1934; see also 27 Jan., 17 June 1934.

79   Ibid., 3 March 1934.

80   Ibid., 13 Jan., 17 March 1934.

81   *Irish Independent*, 3 June 1934.

82   *United Ireland*, 7 July 1934.

83   Cronin, *Blueshirts*, 56.

84   Lee, *Ireland*, 183.

85   Cronin, *Blueshirts*, 48. See also Dolan, *Civil War*, 172; Regan, *Counter-Revolution*, 342.

86   *United Ireland*, 29 July 1933.

87   Ibid., 7 April 1934.

88   Ibid., 4 Aug. 1934.

89   Ibid., 17 March 1934.

90   *The Round Table*, March 1935, quoted in Manning, *Blueshirts*, 152.

91   Lyons, *Ireland Since the Famine*, 530.

92   Cronin, *Blueshirts*, 47.

93 *United Ireland*, 17 Feb. 1934.

94 Ibid., 28 April 1934.

95 Resolutions passed at Blueshirt Congress, 18–19 Aug. 1934, UCDA P7b/92.

96 Cronin, *Blueshirts*, 115.

97 Forrest, *Worse*, 138; Cronin, *Blueshirts*, 184–7.

98 Many met future spouses at Blueshirt dances where, one member nostalgically recalled, they could meet the sort of girls who 'were not brought up on free beef' (Cronin, *Blueshirts*, 120, 183).

99 *Anglo-Celt*, 21 Oct. 1933.

100 *United Ireland*, 8 Sept. 1934.

101 Ibid., 7 Sept. 1934.

102 NAI DJ 8/257.

103 *United Ireland*, 9 June 1934.

104 Ibid., 3 March 1934; see also Cronin, *Blueshirts*, 121–2.

105 *United Ireland*, 2 June 1934.

106 NAI DJ 8/258.

107 Cronin, *Blueshirts*, 169–72, 185–7.

108 *United Ireland*, 30 June 1934.

109 Cronin, *Blueshirts*, 184.

110 Fitzpatrick, *Two Irelands*, 190; *United Ireland*, 25 Aug. 1934.

111 *United Ireland*, 17 March 1934.

112 Ibid., 19 May 1934.

113 J. A. Mangan, 'Global Fascism'.

114 For the traditional ideal, see J. A. Mangan and James Walvin (eds), *Manliness and Morality: Middle Class Masculinity in Britain and America, 1890–1940* (Manchester, 1987), 2–4.

115 Collins, 'Return to Manhood', 159.

116 Ibid., 145.

117 *Cork Examiner*, 3 Aug. 1934; Manning, *Dillon*, 72.

118 *United Irishman*, 12, 26 Nov. 1932.

119 *United Ireland*, 10 March 1934.

120 See McGarry, *Irish Politics*, 153–5; Regan, *Counter-Revolution*, 333–6.

121 *United Ireland*, 10 Feb. 1934.

122 UCDA P24/627.

123 Denis Quish, quoted in NAI DJ 8/276.

124 *Irish Press*, 9 May 1934.

125 *United Irishman*, 15 July 1933.

126 *United Ireland*, 4 Aug. 1934, 2 June 1934.

127 *Irish Independent*, 11 May 1934.

128 Manus O'Riordan, 'Anti-Semitism in Irish Politics', *Irish-Jewish Year Book* (1984/85), 23.

129 *Irish Press*, 18 Dec. 1934; Michael Ledeen, *Universal Fascism: The Theory and Practice of the Fascist International, 1928–1936* (New York, 1972), 118–22.

130 *Irish Press*, 18 Dec. 1934; *The Blueshirt*, 22 Dec. 1934.

131 *The Nation*, 29 June 1935.

132 Ibid., 27 July 1935.

133 Ibid., July 1936.

134 R. J. B. Bosworth, *Mussolini* (London, 2002), 133, 147–8.

135 Mary Banta, 'The Red Scare in the Irish Free State, 1925–37', MA thesis (UCD, 1982), 153.

136 Banta, 'Red Scare', 135–8.

137 *Anglo-Celt*, 28 Oct. 1933. (This was a reference to the Communist Party branch—composed of Castlecomer miners—led by Nicholas Boran.) Banta, *Red Scare*, 162.

138 *Anglo-Celt*, 25 Nov. 1933.

139 *DD*, 17 Feb. 1934.

140 Regan, *Counter-Revolution*, 349.

141 *Irish Independent*, 25 June 1934.

142 *Anglo-Celt*, 20 May, 13 July, 1933; NAI D/J 8/337.

143 UCDA P24/628.

144 Banta, 'Red Scare', 169–70.

145 Cronin, *Blueshirts*, 133.

146 Banta, 'Red Scare', 242; Regan, *Counter-Revolution*, 357–9.

147 *Irish Independent*, 11 May 1934.

148 Regan, *Counter-Revolution*, 352–3; Cronin, *Blueshirts*, 96–7.

149 UCDA P24/680.

150 Regan, *Counter-Revolution*, 353.

151 *Irish Press*, 5 July 1934.

152 Quoted in Keogh, *Ireland and Europe*, 45. The Italian minister in Dublin, Alessandro Mariani, had a greater awareness of O'Duffy's limitations.

153 Keogh, *Ireland and Europe*, 44–5.

154 *Irish Press*, 22 March 1934.

155 Quoted in Fisk, *In Time of War*, 428.

156 Government memo, NAI DT S6433.

157 *Irish Independent*, *Irish Times*, 27 Nov. 1934.

158 MacDermot to EOD, 9 July 1934; EOD to MacDermot, 13 July 1934, NAI 1065/3/1–2; *Irish Times*, 3 Dec. 1934.

159 Quoted in Fisk, *In Time of* War, 427.

160 *United Ireland*, 2 June, 12 May, 20 Jan., 1934.

161 Ibid., 25 Aug. 1934.

162 Garda report, 31 May 1934, NAI DJ 8/154.

163 *Anglo-Celt*, 21 Oct. 1933.

164 *Irish Times*, 18 June 1934.

165 *Irish Press*, 25 June 1934.

166 Police and press reports, NAI DJ 8/125.

167 Cronin, *Blueshirts*, 54.

168 *United Ireland*, 2 June 1934.

169 *United Irishman*, 10 June 1933.

170 Dillon to MacDermot, 1 Oct. 1934, NAI 1065/2/5; Cronin, *Blueshirts*, 55.

171 Special Branch report, 6 Aug. 1934, NAI DJ 8/96.

172 *United Ireland*, 14 July 1934.

173 NAI DJ 8/364.

174 NAI DJ 8/444.

175 *Irish Press*, 11 May 1934.

176 Ibid., 5 July 1934.

177 *United Ireland*, 7 July 1934.

178 Romano Lodi Fé to Ministry of Foreign Affairs, 20 July 1934, Archivio Centrale dello Stato, Ministero della Cultura Popolare, direzione generale propaganda, b. 325, I/27.

179 Regan, *Counter-Revolution*, 357; *United Ireland*, 24 Nov. 1934.

180 Dillon to MacDermot, 1 Oct. 1934, NAI 1065/2/5.

181 *United Ireland*, 18 Aug. 1934; Mark Hull, *Irish Secrets: German Espionage in Ireland 1939–1945* (Dublin, 2003), 54.

182 Regan, *Counter-Revolution*, 355.

183 Dillon to MacDermot, 26 Sept. 1934, NAI 1065/2/4.

184 Walsh memoir, 131–2.

185 *The Blueshirt*, April 1935.

186 Forrest, *Worse*; Cronin, *Blueshirts*, 156–9.

187 Manning, *Blueshirts*, 130–4.

188 *Irish Press*, 25, 29 May, 1 June, 1934; NAI DJ 8/572; NAI DJ 8/490.

189 Manning, *Blueshirts*, 137.

190 *Cork Examiner*, 16 Aug. 1934.

191 UCDA P7a/92; Special Branch report, 20 Aug. 1934, NAI DJ 8/276; *United Ireland*, 25 Aug. 1934.

192 Tierney to MacDermot, 29 Aug. 1934, NAI 1065/4/1.

193 Special Branch report, 20 Aug. 1934, NAI DJ 8/276.

194 *Cork Examiner*, 25 Aug. 1934.

195 Tierney to MacDermot, 29 Aug. 1934, NAI 1065/4/1; Dillon to MacDermot, 24 Aug. 1934, NAI 1065/2/1.

196 Tierney to MacDermot, 4 Sept. 1934, NAI 1065/4/2.

197 Note of Cosgrave's speech, 12 Sept. 1934, UCDA P7b/92.

198 'Resolution to Meet Requirements of Present Situation', UCDA P7b/92.

199 Tierney to MacDermot, 4 Sept. 1934, NAI 1065/4/2.

200 Dillon to MacDermot, 26 Sept. 1934, NAI 1065/2/4.

201 Tierney to MacDermot, 4 Sept. 1934, NAI 1065/4/2.

202 National executive official statement, 1 Sept. 1934, NAI DJ 8/276.

203 *Cork Examiner*, 1 Sept. 1934.

204 Ibid., 1 Sept. 1934.

205 Manning, *Blueshirts*, 149.

206 *United Ireland*, 8 Sept. 1934.

207 Tierney to MacDermot, 8 Sept. 1934, 1065/4/3.

208 Manning, *Blueshirts*, 150.

209 Ibid., 151.

210 Cronin, *Blueshirts*, 51.

211 Misc. documents, UCDA P7b/92.

212 *The Blueshirt*, 6 Oct. 1934.

213 EOD to MacEoin, 11 Sept. 1934, UCDA P51/780.

214 *United Ireland*, 18 Oct. 1934.

215 Dillon to MacDermot, 15 Sept. 1934, NAI 1065/2/3.

216 League of Youth statement on O'Duffy resignation, 4 Oct. 1934, UCDA P24/510.

217 Tierney to MacDermot, 27 Sept. 1934, NAI 1065/4/4.

218 Dillon to MacDermot, 26 Sept. 1934, NAI 1065/2/4.

219 Dillon to MacDermot, 26 Sept. 1934, NAI 1065/2/4.

220 *The Blueshirt*, 6 Oct. 1934.

221 Manning, *Blueshirts*, 248; Lyons, *Ireland since the Famine*, 536.

222 Manning, *Blueshirts*, 250.

223 Cronin, *Blueshirts*, 44.

224 John Newsinger, 'Blackshirts, Blueshirts, and the Spanish Civil War', *Historical Journal* (2001), 839. See also John Heatley, 'The Rise and Fall of the Fascist Threat in Ireland', MA thesis (Queen's University Belfast, 1986), 30–1.

225 Bew *et al.*, *Dynamics*, 65.

226 Manning, *Blueshirts*, 224–9; Dermot Keogh, 'Hogan, Communism, and the Challenge of Contemporary History', in Donnchadh Ó Corráin (ed.), *James Hogan: Revolutionary, Historian and Political Scientist* (Dubin, 2001), 75; Cronin, *Blueshirts*, 50, 65, 82, 94, 98–9.

227 See, for example, UCDA P80/1148.

228 Hogan to FitzGerald, n.d., UCDA P80/1148.

229 Bill Kissane, *Explaining Irish Democracy* (Dublin, 2002), 5. Northern Ireland, administered by uninterrupted one-party rule for half a century until the collapse of Stormont, could not be considered fully democratic.

230 Brian Girvin, 'Nationalism', 143.

231 Robert A. Stradling, *The Irish and the Spanish Civil War 1936–1939* (Manchester, 1999), 1.

232 See *The Blueshirts: Patriots to a Man* (broadcast on RTE in 2001) and the response in the opinion and correspondence columns of the *Irish Times* (12, 22 Jan., 1, 10, Feb., 5 March 2001).

233 Jeffrey Prager, *Building Democracy in Ireland: Political Order and Cultural Integration in a Newly Independent Nation* (Cambridge, 1986); Garvin, *1922*.

234 Lee, *Politics*, 180.

Chapter 10

1 EOD, quoted in UCDA LA10/D285.
2 *Irish Independent*, 2 Oct. 1934.
3 *Cork Examiner*, 27 Sept. 1934; Manning, *Blueshirts*, 164–6.
4 *Cork Examiner*, 2 Oct. 1934.
5 *The Blueshirt*, 6 Oct. 1934.
6 Dillon to MacDermot, 1 Oct. 1934, NAI 1065/2/5.
7 EOD to Captain Quinn, 3 Oct. 1934, NAI DJ 8/286.
8 Col. P. J. Coughlan to Capt. Walsh, 31 Dec. 1936, ODP.
9 *The Blueshirt*, 20 Oct. 1934; Cronin, *Blueshirts*, 154.
10 Garda report, 19 Oct. 1934, NAI DJ 8/104.
11 Garda report, 1 Nov. 1934, NAI DJ 8/6.
12 *Irish Press*, 22 Oct. 1934.
13 Ibid., 1 Nov. 1934.
14 *Irish Independent*, 5 Nov. 1934.
15 *Irish Press*, 8, 13 Nov. 1934.
16 *Irish Independent*, 26 Nov. 1934.
17 Ibid., 19 Nov. 1934, *Irish Press*, 20 Nov. 1934.
18 *The Blueshirt*, 5 Jan. 1935.
19 Dillon to MacDermot, 17 Oct. 1934, NAI 1065/2/6.
20 Tierney to MacDermot, 4 Oct. 1934, NAI 1065/4/5.
21 *Irish Independent, Irish Times*, 27 Nov. 1934.
22 Garda report, 11 Dec. 1934, NAI DJ 8/286.
23 EOD, circular letter, 4 Dec. 1934, NAI DJ 8/286.
24 *The Blueshirt*, 22 Dec. 1934.
25 Ibid., 10 Nov. 1934.
26 NAI DJ 8/286.
27 *The Blueshirt*, 6 Oct. 1934, 15 June 1935; EOD, circular letter, 4 Dec. 1934, NAI DJ 8/286.
28 Ledeen, *Universal Fascism*, 104–32; Hans Fredrik Dahl, *Quisling: A Study in Treachery* (Cambridge, 1999), 110–15.
29 *Irish Press*, 29 Dec. 1934.
30 *Irish Independent*, 7 Jan. 1935.
31 Fr McCabe diary, 25 April 1937, NLI Accession 4872, folders 61–2 [hereafter: Fr McCabe diary].
32 Ledeen, *Universal Fascism*, 124–6.
33 Lodi Fé to ministry of foreign affairs, 15 Jan. 1935, ASMAE, serie affari politici, B.2, Irlanda 1935, (1) Rapporti Politici.
34 *Irish Press*, 10 June 1935.
35 Dillon to MacDermot, 1 Jan. 1935, NAI 1065/2/7.
36 See, for example, Dahl, *Quisling*, 169–71.

37 *Irish Press*, 20, 26 Feb. 1935; *Irish Times*, 8 Feb. 1935.

38 EOD, 'The Function of the Blueshirts in a Corporative State', *c*. March 1935, NAI DJ 8/296.

39 NAI DJ 8/617.

40 *The Blueshirt*, 9 Feb. 1935; NAI DJ 8/288, 624, 628, 630.

41 D/O O'Brien to Special Branch, 13 Nov. 1934, NAI DJ 8/518.

42 Garda report, 1 Dec. 1934, NAI DJ 8/287.

43 Cronin, *Blueshirts*, 160.

44 *The Blueshirt*, 8 Nov. 1934.

45 Memo, 15 Oct. 1934, NAI DJ 8/364.

46 Cronin, *Blueshirts*, 155.

47 O'Coillte to secretary, department of justice, 18 June 1935, NAI DJ 8/617.

48 *The Blueshirt*, 1 May 1935.

49 Ibid., 19 Jan. 1935.

50 Ibid., 12 Jan. 1935.

51 Ibid., 1 May 1935; UCDA P24/1326.

52 Ulster Centre of Fascist Studies, *A Brief Introduction to Fascism in Ulster* (n.p., n.d.).

53 Ulster Centre, *Brief Introduction*, 1, 13.

54 James Loughlin, 'Northern Ireland and British Fascism in the inter-war years', *Irish Historical Studies* (Nov. 1995), 548; Manning, *Blueshirts*, 151.

55 Inspector general's office, RUC, to secretary, ministry of home affairs, 12 June 1935, PRONI HA 32/1/615.

56 *The Blueshirt*, 15 June 1935.

57 P. J. Coughlan, *The Truth: The Story of the Blueshirts* (Skibbereen, 1934), 26.

58 Garda report, 1 May 1935, NAI DJ 8/296.

59 *The Nation*, April 1936.

60 Richard English, ' "Paying No Heed to Public Clamour": Irish Republican Solipsism in the 1930s', *Irish Historical Studies* (Nov. 1993); Lodi Fé to ministry of foreign affairs, 16 March 1936, ASMAE, serie affari politici, B.3, Irlanda 1936, (1) rapporti politici.

61 NCP, circular, 18 June 1935, NAI DJ 8/296. For a detailed account of the NCP, see Martin White, 'The Greenshirts: Fascism in the Irish Free State, 1935–45', Ph.D. thesis (University of London, 2004).

62 Lodi Fé to ministry of foreign affairs, 20 July 1936, ASMAE, serie affari politici, B.3, Irlanda 1936, (2) Fascismo Irlanda.

63 *Irish Independent,* 10 June 1935; *The Blueshirt*, 8 June 1935.

64 Special Branch report, 8 June 1935, NAI DJ 8/307.

65 *The Nation*, 3 Aug. 1935.

66 Garda report, 29 Oct. 1935, NAI DJ 8/296.

67 *Irish Press*, 19 Aug. 1935.

68 Garda report, 31 Oct. 1935, NAI DJ 8/296.

69 Misc. documents, NAI DJ 8/296.

70 NCP circular, 7 Aug. 1935, NAI DJ 8/296.
71 Garda report, 31 Oct. 1935, NAI DJ 8/296.
72 NCP bulletin, No. 5, Dec. 1935, NAI DJ 8/296; *Irish Press*, 9 Dec. 1935; *The Nation*, April 1936.
73 *Irish Press*, 30 Sept. 1935.
74 Ibid., 19 Sept. 1935.
75 NCP bulletin, No. 5, Dec. 1935, NAI DJ 8/296; *Irish Press*, 2 Oct. 1935.
76 *The Nation*, April 1936.
77 *Irish Press*, 4 March 1936; NCP Circular No. 14, Nov. 1935, NAI DJ 8/296.
78 A. Raven Thomson to Liam Walsh, 7 May 1936, ODP.
79 Thomson to Walsh, 21 May 1936, ODP; Thurlow, *Fascism in Britain*, 67.
80 Walsh to Thomson, 3 June 1936, ODP.
81 Thomson to Walsh, 4 June 1936, ODP.
82 Garda report, 23 June 1936, NAI DJ 8/296.
83 Special Branch report, 20 July 1936, NAI DJ 8/296.
84 EOD, *Crusade in Spain* (Dublin, 1938), 39.
85 Ibid., 217–18.
86 Walsh memoir, 205.
87 *Irish Independent*, 10 Aug. 1936.
88 Fr McCabe diary, 13 Oct. 1936.
89 Ibid., 12 Oct. 1936.
90 *Irish Independent*, 27 Aug. 1936.
91 Walsh memoir, 205–7.
92 Lodi Fé to ministry of foreign affairs, 30 April, 5 June 1937, ASMAE, serie affari politici, Irlanda B.3, Irlanda 1937, (2) Legione Irlandese.
93 EOD, *Crusade*, 1–10.
94 *Irish Independent*, 17 Nov. 1934.
95 Ibid., 14 Dec. 1936.
96 Ibid., 21 Nov. 1936, *Irish Press*, 29 Aug. 1936.
97 Manning, *Blueshirts*, 200; Stradling, 'Franco's Irish Volunteers', *History Today* (March 1995), 44.
98 *Irish Independent*, 21 Nov. 1936.
99 EOD, *Crusade*, 227.
100 Ibid., 215. Privately, O'Duffy had a more critical view of Franco.
101 EOD, *Crusade*, 60.
102 Ibid., 116; Fr McCabe diary, 17 June 1937.
103 *Irish Independent*, 22 Aug., 26 Nov. 1936.
104 Judith Keene, *Fighting for Franco: International Volunteers in Nationalist Spain During the Spanish Civil War, 1936–1939* (London, 2001), 293.
105 PRO FO W12847/9549/41.
106 Keene, *Fighting for Franco*, 12.
107 *Irish Press*, 30 Sept. 1936; EOD, *Crusade*, 16–24.

108 Keene, *Fighting for Franco*, 117.

109 EOD, *Crusade*, 59.

110 'Agreement between H. E. General Franco and General Eoin O'Duffy', ODP.

111 EOD, *Crusade*, 86–7, 195.

112 Keene, *Fighting for Franco*, 27–29, 101, 113; Paul Preston, *Franco: A Biography* (London, 1993), 27–30, 164–5; Stradling, *Irish and the Spanish*, 49–50.

113 Nationalist telegram, London to Salamanca, 24 Feb. 1937, Archivos del Ministerio de Asuntos Exteriores (hereafter MAE), Madrid, Archivio de Burgos (hereafter AB) R1105–10; Fr McCabe diary, 17 June 1937.

114 Telegrams, Salamanca to London, 1 Dec. 1936, London to Salamanca, 7 Dec. 1936, MAE AB R1105/10.

115 Coughlan to Walsh, n.d., ODP.

116 *Irish Independent*, 12 Dec. 1936.

117 Memo, 18 Dec. 1936, NAI D/FA 241/12.

118 Fr McCabe diary, 17 June, 25 April 1937; McGarry, *Irish Politics*, 31–7.

119 Francis McCullagh, *In Franco's Spain* (London, 1937), 245.

120 EOD, *Crusade*, 65–7.

121 McCullagh, *In Franco's Spain*, 150; Keogh, *Ireland and Europe*, 81.

122 Liam Walsh, 'My Own Impression of Germany', n.d., ODP.

123 Lindsay, *Memories*, 55.

124 *Irish Independent*, 14 Dec. 1936; Stradling, *Irish and the Spanish*, 37–9.

125 Peter Kemp, *Mine Were of Trouble* (London, 1957), 87.

126 Diary of Tom Hayes, quoted in Stradling, *Irish and the Spanish*, 39.

127 EOD, *Crusade*, 92.

128 Irish Brigade diary, 22–4 Nov. 1936, ODP.

129 EOD, *Crusade in Spain*, 94.

130 Irish Brigade diary, 31 Jan. 1936, ODP; see also EOD, *Crusade*, 126–32.

131 EOD, *Crusade*, 92, 109.

132 Fr McCabe diary, 19 May, 4, 6 Jan. 1937.

133 Ibid., 6 Jan., 17 June 1937; Stradling, *Irish and the Spanish*, 117.

134 Ibid., 17 May 1937. But see also McCullagh, *In Franco's Spain*, 280.

135 Fr McCabe, 7 Jan. 1936. Mulrean was described by the Irish legation as 'mysterious', 'secretive', and 'dangerous' (Horan to Cremins, 5 May 1962, NAI D/FA P/350).

136 Fr McCabe diary, 7 Jan., 19 May 1937.

137 Kerney to Walsh, 13 March 1937, NAI D/FA Madrid Embassy 52/1.

138 Kemp, *Mine Were of Trouble*, 86.

139 Fr McCabe diary, 7 Jan. 1937.

140 McCullagh, *In Franco's Spain*, 132, 153; Kemp, *Mine Were of Trouble*, 90–1; Kerney to Joe Walshe, 8 June 1937, NAI D/FA Madrid Embassy 51/1.

141 Kemp, *Mine Were of Trouble*, 109.

142 *Evening Echo*, 4 Sept. 1967.

143 Spanish representative, Lisbon, to EOD, 4 Dec. 1936, ODP.

144 *Irish Independent, Irish Press*, 24 Dec. 1936.

145 McCullagh, *In Franco's Spain*, 150.

146 Col. P. J. Coughlan to Captain Walsh, n.d., ODP.

147 Fr McCabe diary, 1 May 1937.

148 Stradling, *Irish and the Spanish*, 55.

149 Fr McCabe diary, 6 Jan. 1937. McCabe's cynical reflections were influenced by his reservations about the reactionary nature of the Spanish Catholic Church and Nationalist Spain.

150 Fr McCabe diary, 7 Jan. 1937.

151 Ibid., 6 Jan. 1937.

152 McCullagh, *In Franco's Spain*, 235.

153 Kemp, *Mine Were of Trouble*, 87.

154 Mulrean to McCabe, 9 Feb. 1937, NLI Acc. 4872, folder 57.

155 EOD, *Crusade*, 160; McCullagh, *In Franco's Spain*, 292.

156 Matt Beckett, 'The Irish Brigade', Beckett collection, Clew Bay Heritage Centre, Westport, Co. Mayo.

157 Irish Brigade Association (IBA) minute book, 14 Dec. 1937, ODP.

158 Fr McCabe diary, 7 Jan. 1937.

159 Mulrean to McCabe, 9 Feb. 1937, NLI Acc. 4872, folder 57.

160 EOD, *Crusade*, 110.

161 Fr McCabe diary, 30 April 1937.

162 EOD, *Crusade*, 115–16; *The Kerryman*, 30 Jan. 1998.

163 *Irish Independent*, 10 Feb. 1937; EOD, *Crusade*, 126–32.

164 *Irish Independent*, 10 Feb. 1937.

165 Stradling, *Irish and the Spanish*, 57.

166 Keene, *Fighting for Franco*, 54.

167 Ibid., 54.

168 McCullagh, *In Franco's Spain*, 259–60.

169 Kerney to Walshe, 8 April 1937, NAI D/FA Madrid Embassy 51/1; Kerney to Walshe, 9 March 1937, NAI D/FA Madrid Embassy 10/2.

170 Stradling, *Irish and the Spanish*, 60.

171 McCullagh, *In Franco's Spain*, 261.

172 Stradling, *Irish and the Spanish*, 60.

173 Ibid., 63.

174 Irish Brigade diary, 19 Feb. 1937; EOD, *Crusade*, 139.

175 Kemp, *Mine Were of Trouble*, 46; Stradling, *Irish and the Spanish*, 63–6.

176 Irish Brigade diary, 22 Feb. 1937, ODP.

177 Ibid., 21 Feb. 1937, ODP; EOD, *Crusade*, 141.

178 *Irish Independent*, 26 Feb. 1937.

179 Ibid., 1 March 1937.

180 Ibid., 23 Feb., 12 March, 26 Feb. 1937.

181 Stradling, *Irish and the Spanish*, 62.

182 EOD, *Crusade*, 143.

183 Quoted in Stradling, *Irish and the Spanish*, 66.

184 *Irish Times*, 22 June 1937.

185 EOD, *Crusade*, 143.

186 Beckett, 'Irish Brigade'.

187 EOD, *Crusade in Spain*, 200–3.

188 Tom Murphy interview, Imperial War Museum, Sound Archives, Spanish Civil War collection, 805/2; John Dunlop interview, Imperial War Museum, Sound Archives, Spanish Civil War collection, 11355/4.

189 EOD, *Crusade*, 146–8, 166.

190 Irish Brigade diary, 19 Feb.–23 March 1937.

191 Stradling, *Irish and the Spanish*, 72; McCullagh, *In Franco's Spain*, 300–2.

192 EOD, *Crusade in Spain*, 150–2.

193 Stradling, *Irish and the Spanish*, 40–1.

194 Ibid., 69–70; Irish Brigade diary, 24 Feb., 3 March 1937, ODP.

195 Walshe to Kerney, 6 March 1937, NAI D/FA Madrid Embassy 51/1.

196 Kerney to Walshe, 13 March 1937, NAI D/FA Madrid Embassy 51/1; Fr McCabe diary, 10 March 1937.

197 Irish Brigade diary, 3, 9 March 1937, ODP.

198 Kerney to Walsh, 29 Dec. 1939, NAI D/FA Madrid Embassy 19/4.

199 Fr Mulrean to Fr McCabe, 21 April, 4 June 1937, NLI Acc. 4872, folder 57; Fr McCabe diary, 17 June 1937.

200 *Irish Press*, 19 March 1937; Irish Brigade diary, 6, 16 March 1937, ODP; Stradling, *Irish and the Spanish*, 236.

201 McCullagh, *In Franco's Spain*, 222.

202 Fr McCabe diary, 29 April 1937.

203 McCullagh, *In Franco's Spain*, 235. Smith, a Protestant, was disliked by other officers.

204 EOD, *Crusade*, 163; Irish Brigade diary, 19 March 1937, ODP.

205 Irish Brigade diary, 15 March 1937, ODP.

206 Stradling, *Irish and the Spanish*, 76–9.

207 Thomas, *Spanish Civil War*, 602.

208 Seósamh O'Cuinneagáin, *War in Spain* (Enniscorthy, n.d.), 21.

209 Kerney to Walshe, 19 Dec. 1939, NAI D/FA Madrid Embassy 19/4.

210 *Irish Independent*, 3 April 1937.

211 Ibid., 10 March 1937.

212 Ibid., 25 March 1937.

213 McCullagh, *In Franco's Spain*, 263, 265.

214 Irish Crusade against Communism statement, ODP.

215 *Irish Independent*, 7 April 1937.

216 EOD, *Crusade*, 164.

217 *Irish Press*, 26 May 1937.

218 *Evening Echo*, 15 Sept. 1967.

219 *The Kerryman*, 30 Jan. 1998.

220 *Irish Press*, 26 May 1937.

221 Fr McCabe diary, 17 June 1937.

222 IBA minute book, 19 June 1937, ODP; Kerney to Walshe, 19 Dec. 1939, NAI D/FA 19/4.

223 Kerney to Walshe, 8 June 1937, NAI D/FA Madrid Embassy 51/1.

224 Fr McCabe diary, 1 May 1937.

225 Stradling, *Irish and the Spanish*, 100.

226 Fr McCabe diary, 17 June 1937.

227 McCullagh, *In Franco's Spain*, 297.

228 Stradling, *Irish and the Spanish*, 91–2.

229 Keene, *Fighting for Franco*, 2.

230 Yagüe to General Segundo Jefe de la División Reforzada de Madrid, 24 March 1937, Archivo General Militar, Ávila (hereafter AGMA), Cuartel general del Generalísimo (hereafter CGG), L156/24.

231 El Teniente Coronel Ayudante to General Segundo Jefe de Estado Mayor del Cuartel general de S.E. el Generalísimo, Salamanca, 29 March 1937, AGMA CGG L156/24.

232 Irish Brigade diary, 4–5 April 1937, ODP.

233 EOD to Franco, 9 April 1937, AGMA CGG L156/25.

234 Tom Hayes diary, quoted in Stradling, *Irish and the Spanish*, 99.

235 Translation, EOD to Franco, 9 April 1937, AGMA CGG L156/25.

236 Irish Brigade diary, 16–17 April 1937, ODP.

237 Kemp, *Mine Were of Trouble*, 86.

238 Keene, *Fighting for Franco*, 128–9.

239 McCullagh, *In Franco's Spain*, 151.

240 Irish Brigade diary, 24 March–28 April 1937.

241 Fr McCabe diary, 3 May, 25 April, 1937.

242 Irish Brigade diary, 9 April 1937, ODP.

243 Kemp, *Mine were of Trouble*, 86.

244 EOD, *Crusade*, 236.

245 Fr McCabe diary, 1 May 1937; Stradling, *Irish and the Spanish*, 109.

246 Kerney to Walshe, 29 Dec. 1939, NAI D/FA Madrid Embassy 19/4; see also Stradling, *Irish and the Spanish*, 116.

247 Fr McCabe diary, 25 April 1937.

248 Kerney to Walshe, 8 March, 8 April, 12 May 1937, NAI D/FA Madrid Embassy 51/1.

249 McCullagh, *In Franco's Spain*, 150, 264; Fr McCabe diary, 2 May 1937.

250 Fr McCabe diary, 7 Jan. 1937.

251 Report of El Coronel 2 Jefe de E. M., Navalcarnero, 22 April 1937, AGMA CGG L156/24; Yagüe to General 2 Jefe de E.M., 26 April 1937, AGMA CGG L335/100; Stradling, *Irish and the Spanish*, 96–105.

252 Diary of Tom Hayes, quoted in Stradling, *Irish and the Spanish*, 99.

253 IBA minute book, 2 May 1937, ODP.

254 Ibid., 7 May 1937, ODP.

255 Irish Brigade diary, 6 June 1937, ODP.

256 Fr McCabe diary, 21, 25 April 1937; misc. mediation documents, 30 April 1937, NLI Acc. 4872, folders 54–5.

257 Fr McCabe diary, 2 May, 1937.

258 *Irish Independent*, 12 May 1937.

259 Kerney to Walshe, 12 May 1937, NAI D/FA Madrid Embassy 51/1.

260 Kerney to Walshe, 8 June 1937, NAI D/FA Madrid Embassy 51/1.

261 Kerney to Walshe, 9 June 1938, NAI D/FA Madrid Embassy 19/4.

262 Kerney to Walshe, 10 June 1938, NAI D/FA 244/22.

263 EOD, *Crusade*, 242.

264 Lodi Fé to ministry of foreign affairs, 5 June 1937, ASMAE, serie affari politici, Irlanda B.3, Irlanda 1937, (2) Legione Irlandese.

265 Misc. memos, AGMA CGG, L156/24.

266 McCullagh, *In Franco's Spain*, 306.

Chapter 11

1 EOD, 'Ireland's Attitude Towards International Affairs', n.d., ODP.

2 IBA minute book, 19 June 1937, ODP.

3 EOD, *Crusade*, 247; 'H.E. General O'Duffy, Leader Irish Brigade in Spain 1936–1937', June 1937, ODP.

4 *Irish Times, Irish Press*, 22 June 1937.

5 Quoted in Stradling, *Irish and the Spanish*, 105.

6 Keene, *Fighting for Franco*, 127.

7 *Irish Press*, 22 June 1937.

8 Gunning to Desmond FitzGerald, 15 July 1937, UCDA P80/627.

9 McCullagh, *In Franco's Spain*, 49.

10 Anonymous letter to Italian embassy, 17 Aug. 1938, ASMAE, serie affari politici, B.3, Irlanda 1938, (5) Misc.

11 *Irish Catholic*, 24 June 1937.

12 *Church of Ireland Gazette*, 25 June 1937.

13 Garda report, 30 Sept. 1937, NAI DJ 8/437.

14 *Hibernia*, Jan., April 1938.

15 *Sunday Chronicle*, 24 April 1938.

16 IBA minute book, 12 Aug., 14 Dec. 1937, 15 March, 2 July 1938, ODP.

17 EOD, *Crusade*, 218, 220–1, 226, 227.

18 Press cuttings, *c*. Sept.–Oct. 1936, ODP; Stradling, *Irish and the Spanish*, 24.

19 *Hibernia*, April 1938.

20 EOD, *Crusade*, 72, 73, 205.

21 O'Duffy's position as commissioner had made him an influential figure among the clerics, academics, and journalists who formed a vibrant anti-communist subculture in the Free State and with whom (judging from his personal papers) he exchanged sensitive information. The most extreme fringe of this group regarded communism, like the French Revolution and the Protestant Reformation, as a Satanic conspiracy. See McGarry, *Irish Politics*, 152–6.

22 Stephen Lee, *European Dictatorships* 1918–1945 (London, 2000 edn.), 124–5; Bosworth, *Mussolini*, 335.

23 *Irish Independent*, 31 Oct., 1 Nov. 1938, quoted in O'Riordan, 'Anti-Semitism'.

24 *Irish Press*, 2 Aug. 1938.

25 George Orwell, *The New Light Weekly*, Nov. 1938.

26 Walsh memoir, 145.

27 Special Branch report, 3 Sept. 1940, MA G2/0169.

28 Misc. reports, MA G2/0246.

29 Special Branch report, 3 Sept. 1940, MA G2/1069; G2 report, 29 Aug. 1940, NAI D/FA A8.

30 Misc. reports, MA G2/0246.

31 Special Branch memo, 9 Nov. 1939, MA G2/0246.

32 G2 memo, *c.* 1939, MA G2/0246.

33 O'Halpin, *Defending Ireland*, 147; Fisk, *In Time of War*, 88–9; Hull, *Irish Secrets*, 52–9.

34 Hull, *Irish Secrets*.

35 Memo on Oskar (Karl) Pfaus, MA G2/0169.

36 Sectional History of B.1.H, 29–31, PRO KV 4/9. I am grateful to Eunan O'Halpin for alerting me to this and several other intelligence sources.

37 Memo by Dan Bryan, 16 Aug. 1939, MA G2/0169.

38 Memo on O'Duffy, Sept. 1940, MA G2/0169.

39 Memos by Dan Bryan, 28, 29 Aug. 1939, MA G2/0169.

40 Memo on O'Duffy, n.d., G2/0169.

41 Lee, *Ireland*, 246.

42 EOD, 'Ireland's Attitude'.

43 Special Branch report, 1 Aug. 1939, G2 to Special Branch, 25 Aug. 1939, MA G2/X/0093.

44 Sectional History of B.1.H, 32–33, PRO KV 4/9.

45 Memo on O'Duffy, n.d., G2/0169.

46 Irish affairs, 1 Sept. 1943, QRS/204, PRO DO 121/85.

47 Vincenzo Berardis to ministry of foreign affairs, 25 Feb. 1939, ASMAE, serie affari politici, B.4, Irlanda 1939, (1) rapporti politici.

48 Vincenzo Berardis to ministry of foreign affairs, 26 June 1939, ASMAE, serie affari politici, B.4, Irlanda 1939, (1) rapporti politici.

49 Memo on Brennan-Whitmore, 2 Dec. 1943, NAI D/FA A8.

50 Brennan-Whitmore to Walsh, 13 July 1944, ODP.

51   Enno Stephan, *Spies in Ireland* (London, 1965), 22–6.

52   O'Halpin, *Defending Ireland*, 171–3.

53   Sectional History of B.1.H, 16, PRO KV 4/9.

54   O'Halpin, *Defending Ireland*, 152–3.

55   D. K. Kostal, memo, 31 May 1940, NAI D/FA A8.

56   Maffey to Machtig, 16 Feb. 1940, PRO DO 130/12.

57   Memo by Count Balinski, *c.* Jan. 1941, PRO FO 371/29108.

58   Weenick to Dutch ambassador, London, *c.* 10 July 1941, NAI D/FA A8.

59   Misc. reports, PRO FO 371/29108. Both MI5 and Hempel considered Aiken 'actively pro-German' (Summary of Most Secret Information from Dublin, 19 Sept. to 2 Oct., 1943, PRO DO 121/87).

60   Irish affairs, 1 Nov. 1943, PRO DO 121/85, QRS/205; Sectional History of B.1.H, 13, PRO KV 4/9. In 1942 a more optimistic report claimed that 'the overwhelming majority of the people are clearly pro-British at heart' (*Irish Affairs*, 1 May 1942, PRO DO 121/85, QRS/196). A subsequent cynical report noted the effect of Allied success: 'A few months ago "they" were losing the war, now "we" are winning it . . . their ardour being largely attributable to the shortage of supplies' (*Irish Affairs*, 1 Jan. 1943, PRO DO 121/85, QRS/200).

61   MI5 synopsis of Hempel's 'The Irish Problem in the Future' (Oct. 1942), Summary of Most Secret Information from Dublin, 30 May–12 June 1943, PRO DO 121/87.

62   Leaflet, enclosed in Maffey to Machtig, 8 Feb. 1940, PRO DO 130/8.

63   German propaganda article, ODP.

64   Garda report of interview with Maurice O'Connor, 24 July 1940, MA G2/0169.

65   Transcript of Maurice O'Connor interview, 7 June 1940, MA G2/0169.

66   Walsh to O'Connor, quoted in transcript of O'Connor interview, 7 June 1940, Special Branch report, 16 May 1940, MA G2/0169.

67   Garda report, 31 May 1940, UCDA P7a/220.

68   Police report, 8 July 1940, MA G2/0169.

69   Report of an Anti-Christian Association meeting, 14 June 1940, UCDA P7a/220.

70   Bryan to Walshe, 23 Sept. 1942, NAI D/FA A8(i).

71   Cited in Dermot Keogh, *Jews in Twentieth Century Ireland: Refugees, Anti-Semitism and the Holocaust* (Cork, 1998), 149.

72   Memo, n.d., MA G2/X/1091.

73   Hull, *Irish Secrets*, 99.

74   Keogh, *Jews*, 182, 166–7.

75   Donal Ó Drisccoil, *Censorship in Ireland 1939–1945: Neutrality, Politics and Society* (Cork, 1996), 76.

76   Summary of Most Secret Information from Dublin, 16–20 April 1944, PRO DO 121/87.

77   Special Branch report, 31 July 1940, MA G2/0169.

78   O'Halpin, *Defending Ireland*, 223.

79   Memo on O'Duffy, n.d., MA G2/0169.

80 Memo on O'Duffy, Sept. 1940, MA G2/0169.
81 Memo, n.d., MA G2/X/1091.
82 Memo, Sept. 1940, MA G2/0169.
83 IRA army council statement, 1 July 1940, NAI D/FA A12.
84 *War News*, March 1941.
85 Brian Hanley, ' "Here's to Adolph Hitler": The IRA's Support for the Nazis in Context' (unpublished paper).
86 Proposed National Protest against the Presence of U.S. Personnel in the Six Counties, NAI D/FA A8.
87 Memo on O'Duffy, Sept. 1940, MA G2/0169.
88 Special Branch reports, 24, 26, 31 July 1940, MA G2/0169.
89 Special Branch report, 3 Sept. 1940, MA G2/0169.
90 Memo on O'Duffy, n.d., MA G2/0169.
91 Archer note, 3 Oct. 1940, MA G2/0169.
92 Archer to Walshe, 4 Feb. 1941, NAI D/FA A8.
93 O'Halpin, *Defending Ireland*, 242; Sectional History of B.1.H, 41, PRO KV 4/9.
94 McGarry, *Frank Ryan*; O'Halpin, *Defending Ireland*, 193–5.
95 Goertz document, Dec. 1944, NLI MS 22, 984.
96 O'Halpin, *Defending Ireland*, 244. See also Fisk, *In Time of War*, 358–9. Hull (*Irish Secrets*, 75–6), who has researched the subject in most detail, is more sceptical about Goertz's effectiveness.
97 Goertz document, Dec. 1944, NLI MS 22, 984.
98 O'Halpin, *Defending Ireland*, 175.
99 MI5 synopsis of Hempel's, 'The Irish Problem in the Future' (Oct. 1942), Summary of Most Secret Information from Dublin, 30 May–12 June 1943, PRO DO 121/87.
100 O'Halpin, *Defending Ireland*, 245; Sectional History of B.1.H, 71, PRO KV 4/9.
101 Fisk, *In Time of War*, 253.
102 Introduction, Summary of our Most Secret Information from Dublin, 10 Feb. 1943, PRO DO 121/87.
103 O'Halpin, *Defending Ireland*, 178–9; Hull, *Irish Secrets*, 145–6, 173–5.
104 Proposed National Protest against the Presence of U.S. Personnel in the Six Counties, NAI D/FA A8.
105 Lee, *Ireland*, 267.
106 Irish affairs, QRS 197, PRO DO 121/85.
107 Enno Stephan, *Spies*, 249.
108 Quoted in Seán Cronin, *Frank Ryan: The Search for The Republic* (Dublin, 1980), 251; Hull, *Irish Secrets*, 197–8.
109 Summary of Most Secret Information, 10 Feb. 1943, PRO DO 121/87.
110 Ó Drisceoil, *Censorship*, 211.
111 Memo: Stopped by Censor: 22 July 1940, MA G2/0169.
112 Memo on O'Duffy, Sept. 1940, MA G2/0169.
113 Memo by S. O'B, 4 March 1941, MA G2/0169.

114 G2 to Chief Supt. Carroll, 14 May 1941, report on O'Duffy *c.* May 1941, MA G2/0169.

115 'Irish affairs', 1 Sept. 1943, QRS/204, PRO DO 121/85.

116 Brennan-Whitmore to Liam Walsh, 14 Nov. 1943, NAI D/FA A8/1.

117 Walsh memoir, 158.

118 Ibid., 156. O'Duffy's vast collection of diaries and papers disappeared after his death. However, four boxes of valuable documents (apparently retained by Walsh to complete his biography) which recently came to light are now available for consultation in the National Library.

119 Walsh memoir, 156.

120 Ibid., 156.

121 Ibid., 155.

122 Allen, *Garda Síochána*, 108.

123 Walsh memoir, 164.

124 Ibid., 157–9.

125 *Irish Times*, 1 Dec. 1944; Allen, *Garda Síochána*, 107.

126 Walsh memoir, 157.

127 Ibid., 158.

Epilogue

1 Comerford, *Ireland*, 226, 114.

2 Ibid., 114.

3 Corrupt officials, cruel nuns, and hypocritical priests provide the gallery of rogues in recent novels, such as *Angela's Ashes* and *Song for a Raggy Boy*, and movies like *The Magdalene Sisters*.

4 F. S. L. Lyons, *Culture and Anarchy in Ireland 1890–1939* (Oxford, 1979), 147–77.

5 Comerford, *Ireland*, 145. It should not be forgotten that the Irish Ireland movement had always been characterized by glaring contradictions. As Maume (*Moran*, 4) points out: 'the xenophobia, censorship mentality and Gaelic chauvinism which disfigured the post-independence state were present before 1914'.

6 Hobsbawm, *Nations and Nationalism*, 12.

7 Richard Hofstadter, 'The Paranoid Style in American Politics', *Harper's Magazine*, Nov. 1964, 77–86. This mode of thought resembles the more optimistic palingenetic myth identified by Griffin as central to the appeal of fascism: 'The belief that contemporaries are living through or about to live through a "sea-change", a "water-shed" or "turning point" in the historical process. The perceived corruption, anarchy, oppressiveness, iniquities of the present . . . [are] nearing its end, and a new order is about to emerge' (Griffin, *Nature of Fascism*, 35, 186–94).

8 Writing in the 1960s, Hofstadter identified the John Birch Society, which viewed the United Nations as an instrument of Soviet conspiracy, as one example of the paranoid style. Contemporary examples of this resilient tradition include the

survivalist movement, which, like the American extremists of the 1950s, views its own federal government as part of a broader anti-American conspiracy, and neo-conservative Republican ideologues, who have identified a far reaching 'axis of evil' between countries as diverse as North Korea and Syria which must be destroyed to bring about a new world order.

9 Richard Gid Powers, *Secrecy and Power: The Life of J. Edgar Hoover* (New York, 1987).

10 John J. Horgan, *The Round Table*, March 1935, quoted in Manning, *Blueshirts*, 152.

11 Ed Moloney and Andy Pollak, *Paisley* (Dublin, 1986).

12 Lee, *European Dictatorships*, 100.

13 Denis Mack Smith, *Mussolini* (London, 1985).

14 Lee, *European Dictatorships*, 108.

15 Bosworth, *Mussolini*.

16 Preston, *Franco*.

17 Walsh memoir, 160.

18 *The Standard, c*. Dec. 1944, cited in Walsh memoir, 164.

19 Stradling, *Irish and the Spanish*, pp. viii, 2. A gravestone was subsequently erected by family members, but the contrast between O'Duffy's neglected plot and those of his patron, Collins, and his Spanish Civil War nemesis, Frank Ryan (both of which continue to be decorated with fresh flowers), remains striking. See Brian Maye, 'An Irishman's Diary', *Irish Times*, 19 Nov. 2001 (and subsequent letters on 23, 29 Nov.).

20 *Irish Times*, 1 Dec. 1944.

21 *Irish Independent*, 1 Dec. 1944.

22 Stradling, 'Franco's Irish Volunteers', 40.

23 Stradling, *Irish and the Spanish*, 2; see also *Irish Times*, 19 Nov. 2001.

24 The defunct neo-Nazi NSRUS claimed O'Duffy as a hero (*Irish Examiner*, 23 Aug. 2001). Photographs and speeches of O'Duffy can be found on such unsavoury websites as The Friends of Oswald Mosley and the Third Reich Historical Forum. O'Duffy's career continues to provoke discussion and admiration from visitors to websites such as Final Conflict and the Stormfront White Nationalist Community (where the salutation, 'Hoch O'Duffy', remains in use). James K. Warner's history *The Blue Shirts and Gen. Eoin O'Duffy* can be purchased, alongside such titles as *The Truth about the Jews* and *America, Free, White and Christian*, from the Sons of Liberty Books (Conspiracy Archives), a United States-based website.

25 Somhairle Macalastair, 'Ballyseedy befriends Badajoz', in Valentine Cunningham (ed.), *The Penguin Book of Spanish Civil War Verse* (London, 1996 edn.), 385–6.

26 Ronnie Drew, 'O'Duffy's Ironsides', *Guaranteed Dubliner* (Dolphin, 1978); H. Gustav Klaus, 'The Authorship of the Somhairle Macalastair Ballads', *Irish University Review* (Spring/Summer 1996).

27 Christy Moore, 'Viva la Quinte Brigada', *The Christy Moore Collection Part 2* (Columbia, 1997).

28 Stradling, 'Franco's Irish Volunteers', 47.

29 Stradling, *Irish and the Spanish*, 2.

Select Bibliography

Official records

Archivio Centrale dello Stato, Rome
Ministero della Cultura Popolare: direzione propaganda

Archivio Storico Diplomatico del Ministero degli Affari Esteri, Rome
Serie affari politici (Irlanda)

Archivo General Militar, Ávila
Cuartel general del Generalísimo

Archivos del Ministerio de Asuntos Exteriores, Madrid
Archivo de Burgos

Military Archives, Dublin
Bureau of Military History
Intelligence (G2 series)

National Archives, Dublin
Department of justice
Department of foreign affairs
Department of the taoiseach

National Archive, London
Colonial office
Dominions office
Foreign office
Security service (MI5)
War office

Private papers

(Abbreviations: MCM: Monaghan County Museum; NLI: National Library, Dublin; UCDA: University College Dublin Department of Archives.)

Frank Aiken	UCDA
Ernest Blythe	UCDA
Michael Collins	UCDA
Desmond FitzGerald	NLI
Michael Hayes	UCDA

Richard Hayes	NLI
Sean MacEntee	UCDA
Sean MacEoin	UCDA
Marron papers	MCM
Richard Mulcahy	UCDA
Eoin O'Duffy	NLI
Ernie O'Malley	UCDA

Parliamentary and official publications

Dáil Debates
Official Report: Debate on the Treaty between Great Britain and Ireland (Dublin, n.d.)
Report of the committee on the Criminal Law Amendment Acts (1800–85) and juvenile prostitution (Dublin, 1931)

Newspapers and periodicals

Anglo-Celt
An Phoblacht
The Blueshirt
Dundalk Democrat
Garda Review
Iris an Gharda
Irish Independent
Irish Press
Irish Times
The Nation
Nationality
United Ireland
United Irishman

Books and articles

Allen, G., *The Garda Síochána: Policing Independent Ireland 1922–82* (Dublin, 1999).
Banta, M., 'The Red Scare in the Irish Free State, 1925–37', MA thesis (UCD, 1982).
Bew, P., Hazelkorn, E., and Patterson, H., *The Dynamics of Irish Politics* (London, 1989).
Bosworth, R. J. B., *Mussolini* (London, 2002).
Bourke, J., *Dismembering the Male: Men's Bodies, Britain and the Great War* (London, 1996).
——*An Intimate History of Killing: Face-to-face Killing in Twentieth-century Warfare* (London, 1999).

Brady, C., *Guardians of the Peace* (London, 2000 edn.).

Coleman, M., *County Longford and the Irish Revolution 1910–1923* (Dublin, 2003).

Collins, T., 'Return to Manhood: The Cult of Masculinity and the British Union of Fascists', in J. A. Mangan (ed.), *Superman Supreme: Fascist Body as Political Icon— Global Fascism* (London, 2000).

Comerford, R. V., *Ireland* (London, 2003).

Coogan, T. P., *Michael Collins* (London, 1990).

Cronin, M., *The Blueshirts and Irish Politics* (Dublin, 1997).

Cumann Seanchais Chlochair [Fr Lorcan Ó Mearáin, Fr Joseph Duffy, and Fr Peadar Livingstone], *The War of Independence in Monaghan* (n.p., 1966).

Dahl, H. F., *Quisling: A Study in Treachery* (Cambridge, 1999).

Dolan, A., *Commemorating the Irish Civil War: History and Memory, 1923–2000* (Cambridge, 2003).

Dooley, T., *The Decline of Unionist Politics in Monaghan, 1911–23* (Maynooth, 1988).

—— *Inniskeen, 1912–1918: The Political Conversion of Bernard O'Rourke* (Dublin, 2004).

English, R., *Radicals and the Republic: Socialist Republicanism in the Irish Free State 1925–1937* (Oxford, 1994).

—— *Ernie O'Malley: IRA Intellectual* (Oxford, 1998).

Ferriter, D., *The Transformation of Ireland 1900–2000* (London, 2004).

Finnane, M., 'The Carrigan Committee of 1930–31 and the Moral Condition of the Saorstát', *Irish Historical Studies* (Nov. 2001) 519–36.

Fisk, R., *In Time of War: Ireland, Ulster and the Price of Neutrality, 1939–1945* (Dublin, 1983).

Fitzpatrick, D. ' "Unofficial Emissaries": British Army Boxers in the Irish Free State, 1926', *Irish Historical Studies* (Nov. 1996), 206–32.

—— *Politics and Irish Life 1913–1921: Provincial Experience of War and Revolution* (Cork, 1998 edn.).

—— *The Two Irelands 1912–1939* (Oxford, 1998).

—— *Harry Boland's Irish Revolution* (Cork, 2003).

Foster, R. F., *Modern Ireland, 1600–1972* (London, 1988).

—— *Paddy and Mr Punch: Connections in Irish and English History* (London, 1993).

Garvin, T., *Nationalist Revolutionaries in Ireland, 1858–1928* (Oxford, 1987).

—— *1922: The Birth of Irish Democracy* (Dublin, 1996).

Girvin, B., 'Nationalism, Catholicism and Democracy: Hogan's Intellectual Evolution', in D. Ó Corráin (ed.), *James Hogan* (Dublin, 2001).

Griffin, R., *The Nature of Fascism* (London, 1993).

Hanley, B., *The IRA 1926–1936* (Dublin, 2002).

Hart, P., *The IRA and its Enemies: Violence and Community in Cork 1916–23* (Oxford, 1998).

—— *The IRA at War 1916–1923* (Oxford, 2003).

Hobsbawm, E., *Nations and Nationalism since 1780* (Cambridge, 1992 edn.).

Hofstadter, R., *The Paranoid Style in American Politics and Other Essays* (New York, 1965).

Hopkinson, M., *Green against Green: The Irish Civil War* (Dublin, 1988).

—— *The Irish War of Independence* (Dublin, 2002).

Hull, M., *Irish Secrets: German Espionage in Ireland 1939–1945* (Dublin, 2003).

Hutchinson, J., *The Dynamics of Cultural Nationalism: The Gaelic Revival and the Creation of the Irish Nation State* (London, 1987).

Jeal, T., *Baden-Powell* (London, 1989).

Kavanagh, P., *The Green Fool* (London, 1938).

Keene, J., *Fighting for Franco: International Volunteers in Nationalist Spain during the Spanish Civil War, 1936–1939* (London, 2001).

Keogh, D., *Ireland and Europe 1919–48* (Dublin, 1988).

—— *Jews in Twentieth-century Ireland: Refugees, Anti-Semitism and the Holocaust* (Cork, 1998).

Kissane, B., *Explaining Irish Democracy* (Dublin, 2002).

Laffan, M., *The Resurrection of Ireland: The Sinn Féin Party 1916–1923* (Cambridge, 1999).

Lee, J. J., *Ireland, 1912–85: Politics and Society* (Cambridge, 1989).

Lee, S., *European Dictatorships, 1918–1945* (London, 2000 edn.).

Ledeen, M., *Universal Fascism: The Theory and Practice of the Fascist International, 1928–1936* (New York, 1972).

Linz, J., 'Some Notes Towards a Comparative Study of Fascism', in W. Laquer (ed.), *Fascism: A Reader's Guide* (London, 1976).

Livingstone, P., *The Monaghan Story* (Enniskillen, 1980).

Lyons, F. S. L., *Ireland Since the Famine* (London, 1973 edn.).

McCluskey, S., *The G.A.A. in Co. Monaghan . . . a History* (Monaghan, 1984).

MacEoin, U., *The IRA in the Twilight Years* (Dublin, 1997).

McGarry, F., *Irish Politics and the Spanish Civil War* (Cork, 1999).

—— *Frank Ryan* (Dundalk, 2002).

McCullagh, F., *In Franco's Spain* (London, 1937).

McNiffe, L., *A History of the Garda Síochána: A Social History of the Force, 1922–52* (Dublin, 1997).

Mandle, W. F., *The Gaelic Athletic Association and Irish Nationalist Politics, 1884–1924* (London, 1987).

Mangan, J. A., 'Global Fascism and the Male Body', in J. A. Mangan (ed.), *Superman Supreme: Fascist Body as Political Icon—Global Fascism* (London, 2000).

Manning, M., *The Blueshirts* (Dublin, 1987 edn.).

—— *James Dillon: A Biography* (Dublin, 1999).

Maume, P., *D. P. Moran* (Dundalk, 1995).

—— *The Long Gestation: Irish Nationalist Life 1891–1918* (Dublin, 1999).

Mazower, M., *Dark Continent: Europe's Twentieth Century* (London, 1998).

Moran, S. F., *Patrick Pearse and the Politics of Redemption* (Washington, 1997).

Murray, P., *Oracles of God: The Roman Catholic Church and Irish Politics, 1922–37* (Dublin, 2000).

Novick, B., *Conceiving Revolution: Irish Nationalist Propaganda during the First World War* (Dublin, 2001).

Ó Drisceoil, D., *Censorship in Ireland 1939–1945: Neutrality, Politics and Society* (Cork, 1996).

O'Duffy, E., *Crusade in Spain* (Dublin, 1938).

O'Kelly, D., *Salute to the Gardai, 1922–1958* (Dublin, 1959).

O'Halpin, E., *Defending Ireland: The Irish State and its Enemies since 1922* (Oxford, 1999).

O'Riordan, M., 'Anti-Semitism in Irish Politics', *Irish–Jewish Year Book* (1984/85), 23.

Passmore, K., *Fascism: A Very Short Introduction* (Oxford, 2002).

Phoenix, E., *Northern Nationalism: Nationalist Politics, Partition and the Catholic Minority in Northern Ireland 1890–1940* (Belfast, 1994).

Powers, R. G., *Secrecy and Power: The Life of J. Edgar Hoover* (New York, 1987).

Preston, P., *Franco: A Biography* (London, 1993).

Quinn, A., *Patrick Kavanagh: A Biography* (Dublin, 2001).

Regan, J. M., *The Irish Counter-Revolution 1921–1936* (Dublin, 1999).

Sisson, E., *Pearse's Patriots: St Enda's and the Cult of Boyhood* (Cork, 2003).

Stephan, E., *Spies in Ireland* (London, 1965).

Stradling, R. A., *The Irish and the Spanish Civil War 1936–1939* (Manchester, 1999).

Thurlow, R., *Fascism in Britain: A History 1918–85* (Oxford, 1987).

Townshend, C., *Ireland: The 20th Century* (London, 1998).

Valiulis, M. G., *Portrait of a Revolutionary: General Richard Mulcahy and the Founding of the Irish Free State* (Dublin, 1992).

Index

Abbey Theatre 163, 339
Abwehr (German military intelligence)
    322, 324, 331, 334, 336
Abyssinia 281
ACA, *see* Army Comrades Association
Act of Union 20
Action Française 287
Adare 109
Aghabog 67
agriculture, *see* rural agitation
Aiken, Frank 85, 88, 91–2, 193, 253, 257,
    328
  and truce 77, 85
  and Treaty 89, 90
  and northern offensive (1922) 100,
    101–2
  and Civil War 107, 110
  on EOD 90, 92, 116
Ailtirí na hAiséirghe 338, 339
Alcázar 287, 299
Alexandria 201
Algeciras, Duke of 290, 293, 294
All-Purposes Guilds 321, 325
Allen, Gregory 164–5
Amalgamation of Police Forces act (1925)
    172
Amateur Athletics Association of Great
    Britain and Northern Ireland 152
Amateur Athletics Association (UK)
    152–3, 154
Amsterdam 275
An Phoblacht 177, 191, 193, 225, 332
Ancient Order of Hibernians 3, 64, 67,
    72, 244
  before War of Independence 2–3, 11,
    19, 24, 29, 35, 41

War of Independence 41–2, 50, 53–5,
    64, 66–9, 72
anglicization 9, 10, 13, 15, 16, 46, 344
Anglo-Celt 44
Anglo-Irish coal-cattle pact (1934) 277
Anglo-Irish Treaty 74, 77, 85, 87–98,
    100–1, 103–4, 172, 243, 268
  Treaty ports 326
  see also boundary commission; IRA;
    partition
anglophobia 11, 15, 22, 141, 280
anti-annuities campaign 180, 183, 202,
    224, 242, 258, 262
  Blueshirts and 212, 258, 260, 262–3,
    272, 274, 277
anti-communism 268, 320
  EOD and 111, 161, 166, 177, 198, 344
  and land agitation 180, 203
  and IRA 183–4, 185, 196, 223, 324
  red scare *re* Fianna Fáil (1931) 183–4,
    185, 186, 190, 196
  Fianna Fáil government attacked as
    communist 190, 203–4, 210, 231,
    232, 255–6
  Blueshirts and 196, 203–4, 206–7,
    210, 215, 223, 226, 255–6,
    278
  and corporatism 206, 211–12, 223
  and Spain 280, 284–5, 290, 300, 301,
    304, 307, 319–20
  international 184, 268, 279, 320, 345
anti-Semitism 253, 254, 320
  in Ireland 252, 273, 321, 325, 326, 328,
    330
  EOD and 254, 319–20, 330
Anyalla 63

Aontas Gaedheal 254
Arbour Hill prison 229, 266, 272
Arklow 263
Armagh city 80–2, 93
Armagh, Co. 34, 36, 49, 65, 100, 101, 348
Armstrong, Albert 182
Army Comrades Association 187, 191,
    192, 195, 198, 202, 204–6, 207–8,
    214, 221
army mutiny 131–7, 139, 140
Arnold, Thomas 18
Article 2A 184–5, 186, 191, 217, 229, 230,
    231
Ashe, Thomas 38, 39
Asquith, Herbert 20
Athens 165
athletics 15, 126, 145, 147, 150, 152–4, 155,
    159, 200, 214–15
    see also Garda Síochána; NACA
Athlone 230, 339
Aughnacloy 68
Austria 129, 206, 215, 275
Auxiliaries 59, 71, 73, 76, 237
Axis powers 332, 337, 339, 340

Badajoz 350
Baden-Powell, Robert 163, 214
    see also boy scouts
Balbriggan 159, 231
Balfour, Arthur James 218
Ballaghaderreen 205
Ballina 258
Ballsrud, Terje 264
Ballybay 26, 53, 58, 89
Ballybofey 226
Ballyocean 41
Ballyporeen 225
Ballyseedy 113, 317, 350
Ballyshannon 226, 228
Ballytrain 42, 47, 62, 70, 237, 248
Baltinglass 124, 125
bandera, Irish, see Irish Brigade
Bandon 226, 246, 271, 277

Barrett, Frank 84
Barry, John 255
Barry, Tom 225
Basques 283, 288
Bates, Sir Dawson 79, 82
Bawn 68
Béal na mBláth 112, 138, 235, 245, 264,
    278, 281
Beckett, Matt 297
Beggars' Bush barracks 96, 97
Belfast 8, 49, 63, 93, 98, 100, 102, 279
    prison 36, 37, 49
    Belfast boycott 57, 80, 98, 99
    violence in, post-truce 78–9, 80,
        82, 83
Belfast Soccer League 45
Belgium 323
Belton, Paddy 249, 253, 261, 265–6,
    272–3, 277, 284, 286, 318, 319
Berardis, Vincenzo 324–5
Berlin 129, 155, 291, 309, 334, 337, 339
Black and Tans 58–9, 63–4, 76, 93, 179,
    237
Blackrock College 236
Blackshirts 223
Blair, Dr. 143
Bloody Sunday (Belfast) 78
Bloody Sunday (Dublin) 59
The Blueshirt 210, 272, 278, 280
Blueshirts 164, 278, 289, 329, 330, 335,
    350
    sport and athleticism 18, 121, 214–15,
        251, 252, 276
    and nationalism 121, 160, 234–40,
        245, 249–50, 264, 269, 278
    and masculinity 167, 250, 251–2
    anti-communism 190, 215, 223,
        254–6, 268
    and violence 195, 204, 224–7, 229–30,
        232–3, 237, 244, 246–7, 258–60,
        269
    and IRA 195, 204, 212, 223–7, 230,
        232–3, 234–8, 244, 246, 258, 269

origins 202–7, 208, 209, 210
and fascism 204–20, 222–4, 237–8,
    241–2, 243–50, 252–7, 259, 264,
    266–9, 279, 349–50
and economic war 212, 242, 246, 258,
    261–3, 274, 277
and corporatism 205–6, 208, 210–13,
    217, 220, 221–3, 231, 243, 256,
    262, 267, 275–6
Blue blouses 215, 244, 247, 248, 250
proposed march to Dáil 216–18, 244,
    268, 269
government coercion of 218–19, 222,
    226, 228–30, 232, 277, 280
and Fine Gael 219–24, 231, 233,
    234–42, 249, 256, 260–6, 269,
    270–2
EOD's leadership of 224, 228, 231,
    233, 235, 247–50, 256–8, 260,
    264–5, 268
rural agitation 224–5, 236, 240–2,
    248, 258, 261–3, 267, 272, 274,
    277
and Civil War politics 236, 237, 350
social and economic policy 236,
    240–3, 263, 267, 274, 280
racism and anti-Semitism 252–4
EOD's resignation and split 264–6,
    268–9, 270–4, 277–8, 282
and Spanish Civil War 289, 296, 302,
    318
see also ACA; NCP; YIA
Blum, Leon 320
Blythe, Ernest 132, 221, 331
    Protestant Irish speaker 39, 56, 144,
        205, 253
    before 1922 39, 40, 57, 105
    on Civil War 114, 131
    and Garda Siochána 116, 117, 123, 173,
        188
    and planned coup d'état 189, 190
    and fascism 190, 204, 205, 208, 253,
        257, 267, 331, 339

and Blueshirts 202, 204, 205, 206,
    208, 209, 214, 235, 259
on corporate state 206, 223
and Blueshirt split 249, 261, 265–6,
    270–1
Bodenstown 183
Boer War 9
Boland, Harry 21, 106
bolshevism 111, 190, 200, 202–3, 207,
    284, 323, 339
border 61, 98, 99, 101, 139–40, 239, 335
    see also Boundary Commission
Boston Sunday Post 216
Boundary Commission 88, 93, 98, 139
boxing 126, 146, 148, 162, 166
Boy Scouts 163, 167, 214
Boyle 255
Breen, Dan 111
Breffni Park 151
Bremen 129, 327
Brennan, Colonel Austin 202
Brennan, Michael 38, 97, 107–8, 110,
    116–17, 134, 189
Brennan, Paddy 110, 116–17
Brennan-Whitmore, Commandant 324,
    325, 340
Briscoe, Robert 252, 253
British Commonwealth 105, 222, 235,
    239–40, 279, 280, 282
British forces in Ireland 44
    and GAA 11, 36, 45
    and War of Independence 52–3, 58–9,
        64–5, 70–1, 73, 75–6, 78
    and Civil War 106
    post-truce 85, 96
        in Northern Ireland 78–80, 82
    departure post-Treaty 91, 97, 99
    in post-Treaty Northern Ireland 99,
        102
    see also Auxiliaries; Black and Tans;
        RIC
British intelligence 59, 64, 70, 75–6, 77
    see also informers; MI5

British Union of Fascists 220, 252, 264,
        279, 282–3
    see also Oswald Mosley
Brixton prison 92
Bronx Zoo 142–3
Broomfield 4, 31
Broy Harriers 216–17, 261–2
Broy, Ned 195, 196, 201, 216
Brugha, Cathal 26, 52, 82–3, 85–7, 88,
        94, 103, 106
Bruton, John 349
Bulgaria 129
bullfighting 299
Bundoran 226, 331
Burgos 287, 293
Burke, James 190, 223, 329
Byrne, Alfie 316
Byrne, Dr Edward, Archbishop of
        Dublin 184

Cabanellas Ferrer, General Miguel 287
Cáceres 292, 293–5, 297–9, 302, 306, 311,
        313
Cahill, Fr Edward 206
Cahill, Tom 307
Cairo 201
camogie 348
Canaris, Admiral Wilhelm 324
Canary Islands 302
    bandera 303, 309
Carew, Colonel Tom 236, 262, 289, 317
Cargaghdoo 1, 5
Carlist movement 284, 295, 300, 308,
        319
    Requetés 295, 300, 308, 311
Carr, Henry 65, 67
Carragher, Tom 31, 100
Carrickmacross 15, 22, 23, 26, 29, 42,
        270, 340
    in War of Independence 47, 50, 53, 65
Carrigan committee 157, 159
Carroll (detective) 194
Carroll, Kitty 65–6

Carson, Sir Edward 19, 20, 22
Casement, Sir Roger 164
Cashel 279
Castlebar 226
Castleblayney 1, 5, 9, 26, 42, 50, 57, 63
Castlecomer 255
Catalonia 283
Catholic Bulletin 252
Catholic Emancipation Centenary
        (1929) 149
Catholic Standard 205, 348
Catholic Young Men's Society 285
Catholics and Catholic Church
    in Co. Monaghan 2–3, 4, 11, 20–1, 29,
        41, 42, 46
        during War of Independence 44, 47,
            54, 58, 59–61, 66, 67, 69, 70, 75
    and GAA 11, 46, 151
    priests in Sinn Féin 29, 41, 151
    and nationalism 56, 81, 146, 149, 245,
        276, 350
    in Belfast 57, 78–80, 100
    in Northern Ireland 78–80, 98, 100,
        101
    and moral degeneration 157–60
    and anti-communism 184, 185, 196,
        206–7
    right-wing 206–7, 238, 243, 281, 329,
        332, 344
        and corporatism 205–7, 212, 267
    and Blueshirts 210, 212, 227, 245
    and anti-Semitism 210, 252, 253
    and Second World War 323, 327–8
    see also Eucharistic Congress; Garda
        Síochána; Irish Brigade;
        sectarianism; Spain; Spanish
        Civil War
Cavan, Co. 3, 8, 34, 36, 53, 222, 239, 250,
        258, 272
    GAA 14–15, 17, 36, 151
    Blueshirts 222, 239, 250, 258, 272
Celtic Confederation of Occupation
        Guilds 322

Celtic Professional Societies 321
censorship 327, 328, 339
census 3
Centre Party 218, 219, 221–2, 241
Chaplin, Charlie 153
Chicago 322
Childers, Erskine 111, 113
Christian Front, *see* Irish Christian Front
Church of Ireland 2
Church of Ireland Gazette 318
Churchill 53
Churchill, Winston 99, 100, 326
Chute, Dan 302, 303, 306
Ciano, Count Galeazzo 275
Ciempozuelos 301–2, 303–6, 312
citizenship 175, 180, 215, 251
Civic Guard, *see* Garda Síochána
Civil Guards (Spain) 296, 319
civil service 144, 186, 200
Civil War (1922–3) 90, 106, 120, 139,
        172, 192, 269
    attempts to prevent 89, 95–7, 100–1,
        103–5, 106
    North and 101, 102, 103, 107
    in Munster 106–14, 180, 185, 205, 350
    after death of Collins 111–14, 115–16,
        122–6, 131, 350
    Garda Síochána during 116–17,
        122–4, 171, 175
    EOD and 74, 90, 95, 106–14, 122–4,
        205, 336, 350
    EOD on 111, 175, 191
    and Blueshirts 202, 212, 236–7, 245,
        246, 263, 267, 268, 350
    legacy of 114, 131, 170, 175, 180, 201,
        219, 224, 268
    see also Irregulars
Clare, Co. 38, 116–17, 159
    and Civil War 110, 180
    republicans in 180–1, 185, 194
    Blueshirts 219, 259
Clare, Mrs. 44
'cleanliness' 161, 162, 163

Clones 7, 8, 10, 36, 45, 89, 99, 135, 348,
        349
    and Volunteers 10, 26, 28, 34, 35, 36,
        41, 43
    during War of Independence 48, 49,
        53
    and northern offensive (1922)
        99–100, 101
Clonmel 230, 297
Clontibret 14, 36
Coalisland 34
coercion
    by Cumann na nGaedheal of IRA
        171–2, 174–5, 176, 178, 192
    by Fianna Fáil
        of National Guard 216–17, 218–19,
        220, 226
        of Blueshirts 194, 219, 226, 228,
        232–3, 277, 280
        of IRA 280, 325
    see also Public Safety acts
Cohalan, Dr Daniel, Bishop of Cork
        246–7
Cohn, Roy 345
Coimbra 313
Collins, Michael
    personality and dominance 26, 83
    EOD as protegé 26, 27, 32, 75, 83, 97,
        112, 347
    War of Independence 40, 59, 60, 76,
        77, 96, 171
        and Northern Ireland 57, 78,
        80, 81
    intelligence network 75, 172, 195
    and Brugha 85–7
    and Treaty 85, 88–90, 91, 94, 95, 139
    from Treaty to Civil War 77, 81, 96,
        98–104, 100, 104, 105
    Civil War 106–7, 108, 110, 111, 112
    death and funeral 103, 104, 112–13
    EOD and death of 112–13, 115, 176
    EOD and commemoration of 138,
        216, 235–6, 245

Collins, Michael (*cont.*)
  Blueshirts and 207, 216, 221, 235, 245,
    246–7, 346
  EOD as heir to Collins 234, 239–40,
    274
Collinstown aerodrome 119
Cologne 281
Comerford, R.V. 16, 145, 343
Comintern 320
Committee of action for the Universality
    of Rome 275
Communist International 320
Communist Party of Ireland 254
communists and communism 200, 201,
    202, 254, 283, 305, 307, 318
  see also anti-communism
Connacht Tribune 200
Connaught 1, 160
Connemara 130, 245
Connolly, James 332, 350
Connradh Gaolach an Gharda 146
conscription 21, 22, 35
constitution
  1922 90, 105, 221, 232
    emergency legislation and 178, 183,
      185, 230
    EOD's lack of respect for 189, 199,
      209
  1937 280, 344
Coogan, Eamon 123, 166
Cooney, Andy 338
Cootehill 7, 37, 50, 56
Cope, Alfred 79, 82
Córas na Poblachta 332, 338
Corcoran, Timothy 344
Corduff 59, 62
Cork city 68, 143, 281
Cork, Co.
  War of Independence in 32, 71, 73
  Civil War in 109, 110
  and Irish Brigade 280, 296
  and NCP 280–1

and Blueshirts 230–1, 247, 258, 261,
    262
Cork Examiner 264
corporatism 256, 279, 281, 319
  EOD on Gaelic origins of 211–12,
    325
  see also Blueshirts
Corrigan, Patrick 31–2, 64–5
Corvoy 65
Cosgrave, William T. 155, 173, 178, 267,
    274
  and army mutiny 132, 133, 134, 135
  and red scares 184, 190, 255
  on dismissal of EOD 200–1
  on parliamentary democracy 201, 267
  and Blueshirts 207, 263, 264, 267–8,
    277
  replaced by EOD 220–2, 267–8
  on annuities campaign 263, 277
Costello, John A. 230, 232
Coughlan, Colonel Paddy 236, 271,
    273
coup d'état, planned 189–92, 196, 198,
    217, 220, 350
courts, republican 50–1, 67
Coventry 327
Coyle, Packie 31
Coyne, Fr Edward 206
Craig, James, Viscount Craigavon 98–9,
    100, 102, 155
cricket 146
Croke Park 26, 59, 129
Croke, Thomas, Archbishop of Cashel
    15
Crom Castle 8
Cronin, Anthony 165, 166
Cronin, Felix 135
Cronin, Mike 212, 248, 251, 267
Cronin, Ned 109, 245, 253, 263, 264
  and Blueshirts 202, 204, 208, 226,
    245, 259, 261, 266
  and EOD's leadership of 208, 249,

261, 263, 264–6, 270–1
  director of after split 266, 271–2, 273, 277, 280–1
  and Spanish Civil War 287, 296
Crossmaglen 80
Cuchulainn 235, 249
Cullaville 55, 100
cultural nationalism 3, 9, 253, 343–4
  and GAA 3, 15–17, 18, 25, 121
  and revolutionary politics 9–11, 25, 75, 344
  groups most influenced by 10, 29, 75
  and history and mythology 16–17, 248, 249–50
  and Garda Síochána 146, 149
  see also GAA; Gaelic League; Irish language
Cumann na mBan 30, 38, 250
Cumann na nGaedheal 200, 202, 213, 252, 329, 331
  in government 139, 178, 186, 188, 199
  and relationship of party and state 139, 178, 199
  and drift from republican roots 139, 234–7
  and 1932 election 186, 188
  and Fianna Fáil government 190, 191, 202–3
  IRA attacks on 192, 204
  Blueshirts and 202, 208, 210, 219, 241, 248, 251, 261
  decline 206, 221, 231
  and Fine Gael 218–22, 224, 241, 248
Cumann Náisiunta 329
Cumann Poblachta na h-Eireann 279
Cummins, Monsignor 160
Cunningham, Seán 310
Curragh camp 20, 102, 103, 105, 109, 135, 333
Curragh Mutiny 20
Curtin, Superintendent John 182, 202
cycling 152

Cyprus 202
Czechoslovakia 129, 327

Dáil administration
  county councils 50
  courts 50–1, 67
  police 34, 51–2
Dáil Eireann
  before the Treaty 32, 41, 50–1, 57, 77, 85
  and Treaty 90–1, 92–5, 96, 98, 104
  debates 81, 136, 200–1, 209, 213, 231, 232, 269, 284
  Fianna Fáil entry to 172, 178, 179
  and Blueshirts 216–17, 223, 231, 232, 246, 269, 272
Dail Uladh 21
Daily Mail 301
Dalton, Emmet 110, 111, 112
Dalton, Major Patrick 236, 289, 296, 302, 306
Daly, Charlie 96
Daly, Cornelius 247
Daly, Major-General Paddy 131
Davitt, Michael 236, 277
de Valera, Eamon 155, 178, 236, 241, 244, 281, 323, 344, 346
  and North 56, 81, 239, 274, 335
  and Treaty 77, 90–1, 95, 101
  dispute re EOD's position in GHQ 85, 86–7, 116, 191
  EOD's personal enmity towards 91, 149, 191, 336
  and Civil War 104, 111, 113, 131, 172, 263
  enters Dáil 172, 178–9
  in power (1932) 155, 191–2, 195–6, 202, 204, 207
  opposition distrusts 123, 201–3, 216, 219–20, 228, 232, 235, 261, 281
  red scare 190, 202, 255, 256

de Valera, Eamon (*cont.*)
  and EOD's dismissal 191, 197–8,
    200–1, 207, 347
  and IRA 192–3, 203, 216, 261–2, 267,
    279, 332, 334
    moves against 199, 217–18, 256,
      269, 280, 324, 326
  and security forces 193–4, 198, 199,
    200–1, 202, 289
  and Broy Harriers 216–17, 261–2
  and Blueshirts 216–19, 220, 222,
    225–32, 238, 261–2, 269, 279–80
  xenophobic attacks on 227, 232,
    252–3
  1937 constitution 280, 344
  and Spanish Civil War 284, 285, 289,
    290, 292, 300, 302, 305, 319
  and Second World War 323, 326, 328,
    332, 334, 336, 337, 338
  and EOD's funeral 348
Dear Boy 163, 165, 166
Denmark 216
Derrig, Thomas 337
Derry city 99
Derry, Co. 74, 99
Derry Journal 227
Deutscher Fichte-Bund 321, 322, 328
Devlin, Joe 49
Dillon, James 221–2, 255, 258, 260,
  262–6, 271, 273, 276
Document No. 2 91
Doherty, Sergeant 43
Dollfuss, Engelbert 206, 243
Dollymount 150
dominion status 77, 88
Donaghmore 34
Donegal 43, 45, 228, 273, 324
Dooley, Terence 66
Douglas, Joseph 60
Dresden 129
Drew, Ronnie 350
Drohl, Ernest Weber 334

Drum 2, 41
Drumgarra 54
Dublin 131, 165, 180, 181–2, 329–30
  Mansion House 87, 274, 276, 317
  Civil War in 98, 106, 111
  EOD's proposed march on 216–18,
    244, 268, 269
  and Irish Brigade 290, 292, 294, 297,
    308
  see also Easter Rising; Phoenix Park
Dublin Castle 3, 8, 27, 35, 62, 68, 78, 82,
  117, 195
Dublin Metropolitan Police 118, 171, 172
Dublin Trout Anglers Association 150
The Dubliners 350
Duffy, Alice (sister of EOD) 1
Duffy, Bridget (née Fealy, mother of
  EOD) 1, 4, 6, 165, 342
Duffy family ('the Peadar Mores', family
  of EOD) 1, 4, 6
Duffy, Frank ('Red Frank', brother of
  EOD) 1, 6
Duffy, Hugh 69
Duffy, James (brother of EOD) 1, 6
Duffy, Mary (sister of EOD) 1
Duffy, Owen, *see* Eoin O'Duffy
Duffy, Owen (father of EOD) 1, 4,
  5–6
Duffy, Patrick ('Black Pat', brother of
  EOD) 1, 6
Duffy, Peter ('Big Peter', grandfather of
  EOD) 1
Duffy, Peter (brother of EOD) 1, 6
Duggan, Eamon 116
Dun Aengus 291
Dun Laoghaire dog show 150
Dundalk 4, 8, 13, 107, 230
Dundalk Democrat 12, 23, 50, 57, 61,
  65, 72
  on GAA 17, 36
  on Volunteers 21–2, 23, 34
  on the Irish Party 22, 40

on Sinn Féin 29, 34, 40, 41
on War of Independence 42, 50, 57,
   61, 65
Dunne, Joseph 96
Dusseldorf 281

Easter Rising (1916) 11, 21, 23–4, 27,
   28–9, 95, 98, 344, 346
economic war 202, 207, 224, 242, 258,
   260–2, 274, 277
   Fine Gael and 203, 231, 240–2, 260–3,
      267, 272, 277
   see also anti-annuities campaign;
      Blueshirts
Edwards, Hilton 164, 165
Egypt 201–2
elections 2, 81
   general 3, 222–3
      1918 19, 34, 39–41, 48, 49, 68
      1921 76
      1922 104, 105
      1927 178
      1932 186, 188–93, 221
      1933 195, 197, 203, 207, 221
   by-elections
      1918 34
      1925 139
   local
      1920 49–50
      1934 240, 260
Ellis, William Webb 17
The Emergency 326, 328, 340, 348
emergency legislation, see coercion
Emyvale 43, 48
English, Richard 70
Ennis 107, 219
Erne family (Crom Castle) 8
The Ethics of Sinn Féin 121
Eucharistic Congress, International
   (1932) 149, 167, 197, 244, 245
Evening Herald 161
Evora 313

fáinne 120
Fairbanks, Douglas 153
Falange 275, 287, 293, 300, 303,
   319, 325
Farmers' Party 241
Farney 5
fascism 156, 212–14, 234, 238, 242, 243,
   249, 273
   EOD and, before 1939 156, 209–14,
      220, 237–8, 241, 259, 267–9, 273,
      279
   trappings of 204, 209, 218, 223, 231,
      244, 245, 246
   and Catholicism in Ireland 205–7,
      212, 245, 252, 267, 276
   Fine Gael and 212, 224, 269
   in Europe 212, 232, 234, 245, 249,
      275–6, 281, 283, 287, 321
   in Britain 220, 226, 238, 252, 264, 275,
      279, 282–3
   strength of in Ireland 234, 266–8,
      269, 278, 350
   in Ulster 264, 279, 280
   and Spanish Civil War 283, 284, 286,
      318
   in Ireland after 1939 321–6, 327,
      328–30, 332–3, 336, 338–9
   see also Blueshirts; Italy; racialism
Fascist International 275, 281, 338
Fealy, Bridget (later Duffy, mother of
   EOD) 1, 4, 6
Federal Bureau of Investigation 345
Fenians, see IRB
Fennell, Moss 303
Fermanagh, Co. 8, 36, 58, 81, 99, 100,
   101
Fethard 230
Fianna Éireann 34
Fianna Fáil 172, 184, 221, 231, 248, 252,
   285
   in Co. Monaghan 30, 67, 237
   enters Dáil 172, 178–9

Fianna Fáil (*cont.*)
  and Blueshirts 221, 224, 227, 233, 236,
    238, 243, 269
  and IRA 178, 180, 191–3, 196–8,
    202–3, 207, 232, 236, 267, 269,
    279
    moves against 199, 217–18, 256,
      269, 280, 324, 326
    Broy Harriers 216–17, 261–2
  and security forces 188, 193–6, 198–9,
    200–1, 202, 216, 261–2, 289
  plots against 189–92, 196, 198, 217,
    220, 257, 267, 350
  election victories 191, 203, 207, 260
  attacks on 202–3, 207, 210, 232, 255,
    263
  social and economic policies 202–3,
    224, 241, 242–3
  and Fine Gael 240, 243, 267, 272
  see also de Valera
Finance act (1927) 150
Fine Gael 7, 230, 232, 255, 256, 260–1,
    272, 281, 308, 349
  EOD's leadership of 67, 205, 220,
    224, 228, 233, 235, 242–3
    failure to dominate 249, 267, 320,
      349
  merger of conflicting elements
    219–22, 224, 228, 234, 261
  and fascism 212, 253, 267, 279
  and nationalism 222, 228, 235–6,
    239–40, 242, 265
  and Second World War 328, 335
  plans for government 222, 249, 252,
    256
  and Blueshirts 223–4, 228, 233, 245,
    256, 260–3, 265–6, 269, 270–1,
    289
  and rural agitation 203, 231, 240–3,
    260–3, 267, 272, 277
  split and EOD's resignation 261,
    262–6, 270–4

  see also Cumann na nGaedheal; UIP;
    YIA
Fisk, Robert 220
FitzGerald, Desmond 57, 187, 201,
    206–7, 212, 267
FitzGerald-Kenney, James 178, 181, 186,
    201, 232, 255
Fitzpatrick, Noel 295, 296, 310
Fleming, Robert 55
Fleming, William 54–5
Flinn, Hugo 253
Fogarty, Dr Michael, Bishop of Killaloe
    159, 219, 285
Forde, Liam 97
Forrest, Andrew 245
Four Courts 90, 98, 106
France 148–9, 249, 283, 320, 323, 326, 333
  see also Paris
Franco, General Francisco 212, 243,
    347
  and Spanish Civil War 284, 300, 302,
    306–7, 317, 318
  see also Irish Brigade
Franco, Nicolás 314
Freeman, Dr 305
freemasonry 138, 139, 254, 296, 320, 322,
    323, 330, 344
Fribourg 205
Friends of Soviet Russia 183

G Division (Dublin Metropolitan
    Police) 171, 172
G2 (Irish military intelligence) 321,
    322–3, 324, 325, 327, 329–34,
    336–40
GAA, *see* Gaelic Athletic Association
Gaelic Athlete 12, 150
Gaelic Athletic Association 7, 10, 11, 59,
    151–2, 346, 348
  and nationalism 3, 11–12, 15–16, 21,
    27–9, 37, 46, 151
  ban 11, 15–16, 27, 46, 126, 146, 150–1

in Co. Monaghan 12–14, 17, 26, 27–8, 35–7, 44–6, 146, 348

in Ulster 12–15, 17, 28, 36, 45, 49, 150

and EOD's career 12, 14, 26, 27, 147, 271, 343

non-political 16, 27, 36, 151

physical and moral improvement of young men 17–18, 121, 151, 160, 167

and Volunteers 14, 18, 20, 25, 26, 27–9, 35, 37

central council and committees 21, 44, 150, 151

RIC and government harassment of 35–7, 44–5, 49, 98–9, 101

EOD as Garda Commissioner and 118, 126, 129, 142, 146, 150–1, 156

EOD and, after *1932* 215, 251, 332

Gaelic language, *see* Irish language

Gaelic League 3, 5, 7, 8–10, 23, 36, 145, 204

Gaeltacht 144

Gaertner, Dieter 334

Galicia 291

Gallagher, Sergeant 48

Galway city 144, 255, 285

Galway, Co. 17, 231, 263, 285, 291

Garda Museum 164

Garda Review 162, 176, 180, 186–7, 193, 195

Garda Síochána
sport and athletics in 18, 119, 121, 126, 146–7, 150–1, 158, 162

and Civil War 108, 116, 122–5, 171

EOD's appointment as Commissioner 113, 116, 117

unarmed force 116, 122, 123–4, 149, 175–6, 184–5, 186

recruitment to 116–19, 124, 127

discipline in 117–18, 127

nationalist ethos in 118–21, 125, 144–6, 149

and morality 119–21, 127, 144, 146, 158, 170

and temperance 120, 126, 149, 162

Phoenix Park depot 119, 125, 128–9, 143, 146, 147

Catholic ethos in 121, 125–6, 127, 144, 147–50

non-political 122, 123, 132, 171–2, 181, 188, 269

EOD's effective leadership of 127–8, 130, 131, 141, 178, 195, 197, 200–1, 347, 349

EOD's pride in 127–8, 134, 188, 195, 198, 229

EOD's visits abroad as commissioner 129–31, 142–3, 148–9

EOD's relations with government 140, 186, 187–8, 191–9, 202, 204

cult of personality 142–3

Garda band 143

and manliness 162, 165, 167, 168

reports on EOD 166, 217, 218, 219, 229, 258–9, 279, 281, 331, 332, 333, 340

and emergency powers 171–2, 175–6, 178, 179–82, 184–6, 191, 192–4

and IRA 171–85, 186, 188, 192–4, 195–8, 199

internal discipline 173–4, 179–81, 185, 188, 194, 196–7, 198, 199, 201, 262

and red scares 183–4, 185, 186

and attacks on Cumann na nGaedheal meetings 187

EOD's removal from office 197–9, 200–1

and Blueshirts 224–7, 258–9, 260, 261–2, 274

EOD keeps contact with of 257, 331, 339, 389

during Second World War 329–30, 331–2, 333, 334

Garvin, Tom 18, 70, 164

Gate Theatre 163–4, 166, 167
Geary, William 180
Gegan, Capt. James 130
gender 10, 161, 250
Geneva 275, 281
Geoghegan, James 191, 193–5, 196, 201
George V, King 90, 91
'German plot' 35
German-Russian pact 323
Germany
    EOD admires 129, 156, 168, 214–15,
        257
    and Ireland before the Second World
        War 220, 238, 245, 268–9, 276,
        320, 323
    and Spanish Civil War 283, 287, 291,
        292, 300, 312
    EOD's contacts with 322–4, 329,
        331–4, 335–9
    German agents in Ireland 322, 332,
        334–8, 339
    German invasion expected 326, 329,
        330–1, 333, 334, 338
    and Irish attitudes to the war 327–8,
        329–30, 331, 332, 337
    see also Hitler; IFG; IRA; Liam Walsh;
        National Army; Nazism
Gibbs, Joseph 64
Gibraltar 201
Gil Robles, José María 319
Gilmore, George 194
Glasgow 6
Glasnevin Cemetery 348
Glenties 226
Glynch 37
Goebbels, Joseph 309
Goertz, Herman 334–8, 339
golf 146, 147
Gordon, William 60
Gort 125
Government of Ireland act (1920) 78
Government of Ireland bill (1912) 19

Graham, Sergeant 47
Gralton, Jim 254
Grand Visier of Spanish Morocco 304
Grandi, Count Dino 257
Great Northern Railways 8, 57
Great War 11, 20–1, 148, 160, 161, 234,
    268, 323, 346
Greek Orthodox Church 201
Greenan's Cross 12
Greenwood, Sir Hamar 218, 228, 230,
    328, 329
Greyshirts (Norway) 264
Griffin, George 329, 330
Griffin, Roger 214
Griffith, Arthur 216, 235, 240, 242
    career 2, 34, 50, 88, 95, 97, 99, 112
Guadalajara 307
Gunning, Thomas 205, 208, 243, 249
    and EOD 243, 249, 266, 273, 275,
        281, 317
    and Spanish Civil War 287, 295, 299,
        307, 309, 314, 317

habeas corpus 172, 178
Hamburg 129, 321, 322, 327
handball 126, 188, 224
Hanratty (Volunteer) 63
Hart, Peter 64, 71
Haw-Haw, Lord (William Joyce) 327,
    339
Hayes, Stephen 337
Hazlett, Jock 54
Healy, Cahir 10
Healy, T.M. 29
Heimwehr (Austria) 275
Hempel, Dr Eduard 324, 328, 331, 336,
    337, 340
Hibernians, see Ancient Order of
    Hibernians
Hill, Thomas 55
Hitler, Adolf 214
    Blueshirts and 223, 232, 244, 245, 267

EOD and 254, 257–8, 281, 300, 320, 321, 323
Hobsbawm, Eric 154, 344
Hoey, P.V. 340
Hofstadter, Richard 344–5
Hogan, Dan 28, 32, 36–7, 44
  relationship with EOD 28, 44, 88, 95, 129, 168
  and Treaty 88, 95
  and National Army 88, 98–100, 107, 113, 135–6, 137, 191
  War of Independence 47, 59, 60, 63, 75
Hogan, James 190, 191, 196, 205–6, 221–2, 231, 263–4, 267
Hogan, Michael 59, 185, 189, 191, 196–7, 206
Hogan, Patrick 176, 191, 206, 221–2
Hollywood 153–4
Home Rule 2, 3, 9, 10, 19, 20, 21, 24, 78
homophobia 164
homosexuality 163–8, 349
Hoover, J. Edgar 345, 347
Hopkinson, Michael 78
Horan, Bernard 308
Horan, Brigadier-General Eamon 289, 317
House of Commons 76, 100
Hue and Cry 30, 142
Hungary 129
hunger strikes 92, 215
Hyde, Douglas 9
Hyde, Tom 302, 306

IFG, see Irish Friends of Germany
India 334
infanticide 158
informers 43, 63–70, 71, 72, 92, 180, 182
Inniskeen 22, 50
International Action of Nationalisms 275

International Amateur Athletics Federation 152–3
International Brigades 289, 302, 304
International Fascist Movement 321
internment 79, 171, 172, 178, 333, 334, 341
IRA, see Irish Republican Army
IRB, see Irish Republican Brotherhood
Iris an Gharda 120, 127, 128, 142
Irish Amateur Athletics Association 15, 152
Irish Amateur Boxing Association 166
Irish Amateur Handball Association 150, 151
Irish Amateur Handball Union 151
Irish Brigade 288
  EOD raises 284–91
  ICF and 284, 286, 293, 302, 318, 319
  NCP and 284–5, 286, 289, 302, 306
  motives for 285–6, 290, 306, 308
    EOD's political rehabilitation 285–6, 287, 308, 311–12, 314–15, 320, 324
  and Catholic Church 285–6, 288, 289, 290, 294, 296, 299–300, 302–3, 305–6, 308, 314
  General Franco and 287–8, 289, 290–1, 296, 302, 306, 307, 311, 314–15
  EOD's relations with Franco 286, 292, 306–7, 310, 313–15, 319, 347
    meetings between 290, 293, 302, 306, 314
  social side of EOD's war 290, 292–4, 299–301, 311, 313
  EOD spends little time with his men 292, 294, 301, 304, 305, 306, 311, 320
  in Cáceres 292–300, 302, 306, 311, 313
  poor quality of 294–5, 297–8, 305–6, 309–10, 313, 316
  behaviour of 295–8, 307, 309, 310, 313

Irish Brigade (*cont.*)
  tensions within 295–6, 305–6,
      309–10, 313, 316–17, 319
  to the front 301, 306–7, 309–10, 314
  in Ciempozuelos 301–6, 312
  conditions of 304–5, 308, 311, 313
  Titulcia 306–8, 317
  La Marañosa 308–11
  disbanded, departure, and
      homecoming 311, 313–15, 316–18
  and EOD's reputation 312, 324,
      349–50
  veterans 325, 334, 348
  EOD's Spanish diary and memoirs
      285, 292–4, 298, 311, 316, 319–20
Irish Brigade Association 313, 316, 319,
      321
Irish Catholic 318
Irish Christian Front 284, 286, 293, 302,
      318, 319, 329, 332
Irish Crusade against Communism 286,
      302, 385
Irish Football Association 45
Irish Free State Bowling League 150
Irish Friends of Germany 329, 331,
      332–3, 334, 338
Irish Independent 205, 209, 285, 299,
      307, 320, 341, 348, 350
Irish language 18, 343
  in Co. Monaghan 5, 8–9
  EOD and 5, 8, 36, 37, 39, 48, 145–6,
      200, 344
    and Garda Síochána 118–19, 120,
      121, 144–5, 147, 344
  see also Gaelic League
Irish Military Intelligence, *see* G2
Irish Motor Racing Club 150
Irish Olympic Council 150, 153
Irish Parliamentary Party 2–3, 7, 11, 24,
      65
  decline of 19, 21–2, 24, 29, 35, 40–1
Irish Press 238, 306, 320

Irish Republican Army
  EOD's positions in 26, 30, 74–6,
      83–8, 89, 95, 104–5, 106
  1919–21, see War of Independence
  republican police 34, 51–2
  post truce 76–7, 78–83, 83–8, 91
  northern offensive (1922) 98–104
  pro-Treaty IRA, *see* National Army
  anti-Treaty IRA, *see* Irregulars
  after Civil War ('republicans') 132,
      138–9, 161, 170–85, 187, 190, 203,
      208, 252
    see also Blueshirts; Fianna Fáil;
      Garda Síochána
  left wing leaves 256, 279, 325, 326
  EOD and (after 1935) 279–80, 324–6,
      332, 334, 335–6, 338
  and Germany 322, 324, 325–6, 328,
      332, 334–8
  bombing in Britain 324–5, 327
Irish Republican Brotherhood 3, 64, 177
  Collins and 27, 32–3, 83, 85, 89, 94,
      96, 100, 134, 224
  EOD and 83, 85, 89, 94, 96, 100, 134,
      224
    in Monaghan 21, 32–3, 74
  and GAA 9, 11
  and Volunteers 19, 32–3
Irish Times 158, 200, 226, 280, 316, 348
Irish Volunteers 10, 19–23, 26–35, 40–1,
      167, 341
  EOD's arrest and imprisonment
      36–40
  and GAA 14, 18, 20, 25, 26, 27–9, 35,
      37
  Volunteers from 1919, *see* Irish
      Republican Army
The Irish World Review 322
Irish-Americans 153
Iron Guard (Romania) 254, 275, 287
Irregulars 89, 95–8, 100–2, 103, 105–6,
      107–12, 114, 116, 122–3, 151

Italy
    fascism in 156, 212, 223, 248
    influence in Ireland 206, 217, 223,
        267, 269
        on EOD 168, 217, 254, 257, 275–6,
        280, 281–2, 321, 333
    Italian legation
        EOD and 285, 321, 324–5, 331
        reports on EOD 220, 257, 276,
        280, 285, 314, 324–5
        reports on Ireland 205, 219, 266,
        285
    and Spanish Civil War 283, 285, 287,
        292
    see also Mussolini; Rome

Jarama valley 304, 306, 318
jazz 145, 146, 159, 236
Jerusalem 202
Jesuits 31
Jews and Judaism 210, 252–3, 254,
        320, 322, 323, 328–30, 332,
        344
    see also anti-Semitism
Jordan 202
Jordan, John 165
Joyce, James 343
Joyce, William (Lord Haw-Haw) 327,
        339
Ju Jitsu 146
judicial system 172, 177, 179–80, 182,
        183, 184
Juries Protection act 181

Kavanagh, Jim 296
Kavanagh, Patrick 4, 330
Keady 80
Keane, Sean 236
Kelly, Eddie 23
Kelly, Michael 54, 55
Kemp, Peter 295, 312
Kenmare 132

Kenny, Patrick 247
Kent, William 262
Kerney, Leopold 305, 309, 314
Kerry, Co. 84, 109, 113, 123, 131–2, 185,
        186, 317, 318, 334
Kildare, Co. 116, 238
Kilkenny 97, 225, 318
Killarney 110, 130
Killeavy 80
Kilmallock 109, 204
Kilnadrain 54
Kilrush 180, 194
Kindelán Duany, General Alfredo
        291
Kinsale, battle of 285
Kirke, Jimmy 31
Krueger, Paul 9

La Cierva, Juan de 287, 292
La Marañosa 308–11
labour movement 111, 177
Labour Party 191, 196, 201, 218, 284,
        318, 349
Laggan 5
land annuities see anti-annuities
        campaign; economic war
Land Commission 195
Land League 8, 29, 54, 236, 242,
        277
land redistribution 202, 203, 224, 241,
        280
Land War 64, 224, 261
Laragh 5, 10
Larkin, Jim 23, 139, 253
Larmer, Patrick 63, 64, 66–7
Larne 20
Larne gun-running 20
Lavery, Cecil 331
Lawler, Pete 297
Lawton, Sergeant 47, 48
The Leader 200, 232
League of Nations 281

League of Youth (formerly YIA) 228, 231, 249, 251, 256, 258
  and fascist trappings 245, 246, 247
  and EOD's resignation from Fine Gael 262, 264, 266, 270, 271
Lee, Joe 248
Lee, Sergeant Gabriel 306, 308
Leinster 238
Leitrim 3, 185, 193, 254, 255
Lemass, Seán 188, 213, 232, 236, 253
Leo XIII, Pope 212
Lester, George 59–60, 61
Liberal Party 20
Limerick city 97, 107–9, 110
Limerick, Co. 97, 109–10, 259, 272, 273
Limerick War News 108
Lindsay, Patrick 245
Lisbon 292, 296, 297, 299, 315
Lisnaskea 52
Listowel 159, 193
Liverpool 292, 298
Lloyd George, David 24, 77, 99
local government 2, 222
  republican 50
local government board 105
local government reform (1898) 2
London 85, 89, 101, 292, 294
Longford, Co. 101
Los Angeles 152–4, 155
Losset's school 9
Lough Derg 31
Lough Egish 4
Louth 13
Lynch, Fionan 110–11
Lynch, Liam 84, 97, 98, 104, 107–8, 111
Lynch, Michael 247, 262
Lyons, F.S.L. 249

McAdoo, Robert 53
Macalastair, Somhairle 350
McAlister (Sinn Féin truce official) 82
McBride, Maud Gonne 181, 253

McCabe, Alexander 329
McCabe, Fr Alexander 285, 290, 294–7, 298, 305, 309, 311–12
McCabe, John 65
McCarthy, Senator Joseph 345
McCarville, Dr Paddy 62, 101
McCaughey, Sam 298
McCaughey, Seán 326
McCaul, James 54
McCaul, Patrick 54
McCullagh, Francis 297, 301, 306, 308–9, 311, 312, 318
MacDermot, Frank 221, 222, 239, 257–8, 263, 273–4
MacEntee, Seán 40, 50, 92–3, 188, 193, 236
MacEoin, Seán 89, 90, 101, 129, 134, 139, 187, 202, 236, 265
MacEoin, Uinseann 165–6
McGahey, John 63
McGilligan, Patrick 190, 207
McGlade, Charlie 326
McGrath, Joe 133, 141
McGroder, Master 53
McGrory, Patrick 32, 33
McKean, John 3
McKean's Meadow 10
McKelvey, Joe 89, 90
McKenna, Dr Patrick, Bishop of Clogher 7, 13, 37
McKenna, James 31, 48, 60–1
McKenna, John 67
McKenna, Patrick 54–5
Macklin, Henry 57
MacLiammóir, Micheál 163–4, 165–7
MacMahon, Brian 33
McMahon family 102
McMahon, Peadar 134, 135, 189
MacMahon, Seán 115, 136
MacManus, Diarmuid 107
MacNamara, Sean 259, 262
McNamee, Fr 50

MacNeill, Eoin 9, 19, 23, 90, 206
MacNeill, Hugo 129, 135, 187, 189, 191, 289, 293, 331, 333, 336–7
MacNeill, Major Niall 336
McPhillips, Francis 66–7, 72
McPhillips, Seamus 67
Macready, General Sir Neville 82, 106
MacRory, Cardinal Joseph 49, 184, 284, 285
McSweeney, John 308
MacSwiney, Mary 77, 91–2, 94, 141
MacSwiney, Terence 52, 68, 92
Madden, Colonel John 43–4, 50, 54
Madden property 60
Madrid 303, 307, 308, 311, 350
    Madrid front 284, 301
Maffey, Sir John 327
Maghery 80
Maguire, Constable 36
Maguire (ex-RIC) 53
Maguire, Fr Bernard 22–3, 67
mail raids 65, 66
Manchester Guardian 79
Manchester Martyrs 22
Mandle, W.F. 18
manliness, *see* masculinity
Manning, Mary 164
Manning, Maurice 166, 212, 213, 267
March on Dublin, proposed 216–18, 244, 268, 269
March on Rome 216, 217, 244, 269, 287
Maritain, Jacques 207
Markievicz, Constance 57
Marron, Bernard 54
Marron papers 30, 62
Marron, Phil 28, 49
Marx, Dr Wilhelm 129
Marxism 323, 332
masculinity 18, 121, 149, 150, 157, 160, 161–3, 165, 167–9
    and sport and fitness 18, 150, 151–2, 155, 157, 159, 160, 161, 252

and fascism 250, 251–2
Masterson, Canon 160
Mayer, Louis B. 153
Mayo 281
Mé Féin 121
Meade, Captain 314
Meegan family (Cargaghadoo) 1
Metro-Goldwyn Mayer (MGM) 153
Metropolitan Marine Lake Conference 150
Mexico 184, 305
MI5 (British Intelligence) 323, 324, 326, 328, 334, 337, 339, 340
Middle East 201, 203
Military Services Act (1918) 35
military tribunals 184, 185, 218, 229–30, 231
Milligan, Alice 9
Milltown Park 31
Mola, General Emilio 287
Monaghan board of guardians 68
Monaghan Brigade 26, 42, 55, 73
Monaghan, Co. 1–3, 4, 5, 8, 12
    post-truce IRA in 76, 81, 99, 100, 101
    and Treaty 92, 99, 101, 105
    and Garda Síochána under EOD 118, 146
    EOD during army mutiny 135, 136
    see also AOH; Catholics; EOD; GAA; Gaelic League; IRB; Irish Parliamentary Party; Irish Volunteers; Protestants; RIC; Sinn Féin; UIL; Unionists; War of Independence
Monaghan County Council 7, 19, 23, 33, 49–50, 55, 75, 92, 105
    EOD and 7, 43–4, 105
Monaghan County Museum 349
Monaghan rural council 68
Monaghan town 7, 29, 43, 44, 53
Montreux 275
Montreux resolution 254

Moore, Christy 350
Moors, *see* Morocco
morality 14, 138, 146, 150, 157–60, 167,
        170, 214, 341, 343–5
    and sport and fitness 17, 150, 151, 157,
        158–62, 251, 340
    and manliness 157, 160, 161–3, 252
    see also Garda Síochána
Moran, D.P. 161, 232
The Morning Post 82
Morocco
    and Spain 252, 288
    and Spanish Civil War 288, 303–4,
        305
Morrisroe, Patrick, Bishop of Achonry
        229
Moscardó, Colonel José 299
Moscow 183
Mosley, Oswald 220, 238, 264, 275, 279,
        283
Mountjoy prison 39, 49, 196, 227
Moy 34
Moylan, Seán 108–9
Mulcahy, Richard 75, 139, 141
    War of Independence 44, 73, 74–5, 77
    truce to Treaty 78, 82–3, 85, 86–7, 88
    and split 95, 96, 97–8
    Civil War 90, 104–5, 106–7, 108,
        109–10, 112, 115, 131
    army mutiny 131–6, 137
    after *1932* 189, 192, 202, 220, 236
    on EOD's temperament 14, 84, 87,
        106–7, 115
Mulcahy, Risteárd 87
Muldowney, Detective Myles 194
Mullingar 258
Mulrean, Fr J. 295, 297, 298, 305–6, 307,
        312, 316, 319
Munster 73, 84, 95, 97, 102, 106, 107,
        109, 157, 215, 224, 278
Murphy, W.R.E. 110, 113, 118
Muslims 303–4

Mussolini, Benito 214, 254, 275, 281,
        307, 346–7
    EOD compared with 156, 248, 300,
        346
    influence in Ireland 206, 245, 267,
        281–2, 223, 280
    EOD and 211, 213, 222–3, 254, 276,
        300, 319, 323
        EOD meets 148, 211, 275, 281
    March on Rome 216, 217, 244, 269,
        287

NACA, *see* National Athletic and
        Cycling Association
Nangle, Lieutenant Bill 295, 296,
        310
Nasjonal Samling (Norway) 275
The Nation 281
National Army 198, 240, 289, 321
    IRA becomes, and reorganisation 95,
        96, 104–5
    army convention 96, 97–8
    and northern offensive 98–104
    and Civil War 106, 107–14, 131
    divisions between ministers over
        115–16, 132–6
    ex-members in Garda Síochána
        117–19, 124, 127
    low standards in 127, 130–3
    army mutiny 131–7, 139, 140
    and IRB 132, 133, 134
    demobilization 132, 133, 137, 140
    EOD restores order 132, 137–9, 174,
        185, 218
    loses policing role 171–2, 173
    military tribunals 184, 185, 218,
        229–30, 231
    and NDA 187, 191, 202, 236
    coup d'état plotted 189–91, 196
    and ACA 192, 198, 202, 204–6
    Fianna Fáil and 193, 196–7, 202, 204,
        206, 289

and Blueshirts 212, 218, 224, 226, 236, 257, 269
EOD's contacts in 187, 257, 331, 333, 335, 337, 338, 339–40
and Germany during Second World War 335, 336–7, 338
at EOD's funeral 348
National Association 273
National Athletic and Cycling Association 147, 150, 152–3, 156–7, 159, 160–1, 340
National Corporate Party 280–2, 290, 296
and Irish Brigade 284–5, 286, 289, 302, 306
National Defence Association 187, 191, 202, 236
National Guard 208, 209–10, 216, 221, 226, 254, 265, 268, 275
anti-communist 215, 254
coercion of 216–17, 218–19, 220, 226
and Fine Gael 219, 257
National Volunteers 21
Navalcarnero 301, 306, 307
Nazis and Nazism 206, 212, 213, 275, 321
and racialism 254, 320, 329, 330
supporters in Ireland 291, 322, 325, 331, 336
EOD and 323, 324, 332
NCP, see National Corporate Party
NDA, see National Defence Association
Neligan, David 172, 180–1, 189–90, 194, 195, 196–7
Nenagh 108
Neptune Rowing Club 150
Netherlands 275, 328
neutrality 326, 328, 334, 337, 338
New Land League 277
New York 129, 130, 143, 153
New York Evening Post 62, 130
New York Police Department 130, 143, 153

New York Times 229, 242
Newbliss 8, 10, 26, 34, 35, 36–7, 48, 53
Newcastlewest 244, 272
Nixon, District Inspector John W. 80
Nixon, Samuel 60
Northern Ireland 8, 57, 71, 155, 172, 185
EOD on 56, 78, 80–1, 93, 98, 100–1, 102, 104, 116
violence in, post-truce 78–83, 93
and Treaty 88, 89–90, 93, 100–1, 103–4
northern offensive (1922) 89, 98–104
Blueshirts and 209, 274
Fine Gael and 231, 239
fascism in 279, 280
NCP and 282
during Second World War 326, 334, 335, 336, 338
Northern Ireland Amateur Athletics, Cycling and Cross-Country Association 152
Norton, William 201
Norway 264, 275
Nuremberg 244

Obed, Henry 334
O'Brien, Maurice 166
O'Brien, Michael 68
O'Callaghan, Dr Pat 154
O'Connell, Daniel 218, 228, 244, 346
O'Connell, Edward 195, 196, 197
O'Connell, J.J. ('Ginger') 87, 97, 105, 106
O'Connor, Pat 330
O'Daly, Fr 306
O'Daly, P.J. 28, 33, 40, 51
O'Doherty, Dr Thomas, Bishop of Galway 217
O'Donnell, Peadar 180
O'Donovan, James 96, 324, 325, 335, 337–8
O'Duffy Cup 348

O'Duffy, Eoin
  birth, childhood, and family 1, 3–6,
      8–9, 165, 169, 342
  education 5, 6, 7, 75
  appearance 30, 47, 82, 111, 128–9,
      130–1, 248
    after *1932* 198, 216, 221, 225, 312,
      316, 340
  health 128, 198, 312, 318, 320–1, 339,
      340–2
  drinking habits 129, 162, 198, 220,
      228, 229, 305, 323, 331, 333, 339,
      340, 341, 349
  death and funeral 342, 347–8
  character 345, 346–7
    authoritarian, domineering 14, 30,
      129, 199
    conspiratorial and paranoic 112,
      139, 177–8, 228, 344, 345
    craving for popularity 30, 92, 108,
      110, 115, 143, 149, 249
    defensive, false modesty 14, 87, 92,
      105, 115, 154, 310, 319
    difficult 174, 186, 187, 188, 197, 310,
      312, 342
    egomania and cult of personality
      87, 142–3, 149, 249, 286, 345
    energetic and hardworking 13–14,
      30, 39, 44, 49, 73, 128
    extremism, zealotry 158, 162,
      177–8, 198, 344, 345
    flamboyant, pompous 108, 110,
      164, 198, 221, 331, 346
    frugal, austere 30, 31, 113, 341, 342
    genial 198, 249, 312, 342
    judgement of others 163, 197–8,
      237–8, 249, 312
    lonely 128–9, 242, 340
    love of ceremony 149, 213, 244,
      300, 342
    megalomania 110, 143, 155, 213, 248,
      258, 264, 275, 286, 331
    militarism 14, 25, 27, 30, 61–2, 143,
      162, 167–8, 311–12
    piety 31, 39, 147, 149, 300, 342
    'primadonna' 14, 107
    ruthlessness 58, 61, 62–4, 66–72
    self-invention 163, 164, 169, 344,
      347
    sexuality 163–9, 349
    unbalanced 82, 84, 87, 115, 149,
      167, 197, 199, 213, 309, 324
    unscrupulous 14, 89, 92, 141, 199,
      286
    vanity 116, 129, 312, 346
    volatility 87, 107, 169, 228, 264, 312
  and anti-Semitism 254, 319–20, 330
  as Catholic nationalist 56, 81, 146,
      276, 350
  on citizenship 175, 180, 215, 251
  on 'cleanliness' 120–1, 161, 162, 163
  lack of interest in political ideas 39,
      210
  leadership 12, 13–14, 49, 62, 69–73,
      116, 127–8, 137, 249, 311, 312
    disciplinarian 31, 55, 113, 116, 127,
      137
    a steadying influence 42, 123
  nationalism, post-Treaty 228, 234,
      235, 237, 238, 239, 242–3, 264,
      279
  organisational abilities 12–14, 25, 31,
      43, 50, 73, 74–5, 137
    administrative 28, 30–1, 61, 75, 113,
      116, 137, 249, 312, 341
  reputation 62, 342, 348–50
  travels 129–30, 142–3, 148–9, 153–4,
      156, 201–2, 292, 294, 313
  writings and memoirs 3–5, 9, 29,
      318–19, 339
    Crusade in Spain 285, 298, 316, 319,
      320
    Ireland at an Olympiad 153
    Spanish diary 292–4, 311, 312

Why I Resigned from Fine Gael 271
   see also masculinity; morality; sports
O'Duffy, Francis 32
O'Duffy Gaels 29
O'Duffy silver cup 14
O'Ferrall, Captain 309
Official Secrets act 196
O'Halloran, Garda Patrick 124–5
O'Halpin, Eunan 192, 335
O'Hannigan, Donnchadh 107–8
O'Hegarty, P.S. 170
O'Higgins, Dr T.F. 201, 202, 207, 208,
   232, 255, 270, 272
O'Higgins, Kevin 38, 123, 206, 216
   and civil war 122–3, 131
   and Gardaí under EOD 113, 115–17,
      118, 132, 171–2, 173–4, 177, 186
      unarmed and non-political 122,
         123, 175
   and army 115–16, 131–6, 174
   assassination of 176–8, 179, 216
O'Kelly, Seán T. 188, 236
Olympic Games 155, 156
   1912, Stockholm 18
   1932, Los Angeles 152–5
   Irish Olympic team 152, 158
Omagh 8
O'Malley, Ernie 48, 72–3, 77, 84–5, 89,
   96, 97
O'Meara, Chief Supt. 258–9
Ó Murthuile, Seán 27, 75, 77, 81, 89, 115,
   135
O'Neill, Hugh 63
Orange Order 3, 8, 19, 22, 35, 38, 41
   in Northern Ireland 79, 99
   and War of Independence 54, 56
Ordnance Survey Office 190
O'Regan, Willie 166
O'Reilly, Hugh 246–7, 273
Orgaz y Yaldi, General Luis 301
'Oriel House' Criminal Investigation
   Department 171, 174

Orwell, George 320
O'Shiel, Kevin 103, 116
O'Sullivan, Dermot 306, 310, 313, 314
O'Sullivan, Dr 330
O'Sullivan, Gearóid 76, 133, 135
O'Sullivan, John Marcus 206
O'Sullivan, Maureen 153
O'Toole, Luke 26
Ottawa 236

Paisley, Revd Ian 346
Pamplona 287
Paris 148–9, 202, 275, 292, 293, 294
Parnell, Charles Stewart 11, 236, 240,
   248, 273
partition 8, 11, 98, 151, 274, 320, 327
   EOD on 56, 81, 89–90, 209, 288, 320
   and northern offensive (1922) 98,
      100–1, 103
   see also border
Patrickswell 109
Paxton, Robert 213
Pearse, Patrick 22, 24, 161, 168, 236, 240,
   280, 332
   and cultural nationalism 9, 236, 249
Perkins, Constable 58
Pfaus, Oskar 322, 325, 332
Phelan, Edward 22
Phelan, Garda Harry 123, 124
Phoenix Park 119, 155
   see also Garda Síochána
physical fitness 17–18, 155–7, 159–62,
   163, 168, 210, 214, 251–2
   and Garda Síochána 121, 126, 127, 129
Pickford, Mary 153
Pioneer Total Abstinence Association 8,
   120, 148, 193
Pius XI, Pope 148, 149, 184, 200–1, 206,
   212, 231
Plasencia 301
poitín 51–2, 64, 65, 66, 75, 120
Poland 327

Popular Front, French 320
Popular Front, Spanish 283
Port Said 201
Portlaoise 298
Portobello barracks 107
Portugal 212, 296, 305, 313, 321
Potsdam 129
Preetz, Wilhelm 334
Presbyterians 2, 67, 205
Preston, Paul 347
Price, Bob 75
Primo de Rivera, General Miguel
        319
proportional representation 222, 223
protectionism 202, 242
Protestants and Protestantism 39, 71,
        181, 296
    before 1919 2, 4, 8, 9, 66, 71
    during War of Independence 47, 51,
        52–7, 59–61, 66
        executions of 64, 66, 69, 71, 72
    in Northern Ireland 78, 79, 99
    relations with Catholics 15, 20–1, 41,
        46, 57, 66, 93
    see also sectarianism; Unionists
Prout, John 111
Public Safety acts
    1923 171
    1927 176, 178, 179
    1931, see Article 2A
Punchestown 129
Purser, Ellen 330

Quadragesimo Anno (1931) 206, 212
Quinlan, Lieutenant Pa 236
Quinn, Patrick 236, 259, 271
Quish, Denis 236, 253, 259, 273
Quisling, Vidkun 333, 338
Quislings 333, 339, 340

racialism 252, 253, 254, 304, 349
    see also anti-Semitism

Ramírez de Arellano, Count 284, 285,
        287
Rathkeale 109
red scares, see anti-communism
Redemptorists 4
Redmond, John 3, 20, 21, 34, 236
Redmondites 3, 20–3, 29, 31, 35–6, 46,
        50, 53, 64–5, 72, 219
Republican bonds 44
Republican Congress 256, 279
republican courts 50–1, 67
republican police 34, 51–2
Requetés 295, 300, 308, 311
Rerum Novarum (1891) 212
reunification 239
Ribbonmen 54
Rockcorry 56, 63
Roddy, Constable 48
Romania 254, 275, 287
Rome 148–9, 212, 257, 276, 280, 285, 350
    see also March on Rome
Roscommon, Co. 84, 205, 273
Rosscarbery 283
Rosslea 8, 59–61, 64, 72, 99, 100
Royal Irish Constabulary 29, 42, 123,
        126
    before 1919 9, 22, 28–9, 34–7, 40,
        42–4
        boycott of 42, 43
    during War of Independence 48,
        51–3, 55, 57–8, 65, 67, 68, 70, 73,
        116
        assassination policy 42, 58, 68, 71
        barrack attacks 42–3, 47, 53, 62,
            70, 237, 248
        demoralisation of 48, 49, 51–2, 53,
            178
    ex-RIC men in Garda Síochána 116,
        117, 118, 119
    and GAA 36, 37, 126
    in Northern Ireland during truce
        78–9, 81–2

see also informers; Ulster Special
    Constabulary
Royal Ulster Constabulary 100, 102, 279
rugby 16, 17, 146, 150, 151, 211, 236
Rugby School 17, 18
rural agitation 224–5, 240–3, 261–2, 272,
    277, 280
    farmers' grievances 202, 211, 219, 224,
      240–2
    Blueshirts and 224–5, 241–2, 248, 258,
      261–2, 272, 277
    see also anti-annuities campaign;
      economic war; land
      redistribution
Rushe, Denis Carolan 7
Russell, Seán 325, 334
Russia, *see* Soviet Union
Ruttledge, P.J. 94, 196, 197, 217, 218,
    236, 253, 258–9
Ryan, Colonel Jerry 236, 259, 262
Ryan, Dr James 88, 337
Ryan, Frank 304, 317, 334, 350
Ryan, T.J. 181, 194
Ryle, Constable 36

St Enda's school 168
St Josephs Young Priests Society 147
St Patrick's College, Drumcondra 7
Salamanca 285, 290, 292, 293, 294, 297,
    300–1, 305, 309, 311
    Irish College in 284, 294, 314
Salazar, Antonio de Oliveira 212
Saliquet Zumeta, General Andrés 306,
    307
Saor Éire 183, 184, 185
Sarsfield, Patrick 109, 138, 313
Saunderson family 8
Scotland Yard 141
    Special Branch 287
Scotstown 26, 48, 58
Scott medal 127
Scott, Michael 166

Seanad 161, 164, 178, 232
Second World War 268, 321, 322, 323,
    326–8, 329–31, 332–40
    possible British invasion 326, 336
    see also Germany
sectarianism 2, 15, 19, 44, 78, 99, 101, 151,
    280
    and War of Independence 53–61,
      64–5, 69, 71–2
Seville 293, 294
sexual offences 157, 158, 162
sexuality 163–9, 349
Shercock 50, 68
Simon, Walter 334
Sinn Féin 2, 34–5, 49–50, 121, 242–3,
    276
    in Co Monaghan 3, 22–4, 28–30, 32,
      35–7, 40–2, 46, 51
      and county council 50
      execution of SF opponent 68–9
      and Gaelic League 9
      SF courts 50–1, 52
    and Easter rising 23–4, 28
    EOD in 27, 28–30, 32, 34, 37, 44, 46,
      52, 82
      and elections 40–1, 50, 76
    1918 election 19, 40–1
    1921 election 76
    and truce 77
    and North 78, 80
    and Treaty 84, 89, 90, 92, 104
Skibbereen 193, 230
Sligo 255
Sligo Champion 159
Smith, Denis Mack 346
Smith, Paul 165
Smith, T.F. 306
Smithboro 48
soccer 11, 15, 16–17, 45, 146, 150, 151–2
Social Darwinism 17, 160
socialism 183–4, 185, 244, 246, 283, 320,
    326

Society of St Vincent de Paul 329
South Africa 9, 334
Southern Star 200
Soviet Union 183, 200, 226, 252, 256,
       320, 323
   and Spanish Civil War 283–4, 290,
       296, 304, 305, 308
Spain 252, 253, 268, 288, 331
   Catholic Church in 283, 284, 296,
       300
   divisions in 184, 203–4, 255, 269, 275,
       283
   Moroccan campaigns 288
   see also Franco; Spanish Civil War
Spanish Civil War 283–4, 287, 298–9,
       301–11, 303, 318, 319, 320
   foreign aid to Nationalists 283, 285,
       287, 291, 292, 300, 307
   foreign aid to Republicans 283–4,
       287, 289, 290, 302, 304
   brutality and atrocities 284–5, 296,
       303, 304–5, 308, 317
   Catholic Church and 284–6, 288,
       304–5, 308, 350
   Irish attitudes to 284–6, 290, 306, 308
   Irish government and 284, 285, 289,
       290, 292, 300, 302, 305, 319
   Moroccan mercenaries 288, 303–4,
       305
   communists 305, 307
   see also Franco; Irish Brigade
Spanish Foreign Legion, *see Tercio*
Special Branch 172, 174, 177, 188, 191
   and IRA 180–2, 183, 184–5, 188
   and Fianna Fáil in power 189, 193–6,
       198
   and Blueshirts 216, 219, 230, 262,
       280
   and Second World War 321, 329, 333
Special Police Auxiliary, *see* Broy Harriers
Special Powers act, Northern Ireland
       (1922) 102

sport 10, 129, 138, 149, 150, 250, 251, 281,
       339, 343
   foreign 16–17, 45–6, 146, 147, 150–1
   and physical fitness 17, 18, 157,
       159–60, 162, 251–2
   and politics 15, 16, 18, 45–6, 251
   sports administration 12, 150–3, 251,
       340, 341, 348
   see also athletics; boxing; GAA; Garda
       Síochána; Olympics; rugby;
       soccer
S.S. Aguila 296
S.S. Domino 291
S.S. Mozambique 315, 316
S.S. Urundi 291, 292
Stack, Austin 26, 38, 39, 40, 86, 87
Staines, Michael 115, 116, 117, 128
Stockholm 18
Stott, Job 279
Stradling, R.A. 349
Streicher, Julius 254
Studies 206
Sudetenland 320, 323
Sullivan, Jim 63
Sullivan, John 236
Sunday Chronicle 339
Sunday Independent 321
Sweeney, Joe 76, 88, 94
swimming 146, 152
Switzerland 254

Tailte, Queen 16
Tailteann Games 150
Tara 16, 249
Taylor, A.J.P 346
temperance 8, 31, 120–1, 126, 148, 149,
       162, 193
Tercio [de Extranjeros] (Spanish Foreign
       Legion) 288–9, 293, 295–6, 300,
       306, 307, 309–10, 313
Tetuan, Duchess of 291, 313, 314
The Round Table 249

32 Club 278–9
Thomsen, Henning 332, 336
Thomson, Alexander Raven 282–3
Tierney, Michael 205–6, 208, 221–2, 223, 228, 262–4, 273
Timlin, Sergeant-Major 303
Tipperary, Co. 17, 70, 182, 215, 246, 247
Tisdall, Bob 154
Titulcia 306–8, 317
Toal, Thomas 7
Toledo 287, 290, 301
Tone, Theobald Wolfe 24, 56
Torrejón de la Calzada 301
trade unions 284
Trajillo 294
Tralee 225, 302
travel 14
Traynor, Oscar 75, 92, 94, 180
Treanor, Arthur 41, 68–9, 92
Treasonable Offences act (1925) 172
Treaty, see Anglo-Irish Treaty
Tributh, Herbert 334
Trieste 202
Trinity College Dublin 276
Trotskyism 202
Truagh 64
truce (1921) 58, 76–9, 84–5, 86, 91, 99, 238
Tudor, Major General Sir Henry Hugh 79
Tullyallen 34
Tullycorbett 63
Tullyvaragh 55, 65
Tummon family 8
Tummon, Francis 28
Twomey, Moss 326, 338
Tydavnet 48, 64, 65
Tyrone, Co 20, 34, 74, 81, 99, 100, 101

UIP, see United Ireland Party
Ulster 2, 8
    GAA 12–15, 28, 36, 49

political crisis of 1912–14 19–20
    see also Northern Ireland; partition
Ulster Blackshirts 264
Ulster Centre of Fascist Studies 279
Ulster Covenant 19
Ulster Fascists 279, 280
Ulster Special Constabulary 149, 279
    War of Independence 54, 59–61, 69, 70, 215
    in Belfast post-truce 78, 79, 81, 82
    in Northern Ireland (1922) 98, 99–100, 102
Ulster Volunteers 11, 19, 20
Unionism, see also Orange Order
Unionists and Unionism 158, 182, 209, 238, 346
    before 1919 2, 8, 19–20, 35, 41, 43
    War of Independence 48, 50, 53–5, 61, 64, 70, 78–82
    in Northern Ireland 78–82, 93, 99–100, 102
United Ireland 206, 225, 231, 236, 239, 246, 260, 264
United Ireland Party 222, 227, 236, 240, 257, 264
United Irish League 2–3, 11, 12, 29, 68
United Irishman 201, 202–3, 204, 205, 217
United Irishmen 56
United States of America 160, 253, 312, 322, 345
    Irish-Americans 5, 6, 91, 254, 255, 289
    Irish politicians visit 77, 85
    EOD in 129–31, 142–3, 153–4
    Olympics in (1932) 152–5
    and Second World War 322, 338
The Universal Aspects of Fascism 223
University College Cork 190, 205
University College Dublin 206
Upton, Seamus 21
Urbleshanny 58
USSR, see Soviet Union

Valdemoro 301
Valladolid 287
Vatican 148, 155, 267
Venice 202
Victorianism 18, 167, 252
Victory Fund 250, 272
Vienna 155
Vigo 288

Walsh family (Caragaghdoo) 1
Walsh, J.J. 21, 331
Walsh, Liam
    on EOD 6, 14, 29–30, 82, 197, 198,
        208, 211
        on his final years 198, 320, 340–2
    relationship with EOD 6, 316, 317,
        321, 340–2
    and fascism 228–9, 282–3, 317, 321–2,
        324
    corrupt 260, 321, 333
    and Irish Brigade in Spain 291, 308,
        316, 317, 320
    anti-Semitic 319–20, 321, 328–9
    and German agents 321–3, 328–9, 331,
        332
Walsh, Patrick 43, 117, 118
Walshe, Joseph 328
War of Independence 25, 31, 41–4,
        47–73, 74–5, 92, 93, 174, 238,
        348–9
    attack on Ballytrain barracks 42, 47,
        62, 70, 237, 248
    IRA intelligence 43, 52, 53, 65, 67, 70,
        75–6, 79, 83
    raids on mail 43, 65, 67, 70
    arms raids 52–6
    executions by IRA 51, 63–72, 76, 92
    IRA court martials 57, 63, 65–6, 67
    flying columns 59, 102, 124, 168
    see also Royal Irish Constabulary
War of Independence in Monaghan 10,
        51, 69

War News 326, 332
Ward, Dr Conn 28, 31, 32, 40, 43, 44, 59,
        67, 68–9, 94, 237
Ward, Pat 31
Waterford 166, 173, 219, 236, 290
Wattlebridge 28
Wearing of Uniforms bill 232
Weekly Freeman 5
Wembley stadium 155
West Point 161
Western Mail 221
Westmeath, Co. 295
Westminster 20, 66, 100
Westport 228
Wexford 230, 298
Whelan, Leo 30
Whelan, Patrick 12, 14–15, 20, 28, 40, 46
White, John 182
Wickham, Lieutenant-Colonel Sir
        Charles George 81
Wicklow, Co. 84, 238
Wilaghan, Sergeant 58
Wild Geese 285, 291
Willmore, Alfred, see MacLiammóir,
        Micheál
Wilson, Sir Henry 105
Woods, Séamus 103
Wormwood Scrubs 49
Wray, Sergeant 43

Yagüe Blanco, Colonel Juan 288, 293,
        309–10, 313, 314
Yeats, W.B. 207, 213, 246
Young Comrades (National Guard) 215
Young Ireland Association (YIA,
        formerly Blueshirts) 204, 222–4,
        226, 228
    see also League of Youth
Younger, Calton 110
Yugoslavia 129

Zurich 276